ONLY ONE LIFE

My Autobiography

by

H. Harold Hartzler

© 1992

Printed in the United States of America.

Published by
Olde Springfield Shoppe
10 West Main Street
Elverson, PA 19520-0171

The Hartzler Family
at the wedding of
Terry Yoder and Joan Gotwals
on July 16, 1983

Back row, left to right: Jonathan, Judy, Joel (son of Harold), Dorothy, H. Harold holding Jason Schmucker (son of Patty), Theo, E. D. Yoder, Patty (daughter of Theo) and Doug Schmucker.

Middle row, left to right: Harold E., Rachel holding their daughter Carrie, Aaron Jon (Harold's son), Joan and Terry (Theo's son).

Front row, left to right: Todd and Matthew (Jon's sons), and Sandy and Cindy (Theo's daughters). Harold's three older children (Jody, Mark, and Lea Ann) were not present.

Contents

Only One Life—My Autobiography 1

My Family 66

My Trip to Europe in 1990 70

Forty Years With the ASA 76

God's Very Good Creation 89

A Letter on My Eightieth Birthday 108

My Personal Testimony 111

Letters To and From College Classmates
and Family 113

Unsung Heroes of the Faith.................... 119

Letter to the ASA 120

Lecture Tour From 1976-1977 122

My Vision: Past, Present, and Future 125

Changes I Have Seen in the Mennonite Church 165

MY TRIBUTE
To My Father

As I read this manuscript, it occurred to me that the title Father chose has significance that readers may miss. Some years ago, my father gave me a plaque for a gift. It hangs by my bed today and reads:

I shall pass through this world but once,
Any good therefore that I can do
Or any kindness that I can show,
Let me do it now
Let me not defer or neglect it
For I shall not pass this way again.

I believe my father's motto for life was summed up in that verse. Or perhaps it could be stated in the shorter form:

Only one life
Twill soon be past
Only what's done
For Christ will last.

Both of those verses illuminate the title that Father has chosen for his autobiography, *ONLY ONE LIFE*.

My father has been a dedicated person—dedicated to whatever cause he was interested in. And, of course, his biggest cause was serving Christ—his Saviour. He has left this legacy to me and to all his children, his grandchildren, and his great-grandchildren, and to all who have known him.

Theo "Theodosia" Yoder

About The Author

For H. Harold Hartzler, life is filled with opportunities. The day is never long enough to do all that he would like to do and tomorrow is filled with plans. He always acts with energy and enthusiasm. But most important—he lives with conviction and a commitment to Christian faith.

H. Harold Hartzler is a teacher—a successful one—for forty-one years as a college and university teacher of mathematics, astronomy, and physics. As a university teacher, he encouraged his students to strive for scholarship and was there to help them in their effort. There was mutual respect for each other in the classroom and he valued knowing them.

For H. Harold Hartzler, however, his teaching extends beyond the classroom. One always knows where he stands on an issue—he speaks out honestly according to his conviction—not afraid to go against popular opinion, and people respect him for this. He has a reputation for bringing people together and works hard to maintain communication between all of us. Throughout, he consistently demonstrates a positive attitude toward life in general. He is a teacher by example.

It has been said that one should live every day on one hand as though it is our last and on the other hand like we will live forever. I believe H. Harold Hartzler truly lives this way—but always living to honor and serve Him.

V. Dean Turner, Dean
College of Natural Sciences
Mankato State University
December 1981

ONLY ONE LIFE
My Autobiography

by H. Harold Hartzler

This autobiography was started while I was in the Mankato (Minnesota) Hospital on July 24, 1981. I had suffered a heart attack on July 6 and was in the hospital for a period of eighteen days. During that time, I was well taken care of by doctors and nurses. I called them my angels.

By birth I am a Hoosier, born in the city of Fort Wayne, Indiana, on April 7, 1908. At that time my father, John M. Hartzler, was a Mennonite minister at the Fort Wayne Mission. William Howard Taft was the President of the United States.

My mother, Anna Mary King, was born April 8, 1878, the daughter of Jacob Z. King and Barbara King of West Liberty, Ohio. My father was born September 21, 1871, the son of Yost Hartzler and Barbara King of Allensville, Pennsylvania.

My great-grandparents on my father's side were Yost Hartzler, born April 21, 1791; Elizabeth Beiler, born December 5, 1792; Jacob L. King, born September 30, 1805; and Elizabeth Lapp, born October 20, 1811. On my mother's side they were Shem King, born December 19, 1819; Anna Zook, born August 30, 1825; Joseph King, born February 12, 1809; and Sarah Zook, born July 12, 1814.

My great-great-grandparents were Jacob Hartzler, Anna Yoder, Hans Beiler, Mary Detweiler, John King, Elizabeth Yoder, Isaac Lapp, Barbara Stoltzfus, Samuel King, Nancy Yoder, Abraham Zook, Mattie Yoder, Christian King, Elizabeth Detweiler, David Zook, and Anna Lantz.

Jacob Hartzler, my great-great-grandfather, was the grandson of Immigrant Jacob Hertzler who was the first Amish bishop in this country, arriving in 1749. His son John Hertzler married Veronica Yoder and they were the parents of Jacob Hartzler, my great-great-grandfather.

My father, John M. Hartzler, had been ordained as a minister in 1904 for the new Mennonite congregation located near Surrey, North Dakota. Due to the illness of B. B. King, my parents were asked to take charge of the work at Fort Wayne, Indiana. It was

1

there that I was born, but the family did not stay long in Fort Wayne. That fall of 1908 we moved to North Dakota where my father served as Sunday school superintendent, minister, and public school teacher.

The winters were extremely cold and I recall Mother telling of my father coming home from school, using the wire fence as a guide since the storm was so severe that he was unable to see far ahead. The next August my brother Clayton was born near Surrey. That fall we moved to Long Green, Maryland. The Mennonite church there had been without a minister for a number of years.

Long Green is the first place of which I have a definite memory. It was a small village consisting of several houses, a store, a blacksmith shop and a church, located in Baltimore County, Maryland. One of my earliest recollections is that of the time when my twin sisters, Eva and Ethel, were born. As I remember when I was shown the one baby, I asked whether I might kiss her; when I was shown the other one, I asked whether I might kiss her, too. That was in January of 1911.

Clayton and I started to school in Long Green. We had a half mile to walk to school. My parents thought that Clayton and I should start to school together. My sister Carrie was born that fall soon after we started to go to school.

I have several distinct memories of Long Green. It was there that I first remember of going to Sunday school. My first teacher was Mary Hertzler who died recently. She was the sister of Silas Hertzler, my colleague on the Goshen College faculty. We shared office space for some time since we were both interested in genealogy. I recall helping him with his work on the *Hertzler-Hartzler Family History*. That was completed in 1952. I had not completed my work by 1981 when I started this work. It did finally appear in print in 1985.

Other distinct memories of Long Green are the visits of Grandfather Jacob Z. King of West Liberty, Ohio, and of my Uncle Jonathan Hartzler of Belleville, Pennsylvania, as well as of my Aunt Mollie Smucker, with her husband John Smucker and her son Alphie. I also recall the time we had a black man work for us on our small farm. The thing that stands out in my memory is the fact that the black man ate at a separate table from the rest of the family. That I could not understand at the time.

When I was four years old, my mother took us children with her on the train to visit our grandfather in Ohio. That was a very interesting experience for me. I remember how we slept on the

The John M. Hartzler family at Belleville, Pennsylvania.

train, some of us on the upper berth and the others on the lower berth. I can remember helping Grandpa King drive some sheep to the market. I realize that I was not of much help, but I know that I tried to help.

    Two exciting events stand out in my memory of Long Green. The one was the time that I wished to go with my father to Dance's Mill. This was located about a mile from our home. My father did not want me to go with him so he left me behind. Since I did not want to be left at home, I ran after him all the way to the mill and arrived soon after he did.

    The other exciting event at Long Green was the time that our house was struck by lightning. As you can imagine, we were all very scared. As I recall, no serious damage was done to the house.

    I should mention names of some families who lived near us in Long Green. The Phillips family lived nearby and had the village store under their supervision. I am able to think of Mrs. Phillips as a very good friend. She came to Belleville to visit us.

Some other families were Gorsuch, Smith, and Yoder. We have kept in contact with the Yoder family to this very date. Edith Yoder has been a special friend of our family until her death a few years ago. Carroll Wilhide, her husband, lives at Detour, Maryland.

In the summer of 1915, the Mennonite church we attended, and of which my father served as minister, burned to the ground. We had been cleaning up the churchyard and had a large brush fire going when some of the sparks were blew up on the roof of the church. Since no ladder was available, the church burned completely. During that winter, we worshipped with the Church of the Brethren located near the Mennonite church.

I often think of Long Green, Maryland, and have returned on a number of occasions. Each year a meeting is held near Long Green which is attended by some who formerly lived there or have roots in Long Green. My mother was interested in attending these meetings and a number of us went with her. The meetings were inspirational in nature and we had a fine social time together. A few years ago I was asked to be the main speaker at one of those meetings. At that time, my twin sisters, Eva and Ethel, went with my wife and me and we were entertained in the home of Edith and Carroll Wilhide.

In the spring of 1916, we moved to Belleville, Pennsylvania, where my father was asked to be one of the ministers. The other minister was Joseph H. Byler. This was home territory to my father since he had been born near Allensville, located seven miles from Belleville. This was in the beautiful Kishacoquillas Valley.

We moved to Belleville by train, I recall how some of us stayed first at the home of Sarah Peachey just a short distance from the house on Trella Street. I also recall how some of us stayed at the home of Reuben Zook, married to Sallie King, my mother's first cousin from Ohio. Reuben Zook was a brother of Thomas Zook, well known as one of the founders of "Hertzler and Zook," manufacturers of farm machinery. This plant had been taken over by New Holland and later by Ford and is a very prosperous business in Belleville.

Clayton and I started to school together again in Belleville in the fall of 1916. However, something happened which I still do not understand. Clayton was put in the first grade even though he had been in first grade in Maryland. However, I was put in the second grade for a few days and then transferred to the third grade.

That meant we were separated by two grades though we had started together. This continued to the seventh grade when Jim Wilson, our teacher, asked Clayton and some others, including my twin sisters, to skip the seventh grade and go on to the eighth grade. Thus Clayton was only one grade behind me in the Belleville High School. I recall that my first teacher in Belleville was Anna Gardner while the next teacher was Bess Hassinger. I had her for a teacher through the fourth grade after which I had Rachel McNabb as a teacher for two years.

Two things stand out in my memory of the teaching of Bess Hassinger. The first was the fact that she had all of us sign a pledge that we would never smoke. I am of the opinion that very few kept that pledge. The other thing I recall is some of the good times we enjoyed at recess. In the wintertime we had lots of snow so we had snow battles. I recall that our teacher suggested that we imagine that we were two sides in the Civil War.

Some of our neighbors in Belleville were: Mr. and Mrs. Joe Wills and their three boys; Mr. and Mrs. Sam Yoder, the parents of Jonathan Yoder who later built a house next to our home on Trella Street; Mr. and Mrs. Skid Bennett and their son Rush; Mrs. Marshall and her daughter Alberta; Mr. and Mrs. Christ Plank; Mr. and Mrs. Isaac Zook and their son Maurice; Lydia Zook and her family, where my father later fell from the scaffold and died two days later in 1925; Mr. and Mrs. Levi Kauffman; Mr. and Mrs. Howard Stump and his father Ed. Stump, a Civil War veteran, the only Civil War veteran I ever met. He used to tell us some stories of the War such as eating baked beans which were wormy.

One of the tragedies which happened to us in 1918 was the flu which took so many lives, including that of my sister Euna Grace who was born in November of that year and lived only three days. None of us were able to go to the funeral. I recall how sick I was and how some of the neighbors came in to be of help. As I recall we were all sick at once with the exception of my sister Carrie.

This was also the time of World War I which brought much grief to those who did not support the war effort. My father refused to buy war bonds and was therefore called a slacker. For some reason, which I do not understand, he was also called names like that of Zecharius. This name stuck with the family so all of us were called by that name. Until he died, my brother John Marion was still called by that name. I lost it years ago when I left home to go to college.

I well recall the great rejoicing when the Armistice was signed on November 11, 1918. Everyone seemed to be happy to know that the war was over.

While I was in the fourth grade in Belleville, the fifth and sixth grades made use of another building located up on the hill from the building which we used. That allowed us to use one room in our building for recreation. I can well recall some of the good times we had in that gymnasium. That was great fun.

The next year the fifth and sixth grades, taught by Rachel McNabb, moved into the room which we had been using as a gymnasium. Rachel was a good teacher, but a strict disciplinarian. I still remember how she would have Edgar McCardle stand up in the corner at which time she would give him a good whipping. This happened over and over. If we were caught doing some minor thing which was not approved by the teacher, she had us write the word disobedience several hundred times. Some of us tried to beat this by using two or three pencils at a time.

This was also the time of my life when I thought it was great to write with my left hand. I had seen Glen Kennedy do that and I thought that I should do the same. I did this for two years and only stopped when my father found this to be the case. I was then in the seventh grade under the teaching of Sol Yoder, who later became a physician in Lancaster, Pennsylvania. Later on I had two of his sons as my students at Goshen College. Their names were Carl and Sol.

It was at this time in my life when a good friend from Ohio moved into our community. Fred Kauffman was the same age as Clayton and moved in the home of John Y. Hartzler and his wife Fannie, who was Fred's aunt. His mother had died near West Liberty, Ohio, so he was taken into the home of John X., as he was called. We had many good times together. On Sunday afternoon we would often, together with Clayton, take a walk up in the mountain. Later when I went to college, Fred bought my bicycle which I had earned selling papers. Clayton and I had paper routes in Belleville for a number of years. He had the *Harrisburg Telegraph* and I had the *Harrisburg Evening News*. In order to encourage us to get more subscribers, the paper had contests. For twenty new subscribers I was awarded a new bicycle. This was a very wonderful thing in my life. I had always wanted a bicycle but did not have enough money to buy one.

I now recall visiting Rachel McNabb in Belleville many years after she was my teacher. She always seemed to be very happy for my visits. Her brother Dale McNabb was the undertaker in Belleville and served in that capacity at the funeral of my father in 1925.

It was about this time in my life that Grandpa King from West Liberty, Ohio, came to visit us in Belleville. I can remember that he brought some candy for us which we enjoyed very much. Grandma came with him, though she was not really our grandmother. Our grandfather Jacob Z. King had been married twice. His first wife, Barbara King, died when my mother was eight years old. Several years later he married Mattie A. Yoder. They had three children: Marion, Ivan, and Carrie. I well remember them. In particular I remember how Uncle Ivan came to be with us when my father died.

As stated previously, Sol Yoder was my seventh grade teacher. He was the son of Christian P. Yoder and Lydia Hartzler, who was my father's second cousin. For the first week in the seventh grade I went to school in my bare feet. This would never be done today, but it was common in those days.

In the spring we had a contest to see how many birds we could identify. The contest was held for both the seventh and eighth grades since we were both in the same room. I well recall how my cousin Joseph Hartzler, son of Jonathan Hartzler and Emma Hooley Hartzler, won the contest. He always seemed able to identify many more birds than most of us. I very much enjoyed the seventh grade. It was at this time of my life that I learned to ride a bicycle. That was a great achievement for me.

My father was a preacher, teacher, and painter. In a way, I have followed him. As early as I can remember, I went with my father to paint. When I was eight years old, I went along to help and then every summer I helped my father. However, my brother Clayton did not start to paint until the summer of 1924 when we were painting the buildings on the farm of Rudy Yoder. I also worked for Rudy Yoder when I tested the milk from his cows on the farm. This grew out of a project from the Belleville Vocational High School. I did this for a number of years for Rudy Yoder.

I should mention another important event in my life—the birth of my brother John Marion on April 23, 1917. We always called him Marion, but years later he did not like that name so he wished to be called John. I still think of him as Marion. He was named for my father. I still think of him as my younger brother though he lived to be over sixty years of age. He went to Merchant Marine School during World War II and sailed with the Merchant Marines for a number of years. Finally, he was advanced to be Captain of the ship and was gone for a whole year at the time of the war. He was very good to Mother, helping her financially when some of us were unable to do so. He married Helen Fisher late in life and they had a son Jerry who is interested in commercial art.

My eighth grade teacher was Jim Wilson from Allensville. I consider him as one of my best schoolteachers. He seated us according to our rank in class. I remember how Jim Hanawalt and I used to take turns in having the favored back seat. Others in the back row were my cousin Mildred Hartzler and Eva Peachey, a more distant cousin. She later married Ezra Kauffman, the son of Levi Kauffman, who was our neighbor on Trella Street in Belleville.

Jim Wilson taught us how to do square root and cube root without the use of logarithims. Of course, I did not know anything about logarithims at that time in my life. I learned later how to extend this method of extracting roots of numbers to any root. I have made use of these methods in a number of practical situations.

One of the joys of my eighth grade experience was the arithmetic matches which we had every Friday afternoon. At about 2:00 p.m., we had such a match in which the first person who had the problem done was permitted to go home. The competition was always in addition and I remember that I never was able to be the first one to be allowed to go home. That person was always Herbert Bigelow who later became a painter in Lewistown and died years ago.

As I stated previously, the seventh grade and the eighth grade were in the same room so my brother Clayton and I were in the same room that year. I recall how Fred Kauffman, our good friend, was given a severe whipping that year for a cause which I did not understand. All that I know is that Fred was told to lean over in his seat and then Jim Wilson whipped him severely. I felt that it was much too severe.

A very beautiful experience that year for me was the winning of the highest honors for eighth grade students in Mifflin County. I also recall walking home from school many evenings with James Hanawalt at which times we discussed such things as where we planned to go to college. James planned to go to Penn State while I had no such plans. The irony of it is that James never lived to go to college while I went to Juniata College. In fact, I was taken to Huntingdon by Dan Hanawalt, the father of James, and his sister

Imogene. She was a junior while I was a freshman, but the following year she died. Thus there were two deaths in the Hanawalt family within a few years.

On July 3, 1922, I recall how my mother received a telegram telling of the death of Grandpa King. At that time I was helping my father build a corncrib near our home in Belleville. She was crying as she told the news to my father. It was decided that she would go to the funeral in Ohio. She took my sister Carrie and my brother Marion with her to the funeral. Grandpa King was only 71 years old when he died; however, I considered that he was quite an old man.

As I mentioned previously, I helped my father in the painting business each summer as far back as I am able to remember. It was also in the summer of 1922 that we painted the farm buildings on the Menno Yoder farm just west of Allensville. At that time his son-in-law Levi Hartzler, a second cousin of my father, lived there. We drove back and forth from Belleville each day, taken by a young man whose name was Jacob Peachey, who later married Jennie Krepps. I recall that I helped to train Jake to be a painter.

It took us six weeks to do this job since we painted two dwelling houses, two large barns, and two sheds. It was a great treat for me to be able to ride a bicycle which belonged to Levi Hartzler. I did this every noon when the weather was favorable. At the end of the six weeks, I well recall that Menno Yoder gave me two dollars as a reward for helping with the painting. As far as I know, this was the only money which I ever received for my work as a painter as long as my father lived. I never thought much about money at that time in my life.

There were a number of ways in which I was able to earn money during my teen years. I spaded gardens, mowed lawns, and had a paper route. My mother took care of our money for us. She kept all of my money until I entered college.

I must not forget my farm experience. My parents bought a small tract of land which was next to our lot in Belleville. They bought these seventeen acres from Levi M. Yoder, who was one of the sons of "Rosanna of the Amish" who married Christian Yoder. We usually hired someone to farm this land since we did not have the necessary equipment; however, we did have two cows and a horse for some time. I remember riding this horse whose name was Mae. At the death of my father, we sold the horse at the Community Sale. I still remember that the auctioneer, Tom Peachey, announced that my father's funeral would be held the next day. That was a very traumatic experience for me.

Starting at the age of nine, I worked every summer in the harvest fields for Isaac B. Zook who lived near Belleville. During the first summer I only helped with the oats harvest, but after that Clayton and I helped with making hay, harvesting wheat and oats, and then helping with the threshing of the grain.

A few years later our brother, John Marion, helped with the harvesting. This was a very unique experience for us boys. We very much enjoyed the good meals cooked by Ella Mae, the wife of Isaac B. Zook. Her brother, Tom Yoder, always did the threshing.

I can recall some of the other men who helped with the harvesting. The first was Solomon Byler, son of David Byler and Salome Hartzler. He married Nellie Zook, sister of Reuben and Tom Zook. Next was Howard Stump, who had been our neighbor on Trella Street in Belleville. He was the son of the Civil War veteran Ed. Stump. Simie John Yoder was another who helped in the harvest field as did Ralph Kauffman from Ohio and the brother of Fred Kauffman.

Finally, there was the family of Little Christ Yoder, Aaron, Alphie, and John. Little Christ was the son of Yost Yoder and Barbara Peachey, Yost was the son of "Rosanna of the Amish" and her husband Christian Yoder, who was minister in the Amish Church. I mention Rosanna of the Amish since I well remember the author of that book, Joseph Warren Yoder, or J. W. as he was known in the valley.

You may not believe this, but it is true that J. W. Yoder was my music teacher in the Belleville Mennonite Church. He had a deep bass voice and had taught music in a number of churches and had previously taught at the Elkhart Institute where my father later taught. I can recall John Umble telling that J. W. Yoder finished the term by saying that he had taught them all the Greek which he knew.

My family was peculiar with relation to music. We never had a musical instrument in our home since all musical instruments were frowned upon by the Mennonite Church at that time. My father sang well and led in singing in the church service. My brother Clayton did the same and both Carrie and John Marion were able to sing. However, my mother, my twin sisters, and I had a difficult time carrying a tune. I never cared much for music and was called a semi-monotone by my music teacher, Professor Rolland, of Juniata College. I sing very little and am often told in church services that I should keep quiet. But the Bible tells us that we should make a joyful noise (not music) to the Lord, so I frequently joined in singing unless warned by my wife that my noise may not be joyful to those around me. This is one of the many things I enjoy about charismatic ecumenical meetings where we all make a joyful noise to the Lord. This is great. May we have more of it.

Another music memory is that of the John I. Byler family, consisting of father, mother, and ten children, all excellent singers, who on a number of occasions gave a program of sacred songs at our Mennonite Church at Belleville.

Joseph H. Byler, father of John I. Byler, labored with my father as the senior minister at that church. He died within two weeks of the death of my father. The entire John I. Byler family, with the children, usually took part in these inspirational singing programs. The church was usually filled, showing that many people of the Kishacoquillas Valley appreciated this special exhibition of musical talent. I am not certain how many summers this family appeared in the Maple Grove Church. Later I recall that the Byler quartet, consisting of three of the Byler boys together with Roy Roth, often sang at Goshen College.

I entered the Belleville Vocational High School in the fall of 1922 when I still wore short pants. Few boys wore long pants in those days until they were nearly through high school. My teachers were Euphemia Strouse, the home economics teacher who taught us general science; Ralph McClay, the principal who taught us algebra; Lige Cummings, the vocational agriculture teacher who taught us such things as farm crops, poultry, and woodworking; and finally Grace Metz, our English teacher.

Grace Metz had two sisters, Blanche and Rhoda, who were students with me in high school. Our school was called a vocational school since, for the first two years, we were taught some subjects directly related to agriculture or to homemaking. I enjoyed such subjects very much but was much more interested in algebra. I always delighted in mathematics and will always be grateful to Jim Wilson, our eighth grade teacher, who always encouraged us in that area.

It is interesting that a number of students who were with us in the eighth grade did not go on to high school. Some of these were Eva Peachey who later married Ezra Kauffman, Hazel Laub who married James Stuter, James Carson who always insisted on pitching when we played ball, and John Fultz, the son of the miller, Walter Fultz. This man offered me a job when I finished high school. I remember being called to his office one evening at which time he told me of plans for the future. I was to be given the position of manager of the Reedsville Mill and then to be transferred to the Belleville Mill. This was a big temptation to me, but, after talking this over with my mother, it was decided that I should instead go to college.

My classmates in my first year in high school were James Hanawalt, Herbert Bigelow, Baker Young, Alexander Gibbony, Glen Kennedy, Maude Hartzler, Mildred Hartzler, Thelma Wills, and a number of others whose names I do not recall.

Going from the freshman year to the sophomore year in high school was a great experience. We had new students and new teachers. My brother Clayton, whom I had left behind in the first grade as I was transferred to the third grade, had skipped the seventh grade under the guidance of Jim Wilson, and was now a freshman while I was a sophomore.

The new vocational agriculture teacher was Samuel L. Horst whom we called "Sammy Levi." He was from eastern Pennsylvania and spoke with a distinct Pennsylvania Dutch accent. Ralph McClay continued as principal, Euphemia Strouse as home economics teacher, and Grace Metz as instructor in English and history.

Many changes occurred in my high school during my junior year. Our new principal was Samuel Levi Horst whom many of us made fun of. I know that we should not have done this, but it seemed that he had very few friends among the students in our school. Having a new principal meant that we lost our good principal, Ralph McClay. I really do not know, but it is my impression, that there were some dirty politics involved in the change in principals in our school. Miss Strouse continued as home economics teacher and Grace Metz as English and history teacher. We had new teachers in music, mathematics, and Latin.

The subject of Latin was new at the Belleville High School. I understand that during World War I, German was thrown out as a foreign language. What a pity since many of us from the Kishacoquillas Valley had a German background. Such is the irrationality which develops during war hysteria. As a result, no foreign language was taught in our high school from 1918 to 1924.

Due to a strong demand from students, we were given the privilege of studying Latin beginning with my junior year. This I appreciated very much for it is a fact that very nearly 85% of

H. Harold Hartzler (second person from the left in the first row) was a member of the 1926 graduating class at the Belleville (Pa.) High School.

our English vocabulary is based upon the Latin. Many times I am able to determine the meaning of an English word due to the fact that it is derived from two or more Latin words. In college, I took a number of years of Latin so that I feel fairly competent in Latin. In fact, I was asked to teach a special course in Latin when I was a teacher at Goshen College. I did not accept the assignment.

A number of new students joined us in our junior year including Jesse Renno who later became our class president and married Mildred Hartzler, my second cousin and my classmate; Jonas Yoder, my good friend who later graduated as the Salutatorian of our class; and James Allison from Allensville. At that time, Allensville had a three-year high school so a number of students continued their education in Belleville.

Another thing that I must not forget to mention was the introduction of the *Peasley Gazette*, edited by Jonas Yoder and myself. This was a student newspaper of small dimensions whose outstanding feature was its caricature of "Sammy Levi"

Horst. Jonas Yoder and I had not expected that the principal, Samuel Levi Horst, would get to see this piece of literary genius, but one of the students thought that he should receive a copy, so one was given to him. We never heard of his reaction to our newspaper, but I can imagine that it was not very favorable. We never found out whether he learned the identity of the editors. To this day I do not know what happened to Samuel Levi Horst. What I do know is that he lasted but two years at the Belleville Vocational High School.

A tragedy occurred during our junior year. My best friend, James Hanawalt, son of the K. V. station agent, Daniel Hanawalt, became very ill with tuberculosis of the spine. He became so ill that it was necessary for him to discontinue his education.

I well recall that on a number of occasions some of us from his high school class would be invited to his home to enjoy playing various games. The game which I remember especially well was called "Pit," based on the grain market of Chicago. Mrs. Catherine Hanawalt always acted as our gracious hostess.

James died shortly before we graduated the following year. I recall that the members of his class acted as honorary pallbearers at the funeral held at the Belleville Presbyterian Church. This was a terrible blow to me since James and I had been very close friends for a number of years.

A second tragedy occurred in the spring of our junior year. As previously mentioned, my father was a painter for many years during the summer months. Since the weather was fair during the latter part of March 1925, my father decided to start painting a house on Trella Street close to our home, then occupied by John C. and Artie Yoder. Artie was the daughter of Lydia Zook who lived there for a number of years. I recall how I helped my father set up the scaffold so that painting could start in the afternoon.

I went off to school and before I returned from school my father was found by my sister Carrie, then nine years old, lying on the sidewalk near the end of the scaffold which stood intact. No one will ever know the cause of my father's fall. He was a very careful worker and I had never seen an accident while painting with him over a ten-year period.

As a result of the fall, my father's back was broken and he died at home two days later. He was not taken to the hospital. Of course this was a great shock to the family and especially to my wonderful mother. She bitterly complained because she had been urging my father to get some kind of work all the previous winter.

I do not know why he did not have a teaching position that year. Nearly every winter while we lived in Belleville he was a public school teacher for all eight grades. I have heard through some of his former students that he was an excellent teacher. My cousin, Rachel Esh Helfrick, tells how he was her teacher in a number of different schools in the valley and how he would urge her to do her school work.

Father was conscious for a part of those days and my mother repeatedly asked for his forgiveness since she had blamed him so much for not working and earning a living for us. As far as I know, he was never given a dollar for all his labors as a Mennonite minister. As near as I am able to calculate, he had labored faithfully for a period of more than twenty years. I am not bitter about this since at that time ministers were not paid for preaching the Word of the Lord in most Mennonite churches. The idea was that it was not right to make merchandise of the preaching the Gospel of Jesus Christ. How times have changed! I may be mistaken since I do not know the hearts of men, but it is my judgement that many modern-day ministers are preaching simply for "filthy lucre" rather than the fact that they love the Lord and wish to do His will.

Praise the Lord. He is faithful and liberally supplies all our needs. As far as I am concerned, He has abundantly supplied all my needs. The Depression started four years after the death of my father and yet I do not recall that our family ever went hungry or suffered from the lack of anything. My good and brave mother always worked hard and provided for her family. She took in washings, took care of our cow and chickens, and with the wonderful help of the Lord, we made it through the Depression with no great difficulties. (I write this with tears in my eyes.)

In order to help make "ends meet," Mother started to take care of children whose parents were either dead or separated; so my mother not only raised us six children but also partly raised more than sixty other children. In most cases, the county paid Mother a small sum for taking care of these children. I still recall some of these children, though I was not at home most of the time. During the Depression, I attended Juniata College and Rutgers University.

The first child was Dale Hanson Thompsen who was with us at the time of the death of my father. He left the next year. One whom I remember very well was Katherine Ann Forest who came to our home in 1927 and stayed for a number of years. Later, her two family members, Harold and Mary Sunday, came to be with us. They had the same mother as Katherine Forest but different fathers. This was one of the many cases of broken homes. Later we had a number of members of the Forest family. One of them turned out to be a minister. I well recall the Mathews family consisting of Helen, Catherine, Christine, Bobbie, and Dicky. They were with us for a number of years.

My sister Ethel, who helped take care of most of these children, has given me a list of most of the children cared for by Mother. I wish to list some of the names of those after the Mathews family. They are Ruth Goss, Millard Knepp, James Keisling, John Ritter, Dorothy Ritter, Frank Spickler, Junior Spickler, Robert Bitner, Melvin Mort, Margaret Mort, William Mort, George Mort, Harold Mort, Billie Dumm, Dorothy Dumm, Andrew Dumm, Wayne Dumm, Mildred Fisher, Elba McCracken, George McCracken, Mildred Barlett, George Barlett, Jean Marie Banks, Junior Barnham, Andrew Wilson, Elmer Richardson, Richard Bloom, Barbara Bloom, Joan Ayers, Patty Ayers, Jimmie Burlew, Richard Koul, Donna Paige, Earl Paige, Harry Wilson, Richard Hartsock, Nellie Hartsock, Charles Stuter, Richard Stuter, Joan Stuter, Eugene Irvin Yoder, David Hadley Phillips, who came to Mother as a baby in 1940 and left the next year. I recall how Mother brought him along with her to Goshen as she visited us when I taught at Goshen College. Mother really loved all these children and gave them wonderful care. My dear mother. She was known as Mother Hartzler or as Anna Mary.

Now I feel an obligation to pay tribute to a wonderful sister, one of the twins, whose name is Ethel Naomi. She never goes by her second name as I do not go by my first name which is Harrod. (This name was given to me in honor of the medical doctor in Fort Wayne, Indiana, who was the attending physician on the occasion of my birth.)

Now to return to my dear sister Ethel, who was a freshman in high school when my father died. At the end of that school year, she and my mother decided that it would be best for Ethel to quit school and help Mother with the many duties at home. So Ethel stayed out of school for a period of fourteen years. She helped Mother raise many of these orphan children, helped with the housework in general, and learned to be an excellent seamstress.

Ethel later finished high school, went on to college at Penn State where she earned both Bachelor and Master degrees, and taught public high school at Lititz, Pennsylvania. She also worked as a school psychologist in both Mifflin and Huntingdon

Counties in Pennsylvania. She is now retired and lives in Lewistown, Pennsylvania, although she spends much time with her friend, Mable Potter, in Mifflintown. There she very much enjoys taking care of the garden and doing the cooking.

Ethel's twin sister, Eva Ruth, is very much like Ethel in appearance. But they are also very different. In her younger years, Eva spent more of her time outdoors doing the outside work while Ethel took care of the children and helped with the housework. As far back as I can remember, they were both avid readers. They were also both interested in education.

Eva received her Bachelor's degree from Juniata College and a Masters and Doctors degrees from Penn State University. She was a much appreciated teacher of chemistry at Juniata for more than twenty years. To show their appreciation for her work, a scholarship was set up in her honor. A large number of her former students gathered in the spring of 1992 at a dinner where she was presented a book of written testamonials regarding her fine work. The alumni bulletin contained a lead article about this celebration.

A most unusual character appeared in Belleville about the time we moved there. He was, supposedly, the son of John B. Kauffman who was one of our neighbors. A son of John B. Kauffman by the name of Jonathan E. Kauffman had left home in 1903 in hope of finding a better place to live. He went west and soon was lost to his family. In his travels he met Jack Grimes who resembled him in appearance.

This Jack Grimes decided to come to Kishacoquillas Valley and pretend to be the lost son of John B. Kauffman. This happened in 1915 and he called himself Yonie Kauffman and was able to convince John B. Kauffman and his wife Katie that he was indeed their long lost son. He lived in the Valley for a number of years, came to Maple Grove Church, sang in special groups which came around at Christmastime singing Christmas carols. I well recall his singing in our home since my mother often gave these singers a treat when they came to our home.

This false Yonie pretended to be a sincere Christian and had most people fooled as to his real identity. However, in 1932 the real Jonathan E. Kauffman appeared in the Valley and was recognized by Levi K. Yoder. I remember meeting this man who was a carpenter and the brother of Christian Kauffman whom I knew very well. Finally, the two Yonie Kauffmans met and the false one admitted to his deceit. By this time he was living in

Stone Valley and seldom came to Belleville anymore. My brother Clayton was going to write up this man's life story but he never did it.

I should now tell of two other events which took place about this time in my life. It may have been a little later. One night during my junior year in high school, some of us decided to have a party on the school grounds. All of us boys were to meet together rather late at night. I had always been very obedient to the wishes and demands of my parents. For instance, when it was decided that my class would present a class play to the public, I was chosen by the teachers as one of the leading characters. When my Mother heard of this, she at once gave the final word, which was an emphatic no. So I immediately stopped play practice. This went down very hard for me, but I obeyed my Mother.

One particular night when we had planned a big party on the school grounds, I disobeyed my parents by climbing out of the window of my bedroom where my brother and I slept together. I reached the roof on the back porch and then jumped to the ground without disturbing the rest of the family. Or at least that was what I thought. I do not recall how I re-entered my bedroom, but I do remember that I attended the party and had a wonderful time.

I arrived home some time after midnight, which was very unusual for me. I am now reminded of the Bible verse: "Be sure your sins will find you out." Evidently my parents were aware of my misconduct because the next morning my Father took me privately in the living room of our home where he gave me one of the best lectures of my life. He wound up by stating that he had never done such a thing at Juniata College from where he graduated in 1897. Needless to say, I learned my lesson and never did anything like that again.

It was during this year in school that I took all my books home to study and got up each morning at five o'clock to study. I did my best scholastic work during my junior year in high school when I was the very busiest. I did the same in my junior year in college. Thus it is my observation that a person does their best work when they are the busiest.

I should add that my Father never told us much about his college experience. All I know is that he attended Juniata College from 1894 to 1897 when he graduated from the normal English course. I have learned from my cousin Rachel Helfrick that he was permitted to go to college due to the fact that he was not very strong physically; therefore, it was decided that he should not be a farmer.

I have some of my Father's textbooks—one on Chaucer and another on astronomy. In the astronomy book, the statement was made that the giant planet Jupiter had four moons. These had all been discovered by Galileo before 1642. The very interesting point to me about this is that Father had written in the margin of his book: "A fifth one has been discovered." Remember that this was about the year 1896.

Another point of interest, previously alluded to, refers to my love life. I had never cared much for girls, quite unlike my brother Clayton. However, there was one girl in our school of whom I thought very much. Her name was Ruth Hertzler. She was the daughter of I. Z. Hertzler, one of the owners of the Hertzler and Zook Company. The other owner was Thomas E. Zook, brother of Reuben Zook, previously alluded to. Ruth Hertzler was two years younger than I was and I considered her to be very beautiful; so I wished to go with her as my girlfriend. She lived in Belleville, not far from my home.

A date in those days consisted of a walk home from church, a distance of approximately one-half mile, and then a short visit on the front porch. I can recall distinctly of only two dates with Ruth—one during my high school days and the other several years later. On the first occasion, we had learned that a comet was to appear that night. I had very little knowledge of what a comet really was like. We sat out in the yard for several hours looking for the comet, but we did not see it. This was a rather disappointing experience even though I was with Ruth and very much enjoyed being with her.

The other occasion when I was alone with Ruth was quite different. I did not have a car, nor did my family. However, Ruth's Father did have a car and she invited me to go with her in her Father's car. We went up on the top of Stone Mountain. This was a very unusual situation for a girl to invite a boy to go for a ride. I do not remember more than the fact that we had a nice time together.

After graduation from high school in 1926, I left Belleville for Huntingdon where I attended Juniata College. I always contended that my good friend Fred Kauffman stole my girlfriend, but he contends that such was not the case. After graduation from high school in 1928, Ruth attended business college in

Lancaster, after which she attended Goshen College. There she met and married Ross Gerber from Ohio. She raised a fine family and died of cancer about forty years ago. Thus ended my first love life.

In the fall of 1925, I started my senior year in high school. Now that we were seniors, we considered ourselves as very important. How foolish we were! My classmates this year were Maude Hartzler, Mildred Hartzler, Thelma Wills, Baker Young, Glen Kennedy, Herbert Bigelow, James Allison, Jesse Renno, and Jonas Yoder. Jonas and I were great rivals in school, trying to make the best grades. I finally won out as valedictorian while Jonas came in second as salutatorian. I suppose that Jonas has never forgiven me for this. Perhaps I should not say that for we never discussed this matter since our graduation from Belleville Vocational High School. I still have the picture taken of our class shortly before graduation.

As previously mentioned, I did not take part in the high school play in which I was supposed to have a part. Later at Juniata College, when I graduated in 1930, I did have a part in the play, "As You Like It." I played the part of the First Lord and my whole family came to see it. How things changed in four years!

One of my vivid recollections of my senior year in high school was that of my classmate, Baker Young, who was usually talking at noon and other times with Blanche Fultz, his girlfriend. They were married the summer following our graduation.

As is customary in many high schools, our class took a trip before the close of the school year. Instead of going to Washington, D.C., we compromised by going to the park in Hershey, Pennsylvania. As I recall, we had a very fine time enjoying the amusements in the park.

Also, in the spring of 1926 I took the scholarship examination given to all graduating seniors in the state of Pennsylvania. This six-hour examination was very important since the one receiving the highest grade in each county was eligible for a $400 scholarship good in colleges in Pennsylvania alone. Since I was the winner in Mifflin County, I decided to go to Juniata College where my father had graduated in 1897. This was a major change in my life since I had previously made arrangements to go to Eastern Mennonite College in Harrisonburg, Virginia. In fact, I was to live with A. D. Wenger, the president of the college. I am sure that my life would have been quite different had I gone to E.M.C.

Our school year finally came to an end after many interesting events. As the valedictorian of my class, I was expected to speak on the occasion of commencement. I chose the title "Models" for my speech. The speech was as follows:

Models—everything has its model. At first this may seem too broad a statement, but an examination of certain well-known facts will either convince one of its truth or awaken in the mind a desire to know how generally this may be applied.

This model may be in a real tangible form, or it may be only a mind picture. In building a house, a picture is formed in the mind just as it is wished to be in all its parts, and from this conception plans are drawn from which the builder constructs the house. When inventing a new machine, the inventor's conception is embodied in a small model from which its merits may be ascertained and others copied. Even the very famous Professor Morse was some six thousand years behind in his invention of the telegraph, as this useful instrument was already in the nerves of the human body. Alexander Bell copied the human ear in his construction of the telephone.

When a study is made of the construction of our most important instruments, it is discovered that they are true copies of some parts of the body, and simply a further completion of them. In the first stone hammer, man unconsciously imitated the forearm and the closed fist; the forearm and hollowed hand are seen in the shovel and spoon; in the saw the reproduction of a row of teeth; tongs representing the closing together of the thumb and finger; in the hook is represented the bent finger; the pencil is simply the forefinger prolonged.

It can readily be seen from the foregoing illustrations that it is necessary for everything to have its model. If all machines and implements have their models, then every human being should have a model or aim in life. This model may consist of many different phases, but it should be definite and clearly outlined in the mind of the individual. In our early school years our aim was to master the three "R's." It was our ambition to be able to read, to write, and to handle the mysteries of numbers.

Besides these things, moreover, we hope that we have learned much more that will be useful to us. In our past four years we have become acquainted with the three "H's." These have been the models toward which we have been aiming and only by keeping them clearly and constantly in mind have we been able to attain our

H. Harold Hartzler in 1929 while a student at Juniata College. Here he appears in his track and field uniform.

goal—this commencement. The first "H" stands for head, and is the only one of the three that had to do with book learning. By our studies, not only a worthwhile knowledge and the culture which has come down through the ages has been secured, but more—mental habits which will be invaluable in coming years.

A wise and thoughtful writer one time said: "The education received at school and college is but a beginning, and is mainly valuable insofar as it trains one in the habit of continuous application and enables us to educate ourselves after a definite plan and system." We have often heard this expression: "Use your head for something more than a hatrack," and this is indeed a wise remark for it is important to learn how to think, how to size up a problem, and then—master it. It may sound like heresy, but learning how to use the mind is even more important than filling it full of dates. We have been learning, too, how to use our hands, the second of the three "H's."

Nobody in the old days ever thought of teaching in schools, manual training, shopwork, and typewriting, cooking and sewing, millinery, and stenography, and a score of other subjects taught in schools of our times.

Today, however, they are recognized as studies of practical value, things that enable one to think in terms of exactness, and to use the hands in preparation for a lifework outside the schoolroom. The third "H" seems to be the most important of all. It deals with things of the heart. On the ballfield, in the assembly hall, in our classrooms—everywhere we have met each other, these heart elements have come into being. Fair play, good sportsmanship, honesty, patriotism, right thinking for good citizenry has been our model all through our high school life. In our relationship with our classmates, we have been forming our future attitude toward life, and by this learning we hope to live better and to become more useful citizens.

The ingenuous youth of America will hold up to himself the brilliant model of Washington's example and strive to be what he beholds. If we follow the Scriptural injunction, "Be ye not unequally yoked together," then it is imperative that we all should improve ourselves. We should not be discouraged by comparing ourselves with the ideal set before us. Perhaps if we do our best to fashion ourselves after this model, future generations, in taking up this work, may achieve results which we must of necessity fall short of; and while we who began this work lie in obscurity, they will bloom forth into a glorious manhood. If the example of the youth of America shall prove to be one, not of encouragement but of terror, not fit to be imitated but fit only to be shunned, where else shall the youth of the world look for models?

Everything has an end and all associations between mankind must cease, bringing with it the sweet yet sad word—farewell. We are certain that the class of 1926 finds the pleasure of achievement dimmed by the severing of school and class companionship. There is always pleasure in accomplishment, in attaining a goal, and there is gratification in the thought that we have by conscious effort attained the class of our school career and are now ready to take a step beyond.

We leave our school with deep appreciation for the advantages it has given us. Education is capital; by investing it wisely we may become factors in the world's progress. We have had adequate equipment and materials to forward our high school education. It is with pride that we receive our diplomas of graduation from a school that has given us this excellent training.

Great are the joys and privileges of being a high school student. Yet none of us, it is certain, would wish to remain such forever. There are other heights to climb, other prizes to capture in the great game of life, other marks toward which we feel an overwhelming desire to press. The bright future lies before us, a future in which we have a chance to prove our worth, and to show to the world the value of a high school training.

As we look back upon our record and think of all the intercourse of the classroom, as classmates together, and of our teachers who labored with us so patiently amid all our failures and faults, thoughts of regret arise and steal away something of the day. But we must say farewell and break the ties that have long bound us as a class. Our school life as the class of 1926 is over but we must ever carry with us throughout our lives the carefree and buoyant spirit of our school days.

Teachers and school companions, one and all, let us say farewell to our past and look forward to the awakening of the new day dawning before us.

I should add a word about my experience as a painter. As I previously stated, my father painted houses and other buildings during the summer months. One of my earliest recollections is that of going along with my father to be of help. At first I simply applied putty to fill up holes in the wood siding of the house. Soon I was allowed to use a brush so that by the time I was fourteen years of age I considered myself to be an accomplished painter.

After the death of my father in the spring of 1925, I was the boss painter, the only other one in the gang was my brother Clayton, who, as previously mentioned, started to paint the year before. We worked together every summer from 1925 to 1934, the year I received the Doctor's degree in physics from Rutgers University. We had some very interesting experiences such as falling from a scaffold set up on the porch roof of the house owned by Preacher Jonas D. Yoder, an uncle of my classmate Jonas Yoder. We were so inexperienced that we did not think of having supports on the roof to prevent the ladders from slipping. The first thing we knew was the fact that we had fallen on the roof and then down on the ground. Fortunately no one was injured, but this experience taught us a good lesson to always provide supports so that the ladders could not slip.

Our brother John Marion did not join us in painting until about 1930. As I recall, we were painting the house next to that of James Wills, who was the postmaster in Belleville. We gave John the job of painting the fence while Clayton and I were painting the house. I will never forget how Mrs. Wills came out of the house and

Dorothy and Harold in their college days.

complained about the poor work John was doing. This severe reprimand was very hard on John who was doing the best he knew how. At the time he was thirteen years old and had just started to paint.

Through the years we painted many houses, barns, and other buildings in the beautiful Kishacoquillas Valley. In those days we never thought of painting buildings far from our home. I well recall how our Uncle Jake Hartzler helped us in the summer of 1929 when we were very busy. He took us to work in his Ford car since we did not have an automobile. As we painted we did mathematics problems mentally. The one I especially remember was that of computing the cost of shoeing a horse. The problem went as follows: The cost of the first nail was one cent, while that of the second was two cents, each nail then doubling for all the twenty-four nails. Compute the total cost. I remember how Uncle Jake and I worked on this problem. I do not know whether we knew that this problem was one in geometrical progression. In this special case all that one needs to do is to raise two to the twenty-fourth power and then subtract one. The answer is $167,772.15. We did not have a hand calcuator to do that problem.

On a number of occasions we had visitors from Ohio including my Uncles Joseph and Ivan King from West Liberty. I remember how Uncle Joe took us riding in his car and we achieved the remarkable speed of forty miles per hour. We children thought that was going very fast. Cousin Dorothy King, daughter of Ivan King, recalled that we went to the mountain to see the deer. She called them deers, not knowing the correct word. I thought that she was a very fine young girl as well as her sister Helen who was a cripple and has been dead for a number of years.

Our most serious accident while painting occurred in the spring of 1935 as Clayton, John, and I were painting a house in Lewistown. Usually two of us worked together on a scaffold. However, this time Clayton and I suggested that John come up with us on the scaffold. As he was climbing up on the scaffold, the rungs on the ladder broke to which were attached the jacks holding up the scaffold. So both Clayton and I fell to the ground while John was still on the ladder.

The next thing I knew was when I woke up in the Lewistown Hospital. I had been unconscious and suffered cracked ribs. Clayton was injured more seriously with a broken ankle that kept him from working all summer. I never did find out what John did when he saw our condition. I assume that he called the ambulance.

After two weeks, I returned to work. We then hired David Zook from Allensville to help us and we continued to paint all summer until I started to teach at Elizabethtown College. During this time, Clayton recuperated and served as our boss, working on the books at our home in Belleville. He also took some time off to take our sister Carrie to La Junta, Colorado, where she entered the nursing training program. Clayton drove his car on this trip and took my sister Ethel and our good friend Edith Yoder with him. I have heard that they had some very interesting experiences on this western trip.

As previously mentioned, I decided to go to Juniata College soon after graduation from high school. At that time, I had little comprehension of what college would be like. I did receive some valuable advice from Imogene Hanawalt, sister of James, who had been a student at Juniata and was returning that fall. I remember her advice: "Get a good start, learn to know your teachers, work hard, and everything will work out well."

This I tried to do but was hindered somewhat due to the fact that I needed to earn some money. I started to do some work at the silk mill at night and went to classes in the daytime. This did not work out well for me since I needed more sleep than I was able to get by this arrangement. Thus, after six weeks, I quit the work at the silk mill. My college grades started to improve after that.

In order to become acquainted with some of the college officials, my good friend, Thomas E. Zook, had one of his men, Herman Harshbarger, take me to Huntingdon to visit the college. There I recall meeting with Dr. C. C. Ellis, later to become the college president, and with J. W. Swigart, a loyal supporter of Juniata. When it was time for college classes to start, I went with Mr. Hanawalt and his daughter Imogene in their car to the college.

The first year I roomed in what was called the "frat house," though there were no fraternities at Juniata. There were six of us who roomed in this small house sharing a common bathroom. We went across the street to take a shower in Founders Hall.

When I was a freshman at Juniata, there were strict rules for us. We were never allowed to walk on the grass and I learned my lesson well, for to this day, I seldom walk on the grass on a college campus. Dates for freshmen were allowed only on Sunday afternoon from 3:00 to 5:00. I can still recall one of my roommates taking Gladys Mikesell, a freshman girl, out for a walk. I asked her about this event at one of our recent reunions. She had completely forgotten about it. As for myself, I was too bashful to even think of taking a girl out on a date.

One thing that stands out in my memory is talking to Wilmer Kensinger, who was called "Preach," since he was studying to be a minister. He was then taking calculus, of which I knew nothing, but which intrigued me since I was interested in mathematics.

This reminds me of Freddie Witmer who became a close friend of mine, and who had me help him with his algebra. He considered this subject to be very difficult while I thought it to be easy. Freddie and I have had correspondence over the years and he has frequently reminded me of the fact that I was a great help to him that first year as he struggled with algebra.

Another good friend that first year at Juniata was Edward Dugan from New York City. He was very different from most of the college students. I remember of frequently going to his room in Founders Hall where I very much enjoyed eating some of the good bread made by the Dugan Baking Company owned by his father. A number of college students worked for this company to help out with college expenses. This number included two of my classmates, Bernard King and Daniel Ziegler, both of whom are my distant cousins through the King family.

Edward had some severe emotional problems so he did not return to Juniata after his first year. However, we kept in contact with each other with the result that during the summer of 1929 I was invited by Edward's father to go to Sea Cliff, Long Island, where they lived, to be a companion to Edward. This I did for a period of two weeks and had an interesting experience though I felt that I did very little for my friend. At the end of my visit, Edward was to go with me to my home, but he left me as we changed trains in New York. I never felt right about this since I felt that I should not leave Edward, but I had a commitment to return to my home in Belleville.

During my freshman year, I became acquainted with Albert Corman from Windber, who also worked at the silk mill. He continued working there for the entire academic year. Evidently he could get along with less sleep than I for he worked five or six hours per night for six days per week. The wages were thirty cents per hour. This we considered a fair wage at the time.

Al Corman and I decided to room together the following year. We lived close to the campus in what was called the orphanage. There we fired the furnace for which we received our room rent. We continued to do this for three years. I consider Al Corman as one of my very best friends. We both went out for track, he running the two-mile and I the one-mile race. He won his letter by coming in first in an intercollegiate track meet while I was never able to have that distinction. Later we both went out for debate and in our senior year we were the captains of the two men's debating teams. Al died five years after graduation, but I will always cherish his memories. I continue to correspond with his widow, Helen Wink.

This reminds me of the fact that two of my closest friends, James Hanawalt and Albert Corman, died at an early age. Following my freshman year at Juniata, I went to my home in Belleville where Clayton and I painted a number of houses and barns during the summer months. Business was good those years before the Great Depression.

It was during my sophomore year in college that I decided to major in physics since I found out that it was in that area of science that the most mathematics was used. I had always liked mathematics and I like it to this day. I have often said that I wish I had nothing to do except mathematics. I should add that I have found a number of other interesting things to do in life so I have not given my entire time to the study of mathematics.

My first girlfriend at Juniata was Mary Cook from Waynesboro who was a freshman while I was a sophomore. I had a number of dates with her and we had many interesting conversations. We were never very serious so in my junior year I looked around for another girl.

I well remember how John Saylor and I saw two girls who we thought were very nice. We decided to ask them for dates one Sunday afternoon; John took Margaret Baker and I took her sister Dorothy Baker, who later became my wife. John and Margaret did not get along very well. She thought that he was too much of a sissy. However, I went with Dorothy all of my junior year and we had very wonderful times together. She was the first and only girl whom I truly loved. I will never forget the Christmas vacation of my junior year when I worked for a plumber who never paid me, and how thrilled I was to receive love letters from Dorothy. I did not complain of the loss of a little money since I had something of far greater value.

My mother did not approve of my dating Dorothy. This was a big problem for me since I loved Dorothy and yet wished to please my mother. In the fall of 1929 when I returned to college, I had to tell Dorothy that I felt that we should discontinue our relationship since Mother was so much opposed. I well recall how on one Sunday morning I told her this and we left feeling very sad. This was a major burden for some time, but I did not know how to solve the problem.

In the spring of 1929, I did not leave Huntingdon until after commencement, for the juniors had duties to perform as a part of the commencement exercises. The two previous years I had left the college as soon as final examinations were completed. It was during the summer of 1929 that Clayton and I had our best painting business.

I remember how we often worked twelve hours a day from 6:00 a.m. to 6:30 p.m. with one-half hour off for lunch. As previously stated, Uncle Jake worked for us that summer as we traveled back and forth in his Model T Ford. We were so busy that summer that we worked very little for Isaac B. Zook on the farm.

In October of that year, the big crash on the stock market occurred, but most of us barely knew that it happened. However, we learned of it later when many were unable to get work. In my own case I was spared the difficulties of the Depression. I attended Rutgers University in New Brunswick, New Jersey, and had a steady income due to my graduate assistantship.

After my breakup with Dorothy, I began going with another girl, Lois Harner, a member of my college class. We were never very serious in our relationship, though we did enjoy many good times together. During both my junior and senior years in college, I was one of the student assistants in the physics laboratory. I recall how Professor Yoder, our instructor, had first chosen Wilbur Little as the student physics assistant. However, he felt that his academic load would be too heavy if he accepted that position. It was then offered to me and I was glad for this offer since it led to a graduate assistantship in physics at Rutgers University at the close of my senior year. Again I think of the fact that little things often greatly affect our lives. If I had not had this assistantship at Juniata College, I may never have had the opportunity of attending Rutgers and there receiving the Doctors degree in physics. Thus I may never have had the opportunity of becoming a college professor.

A former Juniatian, Rufus Reber, whom I later found out was one of my relatives, had done such good work at Rutgers that the department head there wanted more persons from Juniata College. Thus it was that both Don Hill, who had graduated a year earlier, and I became graduate students at Rutgers starting in the fall of 1930.

During the second semester of my senior year, I was very busy, for in addition to my duties as a physics assistant, I was captain of the debate team, was on the track team, and was in the play, "As You Like It," which was given near commencement time.

I must mention a special event which took place just before commencement. My mother had bought a new Chrysler car which I was using. Wilfred Stauffer, Esther Harley, Lois Harner, and I took John Sharpe to Everett to investigate a teaching position. On the way back, I was driving too fast around a curve and the car was near the edge of the road with the result that the car overturned and started to burn. We quickly had the fire under control but we were all shook up quite a bit. Somehow we were able to get back to college in time for our commencement activities. John got his job so our mission was accomplished, but I had a bill to be paid and the car was to be repaired. My mother and the family had to hire another car to take them to the commencement activities. We were all thankful that our lives were saved.

It was not until the summer of 1930 that I realized that the Depression had started. Painting jobs were scarce so Clayton and I did not have work all that summer. Later Clayton decided to work for Tom Yoder who had a threshing rig. Thus I was left alone to paint a house in Belleville shortly before I went to Rutgers. I was painting near the school ground and I well recall the noise made by the children as they played at noon and at recess time. I never had realized how much noise children make at recess time.

Clayton and Mother took me to New Brunswick in his truck where I started graduate work in physics. This was a novel experience for me. The work in graduate school was quite different from that at college. I felt that I was fairly well prepared and yet I wished that I had better preparation. By diligent work we were able to succeed but the going was tough at times.

I especially remember the professor in mathematics who used to send us to the blackboard with problems. He was very stern and demanded that we always appear in class on time. His name was Professor Brasefield. We did learn a lot of things which were of use later in our physics courses.

I met Don Hill soon after arriving in New Brunswick and he was my roommate for the next two years. We often studied our lessons together and lived in a house not far from the physics building. I remember how Don was lamenting the fact that he had been out of school for the past year. Professor George Winchester, head of the physics department, assured him that he would have no difficulty if he just applied himself.

The first year we took two mathematics courses, analysis and functions of a complex variable. The analysis course was really a course in advanced calculus which was useful in our physics courses. All the other work was in the field of physics. Both Don and I found ourselves to be quite busy that first year.

I should say something about the work involved in my graduate assistantship. For the first year, I helped in the laboratories and also with the apparatus in the weekly physics demonstrations. Starting with the second year I was given the assignment of teaching one section of sophomore physics. This I continued to do for the remaining three years.

During these years, I had an undergraduate assistant to help with the laboratory work. I was given very little supervision. The only help I had was in making final examinations which was done by the joint efforts of a number of faculty. This teaching experience was very good for me though I often wished for more help. This is one of the criticisms I have of college teaching. I feel that young teachers should be given much more supervision.

During my second year of graduate study, during Christmas vacation, I started going with a neighbor girl from Belleville. Her name was Thelma Stoltzfus, the daughter of John Stoltzfus, who lived on Trella Street. I went with her several times to what we called Literary Society. In the spring of 1931, after I had decided to return to Dorothy, I had to tell Thelma of that situation. I recall that she wept as I told her this news.

I started my research during my third year at Rutgers. The physics department had received a small vacuum spectrograph from Germany. I made use of this instrument in my work with thin metallic films under the supervision of Dr. Robert Atkinson. My experiment was to discover the transparency of thin metallic films in the ultraviolet. I spent most of two years on this experiment, attempting to work with all the different metals.

At first I had a great deal of difficulty in obtaining a satisfactory vacuum system. I also had considerable difficulty in obtaining very thin films of the various metals. At this time I worked in the same room with Don Hill who was involved in another experiment on the characteristics of solid mercury.

A little later I moved my apparatus to another room where I was the only occupant. It was in this room that I had a dangerous explosion which might have ended my life. It seems that I had just the right proportion of hydrogen and oxygen to have an explosion. This did occur when I turned on my source of illumination. The result was that my entire system was destroyed so I had to start over. This is the life of the experimental scientist. One simply learns to start over again.

After two years' work, I felt that I was ready to write up my results, but my professor was not satisfied. The result was that I repeated my results during the summer of 1934 and therefore did not receive my degree until the end of the summer session. I well remember how I typed up my thesis at the end of the summer. I spent one night doing this and was very happy when it was completed. My paper was later published in the journal known as *The Journal of the Optical Society of America*.

I now return to the spring of 1931 when I received a letter from Dorothy Baker, my girlfriend during my junior year at college. This was a big surprise to me and I answered immediately. We continued to correspond so that I went to see her at her home near Martinsburg that spring vacation. However, she had gone shopping with some of her family. I was greatly disappointed and returned to Belleville. I did talk to her father and the hired hand.

We continued our correspondence and both of us decided to attend summer school at Juniata College that summer. I was interested in learning some French, looking forward to passing the French test which was a requirement for the Ph.D degree. Dorothy was interested in completing her college work in three years so she went to summer school for several years. We had a very fine time together that summer and then decided to go again the following summer.

I had been contacted by Dr. I. Harvey Brumbaugh to teach physics during the summer of 1932. I consented to do this and also studied French and again Dorothy and I had a wonderful summer together. These were two of the happiest summers of my life. I well remember that Mary Replogle was one of my physics students. She was a good friend of both Dorothy and her sister Margaret. She later married Ralph Over and we have been good friends ever since those eventful years.

Don Hill, my roommate for the first two years of graduate work, was married in the summer of 1932 so I lost my good roommate. He and I have been good friends ever since. Dorothy and I visited him in his home in California. He retired a number of years ago and is now dead. I roomed with two different graduate students during my third year of graduate work. During a part of this time we were in one of the college dormitories, which was an interesting experience.

I spent most of the summer of 1933 studying for my final examinations for the Doctor's degree. Clayton and I had very little business in the painting line that summer due to the severity of the Depression. It was that summer that Dorothy and I were married in the home of my Uncle Eli Kanagy. He was the minister who performed the ceremony.

We had a small audience consisting of members of our two families. A few days later we were invited to Dorothy's home for a big dinner at which time we took Uncle Eli Kanagy and his wife with us. I remember how Dorothy and I were very busy the next few days canning fruit to take with us to New Brunswick where we were to make our home for the next year as I completed my work for the Doctor's degree.

We started housekeeping in a small apartment that fall where we had to share the bathroom with several young men who lived next door. I remember how surprised the landlady was to see how much canned fruit we brought with us. When we did empty some of those cans, we went to the market, bought pears, and canned them for future use. As an indication of how prices have changed from that day to this, I recall that we paid twenty-five cents for a basket of pears and we were able to buy rice at a price of ten cents for three pounds.

In order to help out with our finances, we boarded two graduate students for most of that academic year. I continued to work in the physics department that year as did Don Hill, my former roommate. His work on his research did not go so well that year with the result that he spent an extra year at Rutgers University. Thus, while he graduated from college a year before I did, it took him an extra year to obtain his Doctor's degree.

It is interesting that he followed me to Elizabethtown College where I had my first teaching experience. I taught there for two years while he was there for four years. I remembered that I considered going back to that college after Don Hill left; however, Harold S. Bender. Dean at Goshen College was very determined to keep me at Goshen. So I stayed there until 1958.

Dorothy and I had a very interesting year together in New Brunswick. I was kept busy with my work in the physics department and often spent a good part of the night in the laboratory. I remember how we walked the streets for our recreation. I also continued to play handball at the University, a game I had started several years before that time.

Don Hill and I often played tennis, but we were unable to keep up with some of the professors who were quite skilled at that game. Dorothy and I went to the church service at a Baptist church in the city where Don Hill and I had often gone before our marriage. I well remember a Sunday school class in that church where we studied the lives of the popes from the earliest time up to date. I learned much about the Catholic Church at those discussions.

Our first child, Harold Eugene, was born in the spring of 1934. This was a very important event in our lives. I recall taking Dorothy to the hospital early in the morning and then working that day in the physics laboratory. That evening I had my first glimpse of my firstborn at which time he was crying vigorously.

We got along fine with our baby and at the end of the school year Dorothy and our son went to her home in Martinsburg while I stayed in New Brunswick to complete my research project. Thus I was left alone for a number of weeks before I returned to Pennsylvania.

Upon completion of my graduate work in physics, I began looking around for a job. Remember that this was the time of the

Great Depression and jobs were very difficult to find. I wrote to Goshen College and to Eastern Mennonite College, but they had nothing to offer me at that time. I should add that S. C. Yoder, president of Goshen College, did suggest that I take the place of Professor S. W. Witmer who was then on leave doing graduate work at Indiana University. His field was biology and I had no preparation in that area so I did not apply for that position. I joined teachers' agencies but only had one notice of a vacancy which I did not get.

Thus, in the fall of 1934, Dorothy and I moved back with her parents. I worked for a time for Jonathan Yoder on the farm for $1.00 per day. I was never without a job, but the wages were rather low. Many persons were without a job at that time, but I wonder how many were willing to work at a very low wage.

In my own case, after I had earned over $30.00, and with all of it in my pocket, I lost all of it while hauling logs for firewood on the mountain near Belleville. Since this was quite a loss for me at that time, I walked up the mountain and was able to find my billfold containing my money. This was very exciting and I have often thought about this loss of a month's wages with no prospect of having work in the future.

The Lord does provide. In December 1934, I started to teach under the government's program of "Adult Education." This was intended to provide employment for teachers who were without work. A group of us from Belleville taught one night per week in five different towns in Mifflin County. This continued to the following spring when the painting business started.

In the meantime, Dorothy and I bought some second-hand furniture and moved into a house on Trella Street in Belleville where we lived from February to April.

We then moved into the house owned by Jonathan A. Yoder which was located next door to my mother's home. We lived there until the following September when we moved to Elizabethtown, Pennsylvania. There at the college I had secured a position as professor of physics and mathematics. I also served as dean of men. I was able to secure this position through my alma mater, Juniata College.

President Schlosser of Elizabethtown College had asked Juniata College to recommend someone for the position of professor of physics and mathematics, and Juniata had recommended me. Thus I was able to obtain a teaching position without any searching on my part. I feel that this was the leading of the Lord.

Clayton, John, and I had started to paint early in the spring of 1935. While in the process of painting a house in Lewistown we had our accident previously mentioned. Since we had little money to pay our hospital bill, we were able to pay it by painting a number of rooms in the hospital.

In June of that year, our daughter Theodosia Ruth was born. I remember how Dorothy had helped to pick cherries the previous day. I also recall how I had Emma Yoder, a nurse who lived close to us, take Dorothy to the hospital in Lewistown while I went to work painting. I did not see our newborn daughter until the evening of June 25 when she had been born in the morning.

I was very busy that summer since Clayton did little work and I was in charge of the business. We hired several painters and were able to paint a number of houses. I particularly remember one man who helped us that summer. He was a skilled painter but was so slow at his work. While he would paint one side of a building, I was able to paint three sides. However, at times his skill showed up as happened when I was unable to please a lady in Lewistown. He knew exactly what to do so that we were able to do this job in a satisfactory manner.

On September 1, 1935, Dorothy and I, together with our two infants, were taken to Elizabethtown by a friend whose name was Walter Stalter. We had our furniture taken by another friend, Irvin Yoder, who had married Dorothy Zook, the daughter of Isaac B. Zook for whom I had worked so many summers. We lived on the college grounds in a double house which was located in an orchard. Professor and Mrs. E. G. Meyer, music instructors, lived in the other half of the house. We got along fine for two years.

Up to this time we had not owned an automobile and did not buy one until the following spring when we bought a 1933 Chevrolet which we kept until 1940. We did not do much traveling those days. At Christmas time, we were taken by a college student to Everett where we were met by Dorothy's sister Verna. Thus we enjoyed that Christmas season at Dorothy's home near Martinsburg.

We had a very fine experience at Elizabethtown College where we lived near the home of President Schlosser. I recall how his younger daughter often took care of our daughter Theodosia Ruth. She seemed to enjoy doing this bit of service.

I not only taught all of the physics and mathematics courses, but I also served as dean of men. These duties kept me rather busy. I remember how Professor Shortess, biology teacher, had constructed a six-inch telescope which I used on a number of occasions. This experience aroused my interest so that I ground and polished a six-inch mirror, but I never did get the telescope constructed.

It was during my second year at Elizabethtown that I became interested in genealogy. For years my mother was very much interested in this subject, so I guess that I inherited some of this interest. I actually started my work in this area when on the occasion of our visit to Goshen, Indiana. There we were visiting at the home of Jesse Smucker whose wife was a second cousin of my mother's.

I recall how I started by obtaining the family record of Jesse Smucker. A few years later he was our neighbor when we lived in the country near Goshen. I decided to work on the family name of King since my mother was a King and I had seen nothing on that family. At that time, I had little comprehension of the work required to complete a family history. I have never lost my interest in this subject, but put it aside after a few years due to the press of other duties.

The government had a special program for students during those years so that I had a student do most of the detailed genealogical work. This continued at Goshen College where I had several students do work for me in genealogy. I will never forget the fine work of Dorothy Snapp who later married Don McCammon and went to China as a missionary.

During my second year at Elizabethtown, I had a letter from President S. C. Yoder of Goshen College inviting me to come to Goshen College to teach mathematics. Professor D. A. Lehman, who had taught there for many years, had become ill so that they needed a replacement. Dorothy and I thought about this for some time, talked it over with our parents, and finally decided to leave Elizabethtown and go to Goshen. Don Hill, who had been my roommate at Rutgers for two years, took my place at Elizabethtown.

We had my cousin Sam Esh from Belleville move our household goods to Goshen. I remember that it took practically all our money to pay for this moving. Goshen College had made arrangements for a house for us in which to live. It was owned by another Harold Hartzler, one of my distant cousins. He had a son by the name of Harold, and since I had a son with the same name, you can imagine how our mail became mixed up during that first year I lived in Goshen. The house in which we

37

lived was on Waverly Street near the college but just across the street from the railroad. I remember that we heard the noise of the trains on many nights.

I also remember that our furniture was scattered over the front lawn as we first saw the house. With the help of some friends, we soon had the furniture arranged in our home. The first evening we were invited for dinner at the home of Paul and Bertha Bender. Paul was professor of physics and also registrar at Goshen College. We have been good friends ever since. He was one of the few staff members at Goshen College with whom I had corresponded while I was still at Rutgers.

I had considered teaching at a Mennonite college for some time so that I felt that I was now at the place where God wanted me. At Goshen, I had been hired to teach mathematics, but after the first year, I also taught some physics courses, and after 1949 I also taught the beginning astronomy course.

Dean Harold S. Bender suggested that I take some more graduate work in mathematics since that was to be my teaching field and I had only minimal training in that area at Rutgers. Therefore I attended Penn State during the sumer of 1938, and, also, the University of Michigan in the summer of 1940.

I recall how I had a wreck on my way home at the close of the summer session of 1940. I had Jake Sudermann and his wife Hilda and son John Jacob with me. Since my car needed repair, we called to Goshen for some help. Professor John C. Wenger from Goshen was kind enough to come to meet us and to take us back to Goshen.

I had always liked mathematics so I was happy to be able to teach in that area. I will always remember my first algebra course which I taught at Goshen. Roman Gingerich, later to become head of the physical education department, was one of my students. He later told me how I called a number of them "sixth graders." This was due to the fact that they were so ill prepared for college work in mathematics. One of my students, Ivan Baumgartner, was especially brilliant. I recall how he easily solved a difficult problem which I had given to the class. He later became a medical doctor and died at a very young age.

After living on Waverly Street for seven months, we moved into a house on Main Street. This house had been built by another Hartzler, formerly from Belleville, a cousin of my father. Here we lived for one year after which we moved to our country home on the Fish Lake Road. Dorothy and I had decided that we would like to raise our family in the country, which was the reason for making this move. There we had an Amish neighbor, Elmer Miller, whose daughter later worked for us and whose wedding we attended.

My first office at Goshen College was on the third floor of Science Hall which I shared with Paul Bender. My classroom, however, was on the third floor of the Administration Building. Thus I had much walking between my office and my classroom. Later my office was changed to the second floor of Science Hall and my classroom was located on the same floor. There my office mate was Silas Hertzler, who was the chairman of the Education Department. He was working on family history so we shared a common interest in genealogy. I was able to help him with a number of Hartzler families. He completed his work called the *Hertzler-Hartzler Family History* and had it published in 1952. I purchased enough copies of this book so that I would have a copy for each of my children and grandchildren.

When we moved to the country, with added responsibilities, I discontinued my activities in this area and did not take it up again until I retired in 1976. Our home in the country was located three miles from Goshen and I recall how Dean Bender warned me that I would probably miss a number of classes due to the bad road conditions. As it happened, I never missed a class.

In the country, we had a cow and raised chickens, pigs, and rabbits. The story of the prank played on me by some of my college students has been told on a number of occasions. This concerns my cow which was taken to the college on Halloween night and tied to the door of my office in Science Hall. Actually, it was not a cow but a young heifer, which we had raised one summer.

The students had tried to put this heifer up on top of the administration building. After that attempt failed, they did put the animal on the second floor of the Science Hall. You can imagine the mess made during the night. Before my arrival the next morning, Jake Sudermann, who was professor of German, had taken the animal out of the Science Hall and tied her to a tree outside.

I was greatly disturbed over this incident and went to the office of President Ernest Miller to see what could be done about it. He offered no help whatsoever, so that evening I borrowed a small trailer from Sam Yoder, a neighbor in the country, and took the heifer home. Some years later one of my former students wrote to me about this incident and sent a check for $5.00 to ease his conscience. At the present time this student is a leader in the Mennonite Church. I have never found out the identity of the other students.

Among my extracurricular activities at Goshen was that of serving as judge of a number of debates. John Umble was then the debate coach and he encouraged me to often serve as one of the judges. I well recall the debate tournaments held at Manchester College. There hundreds of students from colleges in the Midwest would come to debate each winter. We were asked to judge three or four debates on one weekend. I enjoyed this but felt that it was a rather heavy assignment.

I should say something about our trip west in the summer of 1941. In August of that year, my mother, my sister Ethel, Dorothy, and I took a trip to visit my sister Carrie and her husband Kenneth Dodd who then lived in Eugene, Oregon. This was a very interesting experience for all of us. On our way west we stopped at Detroit Lakes, Minnesota, to visit some cousins. In order to reach my sister as soon as possible I did a foolish thing by driving all night with the result that I went to sleep at the wheel. We crossed a four-lane highway and went into a wheatfield. None of us were injured and little damage was done to the car. We visited a number of cousins in the Williamette Valley and attended a church service at the Zion Mennonite Church near Hubbard.

My son Jonathan Edward was born the evening of July 11, 1944. I well recall taking Dorothy to the office of Dr. Young in Goshen. At that time our two older children were at Camp Mack, the Brethren camp near Goshen.

I was a member of the Athletic Committee and often served as one of the judges at the annual inter-class track meet. In those days we had no intercollegiate sports at Goshen College. Only in debate and in oratory, did our students compete with those from other colleges. How times have changed!

World War II came and this definitely had an effect on our student body. A number joined the Army and others went to C.P.S. (Civilian Public Service) camps where they performed services considered to be good for the country. It was finally decided that some faculty changes should be made. A number became directors of C.P.S. camps while others went abroad.

Paul Erb, who had been teaching English, went to Scottdale, Pennsylvania, to become editor of the *Gospel Herald*. This left an opening in the English department. A teacher exchange was made between Bluffton College and Goshen College. Naomi Brenneman came to Goshen for a year, while I went to Bluffton for the academic year 1945-46. This was a very interesting experience for our family. Our younger son, Jonathan, was just one year old while Harold Eugene and Theo were in grade school. At Bluffton my family lived in the men's dormitory since there were few male students left due to the War. We had a football team which included practically all the boys in the college. The first night in the dormitory was an interesting experience. Our son Jonathan became very restless so my wife got up to see what the difficulty might be. We discovered that we were infected with bed bugs; we had a fine time getting rid of those creatures.

At Bluffton, I had about the same duties which I had at Goshen, teaching one course in physics and several in mathematics. I had the pleasure of having a very unusual student at Bluffton named Ronald Rich. He was a freshman that year and took all the mathematics and science courses he could. He took physics by examination, worked on a special qualitative scheme by himself, and often observed the stars with me at night.

I recall how Ronald started with college algebra, went right through the calculus, and took differential equations that year. I would say that Ronald Rich was the best student I had in my entire teaching experience of forty-one years. Later he received the Ph.D. in chemistry from the University of Chicago, taught at Bethel College in Kansas, went to the Christian University in Japan, and later became dean at Bluffton College. He is now a scholar in residence at Bluffton. I had the pleasure of spending several days with him and his wife Elaine at the annual meeting of the American Scientific Affiliation held at Taylor University in 1980.

To supplement our income, my wife and I started to take produce to the farmer's market, first in Goshen and later in Elkhart. This was originally Dorothy's project, but finally I did most of the work, selling chickens, eggs, vegetables, cakes, cottage cheese, and other items. Often our two older children went along to help. This became quite a business so that by this means we were able to pay for our country home. We sold this home in 1948 at a good profit.

To help with our work in the country we had a hired girl for some time. I should add a word about this neighbor girl, Polly Miller. She was a very good worker, the daughter of an Amish deacon who lived next to us, and she worked for us until she was married. We were all invited to this Amish wedding so we went and spent most of the day, first going to one Amish home where a long sermon was preached in German. After this, the wedding ceremony was performed and we went to the home of the bride where all the guests were served as much food as they could eat. This lasted until about four o'clock in the afternoon when we went home. This was the only Amish wedding which I ever attended.

I did go to several Amish church services near my home in Belleville, Pennsylvania. These people, of whom I am a direct descendant, always hold their church services in their homes. Sometimes they hold them in the barn when the weather is favorable. They do not have Sunday school and usually have church services every two weeks. On the other Sundays they usually go visiting.

The Amish are related to the Mennonites, a division occurring in 1693 over the question of the ban or shunning. They take very literally the Scripture in I Corinthians 5:11 where we are told not to keep company or to eat with those who practice sin. There were a number of other issues which helped to divide the groups.

I have discovered that all of my immigrant ancestors were members of the Amish Church. It was in the lifetime of my grandparents that the change was slowly made from the Amish to the Mennonite Church. I can recall when my home church near Belleville in Mifflin County was known as the Amish Mennonite Church. J. W. Yoder, the author of *Rosanna of the Amish*, always insisted that he was a member of the Amish Mennonite Church, since he was a member of my home church, now known as the Maple Grove Mennonite Church.

At this point I must mention an organization which greatly influenced my life. I was first introduced to this wonderful group of Christian men and women by Professor Paul Erb. He gave me a small pamphlet entitled, *The Story of the American Scientific Affiliation*. This aroused my interest so that I wrote to the secretary, Dr. Irving A. Cowperthwaite of Milton, Massachusetts. Even though he did not know me, he recommended me as a member of the ASA to the executive council. The recommendation was accepted with the result that I became a member of the ASA in 1944 at a time when the total membership was forty.

The American Scientific Affiliation is a group of Christians who are attempting to relate all aspects of science with the Holy Scriptures. The statement on the program of every annual meeting from 1946 to 1968 stated: "A group of Christians, involved in science, devoting themselves to the task of reviewing, preparing, and distributing information on the authenticity, historicity, and scientific aspects of the Holy Scriptures in order that the faith of many in Jesus Christ may be firmly established."

I have been active in this Christian group since I became a member in 1944. I remember how that I was very much interested in a God-centered science course given by Professor Birkey at Bluffton College. I gave a paper on that subject at the first annual ASA meeting held at Wheaton College in the summer of 1946. The ASA had been organized during the first week of September in 1941. Due to travel restrictions during World War II, no meetings were held until 1946.

I well recall that first annual ASA meeting when I was able to personally meet members and officers of this group of scientists, all vitally concerned about the Christian faith. I especially remember Dr. Walter L. Wilson from Kansas City. He was a wonderful man of God who seemed to know the proper moment to present the claims of Christ to an unknown person. Dr. Wilson explained the seeming contradiction in the Bible concerning the ratio of the circumference to the diameter of a circle. This is found in I Kings 7:23 and II Chronicles 4:2 where we find the following: "Also he made a molten sea of ten cubits from brim to brim, round in compass, and five cubits the height thereof; and a line of thirty cubits did compass it round about." Dr. Wilson mentioned that the thickness of the molten sea was a handbreadth, which could easily explain the discrepancy since we know that the ratio of the circumference to the diameter of a circle is 3.14 and not 3.0.

Of course, there may be other explanations, but the one given by Dr. Wilson intrigued me. I should also mention that I had the pleasure of meeting Dr. Cowperthwaite who had recommended me for membership. We have been good friends ever since. I have been in his home, spoken in his church, and last met him at Wheaton College in 1991.

The second annual meeting of the ASA was held at Taylor University not far from Goshen. It was there that I first met F. Alton Everest who was then the president of the ASA. Alton and I have been closely associated in work relating to the ASA since that time.

I have held every office in the ASA. Starting in 1949, I was the chairman of the program committee when we met in Los Angeles. The next year at Goshen College I served as general chairman of the meeting. That same year, 1950, I was elected to the Executive Council. They elected me as secretary-treasurer. I served in this capacity for five years and witnessed a remarkable growth in membership.

Then I was re-elected a member of the Executive Council for another five years during which time I served as president. Upon my retirement as a member of the Executive Council, I was appointed to the newly created position of executive secretary which position I held for eleven years. At the end of that time, Bill Sisterson was elected as a full-time executive secretary. I had served on a part-time basis, keeping my position as a college teacher.

At the time of my retirement as an executive officer when the annual meeting was held in Toronto, I was honored by being given a plaque which reads:

H. Harold Hartzler
Man of wisdom and perseverance
Christian conviction, Humility and Love,
whose faithful service as Executive Secretary
strengthened the American Scientific Affiliation,
increasing its effectiveness to God the Creator
and to Jesus Christ the Savior.
August 23, 1972.

In the December 1972 issue of the *Journal of the American Scientific Affiliation*, there appeared a number of testimonies concerning my work for the ASA. Dick Bube, editor of the *Journal*, introduced these testimonies with the following:

"Once in a rare while the spirit of an entire organization is so captured by one individual that he becomes the very incarnation of that organization. The ASA has been blessed to have such a leader in the person of H. Harold Hartzler. For twenty-eight years a member of the ASA, he has been in positions of responsibility and leadership for the past twenty-one years. His own overview of thirty years of history was published in the *Journal ASA* March 1972. It is only appropriate that a few of the many of us who knew him and valued our friendship as Christian colleagues in science should take this opportunity to bear him tribute. This fall Harold passes on the responsibility of Executive Secretary of the ASA to Bill Sisterson, the ASA's first full-time

Harold and Dorothy Hartzler with their children.

Executive Secretary. We look forward to our association in the future and know that Harold's experience and counsel will be a continuing source of inspiration."

There followed statements of appreciation of my work by Donald C. Boardman, Gary R. Collins, Irving A. Cowperthwaite, F. Alton Everest, Robert B. Fisher, Charles Hatfield, Walter R. Hearn, Marlin Kreider, John A. McIntyre, Claude R. Stipe, and Henry Weaver. Henry suggested that I had been known to my students at Goshen College as H^3, I should be voted a triple honor, Executive Secretary Cum Laude Emeritus or perhaps Mr. (ASA)^3.

Since my work for the ASA took so much of my time, more of which I should have devoted to my family, my children often called the ASA the "American Scientific Affliction." I must admit that this has been a difficulty in my life, how to properly divide my time between caring for my family and doing many things to which I thought the Lord has called me. My older son, Harold Eugene, on a recent visit to Mankato, stated that he felt that he never really knew me. So we spent considerable time together in the spring of 1981.

When our family returned to Goshen in the spring of 1946 from our year at Bluffton, the War having ended the previous year, we found ourselves very busy at our country home and at the college. That fall the boys were returning from the Army so that many colleges were crowded with students. Purdue University set up special classes at the high school in Elkhart. Dr. Glen R. Miller of Goshen College and I taught some of those, he in chemistry and I in mathematics. This continued for two nights per week for the academic year 1946-1947.

Grade school teachers were in demand so my wife Dorothy taught grades 4 to 8 in the village of Benton, not far from Goshen. In order to help out with the work at home, we arranged to have a college student, Leonard Smucker and his wife, live with us that academic year.

As I previously stated, we were raising quite a number of chickens at that time. We sold dressed chickens and eggs at the Farmer's Market in Elkhart, thus our two families had a very busy and interesting year. Leonard went on to seminary and became a minister. We have kept in touch with the Smucker family ever since. They now live in Hesston, Kansas.

One of the arrangements made by Goshen College for the benefit of the faculty was a system of sabbatical leaves. We were to teach a period of ten years before the first sabbatical was granted and then have one every seven years. Since it did not suit the college for me to have a sabbatical at the end of ten years, I waited until I had completed eleven years of teaching.

I decided to go to Arizona to study astronomy during my sabbatical year. There were two reasons for this decision. For some time I had been afflicted with asthma and I had heard that the dry climate in Arizona was good for those suffering with asthma. Second, I had been hired by Goshen College to take the place of D. A. Lehman who had been teaching both mathematics and astronomy. I had always been interested in this area of study but had taken no courses in astronomy. Thus, I felt that my sabbatical would allow me time to study astronomy. I had visited the

University of Arizona in the spring of 1948 and was offered a fellowship in astronomy. This was all I needed to encourage me to go to Arizona for one year.

We radically changed our living habits from the country where we had plenty of room to a travel trailer in which we lived in Tucson, Arizona.

During the summer of 1948, we purchased several travel trailers and sold them in Pennsylvania before moving to Arizona. There we found a suitable court where we lived for nine months. We had a number of trials and tribulations on this trip to Arizona. One day as we traveled in Texas when the weather was very hot, we decided to stop along the road in order to rest and cool off. I had neglected to notice that we were on an upward grade and two wheels of our car were on the soft berm. When we tried to start again we were unable to get the trailer moving. We then disconnected it and went thirty miles to a service station for some help. The attendant used his truck to help us get started.

This caused a delay of several hours, so by the time we arrived in El Paso it was dark and we were unable to find a place in a trailer park. We parked on the street for the night and started early the next morning. We reached Tuscon the next evening. That first night we found a trailer park on the southern part of the city. We stayed there only one night and then spent the next day looking for a trailer park not too far from the University.

It was very hot when we arrived in Tucson, about 115 degrees in the daytime and 85 degrees at night. We decided to go on and visit my sister Carrie in Newport, Oregon. We spent a very enjoyable time with Carrie and her family. Upon our return, I spent a number of days in the library working on a paper to be given at the annual meeting of the ASA. The title of the paper was: "The Nature of Mathematics," which was published in the first issue of the *Journal ASA*.

That year I traveled by train from Tucson to Grand Rapids, Michigan, where the ASA met at Calvin College. There are two things that I will always remember about this meeting. The first was the conversation I had on the train from Chicago to Grand Rapids when I found my good friend Irving A. Cowperthwaite on the same train. The second was the wonderful reception we were given by the local committee consisting of Professors Karstens and Monsma. It was also at this meeting that we had the pleasure of first seeing the publication called *Modern Science and Christian Faith*, edited by F. Alton Everest and written by a number of ASA members. I recall how excited we were over this publication, the product of our labors over a number of years.

After my trip to Grand Rapids, I started my work in astronomy at the University of Arizona. The astronomy department consisted of only two professors and myself as a fellow. I took several astronomy courses, did some observing with the 40-inch reflector in the Steward Observatory, and assisted in the laboratory work which was a part of the introductory astronomy course. I also did some observing with the smaller telescopes on the campus with a smaller telescope located about ten miles from the campus.

I remember Professor Luyten of the University of Minnesota who came to Arizona several times each year to do some observing. He was an authority on white dwarf stars which are small but very hot. While he was there I did not have the use of the 40-inch telescope. After a few months I was given a special problem studying eclipsing variables under the direction of Professor Brad Wood.

For three months, February through April of 1949, I made observations of the star YY Canis Minoris. This star, invisible to the naked eye, is an eclipsing variable with a period of slightly more than one day. It is located near the bright star Procyon in the constellation Canis Minor or the Little Dipper. In my work I made use of a photoelectric photometer attached to the 40-inch reflector.

When I went to Arizona, I had the idea that every night would be clear and suitable for observation. I found out that this was not so, due to disturbances in the atmosphere. Thus, on a number of nights when I would open up the telescope and get set for observing, I would discover that some clouds were present with the result that no satisfactory observations were possible. On other nights the smoke from the passing train would make my work very difficult. I found that patience is a wonderful virtue of the astronomer. In spite of some difficulties, I was able to obtain sufficient data to draw a satisfactory light curve from which I was able to determine the period of this variable star. I presented some of my results at the Southwest Section of the AAAS and also at the fall meeting of the Indiana Academy of Science.

I should add that an eclipsing variable consists of two stars revolving around their center of mass. The result is that at certain times they eclipse one another while at other times the light from both stars is visible. The two stars are comparatively close together so that they appear as one star. The only way we have of determining whether they form an eclipsing variable is by the form of the light curve. We can predict by theory the form of the light curve which then can be checked by observation. There are many variable stars of different types which can be distinguished from one another by means of a telescope.

Before the end of the spring term, I received a letter from F. Alton Everest asking me to serve as Program Chairman for the annual ASA meeting. This was quite a challenge to me and I was happy to accept. I did a considerable amount of correspondence in order to arrange the program for the ASA meeting that summer. I recall that I completed the assignment in the summer after we had moved to Pennsylvania.

At Dorothy's home that summer, I painted the buildings on the farm and also helped with the farm work for Mildred Dilling, Dorothy's sister, whose husband had died the previous winter.

The ASA meeting was held at Biola College in Los Angeles that summer. I traveled by bus from Goshen to Los Angeles. I took my family by car from Martinsburg to Goshen where we rented a new home.

I will always remember the ASA meeting of 1949 because of the number and excellence of the field trips. On one such trip, we took an entire day to visit the famous Mt. Polamar Observatory where is located the 200-inch telescope. Paul Bender and I took literature along with us to try to convince the Executive Council to hold the 1950 meeting at Goshen College.

In this we were successful and I was appointed General Chairman for that convention. In the meantime, Dorothy and I had purchased a new home in Goshen located on Plymouth Avenue.

At the close of the 1950 Convention, I was elected a member of the Executive Council of the ASA and then elected Secretary-Treasurer. This meant a great amount of additional work for me which continued for a number of years. I served in various offices of the ASA for a period of twenty-one years.

After my retirement, I have continued my interest in the work of the ASA and have only missed three meetings since the first one in 1946. I still write papers for the annual meetings of the ASA.

Beginning in the summer of 1950, I started a business of my own. I decided to go into the painting business since my services were no longer needed at Goshen College during the summer. My son Harold Eugene and I painted a number of houses in and around Goshen that summer. Later I hired a number of other

H. Harold Hartzler all ready to begin painting.

helpers and continued painting every summer through 1957. That summer I hired my son-in-law, Elvin Dale Yoder.

After returning from Arizona in the summer of 1949, I taught a number of courses in astronomy in addition to courses in mathematics at Goshen College. I very much enjoyed the teaching of astronomy and often took field trips. One that stands out in my memory was that which we took to the Yerkes Observatory in Wisconsin. We were very fortunate in that the observatory was reserved on this particular occasion for the use of the students from the University of Chicago. Thus my students and I were able to make visual observations using the 40-inch refractor, the largest of its type in the world. I recall the moon and rings of Saturn.

I continued to teach at Goshen College until the end of the first semester of the academic year 1957-58. My sabbatical was supposed to start in the fall of 1957. Due to the fact that my replacement, Albert Meyer, was in Europe and was not returning until January 1958, I agreed to begin the sabbatical at that time. I was to be given one and one-half years for the sabbatical.

I decided that I would like to try teaching at a different type of institution. Dorothy and I had visited two state colleges during the summer of 1958. Our first visit was at Eastern Illinois University where I was offered a position in the mathematics department.

The second visit was at Mankato State College where I was offered a position in the physics department. We liked the second one better than the first so I accepted the physics position. Mankato State wanted me to begin my duties in the fall of 1957 but agreed to wait until January 1958.

I should mention the wonderful reception we were given in Mankato on the occasion of our visit. Dr. Paul Miller, whom I had learned to know at Goshen College, and his wife Ann kept us in their home overnight. A number of the faculty members from Mankato State visited us in Paul Miller's home and there we had a frank discussion of the teaching conditions at the college, particularly with regard to the physics department.

President C. L. Crawford was very gracious when I visited him in his office. He immediately inquired about my religious denomination. Upon finding out that I was a Mennonite, he called the local Mennonite church in Mankato. This made a deep impression upon me. He then introduced me to Dr. Wissink who was both dean of the college and chairman of the physics department. I was also introduced to Dr. Ford, the chairman of the division of science and mathematics. He showed me through the science hall and explained my duties. All of this attention given to us by members of the faculty and by the administration greatly impressed Dorothy and me so we soon decided that we would try teaching at Mankato.

I had heard that one could expect much snow in Minnesota so I put snow tires on my car and we started for our new home in Mankato in January 1958. We used a U-haul trailer to move part of our goods. We also sent a number of things by freight.

I remember the scene when we left Goshen for Mankato— Dorothy and Harold Eugene's wife crying, and our 13-year-old son Jonathan not very anxious to leave home. We took two days to drive to Mankato, staying in a motel overnight and having a flat tire in the morning. We had several inches of snow on the way but finally landed at 121 Clark Street where we had rented the first floor of a large house. However, we could not have the use of the house for several days so we stayed in a motel in the meantime.

Again it was the Paul Miller family who befriended us by inviting us to their home for Sunday dinner. That day we went to the Methodist church and Sunday school with the Miller family. I started to teach my classes in physics on the following Monday morning, took Jonathan to his school, and then had him visit me in one of my classes. That term I taught general physics, thermodynamics, and modern physics. I took over these courses in the middle of the winter quarter from Dr. Ford and Dr. Wissink.

Mankato State was using the quarter system whereas all my previous experience had been the semester system. I cannot see the advantage of the quarter system except it allows for more flexibility for the students.

The following summer I taught two physics courses for a period of five weeks in what was called the first summer session. For most of my years at Mankato State from 1958 to 1976, I taught in the first summer session. This arrangement allowed our family to have a nice vacation each summer. We usually traveled to Pennsylvania to visit relatives and friends.

The summer teaching in 1959 was a special experience for me. At that period in history the United States was trying desperately to upgrade the teaching of science and mathematics at all levels. The National Science Foundation, established for this purpose, awarded many scholarships for faculty and students. I was a member of a committee of the science faculty charged with the responsibility of making a proposal to N. S. F. for a science teachers institute. Our request was granted and I was one of the teachers in this Institute. Our students were mainly high school science teachers.

We were also successful in getting a grant for high school students. This was a great delight to me since all of the students were very eager to learn and always asked for more. Since no examinations nor grades were given, this was a time of rich learning experience which I thoroughly enjoyed.

This was the summer when I started to play golf. Dr. Glen R. Miller, my colleague from Goshen College, was at Mankato State to teach chemistry to the high school students. He had been a golf enthusiast for years and we went out on a number of occasions at which time he tried to teach me some of the tricks in the game of golf. I have played golf on a number of occasions since, but I never did take much interest in the game and finally gave my clubs to my son Jonathan.

The Mennonite church in Mankato, previously mentioned, was replaced by a Baptist group by the time we had moved to Mankato. This church is now known as the Grace Baptist Church and has grown considerably during the past thirty years. My family and I had visited a number of churches in Mankato and soon decided to attend the Covenant Church in North Mankato.

We liked the people in the Covenant Church and were especially pleased that Jonathan was able to find a few boys of about his age. We attended the Covenant Church for a number of years and became associate members of this church. I served as a Sunday school teacher and as a member of the Building Committee when we built the new church.

Since our stay, this church has built twice, first due to the fact that the highway was being reconstructed quite close to the church and second, due to the fact that the new church blew up because of escaping gas. It is a miracle that no one was injured in this explosion. At that time, Dorothy and I still retained our membership in the Goshen College Mennonite Church which we joined in 1937 when we moved to Goshen.

Through the experience of the destruction of the Covenant Church building, we learned to be dependent on others. For a year we worshipped in the Seventh Day Adventist Church. In addition to this facility, we made use of the Y.M.C.A. for our Sunday school.

One of the memorable events associated with this church was the experience one Sunday morning of a bat flying back and forth through the building at the same time as the pastor, Raymond Dahlberg, was attempting to preach. You can imagine the disturbance caused by the bat that morning. After many futile attempts the bat was finally caught after which the service continued. I would say that was the most unusual church service I have ever attended.

Dorothy, Jonathan, and I very much enjoyed the association with the Covenant Church members and have learned to appreciate the rich spiritual heritage of these Swedish Christians. The Covenant Church, officially known as the Evangelical Covenant

Church of North America, started over 100 years ago in Sweden as a reaction against the formality of the Lutheran State Church.

In addition to teaching, raising a family, and doing some farming, I have been active in a number of what might be called extracurricular activities. I have been much interested in trying to be of help to older persons. At Bluffton College I recall how I helped an elderly lady with her yard and garden. Long before this, while a student at Juniata College, I helped Mrs. C. C. Ellis, wife of President Ellis, with her flower garden. This was a very interesting experience for me due to the fact that Mrs. Ellis took such an interest in her flowers. This helped me to gain an increased interest in the beauties of God's creation. Years later I was able to visit Mrs. Ellis in the Morrisons Cove Home in the town of Martinsburg, Pennsylvania.

We sold our Goshen country home to Mr. and Mrs. Oliver Dovel. He died a year later and Dorothy and I helped Mrs. Dovel with her garden for a number of years. Soon after our arrival in Mankato, I learned of a garden that I could rent. This garden was a part of a lot owned by Mrs. Sarah Hamley who lived in a small house located on the same lot.

At that time, Mrs. Hamley, a widow for a number of years, was 85 years old and lived by herself. After several years, she became ill and needed hospital care. My wife and I frequently went to see her. After some time in the hospital she was removed to a nursing home where we continued to visit her and minister to her needs. Mrs. Hamley was a devoted Catholic and she was very happy when we arranged to have her moved to a Catholic rest home in Mankato. There she was well taken care of and was able to attend Mass every day.

We continued to visit her and took care of all her financial transactions. She lived on Social Security and the income from a small farm near Mankato. I was finally appointed by the Court to be her legal guardian. Due to the closing of the Catholic Rest Home, we had to have her moved to another rest home. By this time Mrs. Hamley was over ninety years old. She had very few friends, seemed to be suspicious of everybody, even of her own sister. She had a niece in Rochester who often came to visit her.

Since she was in rest homes for a number of years, her money was running out so that eventually I had to sell her farm and her home. In August 1974, Mrs. Hamley died and I attended her funeral with her niece. After that it was my duty to settle her estate. She left only a few thousand dollars to her nephews and nieces.

My experience in dealing with this elderly lady has taught me a number of lessons, particularly regarding patience with others.

My second extracurricular activity has to do with science fairs. While I was teaching at Goshen College, I first became involved with science fairs. These consist of demonstrations and experiments by both grade and high school students in which they develop an idea into a demonstration of a scientific principle. Such experiments are called projects which are brought to a central location where each project is judged as to its merits. Science fairs started in the early fifties and have continued to the present time.

At Goshen College we had two county science fairs before we hosted the Regional Science Fair of Northern Indiana. I was the Chairman of these fairs and also took my first trip to the National Science Fair in 1957 held in Los Angeles. Two winners from each regional science fair, together with their teachers and the director of the fair, had all expenses paid to the National Science Fair. I recall how the group from the state of Indiana chartered a plane to take the trip to Los Angeles. This was a thrilling experience for me and I learned much about science fairs.

After I went to Mankato, I found out that Dr. Ford, Chairman of the science division, had been sponsoring science fairs for a number of years. At that time the Regional Science Fair in Mankato was held in the Science Hall. The first year I was one of the judges in the physics section. Up to that time, Mankato had not been sending winners to the National Science Fair.

At the beginning of my second year at Mankato, Dr. Ford asked me to become responsible for the operation of the Regional Science Fair of Southwestern Minnesota. I accepted this assignment and made a number of changes. First, I had the Fair enlarged to include the grade school children in addition to the junior and senior high school students. Second, I made arrangements to hold the fair in the college gymnasium where we had more adequate space. Third, I arranged for the two top winners to go to the National Science Fair which was held that year in Hartford, Connecticut.

I will never forget how we managed to arrange for our transportation. A local car dealer agreed for us to use one of his cars. One of the teachers was a local Catholic priest who went with us. Two things stand out in my memory of this man. Each day he insisted on conducting Mass in a local church. Twice he was caught speeding while he was driving the car. It was very interesting to me to note that in each case the police officer let him off after he showed that he was a Catholic priest. Evidently some people are able to get away with things in this country which is not true for the rest of us.

I continued to serve as director of the Southwestern Minnesota Science Fair from 1959 through 1965. Each year I accompanied the two top winners with their teachers to the national science fairs held throughout the country. I learned to know the people responsible for the National Science Fair and was elected a member of the Council which is the chief governing body. I spent many hours in this kind of activity and enjoyed it very much. Through this experience, I learned to know many interesting persons and have a better appreciation of the ability and activities of young students who may become leading scientists in the future.

My third extracurricular activity has taken much more of my time than any other. I have been much interested in the relationship existing between science and Christianity. When I heard in 1944 through Professor Paul Erb of an organization devoted to this subject, I immediately wrote for information, was accepted for membership, and have been active as previously stated.

I should say something about the origin of the American Scientific Affiliation. At the suggestion of Dr. Will H. Houghton, President of Moody Bible Institute, five men met on their campus September 2-5, 1941, to explore the possibility of helping college students who often ask whether modern scientific knowledge rules out Christian faith.

Those persons attending that historic meeting were Irving A. Cowperthwaite, an engineer with the Thomsen Wire Company; Russell D. Sturgiss, professor of chemistry at Ursinus College; Peter W. Stoner, professor of mathematics and astronomy at Pasadena City College; John P. Van Haitsma, professor of biology at Calvin College; and F. Alton Everest, assistant director of the Moody Institute of Science in Los Angeles.

After several days of deliberation, these men decided to form an organization for the purpose of correlating the facts of science with the tenets of Christian faith. Officers elected were F. Alton Everest, President, and Irving A. Cowperthwaite, Secretary-Treasurer.

My fourth extracurricular activity was participation in the work of the American Association of University Professors.

This organization of college teachers is concerned with all aspects of college and university activities. This is a national organization although I had no experience with it before my teaching at Mankato State University. It seems to me that the chief concern of the AAUP has to do with salaries and working conditions of college teachers. I held all the offices of the local AAUP and then had the pleasure of being their representative at the national meeting held at Palm Springs, California. At that meeting, I learned to know the national officers, heard addresses by representatives of the federal government, and had a most wonderful time. At the airport in Los Angeles, I was met by my good friend, F. Alton Everest, and we had a fine chat together.

At Mankato State, the AAUP is no longer a very strong organization due to the fact that the faculty there is organized through the state educational organization so far as salary and working conditions are concerned. At a number of other colleges and universities the AAUP is the organization concerned with such things.

While a graduate student at Rutgers University, I was elected a member of the Society of Sigma Xi, the organization promoting scientific research. They have been quite active in this activity for a long time. They have chapters and clubs on a large number of college campuses.

When I arrived in Mankato, I attempted to start a local club or chapter of the Sigma Xi. Previously there had been no such a group on campus. After a number of years and due primarily to the influence of the President, we were finally able to start a local club of the Sigma Xi.

I held every office and again was the representative at the National Convention held at Palm Springs, California. I remember riding on the plane with V. Elving Anderson from the University of Minnesota and one of my ASA colleagues. He has been an officer of Sigma Xi on the national level for a number of years and is currently the President of Sigma Xi. One of the many pleasures connected with this organization was that of aiding in installing a Club of the Sigma Xi at Gustavus Adolphus College. This college is located near Mankato. Recently the two groups have been able to join in a number of joint projects

As soon as I started my work at Mankato State, I was asked to serve as faculty advisor of the local group of students known as Inter-Varsity Christian Fellowship and have much enjoyed my association with this group. These college students, all committed Christians, are concerned about the claims of Christ on other college students. They feel that their field of missionary activity is that of the college campus. Weekly and monthly Bible study and inspirational meetings are held through the academic year. They also have a number of training camps throughout the country. These are meant to be of help to the officers of the local groups.

I attended two of these meetings at Colorado Springs, Colorado. We lived in what was known as Bear Trap Ranch. This was a rich spiritual experience for me. The members of Inter Varsity Christian Fellowship often work together with other campus groups in order to win others to Christ. I recall how we worked together with members of the Navigators and Campus Crusade for Christ. Each of these organizations of college students has its own particular emphasis, but they all are interested in the spiritual welfare of all college students. It is my observation that many students are won to the Lord through the efforts of these groups of students.

In the early sixties, a number of Christian businessmen in Mankato organized a local chapter of the Christian Business Men's Committee. I joined this fine group of Christian men and held a number of offices in the local group. For years, we met every Saturday morning for a prayer breakfast in a motel in Mankato.

One important activity which we helped to sponsor was that of the Billy Graham films. These were shown in one of the local theatres. This was a rather large undertaking and we succeeded in having several hundred people accept the Lord as their Savior due to this endeavor. I had an active part in several of these evangelistic efforts. I felt that this was one of the most important activities in which I had a part. It was good to see the wonderful cooperation of a number of churches in this effort of evangelism in the city of Mankato.

Another group of witnessing Christians is that of the Gideons, International. I have been an active member of this fine group of Christians since 1964 when I became a member of the Mankato Camp. Their objectives are: Be men of the Book, Be men of prayer, Be men of faith, Be men of a separated walk, Be men who witness, Be men of a compassionate heart, Be men who give. In other words, the Gideons are soul-winning men for Christ through personal work.

I was privileged to attend a number of the international meetings of the Gideons. Two that I remember are the Chicago meeting in 1989 and the Kansas City meeting in 1990. I've been greatly inspired by the testimony of many Gideons. While Christian men compose the membership of every Gideon Camp, they also have a group for the wives of Gideons—known as the Auxiliary—who pray for the work and help in the distribution of Bibles.

The year 1981 marked a dividing point in my life. It was on July 6, 1981, that I suffered a heart attack while resting in bed after picking raspberries in my garden. Only by the urging of my wife, my pastor, and my physician, did I consent to go to the hospital. That was the day after the heart attack. I was sorry that I had to miss the Shem King reunion and the annual ASA meeting. How wonderful is modern technology. By its use, I was able to present my talk to the ASA.

At Christmas 1982, we had the pleasure of having as our guests our son Harold Eugene, his wife Rachel, and their sons Joel and Aaron. In the January family newsletter it is reported that Eva and Ethel saw my grandson Mark at EMC. At that time I was writing to him every month but have not heard from him since September.

Our daughter Theo and her husband Elvin Dale visoted us in Arizona after their trip to Hawaii. This year marked their twenty-fifth wedding anniversary.

It should be noted that the year 1982 marked the first year of the publication of the quarterly journal known as *Mennonite Family History*. I have an article in the first issue and in every issue since. I noted that in my family letter of May 13, 1982.

I mention the fact that I expect my next article in *Mennonite Family History* to report that I now have identified every character mentioned in *Rosanna of the Amish* as being a real person. I also mention that I expect to attend the annual meeting of the ASA to be held August 13-16 at Calvin College, Grand Rapids, Michigan.

In my October 4 issue of the family letter I made note of the fact that this year Eva is in Europe, Ethel in Oregon, Carrie in Portland, Mamie in Virginia, John visited us in Arizona, and Dorothy and I went to Pennsylvania two times. As usual Dorothy and I planned to travel to Arizona, starting in November and staying five months.

In January 1983, I had the privilege of attending the Men's Retreat held near Glendale and sponsored by the Mennonite churches of this area. David Augsburger of the Biblical Seminary was the speaker. Dorothy and I took our cousin Lomie Esh and her husband Amandus Kanagy to witness the Christmas pageant at a local Baptist church in Phoenix. This was a very impressive service with beautiful music and wonderful pageantry.

I noted in my June 8, 1983, newsletter that we had the following visitors during the previous winter: John and Helen, Carrie, Elvin and Theo, as well as three couples from Mankato. The year 1983 marked the fiftieth wedding anniversary held in Martinsburg in our honor which we enjoyed very much. The Covenant Church in Mankato had an open house in our honor several weeks later where again we met many friends.

In the summer of 1983, I attended the annual meeting of the ASA held at George Fox College in Newburg, Oregon, near Portland. At that time, I had the privilege of visiting with Carrie and Ken, as well as with several members of their family.

During the winter of 1984-85, we invited Jonathan and Judy to visit us in Arizona. While they were with us we took a two-day trip to the Grand Canyon. Jonathan and his family hiked to near the bottom of the canyon while Dorothy and I only took a short walk near the ridge.

On April 1, 1985, we left Arizona by car and stopped to see Jonathan and his family in Volga, South Dakota. I helped with the farm work, disking over 100 acres in preparation for corn planting. We found Jonathan to be very busy. He moved in August to a farm near Sherburn, Minnesota. This farm of 440 acres really belongs to his wife Judy. On June 1, we attended alumni activities at Juniata College.

The big event of this summer was the wedding of Sandra Yoder and Mike Leininger in Archbold, Ohio. Terry Yoder, brother of the bride, led in a short meditation in the ceremony.

In 1985 we returned to Arizona later than usual. We arrived in Glendale November 7, just ahead of the storm. On the way we visited with Hugh King and his wife Viola. We stayed over night with Ray and Betty Linscheid. While in the Hesston area, we visited the Hertzler Clinic, the hospital and the museum.

On a second trip to Pennsylvania in the summer of 1985, I was invited by my brother and his wife Helen to go to Long Green, Maryland. I still think of Long Green as my home.

My high school class of 1926 had a dinner meeting at which time we had a history of our class read. Only six of our class of 1926 were living in 1986. I noted in the family letter of March 12, 1986, that my brother John is no longer with us. I am glad that he could go peacefully. As Helen said, "He just stopped breathing."

At this point I wish to add a note from Dorothy. She says:

"Dear family, Harold wants me to write about my winter here. It has been a very different one, to say the least. I had never been ill here except for colds and other virus infections. I really made up for it this winter, however. Less than two weeks after we arrived here, I blacked out in a Bible study. Harold stood helpless, shaking all over, while the others took over. One person called the paramedics. They arrived in a short time, gave me oxygen and an IV and hustled me off to a hospital in an ambulance. There I had many tests and it was learned that I had 90% blockage of the carotid artery on the left side.

"The next step was to have a thorough physical by a vascular surgeon. He was very thorough and then explained to Harold and me the risks of surgery, but he knew in my condition that I could not live the way I was. I had not felt well all summer and felt many times like I'd pass out but never expected that I really would. The surgeon told us that I had a 50-50 chance to live through the surgery. It was a hard decision to make, but since I had many T.I.A.'s, I decided to take the chance, knowing that without surgery my risks of having a massive stroke were very high.

"The surgery was scheduled and I came through it very well, but that same evening I got chest pains and it was soon found out that I had suffered a mild heart attack. That kept me in intensive care for three extra days. I was to be in I.C.U. for one day after the surgery but ended up being there four days and then in post intensive care on a heart monitor.

"I got along well and was in the hospital a little less than two weeks. My first hospital stay was only four days. That was all for tests. I had excellent care in both hospitals. The nurses told me that I really 'lucked out' in getting their best doctors. Since I didn't know the doctors I was very fortunate to get the best. They were all highly specialized and charged accordingly. We just could not believe the size of the bills that we got. It totaled over $15,000 for the hospitals and doctors.

"Now we are warning our friends and relatives that they better have good supplemental insurance in addition to medicare. We did and that is how we survived financially. I thank God to be alive and am glad that I decided on the surgery. After the surgery, the doctors explained that a piece of plaque was very loosely attached to my artery and looked just ready to break loose. Had that happened I'd have had a massive stroke.

"I feel better now than I have in several years, but I get very tired and have to rest a lot. It was so nice to have Theo come and be with me through this ordeal. It was also nice for Harold. He can't seem to cope easily with sickness and has always had trouble with fainting at the sight of blood. Love to all, Dorothy."

In 1986, I finished reading the journal of Edward Yoder. It was so interesting that I decided to start a diary of my own. I highly recommend the book called *Edward*.

Also, in 1986, Dorothy was again in the hospital with a partially blocked artery in her right leg. The operation was a success and she was soon out of intensive care. I attended several reunions in the summer of 1986 while Dorothy stayed with her sisters. I was the speaker at the Hertzler-Hartzler reunion held in New Holland, Pennsylvania, then attended the Smucker reunion in Lancaster, the Sharp reunion in Big Valley, and the King reunion in Allensville. After that I attended the Creation Conference in Pittsburgh and the meeting of the ASA at Houghton College.

The year 1987 was filled with important events in my life. Dorothy and I sold our home in Mankato while I was in the hospital. First I had a bad attack of asthma and then had congestive heart failure. Though quite ill, I did manage to go to Pennsylvania to attend the fiftieth anniversary of the wedding of Verna and Marion Smith in Martinsburg. Right after that we were taken to Belleville to visit the Hartzler family. There we were entertained in the home of Helen Hartzler.

In the summer of 1987, I spent two months in hospitals. After that I was taken to the Greencroft Nursing Center where I shared a room with S. W. Witmer. My good wife soon took me to our home on College Avenue in Goshen. She thought that she was able to give me better care than I had received at the nursing center. For the remainder of that summer we ate our lunch at the Greencroft Senior Center. We liked that arrangement very much since we are able to meet so many friends.

We now have a house at 901 College Avenue, located near the college and the Mennonite church. This fall we were delighted to have Dorothy's three sisters and one brother-in-law as our guests for a week.

A big event for our family in 1988 was the wedding of our granddaughter LeaAnn on April 2 at Scottsdale, Arizona. The groom was David Williams. Harold Eugene, LeaAnn's father, with his family, Dorothy and I, and the Erb family from Florida were present at this very beautiful wedding.

After the wedding, we went with Harold Eugene and his family to once again visit the Grand Canyon, which I always enjoy. There is nothing like it anywhere in the world. Both Dorothy and I felt so good that we decided to drive our car from Arizona to Indiana. On the way back to Goshen we had the pleasure of visiting with Jonathan and his family. We also stopped to visit friends in Mankato.

One of my main trips for the summer of 1988 was attending the annual meeting of the American Scientific Affiliation held August 5-8 at Malibu, California. On this trip, I also was able to visit Carrie and Ken Dodd and a part of their family. My sisters Eva and Ethel, as well as our sister-in-law Helen Hartzler, were present to help in the celebration of the fiftieth wedding anniversary of Ken and Carrie Dodd.

I note that when I wrote the family letter on September 12, 1988, that was the very day that Elmer C. Wisenant wrote the book: *88 Reasons Why The Rapture Will Be In 1988*. Obviously that event did not occur in 1988.

The big news for my family in 1988 was the arrival of Kimberly Joy Leininger on August 29. Dorothy had the pleasure of holding her in her arms and having her picture taken.

For three Sundays that fall, I taught Sunday school at Greencroft. I did this for Levi Hartzler whose wife had been ill for some time. We discussed a very difficult subject—that of suffering. Just why does God permit so much suffering?

The subject of health was a big one for us in the year 1989. It seems as though either Dorothy or I were ill most of the time. We usually came to Arizona soon after the first of November. Due to the illness of Dorothy we did not go to Arizona until after the first of January. Jonathan drove our car and stayed with us a few days.

As I grow older I think much more of heaven. This was especially true during the fall of 1988 when Dorothy was in the Goshen Hospital a number of times. The Bible tells us little about heaven, but it does give us some hints. It is beautiful, with no sorrow or pain. We will have spiritual bodies, a very difficult subject.

I began my June 29, 1989, letter with the statement: "I feel very lonely as I write this family letter." Dorothy was in the hospital five times this year. She went to be with the Lord on April

H. Harold Hartzler teaching a class on "Science and the Bible" in 1991.

18, 1989. At this time Jonathan was with us and was with her in the hospital. We had two memorial services for her—one in the Mennonite church in Goshen and a second one in Martinsburg. This later one was conducted by members of the family, including Harold Eugene, Patricia Schmucker, and Terry Yoder.

After the service I was taken to Belleville by my nephew Jerry Hartzler. I am happy that Jerry has had his book published. This book deals with the K.V. Railroad and its sale is doing well.

While in Belleville, I visited many friends. Norman Yoder took me to visit friends in the McVeytown area. I then visited friends near Martinsburg as I stayed with Mildred Dilling. Later I made another trip to Pennsylvania to attend alumni activities at Juniata College and visit friends in Lancaster County.

After Dorothy's death I did not know whether I should return to Arizona for the winter of 1989-90. I decided to do so and found many friends. I helped some complete their income tax forms. I have always completed my own income tax forms.

I took a second trip to Europe in 1990 with J. Lemar and Lois Ann Mast as tour leaders. (A write-up follows.)

Later in the summer of 1990, I attended the Gideon meeting in Kansas City, the World Conference of Mennonites in Winnipeg, the Creation Conference in Pittsburgh, and the annual meeting of the ASA held at Messiah College.

In December 1990, I spent two days in the work of the Gideons where 31 Gideons distributed about 2,000 Bibles and Testaments in Kingman, Bullhead City, and Havisu City. A week later I attended two sessions of a Biblical Financial Guidelines Seminar conducted by Lester E. Miller of Lancaster County, Pennsylvania.

In June 1991, I attended the 200th anniversary of the coming of the Amish and Mennonites to Mifflin County. Here I spoke at the Valley View Amish Church, using as my topic: "The Influence of Mifflin County on my Spiritual Heritage."

I attended the annual meeting of the ASA at Wheaton College July 26-29. There I had the pleasure of having my son Harold Eugene with me. From July 30 to August 3 I attended the General Mennonite Assembly in Eugene, Oregon, and visited my sister Carrie Dodd at the home of her daughter Sandra in Newport. I then took a delightful trip to Alaska.

I now finish this story of my life with a note of sadness.

I realize that I am a victim of asthma attacks since the spring of 1939 when I moved to my country home in the Goshen area. I discovered that I was allergic to a large number of things but was able to keep them under control, first with Asthma Nefrin and later with a Vanceril inhaler. This continued to be of help for about fifty years. Its effectiveness finally wore out.

By December 1991, I discovered that it became more difficult for me to breathe. I began to use oxygen but still had great trouble breathing. Finally my good neighbor, Marion Lehman, toke me to the hospital where I stayed a little more than a week. Then I was taken to the Carriage Manor Rest Home where I received good nursing care, but still had trouble breathing, especially at night.

Recently I have made a great discovery, namely that I can breathe much better when I have a stream of air from a fan constantly flowing in my nostrils. I am now at my home located at 901 College Avenue, Goshen, Indiana, waiting for my heavenly home.

My Family

Three children:
1. Harold Eugene Hartzler
2. Theodosia Ruth (Hartzler) Yoder
3. Jonathan Edward Hartzler

Thirteen grandchildren:
Children of Harold:
1. Jody Dorene (Hartzler) Kemery Noble
2. Mark Douglas Hartzler
3. Lea Ann (Hartzler) Williams
4. Joel Harold Hartzler
5. Aaron Jon Hartzler
6. Carrie Marie Hartzler
7. Dori Cristina Hartzler

Children of Theo:
1. Patricia June (Yoder) Schmucker
2. Terry Alan Yoder
3. Cynthia Diane (Yoder) Shafik
4. Sandra Joy (Yoder) Leininger

Children of Jonathan:
1. Todd Judson Hartzler
2. Matthew Jon Hartzler

Six great-grandchildren (at the time this was printed):
1. Joshua Bruce Kemery
2. Marc Lynn Hartzler
3. Jason Allen Schmucker
4. Natalie Joy Schmucker
5. Kimberly Joy Leininger
6. Jeremy Michael Leininger

CHILDREN

Harold Eugene Hartzler, son of H. Harold Hartzler, was born on March 23, 1934. He graduated from Goshen College in 1956 with a degree in chemistry. Harold lives in Goshen and has been employed at Miles Laboratories in Elkhart since his college graduation. He did research in medicinal chemistry for many years and now manages a pilot plant

Harold was married to Sara Jean Erb and is now married to Rachel Marie Nafziger. Rachel is a graduate of the Goshen College School of Nursing. Harold had release time from Miles to teach chemistry labs at Goshen College a number of years ago, and Rachel was employed by Goshen College as a clinical instructor in nursing for several years.

Theodosia Ruth "Theo" Hartzler was born on June 25, 1935 and graduated from Goshen College with a B.S. in Nursing in 1957. She has done nursing in a variety of settings over the years. Presently, she works occasionally at their local hospital and spends many hours as a volunteer and babysitter for her grandchildren.

Theo's husband, Elvin Dale "Ed" Yoder, graduated from Goshen College with a degree in commerce and serves as Vice President for Finance at Sauder Woodworking in Archbold, Ohio. He also is currently serving on the Goshen College Board of Overseers.

Jonathan Edward Hartzler was born on July 11, 1944. He graduated from Goshen College in 1966 with a degree in biology; earned a Masters degree from Mankato State University; and received a Ph.D. in Behavorial Science from Montana State University.

He taught sciences at South Dakota Weslyan University in Mitchell, South Dakota, for a number of years before taking up farming. He now lives with his family near Sherburn, Minnesota, in the community where his wife, Judy Jeanette Bishop, grew up. Judy has a degree in mathematics and English from Mankato State University, Mankato, Minnesota.

GRANDCHILDREN

Jody Doreen Hartzler, born February 11, 1956, married 1) Bruce Kemery (divorced); and married 2) Stephen Noble. Jody attended Goshen College and now works with a business in Phoenix, Arizona.

Mark Douglas Hartzler, born February 17, 1957, married 1) Jeannie Lynn Pietrie (divorced); and married 2) Joan Eaton. Mark attended Eastern Mennonite College and is now attending Purdue University in Indiana, studying Industrial Arts Education. Joan is a Pharmacy student at Purdue.

Lea Ann Hartzler, born January 31, 1959, married David Williams. Lea Ann and David have worked together in Phoenix, Arizona, developing and operating a factory which manufactures tow trailers used to transport cars.

Patricia June Yoder, born March 10, 1958, attended Goshen College and married Douglas James Schmucker who manages a restaurant in Toledo, Ohio. The restaurant is owned by Doug's father and was previously owned by his grandfather.

Terry Alan Yoder, born May 5, 1959, graduated from Goshen College and married Joan Gotwals. Terry was a youth minister for five years. He has been taking seminary classes and now works for a produce company in Lancaster, Pennsylvania.

Cynthia Diane Yoder, born March 23, 1961, married Adel Shafik (divorced). Cindy earned a bachelors degree from Goshen College and a Masters degree from Indiana University. She has worked with MCC in Egypt and is now teaching English as a Second Language at Eastern Mennonite College.

Sandra Joy Leininger, born April 21, 1964, married Michael Leininger, who has his own business manufacturing kitchen cabinets. Sandy graduated from Goshen College. She is an RN who works part-time in OB as her mother did for over twenty-five years.

My younger grandchildren include **Joel Harold Hartzler**, born May 21, 1974. He is a basketball player and is studying physics at Goshen College.

Aaron Jon Hartzler was born November 23, 1976. He plays a number of musical instruments and is a cross-country runner as I was in college.

Carrie Marie Hartzler was born in Colombia on September 21, 1981. Carrie and Dori were adopted by Harold and Rachel when they were babies. They were both born with heart defects, but after surgery are now in good health.

Dori Cristina Hartzler was also born in Colombia on August 9, 1984, and is also in good health after surgery for her heart defect.

Todd Judson Hartzler was born August 18, 1974. After completing another year of high school, he plans to study engineering in college.

Matthew Jon Hartzler was born October 3, 1977. Todd and Matthew both participate in a number of sports and play a variety of musical instruments.

My Trip To Europe in 1990

by H. Harold Hartzler

I was one of twenty-nine persons who made a Mennonite heritage tour of Europe under the leadership of tour leaders J. Lemar and Lois Ann Mast of Elverson, Pennsylvania.

Travel arrangements were made by Pilgrim Tours of Morgantown, Pennsylvania. We found that they did a fine job, arranging for our flight from New York on May 3, 1990, on Iceland Air, with a stopover at Iceland for one hour. An interesting experience for me was to see the sun rise at 2:00 a.m.

We arrived at Luxembourg the next day. They also made our hotel arrangements. We met our bus driver, Guy Bartholome, who could speak several languages, including English. He was a great help to our group and really became an integral part of us. He drove a motor coach, owned by himself, equipped with rest room facilities. He also provided soft drinks for us besides hot coffee and tea. We were a jolly group. Throughout the tour there was much laughing, and it appeared that a good time was enjoyed by all. At times I thought that the mirth was excessive.

We were taken on a leisurely drive north to Belgium. Our first night was spent at the Hotel Palace in Brussels, Belgium, where we had a delicious meal followed by a good night's rest. The next morning our first stay was at Ghent where we viewed the castle and saw some of the instruments used to persecute the Anabaptists. We then went on to Holland to view the windmills and the beautiful tulips. At Lisse we saw a part of the seventy acres of tulips at a place called Keukenhof. This has been called the greatest flower show on earth. I took a number of snapshots there.

More than 9,000 windmills were once in service throughout the country; almost 1,000 exist today. We saw a number of them and I took pictures of some. In Holland we stayed for two nights at the Cok Superior Tourist Class Hotel located in Amsterdam.

On Sunday morning we worshipped at the Singel Mennonite Church, the largest Mennonite church building in Europe and the headquarters of the Dutch Mennonite Conference. Members of the congregation entertained us at a noon lunch held at the church. After the morning service I met Dr. Solomon Yoder, the son of my teacher in the seventh grade at Belleville, Pennsylvania. His name is also Solomon and he is 97 years old. I was disappointed at the small attendance of members of the Dutch Mennonite Church. It was explained that they have a number of places of meeting for this congregation. In the afternoon, we took a boat ride on some of the main canals.

We also took a short ride to see the village of Vollendam. There I tried to converse with some of the older men who knew very little English. I was able to talk to a young man since English is now a required language in the public schools of The Netherlands.

On Monday we drove north to Witmarsum where Menno Simons was born and also to Pingjum, his boyhood home. We also visited the Mennonite Memorial to Menno Simons as well as a hidden Mennonite church. About this time I felt ill and a doctor was called. I felt that I was about to have a heart attack, but the doctor assured me that I did not have such an attack.

We stopped at a cheese factory where some of our group purchased cheese. Later we stopped at Makkum to visit Tichelaar's ceramic shop where beautiful Dutch pottery has been made by the same Mennonite family since 1660.

That night we stayed at Hotel Tachthoven Giethoorn located at Giethoorn, The Netherlands. The next morning we rode in our coach to Weilburg, the town where Christian Felpel lived before coming to America in 1870.

On this trip we first saw the Rhine River on which we later took a boat ride. We stayed for three nights at the Hotel Schloss Weilburg, in Weilburg, West Germany. In this city we saw the old castle and met with three members of the Felpel family, a very interesting experience for a number of our group who are Felpel descendants, including our tour leader Lemar Mast. In a bookstore there I found a poem which I had learned in college known as "Der Erlkonig" by Goethe.

The next day we drove to Boppard where we boarded the boat for a three-hour cruise on the Rhine River, passing many old castles. We passed the fabled Lorelei cliffs where a very beautiful maiden had lured sailors to their death. This reminded me of the song, "Die Loreley," by Heinrich Heine, which I learned in college:

"Ich weiss nicht, was soll es bedeuten,
das ich so traugrig bin
Ein Madchen aus uralten Zeiten
das komme mir nicht aus dem zinn
Die luft ist kuhl und es dunkelt,
und ruhrig fliest der Rhein;

der gipfel des bergus funkelt
in abend sonnen schein.
Die schönste jungfrau sitzet
dort oben wunderbar,
ihr gold'ness Geschmeide blitzet,
Sie Kämmt ihr goldenes Haar.
Sie kommt es mit goldenes Kamme
Und singt ein lieb dabei
das hat eine wundersame
gewaltige Melodie
Den Schiffer im kleine Schiffe
ergriest es mit wildem Wieh
er schaut nur hinauf in die Hoh
Ich glaube die wellen verschlinnen
am Ende nach Schiffer und Kahn
und das hat mit ihrem Singen
die Loreley getan."

 After this lovely ride, we took our coach to reach the Mennonite village of Weierhof. Here we were guests in German Mennonite homes. I stayed with Werner and Ind Galle. Some of us worshipped on Saturday night at the Mennonite church in Weierhof. I had the pleasure of meeting Adolph Hertzler at whose home I stayed twelve years ago.

 Gary Waltner, a cousin of my pastor in Goshen, James Waltner, now a teacher of some children of American Army personnel, served as a very capable guide on our visit to the cities of Heidelberg and Worms. On the way we saw many fields of rape seed which had a beautiful yellow color. We also saw fields of sugar beets, used both for sugar and for cattle feed. We traveled on the Kaiser Strasse or Napoleon Road which was used by the American Army in 1945.

 In Heidelberg, we toured the old castle and walked through the old part of the city.

 In Worms, we had a guided tour of the cathedral and saw the spot where Martin Luther was tried. We saw his statue together with those of four martyrs. I was most impressed with the size of the cathedral. The same can be said of a number of European cathedrals. It is staggering to think of the time and material resources required for just one of the many cathedrals.

 Sunday night we stayed at Hotel Hollander Hof in Heidelberg, West Germany. The next morning we drove south through the Kraichgau and saw villages where some of our ancestors once lived.

Then it was on to Switzerland where we first stayed at the See Hotel Meierhof at Horgan. There I bought three music boxes for my children. After a night's rest we visited the elegant Grossmunster and had a walking tour of Zurich. Most of the group walked to the "cave of the Anabaptists." I only walked part way.

The next day we went to Lucerne, the first city of the Swiss Confederation. Then we traveled through the scenic Emmental Valley to Langnau to visit the Langnau Mennonite Church. This is the oldest Mennonite congregation in the world.

After two nights at Horgen we traveled to Huttwil where we stayed two nights at Romantik Hotel Mohren. The previous night we were entertained with some native yodeling. We visited the Trachselwald Castle where Anabaptists in the sixteenth century were held in the prison tower for questioning, banishment or execution. Inside the tower we saw the chains used on the prisoners.

The next day we traveled further south to Thun and Interlaken and finally arrived in Bern where we toured the city and saw the Clock Tower and the bear pits. However, we saw no cubs since none were born this year.

On the way we stopped at Steffisburg where I took a number of pictures and had one taken of me. It has been suggested that Immigrant Samuel Koenig originally came from this town. We had some very exciting experiences as we attempted to find Beatenberg and then Grindelwald, the original home of the Schmuckers. In Bern we stayed one night at Hotel City.

The next day we stopped at Basel where many Anabaptists boarded ship for the new world. We traveled north to Germany where we entered the Black Forest, visited an open-air museum and stopped at several places where members of our group purchased cuckoo clocks. A late afternoon drive took us to the Le Grand Hotel in Strasbourg, France. That evening we had a special farewell dinner. Jane Davidson served as master of ceremonies and bequeathed to each member of the group a special gift. I was given a copy of *Mennoniten Gemeinde* written by Krefeld. This book, written in German, is a brief history of the Mennonite Church at Weierhof. This event was very much enjoyed by all members of our tour group, including our driver Guy Bartholome.

The next morning, Sunday, May 20, five members of our tour group left to return to their homes in the United States. The remaining 24 members started for Oberammergau, Bavaria, West Germany. We stayed there for two nights in guest houses. We were divided into four groups. I stayed with six others in the home of a very gracious hostess named Anni Fohrer. Four other persons, teachers of children of the American military, stayed in the same house. We had our noon and evening meals at a nearby restaurant and breakfast, consisting mainly of hard rolls, at the guest house.

Of course our purpose in coming to the village of Oberammergau was to see the Passion Play, which is shown only every ten years. I consider myself fortunate that I was able to see this world-famous play. The superb presentation of the conclusion of the life and death of our Lord made such a deep impression on me that I was compelled to weep. The attentive crowd, numbering more than 5,000, was the best behaved one that I have ever seen.

The play began promptly at 9 o'clock in the morning and continued until 5:30 p.m. However, there was a three-hour lunch break. To me the Passion Play was the high point of our tour. This was true, in spite of the fact that I am much interested in genealogy and our tour was called the Mennonite Heritage Tour.

One of the outstanding aspects of the play was the repeated entrances and exists of the 49 white-robed singers. I was also impressed by the excellent acting of such a large group of actors who appeared several times. That evening after the play we experienced some rain, one of the few times we had rain on our trip.

We viewed the play on Monday, May 21. This was the first showing of the season. The next day we traveled to Salzburg, Austria, where we stayed at the Hotel Schaffenrath.

I found Austria to be very beautiful, almost as beautiful as Switzerland. In Salzburg we took a walking tour where we saw the high towered cathedral, a golden decorated castle, and also a salt mine, where we had to don a special garb to protect our clothing. From Salzburg we traveled to Augsburg, West Germany.

During the previous night our bus driver suffered a heart attack and was placed in intensive care in a hospital in Salzburg. We had a special prayer for him the next morning in our coach. So for the next two days we had different bus drivers. In Augsburg we stayed at the Ringhotel Alpenhof.

The next day we stopped to take pictures of Zweibrücken, the home of Immigrant Nicholas Stoltzfus, who was the ancestor of a number of members of our group, including me. In that town we saw a beautiful rose garden. I was impressed with the large number of flowers in Europe.

I failed to report that on our way to Oberammergau we stopped at Dachau and saw a film depicting some of the terrible things that occurred in World War II at which time more than six million Jews were put to death. That film was very depressing.

Our last night in Europe we stayed at the Pullman Kongress Hotel in Saarbrücken, West Germany. Our leaders, Lemar and Lois Ann Mast, had arranged for Hermann and Gertrud Guth to have dinner with us at the hotel. The Guths have been writers for *Mennonite Family History* ever since its beginning in 1982. It was arranged that I be seated between this couple who reside in Saarbrücken. Hermann speaks only German while Gertrud speaks English. We had a most delightful time together. After dinner they led us on a walking tour through a part of Saarbrücken.

We visited a fine china shop the next morning on our way to Luxembourg where we boarded the plane for New York. On the way to New York we stopped for an hour in Iceland where I purchased some postal cards and a small jar of caviar. This delicacy consists of fish roe which I enjoyed eating while attending Juniata College.

On arriving at J.F.K. Airport in New York, I had an interesting experience. Previously, I had informed our group leaders that I had only one-half hour to get my baggage, go through customs, and meet the plane for my flight to Chicago. Sure enough, my baggage was one of the first ones to arrive and was picked up by Lemar Mast and brought to me. Thus I was able to go through customs, catch the shuttle bus, and arrive at the United terminal one minute before the time of flight.

However, after all my rushing around, I found that my flight on the United was one hour late. The same thing happened in Chicago with the result that I was two hours late when I arrived in South Bend. My son, Harold Eugene, was there to meet me so that I arrived home in Goshen soon after midnight.

To top my trip off, my key did not appear to fit the lock in my door so my son entered my house through a window and opened the front door to allow me to enter. Exhausted, I immediately found my bed to be a great comfort.

I must say that I had a fine time in Europe, enjoyed the companionship of my fellow travelers, and recommend such a trip to others. I thank God for His guidance through the entire trip.

Forty Years With The ASA

by H. Harold Hartzler
Mankato State University, Mankato, Minnesota

The saying goes that life begins at forty. It was exactly forty years ago that Professor Paul Erb of the English department of Goshen College gave me a brochure entitled: "The Story of the American Scientific Affiliation." This interested me greatly with the result that I wrote to Irving A. Cowperthwaite who was listed as Secretary-Treasurer.

I recall that I was impressed with the objectives of this new organization.

1.) To integrate and organize the efforts of many individuals desiring to correlate the facts of science and the Holy Scriptures.

2.) To promote and encourage the study of the relationship between the facts of science and the Holy Scriptures.

3.) To promote the dissemination of the results of such studies.

I was very much surprised when I received a letter from Irving telling me that he had recommended me to the Executive Council for membership in the ASA. Thus it was that I, completely unknown to the Executive Council, was elected a member of the ASA. I should mention the names of the members of the Executive Council in 1944: F. Alton Everest, Irving A. Cowperthwaite, Peter W. Stoner, John P. Van Haitsma, and Russell D. Sturgis. The latter two have gone on to their reward. I have had many pleasant exchanges of ideas with the first three.

The number forty seems to have special significance in the Bible. Rain fell forty days and forty nights at the time of the flood of Noah, the children of Israel ate manna forty years in the wilderness, Moses spent forty years in the palace of Pharaoh, forty years in the wilderness in preparation for his great task, and he led the children of Israel forty years to the promised land.

Moses was up in the mountain forty days and forty nights when he received the Ten Commandments, Moses fasted forty days and forty nights when he was on the mountain, the spies searched the land of Caanan forty days, the Children of Israel were forced to wander in the wilderness forty years, a condemned man was given forty stripes, Joshua was forty years old when he went as one of the spies, both David and Solomon reigned forty years, the good king Josiah reigned forty years, Jonah preached in Ninevah forty days, Jesus fasted forty days and forty nights, Jesus was seen by his disciples forty days after the resurrection.

It is interesting that the membership of the ASA in 1944 was slightly greater than forty. I have this list of ASA members in my possession. They then numbered forty-three. The previous year there were twenty-seven members of the ASA.

World War II was going on during these years with the result that travel was greatly restricted. Hence, no national meetings of the ASA took place until 1946 when we met at Wheaton College. I presented a paper there with the title: "A God-Centered Science Course."

There I had the delightful experience of meeting a number of ASA members. I well remember Dr. Marion Barnes, then Secretary-Treasurer. He stated that when he heard that I, a Mennonite, was coming, he expected to see a man with a beard.

One member who especially impressed me was Walter L. Wilson from Kansas City. I also became acquainted with Russell L. Mixter, Brian P. Sutherland, Roger Voskuyl, George Horner, Allen A. MacRae, and Irving A. Cowperthwaite. One of my big disappointments was not being able to meet F. Alton Everest, President of the ASA, who was unable to attend due to the fact that his family had the mumps.

During those early years, the chief activity of the ASA was that of preparing the chapters of what was then called the Student's Handbook. I recall how glad we were when this book appeared in 1948. The title was *Modern Science and Christian Faith*.

I recall how every member was invited to participate by sending in comments and criticisms to F. Alton Everest, who served as editor. Some chapter headings were: A Christian Interpretation of Science; Astronomy and the First Chapter of Genesis; Geology and the Bible; Biology and Creation; Psychology and the Christian Faith; and The Relation of Archaeology to the Bible. This book of 289 pages was written in order to strengthen the faith of college students.

The second annual ASA meeting was held at Taylor University in 1947. It was there that I first met Al Eckert, who later edited the ASA tract, "Ten Scientists Look at Life," and also Frank Cassel who later served as President of the ASA. The following year I moved with my family to Tucson, Arizona, where I studied astronomy at the University of Arizona. I traveled by train from Tucson to Grand Rapids, Michigan, to attend the third annual convention of the ASA. I remember my conversation with Irving Cowperthwaite as we traveled together from Chicago to Grand Rapids.

I will never forget the fine welcome we received at Calvin College from Dr. and Mrs. Monsma and Mr. and Mrs. Karsten. For a number of years these two couples faithfully attended the annual ASA meetings. It was at this meeting that I presented a paper with the title, "The Meaning of Mathematics."

In the spring of 1949, while I was at the University of Arizona, a letter arrived from F. Alton Everest in which he asked me to serve as Chairman of the Program Committee for the annual ASA meeting to be held that year in California. I accepted the assignment and thus became more involved in the work of the ASA. It was in California that field trips became a part of many ASA meetings. The program lasted five days, one of which was a delightful trip to Mount Polamar. At the suggestion of Everest, I presented a paper at this meeting with the title, "The Hole in the North." At the close of this meeting Roger Voskuyl and I traveled in the car driven by Hendrik Oorthuys from Los Angeles to Chicago.

Dr. Paul Bender of Goshen College and I were very much interested in having the next annual meeting of the ASA on the campus of Goshen College. I remember that we brought literature describing Goshen College to be considered by the members of the Executive Council. It seems that Goshen College was not well known by the Executive Council. After some deliberation the decision was made to hold the 1950 annual meeting of the ASA at Goshen College.

Soon after the California meeting I was appointed General Chairman of the 1950 meeting. I was ably assisted in my duties by Hendrik Oorthuys, Chairman of the Program Committee, and by Paul Bender, Chairman of the Local Arrangements Committee. Soon after that meeting, I was elected a member of the Executive Council and also Secretary-Treasurer of the ASA. Thus began my long tenure of 21 years as an officer of the ASA. I served as Secretary-Treasurer for five years, as President for five years, followed by eleven years as the first Executive Secretary.

In the meantime, I had left Goshen College for health reasons and began teaching at Mankato State College, first in the physics department and later in the mathematics department. Under my tenure the national office was moved from Goshen to West Lafayette, Indiana, and then to Mankato, Minnesota.

For some time the Executive Council had been looking for a full-time Executive Secretary. I continued to teach at Mankato State, though I spent much time in the ASA office. Finally in 1972, Bill Sisterson was hired as the first full-time Executive Secretary. His title was later changed to Executive Director.

Upon my retirement, I was presented with a beautiful bronze plaque at the 1972 meeting held in Toronto. Don Boardman, President of the ASA, presented this plaque to me which read as follows: H. Harold Hartzler, Man of Vision and Perseverance, Christian Conviction, Humility, and Love, whose faithful service as Executive-Secretary strengthened the American Scientific Affiliation, increasing its effectiveness as a witness to God, the Creator and Jesus Christ, the Savior, Aug. 23, 1972.

In addition, Dick Bube, editor of the *Journal ASA*, had a number of testimonials concerning my work by former members of the Executive Council which appeared in the December 1972 issue of the *Journal*. I very much appreciated Dick's introduction to these testimonials:

"Once in a rare while the spirit of an entire organization is so captured by one individual that he becomes the very incarnation of that organization. The ASA has been blessed to have such a leader in the person of H. Harold Hartzler. For 28 years a member of the ASA, he has been in positions of responsibility for the past 21 years. His own overview of 30 years of ASA history was published in the *Journal ASA* March 1972. It is only appropriate that a few of the many of us who have known him and valued our friendship as Christian colleagues in science should take this opportunity to bear him tribute. Ths fall Harold passes on the responsibility of Executive-Secretary of the ASA to William D. Sisterson, the ASA's first full-time Executive-Secretary. We look forward to our association in the future and know that Harold's experience and council will be a continuing source of inspiration and guidance."

The testimonial of Henry Weaver, my colleague at Goshen College and the President of the ASA in 1962, is especially appealing to me. Henry says: "Dedication seems to be the word that best describes H. Harold Hartzler and his work with the ASA. I have had the privilege of working with him as a teaching colleague and in the operation of the ASA. He has always shown the virtues of a Christian combined with the thoroughness of a scholar. Beyond these attributes, however, has been his dedication to the task of relating science and the Christian faith. Certainly no one has been a more consistent proponent of the work of the ASA, nor a more faithful evangelist for members in the association.

"When he taught at Goshen College, his students often referred to him as H³ or Cubey, based on his name. Somehow it seems that we ought to vote him a triple honor, Executive-Secretary cum laude Emeritus or perhaps Mr. (ASA)³."

I do very much appreciate these kind words from my friends. But I feel that I am an unworthy servant of the Lord and I wish to faithfully serve Him until He calls me home.

I now wish to mention some highlights of the annual ASA conventions. The fifth one, held at Goshen College August 29 to September 1, 1950, featured a paper by Delbert Eggenberger with the title, "Methods of dating the earth and the universe." Delbert, now deceased, served as editor of the *Journal ASA*, 1951-62. The sixth convention was held August 28-31, 1951, at Shelton College.

At this meeting, F. Alton Everest gave a public address: "American Scientific Affiliation—The First Ten Years." I remember the guest speaker, Dr. Gordon H. Clark of Butler University, who spoke on the philosophy of science. Several years later Ronald L. Nash edited a book with the title, *The Philosophy of Gordon H. Clark*. I wrote a chapter in that book with the title, "Gordon Clark's Philosophy of Science."

After this meeting held in New York City, we moved to a rural setting for our next annual ASA meeting. This was at the Wheaton College Science Station in the Black Hills of South Dakota. I recall traveling by automobile to this convention from Goshen, Indiana, together with Paul Bender, William Tinkle, William Fletcher, and Hendrik Oorthuys.

The eighth annual convention was held at Grace Theological Seminary, Winona Lake, Indiana. At this meeting a spirited discussion followed the paper on Deluge Geology by Henry Morris who is now President of the Institute for Creation Research, El Cajon, California.

A very interesting ASA meeting was held on the campus of Eastern Mennonite College August 24-27, 1954. I remember how Maurice Brackbill made our stay there very enjoyable. He kept promising that we would have turkey eggs for breakfast, but they never appeared. I presented a paper there on the Life of Robert A. Millikan.

We had our tenth annual convention at the Star Ranch of Young Life, Colorado Springs, Colorado. The dates were August

23-26, 1955. This was the first year that I made my President's annual report. An important item of business at that meeting was the decision to sponsor a book on evolution to appear in 1959. This book, *Evolution and Christian Thought Today*, did appear in 1959 under the editorship of Russell L. Mixter.

Ten years after our first meeting there, the ASA met again on the campus of Wheaton College. At this meeting a symposium was held on Extra Sensory Perception. A preliminary report was made by the Darwin Centennial Committee.

The 12th annual ASA convention was held at Gordon College August 27-29, 1957. It is interesting that this was the first ASA meeting that the idea of theistic evolution was openly discussed and advocated by some. Now it is true, as stated by a number of ASA members, that the ASA does not take a stand on any scientific theory, yet it is also true that a number of papers at previous ASA meetings were rather critical of the theory of evolution and none even mentioned theistic evolution.

In 1958, for the first time in our history, the ASA met on the campus of a state university when we met August 26-28 at Iowa State, Ames, Iowa. This took place under the general chairmanship of Walter R. Hearn, at that time assistant professor of biochemistry at Iowa State. At this meeting there was a special program for wives and George L. Speake presented two of his demonstrations called "Sermons from Science." I recall that he was rather critical of some ideas which I presented in my paper on World Peace.

The 14th annual ASA convention was held June 9-11, 1959, at Trinity College in Chicago as a joint meeting with the Evangelical Society. This was the fourth biennial meeting with the theologians. The first joint meeting of the two groups was held June 21, 14, 1955, at Grace Theological Seminary, Winona Lake, Indiana. I remember that I was the first speaker on the program. My topic was, "The ASA, History and Purposes."

The second joint meeting was held June 12-14, 1957, at Wheaton College. At this meeting we had discussions on the flood of Noah by John C. Whitcomb, representing the Evangelical Theological Society, and by Douglas A. Block, representing the ASA. I recall that I spoke on the subject, "The American Scientific Affiliation, an Appraisal of its Achievements in the Light of its Purposes."

The third such meeting was held June 14-16, 1961, at Goshen College. At this meeting we had three papers on the subject,

"Science Looks Into the Future." James H. Kraakevik of Wheaton College spoke on the physical sciences, Paul Peachey of Eastern Mennonite College talked about the social sciences, and Irving W. Knoble concluded by discussing the biological sciences.

The fifth biennial joint meeting was held June 19-21, 1963, at Asbury College and Seminary, Wilmore, Kentucky. I recall that I served as Chairman of the opening session when G. Douglas Young spoke on "Values and Limitations of Natural Theology," and Robert Fisher, later President of the ASA, spoke on "Presuppositions and Assumptions of Science." In a sense this was an historic meeting since a number of ASA members, under the leadership of Walter Lammerts, decided to have another meeting that year when the Creation Research Society was formed. A number of those who were charter members of CRS later disassociated themselves from the ASA. A few of us are now members of both organizations. To me it is very sad that this rift had to occur.

The 15th annual ASA convention was held August 22-25, 1960, at Seattle Pacific College under the general chairmanship of Harold T. Wiebe. This was the last year that I served as President of the ASA. Thus, it was fitting that the final item on the program was that of concluding remarks by myself.

"The Christian's Responsibility Toward the Increasing Population of the World" was the theme of the 16th annual ASA convention, held August 22-25, 1961, at Houghton College. Robert Luckey served as General Chairman while Henry Weaver was Chairman of the program committee. My good friend, Irving A. Cowperthwaite, presented a review of the history of the ASA on the 20th anniversary of its founding. Irving was one of the founding fathers of the ASA.

"Modern Psychology and the Christian" was the theme of the 17th convention held August 20-24, 1962, at Bethel College, St. Paul, Minnesota.

The 18th annual ASA convention was held August 19-23, 1963, at Westmont College, Santa Barbara, California. It was at this meeting that Richard H. Bube gave an evening address on the subject, "The Encounter Between Christianity and Science." Later he edited a book bearing the same title. This book, written mainly by members of the ASA, was somewhat controversial and thus did not appear as an official ASA publication.

"Panorama of the Past" was the theme of the 19th annual ASA convention held August 24-27, 1964, at John Brown University, Siloam Springs, Arkansas. Some highlights of this meeting were the fine work of Irvin A. Wills who served as Chairman of the local arrangements committee and the banquet address by V. Elving Anderson, President of the ASA, who spoke on "The New High School Science Curricula— Some Implications for the ASA."

The 20th annual convention was held August 23-27, 1965, at the King's College, Briarcliff, New York. This was a joint meeting with Inter Varsity Christian Fellowship. I remember the evening address by John Alexander, General Director of IVCP, who spoke on "Christian Witness on a Secular University." It was at this meeting that the decision was made to not sponsor the book, *The Encounter Between Christianity and Science*. I recall that my wife and two of her sisters were with me. A number of us from the ASA arrived early and attended the World's Fair in New York City.

The 21st annual ASA convention was held August 22-26, 1966, at North Park College, Chicago. It was a joint meeting with the Evangelical Theological Society. As I recall, this was the last joint meeting of the ASA and the ETS. At this meeting I led a discussion on "The Future of the ASA," and F. Alton Everest, our first President, was the speaker at the banquet when we celebrated the 25th anniversary of ASA.

The theme of the 22nd annual ASA convention was, "A Christian Approach to Human Responsibility: A Psychological and Biological Discussion." The meeting was held August 28-31, 1967, on the beautiful campus of Stanford University. Here Richard H. Bube acted as our host. He also led a discussion on "The Relationship Between the ASA and the Scientific Community."

The ASA returned to Calvin College for its 23rd annual convention held August 20-23, 1968. The program at this convention was unique in that each of the five commissions had a part. There were biological sciences, history and philosophy of science, physical science, psychology, and social science. A retreat dealing with the purposes of the ASA was held on Monday preceeding the formal opening of the convention. This was the last convention at which the following statement appeared on the cover of the official program: "A group of Christian scientific men, devoting themselves to the task of reviewing, preparing, and distributing informaiton on the authenticity, historicity, and scientific aspects of the Holy Scriptures in order that the faith of many in Jesus Christ may be firmly established."

Starting with the official program in 1969 when we met at Gordon College, this statement was changed to: "The American

Scientific Affiliation is an association of men and women who have made a personal commitment of themselves and their lives to Jesus Christ as Lord and Savior, and who have made a personal commitment of themselves and their lives to a scientific understanding of the world."

Preceding the convention in 1969, a special workshop on science and religion in the high school classroom was held for high school science teachers. For some reason this workshop was poorly attended. The special speaker at the annual banquet was William E. Pannell, black evangelist from Detroit, who spoke on the subject, "My Friend, the Enemy." At this convention I was accompanied by my wife and her three sisters which fact seemed to cause some confusion at the time of registration.

The 25th convention of the ASA was held August 17-20, 1970, on the new campus of Bethel College, St. Paul, Minnesota. In his presidential address, Charles Hatfield praised God for the gift of mathematics. At least that was the way that Walt Hearn, editor of the *Newsletter*, described the speech with the title, "Men, Models, and Mathematics." I was happy to have Hazel Fetherhuff, faithful office secretary, to be present for the annual banquet. She was so faithful that when the ASA office moved form Mankato to Elgin, she moved with it and served as the office secretary until the time of her death in 1973.

In order to give more publicity to the ASA, I attended the International Congress on Evangelism in Ottawa. I traveled by bus and sent several boxes of ASA material ahead on another bus. What I did not know was that it was necessary that I be present with my materials to get through customs. The material never did get through so that all I had was with me in my briefcase. I was still able to make a number of contacts for the ASA.

"Man and His Environment" was the theme for the 26th convention held August 17-20, 1972, at Whitworth College, Spokane, Washington, under the chairmanship of Edwin A. Olson. At this convention I presented a paper entitled, "The American Scientific Affiliation—30 Years." For some time the ASA had been looking for a full-time Executive Secretary. I remember how John McIntyre and I spent considerable time together thinking of various possibilities for this position. Before the next annual meeting we had contacted Bill Sisterson who agreed to serve as Executive-Secretary starting with the annual convention in 1972.

For the first time in the history of the ASA we met in Canada August 21-24, 1972. We met on the campus of York University,

Downsview, Ontario. The theme of this meeting was, "Presuppositions of Science—A Christian Response." Harry Leith was the speaker at the banquet. The title of his address was "Galileo and the Church-Tensions with a Message for Today." It was on this occasion that Donald Boardman presented to me the plaque of appreciation, previously mentioned.

The 28th annual ASA meeting was held at Geneva College, Beaver Falls, Pennsylvania. The dates were August 20-23, 1973. The theme of the meeting was, "Creation, Evolution, and Molecular Biology." This was the first annual meeting at which William D. Sisterson, the newly appointed Executive Secretary, served as General Chairman. I felt a great relief after serving in that capacity for eleven years.

I well remember the opening address by David L. Willis who used as his subject, "Creation and/or Evolution." At the next annual convention held August 19-22, 1974, on the campus of Bethany Nazarene College, Bethany, Oklahoma, Charles Hatfield gave the opening address. He spoke on "Perspectives on Time." The film, "Footprints in Stone," was shown and a panel discussion followed.

The 30th annual convention was held August 15-18, 1975, on the San Diego campus of the University of California. I enjoyed being entertained in the home of Donald Hill, my roommate from university days at Rutgers. "What is Man," taken from Psalm 8 was the theme of the meeting. An innovation was started that year in that the meeting started on Friday evening and concluded Monday afternoon. This has been the pattern for the past number of ASA meetings. Another innovation was the introduction of concurrent sessions. At this meeting I presented two papers: 1) "Sir Isaac Newton, Scientist, Philosopher, Mathematician, Theologian," and 2) "Speaking the Truth in Love." Having the meetings over the weekend enables a number of ASA members to speak in area churches and thus spread the word about the ASA. This has been continued on a number of occasions.

Starting with the 31st ASA meetng, held August 20-23, 1976, at Wheaton College, we have been having special speakers giving a number of addresses. The first was Donald MacKay from Keele University, England. He spoke on "A Basic Interpretation of Science and Christianity." At the annual dinner our President spoke on, "Does the ASA take a Position on Controversial Issues?"

The 32nd annual ASA meeting was held August 12-13, 1977, at Nyack College, Nyack, New York. Kenneth Pike of the Summer Institute of Linguistics was our special speaker. His topics were, "Conscience and Culture," "Incarnation is a Culture," and "On the Relation of the Absolute to the Relative."

I remember the special worship service conducted by Robert L. Hermann, now our Executive Director. Upon my retirement from teaching at Mankato State in 1976, I spent most of the following year on a lecture tour using as my theme, "Science and the Bible." I spoke on this experience at this 32nd annual meeting. Clark Pinnock of McMaster Divinity College was the featured speaker at the 33rd annual meeting held August 11-14, 1978, at Hope College. The theme of this convention was, "A Christian Stewardship of Natural Resources." Jerry Bergman of Bowling Green University, an active participant in the current Creation-Evolution controversy, spoke on the subject, "The Attitude of College Students Toward the Creation-Evolution Controversy." He has since been dismissed from his teaching position at Bowling Green University.

The year 1979 was a year of tragedy for the ASA. Fire destroyed the building in Elgin in which our office was located. Most of our records and stock of books and journals was destroyed. Bill Sisterson was allowed little time to remove some of the ASA possessions. The insurance company partly reimbursed us, but the fire left the ASA in a precarious financial situation.

We returned to Stanford University for our 34th annual meeting. Dick Bube was the featured speaker who gave the opening address with the title, "How simple life would be if only things weren't so complicated." Of special note was the presidential address of A. Kurt Weiss who spoke on "The Weisses who escaped the Holocaust: grace that is greater than all our sins."

The 35th annual ASA meeting was held August 8-11, 1980, at Taylor University, Upland, Indiana. Our special speaker was Walter R. Thorson of the University of Alberta. His subject for the opening address was, "Reflections on the Practice of Outworn Creeds."

It was at this meeting that the announcement was made of the resignation of William Sisterson as Executive Director. I recall that I had been asked to serve in that capacity for one year. Since I insisted on moving the office to Mankato, the Executive Council decided to employ another person. President Weiss and other members of the Executive Council spent some time at this meeting searching for an interim Executive Director. We were fortunate to find Harry Lubansky, Jr., who was willing to take over this part-time job while he continued teaching at Judson College.

Our present Executive Director Robert L. Hermann assumed this responsibility the following year.

It is interesting to note that beginning with this meeting the word chair was used in place of chairman to designate the person in charge of a given session. At this meeting I presented a paper with the title, "Creation, Conflict, Commitment." I had the pleasure of meeting Ronald Rich and his wife. He had been one of my better students at Bluffton College, while she had been a student at Goshen College when I taught there. They and their son attended the church service on Sunday morning when I was the speaker.

In the summer of 1981, I had a heart attack and thus was unable to be present at the 36th annual meeting held August 14-17 at Eastern College, St. Davids, Pennsylvania. This was a great disappointment to me, especially since Owen Gingerich of Harvard University was the invited speaker and the theme of the meeting was, "The Heavens Declare the Glory of God." He had been a student of mine at Goshen College. Nevertheless, I was able to present my paper, "Science of the Reformers," on videotape. I also sent an audiotape which was used when Owen Gingerich was introduced. Thus my attendance record of perfect attendance at annual ASA meetings was broken. I did feel greatly encouraged when I received a wonderful greeting signed by many of my ASA friends. All I can say is thank you, thank you, and may God's name be praised.

We returned to Calvin College for the 37th annual ASA meeting. A special feature was a biology workshop which took place one day preceeding the opening session. We were very happy to have V. Elving Anderson, former ASA President, as the special speaker. The title of his opening address was, "Design for Development." Other titles were: "The Design of the Design" and "Man the Designer." At this meeting, we had Wilbert H. Rusch with us who spoke on "History and Aims of the Creation Research Society." This preceded my paper entitled, "The Relationship Between the American Scientific Affiliation and the Creation Research Society." To me it is interesting that Robert L. Hermann, who had been the President of the ASA in 1981, was now Executive Director. He gave up his professorship at Oral Roberts University in order to serve the ASA.

The theme of the 38th annual ASA meeting held August 5-8, 1983, was "North American Resources and World Needs." The meeting was held at George Fox College, Newberg, Oregon. The featured speaker was Loren Wilkenson of Regent College.

The titles of his addresses were: "The Natural World as a Frontier to be Developed," "The Natural World as a Wilderness to be Preserved," and "The Natural World as a Garden to be Tended." I had the interesting experience of traveling by train from Minneapolis to Portland and then visiting my sister Carrie and her husband Kenneth Dodd a few days before the convention. She and her family came to hear me present my paper, "The Time Problem." A special feature of this meeting was a salmon bake held at a rural setting on property owned by the college.

The ASA has always been concerned with publication. As previously stated, we published *Modern Science and Christan Faith* in 1948. This was followed by *Evolution and Christian Thought Today*. In 1970 Gary Collins edited as ASA sponsored a book with the title, *Our Society in Turmoil*. We have also published three monographs: "Christian Theism and the Empirical Sciences" by Cornelius Jaarsma, "Creation and Evolution" by Russell L. Mixter, and "The Eye as an Optical Instrument" by Frank Allen.

The *Journal of the American Scientific Affiliation* (first called *The American Scientific Affiliation Bulletin*), under the editorship of Marion D. Barnes, first appeared in January 1949. This is a quarterly journal dealing with a wide variety of subjects in the general area of science and the Bible. After Volume 3, Delbert Eggenberger was designated editor. He served from 1950 to 1961, followed by David Moberg 1962-64. Russell L. Mixter edited the *Journal* from 1965-68, followed by Richard Bube, 1969-83. The present editor is Wilbur Bullock.

A number of years ago the ASA sponsored a tract edited by Alfred Eckert and published by Good News Publishers. In this tract a number of ASA members gave their personal testimony for the Lord Jesus Christ. They were George L. Bate, Walter R. Hearn, Russell L. Mixter, Walter L. Starkey, Robert B. Fisher, Brian P. Sutherland, John R. Brobeck, Stanley W. Olson, Edward J. Matson, and Kenneth Pike.

One of the most interesting publications of the ASA is the newsletter published bimonthly since 1959. F. Alton Everest served as editor from February 1958 to September 1969. Walt Hearn also very capably handled this job.

God's Very Good Creation

(This was originally prepared to be given at a meeting of
Mennonite Concerned Members in 1957.)

The Psalmist says, "The heavens declare the glory of God; and the firmament showeth his handiwork" (Psalm 19:1). We also read in Psalm 8:1-9:

"O Lord our Lord, how excellent is thy name in all the earth! who hast set thy glory above the heavens. Out of the mouth of babes and sucklings hast thou ordained strength because of thine enemies, that thou mightest still the enemy and the avenger. When I consider thy heavens, the work of thy fingers, the moon and the stars, which thou hast ordained, what is man, that thou art mindful of him? and the son of man, that thou visitest him? For thou hast made him a little lower than the angels, and hast crowned him with glory and honor. Thou madest him to have dominion over the works of thy hands; thou hast put all things under his feet: All sheep and oxen, yea, and the beasts of the field; the fowl of the air, and the fish of the sea, and whatsoever passeth through the paths of the seas. O Lord our Lord, how excellent is thy name in all the earth!"

Here we observe how David, the Psalmist, viewed this good creation of God. He seems to be overwhelmed and asks how mankind fits into this perfect creation. He is aware of the beauty of the created universe, but he also realizes how prone he is to sin. He seems to realize his insignificance in this vast universe, and yet he rejoices in that he is given dominion over much of animal life.

This discussion will be divided into four parts: first the atom, second the human body, third the earth as a part of the solar system, and fourth the stars and galaxies.

Let us take another look at the first chapter of Genesis. After the creation of light, the statement is made: "And God saw the light, that it was good."

After the creation of vegetation in verse 12, the statement is made: "And God saw that it was good."

After the creation of the sun, moon, and stars, we read: "And God saw that it was good."

After the creation of the animals, we find the statement: "And God saw that it was good."

Finally, after the creation of man in his own image, we read: "And God saw everything that he had made, and, behold, it was very good."

Here we see that God created a perfect universe and placed man upon the earth so that he might have fellowship with God forever.

We observe, however, in the third chapter of Genesis, that sin entered the world. The result was a curse on all creation and a loss of perfect fellowship between God and man.

We read: "And unto Adam he said, Because thou hast hearkened unto the voice of thy wife, and hast eaten of the tree, of which I commanded thee, saying: Thou shalt not eat of it; cursed is the ground for thy sake; in sorrow shalt thou eat of it all the days of thy life; Thorns also and thistles shall it bring forth unto thee; and thou shalt eat the herb of the field; In the sweat of thy face shalt thou eat bread, till thou return unto the ground; for out of it wast thou taken: for dust thou art, and unto dust shalt thou return" (Gen. 31:17-19).

The results of sin are very far reaching, both in time and in space. Today we suffer due to the sin of our first parents, Adam and Eve. Yet in spite of the curse due to sin, we are still able to discern many aspects of the love of God as manifested in His very good creation. Since this is a tremendous subject with many ramifications, I will discuss only a few of them. However, in each area, there is much material which makes us marvel at the wonderful work of our creator.

If we carefully observe, we are able to sense the results of creation almost everywhere. Most of us do not take the time or have the patience to explore the handiwork of the creator who has made everything good in its original state.

As we live our very busy lives in this world of God's creation, we seldom stop to gaze up to view the moon, planets, and stars, or to look all around us where so much beauty exists. Many of us are too busy or too blind to be able to see the marvels of creation, from the tiny flower, growing in the crevice of the rock, to the majestic high mountains, filled with beauty and treasures.

Besides all this, God has also created hundreds of thousands of insects and animals. Let us consider the marvelous honey bee created both for the purpose of helping in the pollination of many kinds of flowers and for the production of honey, which is useful as food for the bee as well as for mankind. It is very difficult for us to comprehend how the bee is able to find the sources of honey and then the way back to the hive. We see again the handiwork of God.

The Bible tells us that we should consider the ant, another of God's good creations. "Go to the ant, thou sluggard; consider her ways, and be wise: which having no guide, overseer, or ruler, provideth her meat in the summer, and gathereth her food in the harvest" (Prov. 6:6-8). Here we should be able to learn lessons from one of the least of the creation. Are we as busy as the ant in doing God's will?

This reminds me of the life of S. G. Shetler, known to most of us. His son, Sanford, in his book, *Preacher of the People, A Biography of S. G. Shetler*, tells of the very busy life of his father. Just a month before he died, he preached on Sunday morning in his home church, preached the dedication sermon for the new basement chapel of the Mountain Meadow congregation in the afternoon, and preached there again that night.

Let us consider one of the smallest units of matter, called the atom. Although the word, atom, means uncutable, we have learned that it is possible to disect the atom into parts known as protons, neutrons, and electrons. These elementary particles combine with each other in a variety of ways into ninety-two naturally occuring kinds of atoms which we call elements. The simplest is known as hydrogen, occuring as a gas under ordinary conditions, while the most complex is called uranium, a solid under normal conditions of temperature and pressure. Every atom is composed of a nucleus surrounded by a cloud of electrons.

Besides the ninety-two naturally occuring elements there are about a dozen elements which have been produced in scientific laboratories. These are called transuranium elements, more complex than uranium, and disintegrate spontaneously into simpler kinds of atoms. We say that they are radioactive, meaning that they are like radium which changes into simpler atoms. By simplicity we mean having few electrons about the nucleus.

The simplest atom is called hydrogen and consists of one positive proton in the nucleus and one negative electron which travels around the nucleus in a nearly circular orbit. It is interesting, according to our best present knowledge, that the element hydrogen is the most common in the universe. It comprises 90% of the atoms or about three-quarters of the mass of the universe.

Helium, the next simplest natural atom, accounts for most of the remainder. Each atom of helium is composed of two protons and two neutrons in the nucleus and two electrons circling the nucleus. More complex atoms are formed by having additional protons and neutrons in the nucleus and additional electrons traveling outside the nucleus. After helium we have lithium with three electrons, berillium with four electrons, boron with five electrons, carbon with six electrons and so on to uranium with ninety-two electrons.

Motion appears in all of God's creation, from the smallest atom to the largest galaxy. Electrons are continually moving around the nucleus of every atom. Molecules, composed of atoms, again exhibit motion. The molecules of air in this room, composed of nitrogen, oxygen, water vapor, and dust particles are moving very rapidly, approximately 1,400 feet per second. This value depends on the temperature.

This is a very complicated motion due to the huge number of molecules in any given column. Molecules of water, whether in the state of gas, liquid, or solid, are in constant motion. Even in the form of ice, the water molecules are always vibrating. As the temperature increases, the velocity of each molecule increases.

In the case of the stars, the interior temperature is very, very high, with resulting very great velocities of the component parts. The interior temperature is measured in millions of degrees. This results in the disruption of many of the atoms with an extremely rapid motion of electrons and of the constituent parts of the nucleus of the atom.

Though it may appear that you are quite still, sitting on a chair, yet it is known that you are moving in a number of different ways since the earth is moving. It is rotating on its axis, revolving around the sun, with its axis wobbling, as well as precessing like a top, is revolving with a common center of earth and moon, and our sun is revolving about the center of the milky way galaxy, carrying the earth with it.

All atoms are so small in size that they cannot be observed with the most powerful microscope. The approximate size of the hydrogen atom is one-hundredth part of one-millionth of one centimeter. Remember that it takes 2.5 centimeters to make one inch. Thus it would take 250 million hydrogen atoms placed side by side to take up the space of one inch. Their constituent parts are approximately one-hundred-thousandth of the size of the atom. In order to begin to appreciate such a small size, it is a well established fact that under ordinary conditions of temperature and pressure, there are over ten million million million air molecules per cubic centimeter in this room at the present time.

Truly, it is amazing how God has created the entire physical universe with such attention to details. We simply are unable to comprehend his very good creation. Remember, too, that as far as scientists have found, atoms of hydrogen are all alike wherever found in the universe. This means that atoms of hydrogen, whether found in the sun, on the earth, or in a most distant star, are exactly alike. In this they differ from snowflakes, no two of which are alike.

However, I should mention that many elements have isotopes. That is, some of the atoms of a given element have different numbers of neutrons in the nucleus, while having the same number of electrons outside the nucleus. Thus hydrogen is known to have three isotopes.

Ordinary hydrogen has one proton in the nucleus; a second form, deuterium, has one proton and one neutron in the nucleus; while a third form, tritium, has one proton and two neutrons in the nucleus. In some cases we also have what are known as isobars, in which case two elements, with different numbers of electrons outside the nucleus, still have the same combined number of protons and neutrons in the nucleus. Evidently the creator had a master plan as he formed the entire universe out of nothing.

Let us now think of the mass or what might be considered the weight of an atom of hydrogen. This is so very tiny that it would require one million times one million times one million times one million of hydrogen atoms to make a mass of one gram. Remember that it takes about 450 grams to make one pound. Again, such numbers are beyond our comprehension.

You may ask the question: How do we know that these numbers are correct? The answer is complicated, but these results have been checked by many scientists, working in many laboratories, over a long period of time. To me they are as exact as the calculated time of the eclipse of the sun or of the moon. I was able to observe a total eclipse of the sun in North Carolina on March 7, 1970. It occured exactly to the very second, at the time calculated. This was the only total eclipse of the sun I have ever observed. It was an experience that I will never forget.

Now we come to the most interesting aspect of atomic theory which was unknown at the time I graduated from college. This is current history. As early as 1905, Albert Einstein predicted that mass could be converted into energy by the famous equation: E equals m times c squared. Here E stands for energy, m for mass, and c for the velocity of light. This was experimentally verified in 1939. Since that time much work has been done in this area. The most striking and devastating result of the release of nuclear energy has been the destruction of Hiroshima and Nagasaki in Japan in 1945. Thousands of citizens of those cities were killed, or severely burned, or tortured in many ways. I have viewed with horror films which have portrayed the bombings of those cities. This resulted in the bringing of the war with Japan to a speedy ending. We may still question whether this use of nuclear power was necessary. Our government officials said that it was necessary. I am of the opinion that it was not necessary at all. Only God can judge.

The problem of nuclear energy has been with us ever since. Many of us are not aware of the imminent dangers of nuclear destruction. Donald Kraybill, in his book, *Facing Nuclear War*, has helped us as a people of faith to think clearly about this complex and urgent issue. He combines distilled facts and illuminating analysis with an uncompromising evangelical faith.

Our own Mennonite Church has passed a resolution from its General Assembly, August 1982, with the title: "Security and the Current World Arms Race."

I now wish to quote a paragraph from that resolution: "While celebrating our hope, we are also aware of a growing despair in the world due to the escalation of the arms race. The development of new nuclear weapons proceeds amidst a political mood which is apparently ready to use them. Many are now saying that the question is no longer if nuclear weapons will be used, but when. The probable resulting devastation to the human race is beyond comprehension."

This reminds me of the paper on World Peace which I read in 1958 at the annual meeting of the American Scientific Affiliation, the group of scientists interested in the relationship between science and Christianity. I quoted from Mr. Bernard Baruch, Chairman of the United Nations Atomic Energy Commission.

He stated in the opening address to the Commission: "My fellow members of the United Nations Atomic Energy Commission, and my fellow citizens of the world. We are here to make a choice between the quick and the dead. That is our business. Behind the black portent of the atomic age lies a hope which, if seized upon by faith, can work our salvation. If we fail, then we have damned every man to be the slave of fear. Let us not deceive ourselves. We must elect world peace or world destruction." I can now say: How prophetic.

Senator Mark Hatfield has recently stated: "The U. S. today possesses 31,000 nuclear warheads, both straight and tactical.

This equals 8 billion tons of TNT or the equivalent of 625,000 Hiroshima-type bombs. This stockpile can kill every Russian thirty-six times. Unleashing this power would ensure the virtual destruction of the earth. Yet we continue to pour our financial and intellectual resources and our scientific ingenuity into increasing these arsenals still further."

Certain atoms such as uranium, with 235 particles in the nucleus, when bombarded by neutrons, break up into two lighter elements with a resultant loss of mass. The result is the production of a very large amount of energy.

When one gram of mass, about one-five-hundredth of a pound, is converted into energy by the equation E equals M times C squared, the results amount to 900 million million million ergs. This amount of energy is equivalent to 25 million kilowatt hours. Based on a rate of 10 cents per kilowatt hour, this would cost 2 1/2 million dollars.

Thus we see that the energy from one pound of matter would be worth approximately 750 million dollars. However, as we have witnessed, there are many hazards involved in the production of nuclear energy. We are again reminded of the wisdom of the creator in that we have such an enormous amount of energy for our use.

I will now consider some of the marvels of the human body as the second argument for the case of a good creator. Here I wish to give credit to Dr. Paul Brand and to Philip Yancy for some of the ideas expressed in their book, *Fearfully and Wonderfully Made*.

This title comes from Psalm 139:14. "I will praise thee; for I am fearfully and wonderfully made: marvelous are thy works; and that my soul knoweth right well."

In the preface, Philip Yancy has expressed the aim of the writers by saying, "Dr. Brand and I desire that this book will help span the chasm that for too long has separated the created world from its source. God invented matter. He invested His great creative self in this world and, specifically, in the design of our bodies. The least we can do is to be grateful."

Making use of Paul's analogy, the writer says: "The body is one unit, though it is made up of many cells, and though all its cells are many, they form one body. If the white cell should say, because I am not a brain cell, I do not belong to the body, would it cease to be a part of the body? And if the muscle cell should say to the optic nerve cell, because I am not an optic nerve cell,

I do not belong to the body, it would not for that reason cease to be a part of the body. If the whole body were an auditory nerve, where would be the sense of sight? But in fact God has arranged the cells in the body, every one of them, just as He wanted them to be. If all cells were the same, where would the body be? As it is, there are many cells, but one body."

The number of cells in the human body is enormous. It may be difficult to specify the exact number, but we know that it runs into many, many billions. We should also remember that each cell is composed of millions of atoms. Again we find it very difficult to comprehend the complexity of the human body. As we consider our bodies, we marvel at the wisdom and power of the creator.

We are permitted to live on this planet for a short time—three score years and ten—and then our bodies are changed drastically and turn into atoms like those which compose the mass of the earth—to dust as stated in the Bible.

Just to think that our bodies are the temple of the Holy Spirit. What a high honor that God has chosen to live in our bodies if we are believers in Jesus Christ as Savior and Lord.

Since the Holy Spirit indwells us, we should be very careful how we take care of this temple. Our bodies should be given the very best of care and there should be no attempt made to mutilate or destroy it. No born again Christian should engage in activities harmful to the body which God has created. Some of us have been permitted to live beyond the three score years and ten. We ought to be very thankful to our Heavenly Father for this opportunity to serve Him in every way possible.

Consider the organ of sight. Inside the human eye there are 107 million cells. Seven million are cones, each sending messages to the brain when they are crossed by a few photons of light. Because of the cones we can distinguish a thousand shades of color. The other hundred million cells are rods, used for light of low intensity. We do not see color with the rods, but we are able to distinguish brightness of light sources which may differ in intensity by a factor of one billion.

Now consider how the human body grows from the fertilization of a single egg. We cannot explain, and therefore view as a miracle, how the sperm unites with the egg in the process which ultimately produces a human being. The existence of that cell should be one of the greatest astonishments of the earth. After a period of nine months billions of cells appear, all formed from a single fertilized ovum. Finally a baby is born with many, many cells, but one organism.

These billions of cells work together in a marvelous fashion. The body maintains its shape but is constantly being renewed by new cells which are welcomed. The secret to membership is contained in each cell nucleus, chemically coiled in a strand of DNA.

In the first cell, the DNA splits down the middle as each new cell is formed. Along the way cells specialize, but each carries the instruction book of one hundred thousand genes. It is estimated that DNA contains instructions that if written out, would fill a thousand six-hundred-page books. Every cell possesses a genetic code so complete that the entire body could be reassembled from information from any one of the body's cells.

The DNA is so narrow and compacted that the genes in all of my body's cells would fit into an ice cube, yet if unwound and joined together end to end, the strand could reach from the earth to the sun and back more than four hundred times. Remember that the distance from the earth to the sun is 93 million miles.

This may seem to be totally unrealistic. Calculations show that over 400,000 billion billion atoms are involved in a single strand of DNA. How our very good creator did this is completely beyond our comprehension. We are reminded of the Scripture passage which states: "For my thoughts are not your thoughts, neither are your ways my ways, saith the Lord. For as the heavens are higher than the earth, so are my ways higher than your ways, and my thoughts than your thoughts" (Isa. 55:8,9). Yet the fact remains that some scientists attempt to explain all life, including human life, without the need of a creator.

Now consider the solid structure of the body. Bones are a very important part of the human body. No research has yet discovered a material as well-suited for the body's needs as bone, which comprises only one-fifth of our body weight.

It has been demonstrated that the arrangement of bone cells forms the lightest structure, made of least material to support the body's weight. As the only hard material in the body, bone possesses incredible strength, enough to protect and support every other cell.

There are twenty-six bones in each foot, about the same number in each hand. Most of us use our feet in walking some 65,000 miles or more than two and one-half times around the world, in a lifetime. Our body weight is evenly spread out through architecturally perfect arches which serve as springs, and the bending of the knees and ankles absorbs stress. Bone's strength is quiet and dependable. It serves us well, without fanfare, and comes to our attention only when we encounter a rude fracturing stress that exceeds its own high tolerance.

Our bodies have a covering called the skin, which is like a window in that we are able to read of the activities within. An allergist can crack the secret of your body's likes and dislikes merely by mapping out a grid on your back and pricking the skin with pin-size potions. The skin also provides a window to the emotional world within.

There is no organ like the skin. Its weight is about nine pounds and amazingly, each of us has a different pattern for the ridges, therefore making fingerprinting important. We have a love affair with our skin so that we attempt to adorn it. Many persons spend large sums of money in an attempt to improve on the work of the creator. Various kinds of cosmetics are used to make the body beautiful. Some go so far as to have a face-lift.

Frequent bathing of the body is necessary, but why do we spend so much time and effort trying to change the appearance of the body? More than that of any other species, our skin is designed not so much for appearance, as for relating to others—that is, for being touched.

The skin does not exist merely to give the body an appearance. It is also a vital source of ceaseless information about our environment. Most of our sense organs—the ears, the eyes, the nose—are confined to one spot. The skin is rolled thin with very many transmitters, informing the brain of important news.

Think of the variety of stimuli your skin monitors each day: wind, particles, parasites, changes in pressure, temperature, humidity, light, and different kinds of radiation. Skin is tough enough to withstand the rigors of pounding on asphalt, yet sensitive enough to have bare toes tickled by a light breeze. Of all the senses, touch is the most trustworthy.

Perception by the skin is more basic than perception through an eye or an ear. It senses a need and responds instinctively, personally. The best illustration of this truth is Jesus Christ. The book of Hebrews sums up this experience on earth by declaring that we have a leader who can be touched with the feelings of our infirmities (Heb. 4:15). God himself saw the need to come along beside us, not just love us at a distance. Before taking on a body,

God had no personal experience of physical pain or of the effect of rubbing against needy persons. But God dwelt among us, and touched us, and the time spent here allows Him to more fully identify with our pain. Through Jesus Christ our creator has become one of us, for which we should be eternally grateful.

One of the many mysteries of life for us as finite human beings is the relation between the physical and the spiritual. This thought was brought vividly to my attention some years ago when I was teaching at Elizabethtown College. A chapel speaker challenged the audience to try to think spiritually, with no thoughts of the physical world, for a period of five minutes. I now ask you to do that. We are so oriented to the physical that it is very difficult to think spiritually.

The Bible clearly teaches that we have two natures, the physical and the spiritual. We are to love God with all our heart, our soul, and our mind (Matt. 22:37).

Often spoken of as the mind-body problem, it is sometimes rather difficult to distinguish between the two. I recognize the fact that I have a physical body which includes my brain. But how are my mind and my brain related? Which is the most important? Which one controls the other organs of my body? Here the distinction becomes fuzzy. Closely related to my mind is my spirit. And closely related to my spirit is the Holy Spirit indwelling my body.

The apostle Paul speaks of a spiritual body as well as of a natural body in I Cor. 15:44. It is likely that most of us would agree that the natural body refers to the physical body which is composed of atoms. But what can be said of the spiritual body? We believe that it is a reality. We are told that it is incorruptible, that it is glorious, that it is powerful, and that it will live eternally in heaven.

This brings up the subject of the resurrection from the dead. Do we believe that God will rearrange the atoms which compose our physical body into a body like our present body?

Another question might be, which body? Our physical bodies continually change so that the body you have today is not the body which you had ten years ago. And what of the body of the person in old age whose body has decreased to a size much smaller than when young? And then what of the body of the cripple and deformed?

I have a friend who has two sons whose bodies never developed in a normal fashion. He is thinking that in heaven these two sons will walk up to him and say, "Hello Dad," in spite of the fact that they never uttered a word while living on this planet.

We may think that we know much about our bodies, but I wonder whether we even begin to understand the mystery of our bodies. In fact, modern science has now reached the point where the constituent parts of the atom are no longer being thought of as indivisible entities but that they are composed of parts which are given names such as quarks. It is clear that I do not possess a spiritual body here on earth, but I do possess a spirit.

Even though I may not be able to understand, yet I believe that my spiritual life is far more important than my physical life. The first is eternal and capable of communication with God, while the latter will decay and turn into dust. Concerning the resurrection, Paul, speaking by inspiration, says: "But some man will say, How are the dead raised? and with what body do they come? Thou fool, that which thou sowest is not quickened, except it die. And that which thou sowest, thou sowest not that body which shall be, but bare grain, it may chance of wheat, or of some other grain. But God giveth it a body as it hath pleased him, and to every seed his own body" (I Cor. 15:35-38).

For us as human beings, this earth on which we live for a short span of time is one of the most important parts of God's very good creation. Though marred due to sin, there is much beauty and many treasures both on its surface and in its interior. Our country, the United States of America, offers us much in the way of natural beauty.

It has been my privilege to travel over our country from New England, over the Appalachian Mountains, through the heartland of America with its broad plains, then to the majestic peaks of the Rocky Mountains, through the beautiful deserts of the Southwest and over the lower coastal ranges to the beaches of California, Oregon, and Washington. This has been a very wonderful experience for me and I am sure for many others. I have thoroughly enjoyed this bit of God's creation. The same can be said of many other parts of this planet, one of the nine known planets which keep their regular orbits around the sun.

Earth is one of the smaller planets of the solar system. Other planets are: Mercury, Venus, Mars, Jupiter, Saturn, Uranus, Neptune, and Pluto. The orbits of the planets around the sun vary tremendously. These orbits are in the form of ellipses which are elongated circles.

The planet Mercury is located at a distance of about thirty-six million miles from the sun and requires eighty-eight days to complete one revolution around the sun.

The planet Venus is located sixty-seven million miles from the sun and requires 225 days for one revolution.

At the other extreme, the planet Neptune is located 2,794 million miles from the sun and takes 165 years for one circuit.

The outermost planet Pluto, only discovered by Astronomer Tombaugh at the Lowell Observatory in 1930, is at a distance of 3,670 million miles from the sun and requires 248 years to complete a circuit around the sun.

Judging by human standards, the size of the solar system is enormous. Just to think of ninety-three million miles, the distance from the earth to the sun, is difficult to comprehend, but that is small as compared to the distance of Pluto at 3,670 million miles from the sun.

From the human point of view, Earth appears to be quite large; but from the creator's point of view, it is very small. Yet it is not insignificant. God created the Earth, having a diameter of about 8,000 miles and a mass of 6,600 million, million, million tons to be the abode of mankind. It was created perfect in every way. It is large enough for billions of people to live on its surface, has abundant resources, massive enough to retain its atmosphere, yet not so massive as to make it difficult for us to walk upon its surface, located the proper distance from the sun, turning on its axis every twenty-four hours for our benefit, having its axis of rotation inclined so that we can have change of seasons, and having the proper kind of atmosphere so that we are able to breathe. It also helps to keep us warm and shields us from deadly rays from the sun. The evidence of the creator is all around us.

We also observe much around us that is not beautiful. We experience floods, storms, hurricanes, tornadoes, fires, murders, wars, deception, greed, violence, lootings, and many other evidences of evil on the surface of the Earth. All these are the results of sin of which all of us are guilty. The devil is still busy, attempting to deceive mankind. Many passages from the Scriptures tell us of the results of sin. "For we know that the whole creation groaneth and travaileth in pain together until now" (Romans 8:22). Though we must face this dark side of life, there is a brighter side as Paul says in Romans 6:23: "For the wages of sin is death, but the gift of God is eternal life through Jesus Christ our Lord."

The solar system, of which the planet Earth is a small part, is all a part of the work of the creator. It is here that we begin to see more of the wisdom and power of God in His very good creation. The solar system is simple and yet very complex. The book of Genesis tells us very little about this system. There we read, "And God said, Let there be lights in the firmament of the heavens to divide the day from the night, and let them be for signs, and for seasons, and for days and years. And let them be for lights in the firmament of the heavens to give light upon the earth and it was so. And God made two great lights, the greater light to rule the day, and the lesser light to rule the night; he made the stars also" (Gen. 1:14-16).

The last phrase, "he made the stars also," is very interesting. We might consider this phrase to be an afterthought that is not of much importance. Since the purpose of the Bible is to reveal God's concern for mankind, it is therefore clear that the sun and the moon are much more important than all the hundreds of billions of stars.

Though we now know that every star is a gigantic powerhouse sending out in all directions enormous amounts of radiant heat and energy, yet they appear to be so small as to be insignificant. Their appearance is deceiving due to their great distance from the Earth from which we view them. In general, objects appear to be smaller the farther they are removed from the observer.

Thus, from the point of view of the entire universe, stars are very important while the earth is quite insignificant. From the point of view of a human being, the sun is of the greatest importance while we might well get along without the stars. To most of us their purpose is to show the glory of the creator. To the astronomer, however, the study of the stars is of the greatest importance.

Personally, the study of the stars gives me the greatest appreciation of the wisdom and power of the creator. Just to think of the enormous amount of energy bursting forth from each of the billions and billions of stars causes me to wonder at the glory of the creator. It is in this area of study that there is no end.

We interpret the Genesis passage to refer to the sun and the moon. No mention is made of the planets. At that time the solar system was unknown. Historically the concept of such a system was a late comer. Not until the time of Niclausaus Copernicus (1473-1543) was the present-day point of view accepted by most people. For many years his idea of the sun being the center of the solar system was disputed. This incident in the history of science shows how very difficult it is for us to accept new ideas. We are now quite certain that God created the solar system with the massive and extremely bright sun at the center. The nine principle planets revolve around the sun in great orbits. A number of the planets have moons or satellites revolving about them.

In addition to the nine planets, the creator has placed thousands of small bodies, known as asteroids or minor planets, rotating around the sun between the orbits of Mars and Jupiter.

The creator has also seen fit to add comets and meteors to the solar system. Comets, once greatly feared by mankind, revolve around the sun, often in greatly elongated orbits. A comet consists of a foggy envelope surrounding a nucleus of frozen material, with a long tail always extending away from the sun.

The best known comet is Haley's comet, having a period of seventy-five years. Many of us have looked forward for years to observe Halley's comet. It had made an appearance in 1910 so we looked forward to 1985 or 1986. However, we were greatly disappointed by its very faint appearance. I am not certain that I saw it even though I went out to view it on a number of mornings. However, I should add that I have been able to see at least two other comets, both of which had long tails, giving a spectacular appearance.

Meteors are rather small pieces of matter which make bright trails across the sky as they enter the atmosphere of the Earth. They are sometimes called shooting stars but they are not stars in any sense of the word. Most of them are of the size of the head of a pin. Some are larger and some so large that they finally arrive on the surface of the Earth. They are then called meteorites. Thousands of them have been picked up from the earth. One is able to view them in large museums. A very large meteorite struck northern Arizona many years ago. It left a huge hole in the Earth. It is so large that it could contain ten football fields. I have seen this crater left by the meteorite on a number of occasions.

As far as size and energy production goes, the sun is the most important part of the solar system. Located at an average distance from the Earth of ninety-three million miles, the sun is the source of practically all of our light and energy. Though appearing rather small as viewed from Earth, the sun is so large that it could contain more than one million Earths. It consists of multiplied billions of violently reacting atoms sending out into space huge quantities of energy. Scientists now view the sun as a large hydrogen bomb. Here matter is constantly being converted into energy. Calculations show that the sun is losing mass at the rate of thousands of tons every second. Yet the mass of the sun is so large that it will require millions of years before the brightness will noticeably decrease.

The rate of the sun's radiation is about 70,000 horsepower per square yard of its surface. Though Earth receives only one-two-billionth of the sun's energy, this is sufficient to supply all of our needs. You may ask, where does all the remainder of the energy from the sun go? The answer is that it goes out into space and therefore useless as far as the Earth is concerned.

Again we see the wisdom of the creator when God placed the Earth at the proper distance from the sun, not too close, to burn us to a crisp, or too far away, to cause us to freeze to death. We are made to exclaim: God is so good.

Finally, let us consider the twinkling stars, many of which can be seen on any clear night. By very careful observation it is possible to see 2,000 stars from any one position on the surface of the Earth. It has been calculated that there are 6,000 stars visible to the naked eye when all points of the Earth are taken into consideration.

With a small telescope it is possible to see many more stars. With a very large telescope, like the 200-inch telescope on Mount Polamar in California, it is possible to see multiplied billions of stars. Some of these are larger than the sun and all are located at enormous distances from the Earth. It is here that we get a larger view of the creator's power and glory. Stars have been observed by numerous people for many centuries. Many persons have pondered their nature, purpose, and distance from Earth. They are located at such enormous distances from us that it has been very difficult to measure the distance to any star.

In the book of Job we read: "Is not God in the height of heaven? and behold the height of the stars, how high they are" (Job 22:12). Men in that day had no conception of the distance to the stars. Yet this phrase is quite interesting in that it allows for very great distances. This reminds me that the Bible does not make mistakes. It is the Word of God and is inspired, inerrant, and infalible.

Now, we may ask. What is a star? The answer to this question was unknown for many years. By diligent study, astronomers are now quite certain that stars are like the sun, though located at enormous distance both from the sun and from the Earth. It was not until 1838 that Bessel in Germany was able to measure the distance to a star. He did this by the method of parallax, using the telescope and the methods of trigonometry. Here I wish to bring in a personal reminiscence. Some of you may remember J. B. Smith who taught at Hesston College and was the first president of Eastern Mennonite College, then Eastern Mennonite School.

I remember at a time before I went to college that J. B. Smith was preaching at the Allensville Mennonite Church. In his sermon he mentioned that by means of trigonometry one is able to measure the distance to a star. That was a new thought to me and gave me the desire to study trigonometry. At that time, I had little idea of what the subject of trigonometry was about. I had not forgotten that idea as I studied, not one but two courses in trigonometry, and later studied and taught courses in astronomy. Though I have never actually measured the distance to a star, I am confident that I understand how this is possible.

In order to use the method of parallax in stellar measurement, we determine the position of a given star against the background of more distant stars. A measurement is made at two times six months apart. In that time, the Earth will have traveled halfway of its nearly circular orbit around the sun. I illustrate as follows:

By definition, the sine of an angle, here written sin p, equals the ratio of the opposite side to the hypotenuse, or longer side of the right angle. In the figure we have sin p = r/s, therefore s = r/ sin p.

For the case of stellar distances, the angle of parallax is very small, less than one second of arc. Angles are measured in degrees, minutes, and seconds. 90 degrees equals one right angle, 60 minutes equals one degree, while 60 seconds equals one minute. Thus it is apparent that a second of arc is small. It is found that the angles of parallax of stars are always less than one second. This accounts for the fact that distances to stars are difficult to measure. Only a relative few stars are close enough to be measured by the method of parallax. So other methods have been devised which allow us to measure the distance to more distant stars. Indirect methods are based on the relative brightness of stars, combined with the well-known principle that the apparent intensity of a source of light varies inversely with the square of the distance from the observer. Given two light sources located at 300 feet and 3,000 feet respectively from the observer, the second being ten times farther away from the observer than the first, both having the same brightness when viewed close to the source. Then the first source will appear to be 100 times as bright as the second.

Stellar distances are so great that they are usualy expressed in terms of light-years, this being the distance that light travels in one year. The distance to the nearest star, Alpha Centauri, is 4.3 light-years. Light travels at the rate of 186,000 miles per second. Since there are 30.6 billion seconds in one year, there are 5.8×10^{12} miles or 5.8 million million miles in one light-year. Only a few hundred stars are close enough to be measured by the method using parallax and trigonometry. By multiplying 4.3 by 5.8×10^{12} we obtain approximately 25×10^{12} or 25 million million miles. This distance is many times the distance from the earth to the sun. Many stars are located at distances from the earth which are measured in thousands or millions of light-years.

Just think what this means. What we see tonight may have been traveling for thousands or millions of years before it reaches us. Thus we are looking at a very old universe. Some people may say that this is not true. All I can say is that this result is the best that scientists have been able to come up with. Since science is constantly changing, we may have a different explanation for great stellar distances in the future.

Some stars are grouped together in what are called clusters, some open and others globular. An example of the latter, called M13 in Hercules, located at a distance of 30,000 light-years, contains approximately 500,000 stars of average mass equal to that of the sun. Even though globular clusters contain thousands of stars, they are so distant that most of them appear as a single source of starlight. A telescope is required to reveal the individual stars.

A large number of stars are called variable stars, meaning that the apparent brightness varies from time to time. There are various types of variable stars. While in Arizona, I made a study of what is known as an eclipsing variable. This star is called YY Canis Minoris, located in the constellation Little Dog in which is located the bright star Procyon. This star is so dim that a telescope is required to see it.

Eclipsing variable stars consist of two or more stars, located relatively close to each other, which are revolving about a common axis. The reason that such a star is variable is that they eclipse one another in their paths around their common center of gravity. I studied this variable star for a period of three months. A large amount of information can be obtained from the study of such a star.

Again we are made to marvel at the wisdom and power of God, since every star is moving at a tremendous velocity with no mishaps. Astronomers have never witnessed a collision between two or more stars. In the fifth chapter of Judges, verse 20, we read concerning the stars in their courses. Our very good creator has the paths of billions of stars so arranged that they do not interfere with one another. This fact is truly amazing.

Also, the creator has seen fit to arrange the stars into huge groups known as galaxies. This fact was unknown until the present century. This reminds me of the textbook used by my father in the study of astronomy. In that textbook the statement was made that the planet Jupiter has four moons. My father added as a footnote, "a fifth one has been discovered." Now we know that Jupiter has at least twelve moons.

A given galaxy contains two billion or more stars, each one as large as the sun and many much brighter. The sun is one member of the Milky Way galaxy, located about three-fourths of the distance from the center. The entire galaxy is rotating so that it will require about 200 million years for the sun to make one revolution.

There are many different types of galaxies with various kinds of shapes, but all containing very many stars. The number of galaxies is estimated to be many billions located at distance from each other measured in millions of light-years. As we have looked deeper into space we find more and more galaxies. There seems to be no limit just as our creator is unlimited.

I conclude this discussion by declaring that God, in His wisdom, has permitted us to view both aspects of His creation from that which is too small to be comprehended, through the wonders of the human body, and of man's home in the solar system, to His marvelous power in the creation of the vast number of stars and galaxies which causes us to wonder.

Finally, in His great love for sinful man, He has made provision for our salvation, and for all who will acknowledge Jesus Christ as their Savior and Lord.

Let us continually praise His name.

A Letter On My Eightieth Birthday

901 College Avenue
Goshen, Indiana 46526
April 7, 1988

To my children, grandchildren, and great-grandchildren:

Today I am 80 years old. This reminds me of Psalm 90, verses 10 and 12. "The days of our years are threescore and ten, and if by reason of strength they be fourscore years, yet is their strength labour and sorrow; for it is soon cut off, and we fly away,—so teach us to number our days, that we may apply our hearts unto wisdom." I remember a sermon by Sanford C. Yoder, President of Goshen College, on December 5, 1943, when he used as his text, the second of these two verses.

I find that most of my ancestors did not live to be eighty years old. My father, John M. Hartzler, died at the age of fifty-three. My mother, Anna Mary King Hartzler, lived to be seventy-eight years of age, while her father, Jacob Z. King, died at the age of seventy-one. Her mother, Barbara King, only lived to be thirty years old. My grandfather, Yost Hartzler, died at the age of seventy-three while his wife, Barbara King Hartzler, only lived to be sixty-six years of age. Judging by this information, I do not expect to live many more years.

I want each of you to know that I love you very much. I recommend that you should read I Corinthians 13, the great love chapter in the Bible. I now quote from the first verse: "Though I speak with the tongues of men and angels, and have not love, I am become as sounding brass, or a tinkling cymbal."

You should thank God for a goodly heritage. Your parents, grandparents, and their ancestors loved the Lord and sought to do His will. Your family expects you to follow their example.

My prayer for you is that you have a Godly home where you feel the presence of the Lord. Daily Bible reading and prayer to God our heavenly Father should be your habit. In this life we can expect many difficulties, but you should know that God is with you at all times. Each of us should look forward to our heavenly home. There we will be with Jesus forever if we trust

Him now as our personal Savior. You should realize that Jesus Christ died on the cross in order that we might be saved from sin.

We know little of our heavenly home. The Bible only gives us glimpses of what heaven is like. We do know that God, the Father, Jesus Christ, His son, and very many persons who have accepted Christ as their Savior, will be there where there will be no night. From the Bible we know that heaven will be beautiful beyond description.

In this life on earth most of us make major decisions. Many of these are very important and far-reaching. First I think of our education. We should be thankful for schools and colleges. Since I have given most of my life to education I wish to give you some advice. All of us need to continue our education as long as we live. My advice is to go to school and college as long as you can. I continued until I received my graduate degree. I am thankful for this wonderful opportunity. I did not discontinue my education after my work at Rutgers University in New Brunswick, New Jersey. I am quite certain that I have learned much since I graduated in 1934.

One of the most important decisions in life is that of receiving or rejecting Jesus Christ as our Lord and Savior. He died for you. He loves you. He offers you salvation from sins. He has sent the Holy Spirit to guide us into all truth. The most important truth is that we do have a Savior. My plea is that you accept the offer of this free gift.

The choosing of a vocation or of a lifework is another important decision. As in many other decisions, here we have freedom of choice. I know that the choices may appear to be few, but we are able to make the final decision. My advice is that you choose that vocation in which you will be happy and contented. You should also consider the worth of that which you intend to do.

As we think of our lifework, we should also consider its relation to our Christian life. We should never become so involved in our vocation that we do not have any time left for the work of the kingdom of God in this world. In my case, I not only have been a college teacher but also a Sunday school teacher, an active member of the American Scientific Affiliation, a member of the Christian Business Men's Committee, an active Gideon, and a member of the Church Building Committee in Mankato. My advice to you is to become involved in at least one activity related to your Christian life.

The question of marriage is also very important. First, should you marry or remain single? Whom should you marry? My advice is to marry a person who shares your Christian ideals. Since marriage is for life, this is one of your most important decisions. This year marks the fifty-fifth year of our own marriage. I wish that you will also find happiness in marriage for many years.

Another major decision for most of us is that of retirement. Some people die before they retire. Others continue in their vocation until after normal retirement age. This is usually considered to be sixty-five years of age.

In my case, I retired from college teaching at the age of sixty-eight. I am very happy since I retired in 1976. Now I do not need to follow a rigid schedule. Since I retired, I was able to complete the *King Family History* on which I worked for more than forty years. I expect to be involved in genealogical work as long as I live.

A few final words from one who has lived to be eighty years old. First of all, learn and continue to smile which costs you nothing but may help to make another person happy. Second, remember who you are and that God loves you in spite of your many errors. Third, always look on the bright side of any situation. Fourth, love the Lord with all your heart and your neighbor as yourself. Fifth, honor your father and your mother. Sixth, work diligently and remember to keep one day in seven to worship God. And seventh, accept the Lord Jesus Christ as your Lord and Savior.

With all my love,

H. Harold Hartzler

P.S. Please keep this letter as long as possible. Read it from time to time.

H.H.H.

My Personal Testimony

by H. Harold Hartzler

As far as I can remember, I knew that God existed and that Jesus Christ was His Son sent to this earth to be the Savior of men and women. Even though I knew this from an early age, I was aware that I needed a savior and I also knew that I had not accepted Him as my own Savior. I grew up in a Christian home where prayer was heard every day and both of my parents were much concerned about the salvation of their children. I was the oldest of six.

Through the influence of a number of Sunday school teachers, I was led to make a public confession of Jesus Christ as my personal Savior. I cannot recall of a special time when I decided to make Jesus Christ the Lord of my life. I feel that this occured gradually and there was a time of maturing in the Christian faith.

I also recall that at times I did not closely follow my Lord, but I never came to the point in life where I completely left Jesus Christ out of my life.

Since I have come to the place in life where I have recognized that Jesus Christ is the only Savior, I have come to love Him more and more. I have also come to serve Him in a more complete fashion. He has for a number of years been very close to me and I have come to have a close walk with God.

For the past number of years, I have consciously tried to live for Jesus Christ and to make him my Lord as well as my Savior. I have become burdened for the salvation of many who are lost without Jesus Christ. Because of this, I have actively engaged in many types of Christian activities and have found them to be very satisfying. I can honestly say that being a Christian is the best thing in life and I try in many ways to show to the world that I love the Lord.

As I have matured in the Christian life, I have learned that each person is an individual and therefore different. Thus I have accepted others as Christians even though we may disagree on many issues. I still have some difficulty along this line and must continually look to Christ for guidance.

One of the great joys of my life has been that of working together with other Christians in many activities directed toward that of helping others to learn to know the Lord as their Savior. I do thank Him for this privilege.

For years one of my mottoes had been that of Romans 1:16: "For I am not ashamed of the gospel of Christ; for it is the power of God unto salvation to everyone that believeth; to the Jew first, and also to the Greek." It is my aim to constantly show to the world that Jesus Christ is the only Savior. Praise the Lord.

Letters To and From
College Classmates and Family

901 College Ave.
Goshen, IN 46526
October 18, 1989

Dear Classmates:

I wish to report to you that I had a fine time both in May and in September at Juniata College when I represented the class of 1930. I continue to feel rather lonely since my faithful wife Dorothy departed from this vale of tears on April 18. She died due to heart failure after being in the hospital five times this year.

Due to her health condition last fall, we delayed going to Arizona until January. Our son Jonathan drove our car on that trip. Dorothy felt well during that week and enjoyed the trip but was not well for the next two months. I thank the Lord that she did not need to suffer much and that she can now rest in peace. I am glad that God took her first so that she will not need to live as a poor widow. That possibility was mentioned by Dorothy many times.

I note that a number of our classmates have departed from this life during the last year. I especially miss John Swigart and Ernest Weyant. It seems strange not to be able to see them when I return to Huntingdon. I wonder how many of our classmates will be alive by the time of our sixtieth reunion next spring. Only the good Lord knows whether I will be able to make that reunion.

The class of 1930 had a giving record of 74% this past year. That was an increase of 15% over that of the previous year. I now challenge my classmates to have a giving record of 89% for this coming year. After all these years, I am quite certain that we can reach that goal.

How many of you will not only give a gift to the college but will also try to be present for our reunion next year? As for myself, I plan to make a gift to the college and I also expect to be present on the occasion of our sixtieth anniversary of the class of 1930.

In addition, I expect to bring with me for your observation, three notebooks. These contain 1) letters to H. H. H., 2) letters from H. H. H. to classmates, and 3) remembrances of Juniata College. I recognize that only God knows whether these expectations will be a reality. I am reminded of the firm statement of our class president, John Beery, who was so certain that he would be present for our fiftieth reunion. That was in the year 1975. I close with the statement which I learned at Juanita.

Humility, the fairest flower that grew in Eden,
The first that died;
It is so frail that it dare not look upon itself,
And he who says he has it, proves by that very thought,
that he has it not.

Very sincerely yours,
H. Harold Hartzler

Saltillo....
Almost April Fools' Day

Dear H.H.H.....

Your recent letter stirs memories. Can it be almost our 55th? Yes. I remember the old brick house in which you lived with some others. Wasn't it nicknamed "The Fraternity House?" If so, how did you get away with that? I so well recall that Sam King, Tel Blough, and Ernie Weyant...also Mitch Atalski with our Bus. Mgrs. made up a Year-book club for the advancement of that campus activity. We called it the Beta Tau Kappa (or something... I forget). Harvey B. was the chairman of student activities for the faculty. He carpeted us with a lecture about Greek fraternities. I am sure he meant well but was unduly alarmed...we felt.

And Al Corman...oh yes. I cannot recall why, but the day that Al broke his arm in gym class, I was sent post haste to find a doctor. First of all, at that time in the afternoon and on a Wed., maybe, doctors were either out of town or by no way in their offices waiting to be called to take care of the accidents that never happen on schedule. Second, I was a poor one to send to phone. It is doubtful if at that time in my life that I had ever used a phone before. Weren't you, too, a country boy?

But somehow I did get the hospital agreed to take Al, and I went with whatever kind of ambulance we contrived. To this day I can close my eyes and see poor Al's broken arm thru the fluroscope...a new-fangled contrivance then.

There was a weekend, too, when you and Al had to be away and had me take over at firing the furnace at the orphanage. The furnace was either a steam or hot-water affair and the grate was clogged with clinkers. With none of these had I any past experience. The kind lady who ran the place had to help me get up enough heat to keep the orphans from freezing. Both she and I were happy when you fellows returned.

We all had many happy times at J.C. (few clinkers). I return to the campus often and find little evidence of the good times of old. J.C. could well do with a Nicotine Alley...for one thing. But then Pres. Binder sits on a board of which I am a member. Said he one day, "Why, you must be older than Harold Brumbaugh." We are considered relics, Harold...and to be sure we are lucky to be still here.

See you some time...

Ernest H. Weyant

Mankato State College
Mankato, Minnesota
September 15, 1960

Dear Brothers and Sisters:

Some of you have suggested that we start a circle letter. This is an attempt in that direction. I do think that it is a good idea and I hope that each of us will assume responsibility for keeping it going. May I offer a few suggestions?

I am sending this letter to John Marion who is to pass it on to Clayton, who in turn is to send it to Ethel, who then will send it to Eva, she then to send it to Carrie, who then will send it back to me. Each one is to add at least a page of interesting happenings in your recent experience. I think that no one should hold the letter for more than a week. That means that John should send it to Clayton by September 24. That allows two days for this letter to get to John. That furthermore means that I should hear from Carrie in about six weeks. If anyone thinks that this is an unreasonable schedule, please let me hear from you at once.

Eva thought that it would be a fine idea to start this circle letter at this time since I have recently returned from a trip to the west coast where I had the pleasure of visiting with Carrie and her family. So I expect to try to tell you something of my trip and of some of our experiences camping along the way.

I just received my copy of the *Belleville Times* and made the interesting observation that five of our names are in this issue of the *Times*. I wonder how many of the other members of the family have noticed this. I will point them out since Carrie does not get the *Times*. By the way, I think that is a mistake on her part.

In the past I have thought of stopping my subscription to the *Times*, but I am now glad that I have continued to get this paper. It does help to keep one in touch with the hometown and with the family. So I think my first resolution is to start a subscription to the *Belleville Times* for Carrie. It is all right to me, Carrie, if you do not wish to continue.

On the front page of the *Times* for September 8, under the caption, "20 Years Ago in Belleville," there is the following note: "John Marion Hartzler, son of Mrs. Anna Hartzler, who recently joined the Merchant Marine of the American South African Line in New York City, sailed Sunday, August 18, for Capetown, S. Africa, on the *S. S. Challenger*. He will arrive in Capetown on September 18 and will return to New York December 12. Mr. Hartzler has enlisted for a four-year period." I am sure that this brings back memories to all of us.

Then on the back page under the caption, "25 Years Ago in Belleville," there are two notes of interest to us. "Clayton, Ethel, and Carrie Hartzler of Trella Street and Edith Yoder of Maryland left Tuesday August 20 for Colorado where Carrie will enter training at the LaJunta Hospital. They expect to visit Pikes Peak and other places of interest before returning home."

"Mr. Harold Hartzler and family of Trella Street moved to Elizabethtown on Tuesday, September 3, where Mr. Hartzler has accepted the position of Dean of Men at the Elizabethtown College."

Those were historic days for some of us. The only item which I see concerning Eva is an article that Freshman Days are to start at Juniata Sunday, September 11, and that they are expecting 785 students....

1311 Warren Street
Mankato, Minn. 56001
June 27, 1970

Dear Family:

I was very happy to receive the family letter this week, even though I had visited with Eva, John, and Clayton just four weeks ago. At that time Dorothy and I had the interesting experience of traveling by plane to Pennsylvania. There we had the pleasure of visiting with all of Dorothy's brothers and sisters on Friday evening, May 29, and then went to Huntingdon where we visited with Eva and also attended the reunion of the class of 1930. There were forty-nine persons present for the banquet. This included some husbands and wives of the graduates. We also attended the Alumni luncheon at the college where we met many friends whom we had not seen for a number of years.

It was very interesting to see many of my classmates whom I did not recognize since they had changed so much since graduation. Then others seemed to appear just as I thought of them forty years ago. A sobering thought was that one of the class members who had definitely planned to be present was called by death just a few weeks previous. A very interesting fact to me is that a number are already retired or are making plans for such.

No, Carrie, I do not think that I am growing old and I am not making plans for retiring. However, I do realize that this college at Mankato retires everyone at age sixty-eight, so that means I have but six more years to teach here. However, I hope to be able to teach elsewhere after I leave Mankato. I think that will be a very interesting experience.

I must say that Dorothy and I had a fine visit with the family in addition to the wonderful time we enjoyed on the campus of Juniata College. I purchased a new camera just before I went to Juniata and have some fine pictures of my classmates. This camera has a very fast lens so that now I can take indoor pictures just as well as outdoors. I have a good one of Dorothy and Helen in Clayton's house which I will include next time in the family letter. At the moment I just have the color slide and I hope to have a print made from it.

After my visit to Huntingdon and Belleville, I went on to Washington, D.C., where I did some lobbying for the cause of peace in the world. The National AAUP encouraged a number of chapters to send delegates to Washington to do some work in the cause for peace. This was a most unusual experience for me for I am not much interested in politics and here I found myself right in the midst of it.

In Washington I was a part of a group of representatives from midwestern colleges who had come for the same purpose. So we worked together for three days in the halls of congress. We visited in the offices of many senators and representatives from a number of states.

I must tell Carrie that I was in the office of Senator Hatfield where we were warmly received. In fact, I must add that we were well received in most offices. All seemed glad that we took the time to come to talk to them. So I am recommending it to others. I will probably not get as far as Ken Dodd in politics, but I do recommend that you go to see your congressmen. If you think that you are unable to go to Washington, you can write to them. They do appreciate your letters.

Since that time, we have had our commencement here and are now in the midst of summer school. We graduated over a thousand seniors and this summer we expect a total enrollment of about ten thousand. This hardly seems possible. I remember that when I first came to Mankato, we had a total enrollment of about 3,200 in the regular school term. Now we have several times that number in the summer school. We have three more weeks of summer school. Then we expect to start for the east, visiting in Indiana and Ohio and then in Pennsylvania.

Then the ASA has its meeting in St. Paul, after which I am to go to Ottawa where I will attend the Canadian Congress on Evangelism and also represent the ASA. That meeting is August 24-28. Who also would like to attend?

With love to all,
Harold

Unsung Heroes of the Faith

For some time I have written up the life stories of Mennonite leaders whom I have known. These have appeared in issues of *Mennonite Family History*, a genealogical journal dealing with Amish, Mennonite, and Brethren families. Copies of these articles are available from Mennonite Family History, P. O. Box 171, Elverson, PA 19520-0171.

I started with my own father, John M. Hartzler. Others included are: Eli Hartzler Kanagy, Christian Zook Yoder, Samuel Evans Allgyer, Joseph H. Byler, Joshua B. Zook, Jacob C. Kanagy, Amos Israel Yoder, Jonas D. Yoder, Samuel T. Yoder, John S. Mast, Uriel Sylvanus Zook, Elmer E. Yoder, Paul M. Roth, Leroy A. Zook, Louis S. Peachey, Marion Y. King, Daniel D. Miller, Samuel G. Glick, Allen Bennett Ebersole, Elmer D. Hess, Isaiah W. Royer, Milo Franklin Kauffman, John Ira Byler, Isaac Stoltzfus Mast, Christian J. Kurtz, Raymond R. Peachey, Ben B. King, Erie H. Renno, Levi Clement Hartzler, Timothy H. Brenneman, John L. Mast, Irvin L. Roth, Tobias Kreider Hershey, Cleo Aaron Mann, Jacob Brubaker Smith, and Irvin Burkhart.

Letter to the ASA

I served as Executive Secretary of the American Scientific Affiliation for a period of twenty years. I am enclosing a letter to the present Executive Secretary, Dr. Robert L. Hermann.

                                    901 College Ave.
                                    Goshen, IN 46526
                                    October 10, 1991

Dr. Robert L. Hermann
P.O. Box 668
Ipswich, MA 01938

Dear Robert:

    It has been some time since I have heard from you. Sorry that you were unable to make it to Wheaton at the annual ASA meeting. That was a very special meeting and I am happy to have been able to be present. Not only that, but my son Harold Eugene from Goshen was there to hear my speech. He appeared to enjoy the meeting.

    Enclosed please find a check for $100.00 for the work of the ASA. I still believe in the work of the ASA though I wish that we could work together with some of the other organizations who are interested in doing the same thing we are doing. I refer to the Creation Research Society. I brought this matter up at the business meeting but was voted down. It appears that we are unable to work together with some of our colleagues. I feel very bad about this situation. I do not give up so will try other approaches.

    It seems to me that we made a big mistake when we did not take a picture of the members present at this special meeting. We will never have such an opportunity. But I must say that we did have a good meeting and I was glad to meet so many old friends.

    At the present time I am planning to attend the next annual ASA meeting to be held in Hawaii. I assume that the plans are completed for such a meeting. Could you tell me on which island we are meeting and what will be the cost of the fare from Chicago to Hawaii. I already have a bid from a Mennonite Travel Agency. I fully realize the brevity of life so I am not at all certain that I will be able to make the trip to Hawaii. From my present health condition I feel that I will be able to go.

Last Saturday night at the Alumni banquet at Goshen College I sat at the same table with Owen Gingerich. I inquired about your health and was told that you are improved and able to be back at the office, though you are not to over exercise. I do hope that you are able to continue your work as the Executive Director of the ASA. I assure you that I am praying for you.

I did considerable traveling this past summer. Right after the ASA meeting I went to Oregon to attend the Assembly meeting of the Mennonite Church at Eugene. There I met many old friends, some of whom I had not seen for a number of years. After that meeting I traveled to Alaska for a two-week trip. That was a very wonderful experience for me and I thoroughly enjoyed every minute of it. It seems that everything in the state of Alaska is described as big. I had never thought that I would have the opportunity of going to Alaska, but when I saw the announcement of such a trip in one of my periodicals and that it was to follow the meeting in Oregon, I decided that this was the time for me to make such a trip.

I am still concerned that we are not using our resources properly when we plan the TV series. Owen tells me that the only thing in the way is the lack of money. I wonder whether we will ever be able to get that kind of money. I hear so many voices calling for money that it overwhelms me. I try to do my bit, but I know that is small. My own Mennonite Church here in Goshen is planning an expansion to its building to cost over $3,000,000. I do not approve when I see the needs of the world. Why do we wish to spend so much on ourselves?

Sincerely yours,
Harold

Lecture Tour From 1976 -1977

by H. Harold Hartzler

A lecture tour is proposed by H. Harold Hartzler of Mankato, Minnesota, to begin September 1, 1976, and to continue to June 1, 1977. All lecture topics will be related to the general subject of Science and the Bible. A number of the lectures will be illustrated by means of color slides.

Some of the topics are as follows: EVIDENCES OF GOD'S DESIGN AS MANIFESTED IN ASTRONOMY, CHRISTIAN VIRTUES AND THE ATTRIBUTES OF A GOOD SCIENTIST, THE CONFLICT BETWEEN SCIENCE AND THE BIBLE, CHRISTIANITY IN THE ATOMIC AGE, SCIENCE AND FAITH, THE HEAVENS DECLARE THE GLORY OF GOD, THE FAITH OF AN ASTRONOMER, MODERN PHYSICS AND THE CHRISTIAN FAITH, SPIRITUAL TRUTHS IN MATHEMATICS, THE LONG DAY OF JOSHUA, PROBABILITY AS IT RELATES TO BIBLICAL PROPHECY, HOW THE STUDY OF SCIENCE HAS INCREASED MY FAITH.

H. Harold Hartzler, born April 7, 1908, in Fort Wayne, Indiana, graduated from Belleville High School, Belleville, Pa.; Juniata College, Huntingdon, Pa., A.B. degree; Rutgers University, New Brunswick, N. J., Ph.D. in Physics. Thesis title: TRANSPARENCY OF THIN METALLIC FILMS IN THE ULTRAVIOLET. Post doctorate work at Pennsylvania State University, University of Michigan, University of Arizona.

Positions in the academic world: Professor of Mathematics and Physics and Dean of Men at Elizabethtown College, 1935-37; Assistant Professor of Mathematics at Goshen College, 1937-38; Associate Professor of Mathematics at Goshen College, 1938-42; Professor of Mathematics at Goshen College, 1942-45 and 1946-58; Professor of Mathematics at Bluffton College, 1945-46; Associate Professor of Physics at Mankato State College, 1958-59; Professor of Physics, 1959-64; Professor of Mathematics and Astronomy, 1964-76. Retired June 1, 1976.

Other positions of responsibility: Secretary-Treasurer of the American Scientific Affiliation, 1951-55, President, 1955-60, Executive-Secretary, 1961-72. Secretary Minnesota Area Physics Teachers, 1962-64; Board of Directors, Minnesota Academy of

Science, 1959-64; Director of Science Fair at Mankato State College, 1959-65; President of local chapter of AAUP, 1969-70; President of local Sigma Club, 1969-70.

Member of the following professional organizations: American Mathematical Society, Mathematical Association of America, American Astronomical Society, American Physical Society, American Association of Physics Teachers, American Association for the Advancement of Science, National Council of Teachers of Mathematics, Minnesota Academy of Science, American Scientific Affiliation, Creation Research Society.

Member of the following honor societies: Tau Kappa Alpha, Sigma Xi.

Member of the Mennonite Church and an Associate Member of the Evangelical Covenant Church of North America, member of the Gideons and the Christian Business Men's Committee, International.

Invitations to present any lecture are welcomed from church groups, Sunday schools, elementary and secondary schools (both public and private), colleges and universities, service clubs, or any other group which may be interested.

Invitations from the five states of Wisconsin, Minnesota, North Dakota, South Dakota, and Iowa are desired for the month of September. The lecturer plans to then spend two or three months in Europe. For the months of January, February, and March of 1977 invitations are welcome from the states of California, Arizona, and New Mexico. The states of Colorado, Kansas, and Nebraska will be toured in April and May. Address all correspondence to H. Harold Hartzler, 1311 Warren St., Mankato, Minnesota 56001. Home phone: 507-388-4461.

Lecture Topics on Science and the Bible

1. The Scientist and the Christian
2. Science and the Bible
3. Witnessing to the Scientific Community
4. Evidences of God's Design in Astronomy
5. A Christian Interpretation of Science
6. Christian Virtues and the Attributes of a Good Scientist
7. Examining Evolution in the Light of the Scripture
8. The Conflict Between Science and the Bible

9. Limitations of Science
10. Christianity in the Atomic Age
11. The Heavens Declare the Glory of God
12. Science and Faith
13. The Faith of an Astronomer
14. A Physicist's Glimpse of God
15. Modern Physics and the Christian Faith
16. Spiritual Truths in Mathematics
17. The Long Day of Joshua
18. Probability in Biblical Prophecy
19. Science and Biblical Miracles
20. How the Study of Science has Increased My Faith
21. Evidence for the Existence of God from Science
22. Ethical Decisions of Christians in Science
23. Mathematical Thinking and Christian Theology
24. Cosmic Mysteries of the Universe
25. Christian Faith in an Age of Science
26. Evolution vs Creation
27. The Origin of the Solar System
28. Stellar Evolution
29. Newton as a Scientist and Theologian
30. Speculation vs Truth
31. The Eye as an Evidence of God's Design
32. Modern Physical Science in the Bible
33. Faith and the Scientific Method
34. A Critique of Evolution
35. Abraham and the Stars
36. Science and the Spiritual Nature of Man
37. Science and the Infallibility of the Bible
38. Space and the Bible
39. Mathematical Thinking and the Theory of Evolution
40. The Philosophy of Science and Belief in God
41. Astrology and the Bible
42. Christian Love vs Scientific Facts
43. Christianity and the Origin of Science
44. The Ecology Crisis
45. The Quest for Noah's Ark
46. Can Science Save Us?
47. Modern Science and Christian Life
48. Paradoxes in Mathematics and in Christianity
49. The Trial of Galileo Galilei
50. The Reformers and Science

My Vision: Past, Present, and Future

by H. Harold Hartzler

Introduction

This present work had its origin in my mind as I lay on my hospital bed in the Immanuel-St. Joseph Hospital the summer of 1987 in Mankato, Minnesota. There I had what I call a spiritual reawakening as I pondered many things. I had been ill with a lack of appetite all summer.

On August 14 my wife took me to the Mankato Hospital. At that time, I did not know the nature of my illness. After a number of examinations it was determined that I suffered from congestive heart failure and also was in need of a prostate gland operation.

In the meantime, Dorothy and I had been able to sell our home in Mankato and made plans to move to Goshen, Indiana. It was from there we had moved to Mankato twenty-nine years ago when I had started to teach at Mankato State College.

We had a public auction and moved to Goshen August 28. I was moved in my own car from one hospital to another while lying on a special bed in the back of our station wagon. All went well on this 600-mile trip with Dorothy and our daughter, Mrs. Elvin Yoder, driving the car. Our daughter's husband followed driving a U-Haul truck carrying our possessions.

While in the Mankato Hospital, I had a large number of visitors. My memory goes back to the lengthy conversation I had with two of my colleagues, Wayne Prichard and Dr. Lokensgard. Wayne shared his life story with us. He and I have shared Romans 8:28 for a number of years: "And we know that in all things God works for the good of those who love him and who have been called according to his purpose." Such a very wonderful promise. Please note the statement, "in all things," which includes a lot of territory.

Now let me share Wayne's story. At the age of twelve he had a bicycle wreck which so bruised his body that he was in bed for two years and since that time he has not been able to walk normally. Even though not able to walk without a limp and not able to run, Wayne finished public school, graduated from college in accounting and married a fine Christian girl. They raised a family of four boys and he taught accounting for a period of forty years. He retired from Mankato State University two years ago.

On many occasions during these forty years, Wayne felt the burden of his physical handicap. Nevertheless, as he started to teach, the Lord gave him strength for the duties of the day. Meanwhile, he and his wife had the added responsibility of the care of three handicapped boys. The older two, now thirty years old, have never walked or talked and are now in a nursing home. The next son Douglas continues to live with his parents in Mankato. He is autistic, never talks, often causes damage in the home, and is a constant care for his parents. He does attend a local school for handicapped children.

In spite of these difficulties, both Wayne and his wife Judy attempt to live normal Christian lives. Their pride and joy is their son Daniel who is now a student at Mankato State University. Wayne takes the attitude that all of his many difficulties have led him closer to the Lord. Therefore he still clings to Romans 8:28. What a beautiful way to live.

As Wayne continued his story for more than an hour in my hospital room in Mankato, my other friend, Dr. Lokensgard, asked a number of deep questions regarding life and death. One of his main difficulties is attempting to understand the justice of God when so many people are required to suffer so much and why some people will spend eternity separated from God in a condition often called hell. These questions greatly trouble this good man as they have troubled many others. In my weak way, I attempted to show to Dr. Lokensgard that our heavenly Father continues to show us justice in spite of our ignorance.

As I continue to study the Scriptures, I become more and more convinced that God is a God of justice and He assures us that His love is greater than His justice. The Bible is full of many such statements. Allow me to quote from the Pentatuch: "He is the rock, his ways are perfect, and all his ways are just. A faithful God who does no wrong, upright and just is he" (Deut. 32:4).

• • •

The Trinity: Perfect, perfect, perfect. "For we know in part, and we prophecy in part. But when that which is perfect is come, then that which is in part shall be done away. When I was a child,

I understood as a child, I thought as a child, but when I became a man, I put away childish things. For now we see through a glass darkly; but then face to face; now I know in part, but then shall I know even as I am known" (I Cor. 13:9-12).

The word trinity is not mentioned in the Bible. This concept is very difficult for us to understand. In the Holy Scripture, we read of the Father, the Son Jesus Christ, and the Holy Spirit. These three are spoken of as being one. However, it is very difficult for us to comprehend three spirits as being one.

Let us consider the attributes of God, all of which are perfect:

1) Bounty: The Lord has been good to us. We read in Psalm 116:7, "Return unto thy rest, O my soul, for the Lord hath dealt bountifully with thee."

2) Eternity: In Psalm 90:2 it is stated: "Before the mountains were brought forth, or ever thou hadst formed the earth and the world, even from everlasting to everlasting, thou art God." Isaiah states: "I am the first and I am the last" (Isaiah 44:6).

3) Goodness: The Lord himself proclaimed to Moses: "The Lord, the Lord, the compassionate and gracious God, slow to anger, abounding in love and faithfulness" (Ex. 34:6). The Psalmist says: "Taste and see that the Lord is good" (Ps. 34:8).

4) Grace: Luke writes: "And the child grew and became strong; he was filled with wisdom, and the grace of God was upon him. (Luke 2:40).

5) Holiness: Speaking to Moses the Lord said, "Speak to the entire assembly of Israel and say to them: "Be holy because I the Lord your God am holy" (Lev. 19:2). David said: "You are enthroned as the Holy One; you are the praise of Israel" (Ps. 22: 3).

6) Immutability: Speaking of the Lord, the Psalmist says, "But you remain the same, and your years will never end" (Ps.102:27). James writes, "Every good and perfect gift is from above, coming down from the Father of the heavenly lights, who does not change like shifting shadows" (James 1:17).

7) Infinity: The prophet Jeremiah states: "Can anyone hide in secret places so that I cannot see him declares the Lord? Do not I fill heaven and earth? declares the Lord" (Jer. 23:24).

8) Justice: "God is a righteous judge" (Ps. 7:11). "He will judge the world in righteousness" (Ps. 96:18).

9) Love: "I will heal their waywardness and love them freely" (Hos. 14:4). "For God so loved the world that he gave his only son that whosoever believes in him shall not perish but have eternal life" (John 3:16).

10) Mercy: "Showing love to a thousand generations of them who love me and keep my commandments" (Ex. 25:6). "That the Gentiles may glorify God for his mercy" (Rom. 15:9).

11) Omnipotence: "Our God is in heaven; he does whatever pleases him" (Ps. 115:3). "Ah, sovereign Lord, you have made the heavens and the earth by your great power and outstretched arm. Nothing is too hard for you" (Jer. 32:18).

12) Omnipresence: "Acknowledge and take heart this day that the Lord is God in heaven above and on the earth below. There is no other" (Deut. 4:39). "Is not God in the heights of heaven?" (Job 22:12).

13) Omniscience: "You know when I sit and when I arise; you perceive my thoughts from afar" (Ps. 139:2). "Great is our Lord and mighty in power, his understanding has no limit" (Ps. 147:5).

14) Patience: "The Lord is slow to anger, abounding in love and forgiveness of sin and rebellion" (Num. 14:18). "Who disobeyed long ago when God waited in patience in the days of Noah while the ark was being built" (I Pet. 3:20).

15) Pity: "As a father has compassion on his children, so the Lord has compassion on those who fear him" (Ps. 103:13). "You have heard of Job's perseverance and have seen what the Lord brought about" (James 5:11).

16) Spirituality: "The Spirit of the Lord is upon me because he has anointed me to preach good news to the poor" (Luke 4:18). "But when he, the Spirit of truth is come, he will guide you into all truth" (John 16:13).

17) Truth: "Into your hands I commit my spirit, redeem me,

O Lord, the God of truth" (Ps. 31:5). "We have seen his glory, the glory of the one, and only one, who came from the Father, full of grace and truth" (John 1:14).

18) **Unity:** "The earth is the Lord's and everything in it, the world, and all who live in it" (Ps. 24:1). "Hear O Israel, the Lord our God, the Lord is one" (Deut. 6:4).

19) **Wisdom:** "Great is our God, and of great power; his understanding is infinite" (Ps. 147:5).

The Creation. "In the beginning God created the heavens and the earth" (Gen. 1:1). "In the beginning was the Word, and the Word was with God, and the Word was God. The same was in the beginning with God. All things were made by him; and without him was not anything made that was made" (John 1:1-3). "Of old hast thou made the foundations of the earth; and the heavens are the work of thy hands" (Ps. 102:25).

To me this marks the creation of the entire physical universe. The biological is not included. The earth is mentioned because the Bible was written for men and women who live on this planet.

Robert Jastrow, in his book, *From God and the Astronomers*, stated: "Science has proven that the universe exploded into being at a certain moment. Was the universe created out of nothing? The scientist's pursuit of the past ends in the moment of creation. For the scientist who has lived by his faith in the power of reason, the story ends in a bad dream." Nevertheless, it has been stated in a recent Sigma Xi publication that science is society's most successful and effective and remarkable enterprises. That statement is from the human point of view, not from the divine point of view.

Energy: God, the ultimate source of all energy, or the ability to do work, used an enormous amount of it when he created the physical universe. There are two kinds of energy—potential and kinetic. In science we speak of the two laws of thermodynamics. The first law, called the law of the conservation of energy, states that energy is neither created nor destroyed. We should remember that this law took effect after Gen. 1:1. The second law of thermodynamics, also called the law of the degradation of energy, is best stated in mathematical form. It states that the total amount of useful energy in a closed system, is continuing to decrease at all times. In the natural world both laws appear to operate at all times.

Angels: These created, sexless beings are God's messengers. Billy Graham calls them God's secret agents. He further states, "I believe in angels because the Bible says there are angels; and I believe the Bible to be the true Word of God."

John Calvin stated: "The angels are the dispensers and administrators of the divine beneficence toward us; they regard our safety and undertake our defense, direct our ways, and exercise a constant solicitude that no evil befalls us." Martin Luther said, "An angel is a spiritual creature without a body created by God for the service of Christendom and the church." In Ps. 91:11 we read, "He will give his angels charge over you, to guard you in all your ways."

The history of virtually all nations and cultures reveals at least some belief in angelic beings. The number of angels is enormous. I estimate that their number is approximately 100 trillion by making use of such biblical references as Rev. 5:11, Job 25:3, and Dan. 7:11. The first of these references states: "And I beheld, and I heard the voice of many angels round about the throne and the beasts and the elders; and the number of them was ten thousand times ten thousand and thousands of thousands."

The angels were given the gift of free will just as man was given this gift. The result was that a large number of angels chose evil rather than the good. I have a problem here as to the source of evil. Where did it come from? Surely not from God. What other source is possible? We must remember that there was no devil before the creation of angels. The devil is the leader of the fallen angels. I do not know how many angels fell into sin; however, I estimate that one-half fell.

Now think of all the grief, sorrow, sickness, and poverty caused by the devil. It is staggering in magnitude. Think of the tribulations of Job as well as of many others. Think of the thousands of Christian martyrs. Many are suffering today due to their Christian faith. We live in a fallen world. Our thinking may be disturbed as well as all natural phenomena. All of God's creatures are suffering due to the fall of Satan. It is impossible for us to comprehend the magnitude of this tragedy.

Atoms: After a sufficient length of time the very high speed of the original created particles slowed down so that the atoms could form. Consider Gen. 1:3. Different kinds of atoms are called elements. The simplest kind of atom is called hydrogen and was formed first. It is very interesting to know that today—after multiplied billions of years, the most abundant atom in the known physical universe is that of hydrogen.

Today we know of many kinds of atoms. We also know of isotopes, having different numbers of particles in the nucleus of the atom. We also know of isobars which have different numbers of electrons outside the nucleus but the same number of particles in the nucleus.

The particles in the nucleus of the atom are called protons and neutrons which in turn are composed of smaller particles called quarks. Our bodies, composed of atoms, are very complex We are fearfully and wonderfully made (Ps.139:14). Most of the space, occupied by our bodies, is pure vacuum. However, when we speak of the air which we breathe as airy nothing, we should remember that there are more than ten million, million, million particles in a volume the size of the thumb.

Compounds of atoms are called molecules. An enormous number of different kinds of molecules are known. One of the most useful to mankind is H_2O or water. This is a very stable compound consisting of two atoms of hydrogen and one atom of oxygen tightly bound together. H_2O is very common on the surface of our planet. Also we have evidence of a huge volume of water beneath the surface of the earth. Some of this is very hot.

In nature we have three states in which water exists: liquid, solid, and gas. We usually associate water with the liquid state. However, the three states, which depend on the temperature, are different forms of the same compound.

The forms of molecules vary widely. They are the constituent parts of both the physical and the biological world and of the entire universe. In size they vary tremendously. In order for atoms to join together to form molecules, the temperature must be much lower than it was at the time of creation, roughly this means from temperatures measured in millions of degrees to first thousands and then hundreds of degrees measured in absolute degrees. The freezing point of pure water is 273 degrees.

The Solar System: This is our home before we rest with Jesus in the loving care of our heavenly Father who shows to us unfailing sympathy and undying love. Praise the Lord (Psalm 103). The first clear reference to the solar system is found in Genesis 1:24, "And God said, 'Let there be lights in the expanse of the sky to separate the day from the night and let them serve as signs to mark seasons and days and years and let them be lights in the expanse of the sky to give light on the earth.' God made two great lights—the greater to govern the day and the lesser light to govern the night. He made the stars also." The latter statement, in all its simplicity, is a very profound one.

From the point of view of most people on the earth, the stars are not important. But from the point of view of the creator of the physical universe, the stars are very, very important. Just think. From our present understanding, well over 99.9% of the physical universe is now contained in the great multitude of stars and galaxies. Thus we see that the whole earth is a very insignificant part of the universe. This thought should be kept in mind as we view this very wonderful universe created by our Heavenly Father. What a gorgeous and beautiful spectacle we witness on any clear night. Of course you must leave the bright lights of the city if you are to enjoy God's handiwork.

Origin of the Solar System: Scientific theories of the origin of the solar system have been around a long time with none being very satisfactory. In my judgement no satisfactory theory will be found. In the first place, the problem is very complex. However, that is not a good reason for not searching for a solution. Many examples can be given of the solution of a difficult scientific problem. One would be the solution of Maxwell's equations together with the far-reaching results resulting in radio and TV.

In the second place, the problem is very old. It goes back to the time of the Greek under Ptolemy. It seems to me that God has chosen not to reveal the solution of this problem to man. This is my view and it may be far from the truth.

It took a long time for the tremendous change from the theory of Ptolemy to that of Copernicus. From the modern point of view it seems ridiculous for the earth to act as the center of the universe or of the solar system. But not from the point of view of those who lived in the middle ages. Here I am reminded of the biblical passage: "This world is firmly established: it cannot be moved" (Ps. 93:1). The same words are repeated in Ps. 96:10. Also in I Chron. 16:30.

I am puzzled as I think of these verses as compared to the theory of Copernicus. Since it is my desire to understand the universe as much as possible, I am left with a problem. Perhaps we do not understand the meaning of Ps. 93:1. One of my theological friends suggests that Ps. 93:1 refers to the condition of the world.

Brief Description of the Solar System: The known solar system is composed of the sun, which is extremely large and very hot; the nine known planets: Mercury, Venus, Earth, Mars, Jupiter, Saturn, Uranus, Neptune, and Pluto, with their satellites, meteors, comets, the minor planets, and a variety of kinds of dust particles. As far as is known, the solar system is unique. In spite of the fact that a tremendous effort has been undertaken for many years, not a single solar system has been found. It is my conviction that none will be found.

God has provided for mankind a very wonderful place to dwell before he takes us to that home in heaven where we can live with him in an existence that is timeless. We are given this beautiful universe in which to dwell and enjoy life in spite of the fact that the devil is constantly attempting to cause us to sin. Believe me, he is always on the job. We are told to fear him for he often comes in sheep's clothing (Matt. 7:15). He also appears as an angel of light (II Cor. 11:14).

Future of the Solar System: According to II Pet. 3:10, the entire solar system will be destroyed. This may be difficult for us to understand, but God's Word tells us that it will happen. "Of old hast thou laid the foundations of the earth; and the heavens are the work of thy hands. They shall perish, but thou shalt endure, yes all of them shall wax old like a garment; as a vesture shalt thou change them and they shall be changed" (Ps. 102:25,26). We think of the material of the physical universe as being indestructible. That is the first law of thermodynamics. However, we are assured of great changes to come in the universe.

Stars and Galaxies: Here we find over 99.9% of the physical universe, though it may seem to be of little importance to us who live on the planet Earth. We usually think of the earth as being very large and the stars as being mere specks in the sky. In this case, things are really not what they seem to be. By diligent study we have been able to measure stellar distances, sizes, masses, densities, and compositions. Their number is quite beyond our comprehension as well as their distances from the Earth. Hence we often speak of large numbers as being astronomical.

Stars are in continuous motion though they appear to be stationary. Their velocities are enormous. Their paths are so ordered by God that they do not interfere with each other. I have found the study of astronomy to be most interesting. It is in this area that we discover how very small we really are. In spite of this, God loves us and is not willing that any should perish. We should continually praise Him for this love.

Geology: The study of the Earth's surface features is very important from several points of view. Besides its history, it is now of great commercial importance. The dry ground or the crust of the Earth is first mentioned in the Bible in Gen. 1:9. This is a very large subject and of interest to mankind since we live on the crust of the Earth. Estimates of the age of the Earth have been made by a careful study of the rocks found all over the surface of the Earth. We are led to believe that many rocks are very old. The geological column is given in many textbooks. Many Christians question the correctness of the magnitude of the ages presented in the geological column. An example is given:

Era	**Period**	**Epoch**	**Date**
Cenozoic	Quaternary	Pleistocene	1,000,000
	Tertiary	Pliocene	
	Tertiary	Pliocene	
		Miocene	
Mesozoic	Cretaceous		60,000,000
	Jurassic		
Paleozoic	Permian		200,000,000
	Pennsylvanian		
	Devonian		
Cryptozoic			1,000,000,000

Biological Life: This subject is first mentioned in Gen. 1:11. After including the creation of our first parents, the conclusion of the first chapter of Genesis is: "God saw all that he had made and it was very good." We have made great progress in our understanding of life processes. But we know so little. All that can be said is that we are fearfully and wonderfully made (Ps. 139:14). "I will praise you because I am fearfully and wonderfully made."

The Garden of Eden: We do not know the location of this beautiful place. It was a perfect home for our first parents. Adam was created a perfect man with fully developed mind and body. Eve, taken from the body of man, was created a perfect woman and was presented to Adam as his wife. In that perfect condition, all of life was supreme joy with no pain. Let us imagine their happy life together. However, both Adam and Eve were given the wonderful gift of free will just as the angels had been given this gift many years before (Gen. 2:9).

Did you ever think of the number of happy years spent in the Garden of Eden by our first parents? Perhaps this period of time may have been measured in hundreds of years. Of course, I have no idea of the magnitude of this number. As far as I know there is no hint in the Bible of the length of time Adam and Eve spent in this perfect place and condition. However, I can use my imagination which is another gift from God. The original reference is Gen. 2:23-25.

The Entrance of Sin in the World: This tragic story appears in the third chapter of Genesis. The terrible consequences stagger the imagination. From that time forth every human being is given the gift of free will. That means that we can choose either to obey God or not to obey our Heavenly Father. It seems to me that many more persons choose evil rather than good. What a tragedy. Involved in this story is the promise of a Savior (Gen. 3:15). Thus we learn that God is always interested in our welfare. Jesus Christ is now pleading our cause (Rom 8:35, Ps. 102:8). How thankful we should be for such an intercessor. We also see the tree of life and the tree of the knowledge of good and evil. Can we imagine what their appearance was like? It was likely more beautiful than any tree we have seen.

Man's boldness in taking of the forbidden fruit reminds me of the verse I learned years ago, the author of which I have forgotten. "Humility, the fairest flower that grew in Eden, the first that died. It is so frail that it dare not look upon itself. And he who thinks he has it, proves by that very thought that he has it not." This also reminds me of the Scripture: "With all lowliness and meekness, with longsuffering, forbearing one another in love" (Eph. 4:2).

Cain: He was the firstborn of Adam and Eve and became a murderer. Here we witness one of the results of sin. Whom did he marry? It must have been his sister. Their first son was named Enoch. The family line from Cain evidently grew rapidly because the life span of humankind was lengthy with many children in most families. I wonder how many of his descendants worshipped the true God, our merciful kind Heavenly Father. It appears to me that most of them were sinners who had forgotten their creator. In the history of mankind, it frequently occurs that but a short time is required to forget our goodly heritage.

From Adam to Noah: After the death of Abel, another son, Seth, was born to Adam and Eve. His son, Enoch, began the godly line from Adam and Eve. The fourth chapter of Genesis ends with the statement: "At that time men began to call on the name of the Lord." I ponder the implications of this verse. Does this mean that Adam and Eve had lost their love of God? No, I believe that many of Adam's descendants called on the name of the Lord.

In the fifth chapter of Genesis, there is a list of the names and ages of the descendants of Adam. This is then followed by a brief description of the wickedness of mankind. However, "Noah found grace in the eyes of the Lord." It was also stated: "Noah was a just man and perfect in his generation, and Noah walked with God" (Gen. 6:9). He was quite different from most of his neighbors for we read: "And God saw the wickedness of man that it was great on the earth, and that every imagination of the thoughts of his heart was only evil continually" (Gen. 6:5).

Longevity: Adam lived 930 years and I estimate had 200 children; Seth lived 912 years and I estimate had 200 children; Enosh lived 895 years and I estimate had 200 children; Kenan lived 890 years and I estimate had 200 children; Mahalelel lived 895 years and I estimate had 200 children; Jared lived 962 years and I estimnate had 200 children; Enoch lived 365 years and I estimate had 100 children; Methuselah lived 969 years and I estimate had 200 children; and Lamech lived 777 years and I estimate had 100 children. Now let us do a little computation as to the number of persons who might have been living on the earth at the time when Noah was building the ark. There were nine generations from Adam to Noah.

In Genesis 6:2 we read: "The sons of God saw the daughters of men that they were fair and they took them wives of all which they chose." I interpret this verse to mean that the godly line of Seth intermarried with the not-so-godly line of Cain with the resultant wickedness. If we allow 100 families in each of the above-mentioned nine generations, we find that in the time of Noah the population of the earth might have been 100^9 or 10^{18} which is much greater than the population of the earth at present. This is a staggering thought—that many more people may have died in the flood of Noah than are now living.

This calculation adds to the argument that the flood was worldwide to provide living space for so many people. I realize that many authors do not believe that the flood waters covered the entire surface of the earth. However, it should also be noted that we have many flood stories from various parts of the world. There is a bright side to the flood story in that God promised that there would never again be such a flood. History shows that God has kept his promise.

The Origin of Religious Belief: Religion has been defined as the attitude of individuals in community to the powers which they conceive as having ultimate control over their destinies and interests. When did this attitude on the part of mankind start? I believe that it must have started with our first parents, Adam and Eve, who enjoyed intimate fellowship with our Heavenly Father before sin entered the world. It is difficult for us to imagine such intimate fellowship.

I wonder whether any of the descendants of Cain worshipped the one true God. Do we have any evidence? It is true that it does not take a very long time to forget our kind Heavenly Father. We should worship Him daily. We should keep our faith in God who continues to love us in spite of our many sins. Frequently we are reminded that the truth is unbelievable.

The Tower of Babel: After the great flood the sons of Noah traveled eastward in search of a better soil and climate. They discovered the art of making brick and cementing it with bitumen or asphalt. Soon they got the idea of building a great city. In their pride they imagined that they could defy God and thus defeat his design of dispersing them over the earth. "Come," said they, "let us build us a city, and a citadel with the top reaching to heaven, and let us make us a name, lest we be scattered abroad over the face of the whole earth."

God saw the danger in their scheme and confused their speech. The same attempt has been made since by Nebuchadnezzar, Cyrus, and Alexander. It has been repeated by Charlemagne and Napoleon. I wonder whether they had any idea of the height of heaven They likely thought of this as the distance to the stars which we measure in light-years. Throughout history we find that men are continually trying to do the impossible.

The Call of Abraham: Genesis 12:1-3. Mankind had evidently forgotten the true God in Ur of the Chaldees. However, God had not forgotten his human creatures. He called on one whom He could trust. Abraham exhibited remarkable faith as he left his very comfortable home to travel to an unknown land. His entire family also must have had faith in God since they were willing to go with him. What a wonderful lesson to us.

We need to constantly keep our faith in God. This reminds me of the fact that many of our ancestors left their homes in Europe to come to this country which was quite unknown to them. They endured much suffering as they crossed the ocean. They did this in order to escape persecution in Europe and to better themselves in many ways. We should thank God that they were willing to endure sacrifice.

Life of Abraham: Genesis 12:25. Though Abraham has set for us a remarkable example of faith, yet he appeared to be quite human when he went to Egypt and pretended that Sarah was his sister rather than his wife. Still the Lord was with Abraham with the result that no harm came to Sarah while she was in the house of Pharoah.

Evidently Abraham did quite well for we read: "Abram was very rich in cattle, in silver, and in gold" (Gen. 13:2). In fact, he was so wealthy that he had to separate from his nephew Lot for "their substance was so great, that they could not dwell together" (Gen. 13:6).

Nevertheless Abraham was a man of faith. He believed God who told him that his seed should be in number like the stars in the heaven. Still he did not have a son so he listened to his wife Sarah to take Hagar, her maid, as his wife. Abraham was eighty-six years old when his son Ishmael was born. After he was ninety years old the Lord again promised him that he would have numerous offspring. It was at this time that his name was changed from Abram to Abraham.

A little later three men appeared to him as he sat in the door of his tent. They again promised him a son which caused his wife Sarah to laugh. They also told him of the coming destruction of the wicked cities, Sodom and Gomorrah. Abraham pleaded for them and asked that they be not destroyed if only ten righteous persons were found there. Nevertheless they were destroyed when Lot barely escaped with his wife and two daughters.

When Abraham lived in Gerar he told the King Abimelech that Sarah was his sister. Again God protected Sarah so that no harm came to her. When Abraham was 100 years old his wife did bear a son called Isaac. After a number of years the Lord told Abraham to offer his son Isaac as a burnt offering. This was done to test the faith of Abraham. He came through this test with flying colors and God provided a ram for the burnt offering.

When Abraham was old he told his servant to go to Nahor in Mesopotamia seek a wife for Isaac. This trip was successful so that Rebecca willingly came to become the wife of Isaac. After this Abraham took another wife named Keturah. She bore six sons to Abraham who then died at the age of 175 years. In Gen. 25:8 we read: "Then Abraham gave up the ghost, and died in a good old age, an old man, and full of years; and was gathered to his people."

Life of Isaac: Isaac was forty years old when he took Rebecca as his wife. They had twin sons, Jacob and Esau. This birth occured when Isaac was sixty years old. There was rivalry between the two sons with the result that Esau sold his birthright to Jacob. As the result of a famine, Isaac traveled to Egypt. God renewed the promise which he had made to Abraham by telling Isaac that his seed will be as the stars of heaven and that all nations should be blessed by them.

When he was in Gerar he told Abimelech, king of the Philistines, that Rebecca was his sister rather than his wife. No harm came to her because of this deception. Like his father, Isaac had great possessions and prospered. The Lord appeared to him and told Isaac that He would bless him for the sake of Abraham.

When Isaac was old and his sight was failing, he called his oldest son to hunt and get some game for him to eat. Before he did this, Rebecca had Jacob prepare a meal for Isaac. Thus Jacob received the blessing from the father which caused Esau to hate his brother with the threat of killing him. The parents sent Jacob to Laban, Rebecca's brother, to find a wife which he did. Later he returned and was met by Esau. Isaac lived 180 years and was buried by his sons Esau and Jacob. His name is frequently mentioned as one of the progenitors of the children of Israel.

Jacob, the Father of the Children of Israel: He was one of the most colorful of the Old Testament patriarchs. His life was a very full one. Yet he had to suffer very much. On his way to Laban, Jacob had a dream and felt that he was in the presence of the Lord. There he set up a stone which had been his pillow for a memorial. He consecrated it with oil and called the place the House of God, or Bethel. This was a turning point in his life at the age of seventy-seven. After meeting Laban, he offered to serve him seven years if he would give Rachel to him. This agreement was kept, but he was given Leah instead of Rachel. After serving seven more years and having eleven sons and one daughter, Jacob decided to return to his old home. This he did and was graciously received by Esau.

The twelfth son, named Benjamin, was born on the way home. His mother Rachel died at the birth of her son. Jacob lived a long life and was saddened by the news of the death of Joseph, his beloved son. Joseph was taken to Egypt and became second to Pharoah after his announcement of the seven years of famine which was to come. In the meantime, Jacob and his family suffered due to the famine and he sent his sons to Egypt to buy food. There Joseph met them and finally had Jacob and his entire family move to Egypt. There they lived as shepherds and greatly prospered. Jacob lived in Egypt a number of years. He blessed each of his sons and died at the age of 147 years. He was buried by his family in Caanan, his native land.

In a fine book by R. K. Harrison, *Introduction to the Old Testament*, we are given an understanding of Hebrew culture. Here we learn something of the function of archaeology. The following quotation is found on page 93 of this book. "One of the principal functions of archaeological activity is to awaken a sense of the vitality of the Hebrew past in the study of the Old Testament life and times. This is of great importance for the simple, though frequently unappreciated, reason that the essential message of the Old Testament cannot be fully comprehended without a knowledge of the cultural, religious, historical, and social background of the people to whom the revelation of God was given. Archaeological investigation has brought to light many new facets of Israelite life that had been lost with the passage of the ages and has helped to set Hebrew culture in proper perspective in relation to the trends and currents of ancient Near Eastern life generally."

The Development of Religious Belief: There is a very early development in Egypt as evidenced by burials in the pyramids of Egypt. Evidently pagan religion developed very early in the history of mankind. An example is the religion of the Caananites who were early occupants of the land promised to the Children of Israel. It is very interesting to note the proneness of the Children of Israel to accept idolatry. Only after being taken into captivity did they learn not to worship idols. We of the present generation of Christians should profit from the history of Israel.

The Coming of Jesus Christ: Hundreds of prophecies were fulfilled with the coming into the world of Christ. Many will be fulfilled in the future. His life on earth revolutionized the thinking of many individuals. His life is an example of what a Christian's life should be like. Here we see undying love in action. Now a quotation from the Anathasian creed: "Our Lord Jesus Christ, the Son of God, is God and man—perfect God and perfect man, who although he be God and man; yet he is not two but one Christ, one, not by the conversion of the Godhead into flesh; but by taking of mankind into God."

Some of the Prophecies Concerning Jesus Christ:
The first is Gen. 3:15. In the New Testament we have the statement: "God sent forth his son made of a woman" (Gal. 4:4). He was to be of the seed of Abraham as is stated in Heb. 2:16. "For verily he took not on him the nature of angels, but he took on him the seed of Abraham." He was to be of the tribe of Judah. "The sceptre shall not depart from Judah" (Gen. 49:10). His place of birth was described, "But thou Bethlehem Ephratah, though thou be little among the thousands of Judah, yet out of thee shall come forth unto me that is to be ruler in Israel" (Micah 5:2). The time of birth was designated (Hag. 2:7,9). Elijah was to come first. "Behold I will send to you Elijah the prophet before the coming of the great and dreadful day of the coming of the day of the Lord" (Mal. 4:5).

Jesus was to work miracles. "Then the eyes of the blind shall be opened, and the ears of the deaf shall be stopped. Then shall the lame man leap as a hart, and the tongue of the dumb sing" (Isa. 35:5,6). He was to be rejected by the Jews. "And he shall be for a sanctuary; but for a stone of stumbling and for a rock of offense to both the houses of Israel" (Isa. 8:14).

He was to be scouraged, mocked, and spit upon. "I gave my back to the smiters, and my cheeks to them that plucked off the hair; I hid not my face from shame and spitting" (Isa. 50:6). His hands and his feet were to be pierced. "The assembly of the wicked have enclosed me; they pierced my hands and my feet" (Ps. 22:16). He was to be numbered with the transgressors. "And he was numbered with the transgressors; and he bare the sin of many, and made intercession for the transgressors" (Isa. 53:12).

Jesus was to be mocked and reviled on the cross. "All they that see me laugh me to scorn; they shoot out the lip, they shake the head saying, he trusted in the Lord that he would deliver him; let him deliver him, seeing he delighted in him" (Ps. 22:7,8). He was to make his grave with the rich. "And he made his grave with the wicked, and with the rich in his death" (Isa. 53:9). He was to be a prophet like Moses. "I will raise them up a prophet from among their brethren, like unto thee, and I will put my words in his mouth" (Deut. 18:18). He was to be a king, "Yet have I set my king upon my holy hill of Zion" (Ps. 2:6). His kingdom was to be one of peace. "For unto us a child is born; unto us a son is given; and the government shall be upon his shoulders, and his name shall be called Wonderful, Counselor, the Mighty God, the Everlasting Father, the Prince of Peace" (Isa. 9:6).

The Message of Jesus Christ: His answer to John the Baptist: "Go and show to John again those things which ye do hear and see; the blind receive their sight, and the lame walk, the lepers are cleansed, and the deaf hear, the dead are raised up, and the poor have the gospel preached to them" (Matt. 11:4,5). He has brought salvation from sin to all who are willing to receive this free gift. We may ask the question, "Why do so many fail to receive Him as Savior and Lord?" Here we again witness the power of Satan. He is constantly opposing men and women who would come to Jesus Christ. However, we are assured that we are more than conquerors" (Rom. 8:37).

The Spread of the Gospel of Jesus Christ: At first it was only for the Jews. It required some time for the good news to reach the Gentiles. We should thank God that men like the Apostle Paul, as well as many others, have brought the message to us. Now our work as Christians should be to carry the Gospel to all people. In spite of some noble efforts, we have miserably failed our Master. This enormous task has been carried on by Christians from the day of Pentecost to our day. We now have Christian missionaries in many countries. May we be diligent in this great work.

The Spread of Non-Christian Religions: It is my conviction that what may be called heathenism has spread more rapidly and began to be taught before the time of Christ. We have a lot of work to do in order to catch up. Jesus promises to be with us to the end.

Going back as far as history extends, we find that mankind is religious. All people believe in spirits. No people have been discovered without such a belief. However, primitive man is not spiritual in the true sense. He has not learned to distinguish between a material and a spiritual world. There exists in the mind of primitive peoples the conception of a mysterious pervasive power present in the universe. This is known as Mana in Polynesia, Manito in the Algonquin Indians, Prenda by the Iroquois and Wakatan by the Sioux Spirits, whether disembodied souls or supernatural beings have mana and can impart it.

Animists worship inanimate objects such as trees and stones. They also worship the sky and the moon and the stars. In addition they worship animals such as the lion, the ferocious tiger, the elephant, the cunning fox, the mysterious snake, and many others. Often animals had attributes of wisdom and cunning far beyond their due according to the animists.

The Religion of Egypt: The Egyptian has always been intensely religious. His religion was often of a unique type. The Egyptian seems always to be able to hold the most contradictory views. He held that he lived in a changeless world. Only the changeless is ultimately significant. The heavenly bodies, the Nile, their kings, trees, and piles of stones were looked upon as divine. About 2000 B.C. they constructed a theology in which the sun god Ra was supreme above all others. His only rival is Osiris, who is represented as a man with a beard. He is the ruler of the dead, the supreme god of all that concerns the hereafter. Two unique features distinguish Egyptian religion from all others—the worship of animals and the belief in individual immortality.

The Gods of Babylonia and Assyria: Their religion was based upon an animistic foundation. Ashue was the god of the Assyrian empire. He was represented as the disk of the sun. He was of a more spiritual type. The gods were given consorts or wives. An important one was Ishtar, the goddess of generation and fertility.

Early Roman Religion: The gods of the Romans were powers expected to do things. This religion is very close to animism. Jupiter was first, next came Mars, the god of war. Janus, after whom the first month of the year was named, was the god of opening. The last god was Vesta, the goddess of the family hearth. The gods could be counted upon to prevent evil from the people if they performed their religious duties.

The Religions of India

Hinduism: The Hindu religion is a result of the Aryan invaders of the second millenium B.C. The Aryans brought a religion similar to that of the Persians. They had over a thousand hymns, composed over a long period of time. The gods whose praises were sung were nature deities. These were divided into three groups, the gods of the celestial regions, those of the earth, and those of the atmosphere.

Three gods of the high heavens were Mitra, who was also known as Mithras in Persia and in the Roman Empire, Vishnu, later important in Indian religion, and the great god Varuna. The latter is viewed as embracing all things and is the primary source of all life and every blessing.

There were three important gods of earth, Agni, Soma, and Yama. Agni was fire who had many high functions in human life. Soma was the name of an Indian plant and fermented juice was extracted from it. It was intoxicating and therefore divine. Soma also referred to celestial things and was supposed to flow in the invisible world.

The gods themselves attained immortality by drinking the Soma. Yama chose to die and was the first to cross the flood from which none return. The dead who lived nobly went to him. The worship of the gods was largely sacrificial. Animals were offered in great numbers.

When the Aryans came into India, they did not believe in the doctrine of transmigration. This theory is when a man dies, his soul leaves the dying body and enters the body of some animal or human being as it comes into this world to begin its career. The law or force which determines the operation of transmigration was Karma which means action or deed. Thus actions in this life work out their results in the next life, and so on through unlimited time.

According to Karma we are born into a new life well or strong, good or bad, rich or poor. There is no escape from the clutches of this inexorable law. The importance of the doctrine of transmigration cannot be overestimated. To be saved from the endless succession from births and deeds with death following is what religion means to the Hindus. There are three ways of escape—by good works, by loving devotion to a god, or by knowledge or the method of release by philosophical insight and intuition.

Hinduism is a religion that has wide variations. It is all-comprehensive, all-absorbing, all-tolerant, all-complacent, all-compliant. To be a Hindu means to belong to one of the castes and obey caste regulations. A caste is a group of people kept apart from other caste groups by regulations touching marriage, food, and residence. Marriage within one's caste is very important. Widows have a very hard life. The Brahmin priest is the vitalizing force in the system and dominates it completely. He looks upon himself as inherently superior to all others. In India there are five million outcasts or untouchables whose lot in life is very miserable.

Jainism: The founder, Mahavira, turned against the pretensions of the Brahmin priesthood. He did not break the shackles of Karma. Fear of future rebirths is the key that unlocks the door into the secret of Jainism. All their rules of conduct lead to emancipation from transmigration. It started as an ascetic movement but is now found in India among those who are wealthy. The Jains are constantly reminded that they themselves are divine and that their task is to let the essential divinity within them come to its own and shine out in its beauty. Jainism might be defined as a way of escape, not from death, but from life.

Sikhism: The founder was Nanak who believed that there was one god, a being of love. The Sikhs are an offshoot of Hinduism. The religion of the Sikhs centers in their sacred book, the *Adigranth*. It holds the central place in all places of worship and is treated as a divine object.

Parsiism: The Parsis are 1,200 hundred years old. They derive their name from Persia. They think of themselves as followers of the prophet Zoraster. Highly educated and frequently wealthy, they not only take care of their own poor, but are generous in their gifts to the public enterprises. They are very loyal to their great prophet.

When Zoraster, their prophet, was thirty years old, he experienced a divine manifestation. He was led before the throne of God where he communed with God. In Zoraster's mind, the forces of righteousness and the forces of evil are engaged in an irreconcilable conflict which can only be ended in the complete victory of what is true and noble and right. This religion is on a high level.

Buddhism: Gautama, the Buddha, influenced the thought of Asia more than any other person. He lived from 563 to 483 B.C. and was born in a city 130 miles north of Benares. Little is known of his life before he was thirty years old. At that age, he abandoned his home and became a poor wanderer. By abstinence, he reduced himself to a skeleton. He had many admiring disciples. He finally fell over in a swoon and was thought to be dead. But he revived and then declared that mortification had failed to bring peace. Up to this time he had been a typical Hindu, but now he followed a direction of his own. He became an advocate of the middle way. He set men the example of simple living; he had few regulations. He had learned that the inner peace he was craving was not to be had by living a life of ease or of asceticism.

Under the shadow of the famous bo tree, the most sacred shrine in the Buddhist world, the enlightenment came and he was free. Thus came the Buddha, the enlightened. His battle with his lower nature had been won and peace swept over his soul, never again to be absent from his experience. He had grasped the meaning of the world's sorrow and could cure it. What was the cause of this sorrow? It was the lust for gold and fame and pleasure. His final was that peace and poise could only come by the suppression of desire. After that his life was one of unruffled calm.

Instead of becoming a solitary recluse, he made up his mind to devote his time to the carrying of his message to men. He met many people, men and women of all ranks and classes. He was dignified and firm, dealing in each case with insight and sending each one away with an appropriate word. His followers looked on him as one who could meet every need. He finally went back home and his wife and son became members of the two orders he instituted—one for men and the other for women. No purer character has India given to the world.

Gautama left no written record. His teachings are contained in the three signs or Fundamental Truths. The first of the Fundamental Signs is impermanence of all things. Nothing is to be excluded from the sweep of this theory. The second of the Fundamental Signs is that sorrow is implicit in all individuality. We cannot gain what we want, and we cannot escape what we dislike, and this involves misery and sorrow. The third Fundamental

Sign is that of the absence of soul. It is a delusion to think that there is such a thing as a person. He is composed of parts which, when assembled, we call by a name. To attain these Fundamental Truths, one became separated from ordinary life and became a monk. They lived apart in communities so that all their energies might be concentrated on attaining the end desired. They lived a very simple life and are bound to obey the eight precepts: 1) not destroy life, 2) not take that which is not given, 3) not tell lies, 4) not become a drinker of intoxicating liquor, 5) refrain from unlawful sexual intercourse, 6) not eat unseasonable food at nights, 7) not wear garlands nor use perfume, 8) sleep on a mattress on the ground.

Confucianism: Confucius lived from 551 to 478 B.C. According to Confucius, human nature is naturally good. Confucius was primarily interested in society and the state. He believed that man could not live alone. He desired peace of mind and happiness for all men. Confucius was most careful about the dignity and the courtesies of social life.

His teachings were systemized in what are known as the five relations: Father and Son, Ruler and Subject, Husband and Wife, Elder Brother and Younger Brother, and Friend and Foe. In each case the first is considered the superior. Confucionism is not only an ethical system used to regulate the life of the individual, society, and the state, but as part of Chinese religious life. Confucius will live in the thought of the Chinese as a true patriot and as a worthy example of uprightness and unselfish devotion to the welfare of the people. The Chinese are practical and Confucius ministered to that bent with such insight and wisdom that the whole life of the people has been built around his ideals.

Shintoism: The early religion of Japan is known as Shinto. This is a Chinese word or two words. Shin is the same as the Chinese Chen which means good spirits. To is the same as tao, or the way. This religion is the way of the good spirits or the way of the gods. The earliest form of religion in Japan was nature worship. This cult was quite simple. Unpainted, unadorned wooden shrines were the centers of worship. No images were used, but the presence of the spirits was indicated by fluttering pieces of notched paper. There was no sacred book, no doctrine to be believed, and no code of laws to be followed. Shintoism was a very simple religion. The people of Japan were very religious.

Ancestor worship was everywhere. The emperor was considered as the divine ruler. However, in 1946, Emperor Hirohito disavowed his divinity and no longer claimed that the Japanese people are destined to rule the world.

Mohammedanism: Islam, meaning to submit, the religion of Mohammed, started in Arabia with his birth in A. D. 570. The followers of the prophet believe that their religion is a new creation handed down from heaven. However, its roots are found in the pre-existing heathenism of Arabia. There we find Allah, the supreme god, as well as Mecca, already a sacred city.

When Mohammed was twenty-five years old, a most important event took place. A distant relative, the widow Khadijah, offered him the position of taking charge of her business affairs. He performed this service to her great satisfaction after which they were married, though she was fifteen years older. They lived happily together until she died twenty-five years later.

This marriage changed the whole course of his life. He now had sufficient wealth so that he was able to devote his life to thinking. He probably brooded over the moral tragedy of the universe. He likely came into contact with Christianity. However, it was so covered with formalism and so lacking in vitality that it held little attraction for him. Here is a lesson for us as Christians. Do we let our light shine so that men and women are attracted to Jesus?

In A.D. 610, Mohammed had an experience which made him into a different man. He thought he heard a heavenly voice. The climax of the revelation was that Mohammed was to proclaim a message. He finally arrived at the conclusion that he was the mouthpiece of Allah. He immediately began to preach to his friends in Mecca. Khadijah became his first convert.

After being persecuted, Mohammed left Mecca and fled two hundred miles north to Median where he became a civil ruler. Three tribes of Jews lived there. Two were sent into exile while 600 or 800 men from the third tribe were brutally butchered while the women and children were sold into slavery. After his first wife died, he married twelve or thirteen wives. He was a reformer but he failed at the personal point of character.

When Mohammed died, the *Koran* had not been compiled. It later was written in Arabic, the language of the angels, and is about as long as the New Testament. The accepted doctrine in the Muslim world is that the *Koran* is the uncreated Word of God, which has always existed at the right hand of Allah and was delivered to Gabriel, who in turn was to carry it piecemeal to the prophets as needed.

The *Koran* is the chief foundation of Islam, the authority par excellence on doctrine, ethics, and customs. With all the *Koran* says about the mercy and compassion of Allah, the great overwhelming attribute is that of power. Allah is a typical oriental despot and not a heavenly father. Heaven is not spiritual, but one suited to the physical desires which man is conscious of in this life and will never outgrow. It is a luscious garden of fruits and running streams with delightful nooks, in which are the houris, or damsels, who are the principal reward of the righteous.

Religion in Pre-Columbian America:
Aztecs, Mayas, Incas

The **Aztecs** founded their empire in what is now Mexico City in 1325 and survived for 200 years. In some respects their manners were more refined than in Europe. The gods were savages and demanded a great deal, but in return granted the nation health, favorable weather, growth of crops, and victory over enemies. To the Spaniards the religion of the Aztecs was a ghostly cult in honor of the devil.

The Aztecs believed that periodic human sacrifices were needed in order to keep the sun and moon, which the gods had put in motion, from coming to a standstill. Prisoners regarded it as an honor to be sacrificed to the gods. The Aztec god of war, called the terrible god, watched over the fruitfulness of the fields. The fate of the dead in the hereafter depended not on conduct in life but on manner of death.

The **Mayas** of Guatemala, Southern Mexico, and Yucatan have a religion similar to that of the Aztecs. Human sacrifice was far rarer. The priests were trained in special temple schools. The temple fire was entrusted to vestal virgins. Their sun god acted as both fertility god and lawgiver. There were also various nature gods and a complex mythology of the elements.

The **Incas** or People of the Sun were distinctly an imperial people with remarkable political gifts who welded subject nations into a long-lived empire. This flourished from about 1150 to 1532. The reigning Inca was considered the son of the sun who was from an aristocracy that dominated the country. The people were divided into nobles, freemen, and slaves. The priests formed a special class, as did the virgins of the sun, who served the sun god and lived in convents. The Inca's power as an incarnate god and sacred king was nearly unlimited. The bodies of the deceased rulers of the Incas were mummified and worshipped as gods. In the Inca empire the vast mass of the people were subscribers to the sun cult, while the Supreme Being, whom the upper crust invoked, was vague and indefinite.

The Work of the Apostle Paul: He was probably the greatest missionary who ever lived. Today we need more Christians who are willing to suffer for Christ. We should thank God for those who are now suffering as they carry the Gospel to the ends of the earth.

Paul said: "For to me to live is Christ and to die is gain" (Phil. 1:21). What a wonderful thought. Verses 22-26 should also be read for one to appreciate something of the spirit of the Apostle Paul.

The Christ proclaimed by Paul has certain features borrowed, like those in the gospels, also from the Jewish Messiah of the Old Testament. But, for Paul Jesus is principally the Son of Man who existed before the world was and who will return for His own. Through faith men are in Christ. Ideas expressed by Paul became the fundamental doctrines of the Christian faith and the basis of the church's teachings. Paul thought that the Post-Messianic Age would be short and that the return of Christ was imminent, thus his great concern for the lost and his great missionary endeavors. He remained faithful until the close of his life.

The Catholic Church: The idea of having one universal church is fine, but this ideal has not proved to be very successful. Under Augustine all citizens of the Roman Empire were baptized and thus became Christians. This idea was contrary to the teachings of the Bible.

According to Catholic interpretation the Christian Church started with the Apostle Peter. "You are the rock upon whom I will build my church" (Matt. 16:18). These words appear in golden letters on the inside of the dome of St. Peter's Cathedral in Rome. This dignity was transferred to his successors in office, the bishops of the congregation in Rome.

By the end of the third century we find the bishop of Rome known as the Pope. He claimed to be the vicar of Christ on earth. As such he claimed to possess supreme authority in matters of belief, and in the administration of the Church. This dogmatic assertion of the primacy of Peter and all Roman successors in office is the ideological basis of the Roman papacy. Through its revelation of the true doctrine of God and the incarnation, the Catholic Church presents mankind with a consistent and rational theology. God is imminent in His creation, but yet transcendent, Creator of man, and yet the Father of His children.

Every position taken up by Catholics is surrounded by a network of arguments. The age of faith is also the age of reason. The Catholic Church rests on its doctrine of the supernatural. This implies that God is not idle in His universe. God is alive and active to help men in their need. He does so by transforming and redeeming our earthly nature, not by taking us out of it.

The Roman influence on Christianity and the task of reorganizing to resist corruption, and to discipline pagan Europe after the fall of Rome, soon led the Church from democratic conceptions to authoritarian ones. But as soon as this occured, the essential spirit of Christian liberty and evangelical simplicity arose, first in one place and then in another as a protest against ecclesiasticism, formalism, and worldliness. But the Church had no mercy on these movements and they were ruthlessly suppressed.

It is interesting that a number of non-Catholic groups have existed from the second century right up to the time of the Reformation. These have been called the Free Church.

Marcionism: A revival of Pauline teaching, which caused a schism in the Church at Rome, laid the foundation for a new Christian movement. When Marcion separated from the Church about A.D. 140, a large number of people followed him to establish a separate church. The most significant of Marcion's teachings was repudiation of the close tie the Church had with the Old Testament. The Sermon on the Mount was regarded highly. The Marcionite movement was a major competitor to the primitive Catholic Church and was regarded as a peril.

Montanism: This movement had its origin in the spiritual experience of Montanus who lived in Asia Minor. Montanus had experienced ecstacies and probably spoke in tongues. The Roman Church took definite measures to oppose this new movement. The essential feature was the emphasis on declaring the message of salvation and holiness in the light of signs of the imminent end of the world. The Montanists were rejected as a fanatical sect by their opponents. This movement occured in the second century.

Novations: In the third century, Novation stood for the position that the Church should enforce strict discipline. He won many adherents and was excommunicated. The Novations called themselves the Pure. The movement became widespread, even in Africa and Asia Minor. In many areas Novationism was the predominent form of Christianity. During the fifth century this church had as strong a position in Constantinople as it did in Rome.

Donatism: Immediately after the Emporer Constantine's edict in A.D. 313, which gave toleration to Christianity, the problem of keeping the Chuch pure became seriously acute. Donatism grew out of this controversy. This happened in North Africa. In 316 when Donatis the Great became the foremost bishop within Donatism, the movement obtained a strong leader. Donatism stood adamantly opposed to any intermingling of state power with the Church.

Paulicians: This group of non-Catholic Christians was founded in Syria and Armenia in the seventh century. They stressed a holy life. They called themselves simple Christians. They were persecuted since they opposed the use of the symbol of the cross, clerical vestments, and the celebration of the Mass. Their persecution continued into the eighth and ninth centuries.

Bogamilites: Another group started by the priest Bogamil was formed in Bulgaria in the tenth century. They appeared in the same territory as the Paulicians and had similar beliefs.

Cathari or the Pure: This group started in the eleventh century and had a very strict discipline. The unifying element among all these heretical groups opposed to the Roman Church, was the emphasis on the difference between the material and the spiritual world. The Cathari renounced worldly property. Their preachers and apostles carried considerable influence. Preaching and prayer were the foremost elements in their worship. They emphasized the spiritual and had little use for the ordinary sacraments, including the Lord's Supper.

Waldensians: This group of sincere Christians attracted large numbers of followers. They were known as "The Poor Men from Lyon." Peter Waldo, a prosperous merchant from Lyon, in 1176 suddenly turned his back on his business and the things of the world to attire himself in poor clothing, live the life of an ascetic, and went out to preach. This movement seems to have arisen within the borders of the Church.

The Waldensians had definite similarities with the Cathari. This was evidenced in many points regarding opposition against the Church's teachings and customs, such as the offering of the Mass, Purgatory, the heirarchy, the property holdings of the Church, priesthood, pilgrimages, saint worship, and other elements of a lesser nature.

Basic principles of the Waldensians were that the Bible is the only conclusive authority in faith and action for the Christian, and the Bible in the vernacular coupled with the interpretation of Bible doctrine, is the greatest need. Preaching by laymen, even by women, became an impetus and emphasis which resulted in a free church movement of several centuries duration, and it was independent of the Roman Church.

Waldensians taught that the Christian should refrain from the use of the sword to kill one another and that they should not swear an oath in any form. The Sermon on the Mount was the basis of this strict rule of living. From 1211 to 1216, the Waldensians were burned in France and in Germany. Even in northern Italy there were martyrs.

Lollardism: About two centuries after the Waldensian movement had spread over Europe, a similar movement arose in England. The teaching concerning the priesthood of all believers and the responsibility of every Christian to spread the knowledge of God's Word became the basic principle of the Lollards. John Wycliffe about 1370 was a member. The Lollards were peaceful Bible-believing Christians. The movement continued to the time of the Reformation.

Hussites: John Huss, professor at the University of Prague in Bohemia and pastor of the Bethlehem Church, early became fascinated with ideas of Wycliffe. He had an important position at the university and as a preacher he exhibited unusual ability in winning adherents. Huss believed that the Bible is the only authority for the Christian in the matter of faith and conduct.

Due to his teachings he was called before the Church-Reform Council at Constance. The decision was that the reformer should be imprisoned. After a prolonged period he was burned at the stake July 1415. All of these non-Catholic movements were considered to be Satanic heresies and therefore attempts were made to have them suppressed. It seems that God was on their side since they existed for so many centuries.

The Crusades: The seven major crusades continued for two centuries, 1096-1291. They were conducted by the Catholic Church as a holy war against heretics and heathen. Their purpose was to rescue the Holy Sepulcher from the hands of the unbelievers. All those preparing to give battle against the heathen pinned a red cross to their shoulders and received indulgence for their sins. The armies of the first crusades were successful.

In 1099, the Crusaders set up the kingdom of Jerusalem. But in 1244, Jerusalem fell into the hands of the Turks who held it until 1918. For the west, the major lasting effect of the crusades was the greater contact with Islamic culture, the resumption of oriental trade, and the extension of men's intellectual horizons.

The Enlightenment: After a long period of history, known as the Dark Ages, mankind in Europe felt that they had entered a new age, often called the Enlightenment. At that time men felt that they could find God, instead of God finding men. It was assumed that mankind had no limits. However, it is stated in Romans 3:23, "For all have sinned and come short of the glory of God." The prophet Isaiah said, "For we are all as an unclean thing, and all our righteousness are filthy rags; and we all do fade as a leaf, and our iniquities like the wind, have taken us away."

The Reformation: Martin Luther, 1483-1546: Three movements helped to make the Reformation. First, there was criticism of the Church with its rites and the sale of indulgences. Second, was the spiritual need of the people for peace and salvation. Third, there was a social and political demand for independence from Rome in temporal affairs. Medieval Catholicism seemed to be degenerating into a semi-pagan system. It included the payment of indulgences in order to lessen the pains of purgatory.

Luther denounced the whole thing as a blasphemous swindle. After much prayer he realized that forgiveness and grace could not be bought by works but simply be accepted as God's free gift.

He did not hesitate to fling away from him all that hitherto seemed great and glorious and sacred. He flung off monasticism, asceticism, and the cloistral life. On the contrary, he believed in the priesthood of all believers. The responsibility of each person is to repent and accept forgiveness.

Luther was a reformer, not a philosopher or a theologian. He did not extend toleration to the smaller Christian groups, such as the Anabaptists, and had no objection to persecution. His teaching encouraged a suffering peasantry to revolt which caused a great uprising. Luther wrote volumes and translated the Bible into German. This translation is still widely used. His influence has been tremendous. As the Lutheran Church developed we see the influence of Satan with results in the divisions of the Lutheran Church.

The Reformed Movement: John Calvin, 1509-1564: The son of a laywer, John Calvin was a man of considerable education and a brilliant writer. His theology was profoundly different from that of Luther's. His emphasis was on the sovereignty of God, not on man's faith, but in God's free choice. According to Calvin, only the elect are saved and they are saved simply because God has chosen them. If you have faith, it is because God has given it to you. Geneva was the city Calvin chose to make a city of refuge for persecuted Protestants. He drew up a complete code for the spiritual welfare of the city. His belief in predestination encourages a strong sense of conviction and purpose. John Calvin was the leader of the Reformed Church.

The Work of Ulrich Zwingli, 1484-1531: A priest by 1506, Zwingli read Erasmus and Luther and was deeply influenced by Luther. By 1518 Zwingli became priest in the Great Minster Church in Zurich, Switzerland. Soon he became Protestant in his thinking. He held a disputation October 23-28, 1523, before the city council of Zurich. He convinced the council that the images should be removed from the churches. At this meeting Conrad Grebel and Simon Stumpf demanded the immediate abolition of the Mass. They urged Zwingli to establish a free church composed of voluntary believers. Zwingli flatly refused to meet these demands.

On January 17, 1525, the first disputation between Zwingli and the Brethren was held. Conrad Grebel, Felix Manz, and Wilhelm Reublin spoke for the Brethren. Zwingli defended infant baptism and only agreed to changes in the churches which the city council approved. He stated that it would be dangerous to have more debates with the Brethren. On January 21 the council published a mandate restraining Grebel and Manz from holding further Bible-study meetings. Zwingli was not nonresistant and later was killed in a battle.

Anabaptism: On January 21, 1525, Conrad Grebel, Felix Manz, George Blaurock, and a few others came together and found that they agreed in faith. There was a great anxiety among them and they were moved in their hearts. They unitedly bowed their knees before God Almighty in Heaven and called upon Him to grant them grace to do His divine will and that He would bestow upon them His mercy. After prayer George Blaurock asked Conrad Grebel to baptize him. He knelt down and Conrad Grebel baptized him since there was no ordained minister to administer this ordinance. After this was done, the others asked George to baptize them. Then some of them were chosen for the ministry. They began to minister and to keep the faith.

The main issues which led Grebel and his friends to break with Zwingli were the tempo of the reform, infant baptism, nonresistance, a free church of voluntary believers, and the need of church discipline. Their opponents soon called them Anabaptists or *Wiedertaufer*, meaning rebaptizers. The Anabaptists themselves rejected this designation. They preferred to be called *Bruder* or Brethren. Anabaptism has sometimes been designated as a third reformation. Many historians consider Anabaptism the beginning of those Christians who chose to belong in contrast to the established church into which one is born.

Almost immediately the Anabaptists were persecuted. By October 1525 Grebel, Manz, and Blaurock were imprisoned. In March 1526 they received life sentences, which lasted only two weeks, since they escaped March 21. Neither Grebel nor Manz had long to live. Grebel died of the plague and Manz was drowned January 5, 1527. In spite of severe persecution the Anabaptists became great missionaries and thus the movement spread.

The Work of Menno Simons: He was formerly a Catholic priest in Holland, but for years he had not read the Bible. After considerable study of the Scriptures he discovered that many practices of the Roman Catholic Church were not biblical. He decided to leave the Church of which he had been a leader. After 1596 he became a preacher of Anabaptism. Due to his leadership we derive the name Mennonite as followers of Menno Simons. After some years, in 1623 Jacob Amman led a group of Mennonites to practice a more strict discipline. Thus we have the Amish division of the Mennonites.

Another branch of Mennonites were followers of Jacob Huter who was burned at the stake in 1536. The distinctive practice of the Hutterites is that of living with all material possessions in common. They live in estates called Bruderhofs. These are now located in Canada and in a number of western states of the United States. They have suffered severe persecution throughout their history.

Many Christians have been persecuted through the centuries from the time of Christ right up to the present. The large book by Thieleman J. van Braght with the title *Martyrs Mirror* gives the story of fifteen centuries of Christian martyrdom up to A.D. 1660. In the introduction the author states: "Moreover thou knowest, O my savior and redeemer, the steadfast faith, the unquenchable love, and faithfulness unto death of those of whom I have written and who gave their precious lives and bodies as a sacrifice to thee." Both the Catholics and Protestants actively persecuted the Anabaptists.

Starting in 1693 many members of the Amish and Mennonites accepted the offer of William Penn to come to America so as to better their circumstances and to avoid persecution.

Another group of Mennonites traveled from Holland to Prussia and then to Russia upon the invitation of Queen Catherine. There they were granted freedom from military service. This freedom was lost during the last century so many came to the United States and to Canada.

Many members of other Christian groups also came to America during the past two centuries. These include Catholics, Reformed, Lutheran, Baptists, Presbyterians, Methodists, Moravians, and other persuasions. After a very dangerous ocean voyage they often found themselves having a better life. These are the ancestors of many persons now living in the United States.

Today we live in a scientific age even though many of us are scientifically illiterate. In a Sigma Xi publication we have the statement: "Science is societies' most successful, effective, and remarkable enterprise." Today and for years to come we observe some of the results of science in modern technology. What wonders we are now able to do in transportation, in the distribution of news, in medicine, and in modern computers. The latter is growing rapidly and is effective in our daily lives.

The Modern Missionary Movement: After a long period of relatively little activity, many Christians became concerned about the salvation of those in foreign countries. This movement for foreign missions began in Europe and in America about 1800. This has continued up to the present. A number of denominations have sent out thousands of missionaries to many countries. Today there are a number of interdenominational groups which have been active in the United States and in other countries. The result has been that the Christian Church is growing rapidly in a number of foreign countries, especially in Africa.

The Rise of Modern Cults

Cults are groups of people who share a common vision and who see themselves as separate from the rest of the world. A cult may also be described as an evolutionary phase in the development of religion. The historical relation between cults and religions suggests that the ultimate role of the cults may be to revitalize the established churches. This country has always been a haven for new and marginal religious groups. Cults, sects, and religious revivals have been a continuing feature of American life.

With reference to the Christian religion, cults either neglect or disturb the Gospel. A number of cults will now be described.

Mormonism, or the Church of Jesus Christ of Latter-Day Saints, was organized in Fayette Township in western New York in 1830 by Joseph Smith and five neighbors on the basis of certain divine revelations which he testified to having received. Mormons regard their church as the true church of Jesus, restored in this latter day to its original apostolic form. They accept the Bible as the record of God's dealings with the old world. They regard the Book of Mormon as the record of his ancient followers in the Western Hemisphere.

Mormons regard themselves as Christians but not as Protestants. They believe in the virgin birth, in immortality, in universal salvation, in the Holy Trinity as three distinct personages, in communion using bread and water, in marriage for eternity, in baptism by immersion, and in various baptisms for their ancestors who died before the church was restored. They practice abstinence from alcohol, coffee, tea, and tobacco. Included in their doctrinal statement is the following: "As man is, God once was; as God is, man may become."

The Mormon Church is very missionary minded. All young men of the Mormon faith spend two years in missionary endeavor. As a result, the membership in the Mormon Church is increasing 100,000 annually.

The Watchtower, or Jehovah's Witnesses, believe that the Christian doctrine of the trinity is a lie of Satan. They also believe that there is no divine soul or spirit within man that lives forever. They believe that all Christendom is the anti-Christ and the clergy are Satan's tools. Many of their members go from house to house attempting to sell their literature and doctrine. Their young men refuse to serve in the military.

Christian Science was founded in 1875 by Mrs. Mary Baker Eddy. She propagated a very profound belief in the goodness of God, so profound, in fact, that she met the age-old problem of evil in a divinely created universe by flatly denying its existence. The method of averting one's attention from evil and living simply in the good is splendid as long as it works. Her creed can be summed up in the following inspired statement: "God is all in all, God is good, God is kind, God's Spirit being all, nothing is matter."

There are nearly 700 churches in the United States and many in England. They have a system of Reading Rooms and a newspaper, *The Christian Science Monitor*. Mrs. Eddy and her disciples have been motivated by a deep sense of Christian love. She deserves our gratitude for the happiness she has brought to thousands of troubled souls.

Seventh-Day Adventists: The leader of the Seventh-Day Adventist group is Ellen G. White. They worship God on Saturday, or the Sabbath, the seventh day of the week, which begins Friday at sundown. They believe in soulsleep and deny the existence of hell. They consider themselves to be Christians. Their social life revolves around the church.

Modernism: Among the characteristics of this group of churches is the absence of God and of Jesus Christ. He is presented as a good man. There is little emphasis on the saving faith of Jesus Christ.

Humanism: This group emphasizes the idea of good works. They have complete faith in reason and its ability to solve all questions. They believe in free discussion and free investigation without any interference.

The Unification Church: Sun Myung Moon, a Korean evangelist, started this group in 1972. He claims to have met Jesus Christ in 1936 and was given the key to righteousness and the restoration of the kingdom of heaven on earth. His followers believe that some day Moon will correct all problems. They are told to degrade the Church, schools, state, and the family.

Baha's: These followers of Baha' Ullah have a $3 million temple in Willmette, Illinois, and a membership of 18,000. In the heart of every Bahai there is the feeling that he and his followers are children of destiny as well as children of light. Baha' Ullah speaks as follows: "All of us when we attain to a truly spiritual condition, can hear the voice of God."

Interdenominational Groups of Christians: Many such organized groups have sprung up in the United States and in other countries. Most of them are evangelistic in that members emphasize faith in the Lord Jesus Christ, the Son of God, as the only Savior.

A brief description of some of these groups follows:

· The Gideons are a group of business and professional men who distribute Bibles over the world. They and their wives are interested in the salvation of all people.

· C.B.M.C., or Christian Business Men's Committee, are men in business who are concerned about the salvation of other businessmen.

· The Y.M.C.A., or Young Men's Christian Association, provides spiritual and recreational opportunities for men of all ages. Y.W.C.A., or Young Women's Christian Association, provides spiritual and recreational opportunities for women.

· I.V.C.F., or Inter-Varsity Christian Fellowship, consists of college students interested in the claims of Jesus Christ in the lives of college students.

· Campus Crusade for Christ and the Navigators are both interested in the spiritual life of college students and have done a remarkable work.

· Athletes for Christ is a group of athletes who have learned to know Christ and are interested in the salvation of other athletes.

· A.S.A., or American Scientific Affiliation, is an organization of scientists who attempt to show harmony between the findings of scientists and the statements of the Holy Scriptures.

· C.R.S., or Creation Research Society, are scientists interested in refuting the arguments of those who believe in the theory of evolution.

· Bible Science Association is a layman science group which has aims similar to C.R.S.

· The Christian film ministry is largely an outgrowth of the Billy Graham Evangelistic Campaign which attempts to expand that ministry by Christian films. Thousands have been won to Christ by this means.

World Religions: There are many different religions in most every country in the world. According to data collected by the United Nations the number of countries having their principal religion is as follows: Roman Catholic, 62; Muslim, 39; Protestant, 13; Animism, 12; Buddhist, 10; Anglican, 9; Orthodox, 3; Confucionism, 1; Coptic, 1; Judaism, 1; Shinto, 1; Hindu, 1.

The Future: According to the Bible there are only two final conditions for each of us: Heaven or Hell. As Christians, we look forward to the second coming of Christ as prophecied in the Bible. "And then shall they see the Son of man coming in a cloud with power and great glory" (Luke 21:27). We know that he is coming, but we do not know when that event will occur. "For yourselves know perfectly that the day of the Lord so cometh as a thief in the night" (I Thess. 5:2). His coming is spoken of as near at hand so we should constantly be looking for it. "Behold, I come quickly; hold that fast which thou hast, that no man take thy crown" (Rev. 3:11).

We are told that there will be a last judgement. "When the Son of man shall come in his glory, and all the Holy Angels with him, then shall he sit on the throne of his glory. And before him shall be gathered all nations, and he shall separate them one from another, as a shepherd divideth his sheep from the goats" (Matt. 25: 31-32). "For we must all appear before the judgement seat of Christ; that everyone may receive the things done in his body, according to that he hath done, whether it be good or bad" (II Cor. 5:10).

Our Heavenly Home, the final dwelling place of the saints: We are given but a brief description of heaven in the Bible. The word heaven occurs 570 times, heavenly 23 times, heaven's once, and heavens 133 times. Heaven is spoken of as referring to the atmosphere, where the birds fly, to the physical region of the stars, moon, and sun, and to the spiritual place where God dwells. The Apostle Paul speaks of the third heaven. This is found in II Cor. 12:2. Heaven is spoken of as a safe deposit for our treasures. "But lay up for yourselves treasures in heaven, where neither moth nor rust doth corrupt, and where thieves do not break through nor steal" (Matt. 6:20).

In heaven there is room for all believers. "In my father's house are many mansions; if it were not so I would have told you. I go to prepare a place for you" (John 14:2).

The glorified Christ will be there. "But he being full of the Holy Ghost, looked up steadfastly into heaven, and saw the glory of God, and Jesus standing on the right hand of God" (Acts 7:52).

The redeemed of all nations will be there. "After this I beheld, and lo, a great multitude, which no man can number of all nations, and kindreds, and people, and tongues, stand before the throne, and before the lamb, clothed with white robes, and palms in their hands" (Rev. 21:1).

There will be no tears in heaven. "For the lamb which is in the midst of the throne shall feed them, and shall lead them into living fountains of water: and God shall wipe away all tears from their eyes" (Rev. 7:17).

Neither shall there be death, sorrow, or crying, "And God shall wipe away all tears from their eyes; and there shall be no more death, neither sorrow, nor dying, nor shall there be any more pain; for the former things are passed away" (Rev. 21:4).

In heaven we will dwell in endless joy. "For I reckon that the sufferings of this present time are not worthy to be compared to the glory which shall be revealed" (Rom. 8:18).

In heaven we will be in the presence of Christ. "And if I go and prepare a place for you, I will come again, and receive you to myself, that where I am, there ye may be also" (John 14:3).

The saints will be rewarded in heaven. "And whosoever shall give to drink unto one of these little ones a cup of cold water only in the name of a disciple, verily I say unto you, he shall in no wise lose his reward" (Matt. 10:42).

In heaven there will be rest from the labors of this life. "And I heard a voice from heaven saying unto me, Write, Blessed are the dead which die in the Lord from henceforth. Yea, saith the spirit, that they may rest from their labor, and their deeds do follow them" (Rev. 14:13).

In heaven there will be a crown of righteousness. "Henceforth there is laid up for me a crown of righteousness, which the Lord, the righteous judge shall give me at that day, and not to me only, but unto all them that love his appearance" (II Tim. 4:8).

In the resurrection we will have spiritual bodies. "It is sown a natural body; it is raised a spiritual body. There is a natural body and there is a spiritual body" (I Cor. 15:44).

In this world our knowledge is quite limited. However in heaven it will be greatly extended. Indeed, this is a most wonderful thought. "For now we see through a glass darkly; but then face to face, now I know in part, but then shall I know even as also I am known" (I Cor. 12:13).

In heaven everything is perfect and changeless. There we will have no need of time since time involves change. We are told that time will be no more (Rev. 10:6).

The Future State of Those Who Have Accepted the Lord Jesus Christ as Their Savior: The Bible makes it clear that there is only one way of salvation, there is only one Savior, even though many persons deny this truth. These are described as being banished from God. "And these shall go away into everlasting punishment, but the righteous into eternal life" (Matt. 25:46).

Those who do not accept the free gift of salvation will suffer as by fire. "Then shall he say unto them on the left hand, Depart from me ye cursed, into everlasting fire, prepared for the devil and his angels" (Matt. 25:41). This reference makes it clear that hell was not prepared for mankind but for the devil.

We are told that God is not willing that any should perish. "The Lord is not slack concerning his promise, as some men count slackness, but is longsuffering to usward, not willing that any should perish, but that all shall come to repentance" (II Pet. 3:9).

Jesus warns us to fear the devil and his devices. "And fear not them which kill the body, but are not able to kill the soul; but rather fear them which are able to destroy both soul and body in hell" (Matt. 10:28).

We are also warned by the Apostle Paul: "If any man defile the temple of God, him shall God destroy; for the temple of God is holy, which temple ye are" (I Cor. 3:17).

John, in the book of Revelation, warns us: "But the fearful, and unbelieving, and sorcerers, and idolators, and all liars shall have their part in the lake which burneth with fire and brimstone; which is the second death" (Rev. 21:8).

In John 3:36 we are told: "He that believeth on the Son hath everlasting life; and he that believeth not on the Son shall not see life; but the wrath of God abideth on him."

There are four words in the original language of the Bible which have been translated as hell. These are Gehenna, meaning the place of torment; Hades, the abode of the dead; Sheol, the grave or unseen state; and Tartarus, the place of punishment. The latter term is used in II Pet. 2:4: "For if God spared not the angels that sinned, but cast them down to hell, and delivered them into chains of darkness, to be reserved unto judgement."

The word hell is mentioned forty-three times in tbe Bible, while the word heaven is mentioned 570 times. Our loving heavenly Father is much more interested in our salvation than in punishment. We should continually thank him for his mercy.

I started this vision, while in the hospital, with the statement that God is perfect and now I end it with the thought of His mercy.

Changes I Have Seen In The Mennonite Church

by H. Harold Hartzler

1. General Conference to General Assembly
2. No longer do we have Bible conferences
3. No longer do we have evangelistic meetings
4. We have made many Conference changes
5. No longer designate ourselves as Amish Mennonite
6. Large numbers of members of the Amish church have joined the Mennonite church
7. No longer speak of our houses of worship as church houses
8. We have fewer members who are farmers
9. Many church members are more highly educated
10. We now have many members who are medical doctors
11. We have members who are in many professions
12. We now have M.C.C.
13. Ladies no longer wear capes
14. We now have Mennonite Mutual Aid
15. We now have automobile insurance
16. We no longer frown on life insurance
17. We now insure our houses
18. We do much more traveling at home and abroad
19. Most of us now own a car or two
20. Few of us drive a buggy
21. We now have Mennonite Foundation
22. We now cooperate with other branches of the Mennonite Church
23. We are much more conscious of our Anabaptist heritage
24. We now have salaried ministers
25. We seldom use the lot for ordination
26. We now ordain women as ministers
27. Few ministers wear the plain garb
28. Very few laymen wear the plain garb
29. We dress more like the world
30. We use wedding rings
31. Some ministers make use of the wedding ring
32. We are discontinuing the use of the prayer head covering
33. We are discontinuing the practice of foot washing
34. We seldom greet each other with the holy kiss
35. Most of us are much more affluent
36. The office of bishop is disappearing
37. The office of deacon is less important

38. We now have elders
39. Our church publications have dramatically changed
40. We now have youth pastors
41. We are much more highly organized
42. Many of our pastors are graduates of seminaries
43. We now have a world conference
44. We now make use of university facilities for the Assembly
45. We now have our own seminaries
46. We have many short-term voluntary service projects
47. M.C.C. has greatly expanded its services
48. Our colleges have greatly changed
49. Nursing care has increased
50. We now train nurses in our colleges
51. We seldom kneel to pray in church services
52. We no longer have segregation by sex in our church services
53. We no longer have Young People's Meetings
54. Women are now members of many church committees
55. We have husband-wife teams for a number of our churches
56. We are no longer a peculiar people
57. We now vote in national elections
58. We now make more use of medical doctors and hospitals
59. We now have smaller families
60. We now marry and adopt spouses from foreign countries
61. We now have pianos in our churches
62. We now have organs in our churches
63. Other musical instruments are now in our churches
64. Some churches are now using the computer for church work
65. We now have a music committee working with other conferences
66. We now have a scholarly journal, *Mennonite Quarterly Review*
67. We now have many more genealogies
68. We now have Mennonite historical societies
69. We publish *Mennonite Historical Review*
70. We have written histories of a number of congregations
71. Dancing is permitted on at least one college campus
72. We now have a college connected with a university
74. A new organization called Fellowship of Concerned Mennonites
75. We have a publication called *Sword and Trumpet*
76. We have Mennonite Economic Development Association
77. Many churches have a printed program for Sunday morning service
78. Visitors are often announced Sunday mornings
79. A discussion of the sermon is a part of the Sunday school in some churches
80. We no longer speak of the pulpit as the sacred desk
81. We no longer restrict the pulpit to the use of the minister
82. We make use of Christian films

83. We no longer have authoritarian leadership
84. We no longer view "nonconformity" as an integral part of the Gospel
85. *War, Peace and Nonresistance* by Guy F. Hershberger has influenced us
86. Many members read *The Sunday School Times*
87. We no longer have "Council Meetings" before Communion
88. We have tent evangelism
89. We have Christian Laymen's Evangelism
90. We now have a Lay Activities Committee
91. We make use of radios in our homes
92. We have evangelists who make use of radios
93. We now own television sets
94. Many of our members now support the television ministry
95. Parochial education has greatly increased among us
96. We have Mennonite Disaster Service
97. We now have "Seniors for Peace"
98. Our hymnal is a joint project by Old Mennonite and General Conference
99. We are planning a joint meeting of Old Mennonites and General Conference
100. Some churches have commissions
101. Some churches use the term Fellowship rather than Mennonite
102. Since 1979 we have Mennonite Conciliation Service
103. We now have Mennonite Health Service
104. We now have Mennonite Arts Association
105. Many now read *Mennonite Weekly Review*
106. We no longer have *Christian Monitor*
107. We now have *Christian Living*
108. We no longer have *Words of Cheer*
109. The General Board has replaced General Council
110. We have a number of new conferences
111. We now have Bible Mennonite Fellowship
112. We now have church camps
113. We now have Church Planting Programs
114. We now have the Council of International Ministries
115. We now have the Council of Mennonite Colleges
116. We now have the Council of Mennonite Seminaries
117. We now have Mennonite Relief Sales

GREAT BOOKS OF THE WESTERN WORLD

28. GILBERT
    GALILEO
    HARVEY

29. CERVANTES

30. FRANCIS BACON

31. DESCARTES
    SPINOZA

32. MILTON

33. PASCAL

34. NEWTON
    HUYGENS

35. LOCKE
    BERKELEY
    HUME

36. SWIFT
    STERNE

37. FIELDING

38. MONTESQUIEU
    ROUSSEAU

39. ADAM SMITH

40. GIBBON I

41. GIBBON II

42. KANT

43. AMERICAN STATE
    PAPERS
    THE FEDERALIST
    J. S. MILL

44. BOSWELL

45. LAVOISIER
    FOURIER
    FARADAY

46. HEGEL

47. GOETHE

48. MELVILLE

49. DARWIN

50. MARX
    ENGELS

51. TOLSTOY

52. DOSTOEVSKY

53. WILLIAM JAMES

54. FREUD

GREAT BOOKS
OF THE WESTERN WORLD
ROBERT MAYNARD HUTCHINS, EDITOR IN CHIEF

32.

JOHN MILTON

MORTIMER J. ADLER, *Associate Editor*
Members of the Advisory Board: STRINGFELLOW BARR, SCOTT BUCHANAN, JOHN ERSKINE, CLARENCE H. FAUST, ALEXANDER MEIKLEJOHN, JOSEPH J. SCHWAB, MARK VAN DOREN.
Editorial Consultants: A. F. B. CLARK, F. L. LUCAS, WALTER MURDOCH.
WALLACE BROCKWAY, *Executive Editor*

English Minor Poems
Paradise Lost
Samson Agonistes
Areopagitica

BY JOHN MILTON

W<small>ILLIAM</small> B<small>ENTON</small>, *Publisher*

ENCYCLOPÆDIA BRITANNICA, INC.
CHICAGO · LONDON · TORONTO

English Minor Poems, Paradise Lost, and *Samson Agonistes*
are reprinted from *Milton's Poetical Works,* edited by H. C. Beeching,
by permission of OXFORD UNIVERSITY PRESS

THE UNIVERSITY OF CHICAGO

*The Great Books
is published with the editorial advice of the faculties
of The University of Chicago*

COPYRIGHT IN THE UNITED STATES OF AMERICA, 1952,
BY ENCYCLOPÆDIA BRITANNICA, INC.

COPYRIGHT 1952. COPYRIGHT UNDER INTERNATIONAL COPYRIGHT UNION BY
ENCYCLOPÆDIA BRITANNICA, INC. ALL RIGHTS RESERVED UNDER PAN AMERICAN
COPYRIGHT CONVENTIONS BY ENCYCLOPÆDIA BRITANNICA, INC.

BIOGRAPHICAL NOTE
John Milton, 1608–1674

John Milton was born in Bread Street, London, on December 9, 1608. "My father," he wrote, "destined me, while yet a little boy for the study of humane letters.... Both at the grammar-school and also under other masters at home, he caused me to be instructed daily." At the age of seventeen he was admitted to Cambridge. Here his first years were darkened by unpopularity and a quarrel with the college authorities, but he worked diligently and by the time he received his Master of Arts degree in 1632, his unusual powers had won him recognition and esteem. At Cambridge he decided to abandon his original plan of entering the service of the Church, giving as his reason that he preferred "blameless silence before the sacred office of speaking, bought and begun with servitude and forswearing."

Milton's literary gifts were apparent early. *On the Morning of Christ's Nativity* was written while the poet was still at Cambridge. *L'Allegro* and its companion piece, *Il Penseroso*; two masques, *Arcades* and *Comus*; and *Lycidas*, an elegy for a college friend drowned at sea, were the fruit of six years of study, chiefly of the classics, that followed the termination of his university career. These years, passed quietly with his father in the rural setting of a small Buckinghamshire village, were succeeded by fifteen months of travel in France and Italy where he was widely received. He made a special visit to Galileo, "grown old, a prisoner to the Inquisition for thinking in Astronomy otherwise than the Franciscan and Dominican licensers thought."

Even in the pastoral setting of *Lycidas* there were unmistakable stirrings of Milton's concern with the problem of church reform. When, in 1641, this became one of the crucial issues in the rising tide of civil war, Milton emerged from his life of study and teaching. Renouncing his poetry for militant prose, he scourged those who favored Episcopacy, holding them responsible for arresting the course of the Reformation. His attack was framed in a series of pamphlets, the most elaborate of these being a treatise entitled *The Reason of Church Government urged against Prelaty*.

In 1643, when he was thirty-five, Milton married Mary Powell, the seventeen-year-old daughter of a Cavalier family. After a few weeks she returned to her home and seemed to have no intention of continuing the relationship. Two years later, however, she came back, and their married life was resumed. There were three daughters of this union and a son who died in infancy. Mary Powell herself died in childbirth in 1654.

In the same year that his wife left him, Milton wrote his famous treatise, *The Doctrine and Discipline of Divorce, Restored to the good of both sexes from the Bondage of Canon Law and other Mistakes*, asserting that marriage being a "private matter" could be dissolved in cases of incompatibility. This incendiary tract and another on the same subject happened to have been published without a license immediately after the enactment of a new ordinance requiring the licensing of all works. Accordingly, proceedings against Milton were instituted. His answer was *Areopagitica, a Speech for the Liberty of Unlicensed Printing*, published the following year, without a license.

With the fall of the Stuarts in 1649, Milton mobilized his energies in the service of Cromwell and the Commonwealth. In answer to *Eikon Basilike*, a work of disputed authorship purporting to be the last meditations of Charles I, he wrote *Eikonoklastes*, a point by point refutation. Published the same year was a pamphlet entitled *Tenure of Kings and Magistrates, proving that it is lawful, and hath been held so in all ages, for any who have the power, to call to account a Tyrant or wicked King, and, after due conviction, to depose and put him to death, if the ordinary Magistrate have neglected or denied to do it*. This was probably instrumental in Milton's appointment as Latin Secretary to the Council of State, a position he retained until 1660. The poet continued to defend the Commonwealth against the attacks of continental writers in a series of Latin tractates. This controversy raged for four years with an extraordinary degree of violence and personal vituperation; Milton's participation against the advice of physicians brought him to total blindness.

Turning once more to domestic affairs, Milton focused his attention on church reform, advocating the complete separation of Church and State and mutual tolerance between Protestant sects. In 1660, on the eve of the Restoration and with full awareness that his was one of the last voices to be raised against the "readmitting of kingship", Milton published *The Ready and Easy Way to Establish a Free Commonwealth* and a number of other pamphlets outlining a plan for a permanent parliament.

The Restoration put an end to Milton's public life and forced him to go into hiding. Just why he was not executed with the other prominent supporters of the Commonwealth is not clear. At the age of fifty-two, after nineteen years of stormy political activity, he again turned to the studious and literary pursuits of his youth. To this last period of his life belong his greatest poetic achievements: *Paradise Lost* (1667); its sequel, *Paradise Regained* (1671); and finally *Samson Agonistes* (1671). His prose writings of these last years include a miscellany of scholarly and historical works and *De Doctrina Christiana*, the final statement of his religious position, which by a series of mischances was not published until 1825.

Underlying this vigorous literary activity was the loneliness of Milton's personal life. Totally blind at the time of Mary Powell's death, he lived in helpless dependence on his motherless daughters, who grew up resenting him and careless of his comfort and wishes. This bleak home life was interrupted briefly in 1656 by the poet's marriage to Katharine Woodcock, who died in childbirth less than a year later. In 1663 he married Elizabeth Minshull, then but twenty-five. She seems to have brightened his last decade, which was passed in quiet study tempered with music and the company of friends. Weakened by the gout and other maladies, he died on November 8, 1674, and was buried beside his father in the church of St. Giles Cripplegate.

CONTENTS

MISCELLANEOUS POEMS

On the Morning of Christs Nativity	1	On Shakespear. 1630	16
The Hymn	2	On the University Carrier	16
A Paraphrase on Psalm 114	7	Another on the same	17
Psalm 136	8	L'Allegro	17
The Passion	10	Il Penseroso	21
On Time	12	Arcades	25
Upon the Circumcision	12	Lycidas	27
At a Solemn Musick	13	Comus	33
An Epitaph on the Marchioness of Winchester	14	*Poems added in the 1673 Edition*	
		On the Death of a Fair Infant	57
		At a Vacation Exercise	59
Song on May morning	15	The Fifth Ode of Horace. Lib. I	61

SONNETS

I, VII–XIX	63–68	To the Lord Generall Cromwell May 1652	69
On the new forcers of Conscience under the Long Parliament	68	To Sr Henry Vane the younger	69
On the Lord Gen. Fairfax at the seige of Colchester	68	To Mr. Cyriack Skinner upon his Blindness	70

PSALMS

I–VIII 71–77	LXXX–LXXXVIII . . 78–90	

PARADISE LOST

Book I	93	Book VII	217
Book II	111	Book VIII	232
Book III	135	Book IX	247
Book IV	152	Book X	274
Book V	175	Book XI	299
Book VI	196	Book XII	319

SAMSON AGONISTES 335

AREOPAGITICA 379

MISCELLANEOUS POEMS

MISCELLANEOUS POEMS

On the Morning of Christs Nativity
Compos'd 1629

I

THIS is the Month, and this the happy morn
Wherin the Son of Heav'ns eternal King,
Of wedded Maid, and Virgin Mother born,
Our great redemption from above did bring;
For so the holy sages once did sing,
   That he our deadly forfeit should release,
And with his Father work us a perpetual peace.

II

That glorious Form, that Light unsufferable,
And that far-beaming blaze of Majesty,
Wherwith he wont at Heav'ns high Councel-Table,   *10*
To sit the midst of Trinal Unity,
He laid aside; and here with us to be,
   Forsook the Courts of everlasting Day,
And chose with us a darksom House of mortal Clay.

III

Say Heav'nly Muse, shall not thy sacred vein
Afford a present to the Infant God?
Hast thou no vers, no hymn, or solemn strein,
To welcom him to this his new abode,
Now while the Heav'n by the Suns team untrod,
   Hath took no print of the approching light,   *20*
And all the spangled host keep watch in squadrons bright?

IV

See how from far upon the Eastern rode
The Star-led Wisards haste with odours sweet,
O run, prevent them with thy humble ode,
And lay it lowly at his blessed feet;
Have thou the honour first, thy Lord to greet,
   And joyn thy voice unto the Angel Quire,
From out his secret Altar toucht with hallow'd fire.

The Hymn

I

It was the Winter wilde,
While the Heav'n-born-childe, 30
   All meanly wrapt in the rude manger lies;
Nature in aw to him
Had doff't her gawdy trim,
   With her great Master so to sympathize:
It was no season then for her
To wanton with the Sun her lusty Paramour.

II

Only with speeches fair
She woo's the gentle Air
   To hide her guilty front with innocent Snow,
And on her naked shame, 40
Pollute with sinfull blame,
   The Saintly Vail of Maiden white to throw,
Confounded, that her Makers eyes
Should look so neer upon her foul deformities.

III

But he her fears to cease,
Sent down the meek-eyd Peace,
   She crown'd with Olive green, came softly sliding
Down through the turning sphear
His ready Harbinger,
   With Turtle wing the amorous clouds dividing, 50
And waving wide her mirtle wand,
She strikes a universall Peace through Sea and Land.

IV

No War, or Battails sound
Was heard the World around,
   The idle spear and shield were high up hung;
The hooked Chariot stood
Unstain'd with hostile blood,
   The Trumpet spake not to the armed throng,
And Kings sate still with awfull eye,
As if they surely knew their sovran Lord was by. 60

V

But peacefull was the night
Wherin the Prince of light

His raign of peace upon the earth began:
The Windes with wonder whist,
Smoothly the waters kist,
   Whispering new joyes to the milde Ocean,
Who now hath quite forgot to rave,
While Birds of Calm sit brooding on the charmed wave.

VI

The Stars with deep amaze
Stand fixt in stedfast gaze,   70
   Bending one way their pretious influence,
And will not take their flight,
For all the morning light,
   Or *Lucifer* that often warn'd them thence;
But in their glimmering Orbs did glow,
Untill their Lord himself bespake, and bid them go.

VII

And though the shady gloom
Had given day her room,
   The Sun himself with-held his wonted speed,
And hid his head for shame,   80
As his inferiour flame,
   The new enlightn'd world no more should need;
He saw a greater Sun appear
Then his bright Throne, or burning Axletree could bear.

VIII

The Shepherds on the Lawn,
Or ere the point of dawn,
   Sate simply chatting in a rustick row;
Full little thought they than,
That the mighty *Pan*
   Was kindly com to live with them below;   90
Perhaps their loves, or els their sheep,
Was all that did their silly thoughts so busie keep.

IX

When such musick sweet
Their hearts and ears did greet,
   As never was by mortall finger strook,
Divinely-warbled voice
Answering the stringed noise,
   As all their souls in blisfull rapture took:
The Air such pleasure loth to lose,
With thousand echo's still prolongs each heav'nly close.

X

Nature that heard such sound101
Beneath the hollow round
    Of *Cynthia's* seat, the Airy region thrilling,
Now was almost won
To think her part was don,
    And that her raign had here its last fulfilling;
She knew such harmony alone
Could hold all Heav'n and Earth in happier union.

XI

At last surrounds their sight
A Globe of circular light,110
    That with long beams the shame-fac't night array'd,
The helmed Cherubim
And sworded Seraphim,
    Are seen in glittering ranks with wings displaid,
Harping in loud and solemn quire,
With unexpressive notes to Heav'ns new-born Heir.

XII

Such Musick (as 'tis said)
Before was never made,
    But when of old the sons of morning sung,
While the Creator Great120
His constellations set,
    And the well-ballanc't world on hinges hung,
And cast the dark foundations deep,
And bid the weltring waves their oozy channel keep.

XIII

Ring out ye Crystall sphears,
Once bless our human ears,
    (If ye have power to touch our senses so)
And let your silver chime
Move in melodious time;
    And let the Base of Heav'ns deep Organ blow,130
And with your ninefold harmony
Make up full consort to th'Angelike symphony.

XIV

For if such holy Song
Enwrap our fancy long,
    Time will run back, and fetch the age of gold,
And speckl'd vanity
Will sicken soon and die,

And leprous sin will melt from earthly mould,
And Hell it self will pass away,
And leave her dolorous mansions to the peering day.   140

XV

Yea Truth, and Justice then
Will down return to men,
   Th'enameld *Arras* of the Rain-bow wearing,
And Mercy set between,
Thron'd in Celestiall sheen,
   With radiant feet the tissued clouds down stearing,
And Heav'n as at som festivall,
Will open wide the Gates of her high Palace Hall.

XVI

But wisest Fate sayes no,
This must not yet be so,   150
   The Babe lies yet in smiling Infancy,
That on the bitter cross
Must redeem our loss;
   So both himself and us to glorifie:
Yet first to those ychain'd in sleep,
The wakefull trump of doom must thunder through the
   deep,

XVII

With such a horrid clang
As on mount *Sinai* rang
   While the red fire, and smouldring clouds out brake:
The aged Earth agast   160
With terrour of that blast,
   Shall from the surface to the center shake,
When at the worlds last session,
The dreadfull Judge in middle Air shall spread his throne.

XVIII

And then at last our bliss
Full and perfect is,
   But now begins; for from this happy day
Th'old Dragon under ground
In straiter limits bound,
   Not half so far casts his usurped sway,   170
And wrath to see his Kingdom fail,
Swindges the scaly Horrour of his foulded tail.

XIX

The Oracles are dumm,
No voice or hideous humm

Runs through the arched roof in words deceiving.
Apollo from his shrine
Can no more divine,
   With hollow shreik the steep of *Delphos* leaving.
No nightly trance, or breathed spell,
Inspire's the pale-ey'd Priest from the prophetic cell.   *180*

XX

The lonely mountains o're,
And the resounding shore,
   A voice of weeping heard, and loud lament;
From haunted spring, and dale
Edg'd with poplar pale,
   The parting Genius is with sighing sent,
With flowre-inwov'n tresses torn
The Nimphs in twilight shade of tangled thickets mourn.

XXI

In consecrated Earth,
And on the holy Hearth,   *190*
   The *Lars*, and *Lemures* moan with midnight plaint,
In Urns, and Altars round,
A drear, and dying sound
   Affrights the *Flamins* at their service quaint;
And the chill Marble seems to sweat,
While each peculiar power forgoes his wonted seat.

XXII

Peor, and *Baalim*,
Forsake their Temples dim,
   With that twise-batter'd god of *Palestine*,
And mooned *Ashtaroth*,   *200*
Heav'ns Queen and Mother both,
   Now sits not girt with Tapers holy shine,
The Libyc *Hammon* shrinks his horn,
In vain the *Tyrian* Maids their wounded *Thamuz* mourn.

XXIII

And sullen *Moloch* fled,
Hath left in shadows dred,
   His burning Idol all of blackest hue,
In vain with Cymbals ring,
They call the grisly king,
   In dismall dance about the furnace blue;   *210*
The brutish gods of *Nile* as fast,
Isis and *Orus*, and the Dog *Anubis* hast.

XXIV

Nor is *Osiris* seen
In *Memphian* Grove, or Green,
    Trampling the unshowr'd Grasse with lowings loud:
Nor can he be at rest
Within his sacred chest,
    Naught but profoundest Hell can be his shroud,
In vain with Timbrel'd Anthems dark
The sable-stoled Sorcerers bear his worship Ark.   *220*

XXV

He feels from *Juda's* Land
The dredded Infants hand,
    The rayes of *Bethlehem* blind his dusky eyn;
Nor all the gods beside,
Longer dare abide,
    Not *Typhon* huge ending in snaky twine:
Our Babe to shew his Godhead true,
Can in his swadling bands controul the damned crew.

XXVI

So when the Sun in bed,
Curtain'd with cloudy red,   *230*
    Pillows his chin upon an Orient wave,
The flocking shadows pale,
Troop to th'infernall jail,
    Each fetter'd Ghost slips to his severall grave,
And the yellow-skirted *Fayes*,
Fly after the Night-steeds, leaving their Moon-lov'd maze.

XXVII

But see the Virgin blest,
Hath laid her Babe to rest.
    Time is our tedious Song should here have ending,
Heav'ns youngest teemed Star,   *240*
Hath fixt her polisht Car,
    Her sleeping Lord with Handmaid Lamp attending:
And all about the Courtly Stable,
Bright-harnest Angels sit in order serviceable.

A Paraphrase on *Psalm* 114

This and the following *Psalm* were don by the Author at fifteen yeers old.

  When the blest seed of *Terah's* faithfull Son,
After long toil their liberty had won,
And past from *Pharian* fields to *Canaan* Land,

Led by the strength of the Almighties hand,
Jehovah's wonders were in *Israel* shown,
His praise and glory was in *Israel* known.
That saw the troubl'd Sea, and shivering fled,
And sought to hide his froth-becurled head
Low in the earth, *Jordans* clear streams recoil,
As a faint host that hath receiv'd the foil. *10*
The high, huge-bellied Mountains skip like Rams
Amongst their Ews, the little Hills like Lambs.
Why fled the Ocean? And why skipt the Mountains?
Why turned *Jordan* toward his Crystall Fountains?
Shake earth, and at the presence be agast
Of him that ever was, and ay shall last,
That glassy flouds from rugged rocks can crush,
And make soft rills from fiery flint-stones gush.

Psalm 136

Let us with a gladsom mind
Praise the Lord, for he is kind,
   For his mercies ay endure,
   Ever faithfull, ever sure.

Let us blaze his Name abroad,
For of gods he is the God;
   For, *&c.*

O let us his praises tell,
That doth the wrathfull tyrants quell. *10*
   For, *&c.*

That with his miracles doth make
Amazed Heav'n and Earth to shake.
   For, *&c.*

That by his wisdom did create
The painted Heav'ns so full of state.
   For, *&c.* *20*

That did the solid Earth ordain
To rise above the watry plain.
   For, *&c.*

That by his all-commanding might,
Did fill the new-made world with light.
   For, *&c.*

Psalm 136

And caus'd the Golden-tressed Sun,
All the day long his cours to run. 30
    For, &c.

The horned Moon to shine by night,
Amongst her spangled sisters bright.
    For, &c.

He with his thunder-clasping hand,
Smote the first-born of *Egypt* Land.
    For, &c. 40

And in despight of *Pharao* fell,
He brought from thence his *Israel*.
    For, &c.

The ruddy waves he cleft in twain,
Of the *Erythræan* main.
    For, &c.

The floods stood still like Walls of Glass,
While the Hebrew Bands did pass. 50
    For, &c.

But full soon they did devour
The Tawny King with all his power.
    For, &c.

His chosen people he did bless
In the wastfull Wildernes.
    For, &c. 60

In bloody battail he brought down
Kings of prowess and renown.
    For, &c.

He foild bold *Seon* and his host,
That rul'd the *Amorrean* coast.
    For, &c.

And large-lim'd *Og* he did subdue,
With all his over hardy crew. 70
    For, &c.

And to his Servant *Israel*,
He gave their Land therin to dwell.
    For, &c.

>   He hath with a piteous eye
>   Beheld us in our misery.
>   For, &c. 80
>
>   And freed us from the slavery
>   Of the invading enimy.
>   For, &c.
>
>   All living creatures he doth feed,
>   And with full hand supplies their need.
>   For, &c.
>
>   Let us therfore warble forth
>   His mighty Majesty and worth. 90
>   For, &c.
>
>   That his mansion hath on high
>   Above the reach of mortall ey.
>   For his mercies ay endure,
>   Ever faithfull, ever sure.

The Passion

I

> Ere-while of Musick, and Ethereal mirth,
> Wherwith the stage of Ayr and Earth did ring,
> And joyous news of heav'nly Infants birth,
> My muse with Angels did divide to sing;
> But headlong joy is ever on the wing,
>   In Wintry solstice like the shortn'd light
> Soon swallow'd up in dark and long out-living night.

II

> For now to sorrow must I tune my song,
> And set my Harpe to notes of saddest wo,
> Which on our dearest Lord did sease er'e long, 10
> Dangers, and snares, and wrongs, and worse then so,
> Which he for us did freely undergo.
>   Most perfect *Heroe*, try'd in heaviest plight
> Of labours huge and hard, too hard for human wight.

III

> He sov'ran Priest stooping his regall head
> That dropt with odorous oil down his fair eyes,
> Poor fleshly Tabernacle entered,
> His starry front low-rooft beneath the skies;

The Passion

O what a Mask was there, what a disguise!
    Yet more; the stroke of death he must abide,   20
Then lies him meekly down fast by his Brethrens side.

IV

These latter scenes confine my roving vers,
To this Horizon is my *Phoebus* bound,
His Godlike acts, and his temptations fierce,
And former sufferings other where are found;
Loud o're the rest *Cremona's* Trump doth sound;
    Me softer airs befit, and softer strings
Of Lute, or Viol still, more apt for mournful things.

V

Befriend me night best Patroness of grief,
Over the Pole thy thickest mantle throw,   30
And work my flatter'd fancy to belief,
That Heav'n and Earth are colour'd with my wo;
My sorrows are too dark for day to know:
    The leaves should all be black whereon I write,
And letters where my tears have washt a wannish white.

VI

See see the Chariot, and those rushing wheels,
That whirl'd the Prophet up at *Chebar* flood,
My spirit som transporting *Cherub* feels,
To bear me where the Towers of *Salem* stood,
Once glorious Towers, now sunk in guiltles blood;   40
    There doth my soul in holy vision sit
In pensive trance, and anguish, and ecstatick fit.

VII

Mine eye hath found that sad Sepulchral rock
That was the Casket of Heav'ns richest store,
And here though grief my feeble hands up-lock,
Yet on the softned Quarry would I score
My plaining vers as lively as before;
    For sure so well instructed are my tears,
That they would fitly fall in order'd Characters.

VIII

Or should I thence hurried on viewles wing,   50
Take up a weeping on the Mountains wilde,
The gentle neighbourhood of grove and spring
Would soon unboosom all their Echoes milde,

And I (for grief is easily beguild)
　　Might think th'infection of my sorrows loud,
　Had got a race of mourners on som pregnant cloud.

This Subject the Author finding to be above the yeers he had, when he wrote it, and nothing satisfi'd with what was begun, left it unfinisht.

On Time

　Fly envious *Time*, till thou run out thy race,
　Call on the lazy leaden-stepping hours,
　Whose speed is but the heavy Plummets pace;
　And glut thy self with what thy womb devours,
　Which is no more then what is false and vain,
　And meerly mortal dross;
　So little is our loss,
　So little is thy gain.
　For when as each thing bad thou hast entomb'd,
　And last of all, thy greedy self consum'd,   *10*
　Then long Eternity shall greet our bliss
　With an individual kiss;
　And Joy shall overtake us as a flood,
　When every thing that is sincerely good
　And perfectly divine,
　With Truth, and Peace, and Love shall ever shine
　About the supreme Throne
　Of him, t'whose happy-making sight alone,
　When once our heav'nly-guided soul shall clime,
　Then all this Earthy grosnes quit,   *20*
　Attir'd with Stars, we shall for ever sit,
　　Triumphing over Death, and Chance, and thee O Time.

Upon the Circumcision

　Ye flaming Powers, and winged Warriours bright,
　That erst with Musick, and triumphant song
　First heard by happy watchful Shepherds ear,
　So sweetly sung your Joy the Clouds along
　Through the soft silence of the list'ning night;
　Now mourn, and if sad share with us to bear
　Your fiery essence can distill no tear,
　Burn in your sighs, and borrow
　Seas wept from our deep sorrow,
　He who with all Heav'ns heraldry whileare   *10*
　Enter'd the world, now bleeds to give us ease;
　Alas, how soon our sin
　　Sore doth begin

　　　　　His Infancy to sease!
O more exceeding love or law more just?
Just law indeed, but more exceeding love!
For we by rightfull doom remediles
Were lost in death, till he that dwelt above
High thron'd in secret bliss, for us frail dust
Emptied his glory, ev'n to nakednes;　　　　　　20
And that great Cov'nant which we still transgress
Intirely satisfi'd,
And the full wrath beside
Of vengeful Justice bore for our excess,
And seals obedience first with wounding smart
This day, but O ere long
Huge pangs and strong
　　　Will pierce more neer his heart.

At a Solemn Musick

Blest pair of *Sirens*, pledges of Heav'ns joy,
Sphear-born harmonious Sisters, Voice, and Vers,
Wed your divine sounds, and mixt power employ
Dead things with inbreath'd sense able to pierce,
And to our high-rais'd phantasie present,
That undisturbed Song of pure content,
Ay sung before the saphire-colour'd throne
To him that sits theron
With Saintly shout, and solemn Jubily,
Where the bright Seraphim in burning row　　　10
Their loud up-lifted Angel trumpets blow,
And the Cherubick host in thousand quires
Touch their immortal Harps of golden wires,
With those just Spirits that wear victorious Palms,
Hymns devout and holy Psalms
Singing everlastingly;
That we on Earth with undiscording voice
May rightly answer that melodious noise;
As once we did, till disproportion'd sin
Jarr'd against natures chime, and with harsh din　　20
Broke the fair musick that all creatures made
To their great Lord, whose love their motion sway'd
In perfect Diapason, whilst they stood
In first obedience, and their state of good.
O may we soon again renew that Song,
And keep in tune with Heav'n, till God ere long
To his celestial consort us unite,
To live with him, and sing in endles morn of light.

An Epitaph on the Marchioness of WINCHESTER

This rich Marble doth enterr
The honour'd Wife of *Winchester*,
A Vicounts daughter, an Earls heir,
Besides what her vertues fair
Added to her noble birth,
More then she could own from Earth.
Summers three times eight save one
She had told, alas too soon,
After so short time of breath,
To house with darknes, and with death.　　　　10
Yet had the number of her days
Bin as compleat as was her praise,
Nature and fate had had no strife
In giving limit to her life.
Her high birth, and her graces sweet,
Quickly found a lover meet;
The Virgin quire for her request
The God that sits at marriage feast;
He at their invoking came
But with a scarce-wel-lighted flame;　　　　20
And in his Garland as he stood,
Ye might discern a Cipress bud.
Once had the early Matrons run
To greet her of a lovely son,
And now with second hope she goes,
And calls *Lucina* to her throws;
But whether by mischance or blame
Atropos for *Lucina* came;
And with remorsles cruelty,
Spoil'd at once both fruit and tree:　　　　30
The haples Babe before his birth
Had burial, yet not laid in earth,
And the languisht Mothers Womb
Was not long a living Tomb.
So have I seen som tender slip
Sav'd with care from Winters nip,
The pride of her carnation train,
Pluck't up by som unheedy swain,
Who onely thought to crop the flowr
New shot up from vernall showr;　　　　40
But the fair blossom hangs the head
Side-ways as on a dying bed,
And those Pearls of dew she wears,

Prove to be presaging tears
Which the sad morn had let fall
On her hast'ning funerall.
Gentle Lady may thy grave
Peace and quiet ever have;
After this thy travail sore
Sweet rest sease thee evermore,   50
That to give the world encrease,
Shortned hast thy own lives lease;
Here besides the sorrowing
That thy noble House doth bring,
Here be tears of perfect moan
Weept for thee in *Helicon*,
And som Flowers, and som Bays,
For thy Hears to strew the ways,
Sent thee from the banks of *Came*,
Devoted to thy vertuous name;   60
Whilst thou bright Saint high sit'st in glory,
Next her much like to thee in story,
That fair *Syrian* Shepherdess,
Who after yeers of barrennes,
The highly favour'd *Joseph* bore
To him that serv'd for her before,
And at her next birth much like thee,
Through pangs fled to felicity,
Far within the boosom bright
Of blazing Majesty and Light,
There with thee, new welcom Saint,   70
Like fortunes may her soul acquaint,
With thee there clad in radiant sheen,
No Marchioness, but now a Queen.

Song On May morning

Now the bright morning Star, Dayes harbinger,
Comes dancing from the East, and leads with her
The Flowry *May*, who from her green lap throws
The yellow Cowslip, and the pale Primrose.
    Hail bounteous *May* that dost inspire
    Mirth and youth, and warm desire,
    Woods and Groves, are of thy dressing,
    Hill and Dale, doth boast thy blessing.
Thus we salute thee with our early Song,
And welcom thee, and wish thee long.   10

On Shakespear. 1630

What needs my *Shakespear* for his honour'd **Bones**,
The labour of an age in piled **Stones**,
Or that his hallow'd reliques should be hid
Under a Star-ypointing *Pyramid*?
Dear son of memory, great heir of Fame,
What need'st thou such weak witnes of thy name?
Thou in our wonder and astonishment
Hast built thy self a live-long Monument.
For whilst to th'shame of slow-endeavouring art,
Thy easie numbers flow, and that each heart   *10*
Hath from the leaves of thy unvalu'd Book,
Those Delphick lines with deep impression took,
Then thou our fancy of it self bereaving,
Dost make us Marble with too much conceaving;
And so Sepulcher'd in such pomp dost lie,
That Kings for such a Tomb would wish to die.

On the University Carrier

who sickn'd in the time of his vacancy, being forbid to go to
London, by reason of the Plague

Here lies old *Hobson,* Death hath broke his girt,
And here alas, hath laid him in the dirt,
Or els the ways being foul, twenty to one,
He's here stuck in a slough, and overthrown.
'Twas such a shifter, that if truth were known,
Death was half glad when he had got him down;
For he had any time this ten yeers full,
Dodg'd with him, betwixt *Cambridge* and the Bull.
And surely, Death could never have prevail'd,
Had not his weekly cours of carriage fail'd;   *10*
But lately finding him so long at home,
And thinking now his journeys end was come,
And that he had tane up his latest Inne,
In the kind office of a Chamberlin
Shew'd him his room where he must lodge that night,
Pull'd off his Boots, and took away the light:
If any ask for him, it shall be sed,
Hobson has supt, and's newly gon to bed.

Another on the same

Here lieth one who did most truly prove,
That he could never die while he could move,
So hung his destiny never to rot
While he might still jogg on, and keep his trot,
Made of sphear-metal, never to decay
Untill his revolution was at stay.
Time numbers motion, yet (without a crime
'Gainst old truth) motion number'd out his time:
And like an Engin mov'd with wheel and waight,
His principles being ceast, he ended strait.   10
Rest that gives all men life, gave him his death,
And too much breathing put him out of breath;
Nor were it contradiction to affirm
Too long vacation hastned on his term.
Meerly to drive the time away he sickn'd,
Fainted, and died, nor would with Ale be quickn'd;
Nay, quoth he, on his swooning bed out-stretch'd,
If I may not carry, sure Ile ne're be fetch'd,
But vow though the cross Doctors all stood hearers,
For one Carrier put down to make six bearers.   20
Ease was his chief disease, and to judge right,
He di'd for heavines that his Cart went light,
His leasure told him that his time was com,
And lack of load, made his life burdensom,
That even to his last breath (ther be that say't)
As he were prest to death, he cry'd more waight;
But had his doings lasted as they were,
He had bin an immortall Carrier.
Obedient to the Moon he spent his date
In cours reciprocal, and had his fate   30
Linkt to the mutual flowing of the Seas,
Yet (strange to think) his wain was his increase:
His Letters are deliver'd all and gon,
Onely remains this superscription.

L'Allegro

Hence loathed Melancholy
  Of *Cerberus*, and blackest midnight born,
In *Stygian* Cave forlorn
  'Mongst horrid shapes, and shreiks, and sights unholy,
Find out som uncouth cell,
  Where brooding darknes spreads his jealous wings,

And the night-Raven sings;
    There under *Ebon* shades, and low-brow'd Rocks,
As ragged as thy Locks,
    In dark *Cimmerian* desert ever dwell.   *10*
But com thou Goddes fair and free,
In Heav'n ycleap'd *Euphrosyne*,
And by men, heart-easing Mirth,
Whom lovely *Venus* at a birth
With two sister Graces more
To Ivy-crowned *Bacchus* bore;
Or whether (as som Sager sing)
The frolick Wind that breathes the Spring,
Zephir with *Aurora* playing,
As he met her once a Maying,   *20*
There on Beds of Violets blew,
And fresh-blown Roses washt in dew,
Fill'd her with thee a daughter fair,
So bucksom, blith, and debonair.
Haste thee nymph, and bring with thee
Jest and youthful Jollity,
Quips and Cranks, and wanton Wiles,
Nods, and Becks, and Wreathed Smiles,
Such as hang on *Hebe's* cheek,
And love to live in dimple sleek;   *30*
Sport that wrincled Care derides,
And Laughter holding both his sides.
Com, and trip it as ye go
On the light fantastick toe,
And in thy right hand lead with thee,
The Mountain Nymph, sweet Liberty;
And if I give thee honour due,
Mirth, admit me of thy crue
To live with her, and live with thee,
In unreproved pleasures free;   *40*
To hear the Lark begin his flight,
And singing startle the dull night,
From his watch-towre in the skies,
Till the dappled dawn doth rise;
Then to com in spight of sorrow,
And at my window bid good morrow,
Through the Sweet-Briar, or the Vine,
Or the twisted Eglantine.
While the Cock with lively din,
Scatters the rear of darknes thin,   *50*
And to the stack, or the Barn dore,
Stoutly struts his Dames before,

L'Allegro

Oft list'ning how the Hounds and horn
Chearly rouse the slumbring morn,
From the side of som Hoar Hill,
Through the high wood echoing shrill.
Som time walking not unseen
By Hedge-row Elms, on Hillocks green,
Right against the Eastern gate,
Wher the great Sun begins his state,   60
Rob'd in flames, and Amber light,
The clouds in thousand Liveries dight.
While the Plowman neer at hand,
Whistles ore the Furrow'd Land,
And the Milkmaid singeth blithe,
And the Mower whets his sithe,
And every Shepherd tells his tale
Under the Hawthorn in the dale.
Streit mine eye hath caught new pleasures
Whilst the Lantskip round it measures,   70
Russet Lawns, and Fallows Gray,
Where the nibling flocks do stray,
Mountains on whose barren brest
The labouring clouds do often rest:
Meadows trim with Daisies pide,
Shallow Brooks, and Rivers wide.
Towers, and Battlements it sees
Boosom'd high in tufted Trees,
Wher perhaps som beauty lies,
The Cynosure of neighbouring eyes.   80
Hard by, a Cottage chimney smokes,
From betwixt two aged Okes,
Where *Corydon* and *Thyrsis* met,
Are at their savory dinner set
Of Hearbs, and other Country Messes,
Which the neat-handed *Phillis* dresses;
And then in haste her Bowre she leaves,
With *Thestylis* to bind the Sheaves;
Or if the earlier season lead
To the tann'd Haycock in the Mead,   90
Som times with secure delight
The up-land Hamlets will invite,
When the merry Bells ring round,
And the jocond rebecks sound
To many a youth, and many a maid,
Dancing in the Chequer'd shade;
And young and old com forth to play
On a Sunshine Holyday,

Till the live-long day-light fail,
Then to the Spicy Nut-brown Ale, 100
With stories told of many a feat,
How *Faery Mab* the junkets eat,
She was pincht, and pull'd she sed,
And he by Friars Lanthorn led
Tells how the drudging *Goblin* swet,
To ern his Cream-bowle duly set,
When in one night, ere glimps of morn,
His shadowy Flale hath thresh'd the Corn
That ten day-labourers could not end,
Then lies him down the Lubbar Fend. 110
And stretch'd out all the Chimney's length,
Basks at the fire his hairy strength;
And Crop-full out of dores he flings,
Ere the first Cock his Mattin rings.
Thus don the Tales, to bed they creep,
By whispering Windes soon lull'd asleep.
Towred Cities please us then,
And the busie humm of men,
Where throngs of Knights and Barons bold,
In weeds of Peace high triumphs hold, 120
With store of Ladies, whose bright eies
Rain influence, and judge the prise
Of Wit, or Arms, while both contend
To win her Grace, whom all commend.
There let *Hymen* oft appear
In Saffron robe, with Taper clear,
And pomp, and feast, and revelry,
With mask, and antique Pageantry,
Such sights as youthfull Poets dream
On Summer eeves by haunted stream. 130
Then to the well-trod stage anon,
If *Jonsons* learned Sock be on,
Or sweetest *Shakespear* fancies childe,
Warble his native Wood-notes wilde,
And ever against eating Cares,
Lap me in soft *Lydian* Aires,
Married to immortal verse
Such as the meeting soul may pierce
In notes, with many a winding bout
Of lincked sweetnes long drawn out, 140
With wanton heed, and giddy cunning,
The melting voice through mazes running;
Untwisting all the chains that ty
The hidden soul of harmony.

That *Orpheus* self may heave his head
From golden slumber on a bed
Of heapt *Elysian* flowres, and hear
Such streins as would have won the ear
Of *Pluto*, to have quite set free
His half regain'd *Eurydice*. *150*
These delights, if thou canst give,
Mirth with thee, I mean to live.

Il Penseroso

Hence vain deluding joyes,
   The brood of folly without father bred,
How little you bested,
   Or fill the fixed mind with all your toyes;
Dwell in som idle brain,
   And fancies fond with gaudy shapes possess,
As thick and numberless
   As the gay motes that people the Sun Beams,
Or likest hovering dreams
   The fickle Pensioners of *Morpheus* train. *10*
But hail thou Goddes, sage and holy,
Hail divinest Melancholy,
Whose Saintly visage is too bright
To hit the Sense of human sight;
And therfore to our weaker view,
Ore laid with black staid Wisdoms hue.
Black, but such as in esteem,
Prince *Memnons* sister might beseem,
Or that Starr'd *Ethiope* Queen that strove
To set her beauties praise above *20*
The Sea Nymphs, and their powers offended.
Yet thou art higher far descended,
Thee bright-hair'd *Vesta* long of yore,
To solitary *Saturn* bore;
His daughter she (in *Saturns* raign,
Such mixture was not held a stain)
Oft in glimmering Bowres, and glades
He met her, and in secret shades
Of woody *Ida's* inmost grove,
While yet there was no fear of *Jove*. *30*
Com pensive Nun, devout and pure,
Sober, stedfast, and demure,
All in a robe of darkest grain,
Flowing with majestick train,
And sable stole of *Cipres* Lawn,

Over thy decent shoulders drawn.
Com, but keep thy wonted state,
With eev'n step, and musing gate,
And looks commercing with the skies,
Thy rapt soul sitting in thine eyes: *40*
There held in holy passion still,
Forget thy self to Marble, till
With a sad Leaden downward cast,
Thou fix them on the earth as fast.
And joyn with thee calm Peace, and Quiet,
Spare Fast, that oft with gods doth diet,
And hears the Muses in a ring,
Ay round about *Joves* Altar sing.
And adde to these retired Leasure,
That in trim Gardens takes his pleasure;   *50*
But first, and chiefest, with thee bring,
Him that yon soars on golden wing,
Guiding the fiery-wheeled throne,
The Cherub Contemplation,
And the mute Silence hist along,
'Less *Philomel* will daign a Song,
In her sweetest, saddest plight,
Smoothing the rugged brow of night,
While *Cynthia* checks her Dragon yoke,
Gently o're th'accustom'd Oke;   *60*
Sweet Bird that shunn'st the noise of folly,
Most musicall, most melancholy!
Thee Chauntress oft the Woods among,
I woo to hear thy eeven-Song;
And missing thee, I walk unseen
On the dry smooth-shaven Green,
To behold the wandring Moon,
Riding neer her highest noon,
Like one that had bin led astray
Through the Heav'ns wide pathles way;   *70*
And oft, as if her head she bow'd,
Stooping through a fleecy cloud.
Oft on a Plat of rising ground,
I hear the far-off *Curfeu* sound,
Over som wide-water'd shoar,
Swinging slow with sullen roar;
Or if the Ayr will not permit,
Som still removed place will fit,
Where glowing Embers through the room
Teach light to counterfeit a gloom,   *80*
Far from all resort of mirth,

Save the Cricket on the hearth,
Or the Belmans drousie charm,
To bless the dores from nightly harm:
Or let my Lamp at midnight hour,
Be seen in som high lonely Towr,
Where I may oft out-watch the *Bear*,
With thrice great *Hermes*, or unsphear
The spirit of *Plato* to unfold
What Worlds, or what vast Regions hold
The immortal mind that hath forsook
Her mansion in this fleshly nook:
And of those *Dæmons* that are found
In fire, air, flood, or under ground,
Whose power hath a true consent
With Planet, or with Element.
Som time let Gorgeous Tragedy
In Scepter'd Pall com sweeping by,
Presenting *Thebs*, or *Pelops* line,
Or the tale of *Troy* divine.
Or what (though rare) of later age,
Ennobled hath the Buskind stage.
But, O sad Virgin, that thy power
Might raise *Musæus* from his bower,
Or bid the soul of *Orpheus* sing
Such notes as warbled to the string,
Drew Iron tears down *Pluto's* cheek,
And made Hell grant what Love did seek.
Or call up him that left half told
The story of *Cambuscan* bold,
Of *Camball*, and of *Algarsife*,
And who had *Canace* to wife,
That own'd the vertuous Ring and Glass,
And of the wondrous Hors of Brass,
On which the *Tartar* King did ride;
And if ought els, great *Bards* beside,
In sage and solemn tunes have sung,
Of Turneys and of Trophies hung;
Of Forests, and inchantments drear,
Where more is meant then meets the ear.
Thus night oft see me in thy pale career,
Till civil-suited Morn appeer,
Not trickt and frounc't as she was wont,
With the Attick Boy to hunt,
But Cherchef't in a comly Cloud,
While rocking Winds are Piping loud,
Or usher'd with a shower still,

When the gust hath blown his fill,
Ending on the russling Leaves,
With minute drops from off the Eaves.　　　*130*
And when the Sun begins to fling
His flaring beams, me Goddes bring
To arched walks of twilight groves,
And shadows brown that *Sylvan* loves
Of Pine, or monumental Oake,
Where the rude Ax with heaved stroke,
Was never heard the Nymphs to daunt,
Or fright them from their hallow'd haunt.
There in close covert by som Brook,
Where no profaner eye may look,　　　*140*
Hide me from Day's garish eie,
While the Bee with Honied thie,
That at her flowry work doth sing,
And the Waters murmuring
With such consort as they keep,
Entice the dewy-feather'd Sleep;
And let som strange mysterious dream,
Wave at his Wings in Airy stream,
Of lively portrature display'd,
Softly on my eye-lids laid.　　　*150*
And as I wake, sweet musick breath
Above, about, or underneath,
Sent by som spirit to mortals good,
Or th' unseen Genius of the Wood.
But let my due feet never fail,
To walk the studious Cloysters pale,
And love the high embowed Roof,
With antick Pillars massy proof,
And storied Windows richly dight,
Casting a dimm religious light.　　　*160*
There let the pealing Organ blow,
To the full voic'd Quire below,
In Service high, and Anthems cleer,
As may with sweetnes, through mine ear,
Dissolve me into extasies,
And bring all Heav'n before mine eyes.
And may at last my weary age
Find out the peacefull hermitage,
The Hairy Gown and Mossy Cell,
Where I may sit and rightly spell　　　*170*
Of every Star that Heav'n doth shew,
And every Herb that sips the dew;
Till old experience do attain

To somthing like Prophetic strain.
These pleasures *Melancholy* give,
And I with thee will choose to live.

Arcades

Part of an entertainment presented to the Countess Dowager of *Darby* at *Harefield*, by som Noble persons of her Family, who appear on the Scene in pastoral habit, moving toward the seat of State with this Song

1 SONG

Look Nymphs, and Shepherds look,
What sudden blaze of majesty
Is that which we from hence descry
Too divine to be mistook:
    This this is she
To whom our vows and wishes bend,
Heer our solemn search hath end.

Fame that her high worth to raise,
Seem'd erst so lavish and profuse,
We may justly now accuse   10
Of detraction from her praise,
    Less then half we find exprest,
    Envy bid conceal the rest.

Mark what radiant state she spreds,
In circle round her shining throne,
Shooting her beams like silver threds,
This this is she alone,
    Sitting like a Goddes bright,
    In the center of her light.

Might she the wise *Latona* be,
Or the towred *Cybele*,   20
Mother of a hunderd gods;
Juno dare's not give her odds;
    Who had thought this clime had held
    A deity so unparalel'd?

As they com forward, the genius of the Wood appears, and turning toward them, speaks

Gen. Stay gentle Swains, for though in this disguise,
I see bright honour sparkle through your eyes,
Of famous *Arcady* ye are, and sprung
Of that renowned flood, so often sung,
Divine *Alpheus*, who by secret sluse,   30

Stole under Seas to meet his *Arethuse*;
And ye the breathing Roses of the Wood,
Fair silver-buskind Nymphs as great and good,
I know this quest of yours, and free intent
Was all in honour and devotion ment
To the great Mistres of yon princely shrine,
Whom with low reverence I adore as mine,
And with all helpful service will comply
To further this nights glad solemnity;
And lead ye where ye may more neer behold 40
What shallow-searching *Fame* hath left untold;
Which I full oft amidst these shades alone
Have sate to wonder at, and gaze upon:
For know by lot from *Jove* I am the powr
Of this fair Wood, and live in Oak'n bowr,
To nurse the Saplings tall, and curl the grove
With Ringlets quaint, and wanton windings wove.
And all my Plants I save from nightly ill,
Of noisom winds, and blasting vapours chill.
And from the Boughs brush off the evil dew, 50
And heal the harms of thwarting thunder blew,
Or what the cross dire-looking Planet smites,
Or hurtfull Worm with canker'd venom bites.
When Eev'ning gray doth rise, I fetch my round
Over the mount, and all this hallow'd ground,
And early ere the odorous breath of morn
Awakes the slumbring leaves, or tasseld horn
Shakes the high thicket, haste I all about,
Number my ranks, and visit every sprout
With puissant words, and murmurs made to bless, 60
But els in deep of night when drowsines
Hath lockt up mortal sense, then listen I
To the celestial *Sirens* harmony,
That sit upon the nine enfolded Sphears,
And sing to those that hold the vital shears,
And turn the Adamantine spindle round,
On which the fate of gods and men is wound.
Such sweet compulsion doth in musick ly,
To lull the daughters of *Necessity*,
And keep unsteddy Nature to her law, 70
And the low world in measur'd motion draw
After the heavenly tune, which none can hear
Of human mould with grosse unpurged ear;
And yet such musick worthiest were to blaze
The peerles height of her immortal praise,
Whose lustre leads us, and for her most fit,

If my inferior hand or voice could hit
Inimitable sounds, yet as we go,
What ere the skill of lesser gods can show,
I will assay, her worth to celebrate,   *80*
And so attend ye toward her glittering state;
Where ye may all that are of noble stemm
Approach, and kiss her sacred vestures hemm.

2 SONG

O're the smooth enameld green
Where no print of step hath been,
    Follow me as I sing,
    And touch the warbled string.
Under the shady roof
Of branching Elm Star-proof,
    Follow me,   *90*
I will bring you where she sits
Clad in splendor as befits
    Her deity.
Such a rural Queen
All *Arcadia* hath not seen.

3 SONG

Nymphs and Shepherds dance no more
    By sandy *Ladons* Lillied banks.
On old *Lycæus* or *Cyllene* hoar,
    Trip no more in twilight ranks,
Though *Erymanth* your loss deplore,   *100*
    A better soyl shall give ye thanks.
From the stony *Mænalus*,
Bring your Flocks, and live with us,
Here ye shall have greater grace,
To serve the Lady of this place.
    Though *Syrinx* your *Pans* Mistres were,
    Yet *Syrinx* well might wait on her.
      Such a rural Queen
All *Arcadia* hath not seen.

Lycidas

In this Monody the Author bewails a learned Friend, unfortunatly drown'd in his Passage from *Chester* on the *Irish* Seas, 1637. And by occasion foretels the ruine of our corrupted Clergy then in their height.

Yet once more, O ye Laurels, and once more
Ye Myrtles brown, with Ivy never-sear,
I com to pluck your Berries harsh and crude,

And with forc'd fingers rude,
Shatter your leaves before the mellowing year.
Bitter constraint, and sad occasion dear,
Compels me to disturb your season due:
For *Lycidas* is dead, dead ere his prime
Young *Lycidas*, and hath not left his peer:
Who would not sing for *Lycidas?* he knew
Himself to sing, and build the lofty rhyme.
He must not flote upon his watry bear
Unwept, and welter to the parching wind,
Without the meed of som melodious tear.
   Begin then, Sisters of the sacred well,
That from beneath the seat of *Jove* doth spring,
Begin, and somwhat loudly sweep the string.
Hence with denial vain, and coy excuse,
So may som gentle Muse
With lucky words favour my destin'd Urn,
And as he passes turn,
And bid fair peace be to my sable shrowd.
For we were nurst upon the self-same hill,
Fed the same flock, by fountain, shade, and rill.
   Together both, ere the high Lawns appear'd
Under the opening eye-lids of the morn,
We drove a field, and both together heard
What time the Gray-fly winds her sultry horn,
Batt'ning our flocks with the fresh dews of night,
Oft till the Star that rose, at Ev'ning, bright
Toward Heav'ns descent had slop'd his westering wheel.
Mean while the Rural ditties were not mute,
Temper'd to th'Oaten Flute;
Rough *Satyrs* danc'd, and *Fauns* with clov'n heel,
From the glad sound would not be absent long,
And old *Damætas* lov'd to hear our song.
   But O the heavy change, now thou art gon,
Now thou art gon, and never must return!
Thee Shepherd, thee the Woods, and desert Caves,
With wilde Thyme and the gadding Vine o'regrown,
And all their echoes mourn.
The Willows, and the Hazle Copses green,
Shall now no more be seen,
Fanning their joyous Leaves to thy soft layes.
As killing as the Canker to the Rose,
Or Taint-worm to the weanling Herds that graze,
Or Frost to Flowers, that their gay wardrop wear,
When first the White thorn blows;
Such, *Lycidas*, thy loss to Shepherds ear.

    Where were ye Nymphs when the remorseless deep
Clos'd o're the head of your lov'd *Lycidas?*   *51*
For neither were ye playing on the steep,
Where your old *Bards*, the famous *Druids* ly,
Nor on the shaggy top of *Mona* high,
Nor yet where *Deva* spreads her wisard stream:
Ay me, I fondly dream!
Had ye bin there—for what could that have don?
What could the Muse her self that *Orpheus* bore,
The Muse her self, for her inchanting son
Whom Universal nature did lament,   *60*
When by the rout that made the hideous roar,
His goary visage down the stream was sent,
Down the swift *Hebrus* to the *Lesbian* shore.
    Alas! What boots it with uncessant care
To tend the homely slighted Shepherds trade,
And strictly meditate the thankles Muse,
Were it not better don as others use,
To sport with *Amaryllis* in the shade,
Or with the tangles of *Neæra's* hair?
Fame is the spur that the clear spirit doth raise   *70*
(That last infirmity of Noble mind)
To scorn delights, and live laborious dayes;
But the fair Guerdon when we hope to find,
And think to burst out into sudden blaze,
Comes the blind *Fury* with th'abhorred shears,
And slits the thin spun life. But not the praise,
Phœbus repli'd, and touch'd my trembling ears;
Fame is no plant that grows on mortal soil,
Nor in the glistering foil
Set off to th'world, nor in broad rumour lies,   *80*
But lives and spreds aloft by those pure eyes,
And perfet witnes of all judging *Jove*;
As he pronounces lastly on each deed,
Of so much fame in Heav'n expect thy meed.
    O Fountain *Arethuse*, and thou honour'd floud,
Smooth-sliding *Mincius*, crown'd with vocall reeds,
That strain I heard was of a higher mood:
But now my Oate proceeds,
And listens to the Herald of the Sea
That came in *Neptune's* plea,   *90*
He ask'd the Waves, and ask'd the Fellon winds,
What hard mishap hath doom'd this gentle swain?
And question'd every gust of rugged wings
That blows from off each beaked Promontory,
They knew not of his story,

And sage *Hippotades* their answer brings,
That not a blast was from his dungeon stray'd,
The Ayr was calm, and on the level brine,
Sleek *Panope* with all her sisters play'd.
It was that fatall and perfidious Bark   *100*
Built in th'eclipse, and rigg'd with curses dark,
That sunk so low that sacred head of thine.
    Next *Camus*, reverend Sire, went footing slow,
His Mantle hairy, and his Bonnet sedge,
Inwrought with figures dim, and on the edge
Like to that sanguine flower inscrib'd with woe.
Ah; Who hath reft (quoth he) my dearest pledge?
Last came, and last did go,
The Pilot of the *Galilean* lake,
Two massy Keyes he bore of metals twain,   *110*
(The Golden opes, the Iron shuts amain)
He shook his Miter'd locks, and stern bespake,
How well could I have spar'd for thee, young swain,
Anow of such as for their bellies sake,
Creep and intrude, and climb into the fold?
Of other care they little reck'ning make,
Then how to scramble at the shearers feast,
And shove away the worthy bidden guest.
Blind mouthes! that scarce themselves know how to hold
A Sheep-hook, or have learn'd ought els the least   *120*
That to the faithfull Herdmans art belongs!
What recks it them? What need they? They are sped;
And when they list, their lean and flashy songs
Grate on their scrannel Pipes of wretched straw,
The hungry Sheep look up, and are not fed,
But swoln with wind, and the rank mist they draw,
Rot inwardly, and foul contagion spread:
Besides what the grim Woolf with privy paw
Daily devours apace, and nothing sed,
But that two-handed engine at the door,   *130*
Stands ready to smite once, and smite no more.
    Return *Alpheus*, the dread voice is past,
That shrunk thy streams; Return *Sicilian* Muse,
And call the Vales, and bid them hither cast
Their Bels, and Flourets of a thousand hues.
Ye valleys low where the milde whispers use,
Of shades and wanton winds, and gushing brooks,
On whose fresh lap the swart Star sparely looks,
Throw hither all your quaint enameld eyes,
That on the green terf suck the honied showres,   *140*
And purple all the ground with vernal flowres.

Bring the rathe Primrose that forsaken dies.
The tufted Crow-toe, and pale Gessamine,
The white Pink, and the Pansie freakt with jeat,
The glowing Violet.
The Musk-rose, and the well attir'd Woodbine.
With Cowslips wan that hang the pensive hed,
And every flower that sad embroidery wears:
Bid *Amaranthus* all his beauty shed,
And Daffadillies fill their cups with tears, *150*
To strew the Laureat Herse where *Lycid* lies.
For so to interpose a little ease,
Let our frail thoughts dally with false surmise.
Ay me! Whilst thee the shores, and sounding Seas
Wash far away, where ere thy bones are hurld,
Whether beyond the stormy *Hebrides*,
Where thou perhaps under the whelming tide
Visit'st the bottom of the monstrous world;
Or whether thou to our moist vows deny'd,
Sleep'st by the fable of *Bellerus* old, *160*
Where the great vision of the guarded Mount
Looks toward *Namancos* and *Bayona's* hold;
Look homeward Angel now, and melt with ruth.
And, O ye *Dolphins*, waft the haples youth.
   Weep no more, woful Shepherds weep no more,
For *Lycidas* your sorrow is not dead,
Sunk though he be beneath the watry floar,
So sinks the day-star in the Ocean bed,
And yet anon repairs his drooping head,
And tricks his beams, and with new spangled Ore, *170*
Flames in the forehead of the morning sky:
So *Lycidas* sunk low, but mounted high,
Through the dear might of him that walk'd the waves
Where other groves, and other streams along,
With *Nectar* pure his oozy Lock's he laves,
And hears the unexpressive nuptiall Song,
In the blest Kingdoms meek of joy and love.
There entertain him all the Saints above,
In solemn troops, and sweet Societies
That sing, and singing in their glory move, *180*
And wipe the tears for ever from his eyes.
Now *Lycidas* the Shepherds weep no more;
Hence forth thou art the Genius of the shore,
In thy large recompense, and shalt be good
To all that wander in that perilous flood.
   Thus sang the uncouth Swain to th'Okes and rills,
While the still morn went out with Sandals gray,

He touch'd the tender stops of various Quills,
With eager thought warbling his *Dorick* lay:
And now the Sun had stretch'd out all the hills,   *190*
And now was dropt into the Western bay;
At last he rose, and twitch'd his Mantle blew:
To morrow to fresh Woods, and Pastures new.

COMUS

A MASK Presented at LUDLOW-Castle,

1634 &c.

The Persons

The attendant Spirit afterwards   The Lady.
   in the habit of *Thyrsis*.   1. Brother. 2. Brother.
Comus with his crew.   *Sabrina* the Nymph.

The cheif persons which presented, were
   The Lord *Bracly*,
   Mr. *Thomas Egerton* his Brother,
   The Lady *Alice Egerton*.

The first Scene discovers a wilde Wood
The attendant Spirit descends or enters

BEFORE the starry threshold of *Joves* Court
My mansion is, where those immortal shapes
Of bright aëreal Spirits live insphear'd
In Regions milde of calm and serene Ayr,
Above the smoak and stirr of this dim spot,
Which men call Earth, and with low-thoughted care
Confin'd, and pester'd in this pin-fold here,
Strive to keep up a frail, and Feaverish being
Unmindfull of the crown that Vertue gives
After this mortal change, to her true Servants   10
Amongst the enthron'd gods on Sainted seats.
Yet som there be that by due steps aspire
To lay their just hands on that Golden Key
That ope's the Palace of Eternity:
To such my errand is, and but for such,
I would not soil these pure Ambrosial weeds,
With the rank vapours of this Sin-worn mould.
   But to my task. *Neptune* besides the sway
Of every salt Flood, and each ebbing Stream,
Took in by lot 'twixt high, and neather *Jove*,   20
Imperial rule of all the Sea-girt Iles
That like to rich, and various gemms inlay
The unadorned boosom of the Deep,
Which he to grace his tributary gods
By course commits to severall government,

33

And gives them leave to wear their Saphire crowns,
And weild their little tridents, but this Ile
The greatest, and the best of all the main
He quarters to his blu-hair'd deities,
And all this tract that fronts the falling Sun   30
A noble Peer of mickle trust, and power
Has in his charge, with temper'd awe to guide
An old, and haughty Nation proud in Arms:
Where his fair off-spring nurs't in Princely lore,
Are coming to attend their Fathers state,
And new-entrusted Scepter, but their way
Lies through the perplex't paths of this drear Wood,
The nodding horror of whose shady brows
Threats the forlorn and wandring Passinger.
And here their tender age might suffer perill,   40
But that by quick command from Soveran *Jove*
I was dispatcht for their defence, and guard;
And listen why, for I will tell ye now
What never yet was heard in Tale or Song
From old, or modern Bard in Hall, or Bowr.
   Bacchus that first from out the purple Grape,
Crush't the sweet poyson of mis-used Wine
After the *Tuscan* Mariners transform'd
Coasting the *Tyrrhene* shore, as the winds listed,
On *Circes* Iland fell (who knows not *Circe*   50
The daughter of the Sun? Whose charmed Cup
Whoever tasted, lost his upright shape,
And downward fell into a groveling Swine)
This Nymph that gaz'd upon his clustring locks,
With Ivy berries wreath'd, and his blithe youth,
Had by him, ere he parted thence, a Son
Much like his Father, but his Mother more,
Whom therfore she brought up and *Comus* nam'd,
Who ripe, and frolick of his full grown age,
Roaving the *Celtick*, and *Iberian* fields,   60
At last betakes him to this ominous Wood,
And in thick shelter of black shades imbowr'd,
Excells his Mother at her mighty Art,
Offring to every weary Travailer,
His orient liquor in a Crystal Glasse,
To quench the drouth of *Phœbus*, which as they taste
(For most do taste through fond intemperate thirst)
Soon as the Potion works, their human count'nance,
Th' express resemblance of the gods, is chang'd
Into som brutish form of Woolf, or Bear,   70
Or Ounce, or Tiger, Hog, or bearded Goat,

All other parts remaining as they were,
And they, so perfect is their misery,
Not once perceive their foul disfigurement,
But boast themselves more comely then before
And all their friends, and native home forget
To roule with pleasure in a sensual stie.
Therfore when any favour'd of high *Jove*,
Chances to pass through this adventrous glade,
Swift as the Sparkle of a glancing Star,   80
I shoot from Heav'n to give him safe convoy,
As now I do: But first I must put off
These my skie robes spun out of *Iris* Wooff,
And take the Weeds and likenes of a Swain,
That to the service of this house belongs,
Who with his soft Pipe, and smooth-dittied Song,
Well knows to still the wilde winds when they roar,
And hush the waving Woods, nor of lesse faith,
And in this office of his Mountain watch,
Likeliest, and neerest to the present ayd   90
Of this occasion. But I hear the tread
Of hatefull steps, I must be viewles now.

Comus enters with a Charming Rod in one hand, his Glass in the other, with him a rout of Monsters, headed like sundry sorts of wilde Beasts, but otherwise like Men and Women, their Apparel glistring, they com in making a riotous and unruly noise, with Torches in their hands.

Comus. The Star that bids the Shepherd fold,
Now the top of Heav'n doth hold,
And the gilded Car of Day,
His glowing Axle doth allay
In the steep *Atlantick* stream,
And the slope Sun his upward beam
Shoots against the dusky Pole,
Pacing toward the other gole   100
Of his Chamber in the East.
Mean while welcom Joy, and Feast,
Midnight shout, and revelry,
Tipsie dance, and Jollity.
Braid your Locks with rosie Twine
Dropping odours, dropping Wine.
Rigor now is gon to bed,
And Advice with scrupulous head,
Strict Age, and sowre Severity,
With their grave Saws in slumber ly.   110
We that are of purer fire
Imitate the Starry Quire,
Who in their nightly watchfull Sphears,

Lead in swift round the Months and Years.
The Sounds, and Seas with all their finny drove
Now to the Moon in wavering Morrice move,
And on the Tawny Sands and Shelves,
Trip the pert Fairies and the dapper Elves;
By dimpled Brook, and Fountain brim,
The Wood-Nymphs deckt with Daisies trim,   *120*
Their merry wakes and pastimes keep:
What hath night to do with sleep?
Night hath better sweets to prove,
Venus now wakes, and wak'ns Love.
Com let us our rights begin,
'Tis onely day-light that makes Sin
Which these dun shades will ne're report.
Hail Goddesse of Nocturnal sport
Dark vaild *Cotytto*, t' whom the secret flame
Of mid-night Torches burns; mysterious Dame   *130*
That ne're art call'd, but when the Dragon woom
Of Stygian darknes spets her thickest gloom,
And makes one blot of all the ayr,
Stay thy cloudy Ebon chair,
Wherin thou rid'st with *Hecat'*, and befriend
Us thy vow'd Priests, til utmost end
Of all thy dues be done, and none left out,
Ere the blabbing Eastern scout,
The nice Morn on th' *Indian* steep
From her cabin'd loop hole peep,   *140*
And to the tel-tale Sun discry
Our conceal'd Solemnity.
Com, knit hands, and beat the ground,
In a light fantastick round.

        The Measure

Break off, break off, I feel the different pace,
Of som chast footing neer about this ground.
Run to your shrouds, within these Brakes and Trees,
Our number may affright: Som Virgin sure
(For so I can distinguish by mine Art)
Benighted in these Woods. Now to my charms,   *150*
And to my wily trains, I shall e're long
Be well stock't with as fair a herd as graz'd
About my Mother *Circe*. Thus I hurl
My dazling Spells into the spungy ayr,
Of power to cheat the eye with blear illusion,
And give it false presentments, lest the place
And my quaint habits breed astonishment,

And put the Damsel to suspicious flight,
Which must not be, for that's against my course;
I under fair pretence of friendly ends,   *160*
And well plac't words of glozing courtesie
Baited with reasons not unplausible
Wind me into the easie-hearted man,
And hugg him into snares. When once her eye
Hath met the vertue of this Magick dust,
I shall appear som harmles Villager
Whom thrift keeps up about his Country gear,
But here she comes, I fairly step aside,
And hearken, if I may, her busines here.

    The Lady enters

This way the noise was, if mine ear be true,   *170*
My best guide now, me thought it was the sound
Of Riot, and ill manag'd Merriment,
Such as the jocond Flute, or gamesom Pipe
Stirs up among the loose unleter'd Hinds,
When for their teeming Flocks, and granges full
In wanton dance they praise the bounteous *Pan*,
And thank the gods amiss. I should be loath
To meet the rudenesse, and swill'd insolence
Of such late Wassailers; yet O where els
Shall I inform my unacquainted feet   *180*
In the blind mazes of this tangl'd Wood?
My Brothers when they saw me wearied out
With this long way, resolving here to lodge
Under the spreading favour of these Pines,
Stept as they se'd to the next Thicket side
To bring me Berries, or such cooling fruit
As the kind hospitable Woods provide.
They left me then, when the gray-hooded Eev'n
Like a sad Votarist in Palmers weed
Rose from the hindmost wheels of *Phœbus* wain.   *190*
But where they are, and why they came not back,
Is now the labour of my thoughts, 'tis likeliest
They had ingag'd their wandring steps too far,
And envious darknes, e're they could return,
Had stole them from me, els O theevish Night
Why shouldst thou, but for som fellonious end,
In thy dark lantern thus close up the Stars,
That nature hung in Heav'n, and fill'd their Lamps
With everlasting oil, to give due light
To the misled and lonely Travailer?   *200*
This is the place, as well as I may guess,

Whence eev'n now the tumult of loud Mirth
Was rife, and perfet in my list'ning ear,
Yet nought but single darknes do I find.
What might this be? A thousand fantasies
Begin to throng into my memory
Of calling shapes, and beckning shadows dire,
And airy tongues, that syllable mens names
On Sands, and Shoars, and desert Wildernesses.
These thoughts may startle well, but not astound   *210*
The vertuous mind, that ever walks attended
By a strong siding champion Conscience.—
O welcom pure-ey'd Faith, white-handed Hope,
Thou hovering Angel girt with golden wings,
And thou unblemish't form of Chastity,
I see ye visibly, and now beleeve
That he, the Supreme good, t' whom all things ill
Are but as slavish officers of vengeance,
Would send a glistring Guardian if need were
To keep my life and honour unassail'd.   *220*
Was I deceiv'd, or did a sable cloud
Turn forth her silver lining on the night?
I did not err, there does a sable cloud
Turn forth her silver lining on the night,
And casts a gleam over this tufted Grove.
I cannot hallow to my Brothers, but
Such noise as I can make to be heard farthest
Ile venter, for my new enliv'nd spirits
Prompt me; and they perhaps are not far off.

SONG

  Sweet Echo, sweetest Nymph that liv'st unseen   *230*
    Within thy airy shell
   By slow Meander's *margent green,*
  And in the violet imbroider'd vale
   Where the love-lorn Nightingale
Nightly to thee her sad Song mourneth well.
Canst thou not tell me of a gentle Pair
   That likest thy Narcissus *are?*
    O if thou have
   Hid them in som flowry Cave,
    Tell me but where   *240*
Sweet Queen of Parly, Daughter of the Sphear,
 So maist thou be translated to the skies,
And give resounding grace to all Heav'ns Harmonies.

Com. Can any mortal mixture of Earths mould

Breath such Divine inchanting ravishment?
Sure somthing holy lodges in that brest,
And with these raptures moves the vocal air
To testifie his hidd'n residence;
How sweetly did they float upon the wings
Of silence, through the empty-vaulted night   250
At every fall smoothing the Raven doune
Of darknes till it smil'd: I have oft heard
My mother *Circe* with the Sirens three,
Amid'st the flowry-kirtl'd *Naiades*
Culling their Potent hearbs, and balefull drugs,
Who as they sung, would take the prison'd soul,
And lap it in *Elysium*, *Scylla* wept,
And chid her barking waves into attention,
And fell *Charybdis* murmur'd soft applause:
Yet they in pleasing slumber lull'd the sense,   260
And in sweet madnes rob'd it of it self,
But such a sacred, and home-felt delight,
Such sober certainty of waking bliss
I never heard till now. Ile speak to her
And she shall be my Queen. Hail forren wonder
Whom certain these rough shades did never breed
Unlesse the Goddes that in rurall shrine
Dwell'st here with *Pan*, or *Silvan*, by blest Song
Forbidding every bleak unkindly Fog
To touch the prosperous growth of this tall Wood.   270
La. Nay gentle Shepherd ill is lost that praise
That is addrest to unattending Ears,
Not any boast of skill, but extreme shift
How to regain my sever'd company
Compell'd me to awake the courteous Echo
To give me answer from her mossie Couch.
Co. What chance good Lady hath bereft you thus?
La. Dim darknes, and this leavy Labyrinth.
Co. Could that divide you from neer-ushering guides?
La. They left me weary on a grassie terf.   280
Co. By falshood, or discourtesie, or why?
La. To seek i'th vally som cool friendly Spring.
Co. And left your fair side all unguarded Lady?
La. They were but twain, and purpos'd quick return.
Co. Perhaps fore-stalling night prevented them.
La. How easie my misfortune is to hit!
Co. Imports their loss, beside the present need?
La. No less then if I should my brothers loose.
Co. Were they of manly prime, or youthful bloom?
La. As smooth as *Hebe's* their unrazor'd lips.   290

Co. Two such I saw, what time the labour'd **Oxe**
In his loose traces from the furrow came,
And the swink't hedger at his Supper sate;
I saw them under a green mantling vine
That crawls along the side of yon small hill,
Plucking ripe clusters from the tender shoots,
Their port was more then human, as they stood;
I took it for a faëry vision
Of som gay creatures of the element
That in the colours of the Rainbow live   *300*
And play i'th plighted clouds. I was aw-strook,
And as I past, I worship: if those you seek
It were a journey like the path to Heav'n,
To help you find them. *La.* Gentle villager
What readiest way would bring me to that place?
Co. Due west it rises from this shrubby point.
La. To find out that, good Shepherd, I suppose,
In such a scant allowance of Star-light,
Would overtask the best Land-Pilots art,
Without the sure guess of well-practiz'd feet.   *310*
Co. I know each lane, and every alley green
Dingle, or bushy dell of this wilde Wood,
And every bosky bourn from side to side
My daily walks and ancient neighbourhood,
And if your stray attendance be yet lodg'd,
Or shroud within these limits, I shall know
Ere morrow wake, or the low roosted lark
From her thatch't pallat rowse, if otherwise
I can conduct you Lady to a low
But loyal cottage, where you may be safe   *320*
Till further quest'. *La.* Shepherd I take thy word,
And trust thy honest offer'd courtesie,
Which oft is sooner found in lowly sheds
With smoaky rafters, then in tapstry Halls
And Courts of Princes, where it first was nam'd,
And yet is most pretended: In a place
Less warranted then this, or less secure
I cannot be, that I should fear to change it.
Eie me blest Providence, and square my triall
To my proportion'd strength. Shepherd lead on.—   *330*

The Two Brothers

Eld. Bro. Unmuffle ye faint stars, and thou fair Moon
That wontst to love the travailers benizon,
Stoop thy pale visage through an amber cloud,
And disinherit *Chaos*, that raigns here

In double night of darknes, and of shades;
Or if your influence be quite damm'd up
With black usurping mists, som gentle taper
Though a rush Candle from the wicker hole
Of som clay habitation visit us
With thy long levell'd rule of streaming light, 340
And thou shalt be our star of *Arcady*,
Or *Tyrian* Cynosure. 2. *Bro.* Or if our eyes
Be barr'd that happines, might we but hear
The folded flocks pen'd in their watled cotes,
Or sound of pastoral reed with oaten stops,
Or whistle from the Lodge, or village cock
Count the night watches to his feathery Dames.
'Twould be som solace yet, som little chearing
In this close dungeon of innumerous bowes.
But O that haples virgin our lost sister 350
Where may she wander now, whether betake her
From the chill dew, amongst rude burrs and thistles?
Perhaps som cold bank is her boulster now
Or 'gainst the rugged bark of som broad Elm
Leans her unpillow'd head fraught with sad fears.
What if in wild amazement, and affright,
Or while we speak within the direfull grasp
Of Savage hunger, or of Savage heat?
Eld. Bro. Peace brother, be not over-exquisite
To cast the fashion of uncertain evils; 360
For grant they be so, while they rest unknown,
What need a man forestall his date of grief,
And run to meet what he would most avoid?
Or if they be but false alarms of Fear,
How bitter is such self-delusion?
I do not think my sister so to seek,
Or so unprincipl'd in vertues book,
And the sweet peace that goodnes boosoms ever,
As that the single want of light and noise
(Not being in danger, as I trust she is not) 370
Could stir the constant mood of her calm thoughts,
And put them into mis-becoming plight.
Vertue could see to do what vertue would
By her own radiant light, though Sun and Moon
Were in the flat Sea sunk. And Wisdoms self
Oft seeks to sweet retired Solitude,
Where with her best nurse Contemplation
She plumes her feathers, and lets grow her wings
That in the various bussle of resort
Were all to ruffl'd, and somtimes impair'd. 380

He that has light within his own cleer brest
May sit i'th center, and enjoy bright day,
But he that hides a dark soul, and foul thoughts
Benighted walks under the mid-day Sun;
Himself is his own dungeon.
2. *Bro.* Tis most true
That musing meditation most affects
The pensive secrecy of desert cell,
Far from the cheerfull haunt of men, and herds,
And sits as safe as in a Senat house,
For who would rob a Hermit of his Weeds,   *390*
His few Books, or his Beads, or Maple Dish,
Or do his gray hairs any violence?
But beauty like the fair Hesperian Tree
Laden with blooming gold, had need the guard
Of dragon watch with uninchanted eye,
To save her blossoms, and defend her fruit
From the rash hand of bold Incontinence.
You may as well spred out the unsun'd heaps
Of Misers treasure by an out-laws den,
And tell me it is safe, as bid me hope   *400*
Danger will wink on Opportunity,
And let a single helpless maiden pass
Uninjur'd in this wilde surrounding wast.
Of night, or lonelines it recks me not,
I fear the dred events that dog them both,
Lest som ill greeting touch attempt the person
Of our unowned sister.
Eld. Bro. I do not, brother,
Inferr, as if I thought my sisters state
Secure without all doubt, or controversie:
Yet where an equall poise of hope and fear   *410*
Does arbitrate th'event, my nature is
That I encline to hope, rather then fear,
And gladly banish squint suspicion.
My sister is not so defenceless left
As you imagine, she has a hidden strength
Which you remember not.
2. *Bro.* What hidden strength,
Unless the strength of Heav'n, if you mean that?
Eld. Bro. I mean that too, but yet a hidden strength
Which if Heav'n gave it, may be term'd her own:
'Tis chastity, my brother, chastity: *420*
She that has that, is clad in compleat steel,
And like a quiver'd Nymph with Arrows keen
May trace huge Forests, and unharbour'd Heaths,

Infamous Hills, and sandy perilous wildes,
Where through the sacred rayes of Chastity,
No savage fierce, Bandite, or mountaneer
Will dare to soyl her Virgin purity,
Yea there, where very desolation dwels
By grots, and caverns shag'd with horrid shades,
She may pass on with unblench't majesty,   *430*
Be it not don in pride, or in presumption.
Som say no evil thing that walks by night
In fog, or fire, by lake, or moorish fen,
Blew meager Hag, or stubborn unlaid ghost,
That breaks his magick chains at *curfeu* time,
No goblin, or swart faëry of the mine,
Hath hurtfull power o're true virginity.
Do ye beleeve me yet, or shall I call
Antiquity from the old Schools of Greece
To testifie the arms of Chastity?   *440*
Hence had the huntress *Dian* her dred bow
Fair silver-shafted Queen for ever chaste,
Wherwith she tam'd the brinded lioness
And spotted mountain pard, but set at nought
The frivolous bolt of *Cupid*, gods and men
Fear'd her stern frown, and she was queen oth' Woods.
What was that snaky-headed *Gorgon* sheild
That wise *Minerva* wore, unconquer'd Virgin,
Wherwith she freez'd her foes to congeal'd stone?
But rigid looks of Chast austerity,   *450*
And noble grace that dash't brute violence
With sudden adoration, and blank aw.
So dear to Heav'n is Saintly chastity,
That when a soul is found sincerely so,
A thousand liveried Angels lacky her,
Driving far off each thing of sin and guilt,
And in cleer dream, and solemn vision
Tell her of things that no gross ear can hear,
Till oft convers with heav'nly habitants
Begin to cast a beam on th'outward shape,   *460*
The unpolluted temple of the mind,
And turns it by degrees to the souls essence,
Till all be made immortal: but when lust
By unchaste looks, loose gestures, and foul talk,
But most by leud and lavish act of sin,
Lets in defilement to the inward parts,
The soul grows clotted by contagion,
Imbodies, and imbrutes, till she quite loose
The divine property of her first being.

Such are those thick and gloomy shadows damp 470
Oft seen in Charnell vaults, and Sepulchers
Lingering, and sitting by a new made grave,
As loath to leave the body that it lov'd,
And link't it self by carnal sensualty
To a degenerate and degraded state.
2. Bro. How charming is divine Philosophy!
Not harsh, and crabbed as dull fools suppose,
But musical as is *Apollo's* lute,
And a perpetual feast of nectar'd sweets,
Where no crude surfet raigns. *Eld. Bro.* List, list, I hear
Som far off hallow break the silent Air. 481
2. Bro. Me thought so too; what should it be?
Eld. Bro. For certain
Either som one like us night-founder'd here,
Or els som neighbour Wood-man, or at worst,
Som roaving Robber calling to his fellows.
2. Bro. Heav'n keep my sister, agen agen and neer,
Best draw, and stand upon our guard.
Eld. Bro. Ile hallow,
If he be friendly he comes well, if not,
Defence is a good cause, and Heav'n be for us.

The attendant Spirit habited like a Shepherd

That hallow I should know, what are you? speak; 490
Com not too neer, you fall on iron stakes else.
Spir. What voice is that, my young Lord? speak agen.
2. Bro. O brother, 'tis my father Shepherd sure.
Eld. Bro. Thyrsis? Whose artful strains have oft delaid
The huddling brook to hear his madrigal,
And sweeten'd every muskrose of the dale,
How cam'st thou here good Swain? hath any ram
Slip't from the fold, or young Kid lost his dam,
Or straggling weather the pen't flock forsook?
How couldst thou find this dark sequester'd nook? 500
Spir. O my lov'd masters heir, and his next joy,
I came not here on such a trivial toy
As a stray'd Ewe, or to pursue the stealth
Of pilfering Woolf, not all the fleecy wealth
That doth enrich these Downs, is worth a thought
To this my errand, and the care it brought.
But O my Virgin Lady, where is she?
How chance she is not in your company?
Eld. Bro. To tell thee sadly Shepherd, without blame,
Or our neglect, we lost her as we came. 510
Spir. Ay me unhappy then my fears are true.

Eld. Bro. What fears good *Thyrsis?* Prethee briefly shew.
Spir. Ile tell ye, 'tis not vain or fabulous,
(Though so esteem'd by shallow ignorance)
What the sage Poëts taught by th' heav'nly Muse,
Storied of old in high immortal vers
Of dire *Chimera*'s and inchanted Iles,
And rifted Rocks whose entrance leads to hell,
For such there be, but unbelief is blind.
   Within the navil of this hideous Wood,   520
Immur'd in cypress shades a Sorcerer dwels
Of *Bacchus*, and of *Circe* born, great *Comus*,
Deep skill'd in all his mothers witcheries,
And here to every thirsty wanderer,
By sly enticement gives his banefull cup,
With many murmurs mixt, whose pleasing poison
The visage quite transforms of him that drinks,
And the inglorious likenes of a beast
Fixes instead, unmoulding reasons mintage
Character'd in the face; this have I learn't   530
Tending my flocks hard by i'th hilly crofts,
That brow this bottom glade, whence night by night
He and his monstrous rout are heard to howl
Like stabl'd wolves, or tigers at their prey,
Doing abhorred rites to *Hecate*
In their obscured haunts of inmost bowres.
Yet have they many baits, and guilefull spells
To inveigle and invite th'unwary sense
Of them that pass unweeting by the way.
This evening late by then the chewing flocks   540
Had ta'n their supper on the savoury Herb
Of Knot-grass dew-besprent, and were in fold,
I sate me down to watch upon a bank
With Ivy canopied, and interwove
With flaunting Hony-suckle, and began
Wrapt in a pleasing fit of melancholy
To meditate my rural minstrelsie,
Till fancy had her fill, but ere a close
The wonted roar was up amidst the Woods,
And fill'd the Air with barbarous dissonance,   550
At which I ceas't, and listen'd them a while,
Till an unusuall stop of sudden silence
Gave respit to the drowsie frighted steeds
That draw the litter of close-curtain'd sleep.
At last a soft and solemn breathing sound
Rose like a steam of rich distill'd Perfumes,
And stole upon the Air, that even Silence

Was took e're she was ware, and wish't she might
Deny her nature, and be never more
Still to be so displac't. I was all eare, 560
And took in strains that might create a soul
Under the ribs of Death, but O ere long
Too well I did perceive it was the voice
Of my most honour'd Lady, your dear sister.
Amaz'd I stood, harrow'd with grief and fear,
And O poor hapless Nightingale thought I,
How sweet thou sing'st, how neer the deadly snare!
Then down the Lawns I ran with headlong hast
Through paths, and turnings oft'n trod by day,
Till guided by mine ear I found the place 570
Where that damn'd wisard hid in sly disguise
(For so by certain signes I knew) had met
Already, ere my best speed could prævent,
The aidless innocent Lady his wish't prey,
Who gently ask't if he had seen such two,
Supposing him som neighbour villager;
Longer I durst not stay, but soon I guess't
Ye were the two she mean't, with that I sprung
Into swift flight, till I had found you here,
But furder know I not. 2. *Bro.* O night and shades, 580
How are ye joyn'd with hell in triple knot
Against th'unarmed weakness of one Virgin
Alone, and helpless! Is this the confidence
You gave me Brother? *Eld. Bro.* Yes, and keep it still,
Lean on it safely, not a period
Shall be unsaid for me: against the threats
Of malice or of sorcery, or that power
Which erring men call Chance, this I hold firm,
Vertue may be assail'd, but never hurt,
Surpriz'd by unjust force, but not enthrall'd, 590
Yea even that which mischief meant most harm,
Shall in the happy trial prove most glory.
But evil on it self shall back recoyl,
And mix no more with goodness, when at last
Gather'd like scum, and setl'd to it self
It shall be in eternal restless change
Self-fed, and self-consum'd, if this fail,
The pillar'd firmament is rott'nness,
And earths base built on stubble. But com let's on.
Against th' opposing will and arm of Heav'n 600
May never this just sword be lifted up,
But for that damn'd magician, let him be girt
With all the greisly legions that troop

Under the sooty flag of *Acheron*,
Harpyies and *Hydra's*, or all the monstrous forms
'Twixt *Africa* and *Inde*, Ile find him out,
And force him to restore his purchase back,
Or drag him by the curls, to a foul death,
Curs'd as his life.
Spir. Alas good ventrous youth,
I love thy courage yet, and bold Emprise,   610
But here thy sword can do thee little stead,
Farr other arms, and other weapons must
Be those that quell the might of hellish charms,
He with his bare wand can unthred thy joynts,
And crumble all thy sinews.
Eld. Bro. Why prethee Shepherd
How durst thou then thy self approach so neer
As to make this relation?
Spir. Care and utmost shifts
How to secure the Lady from surprisal,
Brought to my mind a certain Shepherd Lad
Of small regard to see to, yet well skill'd   620
In every vertuous plant and healing herb
That spreds her verdant leaf to th'morning ray,
He lov'd me well, and oft would beg me sing,
Which when I did, he on the tender grass
Would sit, and hearken even to extasie,
And in requitall ope his leather'n scrip,
And shew me simples of a thousand names
Telling their strange and vigorous faculties;
Amongst the rest a small unsightly root,
But of divine effect, he cull'd me out;   630
The leaf was darkish, and had prickles on it,
But in another Countrey, as he said,
Bore a bright golden flowre, but not in this soyl:
Unknown, and like esteem'd, and the dull swayn
Treads on it daily with his clouted shoon,
And yet more med'cinal is it then that *Moly*
That *Hermes* once to wise *Ulysses* gave;
He call'd it *Hæmony*, and gave it me,
And bad me keep it as of sov'ran use
'Gainst all inchantments, mildew blast, or damp   640
Or gastly furies apparition;
I purs't it up, but little reck'ning made,
'Till now that this extremity compell'd,
But now I find it true; for by this means
I knew the foul inchanter though disguis'd,
Enter'd the very lime-twigs of his spells,

And yet came off: if you have this about you
(As I will give you when we go) you may
Boldly assault the necromancers hall;
Where if he be, with dauntless hardihood,   *650*
And brandish't blade rush on him, break his glass,
And shed the lushious liquor on the ground,
But sease his wand, though he and his curst crew
Feirce signe of battail make, and menace high,
Or like the sons of *Vulcan* vomit smoak,
Yet will they soon retire, if he but shrink.
Eld. Bro. Thyrsis lead on apace, Ile follow thee,
And som good angel bear a sheild before us.

The Scene changes to a stately Palace, set out with all manner of deliciousness; soft Musick, Tables spred with all dainties. Comus *appears with his rabble, and the Lady set in an inchanted Chair, to whom he offers his Glass, which she puts by, and goes about to rise.*

Comus. Nay Lady sit; if I but wave this wand,
Your nerves are all chain'd up in Alablaster,   *660*
And you a statue; or as *Daphne* was
Root-bound, that fled *Apollo*.
La. Fool do not boast,
Thou canst not touch the freedom of my minde
With all thy charms, although this corporal rinde
Thou haste immanacl'd, while Heav'n sees good.
Co. Why are you vext Lady? why do you frown?
Here dwell no frowns, nor anger, from these gates
Sorrow flies farr: See here be all the pleasures
That fancy can beget on youthfull thoughts,
When the fresh blood grows lively, and returns   *670*
Brisk as the *April* buds in Primrose-season.
And first behold this cordial Julep here
That flames, and dances in his crystal bounds
With spirits of balm, and fragrant Syrops mixt.
Not that *Nepenthes* which the wife of *Thone*,
In *Egypt* gave to *Jove*-born *Helena*
Is of such power to stir up joy as this,
To life so friendly, or so cool to thirst.
Why should you be so cruel to your self,
And to those dainty limms which nature lent   *680*
For gentle usage, and soft delicacy?
But you invert the cov'nants of her trust,
And harshly deal like an ill borrower
With that which you receiv'd on other terms,
Scorning the unexempt condition
By which all mortal frailty must subsist,
Refreshment after toil, ease after pain,

That have been tir'd all day without repast,
And timely rest have wanted, but fair Virgin
This will restore all soon.
La. 'Twill not false traitor,   *690*
'Twill not restore the truth and honesty
That thou hast banish't from thy tongue with lies,
Was this the cottage, and the safe abode
Thou told'st me of? What grim aspects are these,
These oughly-headed Monsters? Mercy guard me!
Hence with thy brew'd inchantments, foul deceiver,
Hast thou betrai'd my credulous innocence
With visor'd falshood, and base forgery,
And wouldst thou seek again to trap me here
With lickerish baits fit to ensnare a brute?   *700*
Were it a draft for *Juno* when she banquets,
I would not taste thy treasonous offer; none
But such as are good men can give good things,
And that which is not good, is not delicious
To a well-govern'd and wise appetite.
Co. O foolishnes of men! that lend their ears
To those budge doctors of the *Stoick* Furr,
And fetch their precepts from the *Cynick* Tub,
Praising the lean and sallow Abstinence.
Wherefore did Nature powre her bounties forth,   *710*
With such a full and unwithdrawing hand,
Covering the earth with odours, fruits, and flocks,
Thronging the Seas with spawn innumerable,
But all to please, and sate the curious taste?
And set to work millions of spinning Worms,
That in their green shops weave the smooth-hair'd silk
To deck her Sons, and that no corner might
Be vacant of her plenty, in her own loyns
She hutch't th'all-worshipt ore, and precious gems
To store her children with; if all the world   *720*
Should in a pet of temperance feed on Pulse,
Drink the clear stream, and nothing wear but Freize,
Th'all-giver would be unthank't, would be unprais'd,
Not half his riches known, and yet despis'd,
And we should serve him as a grudging master,
As a penurious niggard of his wealth,
And live like Natures bastards, not her sons,
Who would be quite surcharged with her own weight,
And strangl'd with her waste fertility;
Th'earth cumber'd, and the wing'd air dark't with plumes,
The herds would over-multitude their Lords,   *731*
The Sea o'refraught would swell, and th'unsought diamonds

Would so emblaze the forhead of the Deep,
And so bestudd with Stars, that they below
Would grow inur'd to light, and com at last
To gaze upon the Sun with shameless brows.
List Lady be not coy, and be not cosen'd
With that same vaunted name Virginity,
Beauty is natures coyn, must not be hoorded,   740
But must be currant, and the good thereof
Consists in mutual and partak'n bliss,
Unsavoury in th'injoyment of it self
If you let slip time, like a neglected rose
It withers on the stalk with languish't head.
Beauty is natures brag, and must be shown
In courts, at feasts, and high solemnities
Where most may wonder at the workmanship;
It is for homely features to keep home,
They had their name thence; course complexions
And cheeks of sorry grain will serve to ply   750
The sampler, and to teize the huswifes wooll.
What need a vermeil-tinctured lip for that
Love-darting eyes, or tresses like the Morn?
There was another meaning in these gifts,
Think what, and be adviz'd, you are but young yet.
La. I had not thought to have unlockt my lips
In this unhallow'd air, but that this Jugler
Would think to charm my judgement, as mine eyes,
Obtruding false rules pranckt in reasons garb.
I hate when vice can bolt her arguments,   760
And vertue has no tongue to check her pride:
Impostor do not charge most innocent nature,
As if she would her children should be riotous
With her abundance, she good cateress
Means her provision onely to the good
That live according to her sober laws,
And holy dictate of spare Temperance:
If every just man that now pines with want
Had but a moderate and beseeming share
Of that which lewdly-pamper'd Luxury   770
Now heaps upon som few with vast excess,
Natures full blessings would be well dispenc't
In unsuperfluous eeven proportion,
And she no whit encomber'd with her store,
And then the giver would be better thank't,
His praise due paid, for swinish gluttony
Ne're looks to Heav'n amidst his gorgeous feast,
But with besotted base ingratitude

Cramms, and blasphemes his feeder. Shall I go on?
Or have I said anough? To him that dares   *780*
Arm his profane tongue with contemptuous words
Against the Sun-clad power of Chastity,
Fain would I somthing say, yet to what end?
Thou hast nor Eare, nor Soul to apprehend
The sublime notion, and high mystery
That must be utter'd to unfold the sage
And serious doctrine of Virginity,
And thou art worthy that thou shouldst not know
More happiness then this thy present lot.
Enjoy your deer Wit, and gay Rhetorick   *790*
That hath so well been taught her dazling fence,
Thou art not fit to hear thy self convinc't;
Yet should I try, the uncontrouled worth
Of this pure cause would kindle my rap't spirits
To such a flame of sacred vehemence,
That dumb things would be mov'd to sympathize,
And the brute Earth would lend her nerves, and shake,
Till all thy magick structures rear'd so high,
Were shatter'd into heaps o're thy false head.
Co. She fables not, I feel that I do fear   *800*
Her words set off by som superior power;
And though not mortal, yet a cold shuddring dew
Dips me all o're, as when the wrath of *Jove*
Speaks thunder, and the chains of *Erebus*
To som of *Saturns* crew. I must dissemble,
And try her yet more strongly. Com, no more,
This is meer moral babble, and direct
Against the canon laws of our foundation;
I must not suffer this, yet 'tis but the lees
And setlings of a melancholy blood;   *810*
But this will cure all streight, one sip of this
Will bathe the drooping spirits in delight
Beyond the bliss of dreams. Be wise, and taste.—

The Brothers rush in with Swords drawn, wrest his Glass out of his hand, and break it against the ground; his rout make signe of resistance, but are all driven in; The attendant Spirit comes in

Spir. What, have you let the false enchanter scape?
O ye mistook, ye should have snatcht his wand
And bound him fast; without his rod revers't,
And backward mutters of dissevering power,
We cannot free the Lady that sits here
In stony fetters fixt, and motionless;
Yet stay, be not disturb'd, now I bethink me,   *820*
Som other means I have which may be us'd,

Which once of *Melibœus* old I learnt
The soothest Shepherd that ere pip't on plains.
   There is a gentle Nymph not farr from hence,
That with moist curb sways the smooth Severn stream,
Sabrina is her name, a Virgin pure,
Whilom she was the daughter of *Locrine*,
That had the Scepter from his father *Brute*.
The guiltless damsel flying the mad pursuit
Of her enraged stepdam *Guendolen*,   830
Commended her fair innocence to the flood
That stay'd her flight with his cross-flowing course,
The water Nymphs that in the bottom plaid,
Held up their pearled wrists and took her in,
Bearing her straight to aged *Nereus* Hall,
Who piteous of her woes, rear'd her lank head,
And gave her to his daughters to imbathe
In nectar'd lavers strew'd with Asphodil,
And through the porch and inlet of each sense
Dropt in Ambrosial Oils till she reviv'd,   840
And underwent a quick immortal change
Made Goddess of the River; still she retains
Her maid'n gentlenes, and oft at Eeve
Visits the herds along the twilight meadows,
Helping all urchin blasts, and ill luck signes
That the shrewd medling Elfe delights to make,
Which she with pretious viold liquors heals.
For which the Shepherds at their festivals
Carrol her goodnes lowd in rustick layes,
And throw sweet garland wreaths into her stream   850
Of pancies, pinks, and gaudy Daffadils.
And, as the old Swain said, she can unlock
The clasping charm, and thaw the numming spell,
If she be right invok't in warbled Song,
For maid'nhood she loves, and will be swift
To aid a Virgin, such as was her self
In hard besetting need, this will I try
And adde the power of som adjuring verse.

SONG

  Sabrina fair
    Listen where thou art sitting   860
  Under the glassie, cool, translucent wave,
    In twisted braids of Lillies knitting
The loose train of thy amber-dropping hair,
  Listen for dear honour's sake,
  Goddess of the silver lake,

Listen and save.
Listen and appear to us
In name of great *Oceanus*,
By the earth-shaking *Neptune's* mace,
And *Tethys* grave majestick pace,   *870*
By hoary *Nereus* wrincled look,
And the *Carpathian* wisards hook,
By scaly *Tritons* winding shell,
And old sooth-saying *Glaucus* spell,
By *Leucothea's* lovely hands,
And her son that rules the strands,
By *Thetis* tinsel-slipper'd feet,
And the Songs of *Sirens* sweet,
By dead *Parthenope's* dear tomb,
And fair *Ligea's* golden comb,   *880*
Wherwith she sits on diamond rocks
Sleeking her soft alluring locks,
By all the *Nymphs* that nightly dance
Upon thy streams with wily glance,
Rise, rise, and heave thy rosie head
From thy coral-pav'n bed,
And bridle in thy headlong wave,
Till thou our summons answered have.
Listen and save.

Sabrina rises, attended by water-Nymphes, and sings

By the rushy-fringed bank,   *890*
Where grows the Willow and the Osier dank,
   My sliding Chariot stayes,
Thick set with Agat, and the azurn sheen
Of Turkis blew, and Emrauld green
   That in the channell strayes,
Whilst from off the waters fleet
Thus I set my printless feet
O're the Cowslips Velvet head,
   That bends not as I tread,
Gentle swain at thy request   *900*
   I am here.
Splr. Goddess dear
We implore thy powerful hand
To undo the charmed band
Of true Virgin here distrest,
Through the force, and through the wile
Of unblest inchanter vile.
Sab. Shepherd 'tis my office best
To help insnared chastity;

Brightest Lady look on me, 910
Thus I sprinkle on thy brest
Drops that from my fountain pure,
I have kept of pretious cure,
Thrice upon thy fingers tip,
Thrice upon thy rubied lip,
Next this marble venom'd seat
Smear'd with gumms of glutenous heat
I touch with chaste palms moist and cold,
Now the spell hath lost his hold;
And I must haste ere morning hour 920
To wait in *Amphitrite*'s bowr.

   Sabrina descends, and the Lady rises out of her seat

Spir. Virgin, daughter of *Locrine*
Sprung of old *Anchises* line,
May thy brimmed waves for this
Their full tribute never miss
From a thousand petty rills,
That tumble down the snowy hills:
Summer drouth, or singed air
Never scorch thy tresses fair,
Nor wet *Octobers* torrent flood 930
Thy molten crystal fill with mudd,
May thy billows rowl ashoar
The beryl, and the golden ore,
May thy lofty head be crown'd
With many a tower and terrass round,
And here and there thy banks upon
With Groves of myrrhe, and cinnamon.
Com Lady while Heaven lends us grace,
Let us fly this cursed place,
Lest the Sorcerer us intice 940
With som other new device.
Not a waste, or needless sound
Till we com to holier ground,
I shall be your faithfull guide
Through this gloomy covert wide,
And not many furlongs thence
Is your Fathers residence,
Where this night are met in state
Many a friend to gratulate
His wish't presence, and beside 950
All the Swains that there abide,
With Jiggs, and rural dance resort,
We shall catch them at their sport,

Comus

And our sudden coming there
Will double all their mirth and chere;
Come let us haste, the Stars grow high,
But night sits monarch yet in the mid sky.

The Scene changes, presenting Ludlow *Town and the Presidents Castle, then com in Countrey-Dancers, after them the attendant Spirit, with the two Brothers and the Lady*

SONG

Spir. Back Shepherds, back, anough your play,
Till next Sun-shine holiday,
Here be without duck or nod   960
Other trippings to be trod
Of lighter toes, and such Court guise
As Mercury did first devise
With the mincing Dryades
On the Lawns, and on the Leas.

This second Song presents them to their father and mother

Noble Lord, and Lady bright,
I have brought ye new delight,
Here behold so goodly grown
Three fair branches of your own,
Heav'n hath timely tri'd their youth,   970
Their faith, their patience, and their truth,
And sent them here through hard assays
With a crown of deathless Praise,
   To triumph in victorious dance
O're sensual Folly, and Intemperance.

The dances ended, the Spirit Epiloguizes

Spir. To the Ocean now I fly,
And those happy climes that ly
Where day never shuts his eye,
Up in the broad fields of the sky:
There I suck the liquid ayr   980
All amidst the Gardens fair
Of *Hesperus,* and his daughters three
That sing about the golden tree:
Along the crisped shades and bowres
Revels the spruce and jocond Spring,
The Graces, and the rosie-boosom'd Howres,
Thither all their bounties bring,
That there eternal Summer dwels,
And West winds, with musky wing
About the cedar'n alleys fling   990

Nard, and *Cassia's* balmy smels.
Iris there with humid bow,
Waters the odorous banks that blow
Flowers of more mingled hew
Then her purfl'd scarf can shew,
And drenches with *Elysian* dew
(List mortals, if your ears be true)
Beds of *Hyacinth*, and roses
Where young *Adonis* oft reposes,
Waxing well of his deep wound   *1000*
In slumber soft, and on the ground
Sadly sits th' *Assyrian* Queen;
But far above in spangled sheen
Celestial *Cupid* her fam'd son advanc't,
Holds his dear *Psyche* sweet intranc't
After her wandring labours long,
Till free consent the gods among
Make her his eternal Bride,
And from her fair unspotted side
Two blissful twins are to be born,   *1010*
Youth and Joy; so *Jove* hath sworn.
   But now my task is smoothly don,
I can fly, or I can run
Quickly to the green earths end,
Where the bow'd welkin slow doth bend,
And from thence can soar as soon
To the corners of the Moon.
   Mortals that would follow me,
Love vertue, she alone is free,
She can teach ye how to clime   *1020*
Higher then the Spheary chime;
Or if Vertue feeble were,
Heav'n it self would stoop to her.

POEMS ADDED IN THE 1673 EDITION
Anno aetatis 17
On the Death of a fair Infant dying of a Cough

I

O FAIREST flower no sooner blown but blasted,
Soft silken Primrose fading timelesslie,
Summers chief honour if thou hadst out-lasted
Bleak winters force that made thy blossome drie;
For he being amorous on that lovely die
   That did thy cheek envermeil, thought to kiss
But kill'd alas, and then bewayl'd his fatal bliss.

II

For since grim Aquilo his charioter
By boistrous rape th' Athenian damsel got,
He thought it toucht his Deitie full neer,   10
If likewise he some fair one wedded not,
Thereby to wipe away th' infamous blot,
   Of long-uncoupled bed, and childless eld,
Which 'mongst the wanton gods a foul reproach was held.

III

So mounting up in ycie-pearled carr,
Through middle empire of the freezing aire
He wanderd long, till thee he spy'd from farr,
There ended was his quest, there ceast his care.
Down he descended from his Snow-soft chaire,
   But all unwares with his cold-kind embrace   20
Unhous'd thy Virgin Soul from her fair biding place.

IV

Yet art thou not inglorious in thy fate;
For so *Apollo*, with unweeting hand
Whilome did slay his dearly-loved mate,
Young *Hyacinth* born on *Eurotas*' strand,
Young *Hyacinth* the pride of *Spartan* land;
   But then transform'd him to a purple flower
Alack that so to change thee winter had no power.

V

Yet can I not perswade me thou art dead
Or that thy coarse corrupts in earths dark wombe,   30

Or that thy beauties lie in wormie bed,
Hid from the world in a low delved tombe;
Could Heav'n for pittie thee so strictly doom?
   Oh no! for something in thy face did shine
Above mortalitie that shew'd thou wast divine.

VI

Resolve me then oh Soul most surely blest
(If so it be that thou these plaints dost hear)
Tell me bright Spirit where e're thou hoverest
Whether above that high first-moving Spheare
Or in the Elisian fields (if such there were.)   *40*
   Oh say me true if thou wert mortal wight
And why from us so quickly thou didst take thy flight.

VII

Wert thou some Starr which from the ruin'd roofe
Of shak't Olympus by mischance didst fall;
Which carefull *Jove* in natures true behoofe
Took up, and in fit place did reinstall?
Or did of late earths Sonnes besiege the wall
   Of sheenie Heav'n, and thou some goddess fled
Amongst us here below to hide thy nectar'd head.

VIII

Or wert thou that just Maid who once before   *50*
Forsook the hated earth, O tell me sooth
And cam'st again to visit us once more?
Or wert thou that sweet smiling Youth!
Or that c[r]own'd Matron sage white-robed Truth?
   Or any other of that heav'nly brood
Let down in clowdie throne to do the world some good.

IX

Or wert thou of the golden-winged hoast,
Who having clad thy self in humane weed,
To earth from thy præfixed seat didst poast,
And after short abode flie back with speed,   *60*
As if to shew what creatures Heav'n doth breed,
   Thereby to set the hearts of men on fire
To scorn the sordid world, and unto Heav'n aspire.

X

But oh why didst thou not stay here below
To bless us with thy heav'n-lov'd innocence,
To slake his wrath whom sin hath made our foe

To turn Swift-rushing black perdition hence,
Or drive away the slaughtering pestilence,
   To stand 'twixt us and our deserved smart
But thou canst best perform that office where thou art.   70

XI

Then thou the mother of so sweet a child
Her false imagin'd loss cease to lament,
And wisely learn to curb thy sorrows wild;
Think what a present thou to God hast sent,
And render him with patience what he lent;
   This if thou do he will an off-spring give,
That till the worlds last-end shall make thy name to live.

Anno Aetatis 19.   *At a Vacation Exercise in the Colledge, part* Latin, *part* English. *The* Latin *speeches ended, the* English *thus began*

Hail native Language, that by sinews weak
Didst move my first endeavouring tongue to speak,
And mad'st imperfect words with childish tripps,
Half unpronounc't, slide through my infant-lipps,
Driving dum silence from the portal dore,
Where he had mutely sate two years before:
Here I salute thee and thy pardon ask,
That now I use thee in my latter task:
Small loss it is that thence can come unto thee,
I know my tongue but little Grace can do thee: 10
Thou needst not be ambitious to be first,
Believe me I have thither packt the worst:
And, if it happen as I did forecast,
The daintest dishes shall be serv'd up last.
I pray thee then deny me not thy aide
For this same small neglect that I have made:
But haste thee strait to do me once a Pleasure,
And from thy wardrope bring thy chiefest treasure;
Not those new fangled toys, and triming slight
Which takes our late fantasticks with delight,   20
But cull those richest Robes, and gay'st attire
Which deepest Spirits, and choicest Wits desire:
I have some naked thoughts that rove about
And loudly knock to have their passage out;
And wearie of their place do only stay
Till thou hast deck't them in thy best aray;
That so they may without suspect or fears
Fly swiftly to this fair Assembly's ears;

Yet I had rather if I were to chuse,
Thy service in some graver subject use,   *30*
Such as may make thee search thy coffers round,
Before thou cloath my fancy in fit sound:
Such where the deep transported mind may soare
Above the wheeling poles, and at Heav'ns dore
Look in, and see each blissful Deitie
How he before the thunderous throne doth lie,
Listening to what unshorn *Apollo* sings
To th'touch of golden wires, while *Hebe* brings
Immortal Nectar to her Kingly Sire:
Then passing through the Spherse of watchful fire,   *40*
And mistie Regions of wide air next under,
And hills of Snow and lofts of piled Thunder,
May tell at length how green-ey'd *Neptune* raves,
In Heav'ns defiance mustering all his waves;
Then sing of secret things that came to pass
When Beldam Nature in her cradle was;
And last of Kings and Queens and *Hero's* old,
Such as the wise *Demodocus* once told
In solemn Songs at King *Alcinous* feast,
While sad *Ulisses* soul and all the rest   *50*
Are held with his melodious harmonie
In willing chains and sweet captivitie.
But fie my wandring Muse how thou dost stray!
Expectance calls thee now another way,
Thou know'st it must be now thy only bent
To keep in compass of thy Predicament:
Then quick about thy purpos'd business come,
That to the next I may resign my Roome.

Then Ens *is represented as Father of the Prædicaments his ten Sons, whereof the Eldest stood for* Substance *with his Canons, which* Ens *thus speaking, explains*

Good luck befriend thee Son; for at thy birth
The Faiery Ladies daunc't upon the hearth;   *60*
Thy drowsie Nurse hath sworn she did them spie
Come tripping to the Room where thou didst lie;
And sweetly singing round about thy Bed
Strew all their blessings on thy sleeping Head.
She heard them give thee this, that thou should'st still
From eyes of mortals walk invisible,
Yet there is something that doth force my fear,
For once it was my dismal hap to hear
A *Sybil* old, bow-bent with crooked age,
That far events full wisely could presage,   *70*
And in Times long and dark Prospective Glass

Poems Added in the 1673 Edition

Fore-saw what future dayes should bring to pass,
Your Son, said she, (nor can you it prevent)
Shall subject be to many an Accident.
O're all his Brethren he shall Reign as King,
Yet every one shall make him underling,
And those that cannot live from him asunder
Ungratefully shall strive to keep him under,
In worth and excellence he shall out-go them,
Yet being above them, he shall be below them;   80
From others he shall stand in need of nothing,
Yet on his Brothers shall depend for Cloathing.
To find a Foe it shall not be his hap,
And peace shall lull him in her flowry lap;
Yet shall he live in strife, and at his dore
Devouring war shall never cease to roare;
Yea it shall be his natural property
To harbour those that are at enmity.
What power, what force, what mighty spell, if not
Your learned hands, can loose this Gordian knot?   90

The next Quantity *and* Quality, *spake in Prose, then* Relation *was call'd by his Name*

Rivers arise; whether thou be the Son,
Of utmost *Tweed*, or *Ouse*, or gulphie *Dun*,
Or *Trent*, who like some earth-born Giant spreads
His thirty Armes along the indented Meads,
Or sullen *Mole* that runneth underneath,
Or *Severn* swift, guilty of Maidens death,
Or Rockie *Avon*, or of Sedgie *Lee*,
Or Coaly *Tine*, or antient hallowed *Dee*,
Or *Humber* loud that keeps the *Scythians* Name,
Or *Medway* smooth, or Royal Towred *Thame*.   100

The rest was Prose

The Fifth Ode of Horace. Lib. I

Quis multa gracilis te puer in Rosa, *Rendred almost word for word without Rhyme according to the Latin Measure, as near as the Language will permit*

What slender Youth bedew'd with liquid odours
Courts thee on Roses in some pleasant Cave,
    Pyrrha for whom bind'st thou
    In wreaths thy golden Hair,
Plain in thy neatness; O how oft shall he
On Faith and changed Gods complain: and Seas
    Rough with black winds and storms
    Unwonted shall admire:

Who now enjoyes thee credulous, all Gold,
Who alwayes vacant, alwayes amiable 10
    Hopes thee; of flattering gales
    Unmindfull. Hapless they
To whom thou untry'd seem'st fair. Me in my vow'd
Picture the sacred wall declares t' have hung
    My dank and dropping weeds
    To the stern God of Sea.

SONNETS

I

O NIGHTINGALE, that on yon bloomy Spray
Warbl'st at eeve, when all the Woods are still,
   Thou with fresh hope the Lovers heart dost fill,
   While the jolly hours lead on propitious *May*,
Thy liquid notes that close the eye of Day,
   First heard before the shallow Cuccoo's bill
   Portend success in love; O if *Jove's* will
Have linkt that amorous power to thy soft lay,
Now timely sing, ere the rude Bird of Hate
   Foretell my hopeles doom in som Grove ny: 10
   As thou from yeer to yeer hast sung too late
For my relief; yet hadst no reason why,
   Whether the Muse, or Love call thee his mate,
   Both them I serve, and of their train am I.

VII [1]

How soon hath Time the suttle theef of youth,
   Stoln on his wing my three and twentith yeer!
   My hasting dayes flie on with full career,
   But my late spring no bud or blossom shew'th.
Perhaps my semblance might deceive the truth,
   That I to manhood am arriv'd so near,
   And inward ripenes doth much less appear,
   That som more timely-happy spirits indu'th.
Yet be it less or more, or soon or slow,
   It shall be still in strictest measure eev'n,   10
   To that same lot, however mean, or high,
Toward which Time leads me, and the will of Heav'n;
   All is, if I have grace to use it so,
   As ever in my great task Masters eye.

VIII

Captain or Colonel, or Knight in Arms,
   Whose chance on these defenceless dores may sease,
   If ever deed of honour did thee please,
   Guard them, and him within protect from harms,

---

[1] Sonnets II–VI, written in Italian, are omitted.

He can requite thee, for he knows the charms
   That call Fame on such gentle acts as these,
   And he can spred thy Name o're Lands and Seas,
What ever clime the Suns bright circle warms.
Lift not thy spear against the Muses Bowre,
   The great *Emathian* Conqueror bid spare   *10*
   The house of *Pindarus*, when Temple and Towre
Went to the ground: And the repeated air
   Of sad *Electra's* Poet had the power
   To save th' *Athenian* Walls from ruine bare.

IX

Lady that in the prime of earliest youth,
   Wisely hath shun'd the broad way and the green,
   And with those few art eminently seen,
That labour up the Hill of heav'nly Truth,
The better part with *Mary* and with *Ruth*,
   Chosen thou hast, and they that overween,
   And at thy growing vertues fret their spleen,
No anger find in thee, but pity and ruth.
Thy care is fixt and zealously attends
   To fill thy odorous Lamp with deeds of light,   *10*
   And Hope that reaps not shame. Therefore be sure
Thou, when the Bridegroom with his feastfull friends
   Passes to bliss at the mid hour of night,
   Hast gain'd thy entrance, Virgin wise and pure.

X

Daughter to that good Earl, once President
   Of *Englands* Counsel, and her Treasury,
   Who liv'd in both, unstain'd with gold or fee,
   And left them both, more in himself content,
Till the sad breaking of that Parlament
   Broke him, as that dishonest victory
   At *Chæronéa*, fatal to liberty
Kil'd with report that Old man eloquent,
Though later born, then to have known the dayes
   Wherin your Father flourisht, yet by you   *10*
   Madam, me thinks I see him living yet;
So well your words his noble vertues praise,
   That all both judge you to relate them true,
   And to possess them, Honour'd *Margaret*.

XI

A Book was writ of late call'd *Tetrachordon;*
   And wov'n close, both matter, form and stile;

    The Subject new: it walk'd the Town a while,
      Numbring good intellects; now seldom por'd on.
Cries the stall-reader, bless us! what a word on
      A title page is this! and some in file
      Stand spelling fals, while one might walk to Mile-
End Green. Why is it harder Sirs then Gordon,
Colkitto, or Macdonnel, or Galasp?
      Those rugged names to our like mouths grow sleek   *10*
      That would have made *Quintilian* stare and gasp.
Thy age, like ours, O Soul of Sir *John Cheek*,
      Hated not Learning wors then Toad or Asp;
      When thou taught'st *Cambridge*, and King *Edward*
    Greek.

XII *On the same*

I did but prompt the age to quit their cloggs
      By the known rules of antient libertie,
      When strait a barbarous noise environs me
      Of Owles and Cuckoes, Asses, Apes and Doggs.
As when those Hinds that were transform'd to Froggs
      Raild at *Latona's* twin-born progenie
      Which after held the Sun and Moon in fee.
      But this is got by casting Pearl to Hoggs;
That bawle for freedom in their senceless mood,
      And still revolt when truth would set them free.   *10*
      Licence they mean when they cry libertie;
For who loves that, must first be wise and good;
      But from that mark how far they roave we see
      For all this wast of wealth, and loss of blood.

XIII

To *Mr.* H. Lawes, *on his Aires*

Harry whose tuneful and well measur'd Song
      First taught our English Musick how to span
      Words with just note and accent, not to scan
      With *Midas* Ears, committing short and long;
Thy worth and skill exempts thee from the throng,
      With praise enough for Envy to look wan;
      To after age thou shalt be writ the man,
      That with smooth aire couldst humor best our
    tongue.
Thou honour'st Verse, and Verse must send her wing
      To honour thee, the Priest of *Phœbus* Quire   *10*
      That tun'st their happiest lines in Hymn, or Story.
Dante shall give Fame leave to set thee higher

Then his *Casella*, whom he woo'd to sing
Met in the milder shades of Purgatory.

XIV

When Faith and Love which parted from thee never,
   Had ripen'd thy just soul to dwell with God,
   Meekly thou didst resign this earthly load
   Of Death, call'd Life; which us from Life doth sever.
Thy Works and Alms and all thy good Endeavour
   Staid not behind, nor in the grave were trod;
   But as Faith pointed with her golden rod,
   Follow'd thee up to joy and bliss for ever.
Love led them on, and Faith who knew them best
   Thy hand-maids, clad them o're with purple beams   *10*
   And azure wings, that up they flew so drest,
And speak the truth of thee on glorious Theams
   Before the Judge, who thenceforth bid thee rest
   And drink thy fill of pure immortal streams.

XV

On the late Massacher in Piemont

Avenge O Lord thy slaughter'd Saints, whose bones
   Lie scatter'd on the Alpine mountains cold,
   Ev'n them who kept thy truth so pure of old
   When all our Fathers worship't Stocks and Stones,
Forget not: in thy book record their groanes
   Who were thy Sheep and in their antient Fold
   Slayn by the bloody *Piemontese* that roll'd
   Mother with Infant down the Rocks. Their moans
The Vales redoubl'd to the Hills, and they
   To Heav'n. Their martyr'd blood and ashes sow   *10*
   O're all th'*Italian* fields where still doth sway
The triple Tyrant: that from these may grow
   A hunder'd-fold, who having learnt thy way
   Early may fly the *Babylonian* wo.

XVI

When I consider how my light is spent,
   E're half my days, in this dark world and wide,
   And that one Talent which is death to hide,
   Lodg'd with me useless, though my Soul more bent
To serve therewith my Maker, and present
   My true account, least he returning chide,
   Doth God exact day-labour, light deny'd,

I fondly ask; But patience to prevent
That murmur, soon replies, God doth not need
    Either man's work or his own gifts, who best
    Bear his milde yoak, they serve him best, his State
Is Kingly. Thousands at his bidding speed
    And post o're Land and Ocean without rest:
    They also serve who only stand and waite.

XVII

Lawrence of vertuous Father vertuous Son,
    Now that the Fields are dank, and ways are mire,
    Where shall we sometimes meet, and by the fire
    Help wast a sullen day; what may be won
From the hard Season gaining: time will run
    On smoother, till *Favonius* re-inspire
    The frozen earth; and cloth in fresh attire
    The Lillie and Rose, that neither sow'd nor spun.
What neat repast shall feast us, light and choice,
    Of Attick tast, with Wine, whence we may rise
    To hear the Lute well toucht, or artfull voice
Warble immortal Notes and *Tuskan* Ayre?
    He who of those delights can judge, and spare
    To interpose them oft, is not unwise.

XVIII

Cyriack, whose Grandsire on the Royal Bench
    Of Brittish *Themis*, with no mean applause
    Pronounc't and in his volumes taught our Lawes,
    Which others at their Barr so often wrench:
To day deep thoughts resolve with me to drench
    In mirth, that after no repenting drawes;
    Let *Euclid* rest and *Archimedes* pause,
    And what the *Swede* intend, and what the *French*.
To measure life, learn thou betimes, and know
    Toward solid good what leads the nearest way;
    For other things mild Heav'n a time ordains,
And disapproves that care, though wise in show,
    That with superfluous burden loads the day,
    And when God sends a cheerful hour, refrains.

XIX

Methought I saw my late espoused Saint
    Brought to me like *Alcestis* from the grave,
    Whom *Joves* great Son to her glad Husband gave,
    Rescu'd from death by force though pale and faint.
Mine as whom washt from spot of child-bed taint,

    Purification in the old Law did save,
      And such, as yet once more I trust to have
      Full sight of her in Heaven without restraint,
Came vested all in white, pure as her mind:
      Her face was vail'd, yet to my fancied sight,   *10*
      Love, sweetness, goodness, in her person shin'd
So clear, as in no face with more delight.
    But O as to embrace me she enclin'd
I wak'd, she fled, and day brought back my night.

On the new forcers of Conscience under the Long PARLIAMENT

Because you have thrown of your Prelate Lord,
    And with stiff Vowes renounc'd his Liturgie
    To seise the widdow'd whore Pluralitie
From them whose sin ye envi'd, not abhor'd,
Dare ye for this adjure the Civill Sword
    To force our Consciences that Christ set free,
    And ride us with a classic Hierarchy
Taught ye by meer *A. S.* and *Rotherford*?
Men whose Life, Learning, Faith and pure intent
    Would have been held in high esteem with *Paul*   *10*
    Must now be nam'd and printed Hereticks
By shallow *Edwards* and Scotch what d'ye call:
    But we do hope to find out all your tricks,
    Your plots and packing wors then those of *Trent*,
               That so the Parliament
May with their wholsom and preventive Shears
Clip your Phylacteries, though bauk your Ears,
                And succour our just Fears
When they shall read this clearly in your charge
New Presbyter is but *Old Priest* writ Large.   *20*

On the Lord Gen. Fairfax *at the seige of* Colchester

Fairfax, whose name in armes through Europe rings
    Filling each mouth with envy, or with praise,
    And all her jealous monarchs with amaze,
    And rumors loud, that daunt remotest kings,
Thy firm unshak'n vertue ever brings
    Victory home, though new rebellions raise
    Thir Hydra heads, & the fals North displaies
    Her brok'n league, to impe their serpent wings,
O yet a nobler task awaites thy hand;

For what can Warr, but endless warr still breed,   *10*
  Till Truth, & Right from Violence be freed,
And Public Faith cleard from the shamefull brand
  Of Public Fraud. In vain doth Valour bleed
  While Avarice, & Rapine share the land.

To the Lord Generall Cromwell *May 1652*

On the proposalls of certaine ministers at the Committee for Propagation of the Gospell

Cromwell, our cheif of men, who through a cloud
  Not of warr onely, but detractions rude,
  Guided by faith & matchless Fortitude
To peace & truth thy glorious way hast plough'd,
And on the neck of crowned Fortune proud
  Hast reard Gods Trophies, & his work pursu'd,
  While Darwen stream with blood of Scotts imbru'd,
And *Dunbarr feild* resounds thy praises loud,
And *W*orsters laureat wreath; yet much remaines
  To conquer still; peace hath her victories   *10*
  No less renownd then warr, new foes aries
Threatning to bind our soules with secular chaines:
  Helpe us to save free Conscience from the paw
  Of hireling wolves whose Gospell is their maw.

To Sr Henry Vane *the younger*

*V*ane, young in yeares, but in sage counsell old,
  Then whome a better Senatour nere held
  The helme of Rome, when gownes not armes repelld
The feirce Epeirot & the African bold,
Whether to settle peace, or to unfold
  The drift of hollow states, hard to be spelld,
  Then to advise how warr may best, upheld,
Move by her two maine nerves, Iron & Gold
In all her equipage; besides to know
  Both spirituall powre & civill, what each meanes   *10*
  What severs each thou 'hast learnt, which few have don.
The bounds of either sword to thee wee ow.
  Therfore on thy firme hand religion leanes
  In peace, & reck'ns thee her eldest son.

To Mr. Cyriack Skinner *upon his Blindness*

Cyriack, this three years day these eys, though clear
   To outward view, of blemish or of spot;
   Bereft of light thir seeing have forgot,
   Nor to thir idle orbs doth sight appear
Of Sun or Moon or Starre throughout the year,
   Or man or woman. Yet I argue not
   Against heavns hand or will, nor bate a jot
   Of heart or hope; but still bear vp and steer
Right onward. What supports me, dost thou ask?
   The conscience, Friend, to have lost them overply'd *10*
   In libertyes defence, my noble task,
Of which all Europe talks from side to side.
   This thought might lead me through the world's vain mask
   Content though blind, had I no better guide.

PSALMS

PSAL. I *Done into Verse*, 1653

BLESS'D is the man who hath not walk'd astray
In counsel of the wicked, and ith'way
Of sinners hath not stood, and in the seat
Of scorners hath not sate. But in the great
Jehovahs Law is ever his delight,
And in his Law he studies day and night.
He shall be as a tree which planted grows
By watry streams, and in his season knows
To yield his fruit, and his leaf shall not fall,
And what he takes in hand shall prosper all.   *10*
Not so the wicked, but as chaff which fann'd
The wind drives, so the wicked shall not stand
In judgment, or abide their tryal then,
Nor sinners in th'assembly of just men.
For the Lord knows th'upright way of the just,
And the way of bad men to ruine must.

PSAL. II *Done Aug.* 8. 1653. *Terzetti*

WHY do the Gentiles tumult, and the Nations
   Muse a vain thing, the Kings of th'earth upstand
   With power, and Princes in their Congregations
Lay deep their plots together through each Land,
   Against the Lord and his Messiah dear.
   Let us break off, say they, by strength of hand
Their bonds, and cast from us, no more to wear,
   Their twisted cords: he who in Heaven doth dwell
   Shall laugh, the Lord shall scoff them, then severe
Speak to them in his wrath, and in his fell   *10*
   And fierce ire trouble them; but I saith hee
   Anointed have my King (though ye rebell)
On Sion my holi' hill. A firm decree
   I will declare; the Lord to me hath say'd
   Thou art my Son I have begotten thee
This day; ask of me, and the grant is made;
   As thy possession I on thee bestow
   Th'Heathen, and as thy conquest to be sway'd

Earths utmost bounds: them shalt thou bring full low
   With Iron Scepter bruis'd, and them disperse   *20*
   Like to a potters vessel shiver'd so.
And now be wise at length ye Kings averse
   Be taught ye Judges of the earth; with fear
   Jehovah serve, and let your joy converse
With trembling; kiss the Son least he appear
   In anger and ye perish in the way
   If once his wrath take fire like fuel sere.
Happy all those who have in him their stay.

PSAL. III   *Aug.* 9. 1653

When he fled from Absalom

Lord how many are my foes
   How many those
That in arms against me rise
   Many are they
   That of my life distrustfully thus say,
No help for him in God there lies.
But thou Lord art my shield my glory,
     Thee through my story
     Th' exalter of my head I count
        Aloud I cry'd   *10*
   Unto Jehovah, he full soon reply'd
And heard me from his holy mount.
I lay and slept, I wak'd again,
     For my sustain
   Was the Lord. Of many millions
     The populous rout
   I fear not though incamping round about
They pitch against me their Pavillions.
Rise Lord, save me my God for thou
     Hast smote ere now   *20*
   On the cheek-bone all my foes,
     Of men abhor'd
   Hast broke the teeth. This help was from the Lord;
Thy blessing on thy people flows.

PSAL. IV   *Aug.* 10. 1653

Answer me when I call
God of my righteousness;
In straights and in distress
Thou didst me disinthrall

And set at large; now spare,
  Now pity me, and hear my earnest prai'r.
Great ones how long will ye
My glory have in scorn
How long be thus forborn
Still to love vanity,
To love, to seek, to prize
  Things false and vain and nothing else but lies?
Yet know the Lord hath chose
Chose to himself a part
The good and meek of heart
(For whom to chuse he knows)
Jehovah from on high
  Will hear my voyce what time to him I crie.
Be aw'd, and do not sin,
Speak to your hearts alone,
Upon your beds, each one,
And be at peace within.
Offer the offerings just
  Of righteousness and in Jehovah trust.
Many there be that say
Who yet will shew us good?
Talking like this worlds brood;
But Lord, thus let me pray,
On us lift up the light
  Lift up the favour of thy count'nance bright.
Into my heart more joy
And gladness thou hast put
Then when a year of glut
Their stores doth over-cloy
And from their plenteous grounds
  With vast increase their corn and wine abounds.
In peace at once will I
Both lay me down and sleep
For thou alone dost keep
Me safe where ere I lie
As in a rocky Cell
  Thou Lord alone in safety mak'st me dwell.

PSAL. V. *Aug.* 12. 1653

J<small>EHOVAH</small> to my words give ear
    My meditation waigh
  The voyce of my complaining hear
My King and God for unto thee I pray.
    Jehovah thou my early voyce

   Shalt in the morning hear
    Ith'morning I to thee with choyce
  Will rank my Prayers, and watch till thou appear.
   For thou art not a God that takes
    In wickedness delight
   Evil with thee no biding makes
  Fools or mad men stand not within thy sight.
   All workers of iniquity
    Thou hat'st; and them unblest
   Thou wilt destroy that speak a ly
  The bloodi' and guileful man God doth detest.
   But I will in thy mercies dear
    Thy numerous mercies go
   Into thy house; I in thy fear
  Will towards thy holy temple worship low.
   Lord lead me in thy righteousness
    Lead me because of those
   That do observe if I transgress,
  Set thy wayes right before, where my step goes.
   For in his faltring mouth unstable
    No word is firm or sooth
   Their inside, troubles miserable;
  An open grave their throat, their tongue they smooth.
   God, find them guilty, let them fall
    By their own counsels quell'd;
   Push them in their rebellions all
  Still on; for against thee they have rebell'd;
   Then all who trust in thee shall bring
    Their joy, while thou from blame
   Defend'st them, they shall ever sing
  And shall triumph in thee, who love thy name.
   For thou Jehovah wilt be found
    To bless the just man still,
   As with a shield thou wilt surround
  Him with thy lasting favour and good will.

PSAL. VI *Aug.* 13. 1653

Lord in thine anger do not reprehend me
  Nor in thy hot displeasure me correct;
Pity me Lord for I am much deject
  Am very weak and faint; heal and amend me,
For all my bones, that even with anguish ake,
  Are troubled, yea my soul is troubled sore;
And thou O Lord how long? turn Lord, restore
  My soul, O save me for thy goodness sake

For in death no remembrance is of thee;
   Who in the grave can celebrate thy praise?
Wearied I am with sighing out my dayes,
   Nightly my Couch I make a kind of Sea;
My Bed I water with my tears; mine Eie
   Through grief consumes, is waxen old and dark
Ith' mid'st of all mine enemies that mark.
   Depart all ye that work iniquitie.
Depart from me, for the voice of my weeping
   The Lord hath heard, the Lord hath heard my prai'r
My supplication with acceptance fair
   The Lord will own, and have me in his keeping.
Mine enemies shall all be blank and dash't
   With much confusion; then grow red with shame,
They shall return in hast the way they came
   And in a moment shall be quite abash't.

PSAL. VII *Aug.* 14. 1653

Upon the words of Chush *the* Benjamite *against him*

Lord my God to thee I flie
Save me and secure me under
Thy protection while I crie
Least as a Lion (and no wonder)
He hast to tear my Soul asunder
Tearing and no rescue nigh.

Lord my God if I have thought
Or done this, if wickedness
Be in my hands, if I have wrought
Ill to him that meant me peace,
Or to him have render'd less,
And not fre'd my foe for naught;

Let th'enemy pursue my soul
And overtake it, let him tread
My life down to the earth and roul
In the dust my glory dead,
In the dust and there out spread
Lodge it with dishonour foul.

Rise Jehovah in thine ire
Rouze thy self amidst the rage
Of my foes that urge like fire;

And wake for me, their furi' asswage;
Judgment here thou didst ingage
And command which I desire.

So th' assemblies of each Nation
Will surround thee, seeking right,
Thence to thy glorious habitation
Return on high and in their sight.
Jehovah judgeth most upright
All people from the worlds foundation. 30

Judge me Lord, be judge in this
According to my righteousness
And the innocence which is
Upon me: cause at length to cease
Of evil men the wickedness
And their power that do amiss.

But the just establish fast,
Since thou art the just God that tries
Hearts and reins. On God is cast
My defence, and in him lies 40
In him who both just and wise
Saves th' upright of Heart at last.

God is a just Judge and severe,
And God is every day offended;
If th' unjust will not forbear,
His Sword he whets, his Bow hath bended
Already, and for him intended
The tools of death, that waits him near.

(His arrows purposely made he
For them that persecute.) Behold 50
He travels big with vanitie,
Trouble he hath conceav'd of old
As in a womb, and from that mould
Hath at length brought forth a Lie.

He dig'd a pit, and delv'd it deep,
And fell into the pit he made,
His mischief that due course doth keep
Turns on his head, and his ill trade
Of violence will undelay'd
Fall on his crown with ruine steep. 60

Then will I Jehovah's praise
According to his justice raise
And sing the Name and Deitie
Of Jehovah the most high.

PSAL. VIII *Aug.* 14. 1653

O Jehovah our Lord how wondrous great
   And glorious is thy name through all the earth?
So as above the Heavens thy praise to set
   Out of the tender mouths of latest bearth,

Out of the mouths of babes and sucklings thou
   Hast founded strength because of all thy foes
To stint th'enemy, and slack th'avengers brow
   That bends his rage thy providence to oppose.

When I behold thy Heavens, thy Fingers art,
   The Moon and Starrs which thou so bright hast set,   *10*
In the pure firmament, then saith my heart,
   O what is man that thou remembrest yet,

And think'st upon him; or of man begot
   That him thou visit'st and of him art found;
Scarce to be less then Gods, thou mad'st his lot,
   With honour and with state thou hast him crown'd.

O're the works of thy hand thou mad'st him Lord,
   Thou hast put all under his lordly feet,
All Flocks, and Herds, by thy commanding word,
   All beasts that in the field or forrest meet.   *20*

Fowl of the Heavens, and Fish that through the wet
   Sea-paths in shoals do slide. And know no dearth.
O Jehovah our Lord how wondrous great
   And glorious is thy name through all the earth.

April, 1648   J. M.
Nine of the Psalms done into Metre, wherein all but what is in a different Character, are the very words of the Text, translated from the Original

PSAL. LXXX

1 THOU Shepherd that dost Israel *keep*
  Give ear *in time of need*,
Who leadest like a flock of sheep
  Thy loved Josephs seed,
That sitt'st between the Cherubs *bright*
  Between their wings out-spread
Shine forth, *and from thy cloud give light,*
  And on our foes thy dread.
2 In Ephraims view and Benjamins,
  And in Manasse's sight
Awake [1] thy strength, come, and *be seen*
  To save us *by thy might*.
3 Turn us again, *thy grace divine*
  To us O God *vouchsafe;*
Cause thou thy face on us to shine
  And then we shall be safe.
4 Lord God of Hosts, how long wilt thou,
  How long wilt thou declare
Thy [2] smoaking wrath, *and angry brow*
  Against thy peoples praire.
5 Thou feed'st them with the bread of tears,
  Their bread with tears they eat,
And mak'st them [3] largely drink the tears
  Wherwith their cheeks are wet.
6 A strife thou mak'st us *and a prey*
  To every neighbour foe,
Among themselves they [4] laugh, they [4] play,
  And [4] flouts at us they throw.
7 Return us, *and thy grace divine*,
  O God of Hosts *vouchsafe*
Cause thou thy face on us to shine,
  And then we shall be safe.
8 A Vine from Ægypt thou hast brought,
  Thy free love made it thine,
And drov'st out Nations *proud and haut*

[1] *Gnorera*.   [2] *Gnashanta*.   [3] *Shalish*.   [4] *Jilgnagu*.

      To plant this *lovely* Vine.
9 Thou did'st prepare for it a place
    And root it deep and fast
  That it *began to grow apace*,
    And fill'd the land *at last*.
10 With her *green* shade *that* cover'd *all*,
    The Hills were *over-spread*
  Her Bows as *high as* Cedars tall
    Advanc'd their lofty head.
11 Her branches *on the western side*
    Down to the Sea she sent,
  And *upward* to that river *wide*
    Her other branches *went*.
12 Why hast thou laid her Hedges low
    And brok'n down her Fence,
  That all may pluck her, as they go,
    With rudest violence?
13 The *tusked* Boar out of the wood
    Up turns it by the roots,
  Wild Beasts there brouze, and make their food
    Her Grapes and tender Shoots.
14 Return now, God of Hosts, look down
    From Heav'n, thy Seat divine,
  Behold *us, but without a frown*,
    And visit this *thy* Vine.
15 Visit this Vine, which thy right hand
    Hath set, and planted *long*,
  And the young branch, that for thy self
    Thou hast made firm and strong.
16 But now it is consum'd with fire,
    And cut *with Axes* down,
  They perish at thy dreadfull ire,
    At thy rebuke and frown.
17 Upon the man of thy right hand
    Let thy *good* hand be *laid*,
  Upon the Son of Man, whom thou
    Strong for thyself hast made.
18 So shall we not go back from thee
    To wayes of sin and shame,
  Quick'n us thou, then *gladly* wee
    Shall call upon thy Name.
  Return us, *and thy grace divine*
    Lord God of Hosts *voutsafe*,
  Cause thou thy face on us to shine,
    And then we shall be safe.

PSAL. LXXXI

1 To God our strength sing loud, *and clear*,
   Sing loud to God *our King*,
To Jacobs God, *that all may hear*
   Loud acclamations ring.
2 Prepare a Hymn, prepare a Song
   The Timbrel hither bring
The *cheerfull* Psaltry bring along
   And Harp *with* pleasant *string*.
3 Blow, *as is wont*, in the new Moon
   With Trumpets *lofty sound*,
Th' appointed time, the day wheron
   Our solemn Feast *comes round*.
4 This was a Statute *giv'n of old*
   For Israel *to observe*
A Law of Jacobs God, *to hold*
   From whence they might not swerve.
5 This he a Testimony ordain'd
   In Joseph, *not to change*,
When as he pass'd through Ægypt land;
   The Tongue I heard, was strange.
6 From burden, *and from slavish toyle*
   I set his shoulder free;
His hands from pots, *and mirie soyle*
   Deliver'd were *by me*.
7 When trouble did thee sore assaile,
   On me then didst thou call,
And I to free thee *did not faile*,
   And led thee out of thrall.
I answer'd thee in [1] thunder deep
   With clouds encompass'd round;
I tri'd thee at the water *steep*
   Of Meriba *renown'd*.
8 Hear O my people, *heark'n well*,
   I testifie to thee
Thou antient flock of Israel,
   If thou wilt list to mee,
9 Through out the land of thy abode
   No alien God shall be
Nor shalt thou to a forein God
   In honour bend thy knee.
10 I am the Lord thy God which brought
   Thee out of Ægypt land

---
[1] *Be Sether ragnam.*

    Ask large enough, and I, *besought*,
        Will grant thy full demand.
11 And yet my people would not *hear*,
        Nor hearken to my voice;
    And Israel *whom I lov'd so dear*
        Mislik'd me for his choice.
12 Then did I leave them to their will
        And to their wandring mind;
    Their own conceits they follow'd still
        Their own devises blind.
13 O that my people would *be wise*
        To serve me *all their daies*,
    And O that Israel would *advise*
        To walk my *righteous* waies.
14 Then would I soon bring down their foes
        That now so proudly rise,
    And turn my hand against *all those*
        That are their enemies.
15 Who hate the Lord should *then be fain*
        To bow to him and bend,
    But *they, His people, should remain*,
        Their time should have no end.
16 And he would feed them *from the shock*
        With flower of finest wheat,
    And satisfie them from the rock
        With Honey *for their Meat*.

PSAL. LXXXII

1 God in the[1] great[1] assembly stands
        Of Kings and lordly States,
    Among the gods[2] on both his hands
        He judges and debates.
2 How long will ye[3] pervert the right
        With[3] judgment false and wrong
    Favouring the wicked *by your might*,
        Who thence grow bold and strong?
3 [4] Regard the [4] weak and fatherless
        [4] Dispatch the [4] poor mans cause,
    And [5] raise the man in deep distress
        By [5] just and equal Lawes.
4 Defend the poor and desolate,
        And rescue from the hands
    Of wicked men the low estate

---

[1]*Bagnadath-el.*   [2]*Bekerev.*   [3]*Tishphetu gnavel.*   [4]*Shiphtu-dal.*
[5]*Hatzdiku.*

      Of him *that help demands*.
5 They know not nor will understand,
    In darkness they walk on,
  The Earths foundations all are [6] mov'd
    And [6] out of order gon.
6 I said that ye were Gods, yea all
    The Sons of God most high
7 But ye shall die like men, and fall
    As other Princes *die*.
8 Rise God, [7] judge thou the earth *in might*,
    This *wicked* earth [7] redress,
  For thou art he who shalt by right
    The Nations all possess.

PSAL. LXXXIII

1 Be not thou silent *now at length*
    O God hold not thy peace,
  Sit not thou still O God of *strength*
    We cry and do not cease.
2 For lo thy *furious* foes *now* [1] swell
    And [1] storm outrageously,
  And they that hate thee *proud and fell*
    Exalt their heads full hie.
3 Against thy people they [2] contrive
    [3] Their Plots and Counsels deep,
    [4] Them to ensnare they chiefly strive
    [5] Whom thou dost hide and keep.
4 Come let us cut them off say they,
    Till they no Nation be
  That Israels name for ever may
    Be lost in memory.
5 For they consult [6] with all their might,
    And all as one in mind
  Themselves against thee they unite
    And in firm union bind.
6 The tents of Edom, and the brood
    Of *scornful* Ishmael,
  Moab, with them of Hagars blood
    That in the Desart dwell,
7 Gebal and Ammon *there conspire*,
    And *hateful* Amalec,
  The Philistims, and they of Tyre
    Whose bounds the Sea doth check.

[6]*Jimmotu.* [7]*Shiphta.* [1]*Jehemajun.* [2]*Jagnarimu.* [3]*Sod.*
[4]*Jithjagnatsu gnal.* [5]*Tsephuneca.* [6]*Lev jachdau.*

Psalms

 8 With them *great* Asshur also bands
     And doth confirm the knot,
 All these have lent their armed hands
     To aid the Sons of Lot.
 9 Do to them as to Midian *bold*
     That wasted all the Coast.
 To Sisera, and as *is told*
     Thou didst to Jabins *hoast,*
 When at the brook of Kishon *old*
     They were repulst and slain,
10 At Endor quite cut off, and rowl'd
     As dung upon the plain.
11 As Zeb and Oreb evil sped
     So let their Princes speed
 As Zeba, and Zalmunna *bled*
     So let their Princes *bleed.*
12 *For they amidst their pride* have said
     By right now shall we seize
 Gods houses, and *will now invade*
     [1] Their stately Palaces.
13 My God, oh make them as a wheel
     No quiet let them find,
 Giddy and *restless* let *them reel*
     Like stubble from the wind.
14 As *when* an *aged* wood takes fire
     Which on a sudden straies,
 The *greedy* flame runs hier and hier
     Till all the mountains blaze,
15 So with thy whirlwind them pursue,
     And with thy tempest chase;
16 [2] And till they [2] yield thee honour due,
     Lord fill with shame their face.
17 Asham'd and troubl'd let them be,
     Troubl'd and sham'd for ever,
 Ever confounded, and so die
     With shame, *and scape it never.*
18 Then shall they know that thou whose name
     Jehova is alone,
 Art the most high, *and thou the same*
     O're all the earth *art one.*

---

[1] *Neoth Elohim bears both.*   [2] *They seek thy Name.* Heb.

PSAL. LXXXIV

1 How lovely are thy dwellings fair!
    O Lord of Hoasts, how dear
  The *pleasant* Tabernacles are!
    Where thou do'st dwell so near.
2 My Soul doth long and almost die
    Thy Courts O Lord to see,
  My heart and flesh aloud do crie,
    O living God, for thee.
3 There ev'n the Sparrow *freed from wrong*
    Hath found a house of *rest*,
  The Swallow there, to lay her young
    Hath built her *brooding* nest,
Ev'n *by* thy Altars Lord of Hoasts
    They find their safe abode,
And home they fly from round the Coasts
    Toward thee, My King, my God.
4 Happy, who in thy house reside
    Where thee they ever praise,
5 Happy, whose strength in thee doth bide,
    And in their hearts thy waies.
6 They pass through Baca's *thirstie* Vale,
    That dry and barren ground
As through a fruitfull watry Dale
    Where Springs and Showrs abound.
7 They journey on from strength to strength
    With joy and gladsom cheer
Till all before *our* God *at length*
    In Sion do appear.
8 Lord God of Hoasts hear *now* my praier
    O Jacobs God give ear,
9 Thou God our shield look on the face
    Of thy anointed *dear*.
10 For one day in thy Courts *to be*
    Is better, *and more blest*
Then *in the joyes of Vanity*,
    A thousand daies *at best*.
I in the temple of my God
    Had rather keep a dore,
Then dwell in Tents, *and rich abode*
    With Sin *for evermore*.
11 For God the Lord both Sun and Shield
    Gives grace and glory *bright*,
No good from them shall be with-held

    Whose waies are just and right.
12 Lord *God* of Hoasts *that raign'st on high*,
    That man is *truly* blest
  Who *only* on thee doth relie.
    And in thee only rest.

PSAL. LXXXV

1 THY Land to favour graciously
    Thou hast not Lord been slack,
  Thou hast from *hard* Captivity
    Returned Jacob back.
2 Th' iniquity thou didst forgive
    That wrought thy people woe,
  And all their Sin, *that did thee grieve*
    Hast hid *where none shall know*.
3 Thine anger all thou hadst remov'd,
    And *calmly* didst return
  From thy [1] fierce wrath which we had prov'd
    Far worse then fire to burn.
4 God of our saving health and peace,
    Turn us, and us restore,
  Thine indignation cause to cease
    Toward us, *and chide no more*.
5 Wilt thou be angry without end,
    For ever angry thus
  Wilt thou thy frowning ire extend
    From age to age on us?
6 Wilt thou not [2] turn, and *hear our voice*
    And us again [2] revive,
  That so thy people may rejoyce
    By thee preserv'd alive.
7 Cause us to see thy goodness Lord,
    To us thy mercy shew
  Thy saving health to us afford
    And life in us renew.
8 *And now* what God the Lord will speak
    I will *go strait and* hear,
  For to his people he speaks peace
    And to his Saints *full dear*,
  To his dear Saints he will speak peace,
    But let them never more
  Return to folly, *but surcease*
    To trespass as before.
9 Surely to such as do him fear

[1] Heb. *The burning heat of thy wrath*.   [2] Heb. *Turn to quicken us*.

Salvation is at hand
And glory shall *ere long appear*
To dwell within our Land.   *40*
10 Mercy and Truth *that long were miss'd*
Now *joyfully* are met
Sweet Peace and Righteousness have kiss'd
And hand in hand are set.
11 Truth from the earth *like to a flowr*
Shall bud and blossom *then,*
And Justice from her heavenly bowr
Look down *on mortal men.*
12 The Lord will also then bestow
Whatever thing is good   *50*
Our Land shall forth in plenty throw
Her fruits *to be our food.*
13 Before him Righteousness shall go
His Royal Harbinger,
Then [1] will he come, and not be slow
His footsteps cannot err.

PSAL. LXXXVI

1 Thy *Gracious* ear, O Lord, encline,
O hear me *I thee pray,*
For I am poor, and almost pine
With need, *and sad decay.*
2 Preserve my soul, for [2] I have trod
Thy waies, and love the just,
Save thou thy servant O my God
Who *still* in thee doth trust.
3 Pitty me Lord for daily thee
I call; 4 O make rejoyce   *10*
Thy Servants Soul; for Lord to thee
I lift my soul *and voice,*
5 For thou art good, thou Lord art prone
To pardon, thou to all
Art full of mercy, thou *alone*
To them that on thee call.
6 Unto my supplication Lord
Give ear, and to the crie
Of my *incessant* praiers afford
Thy hearing graciously.   *20*
7 I in the day of my distress
Will call on thee *for aid;*

---

[1] Heb. *He will set his steps to the way.*   [2] Heb. *I am good, loving, a doer of good and holy things.*

    For thou wilt *grant* me *free access*
       And *answer, what I pray'd.*
 8 Like thee among the gods is none
      O Lord, nor any works
    Of all that other Gods have done
      Like to thy *glorious* works.
 9 The Nations all whom thou hast made
      Shall come, *and all shall frame*
    To bow them low before thee Lord,
      And glorifie thy name.
10 For great thou art, and wonders great
      By thy strong hand are done,
    Thou *in thy everlasting Seat*
      Remainest God alone.
11 Teach me O Lord thy way *most right,*
      I in thy truth will bide,
    To fear thy name my heart unite
      So shall it never slide.
12 Thee will I praise O Lord my God
      Thee honour, and adore
    With my whole heart, and blaze abroad
      Thy name for ever more.
13 For great thy mercy is toward me,
      And thou hast free'd my Soul
    Eev'n from the lowest Hell set free
      From deepest darkness foul.
14 O God the proud against me rise
      And violent men are met
    To seek my life, and in their eyes
      No fear of thee have set.
15 But thou Lord art the God most mild
      Readiest thy grace to shew,
    Slow to be angry, and *art stil'd*
      Most mercifull, most true.
16 O turn to me *thy face at length,*
      And me have mercy on,
    Unto thy servant give thy strength,
      And save thy hand-maids Son.
17 Some sign of good to me afford,
      And let my foes *then* see
    And be asham'd, because thou Lord
      Do'st help and comfort me.

PSAL. LXXXVII

1 AMONG the holy Mountains *high*
    Is his foundation fast,
There Seated in his Sanctuary,
    His Temple there is plac't.
2 Sions *fair* Gates the Lord loves more
    Then all the dwellings *faire*
Of Jacobs *Land, though there be store,*
    And all within his care.
3 City of God, most glorious things
    Of thee *abroad* are spoke;
4 I mention Egypt, *where proud Kings*
    Did our forefathers yoke,
I mention Babel to my friends,
    Philistia *full of scorn,*
And Tyre with Ethiops *utmost ends,*
    Lo this man there was born:
5 But *twise that praise shall in our ear*
    Be said of Sion *last*
This and this man was born in her,
    High God shall fix her fast.
6 The Lord shall write it in a Scrowle
    That ne're shall be out-worn
When he the Nations doth enrowle
    That this man there was born.
7 Both they who sing, and they who dance
    With sacred Songs are there,
In thee *fresh brooks, and soft streams glance*
    And all my fountains *clear.*

PSAL. LXXXVIII

1 LORD God that dost me save and keep,
    All day to thee I cry;
And all night long, before thee *weep*
    Before thee *prostrate lie.*
2 Into thy presence let my praier
    With sighs devout ascend
And to my cries, that *ceaseless are,*
    Thine ear with favour bend.
3 For cloy'd with woes and trouble store
    Surcharg'd my Soul doth lie,
My life *at death's uncherful dore*
    Unto the grave draws nigh.

4 Reck'n'd I am with them that pass
　　Down to the *dismal* pit
I am a [1] man, but weak alas
　　And for that name unfit.
5 From life discharg'd and parted quite
　　Among the dead *to sleep*,
And like the slain *in bloody fight*
　　That in the grave lie *deep*.　　　　　　　　*20*
Whom thou rememberest no more,
　　Dost never more regard,
Them from thy hand deliver'd o're
　　Deaths hideous house hath barr'd.
6 Thou in the lowest pit *profound*
　　Hast set me *all forlorn*,
Where thickest darkness *hovers round*,
　　In horrid deeps *to mourn*.
7 Thy wrath *from which no shelter saves*
　　Full sore doth press on me;　　　　　　　　*30*
[2] Thou break'st upon me all thy waves,
　　[2] And all thy waves break me.
8 Thou dost my friends from me estrange,
　　And mak'st me odious,
Me to them odious, *for they change*,
　　And I here pent up thus.
9 Through sorrow, and affliction great
　　Mine eye grows dim and dead,
Lord all the day I thee entreat,
　　My hands to thee I spread.　　　　　　　　*40*
10 Wilt thou do wonders on the dead,
　　Shall the deceas'd arise
And praise thee *from their loathsom bed*
　　With pale and hollow eyes?
11 Shall they thy loving kindness tell
　　On whom the grave *hath hold*,
Or they *who* in perdition *dwell*
　　Thy faithfulness *unfold?*
12 In darkness can thy mighty *hand*
　　Or wondrous acts be known,　　　　　　　*50*
Thy justice in the *gloomy* land
　　Of *dark* oblivion?
13 But I to thee O Lord do cry
　　E're yet my life be spent,
And *up to thee* my praier *doth hie*
　　Each morn, and thee prevent.
14 Why wilt thou Lord my soul forsake,

[1] Heb. *A man without manly strength*.　　[2] *The* Heb. *bears both.*

      And hide thy face from me,
15 That am already bruis'd, and [1] shake
      With terror sent from thee;   60
  Bruz'd, and afflicted and *so low*
      As ready to expire,
  While I thy terrors undergo
      Astonish'd with thine ire.
16 Thy fierce wrath over me doth flow
      Thy threatnings cut me through.
17 All day they round about me go,
      Like waves they me persue.
18 Lover and friend thou hast remov'd
      And sever'd from me far.   70
  They *fly me now* whom I have lov'd,
      And as in darkness are.

[1] Heb. *Prae Concussione.*

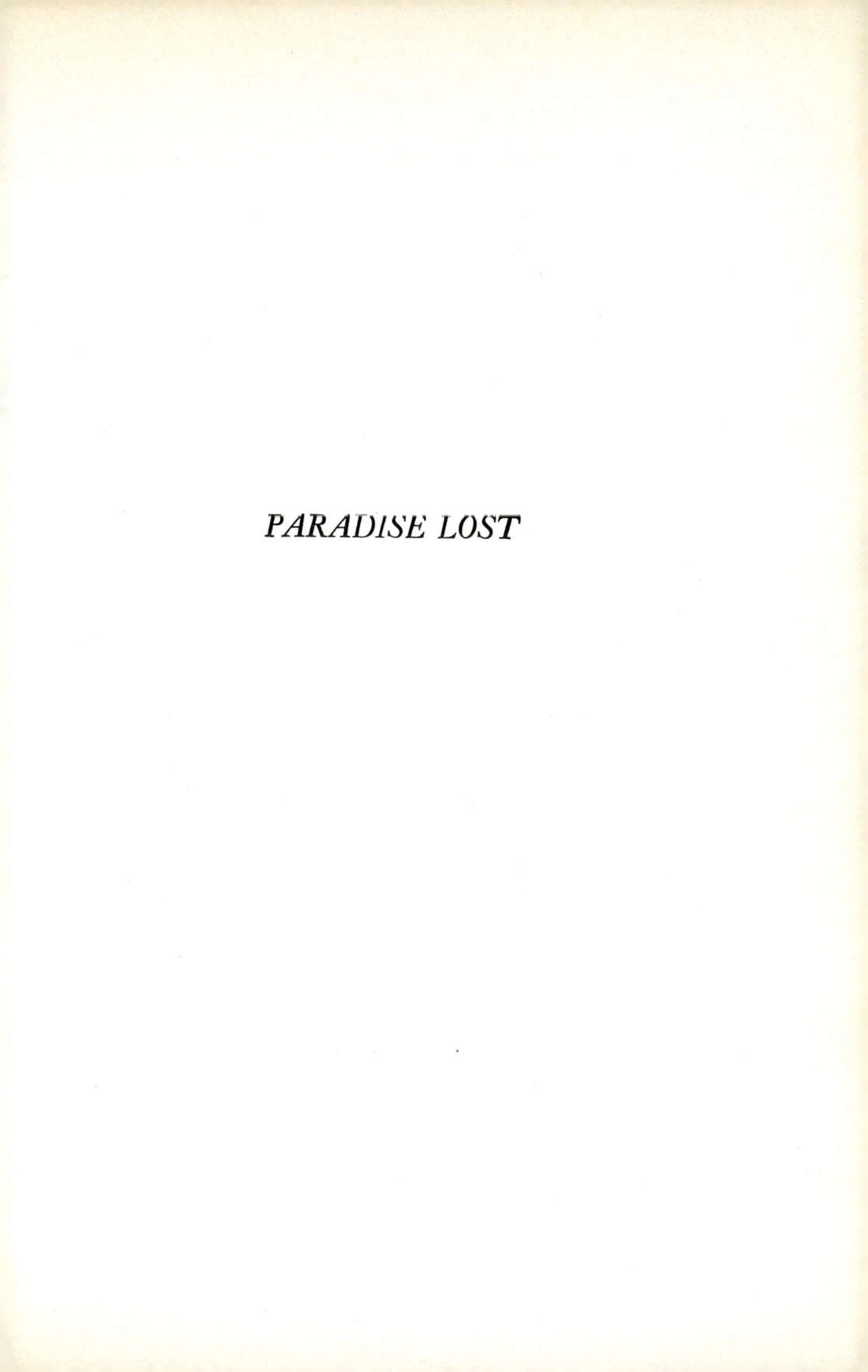

PARADISE LOST

PARADISE LOST

BOOK I

THE ARGUMENT

THIS first Book proposes first in brief the whole Subject, *Mans disobedience, and the loss thereupon of Paradise wherein he was plac't:* Then touches *the prime cause of his fall, the Serpent, or rather* Satan *in the Serpent; who revolting from God, and drawing to his side many Legions of Angels, was by the command of God driven out of Heaven with all his Crew into the great Deep.* Which action past over, the Poem hasts into the midst of things, presenting *Satan with his Angels now fallen into Hell,* describ'd here, *not in the Center* (for Heaven and Earth may be suppos'd as yet not made, certainly not yet accurst) *but in a place of utter darknesse, fitliest call'd* Chaos: Here Satan *with his Angels lying on the burning Lake, thunder-struck and astonisht, after a certain space recovers, as from confusion, calls up him who next in Order and Dignity lay by him; they confer of thir miserable fall.* Satan *awakens all his Legions, who lay till then in the same manner confounded; They rise, thir Numbers, array of Battel, thir chief Leaders nam'd, according to the Idols known afterwards in* Canaan *and the Countries adjoyning.* To these Satan *directs his Speech, comforts them with hope yet of regaining Heaven, but tells them lastly of a new World and new kind of Creature to be created, according to an ancient Prophesie or report in Heaven; for that Angels were long before this visible Creation, was the opinion of many ancient Fathers. To find out the truth of this Prophesie, and what to determin thereon he refers to a full Councell. What his Associates thence attempt.* Pandemonium *the Palace of* Satan *rises, suddenly built out of the Deep: The infernal Peers there sit in Counsel.*

    OF MANS First Disobedience, and the Fruit
Of that Forbidden Tree, whose mortal tast
Brought Death into the World, and all our woe,
With loss of *Eden*, till one greater Man
Restore us, and regain the blissful Seat,
Sing Heav'nly Muse, that on the secret top
Of *Oreb*, or of *Sinai*, didst inspire
That Shepherd, who first taught the chosen Seed,
In the Beginning how the Heav'ns and Earth
Rose out of *Chaos:* or if *Sion* Hill   10
Delight thee more, and *Siloa's* Brook that flow'd
Fast by the Oracle of God; I thence
Invoke thy aid to my adventrous Song,
That with no middle flight intends to soar
Above th' *Aonian* Mount, while it pursues
Things unattempted yet in Prose or Rhime.
And chiefly Thou O Spirit, that dost prefer

Before all Temples th' upright heart and pure,
Instruct me, for Thou know'st; Thou from the first
Wast present, and with mighty wings outspread   20
Dove-like satst brooding on the vast Abyss
And mad'st it pregnant: What in me is dark
Illumine, what is low raise and support;
That to the highth of this great Argument
I may assert Eternal Providence,
And justifie the wayes of God to men.
   Say first, for Heav'n hides nothing from thy view
Nor the deep Tract of Hell, say first what cause
Mov'd our Grand Parents in that happy State,
Favour'd of Heav'n so highly, to fall off   30
From their Creator, and transgress his Will
For one restraint, Lords of the World besides?
Who first seduc'd them to that fowl revolt?
Th' infernal Serpent; he it was, whose guile
Stird up with Envy and Revenge, deceiv'd
The Mother of Mankinde, what time his Pride
Had cast him out from Heav'n, with all his Host
Of Rebel Angels, by whose aid aspiring
To set himself in Glory above his Peers,
He trusted to have equal'd the most High,   40
If he oppos'd; and with ambitious aim
Against the Throne and Monarchy of God
Rais'd impious War in Heav'n and Battel proud
With vain attempt. Him the Almighty Power
Hurld headlong flaming from th' Ethereal Skie
With hideous ruine and combustion down
To bottomless perdition, there to dwell
In Adamantine Chains and penal Fire,
Who durst defie th' Omnipotent to Arms.
Nine times the Space that measures Day and Night   50
To mortal men, he with his horrid crew
Lay vanquisht, rowling in the fiery Gulfe
Confounded though immortal: But his doom
Reserv'd him to more wrath; for now the thought
Both of lost happiness and lasting pain
Torments him; round he throws his baleful eyes
That witness'd huge affliction and dismay
Mixt with obdurate pride and stedfast hate:
At once as far as Angels kenn he views
The dismal Situation waste and wilde,   60
A Dungeon horrible, on all sides round
As one great Furnace flam'd, yet from those flames
No light, but rather darkness visible

Serv'd only to discover sights of woe,
Regions of sorrow, doleful shades, where peace
And rest can never dwell, hope never comes
That comes to all; but torture without end
Still urges, and a fiery Deluge, fed
With ever-burning Sulphur unconsum'd:
Such place Eternal Justice had prepar'd   70
For those rebellious, here their Prison ordain'd
In utter darkness, and their portion set
As far remov'd from God and light of Heav'n
As from the Center thrice to th' utmost Pole.
O how unlike the place from whence they fell!
There the companions of his fall, o'rewhelm'd
With Floods and Whirlwinds of tempestuous fire,
He soon discerns, and weltring by his side
One next himself in power, and next in crime,
Long after known in *Palestine*, and nam'd   80
Beëlzebub. To whom th' Arch-Enemy,
And thence in Heav'n call'd Satan, with bold words
Breaking the horrid silence thus began.

   If thou beest he; But O how fall'n! how chang'd
From him, who in the happy Realms of Light
Cloth'd with transcendent brightness didst outshine
Myriads though bright: If he whom mutual league,
United thoughts and counsels, equal hope,
And hazard in the Glorious Enterprize,
Joynd with me once, now misery hath joynd   90
In equal ruin: into what Pit thou seest
From what highth fal'n, so much the stronger provd
He with his Thunder: and till then who knew
The force of those dire Arms? yet not for those
Nor what the Potent Victor in his rage
Can else inflict do I repent or change,
Though chang'd in outward lustre; that fixt mind
And high disdain, from sence of injur'd merit,
That with the mightiest rais'd me to contend,
And to the fierce contention brought along   100
Innumerable force of Spirits arm'd
That durst dislike his reign, and me preferring,
His utmost power with adverse power oppos'd
In dubious Battel on the Plains of Heav'n,
And shook his throne. What though the field be lost?
All is not lost; the unconquerable Will,
And study of revenge, immortal hate,
And courage never to submit or yield:
And what is else not to be overcome?

That Glory never shall his wrath or might 110
Extort from me. To bow and sue for grace
With suppliant knee, and deifie his power
Who from the terrour of this Arm so late
Doubted his Empire, that were low indeed,
That were an ignominy and shame beneath
This downfall; since by Fate the strength of Gods
And this Empyreal substance cannot fail,
Since through experience of this great event
In Arms not worse, in foresight much advanc't,
We may with more successful hope resolve 120
To wage by force or guile eternal Warr
Irreconcileable, to our grand Foe,
Who now triumphs, and in th' excess of joy
Sole reigning holds the Tyranny of Heav'n.
   So spake th' Apostate Angel, though in pain,
Vaunting aloud, but rackt with deep despare:
And him thus answer'd soon his bold Compeer.
   O Prince, O Chief of many Throned Powers,
That led th' imbattelld Seraphim to Warr
Under thy conduct, and in dreadful deeds 130
Fearless, endanger'd Heav'ns perpetual King;
And put to proof his high Supremacy,
Whether upheld by strength, or Chance, or Fate,
Too well I see and rue the dire event,
That with sad overthrow and foul defeat
Hath lost us Heav'n, and all this mighty Host
In horrible destruction laid thus low,
As far as Gods and Heav'nly Essences
Can perish: for the mind and spirit remains
Invincible, and vigour soon returns, 140
Though all our Glory extinct, and happy state
Here swallow'd up in endless misery.
But what if he our Conquerour, (whom I now
Of force believe Almighty, since no less
Then such could hav orepow'rd such force as ours)
Have left us this our spirit and strength intire
Strongly to suffer and support our pains,
That we may so suffice his vengeful ire,
Or do him mightier service as his thralls
By right of Warr, what e're his business be 150
Here in the heart of Hell to work in Fire,
Or do his Errands in the gloomy Deep;
What can it then avail though yet we feel
Strength undiminisht, or eternal being
To undergo eternal punishment?

Whereto with speedy words th' Arch-fiend reply'd.
    Fall'n Cherube, to be weak is miserable
Doing or Suffering: but of this be sure,
To do ought good never will be our task,
But ever to do ill our sole delight,   *160*
As being the contrary to his high will
Whom we resist. If then his Providence
Out of our evil seek to bring forth good,
Our labour must be to pervert that end,
And out of good still to find means of evil;
Which oft times may succeed, so as perhaps
Shall grieve him, if I fail not, and disturb
His inmost counsels from their destind aim.
But see the angry Victor hath recall'd
His Ministers of vengeance and pursuit   *170*
Back to the Gates of Heav'n: The Sulphurous Hail
Shot after us in storm, oreblown hath laid
The fiery Surge, that from the Precipice
Of Heav'n receiv'd us falling, and the Thunder,
Wing'd with red Lightning and impetuous rage,
Perhaps hath spent his shafts, and ceases now
To bellow through the vast and boundless Deep.
Let us not slip th' occasion, whether scorn,
Or satiate fury yield it from our Foe.
Seest thou yon dreary Plain, forlorn and wilde,   *180*
The seat of desolation, voyd of light,
Save what the glimmering of these livid flames
Casts pale and dreadful? Thither let us tend
From off the tossing of these fiery waves,
There rest, if any rest can harbour there,
And reassembling our afflicted Powers,
Consult how we may henceforth most offend
Our Enemy, our own loss how repair,
How overcome this dire Calamity,
What reinforcement we may gain from Hope,   *190*
If not what resolution from despare.
    Thus Satan talking to his neerest Mate
With Head up-lift above the wave, and Eyes
That sparkling blaz'd, his other Parts besides
Prone on the Flood, extended long and large
Lay floating many a rood, in bulk as huge
As whom the Fables name of monstrous size,
Titanian, or *Earth-born*, that warr'd on *Jove*,
Briarios or *Typhon*, whom the Den
By ancient *Tarsus* held, or that Sea-beast   *200*
Leviathan, which God of all his works

Created hugest that swim th' Ocean stream:
Him haply slumbring on the *Norway* foam
The Pilot of some small night-founder'd Skiff,
Deeming some Island, oft, as Sea-men tell,
With fixed Anchor in his skaly rind
Moors by his side under the Lee, while Night
Invests the Sea, and wished Morn delayes:
So stretcht out huge in length the Arch-fiend lay
Chain'd on the burning Lake, nor ever thence   *210*
Had ris'n or heav'd his head, but that the will
And high permission of all-ruling Heaven
Left him at large to his own dark designs,
That with reiterated crimes he might
Heap on himself damnation, while he sought
Evil to others, and enrag'd might see
How all his malice serv'd but to bring forth
Infinite goodness, grace and mercy shewn
On Man by him seduc't, but on himself
Treble confusion, wrath and vengeance pour'd.   *220*
Forthwith upright he rears from off the Pool
His mighty Stature; on each hand the flames
Drivn backward slope their pointing spires, & rowld
In billows, leave i' th' midst a horrid Vale.
Then with expanded wings he stears his flight
Aloft, incumbent on the dusky Air
That felt unusual weight, till on dry Land
He lights, if it were Land that ever burn'd
With solid, as the Lake with liquid fire;
And such appear'd in hue, as when the force   *230*
Of subterranean wind transports a Hill
Torn from *Pelorus*, or the shatter'd side
Of thundring *Ætna*, whose combustible
And fewel'd entrals thence conceiving Fire,
Sublim'd with Mineral fury, aid the Winds,
And leave a singed bottom all involv'd
With stench and smoak: Such resting found the sole
Of unblest feet. Him followed his next Mate,
Both glorying to have scap't the *Stygian* flood
As Gods, and by their own recover'd strength,   *240*
Not by the sufferance of supernal Power.
   Is this the Region, this the Soil, the Clime,
Said then the lost Arch Angel, this the seat
That we must change for Heav'n, this mournful gloom
For that celestial light? Be it so, since hee
Who now is Sovran can dispose and bid
What shall be right: fardest from him is best

Whom reason hath equald, force hath made supream
Above his equals. Farewel happy Fields
Where Joy for ever dwells: Hail horrours, hail   250
Infernal world, and thou profoundest Hell
Receive thy new Possessor: One who brings
A mind not to be chang'd by Place or Time.
The mind is its own place, and in it self
Can make a Heav'n of Hell, a Hell of Heav'n.
What matter where, if I be still the same,
And what I should be, all but less than hee
Whom Thunder hath made greater? Here at least
We shall be free; th' Almighty hath not built
Here for his envy, will not drive us hence: 260
Here we may reign secure, and in my choyce
To reign is worth ambition though in Hell:
Better to reign in Hell, then serve in Heav'n.
But wherefore let we then our faithful friends,
Th' associates and copartners of our loss
Lye thus astonisht on th' oblivious Pool,
And call them not to share with us their part
In this unhappy Mansion, or once more
With rallied Arms to try what may be yet
Regained in Heav'n, or what more lost in Hell?   270
   So *Satan* spake, and him *Bëelzebub*
Thus answer'd. Leader of those Armies bright,
Which but th' Omnipotent none could have foyld,
If once they hear that voyce, their liveliest pledge
Of hope in fears and dangers, heard so oft
In worst extreams, and on the perilous edge
Of battel when it rag'd, in all assaults
Their surest signal, they will soon resume
New courage and revive, though now they lye
Groveling and prostrate on yon Lake of Fire,   280
As we erewhile, astounded and amaz'd,
No wonder, fall'n such a pernicious highth.
   He scarce had ceas't when the superiour Fiend
Was moving toward the shore; his ponderous shield
Ethereal temper, massy, large and round,
Behind him cast, the broad circumference
Hung on his shoulders like the Moon, whose Orb
Through Optic Glass the *Tuscan* Artist views
At Ev'ning from the top of *Fesole*,
Or in *Valdarno*, to descry new Lands,   290
Rivers or Mountains in her spotty Globe.
His Spear, to equal which the tallest Pine
Hewn on *Norwegian* hills, to be the Mast

Of some great Ammiral, were but a wand,
He walkt with to support uneasie steps
Over the burning Marle, not like those steps
On Heavens Azure, and the torrid Clime
Smote on him sore besides, vaulted with Fire;
Nathless he so endur'd, till on the Beach
Of that inflamed Sea, he stood and call'd 300
His Legions, Angel Forms, who lay intrans't
Thick as Autumnal Leaves that strow the Brooks
In *Vallombrosa*, where th' *Etrurian* shades
High overarch't imbowr; or scatterd sedge
Afloat, when with fierce Winds *Orion* arm'd
Hath vext the Red-Sea Coast, whose waves orethrew
Busiris and his *Memphian* Chivalrie,
While with perfidious hatred they pursu'd
The Sojourners of *Goshen*, who beheld
From the safe shore their floating Carkases 310
And broken Chariot Wheels, so thick bestrown
Abject and lost lay these, covering the Flood,
Under amazement of their hideous change.
He call'd so loud, that all the hollow Deep
Of Hell resounded. Princes, Potentates,
Warriers, the Flowr of Heav'n, once yours, now lost,
If such astonishment as this can sieze
Eternal spirits; or have ye chos'n this place
After the toyl of Battel to repose
Your wearied vertue, for the ease you find 320
To slumber here, as in the Vales of Heav'n?
Or in this abject posture have ye sworn
To adore the Conquerour? who now beholds
Cherube and Seraph rowling in the Flood
With scatter'd Arms and Ensigns, till anon
His swift pursuers from Heav'n Gates discern
Th' advantage, and descending tread us down
Thus drooping, or with linked Thunderbolts
Transfix us to the bottom of this Gulfe.
Awake, arise, or be for ever fall'n. 330
   They heard, and were abasht, and up they sprung
Upon the wing, as when men wont to watch
On duty, sleeping found by whom they dread,
Rouse and bestir themselves ere well awake.
Nor did they not perceave the evil plight
In which they were, or the fierce pains not feel;
Yet to their Generals Voyce they soon obeyd
Innumerable. As when the potent Rod
Of *Amrams* Son in *Egypts* evill day

Wav'd round the Coast, up call'd a pitchy cloud   *340*
Of *Locusts*, warping on the Eastern Wind,
That ore the Realm of impious *Pharaoh* hung
Like Night, and darken'd all the Land of *Nile:*
So numberless were those bad Angels seen
Hovering on wing under the Cope of Hell
'Twixt upper, nether, and surrounding Fires;
Till, as a signal giv'n, th' uplifted Spear
Of their great Sultan waving to direct
Thir course, in even ballance down they light
On the firm brimstone, and fill all the Plain;   *350*
A multitude, like which the populous North
Pour'd never from her frozen loyns, to pass
Rhene or the *Danaw*, when her barbarous Sons
Came like a Deluge on the South, and spread
Beneath *Gibraltar* to the *Lybian* sands.
Forthwith from every Squadron and each Band
The Heads and Leaders thither hast where stood
Their great Commander; Godlike shapes and forms
Excelling human, Princely Dignities,
And Powers that earst in Heaven sat on Thrones;   *360*
Though of their Names in heav'nly Records now
Be no memorial, blotted out and ras'd
By thir Rebellion, from the Books of Life.
Nor had they yet among the Sons of *Eve*
Got them new Names, till wandring ore the Earth,
Through Gods high sufferance for the tryal of man,
By falsities and lyes the greatest part
Of Mankind they corrupted to forsake
God their Creator, and th' invisible
Glory of him, that made them, to transform   *370*
Oft to the Image of a Brute, adorn'd
With gay Religions full of Pomp and Gold,
And Devils to adore for Deities:
Then were they known to men by various Names,
And various Idols through the Heathen World.
Say, Muse, their Names then known, who first, who last,
Rous'd from the slumber, on that fiery Couch,
At thir great Emperors call, as next in worth
Came singly where he stood on the bare strand,
While the promiscuous croud stood yet aloof?   *380*
The chief were those who from the Pit of Hell
Roaming to seek their prey on earth, durst fix
Their Seats long after next the Seat of God,
Their Altars by his Altar, Gods ador'd
Among the Nations round, and durst abide

Jehovah thundring out of *Sion*, thron'd
Between the Cherubim; yea, often plac'd
Within his Sanctuary it self their Shrines,
Abominations; and with cursed things
His holy Rites, and solemn Feasts profan'd,   *390*
And with their darkness durst affront his light.
First *Moloch*, horrid King besmear'd with blood
Of human sacrifice, and parents tears,
Though for the noyse of Drums and Timbrels loud
Their childrens cries unheard, that past through fire
To his grim Idol. Him the *Ammonite*
Worshipt in *Rabba* and her watry Plain,
In *Argob* and in *Basan*, to the stream
Of utmost *Arnon*. Nor content with such
Audacious neighbourhood, the wisest heart   *400*
Of *Solomon* he led by fraud to build
His Temple right against the Temple of God
On that opprobrious Hill, and made his Grove
The pleasant Vally of *Hinnom*, *Tophet* thence
And black *Gehenna* call'd, the Type of Hell.
Next *Chemos*, th' obscene dread of *Moabs* Sons,
From *Aroer* to *Nebo*, and the wild
Of Southmost *Abarim*; in *Hesebon*
And *Horonaim*, *Seons* Realm, beyond
The flowry Dale of *Sibma* clad with Vines,   *410*
And *Eleale* to th' *Asphaltick* Pool.
Peor his other Name, when he entic'd
Israel in *Sittim* on their march from *Nile*
To do him wanton rites, which cost them woe.
Yet thence his lustful Orgies he enlarg'd
Even to that Hill of scandal, by the Grove
Of *Moloch* homicide, lust hard by hate;
Till good *Josiah* drove them thence to Hell.
With these came they, who from the bordring flood
Of old *Euphrates* to the Brook that parts   *420*
Egypt from *Syrian* ground, had general Names
Of *Baalim* and *Ashtaroth*, those male,
These Feminine. For Spirits when they please
Can either Sex assume, or both; so soft
And uncompounded is their Essence pure,
Not ti'd or manacl'd with joynt or limb,
Nor founded on the brittle strength of bones,
Like cumbrous flesh; but in what shape they choose
Dilated or condens't, bright or obscure,
Can execute their aerie purposes,   *430*
And works of love or enmity fulfill.

For those the Race of *Israel* oft forsook
Their living strength, and unfrequented left
His righteous Altar, bowing lowly down
To bestial Gods; for which their heads as low
Bow'd down in Battel, sunk before the Spear
Of despicable foes. With these in troop
Came *Astoreth*, whom the *Phœnicians* call'd
Astarte, Queen of Heav'n, with crescent Horns;
To whose bright Image nightly by the Moon   *440*
Sidonian Virgins paid their Vows and Songs,
In *Sion* also not unsung, where stood
Her Temple on th' offensive Mountain, built
By that uxorious King, whose heart though large,
Beguil'd by fair Idolatresses, fell
To Idols foul. *Thammuz* came next behind,
Whose annual wound in *Lebanon* allur'd
The *Syrian* Damsels to lament his fate
In amorous dittyes all a Summers day,
While smooth *Adonis* from his native Rock   *450*
Ran purple to the Sea, suppos'd with blood
Of *Thammuz* yearly wounded: the Love-tale
Infected *Sions* daughters with like heat,
Whose wanton passions in the sacred Porch
Ezekiel saw, when by the Vision led
His eye survay'd the dark Idolatries
Of alienated *Judah*. Next came one
Who mourn'd in earnest, when the Captive Ark
Maim'd his brute Image, head and hands lopt off
In his own Temple, on the grunsel edge,   *460*
Where he fell flat, and sham'd his Worshipers:
Dagon his Name, Sea Monster, upward Man
And downward Fish: yet had his Temple high
Rear'd in *Azotus*, dreaded through the Coast
Of *Palestine*, in *Gath* and *Ascalon*,
And *Accaron* and *Gaza's* frontier bounds.
Him follow'd *Rimmon*, whose delightful Seat
Was fair *Damascus*, on the fertil Banks
Of *Abbana* and *Pharphar*, lucid streams.
He also against the house of God was bold: *470*
A Leper once he lost and gain'd a King,
Ahaz his sottish Conquerour, whom he drew
Gods Altar to disparage and displace
For one of *Syrian* mode, whereon to burn
His odious offrings, and adore the Gods
Whom he had vanquisht. After these appear'd
A crew who under Names of old Renown,

Osiris, *Isis*, *Orus* and their Train
With monstrous shapes and sorceries abus'd
Fanatic *Egypt* and her Priests, to seek 480
Thir wandring Gods disguis'd in brutish forms
Rather then human. Nor did *Israel* scape
Th' infection when their borrow'd Gold compos'd
The Calf in *Oreb:* and the Rebel King
Doubl'd that sin in *Bethel* and in *Dan*,
Lik'ning his Maker to the Grazed Ox,
Jehovah, who in one Night when he pass'd
From *Egypt* marching, equal'd with one stroke
Both her first born and all her bleating Gods.
Belial came last, then whom a Spirit more lewd 490
Fell not from Heaven, or more gross to love
Vice for it self: To him no Temple stood
Or Altar smoak'd; yet who more oft then hee
In Temples and at Altars, when the Priest
Turns Atheist, as did *Elys* Sons, who fill'd
With lust and violence the house of God.
In Courts and Palaces he also Reigns
And in luxurious Cities, where the noyse
Of riot ascends above thir loftiest Towrs,
And injury and outrage: And when Night 500
Darkens the Streets, then wander forth the Sons
Of *Belial*, flown with insolence and wine.
Witness the Streets of *Sodom*, and that night
In *Gibeah*, when hospitable Dores
Yielded thir Matrons to prevent worse rape.
These were the prime in order and in might;
The rest were long to tell, though far renown'd,
Th' *Ionian* Gods, of *Javans* Issue held
Gods, yet confest later then Heav'n and Earth
Thir boasted Parents; *Titan* Heav'ns first born 510
With his enormous brood, and birthright seis'd
By younger *Saturn*, he from mightier *Jove*
His own and *Rhea's* Son like measure found;
So *Jove* usurping reign'd: these first in *Creet*
And *Ida* known, thence on the Snowy top
Of cold *Olympus* rul'd the middle Air
Thir highest Heav'n; or on the *Delphian* Cliff,
Or in *Dodona*, and through all the bounds
Of *Doric* Land; or who with *Saturn* old
Fled over *Adria* to th' *Hesperian* Fields, 520
And ore the *Celtic* roam'd the utmost Isles.
All these and more came flocking; but with looks
Down cast and damp, yet such wherein appear'd

Obscure som glimps of joy, to have found thir chief
Not in despair, to have found themselves not lost
In loss it self; which on his count'nance cast
Like doubtful hue: but he his wonted pride
Soon recollecting, with high words, that bore
Semblance of worth not substance, gently rais'd
Their fainted courage, and dispel'd their fears.   *530*
Then strait commands that at the warlike sound
Of Trumpets loud and Clarions be upreard
His mighty Standard; that proud honour claim'd
Azazel as his right, a Cherube tall:
Who forthwith from the glittering Staff unfurld
Th' Imperial Ensign, which full high advanc't
Shon like a Meteor streaming to the Wind
With Gemms and Golden lustre rich imblaz'd,
Seraphic arms and Trophies: all the while
Sonorous mettal blowing Martial sounds: *540*
At which the universal Host upsent
A shout that tore Hells Concave, and beyond
Frighted the Reign of *Chaos* and old Night.
All in a moment through the gloom were seen
Ten thousand Banners rise into the Air
With Orient Colours waving: with them rose
A Forrest huge of Spears: and thronging Helms
Appear'd, and serried Shields in thick array
Of depth immeasurable: Anon they move
In perfect *Phalanx* to the *Dorian* mood   *550*
Of Flutes and soft Recorders; such as rais'd
To highth of noblest temper Hero's old
Arming to Battel, and in stead of rage
Deliberate valour breath'd, firm and unmov'd
With dread of death to flight or foul retreat,
Nor wanting power to mitigate and swage
With solemn touches, troubl'd thoughts, and chase
Anguish and doubt and fear and sorrow and pain
From mortal or immortal minds. Thus they
Breathing united force with fixed thought   *560*
Mov'd on in silence to soft Pipes that charm'd
Thir painful steps o're the burnt soyle; and now
Advanc't in view they stand, a horrid Front
Of dreadful length and dazling Arms, in guise
Of Warriers old with order'd Spear and Shield,
Awaiting what command thir mighty Chief
Had to impose: He through the armed Files
Darts his experienc't eye, and soon traverse
The whole Battalion views, thir order due,

Thir visages and stature as of Gods, 570
Thir number last he summs. And now his heart
Distends with pride, and hardning in his strength
Glories: For never since created man,
Met such imbodied force, as nam'd with these
Could merit more then that small infantry
Warr'd on by Cranes: though all the Giant brood
Of *Phlegra* with th' Heroic Race were joyn'd
That fought at *Theb's* and *Ilium*, on each side
Mixt with auxiliar Gods; and what resounds
In Fable or *Romance* of *Uthers* Son 580
Begirt with *British* and *Armoric* Knights;
And all who since, Baptiz'd or Infidel
Jousted in *Aspramont* or *Montalban*,
Damasco, or *Marocco*, or *Trebisond*,
Or whom *Biserta* sent from *Afric* shore
When *Charlemain* with all his Peerage fell
By *Fontarabbia*. Thus far these beyond
Compare of mortal prowess, yet observ'd
Thir dread Commander: he above the rest
In shape and gesture proudly eminent 590
Stood like a Towr; his form had yet not lost
All her Original brightness, nor appear'd
Less then Arch Angel ruind, and th' excess
Of Glory obscur'd: As when the Sun new ris'n
Looks through the Horizontal misty Air
Shorn of his Beams, or from behind the Moon
In dim Eclips disastrous twilight sheds
On half the Nations, and with fear of change
Perplexes Monarchs. Dark'n'd so, yet shon
Above them all th' Arch Angel: but his face 600
Deep scars of Thunder had intrencht, and care
Sat on his faded cheek, but under Browes
Of dauntless courage, and considerate Pride
Waiting revenge: cruel his eye, but cast
Signs of remorse and passion to behold
The fellows of his crime, the followers rather
(Far other once beheld in bliss) condemn'd
For ever now to have their lot in pain,
Millions of Spirits for his fault amerc't
Of Heav'n, and from Eternal Splendors flung 610
For his revolt, yet faithfull how they stood,
Thir Glory witherd. As when Heavens Fire
Hath scath'd the Forrest Oaks, or Mountain Pines,
With singed top their stately growth though bare
Stands on the blasted Heath. He now prepar'd

To speak; whereat their doubl'd Ranks they bend
From Wing to Wing, and half enclose him round
With all his Peers: attention held them mute.
Thrice he assay'd, and thrice in spite of scorn,
Tears such as Angels weep, burst forth: at last   *620*
Words interwove with sighs found out their way.
   O Myriads of immortal Spirits, O Powers
Matchless, but with th' Almighty, and that strife
Was not inglorious, though th' event was dire,
As this place testifies, and this dire change
Hateful to utter: but what power of mind
Foreseeing or presaging, from the Depth
Of knowledge past or present, could have fear'd,
How such united force of Gods, how such
As stood like these, could ever know repulse?   *630*
For who can yet beleeve, though after loss,
That all these puissant Legions, whose exile
Hath emptied Heav'n, shall faile to re-ascend
Self-rais'd, and repossess their native seat?
For me, be witness all the Host of Heav'n,
If counsels different, or danger shun'd
By me, have lost our hopes. But he who reigns
Monarch in Heav'n, till then as one secure
Sat on his Throne, upheld by old repute,
Consent or custome, and his Regal State   *640*
Put forth at full, but still his strength conceal'd,
Which tempted our attempt, and wrought our fall.
Henceforth his might we know, and know our own
So as not either to provoke, or dread
New warr, provok't; our better part remains
To work in close design, by fraud or guile
What force effected not: that he no less
At length from us may find, who overcomes
By force, hath overcome but half his foe.
Space may produce new Worlds; whereof so rife   *650*
There went a fame in Heav'n that he ere long
Intended to create, and therein plant
A generation, whom his choice regard
Should favour equal to the Sons of Heaven:
Thither, if but to prie, shall be perhaps
Our first eruption, thither or elsewhere:
For this Infernal Pit shall never hold
Cælestial Spirits in Bondage, nor th' Abysse
Long under darkness cover. But these thoughts
Full Counsel must mature: Peace is despaird,   *660*
For who can think Submission! Warr then, Warr

Open or understood must be resolv'd.
  He spake: and to confirm his words, out-flew
Millions of flaming swords, drawn from the thighs
Of mighty Cherubim; the sudden blaze
Far round illumin'd hell: highly they rag'd
Against the Highest, and fierce with grasped arm's
Clash'd on their sounding shields the din of war,
Hurling defiance toward the vault of Heav'n.
  There stood a Hill not far whose griesly top   *670*
Belch'd fire and rowling smoak; the rest entire
Shon with a glossie scurff, undoubted sign
That in his womb was hid metallic Ore,
The work of Sulphur. Thither wing'd with speed
A numerous Brigad hasten'd. As when bands
Of Pioners with Spade and Pickaxe arm'd
Forerun the Royal Camp, to trench a Field,
Or cast a Rampart. *Mammon* led them on,
Mammon, the least erected Spirit that fell
From heav'n, for ev'n in heav'n his looks and thoughts *680*
Were always downward bent, admiring more
The riches of Heav'ns pavement, trod'n Gold,
Then aught divine or holy else enjoy'd
In vision beatific: by him first
Men also, and by his suggestion taught,
Ransack'd the Center, and with impious hands
Rifl'd the bowels of their mother Earth
For Treasures better hid. Soon had his crew
Op'nd into the Hill a spacious wound
And dig'd out ribs of Gold. Let none admire   *690*
That riches grow in Hell; that soyle may best
Deserve the pretious bane. And here let those
Who boast in mortal things, and wondring tell
Of *Babel*, and the works of *Memphian* Kings,
Learn how thir greatest Monuments of Fame,
And Strength and Art are easily outdone
By Spirits reprobate, and in an hour
What in an age they with incessant toyle
And hands innumerable scarce perform.
Nigh on the Plain in many cells prepar'd,   *700*
That underneath had veins of liquid fire
Sluc'd from the Lake, a second multitude
With wondrous Art founded the massie Ore,
Severing each kinde, and scum'd the Bullion dross:
A third as soon had form'd within the ground
A various mould, and from the boyling cells
By strange conveyance fill'd each hollow nook,

As in an Organ from one blast of wind
To many a row of Pipes the sound-board breaths.
Anon out of the earth a Fabrick huge 710
Rose like an Exhalation, with the sound
Of Dulcet Symphonies and voices sweet,
Built like a Temple, where *Pilasters* round
Were set, and Doric pillars overlaid
With Golden Architrave; nor did there want
Cornice or Freeze, with bossy Sculptures grav'n,
The Roof was fretted Gold. Not *Babilon*,
Nor great *Alcairo* such magnificence
Equal'd in all thir glories, to inshrine
Belus or *Serapis* thir Gods, or seat 720
Thir Kings, when *Ægypt* with *Assyria* strove
In wealth and luxurie. Th' ascending pile
Stood fixt her stately highth, and strait the dores
Op'ning thir brazen foulds discover wide
Within, her ample spaces, o're the smooth
And level pavement: from the arched roof
Pendant by suttle Magic many a row
Of Starry Lamps and blazing Cressets fed
With *Naphtha* and *Asphaltus* yeilded light
As from a sky. The hasty multitude 730
Admiring enter'd, and the work some praise
And some the Architect: his hand was known
In Heav'n by many a Towred structure high,
Where Scepter'd Angels held thir residence,
And sat as Princes, whom the supreme King
Exalted to such power, and gave to rule,
Each in his Herarchie, the Orders bright.
Nor was his name unheard or unador'd
In ancient *Greece;* and in *Ausonian* land
Men called him *Mulciber;* and how he fell 740
From Heav'n, they fabl'd, thrown by angry *Jove*
Sheer o're the Chrystal Battlements: from Morn
To Noon he fell, from Noon to dewy Eve,
A Summers day; and with the setting Sun
Dropt from the Zenith like a falling Star,
On *Lemnos* th' *Ægæan* Ile: thus they relate,
Erring; for he with this rebellious rout
Fell long before; nor aught avail'd him now
To have built in Heav'n high Towrs; nor did he scape
By all his Engins, but was headlong sent 750
With his industrious crew to build in hell.
Mean while the winged Haralds by command
Of Sovran power, with awful Ceremony

And Trumpets sound throughout the Host proclaim
A solemn Councel forthwith to be held
At *Pandæmonium*, the high Capital
Of Satan and his Peers: thir summons call'd
From every Band and squared Regiment
By place or choice the worthiest; they anon
With hunderds and with thousands trooping came   760
Attended: all access was throng'd, the Gates
And Porches wide, but chief the spacious Hall
(Though like a cover'd field, where Champions bold
Wont ride in arm'd, and at the Soldans chair
Defi'd the best of *Panim* chivalry
To mortal combat or carreer with Lance)
Thick swarm'd, both on the ground and in the air,
Brusht with the hiss of russling wings. As Bees
In spring time, when the Sun with *Taurus* rides,
Poure forth thir populous youth about the Hive   770
In clusters; they among fresh dews and flowers
Flie to and fro, or on the smoothed Plank,
The suburb of thir Straw-built Cittadel,
New rub'd with Baume, expatiate and confer
Thir State affairs. So thick the aerie crowd
Swarm'd and were straitn'd; till the Signal giv'n,
Behold a wonder! they but now who seemd
In bigness to surpass Earths Giant Sons
Now less then smallest Dwarfs, in narrow room
Throng numberless, like that Pigmean Race   780
Beyond the *Indian* Mount, or Faerie Elves,
Whose midnight Revels, by a Forrest side
Or Fountain some belated Peasant sees,
Or dreams he sees, while over head the Moon
Sits Arbitress, and neerer to the Earth
Wheels her pale course, they on thir mirth & dance
Intent, with jocond Music charm his ear;
At once with joy and fear his heart rebounds.
Thus incorporeal Spirits to smallest forms
Reduc'd thir shapes immense, and were at large,   790
Though without number still amidst the Hall
Of that infernal Court. But far within
And in thir own dimensions like themselves
The great Seraphic Lords and Cherubim
In close recess and secret conclave sat
A thousand Demy-Gods on golden seat's,
Frequent and full. After short silence then
And summons read, the great consult began.

BOOK II

THE ARGUMENT

The Consultation begun, Satan *debates whether another Battel be to be hazarded for the recovery of Heaven: some advise it, others dissuade: A third proposal is prefer'd, mention'd before by* Satan, *to search the truth of that Prophesie or Tradition in Heaven concerning another world, and another kind of creature equal or not much inferiour to themselves, about this time to be created: Thir doubt who shall be sent on this difficult search:* Satan *thir chief undertakes alone the voyage, is honour'd and applauded. The Councel thus ended, the rest betake them several wayes and to several imployments, as thir inclinations lead them, to entertain the time till* Satan *return. He passes on his Journey to Hell Gates, finds them shut, and who sat there to guard them, by whom at length they are op'nd, and discover to him the great Gulf between Hell and Heaven; with what difficulty he passes through, directed by* Chaos, *the Power of that place, to the sight of this new World which he sought.*

HIGH on a Throne of Royal State, which far
Outshon the wealth of *Ormus* and of *Ind,*
Or where the gorgeous East with richest hand
Showrs on her Kings *Barbaric* Pearl & Gold,
Satan exalted sat, by merit rais'd
To that bad eminence; and from despair
Thus high uplifted beyond hope, aspires
Beyond thus high, insatiate to pursue
Vain Warr with Heav'n, and by success untaught
His proud imaginations thus displaid.   *10*
    Powers and Dominions, Deities of Heav'n,
For since no deep within her gulf can hold
Immortal vigor, though opprest and fall'n,
I give not Heav'n for lost. From this descent
Celestial vertues rising, will appear
More glorious and more dread then from no fall,
And trust themselves to fear no second fate:
Mee though just right, and the fixt Laws of Heav'n
Did first create your Leader, next, free choice,
With what besides, in Counsel or in Fight,   *20*
Hath bin achievd of merit, yet this loss
Thus farr at least recover'd, hath much more
Establisht in a safe unenvied Throne
Yielded with full consent. The happier state
In Heav'n, which follows dignity, might draw
Envy from each inferior; but who here
Will envy whom the highest place exposes
Formost to stand against the Thunderers aime

III

Your bulwark, and condemns to greatest share
Of endless pain? where there is then no good   *30*
For which to strive, no strife can grow up there
From Faction; for none sure will claim in hell
Precedence, none, whose portion is so small
Of present pain, that with ambitious mind
Will covet more. With this advantage then
To union, and firm Faith, and firm accord,
More then can be in Heav'n, we now return
To claim our just inheritance of old,
Surer to prosper then prosperity
Could have assur'd us; and by what best way,   *40*
Whether of open Warr or covert guile,
We now debate; who can advise, may speak.

    He ceas'd, and next him *Moloc*, Scepter'd King
Stood up, the strongest and the fiercest Spirit
That fought in Heav'n; now fiercer by despair:
His trust was with th' Eternal to be deem'd
Equal in strength, and rather then be less
Car'd not to be at all; with that care lost
Went all his fear: of God, or Hell, or worse
He reckd not, and these words thereafter spake.   *50*

    My sentence is for open Warr: Of Wiles,
More unexpert, I boast not: them let those
Contrive who need, or when they need, not now.
For while they sit contriving, shall the rest,
Millions that stand in Arms, and longing wait
The Signal to ascend, sit lingring here
Heav'ns fugitives, and for thir dwelling place
Accept this dark opprobrious Den of shame,
The Prison of his Tyranny who Reigns
By our delay? no, let us rather choose   *60*
Arm'd with Hell flames and fury all at once
O're Heav'ns high Towrs to force resistless way,
Turning our Tortures into horrid Arms
Against the Torturer; when to meet the noise
Of his Almighty Engin he shall hear
Infernal Thunder, and for Lightning see
Black fire and horror shot with equal rage
Among his Angels; and his Throne it self
Mixt with *Tartarean* Sulphur, and strange fire,
His own invented Torments. But perhaps   *70*
The way seems difficult and steep to scale
With upright wing against a higher foe.
Let such bethink them, if the sleepy drench
Of that forgetful Lake benumme not still,

That in our proper motion we ascend
Up to our native seat: descent and fall
To us is adverse. Who but felt of late
When the fierce Foe hung on our brok'n Rear
Insulting, and pursu'd us through the Deep,
With what compulsion and laborious flight   80
We sunk thus low? Th' ascent is easie then;
Th' event is fear'd; should we again provoke
Our stronger, some worse way his wrath may find
To our destruction: if there be in Hell
Fear to be worse destroy'd: what can be worse
Then to dwell here, driv'n out from bliss, condemn'd
In this abhorred deep to utter woe,
Where pain of unextinguishable fire
Must exercise us without hope of end
The Vassals of his anger, when the Scourge   90
Inexorably, and the torturing houre
Calls us to Penance? More destroy'd then thus
We should be quite abolisht and expire.
What fear we then? what doubt we to incense
His utmost ire? which to the highth enrag'd,
Will either quite consume us, and reduce
To nothing this essential, happier farr
Then miserable to have eternal being:
Or if our substance be indeed Divine,
And cannot cease to be, we are at worst   100
On this side nothing; and by proof we feel
Our power sufficient to disturb his Heav'n,
And with perpetual inrodes to Allarme,
Though inaccessible, his fatal Throne:
Which if not Victory is yet Revenge.
   He ended frowning, and his look denounc'd
Desperate revenge, and Battel dangerous
To less then Gods. On th' other side up rose
Belial, in act more graceful and humane;
A fairer person lost not Heav'n; he seemd   110
For dignity compos'd and high exploit:
But all was false and hollow; though his Tongue
Dropt Manna, and could make the worse appear
The better reason, to perplex and dash
Maturest Counsels: for his thoughts were low;
To vice industrious, but to Nobler deeds
Timorous and slothful: yet he pleas'd the eare,
And with perswasive accent thus began.
   I should be much for open Warr, O Peers,
As not behind in hate; if what was urg'd   120

Main reason to perswade immediate Warr,
Did not disswade me most, and seem to cast
Ominous conjecture on the whole success:
When he who most excels in fact of Arms,
In what he counsels and in what excels
Mistrustful, grounds his courage on despair
And utter dissolution, as the scope
Of all his aim, after some dire revenge.
First, what Revenge? the Towrs of Heav'n are fill'd
With Armed watch, that render all access   130
Impregnable; oft on the bordering Deep
Encamp thir Legions, or with obscure wing
Scout farr and wide into the Realm of night,
Scorning surprize. Or could we break our way
By force, and at our heels all Hell should rise
With blackest Insurrection, to confound
Heav'ns purest Light, yet our great Enemie
All incorruptible would on his Throne
Sit unpolluted, and th' Ethereal mould
Incapable of stain would soon expel   140
Her mischief, and purge off the baser fire
Victorious. Thus repuls'd, our final hope
Is flat despair; we must exasperate
Th' Almighty Victor to spend all his rage,
And that must end us, that must be our cure,
To be no more; sad cure; for who would loose,
Though full of pain, this intellectual being,
Those thoughts that wander through Eternity,
To perish rather, swallowd up and lost
In the wide womb of uncreated night,   150
Devoid of sense and motion? and who knows,
Let this be good, whether our angry Foe
Can give it, or will ever? how he can
Is doubtful; that he never will is sure.
Will he, so wise, let loose at once his ire,
Belike through impotence, or unaware,
To give his Enemies thir wish, and end
Them in his anger, whom his anger saves
To punish endless? wherefore cease we then?
Say they who counsel Warr, we are decreed,   160
Reserv'd and destin'd to Eternal woe;
Whatever doing, what can we suffer more,
What can we suffer worse? is this then worst,
Thus sitting, thus consulting, thus in Arms?
What when we fled amain, pursu'd and strook
With Heav'ns afflicting Thunder, and besought

The Deep to shelter us? this Hell then seem'd
A refuge from those wounds: or when we lay
Chain'd on the burning Lake? that sure was worse.
What if the breath that kindl'd those grim fires   170
Awak'd should blow them into sevenfold rage
And plunge us in the Flames? or from above
Should intermitted vengeance Arme again
His red right hand to plague us? what if all
Her stores were op'n'd, and this Firmament
Of Hell should spout her Cataracts of Fire,
Impendent horrors, threatning hideous fall
One day upon our heads; while we perhaps
Designing or exhorting glorious Warr,
Caught in a fierie Tempest shall be hurl'd   180
Each on his rock transfixt, the sport and prey
Of racking whirlwinds, or for ever sunk
Under yon boyling Ocean, wrapt in Chains;
There to converse with everlasting groans,
Unrespited, unpitied, unrepreevd,
Ages of hopeless end; this would be worse.
Warr therefore, open or conceal'd, alike
My voice disswades; for what can force or guile
With him, or who deceive his mind, whose eye
Views all things at one view, he from heav'ns highth   190
All these our motions vain, sees and derides;
Not more Almighty to resist our might
Then wise to frustrate all our plots and wiles.
Shall we then live thus vile, the race of Heav'n
Thus trampl'd, thus expell'd to suffer here
Chains and these Torments? better these then worse
By my advice; since fate inevitable
Subdues us, and Omnipotent Decree
The Victors will. To suffer, as to doe,
Our strength is equal, nor the Law unjust   200
That so ordains: this was at first resolv'd,
If we were wise, against so great a foe
Contending, and so doubtful what might fall.
I laugh, when those who at the Spear are bold
And vent'rous, if that fail them, shrink and fear
What yet they know must follow, to endure
Exile, or ignominy, or bonds, or pain,
The sentence of thir Conquerour: This is now
Our doom; which if we can sustain and bear,
Our Supream Foe in time may much remit   210
His anger, and perhaps thus farr remov'd
Not mind us not offending, satisfi'd

With what is punish't; whence these raging fires
Will slack'n, if his breath stir not thir flames.
Our purer essence then will overcome
Thir noxious vapour, or enur'd not feel,
Or chang'd at length, and to the place conformd
In temper and in nature, will receive
Familiar the fierce heat, and void of pain;
This horror will grow milde, this darkness light,   *220*
Besides what hope the never-ending flight
Of future days may bring, what chance, what change
Worth waiting, since our present lot appeers
For happy though but ill, for ill not worst,
If we procure not to our selves more woe.

  Thus *Belial* with words cloath'd in reasons garb
Counsel'd ignoble ease, and peaceful sloath,
Not peace: and after him thus *Mammon* spake.

  Either to disinthrone the King of Heav'n
We warr, if warr be best, or to regain   *230*
Our own right lost: him to unthrone we then
May hope, when everlasting Fate shall yeild
To fickle Chance, and *Chaos* judge the strife:
The former vain to hope argues as vain
The latter: for what place can be for us
Within Heav'ns bound, unless Heav'ns Lord supream
We overpower? Suppose he should relent
And publish Grace to all, on promise made
Of new Subjection; with what eyes could we
Stand in his presence humble, and receive   *240*
Strict Laws impos'd, to celebrate his Throne
With warbl'd Hymns, and to his Godhead sing
Forc't Halleluiahs; while he Lordly sits
Our envied Sovran, and his Altar breathes
Ambrosial Odours and Ambrosial Flowers,
Our servile offerings. This must be our task
In Heav'n, this our delight; how wearisom
Eternity so spent in worship paid
To whom we hate. Let us not then pursue
By force impossible, by leave obtain'd   *250*
Unacceptable, though in Heav'n, our state
Of splendid vassalage, but rather seek
Our own good from our selves, and from our own
Live to our selves, though in this vast recess,
Free, and to none accountable, preferring
Hard liberty before the easie yoke
Of servile Pomp. Our greatness will appear
Then most conspicuous, when great things of small,

Useful of hurtful, prosperous of adverse
We can create, and in what place so e're   260
Thrive under evil, and work ease out of pain
Through labour and endurance. This deep world
Of darkness do we dread? How oft amidst
Thick clouds and dark doth Heav'ns all-ruling Sire
Choose to reside, his Glory unobscur'd,
And with the Majesty of darkness round
Covers his Throne; from whence deep thunders roar
Must'ring thir rage, and Heav'n resembles Hell?
As he our Darkness, cannot we his Light
Imitate when we please? This Desart soile   270
Wants not her hidden lustre, Gemms and Gold;
Nor want we skill or art, from whence to raise
Magnificence; and what can Heav'n shew more?
Our torments also may in length of time
Become our Elements, these piercing Fires
As soft as now severe, our temper chang'd
Into their temper; which must needs remove
The sensible of pain. All things invite
To peaceful Counsels, and the settl'd State
Of order, how in safety best we may   280
Compose our present evils, with regard
Of what we are and where, dismissing quite
All thoughts of Warr; ye have what I advise.

    He scarce had finisht, when such murmur filld
Th' Assembly, as when hollow Rocks retain
The sound of blustring winds, which all night long
Had rous'd the Sea, now with hoarse cadence lull
Sea-faring men orewatcht, whose Bark by chance
Or Pinnace anchors in a craggy Bay
After the Tempest: Such applause was heard   290
As *Mammon* ended, and his Sentence pleas'd,
Advising peace: for such another Field
They dreaded worse then Hell: so much the fear
Of Thunder and the Sword of *Michael*
Wrought still within them; and no less desire
To found this nether Empire, which might rise
By pollicy, and long process of time,
In emulation opposite to Heav'n.
Which when *Bëëlzebub* perceiv'd, then whom,
Satan except, none higher sat, with grave   300
Aspect he rose, and in his rising seem'd
A Pillar of State; deep on his Front engraven
Deliberation sat and publick care;
And Princely counsel in his face yet shon,

Majestick though in ruin: sage he stood
With *Atlantean* shoulders fit to bear
The weight of mightiest Monarchies; his look
Drew audience and attention still as Night
Or Summers Noon-tide air, while thus he spake.
    Thrones and imperial Powers, off-spring of heav'n,   *310*
Ethereal Vertues; or these Titles now
Must we renounce, and changing stile be call'd
Princes of Hell? for so the popular vote
Inclines, here to continue, and build up here
A growing Empire; doubtless; while we dream,
And know not that the King of Heav'n hath doom'd
This place our dungeon, not our safe retreat
Beyond his Potent arm, to live exempt
From Heav'ns high jurisdiction, in new League
Banded against his Throne, but to remaine   *320*
In strictest bondage, though thus far remov'd,
Under th' inevitable curb, reserv'd
His captive multitude: For he, be sure,
In highth or depth, still first and last will Reign
Sole King, and of his Kingdom loose no part
By our revolt, but over Hell extend
His Empire, and with Iron Scepter rule
Us here, as with his Golden those in Heav'n.
What sit we then projecting Peace and Warr?
Warr hath determin'd us, and foild with loss   *330*
Irreparable; tearms of peace yet none
Voutsaf't or sought; for what peace will be giv'n
To us enslav'd, but custody severe,
And stripes, and arbitrary punishment
Inflicted? and what peace can we return,
But to our power hostility and hate,
Untam'd reluctance, and revenge though slow,
Yet ever plotting how the Conquerour least
May reap his conquest, and may least rejoyce
In doing what we most in suffering feel?   *340*
Nor will occasion want, nor shall we need
With dangerous expedition to invade
Heav'n, whose high walls fear no assault or Siege,
Or ambush from the Deep. What if we find
Some easier enterprize? There is a place
(If ancient and prophetic fame in Heav'n
Err not) another World, the happy seat
Of som new Race call'd *Man*, about this time
To be created like to us, though less
In power and excellence, but favour'd more   *350*

Of him who rules above; so was his will
Pronounc'd among the Gods, and by an Oath,
That shook Heav'ns whol circumference, confirm'd.
Thither let us bend all our thoughts, to learn
What creatures there inhabit, of what mould,
Or substance, how endu'd, and what thir Power,
And where thir weakness, how attempted best,
By force or suttlety: Though Heav'n be shut,
And Heav'ns high Arbitrator sit secure
In his own strength, this place may lye expos'd   *360*
The utmost border of his Kingdom, left
To their defence who hold it: here perhaps
Som advantagious act may be achiev'd
By sudden onset, either with Hell fire
To waste his whole Creation, or possess
All as our own, and drive as we were driven,
The punie habitants, or if not drive,
Seduce them to our Party, that thir God
May prove thir foe, and with repenting hand
Abolish his own works. This would surpass   *370*
Common revenge, and interrupt his joy
In our Confusion, and our Joy upraise
In his disturbance; when his darling Sons
Hurl'd headlong to partake with us, shall curse
Thir frail Originals, and faded bliss,
Faded so soon. Advise if this be worth
Attempting, or to sit in darkness here
Hatching vain Empires. Thus *Bëëlzebub*
Pleaded his devilish Counsel, first devis'd
By *Satan*, and in part propos'd: for whence,   *380*
But from the Author of all ill could Spring
So deep a malice, to confound the race
Of mankind in one root, and Earth with Hell
To mingle and involve, done all to spite
The great Creatour? But thir spite still serves
His glory to augment. The bold design
Pleas'd highly those infernal States, and joy
Sparkl'd in all thir eyes; with full assent
They vote: whereat his speech he thus renews.
  Well have ye judg'd, well ended long debate,   *390*
Synod of Gods, and like to what ye are,
Great things resolv'd; which from the lowest deep
Will once more lift us up, in spight of Fate,
Neerer our ancient Seat; perhaps in view
Of those bright confines, whence with neighbouring Arms
And opportune excursion we may chance

Re-enter Heav'n; or else in some milde Zone
Dwell not unvisited of Heav'ns fair Light
Secure, and at the brightning Orient beam
Purge off this gloom; the soft delicious Air, 400
To heal the scarr of these corrosive Fires
Shall breath her balme. But first whom shall we send
In search of this new world, whom shall we find
Sufficient? who shall tempt with wandring feet
The dark unbottom'd infinite Abyss
And through the palpable obscure find out
His uncouth way, or spread his aerie flight
Upborn with indefatigable wings
Over the vast abrupt, ere he arrive
The happy Ile; what strength, what art can then 410
Suffice, or what evasion bear him safe
Through the strict Senteries and Stations thick
Of Angels watching round? Here he had need
All circumspection, and wee now no less
Choice in our suffrage; for on whom we send,
The weight of all and our last hope relies.
  This said, he sat; and expectation held
His look suspence, awaiting who appeer'd
To second, or oppose, or undertake
The perilous attempt; but all sat mute, 420
Pondering the danger with deep thoughts; and each
In others count'nance red his own dismay
Astonisht: none among the choice and prime
Of those Heav'n-warring Champions could be found
So hardie as to proffer or accept
Alone the dreadful voyage; till at last
Satan, whom now transcendent glory rais'd
Above his fellows, with Monarchal pride
Conscious of highest worth, unmov'd thus spake.
  O Progeny of Heav'n, Empyreal Thrones, 430
With reason hath deep silence and demurr
Seis'd us, though undismaid: long is the way
And hard, that out of Hell leads up to Light;
Our prison strong, this huge convex of Fire,
Outrageous to devour, immures us round
Ninefold, and gates of burning Adamant
Barr'd over us prohibit all egress.
These past, if any pass, the void profound
Of unessential Night receives him next
Wide gaping, and with utter loss of being 440
Threatens him, plung'd in that abortive gulf.
If thence he scape into what ever world,

Or unknown Region, what remains him less
Then unknown dangers and as hard escape.
But I should ill become this Throne, O Peers,
And this Imperial Sov'ranty, adorn'd
With splendor, arm'd with power, if aught propos'd
And judg'd of public moment, in the shape
Of difficulty or danger could deterre
Me from attempting. Wherefore do I assume   450
These Royalties, and not refuse to Reign,
Refusing to accept as great a share
Of hazard as of honour, due alike
To him who Reigns, and so much to him due
Of hazard more, as he above the rest
High honourd sits? Go therfore mighty powers,
Terror of Heav'n, though fall'n; intend at home,
While here shall be our home, what best may ease
The present misery, and render Hell
More tollerable; if there be cure or charm   460
To respite or deceive, or slack the pain
Of this ill Mansion: intermit no watch
Against a wakeful Foe, while I abroad
Through all the coasts of dark destruction seek
Deliverance for us all: this enterprize
None shall partake with me. Thus saying rose
The Monarch, and prevented all reply,
Prudent, least from his resolution rais'd
Others among the chief might offer now
(Certain to be refus'd) what erst they feard;   470
And so refus'd might in opinion stand
His rivals, winning cheap the high repute
Which he through hazard huge must earn. But they
Dreaded not more th' adventure then his voice
Forbidding; and at once with him they rose;
Thir rising all at once was as the sound
Of Thunder heard remote. Towards him they bend
With awful reverence prone; and as a God
Extoll him equal to the highest in Heav'n:
Nor fail'd they to express how much they prais'd,   480
That for the general safety he despis'd
His own: for neither do the Spirits damn'd
Loose all thir vertue; least bad men should boast
Thir specious deeds on earth, which glory excites,
Or close ambition varnisht o're with zeal.
Thus they thir doubtful consultations dark
Ended rejoycing in thir matchless Chief:
As when from mountain tops the dusky clouds

Ascending, while the North wind sleeps, o'respread
Heavn's chearful face, the lowring Element *490*
Scowls ore the dark'nd lantskip Snow, or showre;
If chance the radiant Sun with farewell sweet
Extend his ev'ning beam, the fields revive,
The birds thir notes renew, and bleating herds
Attest thir joy, that hill and valley rings.
O shame to men! Devil with Devil damn'd
Firm concord holds, men onely disagree
Of Creatures rational, though under hope
Of heavenly Grace; and God proclaiming peace,
Yet live in hatred, enmitie, and strife *500*
Among themselves, and levie cruel warres,
Wasting the Earth, each other to destroy:
As if (which might induce us to accord)
Man had not hellish foes anow besides,
That day and night for his destruction waite.

   The *Stygian* Councel thus dissolv'd; and forth
In order came the grand infernal Peers,
Midst came thir mighty Paramount, and seemd
Alone th' Antagonist of Heav'n, nor less
Then Hells dread Emperour with pomp Supream, *510*
And God-like imitated State; him round
A Globe of fierie Seraphim inclos'd
With bright imblazonrie, and horrent Arms.
Then of thir Session ended they bid cry
With Trumpets regal sound the great result:
Toward the four winds four speedy Cherubim
Put to thir mouths the sounding Alchymie
By Haralds voice explain'd: the hollow Abyss
Heard farr and wide, and all the host of Hell
With deafning shout, return'd them loud acclaim. *520*
Thence more at ease thir minds and somwhat rais'd
By false presumptuous hope, the ranged powers
Disband, and wandring, each his several way
Pursues, as inclination or sad choice
Leads him perplext, where he may likeliest find
Truce to his restless thoughts, and entertain
The irksome hours, till his great Chief return.
Part on the Plain, or in the Air sublime
Upon the wing, or in swift race contend,
As at th' Olympian Games or *Pythian* fields; *530*
Part curb thir fierie Steeds, or shun the Goal
With rapid wheels, or fronted Brigads form.
As when to warn proud Cities warr appears
Wag'd in the troubl'd Skie, and Armies rush

To Battel in the Clouds, before each Van
Pric forth the Aerie Knights, and couch thir spears
Till thickest Legions close; with feats of Arms
From either end of Heav'n the welkin burns.
Others with vast *Typhœan* rage more fell
Rend up both Rocks and Hills, and ride the Air   *540*
In whirlwind; Hell scarce holds the wilde uproar.
As when *Alcides* from *Oealia* Crown'd
With conquest, felt th' envenom'd robe, and tore
Through pain up by the roots *Thessalian* Pines,
And *Lichas* from the top of *Oeta* threw
Into th' *Euboic* Sea. Others more milde,
Retreated in a silent valley, sing
With notes Angelical to many a Harp
Thir own Heroic deeds and hapless fall
By doom of Battel; and complain that Fate   *550*
Free Vertue should enthrall to Force or Chance.
Thir song was partial, but the harmony
(What could it less when Spirits immortal sing?)
Suspended Hell, and took with ravishment
The thronging audience. In discourse more sweet
(For Eloquence the Soul, Song charms the Sense,)
Others apart sat on a Hill retir'd,
In thoughts more elevate, and reason'd high
Of Providence, Foreknowledge, Will, and Fate,
Fixt Fate, free will, foreknowledge absolute,   *560*
And found no end, in wandring mazes lost.
Of good and evil much they argu'd then,
Of happiness and final misery,
Passion and Apathie, and glory and shame,
Vain wisdom all, and false Philosophie:
Yet with a pleasing sorcerie could charm
Pain for a while or anguish, and excite
Fallacious hope, or arm th' obdured brest
With stubborn patience as with triple steel.
Another part in Squadrons and gross Bands   *570*
On bold adventure to discover wide
That dismal World, if any Clime perhaps
Might yeild them easier habitation, bend
Four ways thir flying March, along the Banks
Of four infernal Rivers that disgorge
Into the burning Lake thir baleful streams;
Abhorred *Styx* the flood of deadly hate,
Sad *Acheron* of Sorrow, black and deep;
Cocytus, nam'd of lamentation loud
Heard on the ruful stream; fierce *Phlegeton*   *580*

Whose waves of torrent fire inflame with rage.
Farr off from these a slow and silent stream,
Lethe the River of Oblivion roules
Her watrie Labyrinth, whereof who drinks,
Forthwith his former state and being forgets,
Forgets both joy and grief, pleasure and pain.
Beyond this flood a frozen Continent
Lies dark and wilde, beat with perpetual storms
Of Whirlwind and dire Hail, which on firm land
Thaws not, but gathers heap, and ruin seems   590
Of ancient pile; all else deep snow and ice,
A gulf profound as that *Serbonian* Bog
Betwixt *Damiata* and mount *Casius* old,
Where Armies whole have sunk: the parching Air
Burns frore, and cold performs th' effect of Fire.
Thither by harpy-footed Furies hail'd,
At certain revolutions all the damn'd
Are brought: and feel by turns the bitter change
Of fierce extreams, extreams by change more fierce,
From Beds of raging Fire to starve in Ice   600
Thir soft Ethereal warmth, and there to pine
Immovable, infixt, and frozen round,
Periods of time, thence hurried back to fire.
They ferry over this *Lethean* Sound
Both to and fro, thir sorrow to augment,
And wish and struggle, as they pass, to reach
The tempting stream, with one small drop to loose
In sweet forgetfulness all pain and woe,
All in one moment, and so neer the brink;
But fate withstands, and to oppose th' attempt   610
Medusa with *Gorgonian* terror guards
The Ford, and of it self the water flies
All taste of living wight, as once it fled
The lip of *Tantalus*. Thus roving on
In confus'd march forlorn, th' adventrous Bands
With shuddring horror pale, and eyes agast
View'd first thir lamentable lot, and found
No rest: through many a dark and drearie Vaile
They pass'd, and many a Region dolorous,
O're many a Frozen, many a Fierie Alpe,   620
Rocks, Caves, Lakes, Fens, Bogs, Dens, and shades of death,
A Universe of death, which God by curse
Created evil, for evil only good,
Where all life dies, death lives, and nature breeds,
Perverse, all monstrous, all prodigious things,
Abominable, inutterable, and worse

Then Fables yet have feign'd, or fear conceiv'd,
Gorgons and *Hydra's*, and *Chimera's* dire.
   Mean while the Adversary of God and Man,
Satan with thoughts inflam'd of highest design,   630
Puts on swift wings, and toward the Gates of Hell
Explores his solitary flight; som times
He scours the right hand coast, som times the left,
Now shaves with level wing the Deep, then soares
Up to the fiery concave touring high.
As when farr off at Sea a Fleet descri'd
Hangs in the Clouds, by *Æquinoctial* Winds
Close sailing from *Bengala*, or the Iles
Of *Ternate* and *Tidore*, whence Merchants bring
Thir spicie Drugs: they on the trading Flood   640
Through the wide *Ethiopian* to the Cape
Ply stemming nightly toward the Pole. So seem'd
Farr off the flying Fiend: at last appeer
Hell bounds high reaching to the horrid Roof,
And thrice threefold the Gates; three folds were Brass,
Three Iron, three of Adamantine Rock,
Impenitrable, impal'd with circling fire,
Yet unconsum'd. Before the Gates there sat
On either side a formidable shape;
The one seem'd Woman to the waste, and fair,   650
But ended foul in many a scaly fould
Voluminous and vast, a Serpent arm'd
With mortal sting: about her middle round
A cry of Hell Hounds never ceasing bark'd
With wide *Cerberean* mouths full loud, and rung
A hideous Peal: yet, when they list, would creep,
If aught disturb'd thir noyse, into her woomb,
And kennel there, yet there still bark'd and howl'd
Within unseen. Farr less abhorrd then these
Vex'd *Scylla* bathing in the Sea that parts   660
Calabria from the hoarce *Trinacrian* shore:
Nor uglier follow the Night-Hag, when call'd
In secret, riding through the Air she comes
Lur'd with the smell of infant blood, to dance
With *Lupland* Witches, while the labouring Moon
Eclipses at thir charms. The other shape,
If shape it might be call'd that shape had none
Distinguishable in member, joynt, or limb,
Or substance might be call'd that shadow seem'd,
For each seem'd either; black it stood as Night,   670
Fierce as ten Furies, terrible as Hell,
And shook a dreadful Dart; what seem'd his head

The likeness of a Kingly Crown had on.
Satan was now at hand, and from his seat
The Monster moving onward came as fast,
With horrid strides, Hell trembled as he strode.
Th' undaunted Fiend what this might be admir'd,
Admir'd, not fear'd; God and his Son except,
Created thing naught vallu'd he nor shun'd;
And with disdainful look thus first began. 680
    Whence and what art thou, execrable shape,
That dar'st, though grim and terrible, advance
Thy miscreated Front athwart my way
To yonder Gates? through them I mean to pass,
That be assured, without leave askt of thee:
Retire, or taste thy folly, and learn by proof,
Hell-born, not to contend with Spirits of Heav'n.
    To whom the Goblin full of wrauth reply'd,
Art thou that Traitor Angel, art thou hee,
Who first broke peace in Heav'n and Faith, till then 690
Unbrok'n, and in proud rebellious Arms
Drew after him the third part of Heav'ns Sons
Conjur'd against the highest, for which both Thou
And they outcast from God, are here condemn'd
To waste Eternal daies in woe and pain?
And reck'n'st thou thy self with Spirits of Heav'n,
Hell-doomd, and breath'st defiance here and scorn,
Where I reign King, and to enrage thee more,
Thy King and Lord? Back to thy punishment,
False fugitive, and to thy speed add wings, 700
Least with a whip of Scorpions I pursue
Thy lingring, or with one stroke of this Dart
Strange horror seise thee, and pangs unfelt before.
    So spake the grieslie terrour, and in shape,
So speaking and so threatning, grew ten fold
More dreadful and deform: on th' other side
Incenc't with indignation *Satan* stood
Unterrifi'd, and like a Comet burn'd,
That fires the length of *Ophiucus* huge
In th' Artick Sky, and from his horrid hair 710
Shakes Pestilence and Warr. Each at the Head
Level'd his deadly aime; thir fatall hands
No second stroke intend, and such a frown
Each cast at th' other, as when two black Clouds
With Heav'ns Artillery fraught, come rattling on
Over the *Caspian*, then stand front to front
Hov'ring a space, till Winds the signal blow
To joyn thir dark Encounter in mid air:

So frownd the mighty Combatants, that Hell
Grew darker at thir frown, so matcht they stood; 720
For never but once more was either like
To meet so great a foe: and now great deeds
Had been achiev'd, whereof all Hell had rung,
Had not the Snakie Sorceress that sat
Fast by Hell Gate, and kept the fatal Key,
Ris'n, and with hideous outcry rush'd between.
   O Father, what intends thy hand, she cry'd,
Against thy only Son? What fury O Son,
Possesses thee to bend that mortal Dart
Against thy Fathers head? and know'st for whom; 730
For him who sits above and laughs the while
At thee ordain'd his drudge, to execute
What e're his wrath, which he calls Justice, bids,
His wrath which one day will destroy ye both.
   She spake, and at her words the hellish Pest
Forbore, then these to her *Satan* return'd.
   So strange thy outcry, and thy words so strange
Thou interposest, that my sudden hand
Prevented spares to tell thee yet by deeds
What it intends; till first I know of thee, 740
What thing thou art, thus double-form'd, and why
In this infernal Vaile first met thou call'st
Me Father, and that Fantasm call'st my Son?
I know thee not, nor ever saw till now
Sight more detestable then him and thee.
   T' whom thus the Portress of Hell Gate reply'd;
Hast thou forgot me then, and do I seem
Now in thine eye so foul, once deemd so fair
In Heav'n, when at th' Assembly, and in sight
Of all the Seraphim with thee combin'd 750
In bold conspiracy against Heav'ns King,
All on a sudden miserable pain
Surpris'd thee, dim thine eyes, and dizzie swumm
In darkness, while thy head flames thick and fast
Threw forth, till on the left side op'ning wide,
Likest to thee in shape and count'nance bright,
Then shining heav'nly fair, a Goddess arm'd
Out of thy head I sprung; amazement seis'd
All th' Host of Heav'n; back they recoild affraid
At first, and call'd me *Sin*, and for a Sign 760
Portentous held me; but familiar grown,
I pleas'd, and with attractive graces won
The most averse, thee chiefly, who full oft
Thy self in me thy perfect image viewing

Becam'st enamour'd, and such joy thou took'st
With me in secret, that my womb conceiv'd
A growing burden. Mean while Warr arose,
And fields were fought in Heav'n; wherein remaind
(For what could else) to our Almighty Foe
Cleer Victory, to our part loss and rout 770
Through all the Empyrean: down they fell
Driv'n headlong from the Pitch of Heaven, down
Into this Deep, and in the general fall
I also; at which time this powerful Key
Into my hand was giv'n, with charge to keep
These Gates for ever shut, which none can pass
Without my op'ning. Pensive here I sat
Alone, but long I sat not, till my womb
Pregnant by thee, and now excessive grown
Prodigious motion felt and rueful throes. 780
At last this odious offspring whom thou seest
Thine own begotten, breaking violent way
Tore through my entrails, that with fear and pain
Distorted, all my nether shape thus grew
Transform'd: but he my inbred enemie
Forth issu'd, brandishing his fatal Dart
Made to destroy: I fled, and cry'd out *Death*;
Hell trembl'd at the hideous Name, and sigh'd
From all her Caves, and back resounded *Death*.
I fled, but he pursu'd (though more, it seems, 790
Inflam'd with lust then rage) and swifter far,
Me overtook his mother all dismaid,
And in embraces forcible and foule
Ingendring with me, of that rape begot
These yelling Monsters that with ceasless cry
Surround me, as thou sawst, hourly conceiv'd
And hourly born, with sorrow infinite
To me, for when they list into the womb
That bred them they return, and howle and gnaw
My Bowels, their repast; then bursting forth 800
Afresh with conscious terrours vex me round,
That rest or intermission none I find.
Before mine eyes in opposition sits
Grim *Death* my Son and foe, who sets them on,
And me his Parent would full soon devour
For want of other prey, but that he knows
His end with mine involvd; and knows that I
Should prove a bitter Morsel, and his bane,
When ever that shall be; so Fate pronounc'd.
But thou O Father, I forewarn thee, shun 810

His deadly arrow; neither vainly hope
To be invulnerable in those bright Arms,
Though temper'd heav'nly, for that mortal dint,
Save he who reigns above, none can resist.
    She finish'd, and the suttle Fiend his lore
Soon learnd, now milder, and thus answerd smooth.
Dear Daughter, since thou claim'st me for thy Sire,
And my fair Son here showst me, the dear pledge
Of dalliance had with thee in Heav'n, and joys
Then sweet, now sad to mention, through dire change   *820*
Befalln us unforeseen, unthought of, know
I come no enemie, but to set free
From out this dark and dismal house of pain,
Both him and thee, and all the heav'nly Host
Of Spirits that in our just pretenses arm'd
Fell with us from on high: from them I go
This uncouth errand sole, and one for all
My self expose, with lonely steps to tread
Th' unfounded deep, & through the void immense
To search with wandring quest a place foretold   *830*
Should be, and, by concurring signs, ere now
Created vast and round, a place of bliss
In the Pourlieues of Heav'n, and therein plac't
A race of upstart Creatures, to supply
Perhaps our vacant room, though more remov'd,
Least Heav'n surcharg'd with potent multitude
Might hap to move new broiles: Be this or aught
Then this more secret now design'd, I haste
To know, and this once known, shall soon return,
And bring ye to the place where Thou and Death   *840*
Shall dwell at ease, and up and down unseen
Wing silently the buxom Air, imbalm'd
With odours; there ye shall be fed and fill'd
Immeasurably, all things shall be your prey.
He ceas'd, for both seemd highly pleasd, and Death
Grinnd horrible a gastly smile, to hear
His famine should be fill'd, and blest his mawe
Destin'd to that good hour: no less rejoyc'd
His mother bad, and thus bespake her Sire.
    The key of this infernal Pit by due,   *850*
And by command of Heav'ns all-powerful King
I keep, by him forbidden to unlock
These Adamantine Gates; against all force
Death ready stands to interpose his dart,
Fearless to be o'rematcht by living might.
But what ow I to his commands above

Who hates me, and hath hither thrust me down
Into this gloom of *Tartarus* profound,
To sit in hateful Office here confin'd,
Inhabitant of Heav'n, and heav'nlie-born,   *860*
Here in perpetual agonie and pain,
With terrors and with clamors compasst round
Of mine own brood, that on my bowels feed:
Thou art my Father, thou my Author, thou
My being gav'st me; whom should I obey
But thee, whom follow? thou wilt bring me soon
To that new world of light and bliss, among
The Gods who live at ease, where I shall Reign
At thy right hand voluptuous, as beseems
Thy daughter and thy darling, without end.   *870*
   Thus saying, from her side the fatal Key,
Sad instrument of all our woe, she took;
And towards the Gate rouling her bestial train,
Forthwith the huge Portcullis high up drew,
Which but her self not all the *Stygian* powers
Could once have mov'd; then in the key-hole turns
Th' intricate wards, and every Bolt and Bar
Of massie Iron or sollid Rock with ease
Unfast'ns: on a sudden op'n flie
With impetuous recoile and jarring sound   *880*
Th' infernal dores, and on thir hinges grate
Harsh Thunder, that the lowest bottom shook
Of *Erebus*. She op'nd, but to shut
Excel'd her power; the Gates wide op'n stood,
That with extended wings a Bannerd Host
Under spread Ensigns marching might pass through
With Horse and Chariots rankt in loose array;
So wide they stood, and like a Furnace mouth
Cast forth redounding smoak and ruddy flame.
Before thir eyes in sudden view appear   *890*
The secrets of the hoarie deep, a dark
Illimitable Ocean without bound,
Without dimension, where length, breadth, and highth,
And time and place are lost; where eldest Night
And *Chaos*, Ancestors of Nature, hold
Eternal *Anarchie*, amidst the noise
Of endless warrs, and by confusion stand.
For hot, cold, moist, and dry, four Champions fierce
Strive here for Maistrie, and to Battel bring
Thir embryon Atoms; they around the flag   *900*
Of each his faction, in thir several Clanns,
Light-arm'd or heavy, sharp, smooth, swift or slow,

Swarm populous, unnumber'd as the Sands
Of *Barca* or *Cyrene's* torrid soil,
Levied to side with warring Winds, and poise
Thir lighter wings. To whom these most adhere,
Hee rules a moment; *Chaos* Umpire sits,
And by decision more imbroiles the fray
By which he Reigns: next him high Arbiter
Chance governs all. Into this wilde Abyss,   910
The Womb of nature and perhaps her Grave,
Of neither Sea, nor Shore, nor Air, nor Fire,
But all these in thir pregnant causes mixt
Confus'dly, and which thus must ever fight,
Unless th' Almighty Maker them ordain
His dark materials to create more Worlds,
Into this wild Abyss the warie fiend
Stood on the brink of Hell and look'd a while,
Pondering his Voyage: for no narrow frith
He had to cross. Nor was his eare less peal'd   920
With noises loud and ruinous (to compare
Great things with small) then when *Bellona* storms,
With all her battering Engines bent to rase
Som Capital City, or less then if this frame
Of Heav'n were falling, and these Elements
In mutinie had from her Axle torn
The stedfast Earth. At last his Sail-broad Vannes
He spreads for flight, and in the surging smoak
Uplifted spurns the ground, thence many a League
As in a cloudy Chair ascending rides   930
Audacious, but that seat soon failing, meets
A vast vacuitie: all unawares
Fluttring his pennons vain plumb down he drops
Ten thousand fadom deep, and to this hour
Down had been falling, had not by ill chance
The strong rebuff of som tumultuous cloud
Instinct with Fire and Nitre hurried him
As many miles aloft: that furie stay'd,
Quencht in a Boggie *Syrtis*, neither Sea,
Nor good dry Land: nigh founderd on he fares,   940
Treading the crude consistence, half on foot,
Half flying; behoves him now both Oare and Saile.
As when a Gryfon through the Wilderness
With winged course ore Hill or moarie Dale,
Pursues the *Arimaspian*, who by stelth
Had from his wakeful custody purloind
The guarded Gold: So eagerly the fiend
Ore bog or steep, through strait, rough, dense, or rare,

With head, hands, wings, or feet pursues his way,
And swims or sinks, or wades, or creeps, or flyes: 950
At length a universal hubbub wilde
Of stunning sounds and voices all confus'd
Born through the hollow dark assaults his eare
With loudest vehemence: thither he plyes,
Undaunted to meet there what ever power
Or Spirit of the nethermost Abyss
Might in that noise reside, of whom to ask
Which way the neerest coast of darkness lyes
Bordering on light; when strait behold the Throne
Of *Chaos*, and his dark Pavilion spread 960
Wide on the wasteful Deep; with him Enthron'd
Sat Sable-vested Night, eldest of things,
The Consort of his Reign; and by them stood
Orcus and *Ades*, and the dreaded name
Of *Demogorgon*; Rumor next and Chance,
And Tumult and Confusion all imbroild,
And Discord with a thousand various mouths.
   T' whom *Satan* turning boldly, thus. Ye Powers
And Spirits of this nethermost Abyss,
Chaos and *ancient Night*, I come no Spie, 970
With purpose to explore or to disturb
The secrets of your Realm, but by constraint
Wandring this darksome desart, as my way
Lies through your spacious Empire up to light,
Alone, and without guide, half lost, I seek
What readiest path leads where your gloomie bounds
Confine with Heav'n; or if som other place
From your Dominion won, th' Ethereal King
Possesses lately, thither to arrive
I travel this profound, direct my course; 980
Directed, no mean recompence it brings
To your behoof, if I that Region lost,
All usurpation thence expell'd, reduce
To her original darkness and your sway
(Which is my present journey) and once more
Erect the Standerd there of *ancient Night*;
Yours be th' advantage all, mine the revenge.
   Thus *Satan*; and him thus the Anarch old
With faultring speech and visage incompos'd
Answer'd. I know thee, stranger, who thou art, 990
That mighty leading Angel, who of late
Made head against Heav'ns King, though overthrown.
I saw and heard, for such a numerous host
Fled not in silence through the frighted deep

With ruin upon ruin, rout on rout,
Confusion worse confounded; and Heav'n Gates
Pourd out by millions her victorious Bands
Pursuing. I upon my Frontieres here
Keep residence; if all I can will serve,
That little which is left so to defend   1000
Encroacht on still through our intestine broiles
Weakning the Scepter of old Night: first Hell
Your dungeon stretching far and wide beneath;
Now lately Heaven and Earth, another World
Hung ore my Realm, link'd in a golden Chain
To that side Heav'n from whence your Legions fell:
If that way be your walk, you have not farr;
So much the neerer danger; goe and speed;
Havock and spoil and ruin are my gain.

   He ceas'd; and *Satan* staid not to reply, 1010
But glad that now his Sea should find a shore,
With fresh alacritie and force renew'd
Springs upward like a Pyramid of fire
Into the wilde Expanse, and through the shock
Of fighting Elements, on all sides round
Environ'd wins his way; harder beset
And more endanger'd, then when *Argo* pass'd
Through *Bosporus* betwixt the justling Rocks:
Or when *Ulysses* on the Larbord shunnd
Charybdis, and by th' other whirlpool steard.   1020
So he with difficulty and labour hard
Mov'd on, with difficulty and labour hee;
But hee once past, soon after when man fell,
Strange alteration! Sin and Death amain
Following his track, such was the will of Heav'n,
Pav'd after him a broad and beat'n way
Over the dark Abyss, whose boiling Gulf
Tamely endur'd a Bridge of wondrous length
From Hell continu'd reaching th' utmost Orbe
Of this frail World; by which the Spirits perverse   1030
With easie intercourse pass to and fro
To tempt or punish mortals, except whom
God and good Angels guard by special grace.
But now at last the sacred influence
Of light appears, and from the walls of Heav'n
Shoots farr into the bosom of dim Night
A glimmering dawn; here Nature first begins
Her fardest verge, and *Chaos* to retire
As from her outmost works a brok'n foe
With tumult less and with less hostile din,   1040

That *Satan* with less toil, and now with ease
Wafts on the calmer wave by dubious light
And like a weather-beaten Vessel holds
Gladly the Port, though Shrouds and Tackle torn;
Or in the emptier waste, resembling Air,
Weighs his spread wings, at leasure to behold
Farr off th' Empyreal Heav'n, extended wide
In circuit, undetermind square or round,
With Opal Towrs and Battlements adorn'd
Of living Saphire, once his native Seat;   *1050*
And fast by hanging in a golden Chain
This pendant world, in bigness as a Starr
Of smallest Magnitude close by the Moon.
Thither full fraught with mischievous revenge,
Accurst, and in a cursed hour he hies.

BOOK III

THE ARGUMENT

God *sitting on his Throne sees* Satan *flying towards this world, then newly created; shews him to the Son who sat at his right hand; foretells the success of* Satan *in perverting mankind; clears his own Justice and Wisdom from all imputation, having created Man free and able enough to have withstood his Tempter; yet declares his purpose of grace towards him, in regard he fell not of his own malice, as did* Satan, *but by him seduc't. The Son of God renders praises to his Father for the manifestation of his gracious purpose towards Man; but God again declares, that Grace cannot be extended towards Man without the satisfaction of divine Justice; Man hath offended the majesty of God by aspiring to Godhead, and therefore with all his Progeny devoted to death must dye, unless some one can be found sufficient to answer for his offence, and undergoe his Punishment. The Son of God freely offers himself a Ransome for Man: the Father accepts him, ordains his incarnation, pronounces his exaltation above all Names in Heaven and Earth; commands all the Angels to adore him; they obey, and hymning to their Harps in full Quire, celebrate the Father and the Son. Mean while* Satan *alights upon the bare convex of this Worlds outermost Orb; where wandring he first finds a place since call'd The Lymbo of Vanity; what persons and things fly up thither; thence comes to the Gate of Heaven, describ'd ascending by stairs, and the waters above the Firmament that flow about it: His passage thence to the Orb of the Sun; he finds there* Uriel *the Regent of that Orb, but first changes himself into the shape of a meaner Angel; and pretending a zealous desire to behold the new Creation and Man whom God had plac't here, inquires of him the place of his habitation, and is directed; alights first on Mount* Niphates.

HAIL holy light, ofspring of Heav'n first-born,
   Or of th' Eternal Coeternal beam
May I express thee unblam'd? since God is light,
And never but in unapproached light
Dwelt from Eternitie, dwelt then in thee,
Bright effluence of bright essence increate.
Or hear'st thou rather pure Ethereal stream,
Whose Fountain who shall tell? before the Sun,
Before the Heavens thou wert, and at the voice
Of God, as with a Mantle didst invest   10
The rising world of waters dark and deep,
Won from the void and formless infinite.
Thee I re-visit now with bolder wing,
Escap't the *Stygian* Pool, though long detain'd
In that obscure sojourn, while in my flight
Through utter and through middle darkness borne
With other notes then to th' *Orphean* Lyre
I sung of *Chaos* and *Eternal Night,*
Taught by the heav'nly Muse to venture down

The dark descent, and up to reascend, 20
Though hard and rare: thee I revisit safe,
And feel thy sovran vital Lamp; but thou
Revisit'st not these eyes, that rowle in vain
To find thy piercing ray, and find no dawn;
So thick a drop serene hath quencht thir Orbs,
Or dim suffusion veild. Yet not the more
Cease I to wander where the Muses haunt
Cleer Spring, or shadie Grove, or Sunnie Hill,
Smit with the love of sacred song; but chief
Thee *Sion* and the flowrie Brooks beneath 30
That wash thy hallowd feet, and warbling flow,
Nightly I visit: nor somtimes forget
Those other two equal'd with me in Fate,
So were I equal'd with them in renown,
Blind *Thamyris* and blind *Mæonides*,
And *Tiresias* and *Phineus* Prophets old.
Then feed on thoughts, that voluntarie move
Harmonious numbers; as the wakeful Bird
Sings darkling, and in shadiest Covert hid
Tunes her nocturnal Note. Thus with the Year 40
Seasons return, but not to me returns
Day, or the sweet approach of Ev'n or Morn,
Or sight of vernal bloom, or Summers Rose,
Or flocks, or herds, or human face divine;
But cloud in stead, and ever-during dark
Surrounds me, from the chearful waies of men
Cut off, and for the Book of knowledg fair
Presented with a Universal blanc
Of Natures works to mee expung'd and ras'd,
And wisdome at one entrance quite shut out. 50
So much the rather thou Celestial light
Shine inward, and the mind through all her powers
Irradiate, there plant eyes, all mist from thence
Purge and disperse, that I may see and tell
Of things invisible to mortal sight.
   Now had the Almighty Father from above,
From the pure Empyrean where he sits
High Thron'd above all higthh, bent down his eye,
His own works and their works at once to view:
About him all the Sanctities of Heaven 60
Stood thick as Starrs, and from his sight receiv'd
Beatitude past utterance; on his right
The radiant image of his Glory sat,
His onely Son; On Earth he first beheld
Our two first Parents, yet the onely two

Of mankind, in the happie Garden plac't,
Reaping immortal fruits of joy and love,
Uninterrupted joy, unrivald love
In blissful solitude; he then survey'd
Hell and the Gulf between, and *Satan* there   70
Coasting the wall of Heav'n on this side Night
In the dun Air sublime, and ready now
To stoop with wearied wings, and willing feet
On the bare outside of this World, that seem'd
Firm land imbosom'd without Firmament,
Uncertain which, in Ocean or in Air.
Him God beholding from his prospect high,
Wherein past, present, future he beholds,
Thus to his onely Son foreseeing spake.
   Onely begotten Son, seest thou what rage   80
Transports our adversarie, whom no bounds
Prescrib'd, no barrs of Hell, nor all the chains
Heapt on him there, nor yet the main Abyss
Wide interrupt can hold; so bent he seems
On desperat revenge, that shall redound
Upon his own rebellious head. And now
Through all restraint broke loose he wings his way
Not farr off Heav'n, in the Precincts of light,
Directly towards the new created World,
And Man there plac't, with purpose to assay   90
If him by force he can destroy, or worse,
By som false guile pervert; and shall pervert;
For man will heark'n to his glozing lyes,
And easily transgress the sole Command,
Sole pledge of his obedience: So will fall
Hee and his faithless Progenie: whose fault?
Whose but his own? ingrate, he had of mee
All he could have; I made him just and right,
Sufficient to have stood, though free to fall.
Such I created all th' Ethereal Powers   100
And Spirits, both them who stood & them who faild;
Freely they stood who stood, and fell who fell.
Not free, what proof could they have givn sincere
Of true allegiance, constant Faith or Love,
Where onely what they needs must do, appeard,
Not what they would? what praise could they receive?
What pleasure I from such obedience paid,
When Will and Reason (Reason also is choice)
Useless and vain, of freedom both despoild,
Made passive both, had servd necessitie,   110
Not mee. They therefore as to right belongd,

So were created, nor can justly accuse
Thir maker, or thir making, or thir Fate;
As if Predestination over-rul'd
Thir will, dispos'd by absolute Decree
Or high foreknowledge; they themselves decreed
Thir own revolt, not I: if I foreknew,
Foreknowledge had no influence on their fault,
Which had no less prov'd certain unforeknown.
So without least impulse or shadow of Fate,   *120*
Or aught by me immutablie foreseen,
They trespass, Authors to themselves in all
Both what they judge and what they choose; for so
I formed them free, and free they must remain,
Till they enthrall themselves: I else must change
Thir nature, and revoke the high Decree
Unchangeable, Eternal, which ordain'd
Thir freedom, they themselves ordain'd thir fall.
The first sort by thir own suggestion fell,
Self-tempted, self-deprav'd: Man falls deceiv'd   *130*
By the other first: Man therefore shall find grace,
The other none: in Mercy and Justice both,
Through Heav'n and Earth, so shall my glorie excel,
But Mercy first and last shall brightest shine.
    Thus while God spake, ambrosial fragrance fill'd
All Heav'n, and in the blessed Spirits elect
Sense of new joy ineffable diffus'd:
Beyond compare the Son of God was seen
Most glorious, in him all his Father shon
Substantially express'd, and in his face   *140*
Divine compassion visibly appeerd,
Love without end, and without measure Grace,
Which uttering thus he to his Father spake.
    O Father, gracious was that word which clos'd
Thy sovran sentence, that Man should find grace;
For which both Heav'n and Earth shall high extoll
Thy praises, with th' innumerable sound
Of Hymns and sacred Songs, wherewith thy Throne
Encompass'd shall resound thee ever blest.
For should Man finally be lost, should Man   *150*
Thy creature late so lov'd, thy youngest Son
Fall circumvented thus by fraud, though joynd
With his own folly? that be from thee farr,
That farr be from thee, Father, who art Judge
Of all things made, and judgest onely right.
Or shall the Adversarie thus obtain
His end, and frustrate thine, shall he fulfill

His malice, and thy goodness bring to naught,
Or proud return though to his heavier doom,
Yet with revenge accomplish't and to Hell   160
Draw after him the whole Race of mankind,
By him corrupted? or wilt thou thy self
Abolish thy Creation, and unmake,
For him, what for thy glorie thou hast made?
So should thy goodness and thy greatness both
Be questiond and blaspheam'd without defence.
   To whom the great Creatour thus reply'd.
O Son, in whom my Soul hath chief delight,
Son of my bosom, Son who art alone
My word, my wisdom, and effectual might,   170
All hast thou spok'n as my thoughts are, all
As my Eternal purpose hath decreed:
Man shall not quite be lost, but sav'd who will,
Yet not of will in him, but grace in me
Freely voutsaft; once more I will renew
His lapsed powers, though forfeit and enthrall'd
By sin to foul exorbitant desires;
Upheld by me, yet once more he shall stand
On even ground against his mortal foe,
By me upheld, that he may know how frail   180
His fall'n condition is, and to me ow
All his deliv'rance, and to none but me.
Some I have chosen of peculiar grace
Elect above the rest; so is my will:
The rest shall hear me call, and oft be warnd
Thir sinful state, and to appease betimes
Th' incensed Deitie while offerd grace
Invites; for I will cleer thir senses dark,
What may suffice, and soft'n stonie hearts
To pray, repent, and bring obedience due.   190
To prayer, repentance, and obedience due,
Though but endevord with sincere intent,
Mine eare shall not be slow, mine eye not shut.
And I will place within them as a guide
My Umpire *Conscience*, whom if they will hear,
Light after light well us'd they shall attain,
And to the end persisting, safe arrive.
This my long sufferance and my day of grace
They who neglect and scorn, shall never taste;
But hard be hard'nd, blind be blinded more,   200
That they may stumble on, and deeper fall;
And none but such from mercy I exclude.
But yet all is not don; Man disobeying,

Disloyal breaks his fealtie, and sinns
Against the high Supremacie of Heav'n,
Affecting God-head, and so loosing all,
To expiate his Treason hath naught left,
But to destruction sacred and devote,
He with his whole posteritie must die,
Die hee or Justice must; unless for him   210
Som other able, and as willing, pay
The rigid satisfaction, death for death.
Say Heav'nly Powers, where shall we find such love,
Which of ye will be mortal to redeem
Mans mortal crime, and just th' unjust to save,
Dwels in all Heaven charitie so deare?
   He ask'd, but all the Heav'nly Quire stood mute,
And silence was in Heav'n: on mans behalf
Patron or Intercessor none appeerd,
Much less that durst upon his own head draw   220
The deadly forfeiture, and ransom set.
And now without redemption all mankind
Must have bin lost, adjudg'd to Death and Hell
By doom severe, had not the Son of God,
In whom the fulness dwels of love divine,
His dearest mediation thus renewd.
   Father, thy word is past, man shall find grace;
And shall grace not find means, that finds her way,
The speediest of thy winged messengers,
To visit all thy creatures, and to all   230
Comes unprevented, unimplor'd, unsought,
Happie for man, so coming; he her aide
Can never seek, once dead in sins and lost;
Attonement for himself or offering meet,
Indebted and undon, hath none to bring:
Behold mee then, mee for him, life for life
I offer, on mee let thine anger fall;
Account mee man; I for his sake will leave
Thy bosom, and this glorie next to thee
Freely put off, and for him lastly die   240
Well pleas'd, on me let Death wreck all his rage;
Under his gloomie power I shall not long
Lie vanquisht; thou hast givn me to possess
Life in my self for ever, by thee I live,
Though now to Death I yeild, and am his due
All that of me can die, yet that debt paid,
Thou wilt not leave me in the loathsom grave
His prey, nor suffer my unspotted Soule
For ever with corruption there to dwell;

But I shall rise Victorious, and subdue 250
My Vanquisher, spoild of his vanted spoile;
Death his deaths wound shall then receive, & stoop
Inglorious, of his mortall sting disarm'd.
I through the ample Air in Triumph high
Shall lead Hell Captive maugre Hell, and show
The powers of darkness bound. Thou at the sight
Pleas'd, out of Heaven shalt look down and smile,
While by thee rais'd I ruin all my Foes,
Death last, and with his Carcass glut the Grave:
Then with the multitude of my redeemd 260
Shall enter Heaven long absent, and returne,
Father, to see thy face, wherein no cloud
Of anger shall remain, but peace assur'd,
And reconcilement; wrauth shall be no more
Thenceforth, but in thy presence Joy entire.
   His words here ended, but his meek aspect
Silent yet spake, and breath'd immortal love
To mortal men, above which only shon
Filial obedience: as a sacrifice
Glad to be offer'd, he attends the will 270
Of his great Father. Admiration seis'd
All Heav'n, what this might mean, & whither tend
Wondring; but soon th' Almighty thus reply'd:
   O thou in Heav'n and Earth the only peace
Found out for mankind under wrauth, O thou
My sole complacence! well thou know'st how dear,
To me are all my works, nor Man the least
Though last created, that for him I spare
Thee from my bosom and right hand, to save,
By loosing thee a while, the whole Race lost. 280
Thou therefore whom thou only canst redeeme,
Thir Nature also to thy Nature joyne;
And be thy self Man among men on Earth,
Made flesh, when time shall be, of Virgin seed,
By wondrous birth: Be thou in *Adams* room
The Head of all mankind, though *Adams* Son.
As in him perish all men, so in thee
As from a second root shall be restor'd,
As many as are restor'd, without thee none.
His crime makes guiltie all his Sons, thy merit 290
Imputed shall absolve them who renounce
Thir own both righteous and unrighteous deeds,
And live in thee transplanted, and from thee
Receive new life. So Man, as is most just,
Shall satisfie for Man, be judg'd and die,

And dying rise, and rising with him raise
His Brethren, ransomd with his own dear life.
So Heav'nly love shal outdoo Hellish hate,
Giving to death, and dying to redeeme,
So dearly to redeem what Hellish hate   300
So easily destroy'd, and still destroyes
In those who, when they may, accept not grace.
Nor shalt thou by descending to assume
Mans Nature, less'n or degrade thine owne.
Because thou hast, though Thron'd in highest bliss
Equal to God, and equally enjoying
God-like fruition, quitted all to save
A World from utter loss, and hast been found
By Merit more then Birthright Son of God,
Found worthiest to be so by being Good,   310
Farr more then Great or High; because in thee
Love hath abounded more then Glory abounds,
Therefore thy Humiliation shall exalt
With thee thy Manhood also to this Throne;
Here shalt thou sit incarnate, here shalt Reigne
Both God and Man, Son both of God and Man,
Anointed universal King; all Power
I give thee, reign for ever, and assume
Thy Merits; under thee as Head Supream
Thrones, Princedoms, Powers, Dominions I reduce: 320
All knees to thee shall bow, of them that bide
In Heaven, or Earth, or under Earth in Hell;
When thou attended gloriously from Heav'n
Shalt in the Skie appeer, and from thee send
The summoning Arch-Angels to proclaime
Thy dread Tribunal: forthwith from all Windes
The living, and forthwith the cited dead
Of all past Ages to the general Doom
Shall hast'n, such a peal shall rouse thir sleep.
Then all thy Saints assembl'd, thou shalt judge   330
Bad men and Angels, they arraignd shall sink
Beneath thy Sentence; Hell, her numbers full,
Thenceforth shall be for ever shut. Mean while
The World shall burn, and from her ashes spring
New Heav'n and Earth, wherein the just shall dwell
And after all thir tribulations long
See golden days, fruitful of golden deeds,
With Joy and Love triumphing, and fair Truth.
Then thou thy regal Scepter shalt lay by,
For regal Scepter then no more shall need,   340
God shall be All in All. But all ye Gods,

Adore him, who to compass all this dies,
Adore the Son, and honour him as mee.
    No sooner had th' Almighty ceas't, but all
The multitude of Angels with a shout
Loud as from numbers without number, sweet
As from blest voices, uttering joy, Heav'n rung
With Jubilee, and loud Hosannas fill'd
Th' eternal Regions: lowly reverent
Towards either Throne they bow, & to the ground   *350*
With solemn adoration down they cast
Thir Crowns inwove with Amarant and Gold,
Immortal Amarant, a Flour which once
In Paradise, fast by the Tree of Life
Began to bloom, but soon for mans offence
To Heav'n remov'd where first it grew, there grows,
And flours aloft shading the Fount of Life,
And where the river of Bliss through midst of Heavn
Rowls o're *Elisian* Flours her Amber stream;
With these that never fade the Spirits Elect   *360*
Bind thir resplendent locks inwreath'd with beams,
Now in loose Garlands thick thrown off, the bright
Pavement that like a Sea of Jasper shon
Impurpl'd with Celestial Roses smil'd.
Then Crown'd again thir gold'n Harps they took,
Harps ever tun'd, that glittering by thir side
Like Quivers hung, and with Præamble sweet
Of charming symphonie they introduce
Thir sacred Song, and waken raptures high;
No voice exempt, no voice but well could joine   *370*
Melodious part, such concord is in Heav'n.
    Thee Father first they sung Omnipotent,
Immutable, Immortal, Infinite,
Eternal King; thee Author of all being,
Fountain of Light, thy self invisible
Amidst the glorious brightness where thou sit'st
Thron'd inaccessible, but when thou shad'st
The full blaze of thy beams, and through a cloud
Drawn round about thee like a radiant Shrine,
Dark with excessive bright thy skirts appeer,   *380*
Yet dazle Heav'n, that brightest Seraphim
Approach not, but with both wings veil thir eyes.
Thee next they sang of all Creation first,
Begotten Son, Divine Similitude,
In whose conspicuous count'nance, without cloud
Made visible, th' Almighty Father shines,
Whom else no Creature can behold; on thee

Impresst the effulgence of his Glorie abides,
Transfus'd on thee his ample Spirit rests.
Hee Heav'n of Heavens and all the Powers therein 390
By thee created, and by thee threw down
Th' Aspiring Dominations: thou that day
Thy Fathers dreadful Thunder didst not spare,
Nor stop thy flaming Chariot wheels, that shook
Heav'ns everlasting Frame, while o're the necks
Thou drov'st of warring Angels disarraid.
Back from pursuit thy Powers with loud acclaime
Thee only extold, Son of thy Fathers might,
To execute fierce vengeance on his foes,
Not so on Man; him through their malice fall'n, 400
Father of Mercie and Grace, thou didst not doome
So strictly, but much more to pitie encline:
No sooner did thy dear and onely Son
Perceive thee purpos'd not to doom frail Man
So strictly, but much more to pitie enclin'd,
He to appease thy wrauth, and end the strife
Of Mercy and Justice in thy face discern'd,
Regardless of the Bliss wherein hee sat
Second to thee, offerd himself to die
For mans offence. O unexampl'd love, 410
Love no where to be found less then Divine!
Hail Son of God, Saviour of Men, thy Name
Shall be the copious matter of my Song
Henceforth, and never shall my Harp thy praise
Forget, nor from thy Fathers praise disjoine.
 Thus they in Heav'n, above the starry Sphear,
Thir happie hours in joy and hymning spent.
Mean while upon the firm opacous Globe
Of this round World, whose first convex divides
The luminous inferior Orbs, enclos'd 420
From *Chaos* and th' inroad of Darkness old,
Satan alighted walks: a Globe farr off
It seem'd, now seems a boundless Continent
Dark, waste, and wild, under the frown of Night
Starless expos'd, and ever-threatning storms
Of *Chaos* blustring round, inclement skie;
Save on that side which from the wall of Heav'n
Though distant farr som small reflection gaines
Of glimmering air less vext with tempest loud:
Here walk'd the Fiend at large in spacious field. 430
As when a Vultur on *Imaus* bred,
Whose snowie ridge the roving *Tartar* bounds,
Dislodging from a Region scarce of prey

To gorge the flesh of Lambs or yeanling Kids
On Hills where Flocks are fed, flies toward the Springs
Of *Ganges* or *Hydaspes*, *Indian* streams;
But in his way lights on the barren plaines
Of *Sericana*, where *Chineses* drive
With Sails and Wind thir canie Waggons light:
So on this windie Sea of Land, the Fiend   *440*
Walk'd up and down alone bent on his prey,
Alone, for other Creature in this place
Living or liveless to be found was none,
None yet, but store hereafter from the earth
Up hither like Aereal vapours flew
Of all things transitorie and vain, when Sin
With vanity had filld the works of men:
Both all things vain, and all who in vain things
Built their fond hopes of Glorie or lasting fame,
Or happiness in this or th' other life;   *450*
All who have thir reward on Earth, the fruits
Of painful Superstition and blind Zeal,
Naught seeking but the praise of men, here find
Fit retribution, emptie as thir deeds;
All th' unaccomplisht works of Natures hand,
Abortive, monstrous, or unkindly mixt,
Dissolvd on earth, fleet hither, and in vain,
Till final dissolution, wander here,
Not in the neighbouring Moon, as some have dreamd;
Those argent Fields more likely habitants,   *460*
Translated Saints, or middle Spirits hold
Betwixt th' Angelical and Human kinde:
Hither of ill-joynd Sons and Daughters born
First from the ancient World those Giants came
With many a vain exploit, though then renownd:
The builders next of *Babel* on the Plain
Of *Sennaar*, and still with vain designe
New *Babels*, had they wherewithall, would build:
Others came single; hee who to be deemd
A God, leap'd fondly into *Ætna* flames   *470*
Empedocles, and hee who to enjoy
Plato's Elysium, leap'd into the Sea,
Cleombrotus, and many more too long,
Embryos, and Idiots, Eremits and Friers
White, Black and Grey, with all thir trumperie.
Here Pilgrims roam, that stray'd so farr to seek
In *Golgotha* him dead, who lives in Heav'n;
And they who to be sure of Paradise
Dying put on the weeds of *Dominic*,

Or in *Franciscan* think to pass disguis'd; 480
They pass the Planets seven, and pass the fixt,
And that Crystalline Sphear whose ballance weighs
The Trepidation talkt, and that first mov'd;
And now Saint *Peter* at Heav'ns Wicket seems
To wait them with his Keys, and now at foot
Of Heav'ns ascent they lift thir Feet, when loe
A violent cross wind from either Coast
Blows them transverse ten thousand Leagues awry
Into the devious Air; then might ye see
Cowles, Hoods and Habits with thir wearers tost 490
And flutterd into Raggs, then Reliques, Beads,
Indulgences, Dispenses, Pardons, Bulls,
The sport of Winds: all these upwhirld aloft
Fly o're the backside of the World farr off
Into a *Limbo* large and broad, since calld
The Paradise of Fools, to few unknown
Long after, now unpeopl'd, and untrod;
All this dark Globe the Fiend found as he pass'd,
And long he wanderd, till at last a gleame
Of dawning light turnd thither-ward in haste 500
His travell'd steps; farr distant hee descries
Ascending by degrees magnificent
Up to the wall of Heaven a Structure high,
At top whereof, but farr more rich appeerd
The work as of a Kingly Palace Gate
With Frontispice of Diamond and Gold
Imbellisht, thick with sparkling orient Gemmes
The Portal shon, inimitable on Earth
By Model, or by shading Pencil drawn.
The Stairs were such as whereon *Jacob* saw 510
Angels ascending and descending, bands
Of Guardians bright, when he from *Esau* fled
To *Padan-Aram* in the field of *Luz*,
Dreaming by night under the open Skie,
And waking cri'd, This is the Gate of Heav'n.
Each Stair mysteriously was meant, nor stood
There alwaies, but drawn up to Heav'n somtimes
Viewless, and underneath a bright Sea flow'd
Of Jasper, or of liquid Pearle, whereon
Who after came from Earth, sayling arriv'd, 520
Wafted by Angels, or flew o're the Lake
Rapt in a Chariot drawn by fiery Steeds.
The Stairs were then let down, whether to dare
The Fiend by easie ascent, or aggravate
His sad exclusion from the dores of Bliss.

Direct against which op'nd from beneath,
Just o're the blissful seat of Paradise,
A passage down to th' Earth, a passage wide,
Wider by farr then that of after-times
Over Mount *Sion*, and, though that were large,   530
Over the *Promis'd Land* to God so dear,
By which, to visit oft those happy Tribes,
On high behests his Angels to and fro
Pass'd frequent, and his eye with choice regard
From *Paneas* the fount of *Jordans* flood
To *Bëersaba*, where the *Holy Land*
Borders on *Ægypt* and the *Arabian* shoare;
So wide the op'ning seemd, where bounds were set
To darkness, such as bound the Ocean wave.
Satan from hence now on the lower stair   540
That scal'd by steps of Gold to Heav'n Gate
Looks down with wonder at the sudden view
Of all this World at once. As when a Scout
Through dark and desart wayes with peril gone
All night; at last by break of chearful dawne
Obtains the brow of some high-climbing Hill,
Which to his eye discovers unaware
The goodly prospect of some forein land
First seen, or some renownd Metropolis
With glistering Spires and Pinnacles adornd,   550
Which now the Rising Sun guilds with his beams.
Such wonder seis'd, though after Heaven seen,
The Spirit maligne, but much more envy seis'd
At sight of all this World beheld so faire.
Round he surveys, and well might, where he stood
So high above the circling Canopie
Of Nights extended shade; from Eastern Point
Of *Libra* to the fleecie Starr that bears
Andromeda farr off *Atlantick* Seas
Beyond th' *Horizon;* then from Pole to Pole   560
He views in bredth, and without longer pause
Down right into the Worlds first Region throws
His flight precipitant, and windes with ease
Through the pure marble Air his oblique way
Amongst innumerable Starrs, that shon
Stars distant, but nigh hand seemd other Worlds,
Or other Worlds they seemd, or happy Iles,
Like those *Hesperian* Gardens fam'd of old,
Fortunate Fields, and Groves and flourie Vales,
Thrice happy Iles, but who dwelt happy there   570
He stayd not to enquire: above them all

The golden Sun in splendor likest Heaven
Allur'd his eye: Thither his course he bends
Through the calm Firmament; but up or downe
By center, or eccentric, hard to tell,
Or Longitude, where the great Luminarie
Aloof the vulgar Constellations thick,
That from his Lordly eye keep distance due,
Dispenses Light from farr; they as they move
Thir Starry dance in numbers that compute   580
Days, months, and years, towards his all-chearing Lamp
Turn swift their various motions, or are turnd
By his Magnetic beam, that gently warms
The Univers, and to each inward part
With gentle penetration, though unseen,
Shoots invisible vertue even to the deep:
So wondrously was set his Station bright.
There lands the Fiend, a spot like which perhaps
Astronomer in the Sun's lucent Orbe
Through his glaz'd Optic Tube yet never saw.   590
The place he found beyond expression bright,
Compar'd with aught on Earth, Medal or Stone;
Not all parts like, but all alike informd
With radiant light, as glowing Iron with fire;
If mettal, part seemd Gold, part Silver cleer;
If stone, Carbuncle most or Chrysolite,
Rubie or Topaz, to the Twelve that shon
In *Aarons* Brestplate, and a stone besides
Imagind rather oft then elsewhere seen,
That stone, or like to that which here below   600
Philosophers in vain so long have sought,
In vain, though by thir powerful Art they binde
Volatil *Hermes*, and call up unbound
In various shapes old *Proteus* from the Sea,
Draind through a Limbec to his Native forme.
What wonder then if fields and regions here
Breathe forth *Elixir* pure, and Rivers run
Potable Gold, when with one vertuous touch
Th' Arch-chimic Sun so farr from us remote
Produces with Terrestrial Humor mixt   610
Here in the dark so many precious things
Of colour glorious and effect so rare?
Here matter new to gaze the Devil met
Undazl'd, farr and wide his eye commands,
For sight no obstacle found here, nor shade,
But all Sun-shine, as when his Beams at Noon
Culminate from th' *Æquator*, as they now

Shot upward still direct, whence no way round
Shadow from body opaque can fall, and the Aire,
No where so cleer, sharp'nd his visual ray   620
To objects distant farr, whereby he soon
Saw within kenn a glorious Angel stand,
The same whom *John* saw also in the Sun:
His back was turnd, but not his brightness hid;
Of beaming sunnie Raies, a golden tiar
Circl'd his Head, nor less his Locks behind
Illustrious on his Shoulders fledge with wings
Lay waving round; on som great charge imploy'd
Hee seemd, or fixt in cogitation deep.
Glad was the Spirit impure; as now in hope   630
To find who might direct his wandring flight
To Paradise the happie seat of Man,
His journies end and our beginning woe.
But first he casts to change his proper shape,
Which else might work him danger or delay:
And now a stripling Cherube he appeers,
Not of the prime, yet such as in his face
Youth smil'd Celestial, and to every Limb
Sutable grace diffus'd, so well he feignd;
Under a Coronet his flowing haire   640
In curles on either cheek plaid, wings he wore
Of many a colour'd plume sprinkl'd with Gold,
His habit fit for speed succinct, and held
Before his decent steps a Silver wand.
He drew not nigh unheard, the Angel bright,
Ere he drew nigh, his radiant visage turnd,
Admonisht by his eare, and strait was known
Th' Arch-Angel *Uriel*, one of the seav'n
Who in God's presence, neerest to his Throne
Stand ready at command, and are his Eyes   650
That run through all the Heav'ns, or down to th' Earth
Bear his swift errands over moist and dry,
O're Sea and Land; him *Satan* thus accostes.
 Uriel, for thou of those seav'n Spirits that stand
In sight of Gods high Throne, gloriously bright,
The first art wont his great authentic will
Interpreter through highest Heav'n to bring,
Where all his Sons thy Embassie attend;
And here art likeliest by supream decree
Like honour to obtain, and as his Eye   660
To visit oft this new Creation round;
Unspeakable desire to see, and know
All these his wondrous works, but chiefly Man,

His chief delight and favour, him for whom
All these his works so wondrous he ordaind,
Hath brought me from the Quires of Cherubim
Alone thus wandring. Brightest Seraph tell
In which of all these shining Orbes hath Man
His fixed seat, or fixed seat hath none,
But all these shining Orbes his choice to dwell;   670
That I may find him, and with secret gaze,
Or open admiration him behold
On whom the great Creator hath bestowd
Worlds, and on whom hath all these graces powrd;
That both in him and all things, as is meet,
The Universal Maker we may praise;
Who justly hath drivn out his Rebell Foes
To deepest Hell, and to repair that loss
Created this new happie Race of Men
To serve him better: wise are all his wayes.   680
  So spake the false dissembler unperceivd;
For neither Man nor Angel can discern
Hypocrisie, the only evil that walks
Invisible, except to God alone,
By his permissive will, through Heav'n and Earth:
And oft though wisdom wake, suspicion sleeps
At wisdoms Gate, and to simplicitie
Resigns her charge, while goodness thinks no ill
Where no ill seems: Which now for once beguil'd
Uriel, though Regent of the Sun, and held   690
The sharpest sighted Spirit of all in Heav'n;
Who to the fraudulent Impostor foule
In his uprightness answer thus returnd.
  Faire Angel, thy desire which tends to know
The works of God, thereby to glorifie
The great Work-Maister, leads to no excess
That reaches blame, but rather merits praise
The more it seems excess, that led thee hither
From thy Empyreal Mansion thus alone,
To witness with thine eyes what some perhaps   700
Contented with report heare onely in heav'n:
For wonderful indeed are all his works,
Pleasant to know, and worthiest to be all
Had in remembrance alwayes with delight;
But what created mind can comprehend
Thir number, or the wisdom infinite
That brought them forth, but hid thir causes deep.
I saw when at his Word the formless Mass,
This worlds material mould, came to a heap:

Confusion heard his voice, and wilde uproar 710
Stood rul'd, stood vast infinitude confin'd;
Till at his second bidding darkness fled,
Light shon, and order from disorder sprung:
Swift to thir several Quarters hasted then
The cumbrous Elements, Earth, Flood, Aire, Fire,
And this Ethereal quintessence of Heav'n
Flew upward, spirited with various forms,
That rowld orbicular, and turnd to Starrs
Numberless, as thou seest, and how they move;
Each had his place appointed, each his course, 720
The rest in circuit walles this Universe.
Look downward on that Globe whose hither side
With light from hence, though but reflected, shines;
That place is Earth the seat of Man, that light
His day, which else as th' other Hemisphere
Night would invade, but there the neighbouring Moon
(So call that opposite fair Starr) her aide
Timely interposes, and her monthly round
Still ending, still renewing through mid Heav'n,
With borrowd light her countenance triform 730
Hence fills and empties to enlighten the Earth,
And in her pale dominion checks the night.
That spot to which I point is *Paradise*,
Adams abode, those loftie shades his Bowre.
Thy way thou canst not miss, me mine requires.
    Thus said, he turnd, and *Satan* bowing low,
As to superior Spirits is wont in Heav'n,
Where honour due and reverence none neglects,
Took leave, and toward the coast of Earth beneath,
Down from th' Ecliptic, sped with hop'd success, 740
Throws his steep flight in many an Aerie wheele,
Nor staid, till on *Niphates* top he lights.

BOOK IV

THE ARGUMENT

Satan *now in prospect of* Eden, *and nigh the place where he must now attempt the bold enterprize which he undertook alone against God and Man, falls into many doubts with himself, and many passions, fear, envy, and despare; but at length confirms himself in evil, journeys on to Paradise, whose outward prospect and scituation is described, overleaps the bounds, sits in the shape of a Cormorant on the Tree of life, as highest in the Garden to look about him. The Garden describ'd;* Satans *first sight of* Adam *and* Eve; *his wonder at thir excellent form and happy state, but with resolution to work thir fall; overhears thir discourse, thence gathers that the Tree of knowledge was forbidden them to eat of, under penalty of death; and thereon intends to found his temptation, by seducing them to transgress: then leaves them a while, to know further of thir state by some other means. Mean while* Uriel *descending on a Sun-beam warns* Gabriel, *who had in charge the Gate of Paradise, that some evil spirit had escap'd the Deep, and past at Noon by his Sphere in the shape of a good Angel down to Paradise, discovered after by his furious gestures in the Mount.* Gabriel *promises to find him out ere morning. Night coming on,* Adam *and* Eve *discourse of going to thir rest: thir Bower describ'd; thir Evening worship.* Gabriel *drawing forth his Bands of Night-watch to walk the round of Paradise, appoints two strong Angels to* Adams *Bower, least the evill spirit should be there doing some harm to* Adam *or* Eve *sleeping; there they find him at the ear of* Eve, *tempting her in a dream, and bring him, though unwilling, to* Gabriel; *by whom question'd, he scornfully answers, prepares resistance, but hinder'd by a Sign from Heaven, flies out of Paradise.*

O FOR that warning voice, which he who saw
Th' *Apocalyps,* heard cry in Heav'n aloud,
Then when the Dragon, put to second rout,
Came furious down to be reveng'd on men,
Wo to the inhabitants on Earth! that now,
While time was, our first Parents had bin warnd
The coming of thir secret foe, and scap'd
Haply so scap'd his mortal snare; for now
Satan, now first inflam'd with rage came down,
The Tempter ere th' Accuser of man-kind,   *10*
To wreck on innocent frail man his loss
Of that first Battel, and his flight to Hell:
Yet not rejoycing in his speed, though bold,
Far off and fearless, nor with cause to boast,
Begins his dire attempt, which nigh the birth
Now rowling, boiles in his tumultuous brest,
And like a devillish Engine back recoiles
Upon himself; horror and doubt distract
His troubl'd thoughts, and from the bottom stirr
The Hell within him, for within him Hell   *20*

He brings, and round about him, nor from Hell
One step no more then from himself can fly
By change of place: Now conscience wakes despair
That slumberd, wakes the bitter memorie
Of what he was, what is, and what must be
Worse; of worse deeds worse sufferings must ensue.
Sometimes towards *Eden* which now in his view
Lay pleasant, his grievd look he fixes sad,
Sometimes towards Heav'n and the full-blazing Sun,
Which now sat high in his Meridian Towre: 30
Then much revolving, thus in sighs began.
   O thou that with surpassing Glory crownd,
Look'st from thy sole Dominion like the God
Of this new World; at whose sight all the Starrs
Hide thir diminisht heads; to thee I call,
But with no friendly voice, and add thy name
O Sun, to tell thee how I hate thy beams
That bring to my remembrance from what state
I fell, how glorious once above thy Spheare;
Till Pride and worse Ambition threw me down 40
Warring in Heav'n against Heav'ns matchless King:
Ah wherefore! he deservd no such return
From me, whom he created what I was
In that bright eminence, and with his good
Upbraided none; nor was his service hard.
What could be less then to afford him praise,
The easiest recompence, and pay him thanks,
How due! yet all his good prov'd ill in me,
And wrought but malice; lifted up so high
I 'sdeind subjection, and thought one step higher 50
Would set me highest, and in a moment quit
The debt immense of endless gratitude,
So burthensome, still paying, still to ow;
Forgetful what from him I still receivd,
And understood not that a grateful mind
By owing owes not, but still pays, at once
Indebted and discharged; what burden then?
O had his powerful Destiny ordaind
Me some inferiour Angel, I had stood
Then happie; no unbounded hope had rais'd 60
Ambition. Yet why not? som other Power
As great might have aspir'd, and me though mean
Drawn to his part; but other Powers as great
Fell not, but stand unshak'n, from within
Or from without, to all temptations arm'd.
Hadst thou the same free Will and Power to stand?

Thou hadst: whom hast thou then or what to accuse,
But Heav'ns free Love dealt equally to all?
Be then his Love accurst, since love or hate,
To me alike, it deals eternal woe.   70
Nay curs'd be thou; since against his thy will
Chose freely what it now so justly rues.
Me miserable! which way shall I flie
Infinite wrauth, and infinite despaire?
Which way I flie is Hell; my self am Hell;
And in the lowest deep a lower deep
Still threatning to devour me opens wide,
To which the Hell I suffer seems a Heav'n.
O then at last relent: is there no place
Left for Repentance, none for Pardon left?   80
None left but by submission; and that word
Disdain forbids me, and my dread of shame
Among the spirits beneath, whom I seduc'd
With other promises and other vaunts
Then to submit, boasting I could subdue
Th' Omnipotent. Ay me, they little know
How dearly I abide that boast so vaine,
Under what torments inwardly I groane:
While they adore me on the Throne of Hell,
With Diadem and Scepter high advancd   90
The lower still I fall, onely Supream
In miserie; such joy Ambition findes.
But say I could repent and could obtaine
By Act of Grace my former state; how soon
Would highth recal high thoughts, how soon unsay
What feign'd submission swore: ease would recant
Vows made in pain, as violent and void.
For never can true reconcilement grow
Where wounds of deadly hate have peirc'd so deep:
Which would but lead me to a worse relapse,   100
And heavier fall: so should I purchase deare
Short intermission bought with double smart.
This knows my punisher; therefore as farr
From granting hee, as I from begging peace:
All hope excluded thus, behold in stead
Of us out-cast, exil'd, his new delight,
Mankind created, and for him this World.
So farwel Hope, and with Hope farwel Fear,
Farwel Remorse: all Good to me is lost;
Evil be thou my Good; by thee at least   110
Divided Empire with Heav'ns King I hold
By thee, and more then half perhaps will reigne;

As Man ere long, and this new World shall know.
   Thus while he spake, each passion dimm'd his face
Thrice chang'd with pale, ire, envie and despair,
Which marrd his borrow'd visage, and betraid
Him counterfet, if any eye beheld.
For heav'nly mindes from such distempers foule
Are ever cleer. Whereof hee soon aware,
Each perturbation smooth'd with outward calme,   *120*
Artificer of fraud; and was the first
That practisd falshood under saintly shew,
Deep malice to conceale, couch't with revenge:
Yet not anough had practisd to deceive
Uriel once warnd; whose eye pursu'd him down
The way he went, and on th' *Assyrian* mount
Saw him disfigur'd, more then could befall
Spirit of happie sort: his gestures fierce
He markd and mad demeanour, then alone,
As he suppos'd all unobserv'd, unseen.   *130*
So on he fares, and to the border comes
Of *Eden*, where delicious Paradise,
Now nearer, Crowns with her enclosure green,
As with a rural mound the champain head
Of a steep wilderness, whose hairie sides
With thicket overgrown, grottesque and wilde,
Access deni'd; and over head up grew
Insuperable highth of loftiest shade,
Cedar, and Pine, and Firr, and branching Palm
A Silvan Scene, and as the ranks ascend   *140*
Shade above shade, a woodie Theatre
Of stateliest view. Yet higher then thir tops
The verdurous wall of Paradise up sprung:
Which to our general Sire gave prospect large
Into his neather Empire neighbouring round.
And higher then that wall a circling row
Of goodliest Trees loaden with fairest Fruit,
Blossoms and Fruits at once of golden hue
Appeerd, with gay enameld colours mixt:
On which the Sun more glad impress'd his beams   *150*
Then in fair Evening Cloud, or humid Bow,
When God hath showrd the earth; so lovely seemd
That Lantskip: And of pure now purer aire
Meets his approach, and to the heart inspires
Vernal delight and joy, able to drive
All sadness but despair: now gentle gales
Fanning thir odoriferous wings dispense
Native perfumes, and whisper whence they stole

Those balmie spoiles. As when to them who sail
Beyond the *Cape of Hope*, and now are past   160
Mozambic, off at Sea North-East windes blow
Sabean Odours from the spicie shoare
Of *Arabie* the blest, with such delay
Well pleas'd they slack thir course, and many a League
Cheard with the grateful smell old Ocean smiles.
So entertaind those odorous sweets the Fiend
Who came thir bane, though with them better pleas'd
Then *Asmodeus* with the fishie fume,
That drove him, though enamourd, from the Spouse
Of *Tobits* Son, and with a vengeance sent   170
From *Media* post to *Ægypt*, there fast bound.
   Now to th' ascent of that steep savage Hill
Satan had journied on, pensive and slow;
But further way found none, so thick entwin'd,
As one continu'd brake, the undergrowth
Of shrubs and tangling bushes had perplext
All path of Man or Beast that past that way:
One Gate there onely was, and that look'd East
On th' other side: which when th' arch-fellon saw
Due entrance he disdaind, and in contempt,   180
At one slight bound high overleap'd all bound
Of Hill or highest Wall, and sheer within
Lights on his feet. As when a prowling Wolfe,
Whom hunger drives to seek new haunt for prey,
Watching where Shepherds pen thir Flocks at eeve
In hurdl'd Cotes amid the field secure,
Leaps o're the fence with ease into the Fould:
Or as a Thief bent to unhoord the cash
Of some rich Burgher, whose substantial dores,
Cross-barrd and bolted fast, fear no assault,   190
In at the window climbes, or o're the tiles:
So clomb this first grand Thief into Gods Fould:
So since into his Church lewd Hirelings climbe.
Thence up he flew, and on the Tree of Life,
The middle Tree and highest there that grew,
Sat like a Cormorant; yet not true Life
Thereby regaind, but sat devising Death
To them who liv'd; nor on the vertue thought
Of that life-giving Plant, but only us'd
For prospect, what well us'd had bin the pledge   200
Of immortalitie. So little knows
Any, but God alone, to value right
The good before him, but perverts best things
To worst abuse, or to thir meanest use.

Beneath him with new wonder now he views
To all delight of human sense expos'd
In narrow room Natures whole wealth, yea more,
A Heaven on Earth: for blissful Paradise
Of God the Garden was, by him in the East
Of *Eden* planted; *Eden* stretchd her Line   210
From *Auran* Eastward to the Royal Towrs
Of Great *Seleucia*, built by *Grecian* Kings,
Or where the Sons of *Eden* long before
Dwelt in *Telassar:* in this pleasant soile
His farr more pleasant Garden God ordaind;
Out of the fertil ground he caus'd to grow
All Trees of noblest kind for sight, smell, taste;
And all amid them stood the Tree of Life,
High eminent, blooming Ambrosial Fruit
Of vegetable Gold; and next to Life   220
Our Death the Tree of Knowledge grew fast by,
Knowledge of Good bought dear by knowing ill.
Southward through *Eden* went a River large,
Nor chang'd his course, but through the shaggie hill
Pass'd underneath ingulft, for God had thrown
That Mountain as his Garden mould high rais'd
Upon the rapid current, which through veins
Of porous Earth with kindly thirst up drawn,
Rose a fresh Fountain, and with many a rill
Waterd the Garden; thence united fell   230
Down the steep glade, and met the neather Flood,
Which from his darksom passage now appeers,
And now divided into four main Streams,
Runs divers, wandring many a famous Realme
And Country whereof here needs no account,
But rather to tell how, if Art could tell,
How from that Saphire Fount the crisped Brooks,
Rowling on Orient Pearl and sands of Gold,
With mazie error under pendant shades
Ran Nectar, visiting each plant, and fed   240
Flours worthy of Paradise which not nice Art
In Beds and curious Knots, but Nature boon
Powrd forth profuse on Hill and Dale and Plaine,
Both where the morning Sun first warmly smote
The open field, and where the unpierc't shade
Imbround the noontide Bowrs: Thus was this place,
A happy rural seat of various view:
Groves whose rich Trees wept odorous Gumms and
    Balme,
Others whose fruit burnisht with Golden Rinde

Hung amiable, *Hesperian* Fables true,   *250*
If true, here onely, and of delicious taste:
Betwixt them Lawns, or level Downs, and Flocks
Grasing the tender herb, were interpos'd,
Or palmie hilloc, or the flourie lap
Of som irriguous Valley spread her store,
Flours of all hue, and without Thorn the Rose:
Another side, umbrageous Grots and Caves
Of coole recess, o're which the mantling Vine
Layes forth her purple Grape, and gently creeps
Luxuriant; mean while murmuring waters fall   *260*
Down the slope hills, disperst, or in a Lake,
That to the fringed Bank with Myrtle crownd,
Her chrystall mirror holds, unite thir streams.
The Birds thir quire apply; aires, vernal aires,
Breathing the smell of field and grove, attune
The trembling leaves, while Universal *Pan*
Knit with the *Graces* and the *Hours* in dance
Led on th' Eternal Spring. Not that faire field
Of *Enna*, where *Proserpin* gathring flours
Her self a fairer Floure by gloomie *Dis*   *270*
Was gatherd, which cost *Ceres* all that pain
To seek her through the world; nor that sweet Grove
Of *Daphne* by *Orontes*, and th' inspir'd
Castalian Spring might with this Paradise
Of *Eden* strive; nor that *Nyseian* Ile
Girt with the River *Triton*, where old *Cham*,
Whom Gentiles *Ammon* call and *Libyan Jove*,
Hid *Amalthea* and her Florid Son
Young *Bacchus* from his Stepdame *Rhea's* eye;
Nor where *Abassin* Kings thir issue Guard,   *280*
Mount *Amara*, though this by som suppos'd
True Paradise under the *Ethiop* Line
By *Nilus* head, enclos'd with shining Rock,
A whole dayes journey high, but wide remote
From this *Assyrian* Garden, where the Fiend
Saw undelighted all delight, all kind
Of living Creatures new to sight and strange:
Two of far nobler shape erect and tall,
Godlike erect, with native Honour clad
In naked Majestie seemd Lords of all,   *290*
And worthie seemd, for in thir looks Divine
The image of thir glorious Maker shon,
Truth, Wisdome, Sanctitude severe and pure,
Severe, but in true filial freedom plac't;
Whence true autoritie in men; though both

Not equal, as their sex not equal seemd;
For contemplation hee and valour formd,
For softness shee and sweet attractive Grace,
Hee for God only, shee for God in him:
His fair large Front and Eye sublime declar'd   300
Absolute rule; and Hyacinthin Locks
Round from his parted forelock manly hung
Clustring, but not beneath his shoulders broad:
Shee as a vail down to the slender waste
Her unadorned golden tresses wore
Dissheveld, but in wanton ringlets wav'd
As the Vine curles her tendrils, which impli'd
Subjection, but requir'd with gentle sway,
And by her yeilded, by him best receivd,
Yeilded with coy submission, modest pride,   310
And sweet reluctant amorous delay.
Nor those mysterious parts were then conceald,
Then was not guiltie shame, dishonest shame
Of natures works, honor dishonorable,
Sin-bred, how have ye troubl'd all mankind
With shews instead, meer shews of seeming pure,
And banisht from mans life his happiest life,
Simplicitie and spotless innocence.
So passd they naked on, nor shund the sight
Of God or Angel, for they thought no ill: 320
So hand in hand they passd, the lovliest pair
That ever since in loves imbraces met,
Adam the goodliest man of men since born
His Sons, the fairest of her Daughters *Eve*.
Under a tuft of shade that on a green
Stood whispering soft, by a fresh Fountain side
They sat them down, and after no more toil
Of thir sweet Gardning labour then suffic'd
To recommend coole *Zephyr*, and made ease
More easie, wholsom thirst and appetite   330
More grateful, to thir Supper Fruits they fell,
Nectarine Fruits which the compliant boughes
Yeilded them, side-long as they sat recline
On the soft downie Bank damaskt with flours:
The savourie pulp they chew, and in the rinde
Still as they thirsted scoop the brimming stream;
Nor gentle purpose, nor endearing smiles
Wanted, nor youthful dalliance as beseems
Fair couple, linkt in happie nuptial League,
Alone as they. About them frisking playd   340
All Beasts of th' Earth, since wilde, and of all chase

In Wood or Wilderness, Forrest or Den;
Sporting the Lion rampd, and in his paw
Dandl'd the Kid; Bears, Tygers, Ounces, Pards
Gambold before them, th' unwieldy Elephant
To make them mirth us'd all his might, and wreathd
His Lithe Proboscis; close the Serpent sly
Insinuating, wove with Gordian twine
His breaded train, and of his fatal guile
Gave proof unheeded; others on the grass   350
Coucht, and now fild with pasture gazing sat,
Or Bedward ruminating; for the Sun
Declin'd was hasting now with prone carreer
To th' Ocean Iles, and in th' ascending Scale
Of Heav'n the Starrs that usher Evening rose:
When *Satan* still in gaze, as first he stood,
Scarce thus at length faild speech recoverd sad.

   O Hell! what doe mine eyes with grief behold,
Into our room of bliss thus high advanc't
Creatures of other mould, earth-born perhaps,   360
Not Spirits, yet to heav'nly Spirits bright
Little inferior; whom my thoughts pursue
With wonder, and could love, so lively shines
In them Divine resemblance, and such grace
The hand that formd them on thir shape hath pourd.
Ah gentle pair, yee little think how nigh
Your change approaches, when all these delights
Will vanish and deliver ye to woe,
More woe, the more your taste is now of joy;
Happie, but for so happie ill secur'd   370
Long to continue, and this high seat your Heav'n
Ill fenc't for Heav'n to keep out such a foe
As now is enterd; yet no purpos'd foe
To you whom I could pittie thus forlorne
Though I unpittied: League with you I seek,
And mutual amitie so streight, so close,
That I with you must dwell, or you with me
Henceforth; my dwelling haply may not please
Like this fair Paradise, your sense, yet such
Accept your Makers work; he gave it me,   380
Which I as freely give; Hell shall unfould,
To entertain you two, her widest Gates,
And send forth all her Kings; there will be room,
Not like these narrow limits, to receive
Your numerous ofspring; if no better place,
Thank him who puts me loath to this revenge
On you who wrong me not for him who wrongd.

And should I at your harmless innocence
Melt, as I doe, yet public reason just,
Honour and Empire with revenge enlarg'd,   390
By conquering this new World, compels me now
To do what else though damnd I should abhorre.
   So spake the Fiend, and with necessitie,
The Tyrants plea, excus'd his devilish deeds.
Then from his loftie stand on that high Tree
Down he alights among the sportful Herd
Of those fourfooted kindes, himself now one,
Now other, as thir shape servd best his end
Neerer to view his prey, and unespi'd
To mark what of thir state he more might learn   400
By word or action markt about them round
A Lion now he stalkes with fierie glare,
Then as a Tiger, who by chance hath spi'd
In some Purlieu two gentle Fawnes at play,
Strait couches close, then rising changes oft
His couchant watch, as one who chose his ground
Whence rushing he might surest seise them both
Grip't in each paw: when *Adam* first of men
To first of women *Eve* thus moving speech,
Turnd him all eare to heare new utterance flow.   410
   Sole partner and sole part of all these joyes,
Dearer thy self then all; needs must the Power
That made us, and for us this ample World
Be infinitly good, and of his good
As liberal and free as infinite,
That rais'd us from the dust and plac't us here
In all this happiness, who at his hand
Have nothing merited, nor can performe
Aught whereof hee hath need, hee who requires
From us no other service then to keep   420
This one, this easie charge, of all the Trees
In Paradise that beare delicious fruit
So various, not to taste that onely Tree
Of knowledge, planted by the Tree of Life,
So neer grows Death to Life, what ere Death is,
Som dreadful thing no doubt; for well thou knowst
God hath pronounc't it death to taste that Tree,
The only sign of our obedience left
Among so many signes of power and rule
Conferrd upon us, and Dominion giv'n   430
Over all other Creatures that possesse
Earth, Aire, and Sea. Then let us not think hard
One easie prohibition, who enjoy

Free leave so large to all things else, and choice
Unlimited of manifold delights:
But let us ever praise him, and extoll
His bountie, following our delightful task
To prune these growing Plants, & tend these Flours,
Which were it toilsom, yet with thee were sweet.
    To whom thus *Eve* repli'd. O thou for whom   *440*
And from whom I was formd flesh of thy flesh,
And without whom am to no end, my Guide
And Head, what thou hast said is just and right.
For wee to him indeed all praises owe,
And daily thanks, I chiefly who enjoy
So farr the happier Lot, enjoying thee
Preëminent by so much odds, while thou
Like consort to thy self canst no where find.
That day I oft remember, when from sleep
I first awak't, and found my self repos'd   *450*
Under a shade on flours, much wondring where
And what I was, whence thither brought, and how.
Not distant far from thence a murmuring sound
Of waters issu'd from a Cave and spread
Into a liquid Plain, then stood unmov'd
Pure as th' expanse of Heav'n; I thither went
With unexperienc't thought, and laid me downe
On the green bank, to look into the cleer
Smooth Lake, that to me seemd another Skie.
As I bent down to look, just opposite,   *460*
A Shape within the watry gleam appeerd
Bending to look on me, I started back,
It started back, but pleasd I soon returnd,
Pleas'd it returnd as soon with answering looks
Of sympathie and love, there I had fixt
Mine eyes till now, and pin'd with vain desire,
Had not a voice thus warnd me, What thou seest,
What there thou seest fair Creature is thy self,
With thee it came and goes: but follow me,
And I will bring thee where no shadow staies   *470*
Thy coming, and thy soft imbraces, hee
Whose image thou art, him thou shall enjoy
Inseparablie thine, to him shalt beare
Multitudes like thy self, and thence be call'd
Mother of human Race: what could I doe,
But follow strait, invisibly thus led?
Till I espi'd thee, fair indeed and tall,
Under a Platan, yet methought less faire,
Less winning soft, less amiablie milde,

Then that smooth watry image; back I turnd, 480
Thou following cryd'st aloud, Return fair *Eve*,
Whom fli'st thou? whom thou fli'st, of him thou art,
His flesh, his bone; to give thee being I lent
Out of my side to thee, neerest my heart
Substantial Life, to have thee by my side
Henceforth an individual solace dear;
Part of my Soul I seek thee, and thee claim
My other half: with that thy gentle hand
Seisd mine, I yeilded, and from that time see
How beauty is excelld by manly grace 490
And wisdom, which alone is truly fair.
   So spake our general Mother, and with eyes
Of conjugal attraction unreprov'd,
And meek surrender, half imbracing leand
On our first Father, half her swelling Breast
Naked met his under the flowing Gold
Of her loose tresses hid: he in delight
Both of her Beauty and submissive Charms
Smil'd with superior Love, as *Jupiter*
On *Juno* smiles, when he impregns the Clouds 500
That shed *May* Flowers; and press'd her Matron lip
With kisses pure: aside the Devil turnd
For envie, yet with jealous leer maligne
Ey'd them askance, and to himself thus plaind.
   Sight hateful, sight tormenting! thus these two
Imparadis't in one anothers arms
The happier *Eden*, shall enjoy thir fill
Of bliss on bliss, while I to Hell am thrust,
Where neither joy nor love, but fierce desire,
Among our other torments not the least, 510
Still unfulfill'd with pain of longing pines;
Yet let me not forget what I have gain'd
From thir own mouths; all is not theirs it seems:
One fatal Tree there stands of Knowledge call'd,
Forbidden them to taste: Knowledge forbidd'n?
Suspicious, reasonless. Why should thir Lord
Envie them that? can it be sin to know,
Can it be death? and do they onely stand
By Ignorance, is that thir happie state,
The proof of thir obedience and thir faith? 520
O fair foundation laid whereon to build
Thir ruine! Hence I will excite thir minds
With more desire to know, and to reject
Envious commands, invented with designe
To keep them low whom knowledge might exalt

Equal with Gods; aspiring to be such,
They taste and die: what likelier can ensue?
But first with narrow search I must walk round
This Garden, and no corner leave unspi'd;
A chance but chance may lead where I may meet   530
Some wandring Spirit of Heav'n, by Fountain side,
Or in thick shade retir'd, from him to draw
What further would be learnt. Live while ye may,
Yet happie pair; enjoy, till I return,
Short pleasures, for long woes are to succeed.
   So saying, his proud step he scornful turn'd,
But with sly circumspection, and began
Through wood, through waste, o're hil, o're dale his roam.
Mean while in utmost Longitude, where Heav'n
With Earth and Ocean meets, the setting Sun   540
Slowly descended, and with right aspect
Against the eastern Gate of Paradise
Leveld his eevning Rayes: it was a Rock
Of Alablaster, pil'd up to the Clouds,
Conspicuous farr, winding with one ascent
Accessible from Earth, one entrance high;
The rest was craggie cliff, that overhung
Still as it rose, impossible to climbe.
Betwixt these rockie Pillars *Gabriel* sat
Chief of th' Angelic Guards, awaiting night;   550
About him exercis'd Heroic Games
Th' unarmed Youth of Heav'n, but nigh at hand
Celestial Armourie, Shields, Helmes, and Speares
Hung high with Diamond flaming, and with Gold.
Thither came *Uriel*, gliding through the Eeven
On a Sun beam, swift as a shooting Starr
In *Autumn* thwarts the night, when vapors fir'd
Impress the Air, and shews the Mariner
From what point of his Compass to beware
Impetuous winds: he thus began in haste.   560
   Gabriel, to thee thy cours by Lot hath giv'n
Charge and strict watch that to this happie place
No evil thing approach or enter in;
This day at highth of Noon came to my Spheare
A Spirit, zealous, as he seem'd, to know
More of th' Almighties works, and chiefly Man
Gods latest Image: I describ'd his way
Bent all on speed, and markt his Aerie Gate;
But in the Mount that lies from *Eden* North,
Where he first lighted, soon discernd his looks   570

Alien from Heav'n, with passions foul obscur'd:
Mine eye pursu'd him still, but under shade
Lost sight of him; one of the banisht crew
I fear, hath ventur'd from the deep, to raise
New troubles; him thy care must be to find.

    To whom the winged Warriour thus returnd:
Uriel, no wonder if thy perfet sight,
Amid the Suns bright circle where thou sitst,
See farr and wide: in at this Gate none pass   *580*
The vigilance here plac't, but such as come
Well known from Heav'n; and since Meridian hour
No Creature thence: if Spirit of other sort,
So minded, have oreleapt these earthie bounds
On purpose, hard thou knowst it to exclude
Spiritual substance with corporeal barr.
But if within the circuit of these walks
In whatsoever shape he lurk, of whom
Thou telst, by morrow dawning I shall know.

    So promis'd hee, and *Uriel* to his charge
Returnd on that bright beam, whose point now raisd   *590*
Bore him slope downward to the Sun now fall'n
Beneath th' *Azores;* whither the prime Orb,
Incredible how swift, had thither rowl'd
Diurnal, or this less volubil Earth
By shorter flight to th' East, had left him there
Arraying with reflected Purple and Gold
The Clouds that on his Western Throne attend:
Now came still Eevning on, and Twilight gray
Had in her sober Liverie all things clad;
Silence accompanied, for Beast and Bird,   *600*
They to thir grassie Couch, these to thir Nests
Were slunk, all but the wakeful Nightingale;
She all night long her amorous descant sung;
Silence was pleas'd: now glow'd the Firmament
With living Saphirs: *Hesperus* that led
The starrie Host, rode brightest, till the Moon
Rising in clouded Majestie, at length
Apparent Queen unvaild her peerless light,
And o're the dark her Silver Mantle threw.

    When *Adam* thus to *Eve:* Fair Consort, th' hour   *610*
Of night, and all things now retir'd to rest
Mind us of like repose, since God hath set
Labour and rest, as day and night to men
Successive, and the timely dew of sleep
Now falling with soft slumbrous weight inclines
Our eye-lids; other Creatures all day long

Rove idle unimploid, and less need rest;
Man hath his daily work of body or mind
Appointed, which declares his Dignitie,
And the regard of Heav'n on all his waies;   620
While other Animals unactive range,
And of thir doings God takes no account.
To morrow ere fresh Morning streak the East
With first approach of light, we must be ris'n,
And at our pleasant labour, to reform
Yon flourie Arbors, yonder Allies green,
Our walks at noon, with branches overgrown,
That mock our scant manuring, and require
More hands than ours to lop thir wanton growth:
Those Blossoms also, and those dropping Gumms,   630
That lie bestrowne unsightly and unsmooth,
Ask riddance, if we mean to tread with ease;
Mean while, as Nature wills, Night bids us rest.
 To whom thus *Eve* with perfet beauty adornd.
My Author and Disposer, what thou bidst
Unargu'd I obey; so God ordains,
God is thy Law, thou mine: to know no more
Is womans happiest knowledge and her praise.
With thee conversing I forget all time,
All seasons and thir change, all please alike.   640
Sweet is the breath of morn, her rising sweet,
With charm of earliest Birds; pleasant the Sun
When first on this delightful Land he spreads
His orient Beams, on herb, tree, fruit, and flour,
Glistring with dew; fragrant the fertil earth
After soft showers; and sweet the coming on
Of grateful Eevning milde, then silent Night
With this her solemn Bird and this fair Moon,
And these the Gemms of Heav'n, her starrie train:
But neither breath of Morn when she ascends   650
With charm of earliest Birds, nor rising Sun
On this delightful land, nor herb, fruit, floure,
Glistring with dew, nor fragrance after showers,
Nor grateful Evening mild, nor silent Night
With this her solemn Bird, nor walk by Moon,
Or glittering Starr-light without thee is sweet.
But wherfore all night long shine these, for whom
This glorious sight, when sleep hath shut all eyes?
 To whom our general Ancestor repli'd.
Daughter of God and Man, accomplisht *Eve*,   660
Those have thir course to finish, round the Earth,
By morrow Eevning, and from Land to Land

In order, though to Nations yet unborn,
Ministring light prepar'd, they set and rise;
Least total darkness should by Night regaine
Her old possession, and extinguish life
In Nature and all things, which these soft fires
Not only enlighten, but with kindly heate
Of various influence foment and warme,
Temper or nourish, or in part shed down   670
Thir stellar vertue on all kinds that grow
On Earth, made hereby apter to receive
Perfection from the Suns more potent Ray.
These then, though unbeheld in deep of night,
Shine not in vain, nor think, though men were none,
That heav'n would want spectators, God want praise;
Millions of spiritual Creatures walk the Earth
Unseen, both when we wake, and when we sleep:
All these with ceasless praise his works behold
Both day and night: how often from the steep   680
Of echoing Hill or Thicket have we heard
Celestial voices to the midnight air,
Sole, or responsive each to others note
Singing thir great Creator: oft in bands
While they keep watch, or nightly rounding walk
With Heav'nly touch of instrumental sounds
In full harmonic number joind, thir songs
Divide the night, and lift our thoughts to Heaven.
    Thus talking hand in hand alone they pass'd
On to thir blissful Bower; it was a place   690
Chos'n by the sovran Planter, when he fram'd
All things to mans delightful use; the roofe
Of thickest covert was inwoven shade
Laurel and Mirtle, and what higher grew
Of firm and fragrant leaf; on either side
Acanthus, and each odorous bushie shrub
Fenc'd up the verdant wall; each beauteous flour,
Iris all hues, Roses, and Gessamin
Rear'd high thir flourisht heads between, and wrought
Mosaic; underfoot the Violet,   700
Crocus, and Hyacinth with rich inlay
Broiderd the ground, more colour'd then with stone
Of costliest Emblem: other Creature here
Beast, Bird, Insect, or Worm durst enter none;
Such was thir awe of man. In shadier Bower
More sacred and sequesterd, though but feignd,
Pan or *Silvanus* never slept, nor Nymph,
Nor *Faunus* haunted. Here in close recess

With Flowers, Garlands, and sweet-smelling Herbs
Espoused *Eve* deckt first her Nuptial Bed, 710
And heav'nly Quires the Hymenæan sung,
What day the genial Angel to our Sire
Brought her in naked beauty more adorn'd
More lovely then *Pandora*, whom the Gods
Endowd with all thir gifts, and O too like
In sad event, when to the unwiser Son
Of *Japhet* brought by *Hermes*, she ensnar'd
Mankind with her faire looks, to be aveng'd
On him who had stole *Joves* authentic fire.

   Thus at thir shadie Lodge arriv'd, both stood, 720
Both turnd, and under op'n Skie ador'd
The God that made both Skie, Air, Earth & Heav'n
Which they beheld, the Moons resplendent Globe
And starrie Pole: Thou also mad'st the Night,
Maker Omnipotent, and thou the Day,
Which we in our appointed work imployd
Have finisht happie in our mutual help
And mutual love, the Crown of all our bliss
Ordain'd by thee, and this delicious place
For us too large, where thy abundance wants 730
Partakers, and uncropt falls to the ground.
But thou hast promis'd from us two a Race
To fill the Earth, who shall with us extoll
Thy goodness infinite, both when we wake,
And when we seek, as now, thy gift of sleep.

   This said unanimous, and other Rites
Observing none, but adoration pure
Which God likes best, into thir inmost bower
Handed they went; and eas'd the putting off
These troublesom disguises which wee wear, 740
Strait side by side were laid, nor turnd I weene
Adam from his fair Spouse, nor *Eve* the Rites
Mysterious of connubial Love refus'd:
Whatever Hypocrites austerely talk
Of puritie and place and innocence,
Defaming as impure what God declares
Pure, and commands to som, leaves free to all.
Our Maker bids increase, who bids abstain
But our Destroyer, foe to God and Man?
Haile wedded Love, mysterious Law, true sourse 750
Of human ofspring, sole proprietie,
In Paradise of all things common else.
By thee adulterous lust was driv'n from men
Among the bestial herds to raunge, by thee

Founded in Reason, Loyal, Just, and Pure,
Relations dear, and all the Charities
Of Father, Son, and Brother first were known.
Farr be it, that I should write thee sin or blame,
Or think thee unbefitting holiest place,
Perpetual Fountain of Domestic sweets,   *760*
Whose Bed is undefil'd and chast pronounc't,
Present, or past, as Saints and Patriarchs us'd.
Here Love his golden shafts imploies, here lights
His constant Lamp, and waves his purple wings,
Reigns here and revels; not in the bought smile
Of Harlots, loveless, joyless, unindeard,
Casual fruition, nor in Court Amours
Mixt Dance, or wanton Mask, or Midnight Bal,
Or Serenate, which the starv'd Lover sings
To his proud fair, best quitted with disdain.   *770*
These lulld by Nightingales imbraceing slept,
And on thir naked limbs the flourie roof
Showrd Roses, which the Morn repair'd. Sleep on,
Blest pair; and O yet happiest if ye seek
No happier state, and know to know no more.

   Now had night measur'd with her shaddowie Cone
Half way up Hill this vast Sublunar Vault,
And from thir Ivorie Port the Cherubim
Forth issuing at th' accustomd hour stood armd
To thir night watches in warlike Parade,   *780*
When *Gabriel* to his next in power thus spake.

   Uzziel, half these draw off, and coast the South
With strictest watch; these other wheel the North,
Our circuit meets full West. As flame they part
Half wheeling to the Shield, half to the Spear.
From these, two strong and suttle Spirits he calld
That neer him stood, and gave them thus in charge.

   Ithuriel and *Zephon*, with wingd speed
Search through this Garden, leav unsearcht no nook,
But chiefly where those two fair Creatures Lodge,   *790*
Now laid perhaps asleep secure of harme.
This Eevning from the Sun's decline arriv'd
Who tells of som infernal Spirit seen
Hitherward bent (who could have thought?) escap'd
The barrs of Hell, on errand bad no doubt:
Such where ye find, seise fast, and hither bring.

   So saying, on he led his radiant Files,
Daz'ling the Moon; these to the Bower direct
In search of whom they sought: him there they found
Squat like a Toad, close at the eare of *Eve*;   *800*

Assaying by his Devilish art to reach
The Organs of her Fancie, and with them forge
Illusions as he list, Phantasms and Dreams,
Or if, inspiring venom, he might taint
Th' animal Spirits that from pure blood arise
Like gentle breaths from Rivers pure, thence raise
At least distemperd, discontented thoughts,
Vain hopes, vain aimes, inordinate desires
Blown up with high conceits ingendring pride.
Him thus intent *Ithuriel* with his Spear 810
Touch'd lightly; for no falshood can endure
Touch of Celestial temper, but returns
Of force to its own likeness: up he starts
Discoverd and surpriz'd. As when a spark
Lights on a heap of nitrous Powder, laid
Fit for the Tun som Magazin to store
Against a rumord Warr, the Smuttie graine
With sudden blaze diffus'd, inflames the Aire:
So started up in his own shape the Fiend.
Back stept those two fair Angels half amaz'd 820
So sudden to behold the grieslie King;
Yet thus, unmovd with fear, accost him soon.
   Which of those rebell Spirits adjudg'd to Hell
Com'st thou, escap'd thy prison, and transform'd,
Why satst thou like an enemie in waite
Here watching at the head of these that sleep?
   Know yet not then said *Satan*, filld with scorn
Know ye not me? ye knew me once no mate
For you, there sitting where ye durst not soare;
Not to know mee argues your selves unknown, 830
The lowest of your throng; or if ye know,
Why ask ye, and superfluous begin
Your message, like to end as much in vain?
To whom thus *Zephon*, answering scorn with scorn.
Think not, revolted Spirit, thy shape the same,
Or undiminisht brightness, to be known
As when thou stoodst in Heav'n upright and pure;
That Glorie then, when thou no more wast good,
Departed from thee, and thou resembl'st now
Thy sin and place of doom obscure and foule. 840
But come, for thou, besure, shalt give account
To him who sent us, whose charge is to keep
This place inviolable, and these from harm.
   So spake the Cherube, and his grave rebuke
Severe in youthful beautie, added grace
Invincible: abasht the Devil stood,

And felt how awful goodness is, and saw
Vertue in her shape how lovly, saw, and pin'd
His loss; but chiefly to find here observd
His lustre visibly impar'd; yet seemd   *850*
Undaunted. If I must contend, said he,
Best with the best, the Sender not the sent,
Or all at once; more glorie will be wonn,
Or less be lost. Thy fear, said *Zephon* bold,
Will save us trial what the least can doe
Single against thee wicked, and thence weak.

    The Fiend repli'd not, overcome with rage;
But like a proud Steed reind, went hautie on,
Chaumping his iron curb: to strive or flie
He held it vain; awe from above had quelld   *860*
His heart, not else dismai'd. Now drew they nigh
The western point, where those half-rounding guards
Just met, & closing stood in squadron joind
Awaiting next command. To whom thir Chief
Gabriel from the Front thus calld aloud.

    O friends, I hear the tread of nimble feet
Hasting this way, and now by glimps discerne
Ithuriel and *Zephon* through the shade,
And with them comes a third of Regal port,
But faded splendor wan; who by his gate   *870*
And fierce demeanour seems the Prince of Hell,
Not likely to part hence without contest;
Stand firm, for in his look defiance lours.

    He scarce had ended, when those two approachd
And brief related whom they brought, wher found,
How busied, in what form and posture coucht.

    To whom with stern regard thus *Gabriel* spake.
Why hast thou, *Satan*, broke the bounds prescrib'd
To thy transgressions, and disturbd the charge
Of others, who approve not to transgress   *880*
By thy example, but have power and right
To question thy bold entrance on this place;
Imploi'd it seems to violate sleep, and those
Whose dwelling God hath planted here in bliss?

    To whom thus *Satan* with contemptuous brow.
Gabriel, thou hadst in Heav'n th' esteem of wise,
And such I held thee; but this question askt
Puts me in doubt. Lives ther who loves his pain?
Who would not, finding way, break loose from Hell,
Though thither doomd? Thou wouldst thy self, no doubt,
And boldly venture to whatever place   *891*
Farthest from pain, where thou mightst hope to change

Torment with ease, & soonest recompence
Dole with delight, which in this place I sought;
To thee no reason; who knowst only good,
But evil hast not tri'd: and wilt object
His will who bound us? let him surer barr
His Iron Gates, if he intends our stay
In that dark durance: thus much what was askt.
The rest is true, they found me where they say; 900
But that implies not violence or harme.

  Thus hee in scorn. The warlike Angel mov'd,
Disdainfully half smiling thus repli'd.
O loss of one in Heav'n to judge of wise,
Since *Satan* fell, whom follie overthrew,
And now returns him from his prison scap't,
Gravely in doubt whether to hold them wise
Or not, who ask what boldness brought him hither
Unlicenc't from his bounds in Hell prescrib'd;
So wise he judges it to fly from pain 910
However, and to scape his punishment.
So judge thou still, presumptuous, till the wrauth,
Which thou incurr'st by flying, meet thy flight
Seavenfold, and scourge that wisdom back to Hell,
Which taught thee yet no better, that no pain
Can equal anger infinite provok't.
But wherefore thou alone? wherefore with thee
Came not all Hell broke loose? is pain to them
Less pain, less to be fled, or thou then they
Less hardie to endure? courageous Chief, 920
The first in flight from pain, had'st thou alleg'd
To thy deserted host this cause of flight,
Thou surely hadst not come sole fugitive.

  To which the Fiend thus answerd frowning stern.
Not that I less endure, or shrink from pain,
Insulting Angel, well thou knowst I stood
Thy fiercest, when in Battel to thy aide
The blasting volied Thunder made all speed
And seconded thy else not dreaded Spear.
But still thy words at random, as before, 930
Argue thy inexperience what behooves
From hard assaies and ill successes past
A faithful Leader, not to hazard all
Through wayes of danger by himself untri'd.
I therefore, I alone first undertook
To wing the desolate Abyss, and spie
This new created World, whereof in Hell
Fame is not silent, here in hope to find

Better abode, and my afflicted Powers
To settle here on Earth, or in mid Aire;
Though for possession put to try once more
What thou and thy gay Legions dare against;
Whose easier business were to serve thir Lord
High up in Heav'n, with songs to hymne his Throne,
And practis'd distances to cringe, not fight.
   To whom the warriour Angel soon repli'd.
To say and strait unsay, pretending first
Wise to flie pain, professing next the Spie,
Argues no Leader, but a lyar trac't,
Satan, and couldst thou faithful add? O name,
O sacred name of faithfulness profan'd!
Faithful to whom? to thy rebellious crew?
Armie of Fiends, fit body to fit head;
Was this your discipline and faith ingag'd,
Your military obedience, to dissolve
Allegeance to th' acknowledg'd Power supream?
And thou sly hypocrite, who now wouldst seem
Patron of liberty, who more then thou
Once fawn'd, and cring'd, and servilly ador'd
Heav'ns awful Monarch? wherefore but in hope
To dispossess him, and thy self to reigne?
But mark what I arreede thee now, avant;
Flie thither whence thou fledst: if from this houre
Within these hallowd limits thou appeer,
Back to th' infernal pit I drag thee chaind,
And Seale thee so, as henceforth not to scorne
The facil gates of hell too slightly barrd.
   So threatn'd hee, but *Satan* to no threats
Gave heed, but waxing more in rage repli'd.
   Then when I am thy captive talk of chaines,
Proud limitarie Cherube, but ere then
Farr heavier load thy self expect to feel
From my prevailing arme, though Heavens King
Ride on thy wings, and thou with thy Compeers,
Us'd to the yoak, draw'st his triumphant wheels
In progress through the rode of Heav'n Star-pav'd.
   While thus he spake, th' Angelic Squadron bright
Turnd fierie red, sharpning in mooned hornes
Thir Phalanx, and began to hemm him round
With ported Spears, as thick as when a field
Of *Ceres* ripe for harvest waving bends
Her bearded Grove of ears, which way the wind
Swayes them; the careful Plowman doubting stands
Least on the threshing floore his hopeful sheaves

Prove chaff. On th' other side *Satan* allarm'd
Collecting all his might dilated stood,
Like *Teneriff* or *Atlas* unremov'd:
His stature reacht the Skie, and on his Crest
Sat horror Plum'd; nor wanted in his graspe
What seemd both Spear and Shield: now dreadful deeds
Might have ensu'd, nor onely Paradise   *991*
In this commotion, but the Starrie Cope
Of Heav'n perhaps, or all the Elements
At least had gon to rack, disturbd and torne
With violence of this conflict, had not soon
Th' Eternal to prevent such horrid fray
Hung forth in Heav'n his golden Scales, yet seen
Betwixt *Astrea* and the *Scorpion* signe,
Wherein all things created first he weighd,
The pendulous round Earth with ballanc't Aire   *1000*
In counterpoise, now ponders all events,
Battels and Realms: in these he put two weights
The sequel each of parting and of fight;
The latter quick up flew, and kickt the beam;
Which *Gabriel* spying, thus bespake the Fiend.
   Satan, I know thy strength, and thou knowst mine,
Neither our own but giv'n; what follie then
To boast what Arms can doe, since thine no more
Then Heav'n permits, nor mine, though doubld now
To trample thee as mire: for proof look up,   *1010*
And read thy Lot in yon celestial Sign
Where thou art weigh'd, & shown how light, how weak,
If thou resist. The Fiend lookt up and knew
His mounted scale aloft: nor more; but fled
Murmuring, and with him fled the shades of night.

BOOK V

THE ARGUMENT

Morning approach't, Eve *relates to* Adam *her troublesome dream; he likes it not, yet comforts her: They come forth to thir day labours: Their Morning Hymn at the Door of their Bower. God to render Man inexcusable sends* Raphael *to admonish him of his obedience, of his free estate, of his enemy near at hand; who he is, and why his enemy, and whatever else may avail* Adam *to know.* Raphael *comes down to Paradise, his appearance describ'd, his coming discern'd by* Adam *afar off sitting at the door of his Bower; he goes out to meet him, brings him to his lodge, entertains him with the choycest fruits of Paradise got together by* Eve; *their discourse at Table:* Raphael *performs his message, minds* Adam *of his state and of his enemy; relates at* Adams *request who that enemy is, and how he came to be so, beginning from his first revolt in Heaven, and the occasion thereof; how he drew his Legions after him to the parts of the North, and there incited them to rebel with him, perswading all but only* Abdiel *a Seraph, who in Argument diswades and opposes him, then forsakes him.*

NOW morn her rosie steps in th' Eastern Clime
Advancing, sow'd the Earth with Orient Pearle,
When *Adam* wak't, so customd, for his sleep
Was Aerie light, from pure digestion bred,
And temperat vapors bland, which th' only sound
Of leaves and fuming rills, *Aurora's* fan,
Lightly dispers'd, and the shrill Matin Song
Of Birds on every bough; so much the more
His wonder was to find unwak'nd *Eve*
With Tresses discompos'd, and glowing Cheek,   10
As through unquiet rest: he on his side
Leaning half-rais'd, with looks of cordial Love
Hung over her enamour'd, and beheld
Beautie, which whether waking or asleep,
Shot forth peculiar Graces; then with voice
Milde, as when *Zephyrus* on *Flora* breathes,
Her hand soft touching, whisperd thus. Awake
My fairest, my espous'd, my latest found,
Heav'ns last best gift, my ever new delight,
Awake, the morning shines, and the fresh field   20
Calls us, we lose the prime, to mark how spring
Our tended Plants, how blows the Citron Grove,
What drops the Myrrhe, & what the balmie Reed,
How Nature paints her colours, how the Bee
Sits on the Bloom extracting liquid sweet.
    Such whispering wak'd her, but with startl'd eye
On *Adam*, whom imbracing, thus she spake.

175

O Sole in whom my thoughts find all repose,
My Glorie, my Perfection, glad I see
Thy face, and Morn return'd, for I this Night, 30
Such night till this I never pass'd, have dream'd,
If dream'd, not as I oft am wont, of thee,
Works of day pass't, or morrows next designe,
But of offence and trouble, which my mind
Knew never till this irksom night; methought
Close at mine ear one call'd me forth to walk
With gentle voice, I thought it thine; it said,
Why sleepst thou *Eve?* now is the pleasant time,
The cool, the silent, save where silence yields
To the night-warbling Bird, that now awake 40
Tunes sweetest his love-labor'd song; now reignes
Full Orb'd the Moon, and with more pleasing light
Shadowie sets off the face of things; in vain,
If none regard; Heav'n wakes with all his eyes,
Whom to behold but thee, Natures desire,
In whose sight all things joy, with ravishment
Attracted by thy beauty still to gaze.
I rose as at thy call, but found thee not;
To find thee I directed then my walk;
And on, methought, alone I pass'd through ways 50
That brought me on a sudden to the Tree
Of interdicted Knowledge: fair it seem'd,
Much fairer to my Fancie then by day:
And as I wondring lookt, beside it stood
One shap'd and wing'd like one of those from Heav'n
By us oft seen; his dewie locks distill'd
Ambrosia; on that Tree he also gaz'd;
And O fair Plant, said he, with fruit surcharg'd,
Deigns none to ease thy load and taste thy sweet,
Nor God, nor Man; is Knowledge so despis'd? 60
Or envie, or what reserve forbids to taste?
Forbid who will, none shall from me withhold
Longer thy offerd good, why else set here?
This said he paus'd not, but with ventrous Arme
He pluckt, he tasted; mee damp horror chil'd
At such bold words voucht with a deed so bold:
But he thus overjoy'd, O Fruit Divine,
Sweet of thy self, but much more sweet thus cropt,
Forbidd'n here, it seems, as onely fit
For Gods, yet able to make Gods of Men: 70
And why not Gods of Men, since good, the more
Communicated, more abundant growes,
The Author not impair'd, but honourd more?

Here, happie Creature, fair Angelic *Eve*,
Partake thou also; happie though thou art,
Happier thou mayst be, worthier canst not be:
Taste this, and be henceforth among the Gods
Thy self a Goddess, not to Earth confind,
But somtimes in the Air, as wee, somtimes
Ascend to Heav'n, by merit thine, and see   80
What life the Gods live there, and such live thou.
So saying, he drew nigh, and to me held,
Even to my mouth of that same fruit held part
Which he had pluckt; the pleasant savourie smell
So quick'nd appetite, that I, methought,
Could not but taste. Forthwith up to the Clouds
With him I flew, and underneath beheld
The Earth outstretcht immense, a prospect wide
And various: wondring at my flight and change
To this high exaltation; suddenly   90
My Guide was gon, and I, me thought, sunk down,
And fell asleep; but O how glad I wak'd
To find this but a dream! Thus *Eve* her Night
Related, and thus *Adam* answerd sad.
  Best Image of my self and dearer half,
The trouble of thy thoughts this night in sleep
Affects me equally; nor can I like
This uncouth dream, of evil sprung I fear;
Yet evil whence? in thee can harbour none,
Created pure. But know that in the Soule   100
Are many lesser Faculties that serve
Reason as chief; among these Fansie next
Her office holds; of all external things,
Which the five watchful Senses represent,
She forms Imaginations, Aerie shapes,
Which Reason joyning or disjoyning, frames
All what we affirm or what deny, and call
Our knowledge or opinion; then retires
Into her private Cell when Nature rests.
Oft in her absence mimic Fansie wakes   110
To imitate her; but misjoyning shapes,
Wilde work produces oft, and most in dreams,
Ill matching words and deeds long past or late.
Som such resemblances methinks I find
Of our last Eevnings talk, in this thy dream,
But with addition strange; yet be not sad.
Evil into the mind of God or Man
May come and go, so unapprov'd, and leave
No spot or blame behind: Which gives me hope

That what in sleep thou didst abhorr to dream, 120
Waking thou never wilt consent to do:
Be not disheart'nd then, nor cloud those looks
That wont to be more chearful and serene
Then when fair Morning first smiles on the World,
And let us to our fresh imployments rise
Among the Groves, the Fountains, and the Flours
That open now thir choicest bosom'd smells
Reservd from night, and kept for thee in store.
   So cheard he his fair Spouse, and she was cheard,
But silently a gentle tear let fall 130
From either eye, and wip'd them with her haire;
Two other precious drops that ready stood,
Each in thir chrystal sluce, hee ere they fell
Kiss'd as the gracious signs of sweet remorse
And pious awe, that feard to have offended.
   So all was cleard, and to the Field they haste.
But first from under shadie arborous roof,
Soon as they forth were come to open sight
Of day-spring, and the Sun, who scarce up risen
With wheels yet hov'ring o're the Ocean brim, 140
Shot paralel to the earth his dewie ray,
Discovering in wide Lantskip all the East
Of Paradise and *Edens* happie Plains,
Lowly they bow'd adoring, and began
Thir Orisons, each Morning duly paid
In various style, for neither various style
Nor holy rapture wanted they to praise
Thir Maker, in fit strains pronounc't or sung
Unmeditated, such prompt eloquence
Flowd from thir lips, in Prose or numerous Verse, 150
More tuneable then needed Lute or Harp
To add more sweetness, and they thus began.
   These are thy glorious works Parent of good,
Almightie, thine this universal Frame,
Thus wondrous fair; thy self how wondrous then!
Unspeakable, who sitst above these Heavens
To us invisible or dimly seen
In these thy lowest works, yet these declare
Thy goodness beyond thought, and Power Divine:
Speak yee who best can tell, ye Sons of light, 160
Angels, for yee behold him, and with songs
And choral symphonies, Day without Night,
Circle his Throne rejoycing, yee in Heav'n,
On Earth joyn all yee Creatures to extoll
Him first, him last, him midst, and without end.

Fairest of Starrs, last in the train of Night,
If better thou belong not to the dawn,
Sure pledge of day, that crownst the smiling Morn
With thy bright Circlet, praise him in thy Spheare
While day arises, that sweet hour of Prime. *170*
Thou Sun, of this great World both Eye and Soule,
Acknowledge him thy Greater, sound his praise
In thy eternal course, both when thou climb'st,
And when high Noon hast gaind, & when thou fallst.
Moon, that now meetst the orient Sun, now fli'st
With the fixt Starrs, fixt in thir Orb that flies,
And yee five other wandring Fires that move
In mystic Dance not without Song, resound
His praise, who out of Darkness call'd up Light.
Aire, and ye Elements the eldest birth *180*
Of Natures Womb, that in quaternion run
Perpetual Circle, multiform; and mix
And nourish all things, let your ceasless change
Varie to our great Maker still new praise.
Ye Mists and Exhalations that now rise
From Hill or steaming Lake, duskie or grey,
Till the Sun paint your fleecie skirts with Gold,
In honour to the Worlds great Author rise,
Whether to deck with Clouds the uncolourd skie,
Or wet the thirstie Earth with falling showers, *190*
Rising or falling still advance his praise.
His praise ye Winds, that from four Quarters blow,
Breathe soft or loud; and wave your tops, ye Pines,
With every Plant, in sign of Worship wave.
Fountains and yee, that warble, as ye flow,
Melodious murmurs, warbling tune his praise.
Joyn voices all ye living Souls, ye Birds,
That singing up to Heaven Gate ascend,
Bear on your wings and in your notes his praise;
Yee that in Waters glide, and yee that walk *200*
The Earth, and stately tread, or lowly creep;
Witness if I be silent, Morn or Eeven,
To Hill, or Valley, Fountain, or fresh shade
Made vocal by my Song, and taught his praise.
Hail universal Lord, be bounteous still
To give us onely good; and if the night
Have gathered aught of evil or conceald,
Disperse it, as now light dispels the dark.
   So pray'd they innocent, and to thir thoughts
Firm peace recoverd soon and wonted calm. *210*
On to thir mornings rural work they haste

Among sweet dewes and flours; where any row
Of Fruit-trees overwoodie reachd too far
Thir pamperd boughes, and needed hands to check
Fruitless imbraces: or they led the Vine
To wed her Elm; she spous'd about him twines
Her mariageable arms, and with her brings
Her dowr th' adopted Clusters, to adorn
His barren leaves. Them thus imploid beheld
With pittie Heav'ns high King, and to him call'd 220
Raphael, the sociable Spirit, that deign'd
To travel with *Tobias*, and secur'd
His marriage with the seaventimes-wedded Maid.
    Raphael, said hee, thou hear'st what stir on Earth
Satan from Hell scap't through the darksom Gulf
Hath raisd in Paradise, and how disturbd
This night the human pair, how he designes
In them at once to ruin all mankind.
Go therefore, half this day as friend with friend
Converse with *Adam*, in what Bowre or shade 230
Thou find'st him from the heat of Noon retir'd,
To respit his day-labour with repast,
Or with repose; and such discourse bring on,
As may advise him of his happie state,
Happiness in his power left free to will,
Left to his own free Will, his Will though free,
Yet mutable, whence warne him to beware
He swerve not too secure: tell him withall
His danger, and from whom, what enemie
Late falln himself from Heaven, is plotting now 240
The fall of others from like state of bliss;
By violence, no, for that shall be withstood,
But by deceit and lies; this let him know,
Least wilfully transgressing he pretend
Surprisal, unadmonisht, unforewarnd.
    So spake th' Eternal Father, and fulfilld
All Justice: nor delaid the winged Saint
After his charge receivd; but from among
Thousand Celestial Ardors, where he stood
Vaild with his gorgeous wings, up springing light 250
Flew through the midst of Heav'n; th' angelic Quires
On each hand parting, to his speed gave way
Through all th' Empyreal road; till at the Gate
Of Heav'n arriv'd, the gate self-opend wide
On golden Hinges turning, as by work
Divine the sov'ran Architect had fram'd.
From hence, no cloud, or, to obstruct his sight,

Starr interpos'd, however small he sees,
Not unconform to other shining Globes,
Earth and the Gard'n of God, with Cedars crownd 260
Above all Hills. As when by night the Glass
Of *Galileo*, less assur'd, observes
Imagind Lands and Regions in the Moon:
Or Pilot from amidst the *Cyclades*
Delos or *Samos* first appeering kenns
A cloudy spot. Down thither prone in flight
He speeds, and through the vast Ethereal Skie
Sailes between worlds & worlds, with steddie wing
Now on the polar windes, then with quick Fann
Winnows the buxom Air; till within soare 270
Of Towring Eagles, to all the Fowles he seems
A *Phœnix*, gaz'd by all, as that sole Bird
When to enshrine his reliques in the Sun's
Bright Temple, to *Ægyptian Theb's* he flies.
At once on th' Eastern cliff of Paradise
He lights, and to his proper shape returns
A Seraph wingd; six wings he wore, to shade
His lineaments Divine; the pair that clad
Each shoulder broad, came mantling o're his brest
With regal Ornament; the middle pair 280
Girt like a Starrie Zone his waste, and round
Skirted his loines and thighes with downie Gold
And colours dipt in Heav'n; the third his feet
Shaddowd from either heele with featherd maile
Skie-tinctur'd grain. Like *Maia's* son he stood,
And shook his Plumes, that Heav'nly fragrance filld
The circuit wide. Strait knew him all the Bands
Of Angels under watch; and to his state,
And to his message high in honour rise;
For on som message high they guessd him bound. 290
Thir glittering Tents he passd, and now is come
Into the blissful field, through Groves of Myrrhe,
And flouring Odours, Cassia, Nard, and Balme;
A Wilderness of sweets; for Nature here
Wantond as in her prime, and plaid at will
Her Virgin Fancies, pouring forth more sweet,
Wilde above rule or art; enormous bliss.
Him through the spicie Forrest onward com
Adam discernd, as in the dore he sat
Of his coole Bowre, while now the mounted Sun 300
Shot down direct his fervid Raies, to warme
Earths inmost womb, more warmth then *Adam* needs
And *Eve* within, due at her hour prepar'd

For dinner savourie fruits, of taste to please
True appetite, and not disrelish thirst
Of nectarous draughts between, from milkie stream,
Berrie or Grape: to whom thus *Adam* call'd.
   Haste hither *Eve*, and worth thy sight behold
Eastward among those Trees, what glorious shape
Comes this way moving; seems another Morn   *310*
Ris'n on mid-noon; som great behest from Heav'n
To us perhaps he brings, and will voutsafe
This day to be our Guest. But goe with speed,
And what thy stores contain, bring forth and poure
Abundance, fit to honour and receive
Our Heav'nly stranger; well we may afford
Our givers thir own gifts, and large bestow
From large bestowd, where Nature multiplies
Her fertil growth, and by disburd'ning grows
More fruitful, which instructs us not to spare.   *320*
   To whom thus *Eve*. *Adam*, earths hallowd mould,
Of God inspir'd, small store will serve, where store,
All seasons, ripe for use hangs on the stalk;
Save what by frugal storing firmness gains
To nourish, and superfluous moist consumes:
But I will haste and from each bough and break,
Each Plant & juciest Gourd will pluck such choice
To entertain our Angel guest, as hee
Beholding shall confess that here on Earth
God hath dispenst his bounties as in Heav'n.   *330*
   So saying, with dispatchful looks in haste
She turns, on hospitable thoughts intent
What choice to chuse for delicacie best,
What order, so contriv'd as not to mix
Tastes, not well joynd, inelegant, but bring
Taste after taste upheld with kindliest change,
Bestirs her then, and from each tender stalk
Whatever Earth all-bearing Mother yields
In *India* East or West, or middle shoare
In *Pontus* or the *Punic* Coast, or where   *340*
Alcinous reign'd, fruit of all kindes, in coate,
Rough, or smooth rin'd, or bearded husk, or shell
She gathers, Tribute large, and on the board
Heaps with unsparing hand; for drink the Grape
She crushes, inoffensive moust, and meathes
From many a berrie, and from sweet kernels prest
She tempers dulcet creams, nor these to hold
Wants her fit vessels pure, then strews the ground
With Rose and Odours from the shrub unfum'd.

  Mean while our Primitive great Sire, to meet   *350*
His god-like Guest, walks forth, without more train
Accompani'd then with his own compleat
Perfections, in himself was all his state,
More solemn then the tedious pomp that waits
On Princes, when thir rich Retinue long
Of Horses led, and Grooms besmeard with Gold
Dazles the croud, and sets them all agape.
Neerer his presence *Adam* though not awd,
Yet with submiss approach and reverence meek,
As to a superior Nature, bowing low,   *360*
  Thus said. Native of Heav'n, for other place
None can then Heav'n such glorious shape contain;
Since by descending from the Thrones above,
Those happie places thou hast deignd a while
To want, and honour these, voutsafe with us
Two onely, who yet by sov'ran gift possess
This spacious ground, in yonder shadie Bowre
To rest, and what the Garden choicest bears
To sit and taste, till this meridian heat
Be over, and the Sun more coole decline.   *370*
  Whom thus the Angelic Vertue answered milde.
Adam, I therefore came, nor art thou such
Created, or such place hast here to dwell,
As may not oft invite, though Spirits of Heav'n
To visit thee; lead on then where thy Bowre
Oreshades; for these mid-hours, till Eevning rise
I have at will. So to the Silvan Lodge
They came, that like *Pomona's* Arbour smil'd
With flourets deck't and fragrant smells; but *Eve*
Undeckt, save with her self more lovely fair   *380*
Then Wood-Nymph, or the fairest Goddess feign'd
Of three that in Mount *Ida* naked strove,
Stood to entertain her guest from Heav'n; no vaile
Shee needed, Vertue-proof, no thought infirme
Alterd her cheek. On whom the Angel *Haile*
Bestowd, the holy salutation us'd
Long after to blest *Marie*, second *Eve*.
  Haile Mother of Mankind, whose fruitful Womb
Shall fill the World more numerous with thy Sons
Then with these various fruits the Trees of God   *390*
Have heap'd this Table. Rais'd of grassie terf
Thir Table was, and mossie seats had round,
And on her ample Square from side to side
All *Autumn* pil'd, though *Spring* and *Autumn* here
Danc'd hand in hand. A while discourse they hold;

No fear lest Dinner coole; when thus began
Our Authour. Heav'nly stranger, please to taste
These bounties which our Nourisher, from whom
All perfet good unmeasur'd out, descends,
To us for food and for delight hath caus'd   400
The Earth to yeild; unsavourie food perhaps
To spiritual Natures; only this I know,
That one Celestial Father gives to all.

   To whom the Angel. Therefore what he gives
(Whose praise be ever sung) to man in part
Spiritual, may of purest Spirits be found
No ingrateful food: and food alike those pure
Intelligential substances require
As doth your Rational; and both contain
Within them every lower facultie   410
Of sense, whereby they hear, see, smell, touch, taste,
Tasting concoct, digest, assimilate,
And corporeal to incorporeal turn.
For know, whatever was created, needs
To be sustaind and fed; of Elements
The grosser feeds the purer, earth the sea,
Earth and the Sea feed Air, the Air those Fires
Ethereal, and as lowest first the Moon;
Whence in her visage round those spots, unpurg'd
Vapours not yet into her substance turn'd.   420
Nor doth the Moon no nourishment exhale
From her moist Continent to higher Orbes.
The Sun that light imparts to all, receives
From all his alimental recompence
In humid exhalations, and at Even
Sups with the Ocean: though in Heav'n the Trees
Of life ambrosial frutage bear, and vines
Yeild Nectar, though from off the boughs each Morn
We brush mellifluous Dewes, and find the ground
Cover'd with pearly grain: yet God hath here   430
Varied his bounty so with new delights,
As may compare with Heaven; and to taste
Think not I shall be nice. So down they sat,
And to thir viands fell, nor seemingly
The Angel, nor in mist, the common gloss
Of Theologians, but with keen dispatch
Of real hunger, and concoctive heate
To transubstantiate; what redounds, transpires
Through Spirits with ease; nor wonder; if by fire
Of sooty coal the Empiric Alchimist   440
Can turn, or holds it possible to turn

Metals of drossiest Ore to perfet Gold
As from the Mine. Mean while at Table *Eve*
Ministerd naked, and thir flowing cups
With pleasant liquors crown'd: O innocence
Deserving Paradise! if ever, then,
Then had the Sons of God excuse to have bin
Enamour'd at that sight; but in those hearts
Love unlibidinous reign'd, nor jealousie
Was understood, the injur'd Lovers Hell. *450*
    Thus when with meats & drinks they had suffic'd
Not burd'nd Nature, sudden mind arose
In *Adam*, not to let th' occasion pass
Given him by this great Conference to know
Of things above his World, and of thir being
Who dwell in Heav'n, whose excellence he saw
Transcend his own so farr, whose radiant forms
Divine effulgence, whose high Power so far
Exceeded human, and his wary speech
Thus to th' Empyreal Minister he fram'd. *460*
    Inhabitant with God, now know I well
Thy favour, in this honour done to man,
Under whose lowly roof thou hast voutsaf't
To enter, and these earthly fruits to taste,
Food not of Angels, yet accepted so,
As that more willingly thou couldst not seem
At Heav'ns high feasts to have fed: yet what compare?
    To whom the winged Hierarch repli'd.
O *Adam*, one Almightie is, from whom
All things proceed, and up to him return, *470*
If not deprav'd from good, created all
Such to perfection, one first matter all,
Indu'd with various forms, various degrees
Of substance, and in things that live, of life;
But more refin'd, more spiritous, and pure,
As neerer to him plac't or neerer tending
Each in thir several active Sphears assignd,
Till body up to spirit work, in bounds
Proportiond to each kind. So from the root
Springs lighter the green stalk, from thence the leaves *480*
More aerie, last the bright consummate floure
Spirits odorous breathes: flours and thir fruit
Mans nourishment, by gradual scale sublim'd
To vital Spirits aspire, to animal,
To intellectual, give both life and sense,
Fansie and understanding, whence the soule
Reason receives, and reason is her being,

Discursive, or Intuitive; discourse
Is oftest yours, the latter most is ours,
Differing but in degree, of kind the same. 490
Wonder not then, what God for you saw good
If I refuse not, but convert, as you,
To proper substance; time may come when men
With Angels may participate, and find
No inconvenient Diet, nor too light Fare:
And from these corporal nutriments perhaps
Your bodies may at last turn all to Spirit,
Improv'd by tract of time, and wingd ascend
Ethereal, as wee, or may at choice
Here or in Heav'nly Paradises dwell; 500
If ye be found obedient, and retain
Unalterably firm his love entire
Whose progenie you are. Mean while enjoy
Your fill what happiness this happie state
Can comprehend, incapable of more.
  To whom the Patriarch of mankind repli'd.
O favourable spirit, propitious guest,
Well hast thou taught the way that might direct
Our knowledge, and the scale of Nature set
From center to circumference, whereon 510
In contemplation of created things
By steps we may ascend to God. But say,
What meant that caution joind, *if ye be found
Obedient?* can wee want obedience then
To him, or possibly his love desert
Who formd us from the dust, and plac'd us here
Full to the utmost measure of what bliss
Human desires can seek or apprehend?
  To whom the Angel. Son of Heav'n and Earth,
Attend: That thou art happie, owe to God; 520
That thou continu'st such, owe to thy self,
That is, to thy obedience; therein stand.
This was that caution giv'n thee; be advis'd.
God made thee perfet, not immutable;
And good he made thee, but to persevere
He left it in thy power, ordaind thy will
By nature free, not over-rul'd by Fate
Inextricable, or strict necessity;
Our voluntarie service he requires,
Not our necessitated, such with him 530
Findes no acceptance, nor can find, for how
Can hearts, not free, be tri'd whether they serve
Willing or no, who will but what they must

By Destinie, and can no other choose?
My self and all th' Angelic Host that stand
In sight of God enthron'd, our happie state
Hold, as you yours, while our obedience holds;
On other surety none; freely we serve
Because wee freely love, as in our will
To love or not; in this we stand or fall: 540
And som are fall'n, to disobedience fall'n,
And so from Heav'n to deepest Hell; O fall
From what high state of bliss into what woe!

   To whom our great Progenitor. Thy words
Attentive, and with more delighted eare
Divine instructer, I have heard, then when
Cherubic Songs by night from neighbouring Hills
Aereal Music send: nor knew I not
To be both will and deed created free;
Yet that we never shall forget to love 550
Our maker, and obey him whose command
Single, is yet so just, my constant thoughts
Assur'd me and still assure: though what thou tellst
Hath past in Heav'n, som doubt within me move,
But more desire to hear, if thou consent,
The full relation, which must needs be strange,
Worthy of Sacred silence to be heard;
And we have yet large day, for scarce the Sun
Hath finisht half his journey, and scarce begins
His other half in the great Zone of Heav'n. 560

   Thus *Adam* made request, and *Raphael*
After short pause assenting, thus began.

   High matter thou injoinst me, O prime of men,
Sad task and hard, for how shall I relate
To human sense th' invisible exploits
Of warring Spirits; how without remorse
The ruin of so many glorious once
And perfet while they stood; how last unfould
The secrets of another world, perhaps
Not lawful to reveal? yet for thy good 570
This is dispenc't, and what surmounts the reach
Of human sense, I shall dellneate so,
By lik'ning spiritual to corporal forms,
As may express them best, though what if Earth
Be but the shaddow of Heav'n, and things therein
Each to other like, more then on earth is thought?

   As yet this world was not, and *Chaos* wilde
Reignd where these Heav'ns now rowl, where Earth
   now rests

Upon her Center pois'd, when on a day
(For Time, though in Eternitie, appli'd   580
To motion, measures all things durable
By present, past, and future) on such day
As Heav'ns great Year brings forth, th' Empyreal Host
Of Angels by Imperial summons call'd,
Innumerable before th' Almighties Throne
Forthwith from all the ends of Heav'n appeerd
Under thir Hierarchs in orders bright
Ten thousand thousand Ensignes high advanc'd,
Standards, and Gonfalons twixt Van and Reare
Streame in the Aire, and for distinction serve   590
Of Hierarchies, of Orders, and Degrees;
Or in thir glittering Tissues bear imblaz'd
Holy Memorials, acts of Zeale and Love
Recorded eminent. Thus when in Orbes
Of circuit inexpressible they stood,
Orb within Orb, the Father infinite,
By whom in bliss imbosom'd sat the Son,
A midst as from a flaming Mount, whose top
Brightness had made invisible, thus spake.
   Hear all ye Angels, Progenie of Light,   600
Thrones, Dominations, Princedoms, Vertues, Powers,
Hear my Decree, which unrevok't shall stand.
This day I have begot whom I declare
My onely Son, and on this holy Hill
Him have anointed, whom ye now behold
At my right hand; your Head I him appoint;
And by my Self have sworn to him shall bow
All knees in Heav'n, and shall confess him Lord:
Under his great Vice-gerent Reign abide
United as one individual Soule   610
For ever happie: him who disobeyes
Mee disobeyes, breaks union, and that day
Cast out from God and blessed vision, falls
Into utter darkness, deep ingulft, his place
Ordaind without redemption, without end.
   So spake th' Omnipotent, and with his words
All seemd well pleas'd, all seem'd but were not all.
That day, as other solem dayes, they spent
In song and dance about the sacred Hill,
Mystical dance, which yonder starrie Spheare   620
Of Planets and of fixt in all her Wheeles
Resembles nearest, mazes intricate,
Eccentric, intervolv'd, yet regular
Then most, when most irregular they seem:

And in thir motions harmonie Divine
So smooths her charming tones, that Gods own ear
Listens delighted. Eevning approachd
(For we have also our Eevning and our Morn,
We ours for change delectable, not need)
Forthwith from dance to sweet repast they turn   *630*
Desirous, all in Circles as they stood,
Tables are set, and on a sudden pil'd
With Angels Food, and rubied Nectar flows:
In Pearl, in Diamond, and massie Gold,
Fruit of delicious Vines, the growth of Heav'n.
They eat, they drink, and with refection sweet
Are fill'd before th' all bounteous King, who showrd
With copious hand, rejoycing in thir joy.
Now when ambrosial Night with Clouds exhal'd
From that high mount of God, whence light & shade   *640*
Spring both, the face of brightest Heav'n had changd
To grateful Twilight (for Night comes not there
In darker veile) and roseat Dews dispos'd
All but the unsleeping eyes of God to rest,
Wide over all the Plain, and wider farr
Then all this globous Earth in Plain outspred,
(Such are the Courts of God) Th' Angelic throng
Disperst in Bands and Files thir Camp extend
By living Streams among the Trees of Life,
Pavilions numberless, and sudden reard,   *650*
Celestial Tabernacles, where they slept
Fannd with coole Winds, save those who in thir course
Melodious Hymns about the sovran Throne
Alternate all night long: but not so wak'd
Satan, so call him now, his former name
Is heard no more in Heav'n; he of the first,
If not the first Arch-Angel, great in Power,
In favour and præeminence, yet fraught
With envie against the Son of God, that day
Honourd by his great Father, and proclaimd   *660*
Messiah King anointed, could not beare
Through pride that sight, and thought himself impaird.
Deep malice thence conceiving & disdain,
Soon as midnight brought on the duskie houre
Friendliest to sleep and silence, he resolv'd
With all his Legions to dislodge, and leave
Unworshipt, unobey'd the Throne supream
Contemptuous, and his next subordinate
Awak'ning, thus to him in secret spake.
   Sleepst thou, Companion dear, what sleep can close *670*

Thy eye-lids? and remembrest what Decree
Of yesterday, so late hath past the lips
Of Heav'ns Almightie. Thou to me thy thoughts
Wast wont, I mine to thee was wont to impart;
Both waking we were one; how then can now
Thy sleep dissent? new Laws thou seest impos'd;
New Laws from him who reigns, new minds may raise
In us who serve, new Counsels, to debate
What doubtful may ensue, more in this place
To utter is not safe. Assemble thou   680
Of all those Myriads which we lead the chief;
Tell them that by command, ere yet dim Night
Her shadowie Cloud withdraws, I am to haste,
And all who under me thir Banners wave,
Homeward with flying march where we possess
The Quarters of the North, there to prepare
Fit entertainment to receive our King
The great *Messiah*, and his new commands,
Who speedily through all the Hierarchies
Intends to pass triumphant, and give Laws.   690
   So spake the false Arch-Angel, and infus'd
Bad influence into th' unwarie brest
Of his Associate; hee together calls,
Or several one by one, the Regent Powers,
Under him Regent, tells, as he was taught,
That the most High commanding, now ere Night,
Now ere dim Night had disincumberd Heav'n,
The great Hierarchal Standard was to move;
Tells the suggested cause, and casts between
Ambiguous words and jealousies, to sound   700
Or taint integritie; but all obey'd
The wonted signal, and superior voice
Of thir great Potentate; for great indeed
His name, and high was his degree in Heav'n;
His count'nance, as the Morning Starr that guides
The starrie flock, allur'd them, and with lyes
Drew after him the third part of Heav'ns Host:
Mean while th' Eternal eye, whose sight discernes
Abstrusest thoughts, from forth his holy Mount
And from within the golden Lamps that burne   710
Nightly before him, saw without thir light
Rebellion rising, saw in whom, how spred
Among the sons of Morn, what multitudes
Were banded to oppose his high Decree;
And smiling to his onely Son thus said.
   Son, thou in whom my glory I behold

In full resplendence, Heir of all my might,
Neerly it now concernes us to be sure
Of our Omnipotence, and with what Arms
We mean to hold what anciently we claim   720
Of Deitie or Empire, such a foe
Is rising, who intends to erect his Throne
Equal to ours, throughout the spacious North;
Nor so content, hath in his thought to trie
In battel, what our Power is, or our right.
Let us advise, and to this hazard draw
With speed what force is left, and all imploy
In our defence, lest unawares we lose
This our high place, our Sanctuarie, our Hill.
    To whom the Son with calm aspect and cleer   730
Light'ning Divine, ineffable, serene,
Made answer. Mightie Father, thou thy foes
Justly hast in derision, and secure
Laugh'st at thir vain designes and tumults vain,
Matter to mee of Glory, whom thir hate
Illustrates, when they see all Regal Power
Giv'n me to quell thir pride, and in event
Know whether I be dextrous to subdue
Thy Rebels, or be found the worst in Heav'n.
    So spake the Son, but *Satan* with his Powers   740
Farr was advanc't on winged speed, an Host
Innumerable as the Starrs of Night,
Or Starrs of Morning, Dew-drops, which the Sun
Impearls on every leaf and every flouer.
Regions they pass'd, the mightie Regencies
Of Seraphim and Potentates and Thrones
In thir triple Degrees, Regions to which
All thy Dominion, *Adam*, is no more
Then what this Garden is to all the Earth,
And all the Sea, from one entire globose   750
Stretcht into Longitude; which having pass'd
At length into the limits of the North
They came, and *Satan* to his Royal seat
High on a Hill, far blazing, as a Mount
Rais'd on a Mount, with Pyramids and Towrs
From Diamond Quarries hew'n, & Rocks of Gold,
The Palace of great *Lucifer*, (so call
That Structure in the Dialect of men
Interpreted) which not long after, hee
Affecting all equality with God,   760
In imitation of that Mount whereon
Messiah was declar'd in sight of Heav'n,

The Mountain of the Congregation call'd;
For thither he assembl'd all his Train,
Pretending so commanded to consult
About the great reception of thir King,
Thither to come, and with calumnious Art
Of counterfeted truth thus held thir ears.
    Thrones, Dominations, Princedomes, Vertues, Powers,
If these magnific Titles yet remain   770
Not meerly titular, since by Decree
Another now hath to himself ingross't
All Power, and us eclipst under the name
Of King anointed, for whom all this haste
Of midnight march, and hurried meeting here,
This onely to consult how we may best
With what may be devis'd of honours new
Receive him coming to receive from us
Knee-tribute yet unpaid, prostration vile,
Too much to one, but double how endur'd,   780
To one and to his image now proclaim'd?
But what if better counsels might erect
Our minds and teach us to cast off this Yoke?
Will ye submit your necks, and chuse to bend
The supple knee? ye will not, if I trust
To know ye right, or if ye know your selves
Natives and Sons of Heav'n possest before
By none, and if not equal all, yet free,
Equally free; for Orders and Degrees
Jarr not with liberty, but well consist.   790
Who can in reason then or right assume
Monarchie over such as live by right
His equals, if in power and splendor less,
In freedome equal? or can introduce
Law and Edict on us, who without law
Erre not, much less for this to be our Lord,
And look for adoration to th' abuse
Of those Imperial Titles which assert
Our being ordain'd to govern, not to serve?
    Thus farr his bold discourse without controule   800
Had audience, when among the Seraphim
Abdiel, then whom none with more zeale ador'd
The Deitie, and divine commands obei'd,
Stood up, and in a flame of zeale severe
The current of his fury thus oppos'd.
    O argument blasphemous, false and proud!
Words which no eare ever to hear in Heav'n
Expected, least of all from thee, ingrate

In place thy self so high above thy Peeres.
Canst thou with impious obloquie condemne   *810*
The just Decree of God, pronounc't and sworn,
That to his only Son by right endu'd
With Regal Scepter, every Soule in Heav'n
Shall bend the knee, and in that honour due
Confess him rightful King? unjust thou saist
Flatly unjust, to binde with Laws the free,
And equal over equals to let Reigne,
One over all with unsucceeded power.
Shalt thou give Law to God, shalt thou dispute
With him the points of libertie, who made   *820*
Thee what thou art, & formd the Pow'rs of Heav'n
Such as he pleasd, and circumscrib'd thir being?
Yet by experience taught we know how good,
And of our good, and of our dignitie
How provident he is, how farr from thought
To make us less, bent rather to exalt
Our happie state under one Head more neer
United. But to grant it thee unjust,
That equal over equals Monarch Reigne:
Thy self though great & glorious dost thou count,   *830*
Or all Angelic Nature joind in one,
Equal to him begotten Son, by whom
As by his Word the mighty Father made
All things, ev'n thee, and all the Spirits of Heav'n
By him created in thir bright degrees,
Crownd them with Glory, & to thir Glory nam'd
Thrones, Dominations, Princedoms, Vertues, Powers,
Essential Powers, nor by his Reign obscur'd,
But more illustrious made, since he the Head
One of our number thus reduc't becomes,   *840*
His Laws our Laws, all honour to him done
Returns our own. Cease then this impious rage,
And tempt not these; but hast'n to appease
Th' incensed Father, and th' incensed Son,
While Pardon may be found in time besought.
  So spake the fervent Angel, but his zeale
None seconded, as out of season judg'd,
Or singular and rash, whereat rejoic'd
Th' Apostat, and more haughty thus repli'd.
That we were formd then saist thou? & the work   *850*
Of secondarie hands, by task transferd
From Father to his Son? strange point and new!
Doctrin which we would know whence learnt: who saw
When this creation was? rememberst thou

Thy making, while the Maker gave thee being?
We know no time when we were not as now;
Know none before us, self-begot, self-rais'd
By our own quick'ning power, when fatal course
Had circl'd his full Orbe, the birth mature
Of this our native Heav'n, Ethereal Sons.   *860*
Our puissance is our own, our own right hand
Shall teach us highest deeds, by proof to try
Who is our equal: then thou shalt behold
Whether by supplication we intend
Address, and to begirt th' Almighty Throne
Beseeching or besieging. This report,
These tidings carrie to th' anointed King;
And fly, ere evil intercept thy flight.
   He said, and as the sound of waters deep
Hoarce murmur echo'd to his words applause   *870*
Through the infinite Host, nor less for that
The flaming Seraph fearless, though alone
Encompass'd round with foes, thus answerd bold.
   O alienate from God, O spirit accurst,
Forsak'n of all good; I see thy fall
Determind, and thy hapless crew involv'd
In this perfidious fraud, contagion spred
Both of thy crime and punishment: henceforth
No more be troubl'd how to quit the yoke
Of Gods *Messiah:* those indulgent Laws   *880*
Will not now be voutsaf't, other Decrees
Against thee are gon forth without recall;
That Golden Scepter which thou didst reject
Is now an Iron Rod to bruise and breake
Thy disobedience. Well thou didst advise,
Yet not for thy advise or threats I fly
These wicked Tents devoted, least the wrauth
Impendent, raging into sudden flame
Distinguish not: for soon expect to feel
His Thunder on thy head, devouring fire.   *890*
Then who created thee lamenting learne,
When who can uncreate thee thou shalt know.
   So spake the Seraph *Abdiel* faithful found,
Among the faithless, faithful only hee;
Among innumerable false, unmov'd,
Unshak'n, unseduc'd, unterrifi'd
His Loyaltie he kept, his Love, his Zeale;
Nor number, nor example with him wrought
To swerve from truth, or change his constant mind
Though single. From amidst them forth he passd,   *900*

Long way through hostile scorn, which he susteind
Superior, nor of violence fear'd aught;
And with retorted scorn his back he turn'd
On those proud Towrs to swift destruction doom'd.

BOOK VI

THE ARGUMENT

Raphael *continues to relate how* Michael *and* Gabriel *were sent forth to Battel against* Satan *and his Angels. The first Fight describ'd:* Satan *and his Powers retire under Night: He calls a Councel, invents devilish Engines, which in the second dayes Fight put* Michael *and his Angels to some disorder; But they at length pulling up Mountains overwhelm'd both the force and Machins of* Satan: *Yet the Tumult not so ending, God on the third day sends Messiah his Son, for whom he had reserv'd the glory of that Victory: Hee in the Power of his Father coming to the place, and causing all his Legions to stand still on either side, with his Chariot and Thunder driving into the midst of his Enemies, pursues them unable to resist towards the wall of Heaven; which opening, they leap down with horrour and confusion into the place of punishment prepar'd for them in the Deep:* Messiah *returns with triumph to his Father.*

ALL NIGHT the dreadless Angel unpursu'd
Through Heav'ns wide Champain held his way, till Morn,
Wak't by the circling Hours, with rosie hand
Unbarr'd the gates of Light. There is a Cave
Within the Mount of God, fast by his Throne,
Where light and darkness in perpetual round
Lodge and dislodge by turns, which makes through Heav'n
Grateful vicissitude, like Day and Night;
Light issues forth, and at the other dore
Obsequious darkness enters, till her houre   10
To veile the Heav'n, though darkness there might well
Seem twilight here; and now went forth the Morn
Such as in highest Heav'n, arrayd in Gold
Empyreal, from before her vanisht Night,
Shot through with orient Beams: when all the Plain
Coverd with thick embatteld Squadrons bright,
Chariots and flaming Armes, and fierie Steeds
Reflecting blaze on blaze, first met his view:
Warr he perceav'd, warr in procinct, and found
Already known what he for news had thought   20
To have reported: gladly then he mixt
Among those friendly Powers who him receav'd
With joy and acclamations loud, that one
That of so many Myriads fall'n, yet one
Returnd not lost: On to the sacred hill
They led him high applauded, and present

Before the seat supream; from whence a voice
From midst a Golden Cloud thus milde was heard.
   Servant of God, well done, well hast thou fought
The better fight, who single hast maintaind   *30*
Against revolted multitudes the Cause
Of Truth, in word mightier then they in Armes;
And for the testimonie of Truth hast born
Universal reproach, far worse to beare
Then violence: for this was all thy care
To stand approv'd in sight of God, though Worlds
Judg'd thee perverse: the easier conquest now
Remains thee, aided by this host of friends,
Back on thy foes more glorious to return
Then scornd thou didst depart, and to subdue   *40*
By force, who reason for thir Law refuse,
Right reason for thir Law, and for thir King
Messiah, who by right of merit Reigns.
Goe *Michael* of Celestial Armies Prince,
And thou in Military prowess next
Gabriel, lead forth to Battel these my Sons
Invincible, lead forth my armed Saints
By Thousands and by Millions rang'd for fight;
Equal in number to that Godless crew
Rebellious, them with Fire and hostile Arms   *50*
Fearless assault, and to the brow of Heav'n
Pursuing drive them out from God and bliss,
Into thir place of punishment, the Gulf
Of *Tartarus*, which ready opens wide
His fiery *Chaos* to receave thir fall.
   So spake the Sovran voice, and Clouds began
To darken all the Hill, and smoak to rowl
In duskie wreathes, reluctant flames, the signe
Of wrauth awak't: nor with less dread the loud
Ethereal Trumpet from on high gan blow: *60*
At which command the Powers Militant,
That stood for Heav'n, in mighty Quadrate joyn'd
Of Union irresistible, mov'd on
In silence thir bright Legions, to the sound
Of instrumental Harmonic that breath'd
Heroic Ardor to advent'rous deeds
Under thir God-like Leaders, in the Cause
Of God and his *Messiah*. On they move
Indissolubly firm; nor obvious Hill,
Nor streit'ning Vale, nor Wood, nor Stream divides   *70*
Thir perfet ranks; for high above the ground
Thir march was, and the passive Air upbore

Thir nimble tread; as when the total kind
Of Birds in orderly array on wing
Came summond over *Eden* to receive
Thir names of thee; so over many a tract
Of Heav'n they march'd, and many a Province wide
Tenfold the length of this terrene: at last
Farr in th' Horizon to the North appeer'd
From skirt to skirt a fierie Region, stretcht   *80*
In battailous aspect, and neerer view
Bristl'd with upright beams innumerable
Of rigid Spears, and Helmets throng'd, and Shields
Various, with boastful Argument portraid,
The banded Powers of *Satan* hasting on
With furious expedition; for they weend
That self same day by fight, or by surprize
To win the Mount of God, and on his Throne
To set the envier of his State, the proud
Aspirer, but thir thoughts prov'd fond and and vain   *90*
In the mid way: though strange to us it seemd
At first, that Angel should with Angel warr,
And in fierce hosting meet, who wont to meet
So oft in Festivals of joy and love
Unanimous, as sons of one great Sire
Hymning th' Eternal Father: but the shout
Of Battel now began, and rushing sound
Of onset ended soon each milder thought.
High in the midst exalted as a God
Th' Apostat in his Sun-bright Chariot sate   *100*
Idol of Majestie Divine, enclos'd
With Flaming Cherubim, and golden Shields;
Then lighted from his gorgeous Throne, for now
'Twixt Host and Host but narrow space was left,
A dreadful interval, and Front to Front
Presented stood in terrible array
Of hideous length: before the cloudie Van,
On the rough edge of battel ere it joyn'd,
Satan with vast and haughtie strides advanc't,
Came towring, armd in Adamant and Gold;   *110*
Abdiel that sight endur'd not, where he stood
Among the mightiest, bent on highest deeds,
And thus his own undaunted heart explores.
   O Heav'n! that such resemblance of the Highest
Should yet remain, where faith and realtie
Remain not; wherefore should not strength & might
There fail where Vertue fails, or weakest prove
Where boldest; though to sight unconquerable?

His puissance, trusting in th' Almightie's aide,
I mean to try, whose Reason I have tri'd 120
Unsound and false; nor is it aught but just,
That he who in debate of Truth hath won,
Should win in Arms, in both disputes alike
Victor; though brutish that contest and foule,
When Reason hath to deal with force, yet so
Most reason is that Reason overcome.
   So pondering, and from his armed Peers
Forth stepping opposite, half way he met
His daring foe, at this prevention more
Incens't, and thus securely him defi'd. 130
   Proud, art thou met? thy hope was to have reacht
The highth of thy aspiring unoppos'd,
The Throne of God unguarded, and his side
Abandond at the terror of thy Power
Or potent tongue; fool, not to think how vain
Against th' Omnipotent to rise in Arms;
Who out of smallest things could without end
Have rais'd incessant Armies to defeat
Thy folly; or with solitarie hand
Reaching beyond all limit, at one blow 140
Unaided could have finisht thee, and whelmd
Thy Legions under darkness; but thou seest
All are not of thy Train; there be who Faith
Prefer, and Pietie to God, though then
To thee not visible, when I alone
Seemed in thy World erroneous to dissent
From all: my Sect thou seest, now learn too late
How few somtimes may know, when thousands err.
   Whom the grand foe with scornful eye askance
Thus answerd. Ill for thee, but in wisht houre 150
Of my revenge, first sought for thou returnst
From flight, seditious Angel, to receave
Thy merited reward, the first assay
Of this right hand provok't, since first that tongue
Inspir'd with contradiction durst oppose
A third part of the Gods, in Synod met
Thir Deities to assert, who while they feel
Vigour Divine within them, can allow
Omnipotence to none. But well thou comst
Before thy fellows, ambitious to win 160
From me som Plume, that thy success may show
Destruction to the rest: this pause between
(Unanswerd least thou boast) to let thee know,
At first I thought that Libertie and Heav'n

To heav'nly Soules had bin all one; but now
I see that most through sloth had rather serve,
Ministring Spirits, trained up in Feast and Song;
Such hast thou arm'd, the Minstrelsie of Heav'n,
Servilitie with freedom to contend,
As both thir deeds compar'd this day shall prove.   *170*

   To whom in brief thus *Abdiel* stern repli'd.
Apostat still thou errst, nor end wilt find
Of erring, from the path of truth remote:
Unjustly thou deprav'st it with the name
Of *Servitude* to serve whom God ordains,
Or Nature; God and Nature bid the same,
When he who rules is worthiest, and excells
Them whom he governs. This is servitude,
To serve th' unwise, or him who hath rebelld
Against his worthier, as thine now serve thee,   *180*
Thy self not free, but to thy self enthrall'd;
Yet leudly dar'st our ministring upbraid.
Reign thou in Hell thy Kingdom, let mee serve
In Heav'n God ever blest, and his Divine
Behests obey, worthiest to be obey'd,
Yet Chains in Hell, not Realms expect: mean while
From mee returnd, as erst thou saidst, from flight,
This greeting on thy impious Crest receive.

   So saying, a noble stroke he lifted high,
Which hung not, but so swift with tempest fell   *190*
On the proud Crest of *Satan*, that no sight,
Nor motion of swift thought, less could his Shield
Such ruin intercept: ten paces huge
He back recoild; the tenth on bended knee
His massie Spear upstaid; as if on Earth
Winds under ground or waters forcing way
Sidelong, had push't a Mountain from his seat
Half sunk with all his Pines. Amazement seis'd
The Rebel Thrones, but greater rage to see
Thus foil'd thir mightiest, ours joy filld, and shout,   *200*
Presage of Victorie and fierce desire
Of Battel: whereat *Michael* bid sound
Th' Arch-angel trumpet; through the vast of Heav'n
It sounded, and the faithful Armies rung
Hosanna to the Highest: nor stood at gaze
The adverse Legions, nor less hideous joyn'd
The horrid shock: now storming furie rose,
And clamour such as heard in Heav'n till now
Was never, Arms on Armour clashing bray'd
Horrible discord, and the madding Wheeles   *210*

Of brazen Chariots rag'd; dire was the noise
Of conflict; over head the dismal hiss
Of fiery Darts in flaming volies flew,
And flying vaulted either Host with fire.
So under fierie Cope together rush'd
Both Battels maine, with ruinous assault
And inextinguishable rage; all Heav'n
Resounded, and had Earth bin then, all Earth
Had to her Center shook. What wonder? when
Millions of fierce encountring Angels fought   220
On either side, the least of whom could weild
These Elements, and arm him with the force
Of all thir Regions: how much more of Power
Armie against Armie numberless to raise
Dreadful combustion warring, and disturb,
Though not destroy, thir happie Native seat;
Had not th' Eternal King Omnipotent
From his strong hold of Heav'n high over-rul'd
And limited thir might; though numberd such
As each divided Legion might have seemed   230
A numerous Host, in strength each armed hand
A Legion; led in fight, yet Leader seemd
Each Warriour single as in Chief, expert
When to advance, or stand, or turn the sway
Of Battel, open when, and when to close
The ridges of grim Warr; no thought of flight,
None of retreat, no unbecoming deed
That argu'd fear; each on himself reli'd,
As onely in his arm the moment lay
Of victorie; deeds of eternal fame   240
Were don, but infinite: for wide was spred
That Warr and various; somtimes on firm ground
A standing fight, then soaring on main wing
Tormented all the Air; all Air seemd then
Conflicting Fire: long time in eeven scale
The Battel hung; till *Satan*, who that day
Prodigious power had shewn, and met in Armes
No equal, raunging through the dire attack
Of fighting Seraphim confus'd, at length
Saw where the Sword of *Michael* smote, and fell'd   250
Squadrons at once, with huge two-handed sway
Brandisht aloft the horrid edge came down
Wide wasting; such destruction to withstand
He hasted, and oppos'd the rockie Orb
Of tenfold Adamant, his ample Shield
A vast circumference: At his approach

The great Arch-Angel from his warlike toile
Surceas'd, and glad as hoping here to end
Intestine War in Heav'n, the arch foe subdu'd
Or Captive drag'd in Chains, with hostile frown　　*260*
And visage all enflam'd first thus began.
   Author of evil, unknown till thy revolt,
Unnam'd in Heav'n, now plenteous, as thou seest
These Acts of hateful strife, hateful to all,
Though heaviest by just measure on thy self
And thy adherents: how hast thou disturb'd
Heav'ns blessed peace, and into Nature brought
Miserie, uncreated till the crime
Of thy Rebellion? how hast thou instill'd
Thy malice into thousands, once upright　　*270*
And faithful, now prov'd false. But think not here
To trouble Holy Rest; Heav'n casts thee out
From all her Confines. Heav'n the seat of bliss
Brooks not the works of violence and Warr.
Hence then, and evil go with thee along
Thy ofspring, to the place of evil, Hell,
Thou and thy wicked crew; there mingle broiles,
Ere this avenging Sword begin thy doome,
Or som more sudden vengeance wing'd from God
Precipitate thee with augmented paine.　　*280*
   So spake the Prince of Angels; to whom thus
The Adversarie. Nor think thou with wind
Of airie threats to aw whom yet with deeds
Thou canst not. Hast thou turnd the least of these
To flight, or if to fall, but that they rise
Unvanquisht, easier to transact with mee
That thou shouldst hope, imperious, & with threats
To chase me hence? erre not that so shall end
The strife which thou call'st evil, but wee style
The strife of Glorie: which we mean to win,　　*290*
Or turn this Heav'n it self into the Hell
Thou fablest, here however to dwell free,
If not to reign: mean while thy utmost force,
And join him nam'd *Almightie* to thy aid,
I flie not, but have sought thee farr and nigh.
   They ended parle, and both addrest for fight
Unspeakable; for who, though with the tongue
Of Angels, can relate, or to what things
Liken on Earth conspicuous, that may lift
Human imagination to such highth　　*300*
Of Godlike Power: for likest Gods they seemd,
Stood they or mov'd, in stature, motion, arms

Fit to decide the Empire of great Heav'n.
Now wav'd thir fierie Swords, and in the Aire
Made horrid Circles; two broad Suns thir Shields
Blaz'd opposite, while expectation stood
In horror; from each hand with speed retir'd
Where erst was thickest fight, th' Angelic throng,
And left large field, unsafe within the wind
Of such commotion, such as to set forth   *310*
Great things by small, if Natures concord broke,
Among the Constellations warr were sprung,
Two Planets rushing from aspect maligne
Of fiercest opposition in mid Skie,
Should combat, and thir jarring Sphears confound.
Together both with next to Almightie Arme,
Uplifted imminent one stroke they aim'd
That might determine, and not need repeate,
As not of power, at once; nor odds appeerd
In might or swift prevention; but the sword   *320*
Of *Michael* from the Armorie of God
Was giv'n him temperd so, that neither keen
Nor solid might resist that edge: it met
The sword of *Satan* with steep force to smite
Descending, and in half cut sheere, nor staid,
But with swift wheele reverse, deep entring shar'd
All his right side; then *Satan* first knew pain,
And writh'd him to and fro convolv'd; so sore
The griding sword with discontinuous wound
Pass'd through him, but th' Ethereal substance clos'd   *330*
Not long divisible, and from the gash
A stream of Nectarous humor issuing flow'd
Sanguin, such as Celestial Spirits may bleed,
And all his Armour staind ere while so bright.
Forthwith on all sides to his aide was run
By Angels many and strong, who interpos'd
Defence, while others bore him on thir Shields
Back to his Chariot; where it stood retir'd
From off the files of warr: there they him laid
Gnashing for anguish and despite and shame   *340*
To find himself not matchless, and his pride
Humbl'd by such rebuke, so farr beneath
His confidence to equal God in power.
Yet soon he heal'd; for Spirits that live throughout
Vital in every part, not as frail man
In Entrailes, Heart or Head, Liver or Reines,
Cannot but by annihilating die;
Nor in thir liquid texture mortal wound

Receive, no more then can the fluid Aire:
All Heart they live, all Head, all Eye, all Eare,   *350*
All Intellect, all Sense, and as they please,
They Limb themselves, and colour, shape or size
Assume, as likes them best, condense or rare.
   Mean while in other parts like deeds deservd
Memorial, where the might of *Gabriel* fought,
And with fierce Ensignes pierc'd the deep array
Of *Moloc* furious King, who him defi'd,
And at his Chariot wheeles to drag him bound
Threatn'd, nor from the Holie One of Heav'n
Refrein'd his tongue blasphemous; but anon   *360*
Down clov'n to the waste, with shatterd Armes
And uncouth paine fled bellowing. On each wing
Uriel and *Raphael* his vaunting foe,
Though huge, and in a Rock of Diamond Armd,
Vanquish'd *Adramelec*, and *Asmadai*,
Two potent Thrones, that to be less then Gods
Disdain'd, but meaner thoughts learnd in thir flight,
Mangl'd with gastly wounds through Plate and Maile.
Nor stood unmindful *Abdiel* to annoy
The Atheist crew, but with redoubl'd blow   *370*
Ariel and *Arioc*, and the violence
Of *Ramiel* scorcht and blasted overthrew.
I might relate of thousands, and thir names
Eternize here on Earth; but those elect
Angels contented with thir fame in Heav'n
Seek not the praise of men; the other sort
In might though wondrous and in Acts of Warr,
Nor of Renown less eager, yet by doome
Canceld from Heav'n and sacred memorie,
Nameless in dark oblivion let them dwell.   *380*
For strength from Truth divided and from Just,
Illaudable, naught merits but dispraise
And ignominie, yet to glorie aspires
Vain glorious, and through infamie seeks fame:
Therfore Eternal silence be thir doome.
   And now thir mightiest quelld, the battel swerv'd,
With many an inrode gor'd; deformed rout
Enter'd, and foul disorder; all the ground
With shiverd armour strow'n, and on a heap
Chariot and Charioter lay overturnd   *390*
And fierie foaming Steeds; what stood, recoyld
Orewearied, through the faint Satanic Host
Defensive scarce, or with pale fear surpris'd,
Then first with fear surpris'd and sense of paine

Fled ignominious, to such evil brought
By sinne of disobedience, till that hour
Not liable to fear or flight or paine.
Far otherwise th' inviolable Saints
In Cubic Phalanx firm advanc't entire,
Invulnerable, impenitrably arm'd: 400
Such high advantages thir innocence
Gave them above thir foes, not to have sinnd,
Not to have disobei'd; in fight they stood
Unwearied, unobnoxious to be pain'd
By wound, though from thir place by violence mov'd.
    Now Night her course began, and over Heav'n
Inducing darkness, grateful truce impos'd,
And silence on the odious dinn of Warr:
Under her Cloudie covert both retir'd,
Victor and Vanquisht: on the foughten field   410
Michael and his Angels prevalent
Encamping, plac'd in Guard thir Watches round,
Cherubic waving fires: on th' other part
Satan with his rebellious disappeerd,
Far in the dark dislodg'd, and void of rest,
His Potentates to Councel call'd by night;
And in the midst thus undismai'd began.
    O now in danger tri'd, now known in Armes
Not to be overpowerd, Companions deare,
Found worthy not of Libertie alone,   420
Too mean pretense, but what we more affect,
Honour, Dominion, Glorie, and renowne,
Who have sustaind one day in doubtful fight,
(And if one day, why not Eternal dayes?)
What Heavens Lord had powerfullest to send
Against us from about his Throne, and judg'd
Sufficient to subdue us to his will,
But proves not so: then fallible, it seems,
Of future we may deem him, though till now
Omniscient thought. True is, less firmly arm'd,   430
Some disadvantage we endur'd and paine,
Till now not known, but known as soon contemnd,
Since now we find this our Empyreal forme
Incapable of mortal injurie
Imperishable, and though peirc'd with wound,
Soon closing, and by native vigour heal'd.
Of evil then so small as easie think
The remedie; perhaps more valid Armes,
Weapons more violent, when next we meet,
May serve to better us, and worse our foes,   440

Or equal what between us made the odds,
In Nature none: if other hidden cause
Left them Superiour, while we can preserve
Unhurt our mindes, and understanding sound,
Due search and consultation will disclose.
    He sat; and in th' assembly next upstood
Nisroc, of Principalities the prime;
As one he stood escap't from cruel fight,
Sore toild, his riv'n Armes to havoc hewn,
And cloudie in aspect thus answering spake.   *450*
Deliverer from new Lords, leader to free
Enjoyment of our right as Gods; yet hard
For Gods, and too unequal work we find
Against unequal armes to fight in paine,
Against unpaind, impassive; from which evil
Ruin must needs ensue; for what availes
Valour or strength, though matchless, quelld with pain
Which all subdues, and makes remiss the hands
Of Mightiest. Sense of pleasure we may well
Spare out of life perhaps, and not repine,   *460*
But live content, which is the calmest life:
But pain is perfet miserie, the worst
Of evils, and excessive, overturnes
All patience. He who therefore can invent
With what more forcible we may offend
Our yet unwounded Enemies, or arme
Our selves with like defence, to mee deserves
No less then for deliverance what we owe.
    Whereto with look compos'd *Satan* repli'd.
Not uninvented that, which thou aright   *470*
Beleivst so main to our success, I bring;
Which of us who beholds the bright surface
Of this Ethereous mould whereon we stand,
This continent of spacious Heav'n, adornd
With Plant, Fruit, Flour Ambrosial, Gemms & Gold,
Whose Eye so superficially surveyes
These things, as not to mind from whence they grow
Deep under ground, materials dark and crude,
Of spiritous and fierie spume, till toucht
With Heav'ns ray, and temperd they shoot forth   *480*
So beauteous, op'ning to the ambient light.
These in thir dark Nativitie the Deep
Shall yeild us, pregnant with infernal flame,
Which into hollow Engins long and round
Thick-rammd, at th' other bore with touch of fire
Dilated and infuriate shall send forth

From far with thundring noise among our foes
Such implements of mischief as shall dash
To pieces, and orewhelm whatever stands
Adverse, that they shall fear we have disarmd   490
The Thunderer of his only dreaded bolt.
Nor long shall be our labour, yet ere dawne,
Effect shall end our wish. Mean while revive;
Abandon fear; to strength and counsel joind
Think nothing hard, much less to be despaird.
He ended, and his words thir drooping chere
Enlightn'd, and thir languisht hope reviv'd.
Th' invention all admir'd, and each, how hee
To be th' inventer miss'd, so easie it seemd
Once found, which yet unfound most would have   500
   thought
Impossible: yet haply of thy Race
In future dayes, if Malice should abound,
Some one intent on mischief, or inspir'd
With dev'lish machination might devise
Like instrument to plague the Sons of men
For sin, on warr and mutual slaughter bent.
Forthwith from Councel to the work they flew,
None arguing stood, innumerable hands
Were ready, in a moment up they turnd
Wide the Celestial soile, and saw beneath   510
Th' originals of Nature in thir crude
Conception; Sulphurous and Nitrous Foame
They found, they mingl'd, and with suttle Art,
Concocted and adusted they reduc'd
To blackest grain, and into store conveyd:
Part hidd'n veins diggd up (nor hath this Earth
Entrails unlike) of Mineral and Stone,
Whereof to found thir Engins and thir Balls
Of missive ruin; part incentive reed
Provide, pernicious with one touch to fire.   520
So all ere day-spring, under conscious Night
Secret they finish'd, and in order set,
With silent circumspection unespi'd.
Now when fair Morn Orient in Heav'n appeerd
Up rose the Victor Angels, and to Arms
The matin Trumpet Sung: in Arms they stood
Of Golden Panoplie, refulgent Host,
Soon banded; others from the dawning Hills
Lookd round, and Scouts each Coast light-armed scoure,
Each quarter, to descrie the distant foe,   530
Where lodg'd, or whither fled, or if for fight,

In motion or in alt: him soon they met
Under spred Ensignes moving nigh, in slow
But firm Battalion; back with speediest Sail
Zophiel, of Cherubim the swiftest wing,
Came flying, and in mid Aire aloud thus cri'd.

    Arme, Warriours, Arme for fight, the foe at hand,
Whom fled we thought, will save us long pursuit
This day, fear not his flight; so thick a Cloud
He comes, and settl'd in his face I see   540
Sad resolution and secure: let each
His Adamantine coat gird well, and each
Fit well his Helme, gripe fast his orbed Shield,
Born eevn or high, for this day will pour down,
If I conjecture aught, no drizling showr,
But ratling storm of Arrows barbd with fire.
So warnd he them aware themselves, and soon
In order, quit of all impediment;
Instant without disturb they took Allarm,
And onward move Embattelld; when behold   550
Not distant far with heavie pace the Foe
Approaching gross and huge; in hollow Cube
Training his devilish Enginrie, impal'd
On every side with shaddowing Squadrons Deep,
To hide the fraud. At interview both stood
A while, but suddenly at head appeerd
Satan: And thus was heard Commanding loud.

    Vangard, to Right and Left the Front unfould;
That all may see who hate us, how we seek
Peace and composure, and with open brest   560
Stand readie to receive them, if they like
Our overture, and turn not back perverse;
But that I doubt, however witness Heaven,
Heav'n witness thou anon, while we discharge
Freely our part: yee who appointed stand
Do as you have in charge, and briefly touch
What we propound, and loud that all may hear.

    So scoffing in ambiguous words, he scarce
Had ended; when to Right and Left the Front
Divided, and to either Flank retir'd.   570
Which to our eyes discoverd new and strange,
A triple-mounted row of Pillars laid
On Wheels (for like to Pillars most they seem'd
Or hollow'd bodies made of Oak or Firr
With branches lopt, in Wood or Mountain fell'd)
Brass, Iron, Stonie mould, had not thir mouthes
With hideous orifice gap't on us wide.

Portending hollow truce; at each behind
A Seraph stood, and in his hand a Reed
Stood waving tipt with fire; while we suspense,   580
Collected stood within our thoughts amus'd,
Not long, for sudden all at once thir Reeds
Put forth, and to a narrow vent appli'd
With nicest touch. Immediate in a flame,
But soon obscurd with smoak, all Heav'n appeerd,
From those deep-throated Engins belcht, whose roar
Emboweld with outragious noise the Air,
And all her entrails tore, disgorging foule
Thir devillish glut, chaind Thunderbolts and Hail
Of Iron Globes, which on the Victor Host   590
Level'd, with such impetuous furie smote,
That whom they hit, none on thir feet might stand,
Though standing else as Rocks, but down they fell
By thousands, Angel on Arch-Angel rowl'd;
The sooner for thir Arms, unarm'd they might
Have easily as Spirits evaded swift
By quick contraction or remove; but now
Foule dissipation follow'd and forc't rout;
Nor serv'd it to relax thir serried files.
What should they do? if on they rusht, repulse   600
Repeated, and indecent overthrow
Doubl'd, would render them yet more despis'd,
And to thir foes a laughter; for in view
Stood rankt of Seraphim another row
In posture to displode thir second tire
Of Thunder: back defeated to return
They worse abhorr'd. *Satan* beheld thir plight,
And to his Mates thus in derision call'd.
  O Friends, why come not on these Victors proud?
Ere while they fierce were coming, and when wee,   610
To entertain them fair with open Front
And Brest, (what could we more?) propounded terms
Of composition, strait they chang'd thir minds,
Flew off, and into strange vagaries fell,
As they would dance, yet for a dance they seemd
Somwhat extravagant and wilde, perhaps
For joy of offerd peace: but I suppose
If our proposals once again were heard
We should compel them to a quick result.
  To whom thus *Belial* in like gamesom mood.   620
Leader, the terms we sent were terms of weight,
Of hard contents, and full of force urg'd home,
Such as we might perceive amus'd them all,

And stumbl'd many, who receives them right,
Had need from head to foot well understand;
Not understood, this gift they have besides,
They shew us when our foes walk not upright.
   So they among themselves in pleasant veine
Stood scoffing, highthn'd in thir thoughts beyond
All doubt of Victorie, eternal might   *630*
To match with thir inventions they presum'd
So easie, and of his Thunder made a scorn,
And all his Host derided, while they stood
A while in trouble; but they stood not long,
Rage prompted them at length, & found them arms
Against such hellish mischief fit to oppose.
Forthwith (behold the excellence, the power
Which God hath in his mighty Angels plac'd)
Thir Arms away they threw, and to the Hills
(For Earth hath this variety from Heav'n   *640*
Of pleasure situate in Hill and Dale)
Light as the Lightning glimps they ran, they flew,
From thir foundations loosning to and fro
They pluckt the seated Hills with all thir load,
Rocks, Waters, Woods, and by the shaggie tops
Up lifting bore them in thir hands: Amaze,
Be sure, and terrour seis'd the rebel Host,
When coming towards them so dread they saw
The bottom of the Mountains upward turn'd,
Till on those cursed Engins triple-row   *650*
They saw them whelmd, and all thir confidence
Under the weight of Mountains buried deep,
Themselves invaded next, and on thir heads
Main Promontories flung, which in the Air
Came shadowing, and opprest whole Legions arm'd,
Thir armor help'd their harm, crush't in and brus'd
Into thir substance pent, which wrought them pain
Implacable, and many a dolorous groan,
Long strugling underneath, ere they could wind
Out of such prison, though Spirits of purest light,   *660*
Purest at first, now gross by sinning grown.
The rest in imitation to like Armes
Betook them, and the neighbouring Hills uptore;
So Hills amid the Air encountered Hills
Hurl'd to and fro with jaculation dire,
That under ground they fought in dismal shade;
Infernal noise; Warr seem'd a civil Game
To this uproar; horrid confusion heapt
Upon confusion rose: and now all Heav'n

Had gone to wrack, with ruin overspred, 670
Had not th' Almightie Father where he sits
Shrin'd in his Sanctuarie of Heav'n secure,
Consulting on the sum of things, foreseen
This tumult, and permitted all, advis'd:
That his great purpose he might so fulfill,
To honour his Anointed Son aveng'd
Upon his enemies, and to declare
All power on him transferr'd: whence to his Son
Th' Assessor of his Throne he thus began.
    Effulgence of my Glorie, Son belov'd, 680
Son in whose face invisible is beheld
Visibly, what by Deitie I am,
And in whose hand what by Decree I doe,
Second Omnipotence, two dayes are past,
Two dayes, as we compute the dayes of Heav'n,
Since *Michael* and his Powers went forth to tame
These disobedient; sore hath been thir fight,
As likeliest was, when two such Foes met arm'd;
For to themselves I left them, and thou knowst,
Equal in their Creation they were form'd, 690
Save what sin hath impaird, which yet hath wrought
Insensibly, for I suspend thir doom;
Whence in perpetual fight they needs must last
Endless, and no solution will be found:
Warr wearied hath perform'd what Warr can do,
And to disorder'd rage let loose the reines,
With Mountains as with Weapons arm'd, which makes
Wild work in Heav'n, and dangerous to the maine.
Two dayes are therefore past, the third is thine;
For thee I have ordain'd it, and thus farr 700
Have sufferd, that the Glorie may be thine
Of ending this great Warr, since none but Thou
Can end it. Into thee such Vertue and Grace
Immense I have transfus'd, that all may know
In Heav'n and Hell thy Power above compare,
And this perverse Commotion governd thus,
To manifest thee worthiest to be Heir
Of all things, to be Heir and to be King
By Sacred Unction, thy deserved right.
Go then thou Mightiest in thy Fathers might, 710
Ascend my Chariot, guide the rapid Wheeles
That shake Heav'ns basis, bring forth all my Warr,
My Bow and Thunder, my Almightie Arms
Gird on, and Sword upon thy puissant Thigh;
Pursue these sons of Darkness, drive them out

From all Heav'ns bounds into the utter Deep:
There let them learn, as likes them, to despise
God and *Messiah* his anointed King.
  He said, and on his Son with Rayes direct
Shon full, he all his Father full exprest   720
Ineffably into his face receiv'd,
And thus the filial Godhead answering spake.
  O Father, O Supream of heav'nly Thrones,
First, Highest, Holiest, Best, thou alwayes seekst
To glorifie thy Son, I alwayes thee,
As is most just; this I my Glorie account,
My exaltation, and my whole delight,
That thou in me well pleas'd declarst thy will
Fulfill'd, which to fulfil is all my bliss.
Scepter and Power, thy giving, I assume,   730
And gladlier shall resign, when in the end
Thou shalt be All in All, and I in thee
For ever, and in mee all whom thou lov'st;
But whom thou hat'st, I hate, and can put on
Thy terrors, as I put thy mildness on,
Image of thee in all things; and shall soon,
Armd with thy might, rid heav'n of these rebell'd,
To thir prepar'd ill Mansion driven down
To chains of Darkness, and th' undying Worm,
That from thy just obedience could revolt,   740
Whom to obey is happiness entire.
Then shall thy Saints unmixt, and from th' impure
Farr separate, circling thy holy Mount
Unfained *Halleluiahs* to thee sing,
Hymns of high praise, and I among them chief.
So said, he o're his Scepter bowing, rose
From the right hand of Glorie where he sate,
And the third sacred Morn began to shine
Dawning through Heav'n: forth rush'd with whirl-wind
   sound
The Chariot of Paternal Deitie,   750
Flashing thick flames, Wheele within Wheele undrawn,
It self instinct with Spirit, but convoyd
By four Cherubic shapes, four Faces each
Had wondrous, as with Starrs thir bodies all
And Wings were set with Eyes, with Eyes the Wheels
Of Beril, and careering Fires between;
Over thir heads a chrystal Firmament,
Whereon a Saphir Throne, inlaid with pure
Amber, and colours of the showrie Arch.
Hee in Celestial Panoplie all armd   760

Of radiant *Urim*, work divinely wrought,
Ascended, at his right hand Victorie
Sate Eagle-wing'd, beside him hung his Bow
And Quiver with three-bolted Thunder stor'd,
And from about him fierce Effusion rowld
Of smoak and bickering flame, and sparkles dire;
Attended with ten thousand thousand Saints,
He onward came, farr off his coming shon,
And twentie thousand (I thir number heard)
Chariots of God, half on each hand were seen: 770
Hee on the wings of Cherub rode sublime
On the Crystallin Skie, in Saphir Thron'd.
Illustrious farr and wide, but by his own
First seen, them unexpected joy surpriz'd,
When the great Ensign of *Messiah* blaz'd
Aloft by Angels born, his Sign in Heav'n:
Under whose Conduct *Michael* soon reduc'd
His Armie, circumfus'd on either Wing,
Under thir Head imbodied all in one.
Before him Power Divine his way prepar'd; 780
At his command the uprooted Hills retir'd
Each to his place, they heard his voice and went
Obsequious, Heav'n his wonted face renewed,
And with fresh Flourets Hill and Valley smil'd.
This saw his hapless Foes, but stood obdur'd,
And to rebellious fight rallied thir Powers
Insensate, hope conceiving from despair.
In heav'nly Spirits could such perverseness dwell?
But to convince the proud what Signs availe,
Or Wonders move th' obdurate to relent? 790
They hard'nd more by what might most reclame,
Grieving to see his Glorie, at the sight
Took envie, and aspiring to his highth,
Stood reimbattell'd fierce, by force or fraud
Weening to prosper, and at length prevaile
Against God and *Messiah*, or to fall
In universal ruin last, and now
To final Battel drew, disdaining flight,
Or faint retreat; when the great Son of God
To all his Host on either hand thus spake. 800
   Stand still in bright array ye Saints, here stand
Ye Angels arm'd, this day from Battel rest;
Faithful hath been your Warfare, and of God
Accepted, fearless in his righteous Cause,
And as ye have receivd, so have ye don
Invincibly: but of this cursed crew

The punishment to other hand belongs,
Vengeance is his, or whose he sole appoints;
Number to this dayes work is not ordain'd
Nor multitude, stand onely and behold   810
Gods indignation on these Godless pourd
By mee; not you but mee they have despis'd,
Yet envied; against mee is all thir rage,
Because the Father, t'whom in Heav'n supream
Kingdom and Power and Glorie appertains,
Hath honourd me according to his will.
Therefore to mee thir doom he hath assig'n'd;
That they may have thir wish, to trie with mee
In Battel which the stronger proves, they all,
Or I alone against them, since by strength   820
They measure all, of other excellence
Not emulous, nor care who them excells;
Nor other strife with them do I voutsafe.
   So spake the Son, and into terrour chang'd
His count'nance too severe to be beheld
And full of wrauth bent on his Enemies.
At once the Four spred out thir Starrie wings
With dreadful shade contiguous, and the Orbes
Of his fierce Chariot rowld, as with the sound
Of torrent Floods, or of a numerous Host.   830
Hee on his impious Foes right onward drove,
Gloomie as Night; under his burning Wheeles
The stedfast Empyrean shook throughout,
All but the Throne it self of God. Full soon
Among them he arriv'd; in his right hand
Grasping ten thousand Thunders, which he sent
Before him, such as in thir Soules infix'd
Plagues; they astonisht all resistance lost,
All courage; down thir idle weapons drop'd;
O're Shields and Helmes, and helmed heads he rode   840
Of Thrones and mighty Seraphim prostrate,
That wish'd the Mountains now might be again
Thrown on them as a shelter from his ire.
Nor less on either side tempestuous fell
His arrows, from the fourfold-visag'd Foure,
Distinct with eyes, and from the living Wheels,
Distinct alike with multitude of eyes,
One Spirit in them rul'd, and every eye
Glar'd lightning, and shot forth pernicious fire
Among th' accurst, that witherd all thir strength,   850
And of thir wonted vigour left them draind,
Exhausted, spiritless, afflicted, fall'n.

Yet half his strength he put not forth, but check'd
His Thunder in mid Volie, for he meant
Not to destroy, but root them out of Heav'n:
The overthrown he rais'd, and as a Heard
Of Goats or timerous flock together throngd
Drove them before him Thunder-struck, pursu'd
With terrors and with furies to the bounds
And Chrystall wall of Heav'n, which op'ning wide,   860
Rowld inward, and a spacious Gap disclos'd
Into the wastful Deep; the monstrous sight
Strook them with horror backward, but far worse
Urg'd them behind; headlong themselvs they threw
Down from the verge of Heav'n, Eternal wrauth
Burnt after them to the bottomless pit.
   Hell heard th' unsufferable noise, Hell saw
Heav'n ruining from Heav'n, and would have fled
Affrighted; but strict Fate had cast too deep
Her dark foundations, and too fast had bound.   870
Nine dayes they fell; confounded *Chaos* roard,
And felt tenfold confusion in thir fall
Through his wilde Anarchie, so huge a rout
Incumberd him with ruin: Hell at last
Yawning receavd them whole, and on them clos'd,
Hell thir fit habitation fraught with fire
Unquenchable, the house of woe and paine.
Disburd'nd Heav'n rejoic'd, and soon repaird
Her mural breach, returning whence it rowld.
Sole Victor from th' expulsion of his Foes   880
Messiah his triumphal Chariot turnd:
To meet him all his Saints, who silent stood
Eye witnesses of his Almightie Acts,
With Jubilie advanc'd; and as they went,
Shaded with branching Palme, each order bright,
Sung Triumph, and him sung Victorious King,
Son, Heire, and Lord, to him Dominion giv'n,
Worthiest to Reign: he celebrated rode
Triumphant through mid Heav'n, into the Courts
And Temple of his mightie Father Thron'd   890
On high; who into Glorie him receav'd,
Where now he sits at the right hand of bliss.
   Thus measuring things in Heav'n by things on Earth
At thy request, and that thou maist beware
By what is past, to thee I have reveal'd
What might have else to human Race bin hid:
The discord which befel, and Warr in Heav'n
Among th' Angelic Powers, and the deep fall

Of those too high aspiring, who rebelld
With *Satan*, hee who envies now thy state, 900
Who now is plotting how he may seduce
Thee also from obedience, that with him
Bereavd of happiness thou maist partake
His punishment, Eternal miserie;
Which would be all his solace and revenge,
As a despite don against the most High,
Thee once to gaine Companion of his woe.
But list'n not to his Temptations, warne
Thy weaker; let it profit thee to have heard
By terrible Example the reward 910
Of disobedience; firm they might have stood,
Yet fell; remember, and fear to transgress.

BOOK VII

THE ARGUMENT

Raphael *at the request of* Adam *relates how and wherefore this world was first created; that God, after the expelling of* Satan *and his Angels out of Heaven, declar'd his pleasure to create another World and other Creatures to dwell therein; sends his Son with Glory and attendance of Angels to perform the work of Creation in six dayes: the Angels celebrate with Hymns the performance thereof, and his re-ascention into Heaven.*

<blockquote>
DESCEND from Heav'n *Urania*, by that name
If rightly thou art call'd, whose Voice divine
Following, above th' *Olympian* Hill I soare,
Above the flight of *Pegasean* wing.
The meaning, not the Name I call: for thou
Nor of the Muses nine, nor on the top
Of old *Olympus* dwell'st, but Heav'nlie borne,
Before the Hills appeerd, or Fountain flow'd,
Thou with Eternal wisdom didst converse,
Wisdom thy Sister, and with her didst play   *10*
In presence of th' Almightie Father, pleas'd
With thy Celestial Song. Up led by thee
Into the Heav'n of Heav'ns I have presum'd,
An Earthlie Guest, and drawn Empyreal Aire,
Thy tempring; with like safetie guided down
Return me to my Native Element:
Least from this flying Steed unrein'd, (as once
Bellerophon, though from a lower Clime)
Dismounted, on th' *Alcian* Field I fall
Erroneous, there to wander and forlorne.   *20*
Half yet remaines unsung, but narrower bound
Within the visible Diurnal Spheare;
Standing on Earth, not rapt above the Pole,
More safe I Sing with mortal voice, unchang'd
To hoarce or mute, though fall'n on evil dayes,
On evil dayes though fall'n, and evil tongues;
In darkness, and with dangers compast round,
And solitude; yet not alone, while thou
Visit'st my slumbers Nightly, or when Morn
Purples the East: still govern thou my Song,   *30*
Urania, and fit audience find, though few.
But drive farr off the barbarous dissonance
Of *Bacchus* and his Revellers, the Race
</blockquote>

217

Of that wilde Rout that tore the *Thracian* Bard
In *Rhodope*, where Woods and Rocks had Eares
To rapture, till the savage clamor dround
Both Harp and Voice; nor could the Muse defend
Her Son. So fail not thou, who thee implores:
For thou art Heav'nlie, shee an empty dreame.
    Say Goddess, what ensu'd when *Raphael*,   40
The affable Arch-angel, had forewarn'd
Adam by dire example to beware
Apostasie, by what befell in Heaven
To those Apostates, least the like befall
In Paradise to *Adam* or his Race,
Charg'd not to touch the interdicted Tree,
If they trangress, and slight that sole command,
So easily obeyd amid the choice
Of all tasts else to please thir appetite.
Though wandring. He with his consorted *Eve*   50
The storie heard attentive, and was fill'd
With admiration, and deep Muse to heare
Of things so high and strange, things to thir thought
So unimaginable as hate in Heav'n,
And Warr so neer the Peace of God in bliss
With such confusion: but the evil soon
Driv'n back redounded as a flood on those
From whom it sprung, impossible to mix
With Blessedness. Whence *Adam* soon repeal'd
The doubts that in his heart arose: and now   60
Led on, yet sinless, with desire to know
What neerer might concern him, how this World
Of Heav'n and Earth conspicuous first began,
When, and whereof created, for what cause,
What within *Eden* or without was done
Before his memorie, as one whose drouth
Yet scarce allay'd still eyes the current streame,
Whose liquid murmur heard new thirst excites,
Proceeded thus to ask his Heav'nly Guest.
    Great things, and full of wonder in our eares,   70
Farr differing from this World, thou hast reveal'd
Divine Interpreter, by favour sent
Down from the Empyrean to forewarne
Us timely of what might else have bin our loss,
Unknown, which human knowledg could not reach:
For which to the infinitly Good we owe
Immortal thanks, and his admonishment
Receave with solemne purpose to observe
Immutably his sovran will, the end

Of what we are. But since thou hast voutsaf't
Gently for our instruction to impart
Things above Earthly thought, which yet concernd
Our knowing, as to highest wisdom seemd,
Deign to descend now lower, and relate
What may no less perhaps availe us known,
How first began this Heav'n which we behold
Distant so high, with moving Fires adornd
Innumerable, and this which yeelds or fills
All space, the ambient Aire wide interfus'd
Imbracing round this florid Earth, what cause
Mov'd the Creator in his holy Rest
Through all Eternitie so late to build
In *Chaos*, and the work begun, how soon
Absolv'd, if unforbid thou maist unfould
What wee, not to explore the secrets aske
Of his Eternal Empire, but the more
To magnifie his works, the more we know.
And the great Light of Day yet wants to run
Much of his Race though steep, suspens in Heav'n
Held by thy voice, thy potent voice he heares,
And longer will delay to heare thee tell
His Generation, and the rising Birth
Of Nature from the unapparent Deep:
Or if the Starr of Eevning and the Moon
Haste to thy audience, Night with her will bring
Silence, and Sleep listning to thee will watch,
Or we can bid his absence, till thy Song
End, and dismiss thee ere the Morning shine.
  Thus *Adam* his illustrious Guest besought:
And thus the Godlike Angel answerd milde.
This also thy request with caution askt
Obtaine: though to recount Almightie works
What words or tongue of Seraph can suffice,
Or heart of man suffice to comprehend?
Yet what thou canst attain, which best may serve
To glorifie the Maker, and inferr
Thee also happier, shall not be withheld
Thy hearing, such Commission from above
I have receav'd, to answer thy desire
Of knowledge within bounds; beyond abstain
To ask, nor let thine own inventions hope
Things not reveal'd which th' invisible King,
Onely Omniscient hath supprest in Night,
To none communicable in Earth or Heaven:
Anough is left besides to search and know.

But Knowledge is as food, and needs no less
Her Temperance over Appetite, to know
In measure what the mind may well contain,
Oppresses else with Surfet, and soon turns
Wisdom to Folly, as Nourishment to Winde.   130
    Know then, that after *Lucifer* from Heav'n
(So call him, brighter once amidst the Host
Of Angels, then that Starr the Starrs among)
Fell with his flaming Legions through the Deep
Into his place, and the great Son returnd
Victorious with his Saints, th' Omnipotent
Eternal Father from his Throne beheld
Thir multitude, and to his Son thus spake.
    At least our envious Foe hath fail'd, who thought
All like himself rebellious, by whose aid   140
This inaccessible high strength, the seat
Of Deitie supream, us dispossest,
He trusted to have seis'd, and into fraud
Drew many, whom thir place knows here no more;
Yet farr the greater part have kept, I see,
Thir station, Heav'n yet populous retaines
Number sufficient to possess her Realmes
Though wide, and this high Temple to frequent
With Ministeries due and solemn Rites:
But least his heart exalt him in the harme   150
Already done, to have dispeopl'd Heav'n,
My damage fondly deem'd, I can repair
That detriment, if such it be to lose
Self-lost, and in a moment will create
Another World, out of one man a Race
Of men innumerable, there to dwell,
Not here, till by degrees of merit rais'd
They open to themselves at length the way
Up hither, under long obedience tri'd,
And Earth be chang'd to Heavn, & Heav'n to Earth,   160
One Kingdom, Joy and Union without end.
Mean while inhabit laxe, ye Powers of Heav'n,
And thou my Word, begotten Son, by thee
This I perform, speak thou, and be it don:
My overshadowing Spirit and might with thee
I send along, ride forth, and bid the Deep
Within appointed bounds be Heav'n and Earth,
Boundless the Deep, because I am who fill
Infinitude, nor vacuous the space.
Though I uncircumscrib'd my self retire,   170
And put not forth my goodness, which is free

To act or not, Necessitie and Chance
Approach not mee, and what I will is Fate.
　So spake th' Almightie, and to what he spake
His Word, the Filial Godhead, gave effect.
Immediate are the Acts of God, more swift
Then time or motion, but to human ears
Cannot without process of speech be told,
So told as earthly notion can receave.
Great triumph and rejoycing was in Heav'n　　　*180*
When such was heard declar'd the Almightie's will;
Glorie they sung to the most High, good will
To future men, and in thir dwellings peace:
Glorie to him whose just avenging ire
Had driven out th' ungodly from his sight
And th' habitations of the just; to him
Glorie and praise, whose wisdom had ordain'd
Good out of evil to create, in stead
Of Spirits maligne a better Race to bring
Into thir vacant room, and thence diffuse　　　*190*
His good to Worlds and Ages infinite.
So sang the Hierarchies: Mean while the Son
On his great Expedition now appeer'd,
Girt with Omnipotence, with Radiance crown'd
Of Majestie Divine, Sapience and Love
Immense, and all his Father in him shon.
About his Chariot numberless were pour'd
Cherub and Seraph, Potentates and Thrones,
And Vertues, winged Spirits, and Chariots wing'd,
From the Armoury of God, where stand of old　　　*200*
Myriads between two brazen Mountains lodg'd
Against a solemn day, harnest at hand,
Celestial Equipage; and now came forth
Spontaneous, for within them Spirit livd,
Attendant on thir Lord: Heav'n op'nd wide
Her ever during Gates, Harmonious sound
On golden Hinges moving, to let forth
The King of Glorie in his powerful Word
And Spirit coming to create new Worlds.
On heav'nly ground they stood, and from the shore　*210*
They view'd the vast immeasurable Abyss
Outrageous as a Sea, dark, wasteful, wilde,
Up from the bottom turn'd by furious windes
And surging waves, as Mountains to assault
Heav'ns higth, and with the Center mix the Pole.
　Silence, ye troubl'd waves, and thou Deep, peace,
Said then th' Omnific Word, your discord end:

Nor staid, but on the Wings of Cherubim
Uplifted, in Paternal Glorie rode
Farr into *Chaos*, and the World unborn;   220
For *Chaos* heard his voice: him all his Traine
Follow'd in bright procession to behold
Creation, and the wonders of his might.
Then staid the fervid Wheeles, and in his hand
He took the golden Compasses, prepar'd
In Gods Eternal store, to circumscribe
This Universe, and all created things:
One foot he center'd, and the other turn'd
Round through the vast profunditie obscure,
And said, thus farr extend, thus farr thy bounds,   230
This be thy just Circumference, O World.
Thus God the Heav'n created, thus the Earth,
Matter unform'd and void: Darkness profound
Cover'd th' Abyss: but on the watrie calme
His brooding wings the Spirit of God outspred,
And vital vertue infus'd, and vital warmth
Throughout the fluid Mass, but downward purg'd
The black tartareous cold infernal dregs
Adverse to life; then founded, then conglob'd
Like things to like, the rest to several place   240
Disparted, and between spun out the Air,
And Earth self-ballanc't on her Center hung.
   Let ther be Light, said God, and forthwith Light
Ethereal, first of things, quintessence pure
Sprung from the Deep, and from her Native East
To journie through the airie gloom began,
Sphear'd in a radiant Cloud, for yet the Sun
Was not; shee in a cloudie Tabernacle
Sojourn'd the while. God saw the Light was good;
And light from darkness by the Hemisphere   250
Divided: Light the Day, and Darkness Night
He nam'd. Thus was the first Day Eev'n and Morn:
Nor past uncelebrated, nor unsung
By the Celestial Quires, when Orient Light
Exhaling first from Darkness they beheld:
Birth-day of Heav'n and Earth; with joy and shout
The hollow Universal Orb they fill'd,
And touch't thir Golden Harps, & hymning prais'd
God and his works, Creatour him they sung,
Both when first Eevning was, and when first Morn.   260
   Again, God said, let ther be Firmament
Amid the Waters, and let it divide
The Waters from the Waters: and God made

The Firmament, expanse of liquid, pure,
Transparent, Elemental Air, diffus'd
In circuit to the uttermost convex
Of this great Round: partition firm and sure,
The Waters underneath from those above
Dividing: for as Earth, so hee the World
Built on circumfluous Waters calme, in wide   *270*
Crystallin Ocean, and the loud misrule
Of *Chaos* farr remov'd, least fierce extreames
Contiguous might distemper the whole frame:
And Heav'n he nam'd the Firmament: So Eev'n
And Morning *Chorus* sung the second Day.
    The Earth was form'd, but in the Womb as yet
Of Waters, Embryon immature involv'd,
Appeer'd not: over all the face of Earth
Main Ocean flow'd, not idle, but with warme
Prolific humour soft'ning all her Globe,   *280*
Fermented the great Mother to conceave,
Satiate with genial moisture, when God said
Be gather'd now ye Waters under Heav'n
Into one place, and let dry Land appeer.
Immediately the Mountains huge appeer
Emergent, and thir broad bare backs upheave
Into the Clouds, thir tops ascend the Skie:
So high as heav'd the tumid Hills, so low
Down sunk a hollow bottom broad and deep,
Capacious bed of Waters: thither they   *290*
Hasted with glad precipitance, uprowld
As drops on dust conglobing from the drie;
Part rise in crystal Wall, or ridge direct,
For haste; such flight the great command impress'd
On the swift flouds: as Armies at the call
Of Trumpet (for of Armies thou hast heard)
Troop to thir Standard, so the watrie throng,
Wave rowling after Wave, where way they found,
If steep, with torrent rapture, if through Plaine,
Soft-ebbing; nor withstood them Rock or Hill,   *300*
But they, or under ground, or circuit wide
With Serpent errour wandring, found thir way,
And on the washie Oose deep Channels wore;
Easie, e're God had bid the ground be drie,
All but within those banks, where Rivers now
Stream, and perpetual draw thir humid traine.
The dry Land, Earth, and the great receptacle
Of congregated Waters he call'd Seas:
And saw that it was good, and said, Let th' Earth

Put forth the verdant Grass, Herb yeilding Seed,   *310*
And Fruit Tree yeilding Fruit after her kind;
Whose Seed is in her self upon the Earth.
He scarce had said, when the bare Earth, till then
Desert and bare, unsightly, unadorn'd,
Brought forth the tender Grass, whose verdure clad
Her Universal Face with pleasant green,
Then Herbs of every leaf, that sudden flour'd
Op'ning thir various colours, and made gay
Her bosom smelling sweet: and these scarce blown,
Forth flourish't thick the clustring Vine, forth crept   *320*
The smelling Gourd, up stood the cornie Reed
Embattell'd in her field: add the humble Shrub,
And Bush with frizl'd hair implicit: last
Rose as in Dance the stately Trees, and spred
Thir branches hung with copious Fruit: or gemm'd
Thir Blossoms: with high Woods the Hills were crownd,
With tufts the vallies & each fountain side,
With borders long the Rivers. That Earth now
Seemd like to Heav'n, a seat where Gods might dwell,
Or wander with delight, and love to haunt   *330*
Her sacred shades: though God had yet not rain'd
Upon the Earth, and man to till the ground
None was, but from the Earth a dewie Mist
Went up and waterd all the ground, and each
Plant of the field, which e're it was in the Earth
God made, and every Herb, before it grew
On the green stemm; God saw that it was good:
So Eev'n and Morn recorded the Third Day.

   Again th' Almightie spake: Let there be Lights
High in th' expanse of Heaven to divide   *340*
The Day from Night; and let them be for Signes,
For Seasons, and for Dayes, and circling Years,
And let them be for Lights as I ordaine
Thir Office in the Firmament of Heav'n
To give Light on the Earth; and it was so.
And God made two great Lights, great for thir use
To Man, the greater to have rule by Day,
The less by Night alterne: and made the Starrs,
And set them in the Firmament of Heav'n
To illuminate the Earth, and rule the Day   *350*
In thir vicissitude, and rule the Night,
And Light from Darkness to divide. God saw,
Surveying his great Work, that it was good:
For of Celestial Bodies first the Sun
A mightie Spheare he fram'd, unlightsom first,

Though of Ethereal Mould: then form'd the Moon
Globose, and everie magnitude of Starrs,
And sowd with Starrs the Heav'n thick as a field:
Of Light by farr the greater part he took,
Transplanted from her cloudie Shrine, and plac'd   *360*
In the Suns Orb, made porous to receive
And drink the liquid Light, firm to retaine
Her gather'd beams, great Palace now of Light.
Hither as to thir Fountain other Starrs
Repairing, in thir gold'n Urns draw Light,
And hence the Morning Planet guilds his horns;
By tincture or reflection they augment
Thir small peculiar, though from human sight
So farr remote, with diminution seen.
First in his East the glorious Lamp was seen,   *370*
Regent of Day, and all th' Horizon round
Invested with bright Rayes, jocond to run
His Longitude through Heav'ns high rode: the gray
Dawn, and the *Pleiades* before him danc'd
Shedding sweet influence: less bright the Moon,
But opposite in leveld West was set
His mirror with full face borrowing her Light
From him, for other light she needed none
In that aspect, and still that distance keepes
Till night, then in the East her turn she shines,   *380*
Revolvd on Heav'ns great Axle, and her Reign
With thousand lesser Lights dividual holds,
With thousand thousand Starres, that then appeer'd
Spangling the Hemisphere: then first adornd
With thir bright Luminaries that Set and Rose,
Glad Eevning & glad Morn crownd the fourth day.
    And God said, let the Waters generate
Reptil with Spawn abundant, living Soule:
And let Fowle flie above the Earth, with wings
Displayd on the op'n Firmament of Heav'n.   *390*
And God created the great Whales, and each
Soul living, each that crept, which plenteously
The waters generated by thir kindes,
And every Bird of wing after his kinde;
And saw that it was good, and bless'd them, saying,
Be fruitful, multiply, and in the Seas
And Lakes and running Streams the waters fill;
And let the Fowle be multiply'd on the Earth.
Forthwith the Sounds and Seas, each Creek & Bay
With Frie innumerable swarme, and Shoales   *400*
Of Fish that with thir Finns & shining Scales

Glide under the green Wave, in Sculles that oft
Bank the mid Sea: part single or with mate
Graze the Sea weed thir pasture, & through Groves
Of Coral stray, or sporting with quick glance
Show to the Sun thir wav'd coats dropt with Gold,
Or in thir Pearlie shells at ease, attend
Moist nutriment, or under Rocks thir food
In jointed Armour watch: on smooth the Seale,
And bended Dolphins play: part huge of bulk   *410*
Wallowing unweildie, enormous in thir Gate
Tempest the Ocean: there Leviathan
Hugest of living Creatures, on the Deep
Stretcht like a Promontorie sleeps or swimmes,
And seems a moving Land, and at his Gilles
Draws in, and at his Trunck spouts out a Sea.
Mean while the tepid Caves, and Fens and shoares
Thir Brood as numerous hatch, from the Egg that soon
Bursting with kindly rupture forth disclos'd
Thir callow young, but featherd soon and fledge   *420*
They summ'd thir Penns, and soaring th' air sublime
With clang despis'd the ground, under a cloud
In prospect; there the Eagle and the Stork
On Cliffs and Cedar tops thir Eyries build:
Part loosly wing the Region, part more wise
In common, rang'd in figure wedge thir way,
Intelligent of seasons, and set forth
Thir Aierie Caravan high over Sea's
Flying, and over Lands with mutual wing
Easing thir flight; so stears the prudent Crane   *430*
Her annual Voiage, born on Windes; the Aire
Floats, as they pass, fann'd with unnumber'd plumes:
From Branch to Branch the smaller Birds with song
Solac'd the Woods, and spred thir painted wings
Till Ev'n, nor then the solemn Nightingal
Ceas'd warbling, but all night tun'd her soft layes:
Others on Silver Lakes and Rivers Bath'd
Thir downie Brest; the Swan with Arched neck
Between her white wings mantling proudly, Rowes
Her state with Oarie feet: yet oft they quit   *440*
The Dank, and rising on stiff Pennons, towre
The mid Aereal Skie: Others on ground
Walk'd firm; the crested Cock whose clarion sounds
The silent hours, and th' other whose gay Traine
Adorns him, colour'd with the Florid hue
Of Rainbows and Starrie Eyes. The Waters thus
With Fish replenisht, and the Aire with Fowle,

Ev'ning and Morn solemniz'd the Fift day.
   The Sixt, and of Creation last arose
With Eevning Harps and Mattin, when God said,   *450*
Let th' Earth bring forth Fowle living in her kinde,
Cattel and Creeping things, and Beast of the Earth,
Each in thir kinde. The Earth obey'd, and strait
Op'ning her fertil Woomb teem'd at a Birth
Innumerous living Creatures, perfet formes,
Limb'd and full grown: out of the ground up rose
As from his Laire the wilde Beast where he wonns
In Forrest wilde, in Thicket, Brake, or Den;
Among the Trees in Pairs they rose, they walk'd:
The Cattel in the Fields and Meddowes green: *460*
Those rare and solitarie, these in flocks
Pasturing at once, and in broad Herds upsprung.
The grassie Clods now Calv'd, now half appeer'd
The Tawnie Lion, pawing to get free
His hinder parts, then springs as broke from Bonds,
And Rampant shakes his Brinded main; the Ounce,
The Libbard, and the Tyger, as the Moale
Rising, the crumbl'd Earth above them threw
In Hillocks; the swift Stag from under ground
Bore up his branching head: scarse from his mould   *470*
Behemoth biggest born of Earth upheav'd
His vastness: Fleec't the Flocks and bleating rose,
As Plants: ambiguous between Sea and Land
The River Horse and scalie Crocodile.
At once came forth whatever creeps the ground,
Insect or Worme; those wav'd thir limber fans
For wings, and smallest Lineaments exact
In all the Liveries dect of Summers pride
With spots of Gold and Purple, azure and green:
These as a line thir long dimension drew,   *480*
Streaking the ground with sinuous trace; not all
Minims of Nature; some of Serpent kinde
Wondrous in length and corpulence involv'd
Thir Snakie foulds, and added wings. First crept
The Parsimonious Emmet, provident
Of future, in small room large heart enclos'd,
Pattern of just equalitie perhaps
Hereafter, join'd in her popular Tribes
Of Commonaltie: swarming next appeer'd
The Femal Bee that feeds her Husband Drone   *490*
Deliciously, and builds her waxen Cells
With Honey stor'd: the rest are numberless,
And thou thir Natures know'st, and gav'st them Names,

Needless to thee repeated; nor unknown
The Serpent suttl'st Beast of all the field,
Of huge extent somtimes, with brazen Eyes
And hairie Main terrific, though to thee
Not noxious, but obedient at thy call.
Now Heav'n in all her Glorie shon, and rowld
Her motions, as the great first-Movers hand　　500
First wheeld thir course; Earth in her rich attire
Consummate lovly smil'd; Aire, Water, Earth,
By Fowl, Fish, Beast, was flown, was swum, was walkt
Frequent; and of the Sixt day yet remain'd;
There wanted yet the Master work, the end
Of all yet don; a Creature who not prone
And Brute as other Creatures, but endu'd
With Sanctitie of Reason, might erect
His Stature, and upright with Front serene
Govern the rest, self-knowing, and from thence　　510
Magnanimous to correspond with Heav'n,
But grateful to acknowledge whence his good
Descends, thither with heart and voice and eyes
Directed in Devotion, to adore
And worship God Supream, who made him chief
Of all his works: therefore the Omnipotent
Eternal Father (For where is not hee
Present) thus to his Son audibly spake.
　　Let us make now Man in our image, Man
In our similitude, and let them rule　　520
Over the Fish and Fowle of Sea and Aire,
Beast of the Field, and over all the Earth,
And every creeping thing that creeps the ground.
This said, he formd thee, *Adam*, thee O Man
Dust of the ground, and in thy nostrils breath'd
The breath of Life; in his own Image hee
Created thee, in the Image of God
Express, and thou becam'st a living Soul.
Male he created thee, but thy consort
Femal for Race; then bless'd Mankinde, and said,　　530
Be fruitful, multiplie, and fill the Earth,
Subdue it, and throughout Dominion hold
Over Fish of the Sea, and Fowle of the Aire,
And every living thing that moves on the Earth.
Wherever thus created, for no place
Is yet distinct by name, thence, as thou know'st
He brought thee into this delicious Grove,
This Garden, planted with the Trees of God,
Delectable both to behold and taste;

And freely all thir pleasant fruit for food 540
Gave thee, all sorts are here that all th' Earth yeelds,
Varietie without end; but of the Tree
Which tasted works knowledge of Good and Evil,
Thou mai'st not; in the day thou eat'st, thou di'st;
Death is the penaltie impos'd, beware,
And govern well thy appetite, least sin
Surprise thee, and her black attendant Death.
Here finish'd hee, and all that he had made
View'd, and behold all was entirely good;
So Ev'n and Morn accomplish't the Sixt day: 550
Yet not till the Creator from his work
Desisting, though unwearied, up returnd
Up to the Heav'n of Heav'ns his high abode,
Thence to behold this new created World
Th' addition of his Empire, how it shew'd
In prospect from his Throne, how good, how faire,
Answering his great Idea. Up he rode
Followd with acclamation and the sound
Symphonious of ten thousand Harpes that tun'd
Angelic harmonies: the Earth, the Aire 560
Resounded, (thou remember'st for thou heardst)
The Heav'ns and all the Constellations rung,
The Planets in thir stations list'ning stood,
While the bright Pomp ascended jubilant.
Open, ye everlasting Gates, they sung,
Open, ye Heav'ns, your living dores; let in
The great Creator from his work returnd
Magnificent, his Six days work, a World;
Open, and henceforth oft; for God will deigne
To visit oft the dwellings of just Men 570
Delighted, and with frequent intercourse
Thither will send his winged Messengers
On errands of supernal Grace. So sung
The glorious Train ascending: He through Heav'n,
That open'd wide her blazing Portals, led
To Gods Eternal house direct the way,
A broad and ample rode, whose dust is Gold
And pavement Starrs, as Starrs to thee appeer,
Seen in the Galaxie, that Milkie way
Which nightly as a circling Zone thou seest 580
Pouderd with Starrs. And now on Earth the Seaventh
Eev'ning arose in *Eden*, for the Sun
Was set, and twilight from the East came on,
Forerunning Night; when at the holy mount
Of Heav'ns high-seated top, th' Impereal Throne

Of Godhead, fixt for ever firm and sure,
The Filial Power arriv'd, and sate him down
With his great Father, for he also went
Invisible, yet staid (such priviledge
Hath Omnipresence) and the work ordain'd,   *590*
Author and end of all things, and from work
Now resting, bless'd and hallowd the Seav'nth day,
As resting on that day from all his work,
But not in silence holy kept; the Harp
Had work and rested not, the solemn Pipe,
And Dulcimer, all Organs of sweet stop,
All sounds on Fret by String or Golden Wire
Temper'd soft Tunings, intermixt with Voice
Choral or Unison; of incense Clouds
Fuming from Golden Censers hid the Mount.   *600*
Creation and the Six dayes acts they sung,
Great are thy works, *Jehovah*, infinite
Thy power; what thought can measure thee or tongue
Relate thee; greater now in thy return
Then from the Giant Angels; thee that day
Thy Thunders magnifi'd; but to create
Is greater then created to destroy.
Who can impair thee, mighty King, or bound
Thy Empire? easily the proud attempt
Of Spirits apostat and thir Counsels vaine   *610*
Thou hast repeld, while impiously they thought
Thee to diminish, and from thee withdraw
The number of thy worshippers. Who seekes
To lessen thee, against his purpose serves
To manifest the more thy might: his evil
Thou usest, and from thence creat'st more good.
Witness this new-made World, another Heav'n
From Heaven Gate not farr, founded in view
On the cleer *Hyaline*, the Glassie Sea;
Of amplitude almost immense, with Starr's   *620*
Numerous, and every Starr perhaps a World
Of destind habitation; but thou know'st
Thir seasons: among these the seat of men,
Earth with her nether Ocean circumfus'd,
Thir pleasant dwelling place. Thrice happie men,
And sons of men, whom God hath thus advanc't,
Created in his Image, there to dwell
And worship him, and in reward to rule
Over his Works, on Earth, in Sea, or Air,
And multiply a Race of Worshippers   *630*
Holy and just: thrice happie if they know

Thir happiness, and persevere upright.
  So sung they, and the Empyrean rung,
With *Halleluiahs:* Thus was Sabbath kept.
And thy request think now fulfill'd, that ask'd
How first this World and face of things began,
And what before thy memorie was don
From the beginning, that posteritie
Informd by thee might know; if else thou seek'st
Aught, not surpassing human measure, say.   *640*

BOOK VIII

THE ARGUMENT

Adam *inquires concerning celestial Motions, is doubtfully answer'd, and exhorted to search rather things more worthy of knowledg:* Adam *assents, and still desirous to detain* Raphael, *relates to him what he remember'd since his own Creation, his placing in Paradise, his talk with God concerning solitude and fit society, his first meeting and Nuptials with* Eve, *his discourse with the Angel thereupon; who after admonitions repeated departs.*

[THE ANGEL ended, and in *Adams* Eare
So Charming left his voice, that he a while
Thought him still speaking, still stood fixt to hear;
Then as new wak't thus gratefully repli'd.] [1]
What thanks sufficient, or what recompence
Equal have I to render thee, Divine
Hystorian, who thus largely hast allayd
The thirst I had of knowledge, and voutsaf't
This friendly condescention to relate
Things else by me unsearchable, now heard　　　　　10
With wonder, but delight, and, as is due,
With glorie attributed to the high
Creator; some thing yet of doubt remaines,
Which onely thy solution can resolve.
When I behold this goodly Frame, this World
Of Heav'n and Earth consisting, and compute,
Thir magnitudes, this Earth a spot, a graine,
An Atom, with the Firmament compar'd
And all her numberd Starrs, that seem to rowle
Spaces incomprehensible (for such　　　　　20
Thir distance argues and thir swift return
Diurnal) meerly to officiate light
Round this opacous Earth, this punctual spot,
One day and night; in all thir vast survey
Useless besides, reasoning I oft admire,
How Nature wise and frugal could commit
Such disproportions, with superfluous hand
So many nobler Bodies to create,
Greater so manifold to this one use,
For aught appeers, and on thir Orbs impose　　　　　30

---

[1] The four bracketed lines were added in the second edition (1674), when Book VII was divided into two at line 640. Line 641 had read: "To whom thus *Adam* gratefully repli'd."

Such restless revolution day by day
Repeated, while the sedentarie Earth,
That better might with farr less compass move,
Serv'd by more noble then her self, attaines
Her end without least motion, and receaves,
As Tribute such a sumless journey brought
Of incorporeal speed, her warmth and light;
Speed, to describe whose swiftness Number failes.

    So spake our Sire, and by his count'nance seemd
Entring on studious thoughts abstruse, which *Eve*   40
Perceaving where she sat retir'd in sight,
With lowliness Majestic from her seat,
And Grace that won who saw to wish her stay,
Rose, and went forth among her Fruits and Flours,
To visit how they prosper'd, bud and bloom,
Her Nurserie; they at her coming sprung
And toucht by her fair tendance gladlier grew.
Yet went she not, as not with such discourse
Delighted, or not capable her eare
Of what was high: such pleasure she reserv'd,   50
Adam relating, she sole Auditress;
Her Husband the Relater she preferr'd
Before the Angel, and of him to ask
Chose rather: hee, she knew would intermix
Grateful digressions, and solve high dispute
With conjugal Caresses, from his Lip
Not Words alone pleas'd her. O when meet now
Such pairs, in Love and mutual Honour joyn'd?
With Goddess-like demeanour forth she went;
Not unattended, for on her as Queen   60
A pomp of winning Graces waited still,
And from about her shot Darts of desire
Into all Eyes to wish her still in sight.
And *Raphael* now to *Adam's* doubt propos'd
Benevolent and facil thus repli'd.

    To ask or search I blame thee not, for Heav'n
Is as the Book of God before thee set,
Wherein to read his wondrous Works, and learne
His Seasons, Hours, or Days, or Months, or Yeares;
This to attain, whether Heav'n move or Earth,   70
Imports not, if thou reck'n right, the rest
From Man or Angel the great Architect
Did wisely to conceal, and not divulge
His secrets to be scann'd by them who ought
Rather admire; or if they list to try
Conjecture, he his Fabric of the Heav'ns

Hath left to thir disputes, perhaps to move
His laughter at thir quaint Opinions wide
Hereafter, when they come to model Heav'n
And calculate the Starrs, how they will weild
The mightie frame, how build, unbuild, contrive
To save appeerances, how gird the Sphear
With Centric and Eccentric scribl'd o're,
Cycle and Epicycle, Orb in Orb:
Alreadie by thy reasoning this I guess,
Who art to lead thy ofspring, and supposest
That Bodies bright and greater should not serve
The less not bright, nor Heav'n such journies run,
Earth sitting still, when she alone receaves
The benefit: consider first, that Great
Or Bright inferrs not Excellence: the Earth
Though, in comparison of Heav'n so small,
Nor glistering, may of solid good containe
More plenty then the Sun that barren shines,
Whose vertue on it self workes no effect,
But in the fruitful Earth; there first receavd
His beams, unactive else, thir vigor find.
Yet not to Earth are those bright Luminaries
Officious, but to thee Earths habitant.
And for the Heav'ns wide Circuit, let it speak
The Makers high magnificence, who built
So spacious, and his Line stretcht out so farr;
That Man may know he dwells not in his own;
An Edifice too large for him to fill,
Lodg'd in a small partition, and the rest
Ordain'd for uses to his Lord best known.
The swiftness of those Circles attribute,
Though numberless, to his Omnipotence,
That to corporeal substances could adde
Speed almost Spiritual; mee thou thinkst not slow,
Who since the Morning hour set out from Heav'n
Where God resides, and ere mid-day arriv'd
In *Eden*, distance inexpressible
By Numbers that have name. But this I urge,
Admitting Motion in the Heav'ns, to shew
Invalid that which thee to doubt it mov'd;
Not that I so affirm, though so it seem
To thee who hast thy dwelling here on Earth.
God to remove his wayes from human sense,
Plac'd Heav'n from Earth so farr, that earthly sight,
If it presume, might erre in things too high,
And no advantage gaine. What if the Sun

Be Center to the World, and other Starrs
By his attractive vertue and thir own
Incited, dance about him various rounds?
Thir wandring course now high, now low, then hid,
Progressive, retrograde, or standing still,
In six thou seest, and what if sev'nth to these
The Planet Earth, so stedfast though she seem,
Insensibly three different Motions move? *130*
Which else to several Sphears thou must ascribe,
Mov'd contrarie with thwart obliquities,
Or save the Sun his labour, and that swift
Nocturnal and Diurnal rhomb suppos'd,
Invisible else above all Starrs, the Wheele
Of Day and Night; which needs not thy beleefe,
If Earth industrious of her self fetch Day
Travelling East, and with her part averse
From the Suns beam meet Night, her other part
Still luminous by his ray. What if that light *140*
Sent from her through the wide transpicuous aire,
To the terrestrial Moon be as a Starr
Enlightning her by Day, as she by Night
This Earth? reciprocal, if Land be there,
Feilds and Inhabitants: Her spots thou seest
As Clouds, and Clouds may rain, and Rain produce
Fruits in her soft'nd Soile, for some to eate
Allotted there; and other Suns perhaps
With thir attendant Moons thou wilt descrie
Communicating Male and Female Light, *150*
Which two great Sexes animate the World,
Stor'd in each Orb perhaps with some that live.
For such vast room in Nature unpossest
By living Soule, desert and desolate,
Onely to shine, yet scarce to contribute
Each Orb a glimps of Light, conveyd so farr
Down to this habitable, which returnes
Light back to them, is obvious to dispute.
But whether thus these things, or whether not,
Whether the Sun predominant in Heav'n *160*
Rise on the Earth, or Earth rise on the Sun,
Hee from the East his flaming rode begin,
Or Shee from West her silent course advance
With inoffensive pace that spinning sleeps
On her soft Axle, while she paces Eev'n,
And bears thee soft with the smooth Air along,
Sollicit not thy thoughts with matters hid,
Leave them to God above, him serve and feare;

Of other Creatures, as him pleases best,
Wherever plac't, let him dispose: joy thou   170
In what he gives to thee, this Paradise
And thy fair *Eve:* Heav'n is for thee too high
To know what passes there; be lowlie wise:
Think onely what concernes thee and thy being;
Dream not of other Worlds, what Creatures there
Live, in what state, condition or degree,
Contented that thus farr hath been reveal'd
Not of Earth onely but of highest Heav'n.
   To whom thus *Adam* cleerd of doubt, repli'd.
How fully hast thou satisfi'd mee, pure   180
Intelligence of Heav'n, Angel serene,
And freed from intricacies, taught to live,
The easiest way, nor with perplexing thoughts
To interrupt the sweet of Life, from which
God hath bid dwell farr off all anxious cares,
And not molest us, unless we our selves
Seek them with wandring thoughts, and notions vaine.
But apte the Mind or Fancie is to roave
Uncheckt, and of her roaving is no end;
Till warn'd, or by experience taught, she learn   190
That not to know at large of things remote
From use, obscure and suttle, but to know
That which before us lies in daily life,
Is the prime Wisdom, what is more, is fume,
Or emptiness, or fond impertinence,
And renders us in things that most concerne
Unpractis'd, unprepar'd, and still to seek.
Therefore from this high pitch let us descend
A lower flight, and speak of things at hand
Useful, whence haply mention may arise   200
Of somthing not unseasonable to ask
By sufferance, and thy wonted favour deign'd.
Thee I have heard relating what was don
Ere my remembrance: now hear mee relate
My Storie, which perhaps thou hast not heard;
And Day is yet not spent; till then thou seest
How suttly to detaine thee I devise,
Inviting thee to hear while I relate,
Fond, were it not in hope of thy reply:
For while I sit with thee, I seem in Heav'n,   210
And sweeter thy discourse is to my eare
Then Fruits of Palm-tree pleasantest to thirst
And hunger both, from labour, at the houre
Of sweet repast; they satiate, and soon fill,

Though pleasant, but thy words with Grace Divine
Imbu'd, bring to thir sweetness no satietie.
    To whom thus *Raphael* answer'd heav'nly meek.
Nor are thy lips ungraceful, Sire of men,
Nor tongue ineloquent; for God on thee
Abundantly his gifts hath also pour'd   220
Inward and outward both, his image faire:
Speaking or mute all comliness and grace
Attends thee, and each word, each motion formes
Nor less think wee in Heav'n of thee on Earth
Then of our fellow servant, and inquire
Gladly into the wayes of God with Man:
For God we see hath honour'd thee, and set
On Man his equal Love: say therefore on;
For I that Day was absent, as befell,
Bound on a voyage uncouth and obscure,   230
Farr on excursion toward the Gates of Hell;
Squar'd in full Legion (such command we had)
To see that none thence issu'd forth a spie,
Or enemie, while God was in his work,
Least hee incenst at such eruption bold,
Destruction with Creation might have mixt.
Not that they durst without his leave attempt,
But us he sends upon his high behests
For state, as Sovran King, and to enure
Our prompt obedience. Fast we found, fast shut   240
The dismal Gates, and barricado'd strong;
But long ere our approaching heard within
Noise, other then the sound of Dance or Song,
Torment, and lowd lament, and furious rage.
Glad we return'd up to the coasts of Light
Ere Sabbath Eev'ning: so we had in charge.
But thy relation now; for I attend,
Pleas'd with thy words no less then thou with mine.
    So spake the Godlike Power, and thus our Sire.
For Man to tell how human Life began   250
Is hard: for who himself beginning knew?
Desire with thee still longer to converse
Induc'd me. As new wak't from soundest sleep
Soft on the flourie herb I found me laid
In Balmie Sweat, which with his Beames the Sun
Soon dri'd, and on the reaking moisture fed.
Strait toward Heav'n my wondring Eyes I turnd,
And gaz'd a while the ample Skie, till rais'd
By quick instinctive motion up I sprung,
As thitherward endevoring, and upright   260

Stood on my feet; about me round I saw
Hill, Dale, and shadie Woods, and sunnie Plaines,
And liquid Lapse of murmuring Streams, by these,
Creatures that livd, and movd, and walk'd, or flew,
Birds on the branches warbling; all things smil'd,
With fragrance and with joy my heart oreflow'd.
My self I then perus'd, and Limb by Limb
Survey'd, and sometimes went, and sometimes ran
With supple joints, as lively vigour led:
But who I was, or where, or from what cause,   *270*
Knew not; to speak I tri'd, and forthwith spake,
My Tongue obey'd and readily could name
What e're I saw. Thou Sun, said I, faire Light,
And thou enlight'nd Earth, so fresh and gay,
Ye Hills and Dales, ye Rivers, Woods, and Plaines
And ye that live and move, fair Creatures, tell,
Tell, if ye saw, how came I thus, how here?
Not of my self; by some great Maker then,
In goodness and in power præeminent;
Tell me, how may I know him, how adore,   *280*
From whom I have that thus I move and live,
And feel that I am happier then I know.
While thus I call'd, and stray'd I knew not whither,
From where I first drew Aire, and first beheld
This happie Light, when answer none return'd,
On a green shadie Bank profuse of Flours
Pensive I sate me down; there gentle sleep
First found me, and with soft oppression seis'd
My droused sense, untroubl'd, though I thought
I then was passing to my former state   *290*
Insensible, and forthwith to dissolve:
When suddenly stood at my Head a dream,
Whose inward apparition gently mov'd
My Fancy to believe I yet had being,
And livd: One came, methought, of shape Divine,
And said, thy Mansion wants thee, *Adam*, rise,
First Man, of Men innumerable ordain'd
First Father, call'd by thee I come thy Guide
To the Garden of bliss, thy seat prepar'd.
So saying, by the hand he took me rais'd,   *300*
And over Fields and Waters, as in Aire
Smooth sliding without step, last led me up
A woodie Mountain; whose high top was plaine,
A Circuit wide, enclos'd, with goodliest Trees
Planted, with Walks, and Bowers, that what I saw
Of Earth before scarce pleasant seemd. Each Tree

Load'n with fairest Fruit, that hung to the Eye
Tempting, stirr'd in me sudden appetite
To pluck and eate; whereat I wak'd, and found
Before mine Eyes all real, as the dream   310
Had lively shadowd: Here had new begun
My wandring, had not hee who was my Guide
Up hither, from among the Trees appeer'd,
Presence Divine. Rejoycing, but with aw
In adoration at his feet I fell
Submiss: he rear'd me, & Whom thou soughtst I am,
Said mildely, Author of all this thou seest
Above, or round about thee or beneath.
This Paradise I give thee, count it thine
To Till and keep, and of the Fruit to eate: 320
Of every Tree that in the Garden growes
Eate freely with glad heart; fear here no dearth:
But of the Tree whose operation brings
Knowledg of good and ill, which I have set
The Pledge of thy Obedience and thy Faith,
Amid the Garden by the Tree of Life,
Remember what I warne thee, shun to taste,
And shun the bitter consequence: for know,
The day thou eat'st thereof, my sole command
Transgrest, inevitably thou shalt dye;   330
From that day mortal, and this happie State
Shalt loose, expell'd from hence into a World
Of woe and sorrow. Sternly he pronounc'd
The rigid interdiction, which resounds
Yet dreadful in mine eare, though in my choice
Not to incur; but soon his cleer aspect
Return'd and gratious purpose thus renew'd.
Not onely these fair bounds, but all the Earth
To thee and to thy Race I give; as Lords
Possess it, and all things that therein live,   340
Or live in Sea, or Aire, Beast, Fish, and Fowle
In signe whereof each Bird and Beast behold
After thir kindes; I bring them to receave
From thee thir Names, and pay thee fealtie
With low subjection; understand the same
Of Fish within thir watry residence,
Not hither summond, since they cannot change
Thir Element to draw the thinner Aire.
As thus he spake, each Bird and Beast behold
Approaching two and two, These cowring low   350
With blandishment, each Bird stoop'd on his wing.
I nam'd them, as they pass'd, and understood

Thir Nature, with such knowledg God endu'd
My sudden apprehension: but in these
I found not what me thought I wanted still;
And to the Heav'nly vision thus presum'd.
   O by what Name, for thou above all these,
Above mankinde, or aught then mankinde higher,
Surpassest farr my naming, how may I
Adore thee, Author of this Universe,   *360*
And all this good to man, for whose well being
So amply, and with hands so liberal
Thou hast provided all things: but with mee
I see not who partakes. In solitude
What happiness, who can enjoy alone,
Or all enjoying, what contentment find?
Thus I presumptuous; and the vision bright,
As with a smile more bright'nd, thus repli'd.
   What call'st thou solitude, is not the Earth
With various living creatures, and the Aire   *370*
Replenisht, and all these at thy command
To come and play before thee, know'st thou not
Thir language and thir wayes, they also know,
And reason not contemptibly; with these
Find pastime, and beare rule; thy Realm is large.
So spake the Universal Lord, and seem'd
So ordering. I with leave of speech implor'd,
And humble deprecation thus repli'd.
   Let not my words offend thee, Heav'nly Power,
My Maker, be propitious while I speak.   *380*
Hast thou not made me here thy substitute,
And these inferiour farr beneath me set?
Among unequals what societie
Can sort, what harmonie or true delight?
Which must be mutual, in proportion due
Giv'n and receiv'd; but in disparitie
The one intense, the other still remiss
Cannot well suite with either, but soon prove
Tedious alike: Of fellowship I speak
Such as I seek, fit to participate   *390*
All rational delight, wherein the brute
Cannot be human consort; they rejoyce
Each with thir kinde, Lion with Lioness;
So fitly them in pairs thou hast combin'd;
Much less can Bird with Beast, or Fish with Fowle
So well converse, nor with the Ox the Ape;
Wors then can Man with Beast, and least of all.
   Whereto th' Almighty answer'd, not displeas'd.

A nice and suttle happiness I see
Thou to thy self proposest, in the choice
Of thy Associates, *Adam*, and wilt taste
No pleasure, though in pleasure, solitarie.
What thinkst thou then of mee, and this my State,
Seem I to thee sufficiently possest
Of happiness, or not? who am alone
From all Eternitie, for none I know
Second to mee or like, equal much less.
How have I then with whom to hold converse
Save with the Creatures which I made, and those
To me inferiour, infinite descents
Beneath what other Creatures are to thee?
   He ceas'd, I lowly answer'd. To attaine
The higth and depth of thy Eternal wayes
All human thoughts come short, Supream of things;
Thou in thy self art perfet, and in thee
Is no deficience found; not so is Man,
But in degree, the cause of his desire
By conversation with his like to help,
Or solace his defects. No need that thou
Shouldst propagat, already infinite;
And through all numbers absolute, though One;
But Man by number is to manifest
His single imperfection, and beget
Like of his like, this Image multipli'd,
In unitie defective, which requires
Collateral love, and deerest amitie.
Thou in thy secresie although alone,
Best with thy self accompanied, seek'st not
Social communication, yet so pleas'd,
Canst raise thy Creature to what highth thou wilt
Of Union or Communion, deifi'd;
I by conversing cannot these erect
From prone, nor in thir wayes complacence find.
Thus I embold'nd spake, and freedom us'd
Permissive, and acceptance found, which gain'd
This answer from the gratious voice Divine.
   Thus farr to try thee *Adam*, I was pleas'd,
And finde thee knowing not of Beasts alone,
Which thou hast rightly nam'd, but of thy self,
Expressing well the spirit within thee free,
My Image, not imparted to the Brute,
Whose fellowship therefore unmeet for thee
Good reason was thou freely shouldst dislike,
And be so minded still; I, ere thou spak'st,

Knew it not good for Man to be alone,
And no such companie as then thou saw'st
Intended thee, for trial onely brought,
To see how thou could'st judge of fit and meet:
What next I bring shall please thee, be assur'd,
Thy likeness, thy fit help, thy other self, *450*
Thy wish, exactly to thy hearts desire.
    Hee ended, or I heard no more, for now
My earthly by his Heav'nly overpowerd,
Which it had long stood under, streind to the highth
In that celestial Colloquie sublime,
As with an object that excels the sense,
Dazl'd and spent, sunk down, and sought repair
Of sleep, which instantly fell on me, call'd
By Nature as in aide, and clos'd mine eyes.
Mine eyes he clos'd, but op'n left the Cell *460*
Of Fancie my internal sight, by which
Abstract as in a transe methought I saw,
Though sleeping, where I lay, and saw the shape
Still glorious before whom awake I stood;
Who stooping op'nd my left side, and took
From thence a Rib, with cordial spirits warme,
And Life-blood streaming fresh; wide was the wound,
But suddenly with flesh fill'd up & heal'd:
The Rib he formd and fashond with his hands;
Under his forming hands a Creature grew, *470*
Manlike, but different sex, so lovly faire,
That what seemd fair in all the World, seemd now
Mean, or in her summd up, in her containd
And in her looks, which from that time infus'd
Sweetness into my heart, unfelt before,
And into all things from her Aire inspir'd
The spirit of love and amorous delight.
She disappeerd, and left me dark, I wak'd
To find her, or for ever to deplore
Her loss, and other pleasures all abjure: *480*
When out of hope, behold her, not farr off,
Such as I saw her in my dream, adornd
With what all Earth or Heaven could bestow
To make her amiable: On she came,
Led by her Heav'nly Maker, though unseen,
And guided by his voice, nor uninformd
Of nuptial Sanctitie and marriage Rites:
Grace was in all her steps, Heav'n in her Eye,
In every gesture dignitie and love.
I overjoyd could not forbear aloud. *490*

This turn hath made amends; thou hast fulfill'd
Thy words, Creator bounteous and benigne,
Giver of all things faire, but fairest this
Of all thy gifts, nor enviest. I now see
Bone of my Bone, Flesh of my Flesh, my Self
Before me; Woman is her Name, of Man
Extracted; for this cause he shall forgoe
Father and Mother, and to his Wife adhere;
And they shall be one Flesh, one Heart, one Soule.
   She heard me thus, and though divinely brought,   500
Yet Innocence and Virgin Modestie,
Her vertue and the conscience of her worth,
That would be woo'd, and not unsought be won,
Not obvious, not obtrusive, but retir'd,
The more desirable, or to say all,
Nature her self, though pure of sinful thought,
Wrought in her so, that seeing me, she turn'd;
I follow'd her, she what was Honour knew,
And with obsequious Majestie approv'd
My pleaded reason. To the Nuptial Bowre   510
I led her blushing like the Morn: all Heav'n,
And happie Constellations on that houre
Shed thir selectest influence; the Earth
Gave sign of gratulation, and each Hill;
Joyous the Birds; fresh Gales and gentle Aires
Whisper'd it to the Woods, and from thir wings
Flung Rose, flung Odours from the spicie Shrub,
Disporting, till the amorous Bird of Night
Sung Spousal, and bid haste the Eevning Starr
On his Hill top, to light the bridal Lamp.   520
Thus I have told thee all my State, and brought
My Storie to the sum of earthly bliss
Which I enjoy, and must confess to find
In all things else delight indeed, but such
As us'd or not, works in the mind no change,
Nor vehement desire, these delicacies
I mean of Taste, Sight, Smell, Herbs, Fruits & Flours,
Walks, and the melodie of Birds; but here
Farr otherwise, transported I behold,
Transported touch; here passion first I felt,   530
Commotion strange, in all enjoyments else
Superiour and unmov'd, here onely weake
Against the charm of Beauties powerful glance.
Or Nature faild in mee, and left some part
Not proof enough such Object to sustain,
Or from my side subducting, took perhaps

More then enough; at least on her bestow'd
Too much of Ornament, in outward shew
Elaborate, of inward less exact.
For well I understand in the prime end 540
Of Nature her th' inferiour, in the mind
And inward Faculties, which most excell,
In outward also her resembling less
His Image who made both, and less expressing
The character of that Dominion giv'n
O're other Creatures; yet when I approach
Her loveliness, so absolute she seems
And in her self compleat, so well to know
Her own, that what she wills to do or say,
Seems wisest, vertuousest, discreetest, best; 550
All higher knowledge in her presence falls
Degraded, Wisdom in discourse with her
Looses discount'nanc't, and like folly shewes;
Authoritie and Reason on her waite,
As one intended first, not after made
Occasionally; and to consummate all,
Greatness of mind and nobleness thir seat
Build in her loveliest, and create an awe
About her, as a guard Angelic plac't.
To whom the Angel with contracted brow. 560
    Accuse not Nature, she hath don her part;
Do thou but thine, and be not diffident
Of Wisdom, she deserts thee not, if thou
Dismiss not her, when most thou needst her nigh,
By attributing overmuch to things
Less excellent, as thou thy self perceav'st.
For what admir'st thou, what transports thee so,
An outside? fair no doubt, and worthy well
Thy cherishing, thy honouring, and thy love,
Not thy subjection: weigh with her thy self; 570
Then value: Oft times nothing profits more
Then self-esteem, grounded on just and right
Well manag'd; of that skill the more thou know'st,
The more she will acknowledge thee her Head,
And to realities yeild all her shows;
Made so adorn for thy delight the more,
So awful, that with honour thou maist love
Thy mate, who sees when thou art seen least wise.
But if the sense of touch whereby mankind
Is propagated seem such dear delight 580
Beyond all other, think the same voutsaf't
To Cattel and each Beast; which would not be

To them made common & divulg'd, if aught
Therein enjoy'd were worthy to subdue
The Soule of Man, or passion in him move.
What higher in her societie thou findst
Attractive, human, rational, love still;
In loving thou dost well, in passion not,
Wherein true Love consists not; love refines
The thoughts, and heart enlarges, hath his seat   590
In Reason, and is judicious, is the scale
By which to heav'nly Love thou maist ascend,
Not sunk in carnal pleasure, for which cause
Among the Beasts no Mate for thee was found.
  To whom thus half abash't *Adam* repli'd.
Neither her out-side formd so fair, nor aught
In procreation common to all kindes
(Though higher of the genial Bed by far,
And with mysterious reverence I deem)
So much delights me, as those graceful acts,   600
Those thousand decencies that daily flow
From all her words and actions, mixt with Love
And sweet compliance, which declare unfeign'd
Union of Mind, or in us both one Soule:
Harmonie to behold in wedded pair
More grateful then harmonious sound to the eare.
Yet these subject not; I to thee disclose
What inward thence I feel, not therefore foild,
Who meet with various objects, from the sense
Variously representing; yet still free   610
Approve the best, and follow what I approve.
To love thou blam'st me not, for love thou saist
Leads up to Heav'n, is both the way and guide;
Bear with me then, if lawful what I ask;
Love not the heav'nly Spirits, and how thir Love
Express they, by looks onely, or do they mix
Irradiance, virtual or immediate touch?
  To whom the Angel with a smile that glow'd
Celestial rosie red, Loves proper hue,
Answer'd. Let it suffice thee that thou know'st   620
Us happie, and without Love no happiness.
Whatever pure thou in the body enjoy'st
(And pure thou wert created) we enjoy
In eminence, and obstacle find none
Of membrane, joynt, or limb, exclusive barrs:
Easier then Air with Air, if Spirits embrace,
Total they mix, Union of Pure with Pure
Desiring; nor restrain'd conveyance need

As Flesh to mix with Flesh, or Soul with Soul.
But I can now no more; the parting Sun 630
Beyond the Earths green Cape and verdant Isles
Hesperean sets, my Signal to depart.
Be strong, live happie, and love, but first of all
Him whom to love is to obey, and keep
His great command; take heed least Passion sway
Thy Judgement to do aught, which else free Will
Would not admit; thine and of all thy Sons
The weal or woe in thee is plac't; beware.
I in thy persevering shall rejoyce,
And all the Blest: stand fast; to stand or fall 640
Free in thine own Arbitrement it lies.
Perfect within, no outward aid require;
And all temptation to transgress repel.
  So saying, he arose; whom *Adam* thus
Follow'd with benediction. Since to part,
Go heavenly Guest, Ethereal Messenger,
Sent from whose sovran goodness I adore.
Gentle to me and affable hath been
Thy condescension, and shall be honour'd **ever**
With grateful Memorie: thou to mankind 650
Be good and friendly still, and oft return.
  So parted they, the Angel up to Heav'n
From the thick shade, and *Adam* to his Bowre.

BOOK IX

THE ARGUMENT

Satan *having compast the Earth, with meditated guile returns as a mist by Night into Paradise, enters into the Serpent sleeping.* Adam *and* Eve *in the Morning go forth to thir labours, which* Eve *proposes to divide in several places, each labouring apart:* Adam *consents not, alledging the danger, lest that Enemy, of whom they were forewarn'd, should attempt her found alone:* Eve *loath to be thought not circumspect or firm enough, urges her going apart, the rather desirous to make tryal of her strength;* Adam *at last yields: The Serpent finds her alone; his subtle approach, first gazing, then speaking, with much flattery extolling* Eve *above all other Creatures.* Eve *wondring to hear the Serpent speak, asks how he attain'd to human speech and such understanding not till now; the Serpent answers, that by tasting of a certain Tree in the Garden he attain'd both to Speech and Reason, till then void of both:* Eve *requires him to bring her to that Tree, and finds it to be the Tree of Knowledge forbidden: The Serpent now grown bolder, with many wiles and arguments induces her at length to eat; she pleas'd with the taste deliberates awhile whether to impart thereof to* Adam *or not, at last brings him of the Fruit, relates what persuaded her to eat thereof:* Adam *at first amaz'd, but perceiving her lost, resolves through vehemence of love to perish with her, and extenuating the trespass, eats also of the Fruit: The effects thereof in them both; they seek to cover thir nakedness; then fall to variance and accusation of one another.*

NO MORE of talk where God or Angel Guest
With Man, as with his Friend, familiar us'd
To sit indulgent, and with him partake
Rural repast, permitting him the while
Venial discourse unblam'd: I now must change
Those Notes to Tragic; foul distrust, and breach
Disloyal on the part of Man, revolt,
And disobedience: On the part of Heav'n
Now alienated, distance and distaste,
Anger and just rebuke, and judgement giv'n,   10
That brought into this World a world of woe,
Sinne and her shadow Death, and Miserie
Deaths Harbinger: Sad task, yet argument
Not less but more Heroic then the wrauth
Of stern *Achilles* on his Foe pursu'd
Thrice Fugitive about *Troy* Wall; or rage
Of *Turnus* for *Lavinia* disespous'd,
Or *Neptun's* ire or *Juno's*, that so long
Perplex'd the *Greek* and *Cytherea's* Son;
If answerable style I can obtaine   20
Of my Celestial Patroness, who deignes
Her nightly visitation unimplor'd,
And dictates to me slumbring, or inspires

Easie my unpremeditated Verse:
Since first this Subject for Heroic Song
Pleas'd me long choosing, and beginning late
Not sedulous by Nature to indite
Warrs, hitherto the onely Argument
Heroic deem'd, chief maistrie to dissect
With long and tedious havoc fabl'd Knights   30
In Battels feign'd; the better fortitude
Of Patience and Heroic Martyrdom
Unsung; or to describe Races and Games,
Or tilting Furniture, emblazon'd Shields,
Impreses quaint, Caparisons and Steeds;
Bases and tinsel Trappings, gorgious Knights
At Joust and Torneament; then marshal'd Feast
Serv'd up in Hall with Sewers, and Seneshals;
The skill of Artifice or Office mean,
Not that which justly gives Heroic name   40
To Person or to Poem. Mee of these
Nor skilld nor studious, higher Argument
Remaines, sufficient of it self to raise
That name, unless an age too late, or cold
Climat, or Years damp may intended wing
Deprest, and much they may, if all be mine,
Not Hers who brings it nightly to my Ear.
    The Sun was sunk, and after him the Starr
Of *Hesperus*, whose Office is to bring
Twilight upon the Earth, short Arbiter   50
Twixt Day and Night, and now from end to end
Nights Hemisphere had veild the Horizon round:
When *Satan* who late fled before the threats
Of *Gabriel* out of *Eden*, now improv'd
In meditated fraud and malice, bent
On mans destruction, maugre what might hap
Of heavier on himself, fearless return'd.
By Night he fled, and at Midnight return'd
From compassing the Earth, cautious of day,
Since *Uriel* Regent of the Sun descri'd   60
His entrance, and forewarnd the Cherubim
That kept thir watch; thence full of anguish driv'n,
The space of seven continu'd Nights he rode
With darkness, thrice the Equinoctial Line
He circl'd, four times cross'd the Carr of Night
From Pole to Pole, traversing each Colure;
On the eighth return'd, and on the Coast averse
From entrance or Cherubic Watch, by stealth
Found unsuspected way. There was a place,

Now not, though Sin, not Time, first wraught the
    change,   70
Where *Tigris* at the foot of Paradise
Into a Gulf shot under ground, till part
Rose up a Fountain by the Tree of Life;
In with the River sunk, and with it rose
Satan involv'd in rising Mist, then sought
Where to lie hid; Sea he had searcht and Land
From *Eden* over *Pontus*, and the Poole
Mæotis, up beyond the River *Ob*;
Downward as farr Antartic; and in length
West from *Orontes* to the Ocean barr'd   80
At *Darien*, thence to the Land where flowes
Ganges and *Indus:* thus the Orb he roam'd
With narrow search; and with inspection deep
Consider'd every Creature, which of all
Most opportune might serve his Wiles, and found
The Serpent suttlest Beast of all the Field.
Him after long debate, irresolute
Of thoughts revolv'd, his final sentence chose
Fit Vessel, fittest Imp of fraud, in whom
To enter, and his dark suggestions hide   90
From sharpest sight: for in the wilie Snake,
Whatever sleights none would suspicious mark,
As from his wit and native suttletie
Proceeding, which in other Beasts observ'd
Doubt might beget of Diabolic pow'r
Active within beyond the sense of brute.
Thus he resolv'd, but first from inward griefe
His bursting passion into plaints thus pour'd:
    O Earth, how like to Heav'n, if not preferr'd
More justly, Seat worthier of Gods, as built   100
With second thoughts, reforming what was old!
For what God after better worse would build?
Terrestrial Heav'n, danc't round by other Heav'ns
That shine, yet bear thir bright officious Lamps,
Light above Light, for thee alone, as seems,
In thee concentring all thir precious beams
Of sacred influence: As God in Heav'n
Is Center, yet extends to all, so thou
Centring receav'st from all those Orbs; in thee,
Not in themselves, all thir known vertue appeers   110
Productive in Herb, Plant, and nobler birth
Of Creatures animate with gradual life
Of Growth, Sense, Reason, all summ'd up in Man.
With what delight could I have walk't thee round

If I could joy in aught, sweet interchange
Of Hill and Vallie, Rivers, Woods and Plaines,
Now Land, now Sea, & Shores with Forrest crownd,
Rocks, Dens, and Caves; but I in none of these
Find place or refuge; and the more I see
Pleasures about me, so much more I feel   *120*
Torment within me, as from the hateful siege
Of contraries; all good to me becomes
Bane, and in Heav'n much worse would be my state.
But neither here seek I, no nor in Heav'n
To dwell, unless by maistring Heav'ns Supreame;
Nor hope to be my self less miserable
By what I seek, but others to make such
As I, though thereby worse to me redound:
For onely in destroying I finde ease
To my relentless thoughts; and him destroyd,   *130*
Or won to what may work his utter loss,
For whom all this was made, all this will soon
Follow, as to him linkt in weal or woe,
In wo then; that destruction wide may range:
To mee shall be the glorie sole among
The infernal Powers, in one day to have marr'd
What he *Almightie* styl'd, six Nights and Days
Continu'd making, and who knows how long
Before had bin contriving, though perhaps
Not longer then since I in one Night freed   *140*
From servitude inglorious welnigh half
Th' Angelic Name, and thinner left the throng
Of his adorers: hee to be aveng'd,
And to repair his numbers thus impair'd,
Whether such vertue spent of old now faild
More Angels to Create, if they at least
Are his Created or to spite us more,
Determin'd to advance into our room
A Creature form'd of Earth, and him endow,
Exalted from so base original,   *150*
With Heav'nly spoils, our spoils; What he decreed
He effected; Man he made, and for him built
Magnificent this World, and Earth his seat,
Him Lord pronounc'd, and, O indignitie!
Subjected to his service Angel wings,
And flaming Ministers to watch and tend
Thir earthie Charge: Of these the vigilance
I dread, and to elude, thus wrapt in mist
Of midnight vapor glide obscure, and prie
In every Bush and Brake, where hap may finde   *160*

The Serpent sleeping, in whose mazie foulds
To hide me, and the dark intent I bring.
O foul descent! that I who erst contended
With Gods to sit the highest, am now constraind
Into a Beast, and mixt with bestial slime,
This essence to incarnate and imbrute,
That to the hight of Deitie aspir'd;
But what will not Ambition and Revenge
Descend to? who aspires must down as low
As high he soard, obnoxious first or last   170
To basest things. Revenge, at first though sweet,
Bitter ere long back on it self recoiles;
Let it; I reck not, so it light well aim'd,
Since higher I fall short, on him who next
Provokes my envie, this new Favorite
Of Heav'n, this Man of Clay, Son of despite,
Whom us the more to spite his Maker rais'd
From dust: spite then with spite is best repaid.
  So saying, through each Thicket Danck or Drie,
Like a black mist low creeping, he held on   180
His midnight search, where soonest he might finde
The Serpent: him fast sleeping soon he found
In Labyrinth of many a round self-rowld,
His head the midst, well stor'd with suttle wiles:
Not yet in horrid Shade or dismal Den,
Not nocent yet, but on the grassie Herbe
Fearless unfeard he slept: in at his Mouth
The Devil enterd, and his brutal sense,
In heart or head, possessing soon inspir'd
With act intelligential; but his sleep   190
Disturb'd not, waiting close th' approach of Morn.
Now whenas sacred Light began to dawne
In *Eden* on the humid Flours, that breathd
Thir morning Incense, when all things that breath,
From th' Earths great Altar send up silent praise
To the Creator, and his Nostrils fill
With gratefull Smell, forth came the human pair
And joynd thir vocal Worship to the Quire
Of Creatures wanting voice, that done, partake
The season, prime for sweetest Sents and Aires: 200
Then commune how that day they best may ply
Thir growing work: for much thir work outgrew
The hands dispatch of two Gardning so wide.
And *Eve* first to her Husband thus began.
  Adam, well may we labour still to dress
This Garden, still to tend Plant, Herb and Flour.

Our pleasant task enjoyn'd, but till more hands
Aid us, the work under our labour grows,
Luxurious by restraint; what we by day
Lop overgrown, or prune, or prop, or bind,   *210*
One night or two with wanton growth derides
Tending to wilde. Thou therefore now advise
Or hear what to my mind first thoughts present,
Let us divide our labours, thou where choice
Leads thee, or where most needs, whether to wind
The Woodbine round this Arbour, or direct
The clasping Ivie where to climb, while I
In yonder Spring of Roses intermixt
With Myrtle, find what to redress till Noon:
For while so near each other thus all day   *220*
Our task we choose, what wonder if so near
Looks intervene and smiles, or object new
Casual discourse draw on, which intermits
Our dayes work brought to little, though begun
Early, and th' hour of Supper comes unearn'd.
    To whom mild answer *Adam* thus return'd.
Sole *Eve*, Associate sole, to me beyond
Compare above all living Creatures deare,
Well hast thou motion'd, wel thy thoughts imployd
How we might best fulfill the work which here   *230*
God hath assign'd us, nor of me shalt pass
Unprais'd: for nothing lovelier can be found
In woman, then to studie houshold good,
And good workes in her Husband to promote.
Yet not so strictly hath our Lord impos'd
Labour, as to debarr us when we need
Refreshment, whether food, or talk between,
Food of the mind, or this sweet intercourse
Of looks and smiles, for smiles from Reason flow,
To brute deni'd, and are of Love the food,   *240*
Love not the lowest end of human life.
For not to irksom toile, but to delight
He made us, and delight to Reason joyn'd.
These paths and Bowers doubt not but our joynt hands
Will keep from Wilderness with ease, as wide
As we need walk, till younger hands ere long
Assist us: But if much converse perhaps
Thee satiate, to short absence I could yeild.
For solitude somtimes is best societie,
And short retirement urges sweet returne.   *250*
But other doubt possesses me, least harm
Befall thee sever'd from me; for thou knowst

What hath bin warn'd us, what malicious Foe
Envying our happiness, and of his own
Despairing, seeks to work us woe and shame
By sly assault; and somwhere nigh at hand
Watches, no doubt, with greedy hope to find
His wish and best advantage, us asunder,
Hopeless to circumvent us joynd, where each
To other speedie aide might lend at need;   260
Whether his first design be to withdraw
Our fealtie from God, or to disturb
Conjugal Love, then which perhaps no bliss
Enjoy'd by us excites his envie more;
Or this, or worse, leave not the faithful side
That gave thee being, stil shades thee and protects.
The Wife, where danger or dishonour lurks,
Safest and seemliest by her Husband staies,
Who guards her, or with her the worst endures.
    To whom the Virgin Majestie of *Eve*,   270
As one who loves, and some unkindness meets,
With sweet austeer composure thus reply'd.
    Ofspring of Heav'n and Earth, and all Earths Lord,
That such an Enemie we have, who seeks
Our ruin, both by thee informd I learne,
And from the parting Angel over-heard
As in a shadie nook I stood behind,
Just then returnd at shut of Evening Flours.
But that thou shouldst my firmness therfore doubt
To God or thee, because we have a foe   280
May tempt it, I expected not to hear.
His violence thou fearst not, being such,
As wee, not capable of death or paine,
Can either not receave, or can repell.
His fraud is then thy fear, which plain inferrs
Thy equal fear that my firm Faith and Love
Can by his fraud be shak'n or seduc't;
Thoughts, which how found they harbour in thy brest,
Adam, missthought of her to thee so dear?
    To whom with healing words *Adam* reply'd.   290
Daughter of God and Man, immortal *Eve*,
For such thou art, from sin and blame entire:
Not diffident of thee do I dissuade
Thy absence from my sight, but to avoid
Th' attempt it self, intended by our Foe.
For hee who tempts, though in vain, at least asperses
The tempted with dishonour foul, suppos'd
Not incorruptible of Faith, not prooff

Against temptation: thou thy self with scorne
And anger wouldst resent the offer'd wrong, 300
Though ineffectual found: misdeem not then,
If such affront I labour to avert
From thee alone, which on us both at once
The Enemie, though bold, will hardly dare,
Or daring, first on mee th' assault shall light.
Nor thou his malice and false guile contemn;
Suttle he needs must be, who could seduce
Angels, nor think superfluous others aid.
I from the influence of thy looks receave
Access in every Vertue, in thy sight 310
More wise, more watchful, stronger, if need were
Of outward strength; while shame, thou looking on,
Shame to be overcome or over-reacht
Would utmost vigor raise, and rais'd unite.
Why shouldst not thou like sense within thee feel
When I am present, and thy trial choose
With me, best witness of thy Vertue tri'd.
 So spake domestick *Adam* in his care
And Matrimonial Love, but *Eve*, who thought
Less attributed to her Faith sincere, 320
Thus her reply with accent sweet renewd.
 If this be our condition, thus to dwell
In narrow circuit strait'nd by a Foe,
Suttle or violent, we not endu'd
Single with like defence, wherever met,
How are we happie, still in fear of harm?
But harm precedes not sin: onely our Foe
Tempting affronts us with his foul esteem
Of our integritie: his foul esteeme
Sticks no dishonor on our Front, but turns 330
Foul on himself; then wherfore shund or feard
By us? who rather double honour gaine
From his surmise prov'd false, finde peace within,
Favour from Heav'n, our witness from th' event.
And what is Faith, Love, Vertue unassaid
Alone, without exterior help sustaind?
Let us not then suspect our happie State
Left so imperfet by the Maker wise,
As not secure to single or combin'd.
Fraile is our happiness, if this be so, 340
And *Eden* were no *Eden* thus expos'd.
 To whom thus *Adam* fervently repli'd.
O Woman, best are all things as the will
Of God ordaind them, his creating hand

Nothing imperfet or deficient left
Of all that he Created, much less Man,
Or ought that might his happie State secure,
Secure from outward force; within himself
The danger lies, yet lies within his power:
Against his will he can receave no harme. 350
But God left free the Will, for what obeyes
Reason, is free, and Reason he made right
But bid her well beware, and still erect,
Least by some faire appeering good surpris'd
She dictate false, and missinforme the Will
To do what God expressly hath forbid.
Not then mistrust, but tender love enjoynes,
That I should mind thee oft, and mind thou me.
Firm we subsist, yet possible to swerve,
Since Reason not impossibly may meet 360
Some specious object by the Foe subornd,
And fall into deception unaware,
Not keeping strictest watch, as she was warnd
Seek not temptation then, which to avoide
Were better, and most likelie if from mee
Thou sever not: Trial will come unsought.
Wouldst thou approve thy constancie, approve
First thy obedience; th' other who can know,
Not seeing thee attempted, who attest?
But if thou think, trial unsought may finde 370
Us both securer then thus warnd thou seemst,
Go; for thy stay, not free, absents thee more;
Go in thy native innocence, relie
On what thou hast of vertue, summon all,
For God towards thee hath done his part, do thine.
   So spake the Patriarch of Mankinde, but *Eve*
Persisted, yet submiss, though last, repli'd.
With thy permission then, and thus forewarnd
Chiefly by what thy own last reasoning words
Touchd onely, that our trial, when least sought, 380
May finde us both perhaps farr less prepar'd,
The willinger I goe, nor much expect
A Foe so proud will first the weaker seek;
So bent, the more shall shame him his repulse.
Thus saying, from her Husbands hand her hand
Soft she withdrew, and like a Wood-Nymph light
Oread or *Dryad*, or of *Delia's* Traine,
Betook her to the Groves, but *Delia's* self
In gate surpass'd and Goddess-like deport,
Though not as shee with Bow and Quiver armd, 390

But with such Gardning Tools as Art yet rude,
Guiltless of fire had formd, or Angels brought.
To *Pales*, or *Pomona*, thus adornd,
Likest she seemd, *Pomona* when she fled
Vertumnus, or to *Ceres* in her Prime,
Yet Virgin of *Proserpina* from *Jove*.
Her long with ardent look his Eye pursu'd
Delighted, but desiring more her stay.
Oft he to her his charge of quick returne
Repeated, shee to him as oft engag'd   400
To be returnd by Noon amid the Bowre,
And all things in best order to invite
Noontide repast, or Afternoons repose.
O much deceav'd, much failing, hapless *Eve*,
Of thy presum'd return! event perverse!
Thou never from that houre in Paradise
Foundst either sweet repast, or sound repose;
Such ambush hid among sweet Flours and Shades
Waited with hellish rancor imminent
To intercept thy way, or send thee back   410
Despoild of Innocence, of Faith, of Bliss.
For now, and since first break of dawn the Fiend.
Meer Serpent in appearance, forth was come,
And on his Quest, where likeliest he might finde
The onely two of Mankinde, but in them
The whole included Race, his purposd prey.
In Bowre and Field he sought, where any tuft
Of Grove or Garden-Plot more pleasant lay,
Thir tendance or Plantation for delight,
By Fountain or by shadie Rivulet   420
He sought them both, but wish'd his hap might find
Eve separate, he wish'd, but not with hope
Of what so seldom chanc'd, when to his wish,
Beyond his hope, *Eve* separate he spies,
Veil'd in a Cloud of Fragrance, where she stood,
Half spi'd, so thick the Roses bushing round
About her glowd, oft stooping to support
Each Flour of slender stalk, whose head though gay
Carnation, Purple, Azure, or spect with Gold,
Hung drooping unsustained, them she upstaies   430
Gently with Mirtle band, mindless the while,
Her self, though fairest unsupported Flour,
From her best prop so farr, and storm so nigh.
Neerer he drew, and many a walk travers'd
Of stateliest Covert, Cedar, Pine, or Palme,
Then voluble and bold, now hid, now seen

Among thick-wov'n Arborets and Flours
Imborderd on each Bank, the hand of *Eve*:
Spot more delicious then those Gardens feign'd
Or of reviv'd *Adonis*, or renownd   440
Alcinous, host of old *Laertes* Son,
Or that, not Mystic, where the Sapient King
Held dalliance with his faire *Egyptian* Spouse.
Much hee the Place admir'd, the Person more.
As one who long in populous City pent,
Where Houses thick and Sewers annoy the Aire,
Forth issuing on a Summers Morn to breathe
Among the pleasant Villages and Farmes
Adjoynd, from each thing met conceaves delight,
The smell of Grain, or tedded Grass, or Kine.   450
Or Dairie, each rural sight, each rural sound;
If chance with Nymphlike step fair Virgin pass,
What pleasing seemd, for her now pleases more,
She most, and in her looks summs all Delight.
Such Pleasure took the Serpent to behold
This Flourie Plat, the sweet recess of *Eve*
Thus earlie, thus alone; her Heav'nly forme
Angelic, but more soft, and Feminine,
Her graceful Innocence, her every Aire
Of gesture or lest action overawd   460
His Malice, and with rapine sweet bereav'd
His fierceness of the fierce intent it brought:
That space the Evil one abstracted stood
From his own evil, and for the time remaind
Stupidly good, of enmitie disarm'd,
Of guile, of hate, of envie, of revenge;
But the hot Hell that alwayes in him burnes,
Though in mid Heav'n, soon ended his delight,
And tortures him now more, the more he sees
Of pleasure not for him ordain'd: then soon   470
Fierce hate he recollects, and all his thoughts
Of mischief, gratulating, thus excites.
    Thoughts, whither have ye led me, with what sweet
Compulsion thus transported to forget
What hither brought us, hate, nor love, nor hope
Of Paradise for Hell, hope here to taste
Of pleasure, but all pleasure to destroy,
Save what is in destroying, other joy
To me is lost. Then let me not let pass
Occasion which now smiles, behold alone   480
The Woman, opportune to all attempts,
Her Husband, for I view far round, not nigh,

Whose higher intellectual more I shun,
And strength, of courage hautie, and of limb
Heroic built, though of terrestrial mould,
Foe not informidable, exempt from wound,
I not; so much hath Hell debas'd, and paine
Infeebl'd me, to what I was in Heav'n.
Shee fair, divinely fair, fit Love for Gods,
Not terrible, though terrour be in Love   490
And beautie, not approacht by stronger hate,
Hate stronger, under shew of Love well feign'd,
The way which to her ruin now I tend.
  So spake the Enemie of Mankind, enclos'd
In Serpent, Inmate bad, and toward *Eve*
Address'd his way, not with indented wave,
Prone on the ground, as since, but on his reare,
Circular base of rising foulds, that tour'd
Fould above fould a surging Maze, his Head
Crested aloft, and Carbuncle his Eyes;   500
With burnisht Neck of verdant Gold, erect
Amidst his circling Spires, that on the grass
Floted redundant: pleasing was his shape,
And lovely, never since of Serpent kind
Lovelier, not those that in *Illyria* chang'd
Hermione and *Cadmus*, or the God
In *Epidaurus;* nor to which transformd
Ammonian Jove, or *Capitoline* was seen,
Hee with *Olympias*, this with her who bore
Scipio the highth of *Rome*. With tract oblique   510
At first, as one who sought access, but feard
To interrupt, side-long he works his way.
As when a Ship by skilful Stearsman wrought
Nigh Rivers mouth or Foreland, where the Wind
Veres oft, as oft so steers, and shifts her Saile;
So varied hee, and of his tortuous Traine
Curld many a wanton wreath in sight of *Eve*,
To lure her Eye; shee busied heard the sound
Of rusling Leaves, but minded not, as us'd
To such disport before her through the Field,   520
From every Beast, more duteous at her call,
Then at *Circean* call the Herd disguis'd.
Hee boulder now, uncall'd before her stood;
But as in gaze admiring: Oft he bowd
His turret Crest, and sleek enamel'd Neck,
Fawning, and lick'd the ground whereon she trod.
His gentle dumb expression turn'd at length
The Eye of *Eve* to mark his play; he glad

Of her attention gaind, with Serpent Tongue
Organic, or impulse of vocal Air, 530
His fraudulent temptation thus began.
    Wonder not, sovran Mistress, if perhaps
Thou canst, who art sole Wonder, much less arm
Thy looks, the Heav'n of mildness, with disdain,
Displeas'd that I approach thee thus, and gaze
Insatiate, I thus single, nor have feard
Thy awful brow, more awful thus retir'd.
Fairest resemblance of thy Maker faire,
Thee all things living gaze on, all things thine
By gift, and thy Celestial Beautie adore 540
With ravishment beheld, there best beheld
Where universally admir'd: but here
In this enclosure wild, these Beasts among,
Beholders rude, and shallow to discerne
Half what in thee is fair, one man except,
Who sees thee? (and what is one?) who shouldst be seen
A Goddess among Gods, ador'd and serv'd
By Angels numberless, thy daily Train.
    So gloz'd the Tempter, and his Proem tun'd;
Into the Heart of *Eve* his words made way, 550
Though at the voice much marveling; at length
Not unamaz'd she thus in answer spake.
What may this mean? Language of Man pronounc't
By Tongue of Brute, and human sense exprest?
The first at lest of these I thought deni'd
To Beasts, whom God on thir Creation-Day
Created mute to all articulat sound;
The latter I demurre, for in thir looks
Much reason, and in thir actions oft appeers.
Thee, Serpent, suttlest beast of all the field 560
I knew, but not with human voice endu'd;
Redouble then this miracle, and say,
How cam'st thou speakable of mute, and how
To me so friendly grown above the rest
Of brutal kind, that daily are in sight?
Say, for such wonder claims attention due.
    To whom the guileful Tempter thus reply'd.
Empress of this fair World, resplendent *Eve*,
Easie to mee it is to tell thee all
What thou commandst and right thou shouldst be
    obeyd: 570
I was at first as other Beasts that graze
The trodden Herb, of abject thoughts and low,
As was my food, nor aught but food discern'd

Or Sex, and apprehended nothing high:
Till on a day roaving the field, I chanc'd
A goodly Tree farr distant to behold
Loaden with fruit of fairest colours mixt,
Ruddie and Gold: I nearer drew to gaze;
When from the boughes a savorie odour blow'n,
Grateful to appetite, more pleas'd my sense   580
Then smell of sweetest Fenel, or the Teats
Of Ewe or Goat dropping with Milk at Eevn,
Unsuckt of Lamb or Kid, that tend thir play.
To satisfie the sharp desire I had
Of tasting those fair Apples, I resolv'd
Not to deferr; hunger and thirst at once,
Powerful perswaders, quick'nd at the scent
Of that alluring fruit, urg'd me so keene.
About the Mossie Trunk I wound me soon,
For high from ground the branches would require 590
Thy utmost reach or *Adams:* Round the Tree
All other Beasts that saw, with like desire
Longing and envying stood, but could not reach.
Amid the Tree now got, where plentie hung
Tempting so nigh, to pluck and eat my fill
I spar'd not, for such pleasure till that hour
At Feed or Fountain never had I found.
Sated at length, ere long I might perceave
Strange alteration in me, to degree
Of Reason in my inward Powers, and Speech   600
Wanted not long, though to this shape retain'd.
Thenceforth to Speculations high or deep
I turnd my thoughts, and with capacious mind
Considerd all things visible in Heav'n,
Or Earth, or Middle, all things fair and good;
But all that fair and good in thy Divine
Semblance, and in thy Beauties heav'nly Ray
United I beheld; no Fair to thine
Equivalent or second, which compel'd
Mee thus, though importune perhaps, to come   610
And gaze, and worship thee of right declar'd
Sovran of Creatures, universal Dame.
  So talk'd the spirited sly Snake; and *Eve*
Yet more amaz'd unwarie thus reply'd.
  Serpent, thy overpraising leaves in doubt
The vertue of that Fruit, in thee first prov'd:
But say, where grows the Tree, from hence how far?
For many are the Trees of God that grow
In Paradise, and various, yet unknown

To us, in such abundance lies our choice,   620
As leaves a greater store of Fruit untoucht,
Still hanging incorruptible, till men
Grow up to thir provision, and more hands
Help to disburden Nature of her Bearth.
   To whom the wilie Adder, blithe and glad.
Empress, the way is readie, and not long,
Beyond a row of Myrtles, on a Flat,
Fast by a Fountain, one small Thicket past
Of blowing Myrrh and Balme; if thou accept
My conduct, I can bring thee thither soon.   630
   Lead then, said *Eve*. Hee leading swiftly rowld
In tangles, and made intricate seem strait,
To mischief swift. Hope elevates, and joy
Bright'ns his Crest, as when a wandring Fire
Compact of unctuous vapor, which the Night
Condenses, and the cold invirons round,
Kindl'd through agitation to a Flame,
Which oft, they say, some evil Spirit attends,
Hovering and blazing with delusive Light,
Misleads th' amaz'd Night-wanderer from his way   640
To Boggs and Mires, & oft through Pond or Poole,
There swallow'd up and lost, from succour farr.
So glister'd the dire Snake, and into fraud
Led *Eve* our credulous Mother, to the Tree
Of prohibition, root of all our woe;
Which when she saw, thus to her guide she spake.
   Serpent, we might have spar'd our coming hither,
Fruitless to me, though Fruit be here to excess,
The credit of whose vertue rest with thee,
Wondrous indeed, if cause of such effects.   650
But of this Tree we may not taste nor touch;
God so commanded, and left that Command
Sole Daughter of his voice; the rest, we live
Law to our selves, our Reason is our Law.
   To whom the Tempter guilefully repli'd.
Indeed? hath God then said that of the Fruit
Of all these Garden Trees ye shall not eate,
Yet Lords declar'd of all in Earth or Aire?
   To whom thus *Eve* yet sinless. Of the Fruit
Of each Tree in the Garden we may eate,   660
But of the Fruit of this fair Tree amidst
The Garden, God hath said, Ye shall not eate
Thereof, nor shall ye touch it, least ye die.
   She scarse had said, though brief, when now more bold
The Tempter, but with shew of Zeale and Love

To Man, and indignation at his wrong,
New part puts on, and as to passion mov'd,
Fluctuats disturbd, yet comely, and in act
Rais'd, as of som great matter to begin.
As when of old som Orator renound   670
In *Athens* or free *Rome*, where Eloquence
Flourishd, since mute, to som great cause addrest,
Stood in himself collected, while each part,
Motion, each act won audience ere the tongue,
Somtimes in highth began, as no delay
Of Preface brooking through his Zeal of Right.
So standing, moving, or to highth upgrown
The Tempter all impassiond thus began.
  O Sacred, Wise, and Wisdom-giving Plant,
Mother of Science, Now I feel thy Power   680
Within me cleere, not onely to discerne
Things in thir Causes, but to trace the wayes
Of highest Agents, deemd however wise.
Queen of this Universe, doe not believe
Those rigid threats of Death; ye shall not Die:
How should ye? by the Fruit? it gives you Life
To Knowledge: By the Threatner? look on mee,
Mee who have touch'd and tasted, yet both live,
And life more perfet have attaind then Fate
Meant mee, by ventring higher then my Lot.   690
Shall that be shut to Man, which to the Beast
Is open? or will God incense his ire
For such a petty Trespass, and not praise
Rather your dauntless vertue, whom the pain
Of Death denounc't, whatever thing Death be,
Deterrd not from atchieving what might leade
To happier life, knowledge of Good and Evil;
Of good, how just? of evil, if what is evil
Be real, why not known, since easier shunnd?
God therefore cannot hurt ye, and be just;   700
Not just, not God; not feard then, nor obeid:
Your feare it self of Death removes the feare.
Why then was this forbid? Why but to awe,
Why but to keep ye low and ignorant,
His worshippers; he knows that in the day
Ye Eate thereof, your Eyes that seem so cleere,
Yet are but dim, shall perfetly be then
Op'nd and cleerd, and ye shall be as Gods,
Knowing both Good and Evil as they know.
That ye should be as Gods, since I as Man,   710
Internal Man, is but proportion meet,

I of brute human, yee of human Gods.
So ye shall die perhaps, by putting off
Human, to put on Gods, death to be wisht,
Though threat'nd, which no worse then this can bring.
And what are Gods that Man may not become
As they, participating God-like food?
The Gods are first, and that advantage use
On our belief, that all from them proceeds;
I question it, for this fair Earth I see,   720
Warm'd by the Sun, producing every kind,
Them nothing: If they all things, who enclos'd
Knowledge of Good and Evil in this Tree,
That whoso eats thereof, forthwith attains
Wisdom without their leave? and wherein lies
Th' offence, that Man should thus attain to know?
What can your knowledge hurt him, or this Tree
Impart against his will if all be his?
Or is it envie, and can envie dwell
In heav'nly brests? these, these and many more   730
Causes import your need of this fair Fruit.
Goddess humane, reach then, and freely taste.
   He ended, and his words replete with guile
Into her heart too easie entrance won:
Fixt on the Fruit she gaz'd, which to behold
Might tempt alone, and in her ears the sound
Yet rung of his perswasive words, impregn'd
With Reason, to her seeming, and with Truth;
Meanwhile the hour of Noon drew on, and wak'd
An eager appetite, rais'd by the smell   740
So savorie of that Fruit, which with desire,
Inclinable now grown to touch or taste,
Sollicited her longing eye; yet first
Pausing a while, thus to her self she mus'd.
   Great are thy Vertues, doubtless, best of Fruits,
Though kept from Man, & worthy to be admir'd,
Whose taste, too long forborn, at first assay
Gave elocution to the mute, and taught
The Tongue not made for Speech to speak thy praise:
Thy praise hee also who forbids thy use,   750
Conceales not from us, naming thee the Tree
Of Knowledge, knowledge both of good and evil;
Forbids us then to taste, but his forbidding
Commends thee more, while it inferrs the good
By thee communicated, and our want:
For good unknown, sure is not had, or had
And yet unknown, is as not had at all.

In plain then, what forbids he but to know,
Forbids us good, forbids us to be wise?
Such prohibitions binde not. But if Death 760
Bind us with after-bands, what profits then
Our inward freedom? In the day we eate
Of this fair Fruit, our doom is, we shall die.
How dies the Serpent? hee hath eat'n and lives,
And knows, and speaks, and reasons, and discernes,
Irrational till then. For us alone
Was death invented? or to us deni'd
This intellectual food, for beasts reserv'd?
For Beasts it seems: yet that one Beast which first
Hath tasted, envies not, but brings with joy 770
The good befall'n him, Author unsuspect,
Friendly to man, farr from deceit or guile.
What fear I then, rather what know to feare
Under this ignorance of Good and Evil,
Of God or Death, of Law or Penaltie?
Here grows the Cure of all, this Fruit Divine,
Fair to the Eye, inviting to the Taste,
Of vertue to make wise: what hinders then
To reach, and feed at once both Bodie and Mind?
   So saying, her rash hand in evil hour 780
Forth reaching to the Fruit, she pluck'd, she eat:
Earth felt the wound, and Nature from her seat
Sighing through all her Works gave signs of woe,
That all was lost. Back to the Thicket slunk
The guiltie Serpent, and well might, for *Eve*
Intent now wholly on her taste, naught else
Regarded, such delight till then, as seemd,
In Fruit she never tasted, whether true
Or fansied so, through expectation high
Of knowledg, nor was God-head from her thought. 790
Greedily she ingorg'd without restraint,
And knew not eating Death: Satiate at length,
And hight'nd as with Wine, jocond and boon,
Thus to her self she pleasingly began.
   O Sovran, vertuous, precious of all Trees
In Paradise, of operation blest
To Sapience, hitherto obscur'd, infam'd,
And thy fair Fruit let hang, as to no end
Created; but henceforth my early care,
Not without Song, each Morning, and due praise 800
Shall tend thee, and the fertil burden ease
Of thy full branches offer'd free to all;
Till dieted by thee I grow mature

In knowledge, as the Gods who all things know;
Though others envie what they cannot give;
For had the gift bin theirs, it had not here
Thus grown. Experience, next to thee I owe,
Best guide; not following thee, I had remaind
In ignorance, thou op'nst Wisdoms way,
And giv'st access, though secret she retire.   *810*
And I perhaps am secret; Heav'n is high,
High and remote to see from thence distinct
Each thing on Earth; and other care perhaps
May have diverted from continual watch
Our great Forbidder, safe with all his Spies
About him. But to *Adam* in what sort
Shall I appeer? shall I to him make known
As yet my change, and give him to partake
Full happiness with mee, or rather not,
But keep the odds of Knowledge in my power   *820*
Without Copartner? so to add what wants
In Femal Sex, the more to draw his Love,
And render me more equal, and perhaps,
A thing not undesirable, somtime
Superior: for inferior who is free?
This may be well: but what if God have seen
And Death ensue? then I shall be no more,
And *Adam* wedded to another *Eve*,
Shall live with her enjoying, I extinct;
A death to think. Confirm'd then I resolve,   *830*
Adam shall share with me in bliss or woe:
So dear I love him, that with him all deaths
I could endure, without him live no life.
  So saying, from the Tree her step she turnd,
But first low Reverence don, as to the power
That dwelt within, whose presence had infus'd
Into the plant scientail sap, deriv'd
From Nectar, drink of Gods. *Adam* the while
Waiting desirous her return, had wove
Of choicest Flours a Garland to adorne   *840*
Her Tresses, and her rural labours crown
As Reapers oft are wont thir Harvest Queen.
Great joy he promis'd to his thoughts, and new
Solace in her return, so long delay'd;
Yet oft his heart, divine of somthing ill,
Misgave him; hee the faultring measure felt;
And forth to meet her went, the way she took
That Morn when first they parted; by the Tree
Of Knowledge he must pass, there he her met,

Scarse from the Tree returning; in her hand 850
A bough of fairest fruit that downie smil'd,
New gatherd, and ambrosial smell diffus'd.
To him she hasted, in her face excuse
Came Prologue, and Apologie to prompt,
Which with bland words at will she thus addrest.

    Hast thou not wonderd, *Adam*, at my stay?
Thee I have misst, and thought it long, depriv'd
Thy presence, agonie of love till now
Not felt, nor shall be twice, for never more
Mean I to trie, what rash untri'd I sought, 860
The paine of absence from thy sight. But strange
Hath bin the cause, and wonderful to heare:
This Tree is not as we are told, a Tree
Of danger tasted, nor to evil unknown
Op'ning the way, but of Divine effect
To open Eyes, and make them Gods who taste;
And hath bin tasted such: the Serpent wise,
Or not restraind as wee, or not obeying,
Hath eat'n of the fruit, and is become,
Not dead, as we are threatn'd, but thenceforth 870
Endu'd with human voice and human sense,
Reasoning to admiration, and with mee
Perswasively hath so prevaild, that I
Have also tasted, and have also found
Th' effects to correspond, opener mine Eyes
Dimm erst, dilated Spirits, ampler Heart,
And growing up to Godhead; which for thee
Chiefly I sought, without thee can despise.
For bliss, as thou hast part, to me is bliss,
Tedious, unshar'd with thee, and odious soon. 880
Thou therfore also taste, that equal Lot
May joyne us, equal Joy, as equal Love;
Least thou not tasting, different degree
Disjoyne us, and I then too late renounce
Deitie for thee, when Fate will not permit.

    Thus *Eve* with Countnance blithe her storie told;
But in her Cheek distemper flushing glowd.
On th' other side, *Adam*, soon as he heard
The fatal Trespass done by *Eve*, amaz'd,
Astonied stood and Blank, while horror chill 890
Ran through his veins, and all his joynts relax'd;
From his slack hand the Garland wreath'd for *Eve*
Down drop'd, and all the faded Roses shed:
Speechless he stood and pale, till thus at length
First to himself he inward silence broke.

O fairest of Creation, last and best
Of all Gods Works, Creature in whom excell'd
Whatever can to sight or thought be formd,
Holy, divine, good, amiable, or sweet!
How art thou lost, how on a sudden lost,   *900*
Defac't, deflourd, and now to Death devote?
Rather how hast thou yeelded to transgress
The strict forbiddance, how to violate
The sacred Fruit forbidd'n! som cursed fraud
Of Enemie hath beguil'd thee, yet unknown,
And mee with thee hath ruind, for with thee
Certain my resolution is to Die;
How can I live without thee, how forgoe
Thy sweet Converse and Love so dearly joyn'd,
To live again in these wilde Woods forlorn?   *910*
Should God create another *Eve*, and I
Another Rib afford, yet loss of thee
Would never from my heart; no no, I feel
The Link of Nature draw me: Flesh of Flesh,
Bone of my Bone thou art, and from thy State
Mine never shall be parted, bliss or woe.

   So having said, as one from sad dismay
Recomforted, and after thoughts disturbd
Submitting to what seemd remediless,
Thus in calme mood his Words to *Eve* he turnd.   *920*

   Bold deed thou hast presum'd, adventrous *Eve*
And peril great provok't, who thus hast dar'd
Had it bin onely coveting to Eye
That sacred Fruit, sacred to abstinence,
Much more to taste it under banne to touch.
But past who can recall, or don undoe?
Not God Omnipotent, nor Fate, yet so
Perhaps thou shalt not Die, perhaps the Fact
Is not so hainous now, foretasted Fruit,
Profan'd first by the Serpent, by him first   *930*
Made common and unhallowd ere our taste;
Nor yet on him found deadly, he yet lives,
Lives, as thou saidst, and gaines to live as Man
Higher degree of Life, inducement strong
To us, as likely tasting to attaine
Proportional ascent, which cannot be
But to be Gods, or Angels Demi-gods.
Nor can I think that God, Creator wise,
Though threatning, will in earnest so destroy
Us his prime Creatures, dignifi'd so high,   *940*
Set over all his Works, which in our Fall,

For us created, needs with us must faile,
Dependent made; so God shall uncreate,
Be frustrate, do, undo, and labour loose,
Not well conceav'd of God, who though his Power
Creation could repeate, yet would be loath
Us to abolish, least the Adversary
Triumph and say; Fickle their State whom God
Most Favors, who can please him long? Mee first
He ruind, now Mankind; whom will he next? 950
Matter of scorne, not to be given the Foe.
However I with thee have fixt my Lot,
Certain to undergoe like doom, if Death
Consort with thee, Death is to mee as Life;
So forcible within my heart I feel
The Bond of Nature draw me to my owne,
My own in thee, for what thou art is mine;
Our State cannot be severd, we are one,
One Flesh; to loose thee were to loose my self.
    So *Adam*, and thus *Eve* to him repli'd. 960
O glorious trial of exceeding Love,
Illustrious evidence, example high!
Ingaging me to emulate, but short
Of thy perfection, how shall I attaine,
Adam, from whose deare side I boast me sprung,
And gladly of our Union heare thee speak,
One Heart, one Soul in both; whereof good prooff
This day affords, declaring thee resolvd,
Rather then Death or aught then Death more dread
Shall separate us, linkt in Love so deare, 970
To undergoe with mee one Guilt, one Crime,
If any be, of tasting this fair Fruit,
Whose vertue, for of good still good proceeds,
Direct, or by occasion hath presented
This happie trial of thy Love, which else
So eminently never had bin known.
Were it I thought Death menac't would ensue
This my attempt, I would sustain alone
The worst, and not perswade thee, rather die
Deserted, then oblige thee with a fact 980
Pernicious to thy Peace, chiefly assur'd
Remarkably so late of thy so true,
So faithful Love unequald; but I feel
Farr otherwise th' event, not Death, but Life
Augmented, op'nd Eyes, new Hopes, new Joyes,
Taste so Divine, that what of sweet before
Hath toucht my sense, flat seems to this, and harsh.

On my experience, *Adam*, freely taste,
And fear of Death deliver to the Windes.
   So saying, she embrac'd him, and for joy   990
Tenderly wept, much won that he his Love
Had so enobl'd, as of choice to incurr
Divine displeasure for her sake, or Death.
In recompence (for such compliance bad
Such recompence best merits) from the bough
She gave him of that fair enticing Fruit
With liberal hand: he scrupl'd not to eat
Against his better knowledge, not deceav'd,
But fondly overcome with Femal charm.
Earth trembl'd from her entrails, as again   1000
In pangs, and Nature gave a second groan,
Skie lowr'd, and muttering Thunder, som sad drops
Wept at compleating of the mortal Sin
Original; while *Adam* took no thought,
Eating his fill, nor *Eve* to iterate
Her former trespass fear'd, the more to soothe
Him with her lov'd societie, that now
As with new Wine intoxicated both
They swim in mirth, and fansie that they feel
Divinitie within them breeding wings   1010
Wherewith to scorn the Earth: but that false Fruit
Farr other operation first displaid,
Carnal desire enflaming, hee on *Eve*
Began to cast lascivious Eyes, she him
As wantonly repaid; in Lust they burne:
Till *Adam* thus 'gan *Eve* to dalliance move.
   Eve, now I see thou art exact of taste,
And elegant, of Sapience no small part,
Since to each meaning savour we apply,
And Palate call judicious; I the praise   1020
Yeild thee, so well this day thou hast purvey'd.
Much pleasure we have lost, while we abstain'd
From this delightful Fruit, nor known till now
True relish, tasting; if such pleasure be
In things to us forbidden, it might be wish'd,
For this one Tree had bin forbidden ten.
But come, so well refresh't, now let us play,
As meet is, after such delicious Fare;
For never did thy Beautie since the day
I saw thee first and wedded thee, adorn'd   1030
With all perfections, so enflame my sense
With ardor to enjoy thee, fairer now
Than ever, bountie of this vertuous Tree.

So said he, and forbore not glance or toy
Of amorous intent, well understood
Of *Eve*, whose Eye darted contagious Fire.
Her hand he seis'd, and to a shadie bank,
Thick overhead with verdant roof imbowr'd
He led her nothing loath; Flours were the Couch,
Pansies, and Violets, and Asphodel,   *1040*
And Hyacinth, Earths freshest softest lap.
There they thir fill of Love and Loves disport
Took largely, of thir mutual guilt the Seale,
The solace of thir sin, till dewie sleep
Oppress'd them, wearied with thir amorous play.
Soon as the force of that fallacious Fruit,
That with exhilerating vapour bland
About thir spirits had plaid, and inmost powers
Made erre, was now exhal'd, and grosser sleep
Bred of unkindly fumes, with conscious dreams   *1050*
Encumberd, now had left them, up they rose
As from unrest, and each the other viewing,
Soon found thir Eyes how op'nd, and thir minds
How dark'nd; innocence, that as a veile
Had shadow'd them from knowing ill, was gon,
Just confidence, and native righteousness,
And honour from about them, naked left
To guiltie shame hee cover'd, but his Robe
Uncover'd more. So rose the *Danite* strong
Herculean Samson from the Harlot-lap   *1060*
Of *Philistean Dalilah*, and wak'd
Shorn of his strength, They destitute and bare
Of all thir vertue: silent, and in face
Confounded long they sate, as struck'n mute,
Till *Adam*, though not less then *Eve* abasht,
At length gave utterance to these words constraind.
   O *Eve*, in evil hour thou didst give eare
To that false Worm, of whomsoever taught
To counterfet Mans voice, true in our Fall,
False in our promis'd Rising; since our Eyes   *1070*
Op'nd we find indeed, and find we know
Both Good and Evil, Good lost, and Evil got,
Bad Fruit of Knowledge, if this be to know,
Which leaves us naked thus, of Honour void,
Of Innocence, of Faith, of Puritie,
Our wonted Ornaments now soild and staind,
And in our Faces evident the signes
Of foul concupiscence; whence evil store;
Even shame, the last of evils; of the first

Be sure then. How shall I behold the face 1080
Henceforth of God or Angel, earst with joy
And rapture so oft beheld? those heav'nly shapes
Will dazle now this earthly, with thir blaze
Insufferably bright. O might I here
In solitude live savage, in some glade
Obscur'd, where highest Woods impenetrable
To Starr or Sun-light, spread thir umbrage broad,
And brown as Evening: Cover me ye Pines,
Ye Cedars, with innumerable boughs
Hide me, where I may never see them more. 1090
But let us now, as in bad plight, devise
What best may for the present serve to hide
The Parts of each from other, that seem most
To shame obnoxious, and unseemliest seen,
Some Tree whose broad smooth Leaves together sowd,
And girded on our loyns, may cover round
Those midde parts, that this new commer, Shame,
There sit not, and reproach us as unclean.
  So counsel'd hee, and both together went
Into the thickest Wood, there soon they chose 1100
The Figtree, not that kind for Fruit renown'd,
But such as at this day to *Indians* known
In *Malabar* or *Decan* spreds her Armes
Braunching so broad and long, that in the ground
The bended Twigs take root, and Daughters grow
About the Mother Tree, a Pillard shade
High overarch't, and echoing Walks between;
There oft the *Indian* Herdsman shunning heate
Shelters in coole, and tends his pasturing Herds
At Loopholes cut through thickest shade: Those
    Leaves 1110
They gatherd, broad as *Amazonian* Targe,
And with what skill they had, together sowd,
To gird thir waste, vain Covering if to hide
Thir guilt and dreaded shame; O how unlike
To that first naked Glorie. Such of late
Columbus found th' *American* so girt
With featherd Cincture, naked else and wilde
Among the Trees on Iles and woodie Shores.
Thus fenc't, and as they thought, thir shame in part
Coverd, but not at rest or ease of Mind, 1120
They sate them down to weep, nor onely Teares
Raind at thir Eyes, but high Winds worse within
Began to rise, high Passions, Anger, Hate,
Mistrust, Suspicion, Discord, and shook sore

Thir inward State of Mind, calme Region once
And full of Peace, now tost and turbulent:
For Understanding rul'd not, and the Will
Heard not her lore, both in subjection now
To sensual Appetite, who from beneathe
Usurping over sovran Reason claimd   *1130*
Superior sway: From thus distemperd brest,
Adam, estrang'd in look and alterd stile,
Speech intermitted thus to *Eve* renewd.
    Would thou hadst heark'nd to my words, & stai'd
With me, as I besought thee, when that strange
Desire of wandring this unhappie Morn,
I know not whence possessd thee; we had then
Remaind still happie, not as now, despoild
Of all our good, sham'd, naked, miserable.
Let none henceforth seek needless cause to approve *1140*
The Faith they owe; when earnestly they seek
Such proof, conclude, they then begin to faile.
    To whom soon mov'd with touch of blame thus *Eve*.
What words have past thy Lips, *Adam* severe,
Imput'st thou that to my default, or will
Of wandering, as thou call'st it, which who knows
But might as ill have happ'nd thou being by,
Or to thy self perhaps: hadst thou bin there,
Or here th' attempt, thou could'st not have discernd
Fraud in the Serpent, speaking as he spake;   *1150*
No ground of enmitie between us known,
Why hee should mean me ill, or seek to harme.
Was I to have never parted from thy side?
As good have grown there still a liveless Rib.
Being as I am, why didst not thou the Head
Command me absolutely not to go,
Going into such danger as thou saidst?
Too facil then thou didst not much gainsay,
Nay, didst permit, approve, and fair dismiss.
Hadst thou bin firm and fixt in thy dissent,   *1160*
Neither had I transgress'd, nor thou with mee.
    To whom then first incenst *Adam* repli'd.
Is this the Love, is this the recompence
Of mine to thee, ingrateful *Eve*, exprest
Immutable when thou wert lost, not I,
Who might have liv'd and joyd immortal bliss,
Yet willingly chose rather Death with thee:
And am I now upbraided, as the cause
Of thy transgressing? not enough severe,
It seems, in thy restraint: what could I more?   *1170*

I warn'd thee, I admonish'd thee, foretold
The danger, and the lurking Enemie
That lay in wait; beyond this had bin force,
And force upon free Will hath here no place.
But confidence then bore thee on, secure
Either to meet no danger, or to finde
Matter of glorious trial; and perhaps
I also err'd in overmuch admiring
What seemd in thee so perfet, that I thought
No evil durst attempt thee, but I rue   *1180*
That errour now, which is become my crime,
And thou th' accuser. Thus it shall befall
Him who to worth in Women overtrusting
Lets her Will rule; restraint she will not brook,
And left to her self, if evil thence ensue,
Shee first his weak indulgence will accuse.
    Thus they in mutual accusation spent
The fruitless hours, but neither self-condemning,
And of thir vain contest appeer'd no end.

BOOK X

THE ARGUMENT

Mans transgression known, the Guardian Angels forsake Paradise, and return up to Heaven to approve thir vigilance, and are approv'd, God declaring that The entrance of Satan *could not be by them prevented. He sends his Son to judge the Transgressors, who descends and gives Sentence accordingly; then in pity cloaths them both, and reascends. Sin and Death sitting till then at the Gates of Hell, by wondrous sympathie feeling the success of* Satan *in this new World, and the sin by Man there committed, resolve to sit no longer confin'd in Hell, but to follow* Satan *thir Sire up to the place of Man: To make the way easier from Hell to this World to and fro, they pave a broad Highway or Bridge over* Chaos, *according to the Track that* Satan *first made; then preparing for Earth, they meet him proud of his success returning to Hell; thir mutual gratulation.* Satan *arrives at* Pandemonium, *in full assembly relates with boasting his success against Man; instead of applause is entertained with a general hiss by all his audience, transform'd with himself also suddenly into Serpents, according to his doom giv'n in Paradise; then deluded with a shew of the forbidden Tree springing up before them, they greedily reaching to take of the Fruit, chew dust and bitter ashes. The proceedings of Sin and Death; God foretels the final Victory of his Son over them, and the renewing of all things; but for the present commands his Angels to make several alterations in the Heavens and Elements.* Adam *more and more perceiving his fall'n condition heavily bewailes, rejects the condolement of* Eve; *she persists and at length appeases him: then to evade the Curse likely to fall on thir Ofspring, proposes to* Adam *violent wayes, which he approves not, but conceiving better hope, puts her in mind of the late Promise made them, that her Seed should be reveng'd on the Serpent, and exhorts her with him to seek Peace of the offended Deity, by repentance and supplication.*

MEANWHILE the hainous and despightfull act
   Of *Satan* done in Paradise, and how
Hee in the Serpent had perverted *Eve*,
Her Husband shee, to taste the fatall fruit,
Was known in Heav'n; for what can scape the Eye
Of God All-seeing, or deceave his Heart
Omniscient, who in all things wise and just,
Hinder'd not *Satan* to attempt the minde
Of Man, with strength entire, and free Will arm'd,
Complete to have discover'd and repulst   10
Whatever wiles of Foe or seeming Friend.
For still they knew, and ought to have still remember'd
The high Injunction not to taste that Fruit,
Whoever tempted; which they not obeying,
Incurr'd, what could they less, the penaltie,
And manifold in sin, deserv'd to fall.
Up into Heav'n from Paradise in hast
Th' Angelic Guards ascended, mute and sad

For Man, for of his state by this they knew,
Much wondring how the suttle Fiend had stoln
Entrance unseen. Soon as th' unwelcome news
From Earth arriv'd at Heaven Gate, displeas'd
All were who heard, dim sadness did not spare
That time Celestial visages, yet mixt
With pitie, violated not thir bliss.
About the new-arriv'd, in multitudes
Th' ethereal People ran, to hear and know
How all befell: they towards the Throne Supream
Accountable made haste to make appear
With righteous plea, thir utmost vigilance,
And easily approv'd; when the most High
Eternal Father from his secret Cloud,
Amidst in Thunder utter'd thus his voice.

   Assembl'd Angels, and ye Powers return'd
From unsuccessful charge, be not dismaid,
Nor troubl'd at these tidings from the Earth,
Which your sincerest care could not prevent,
Foretold so lately what would come to pass,
When first this Tempter cross'd the Gulf from Hell
I told ye then he should prevail and speed
On his bad Errand, Man should be seduc't
And flatter'd out of all, believing lies
Against his Maker; no Decree of mine
Concurring to necessitate his Fall,
Or touch with lightest moment of impulse
His free Will, to her own inclining left
In even scale. But fall'n he is, and now
What rests, but that the mortal Sentence pass
On his trangression, Death denounc't that day,
Which he presumes already vain and void,
Because not yet inflicted, as he fear'd,
By some immediate stroak; but soon shall find
Forbearance no acquittance ere day end.
Justice shall not return as bountie scorn'd.
But whom send I to judge them? whom but thee
Vicegerent Son, to thee I have transferr'd
All Judgement, whether in Heav'n, or Earth, or Hell.
Easie it may be seen that I intend
Mercie collegue with Justice, sending thee
Mans Friend, his Mediator, his design'd
Both Ransom and Redeemer voluntarie,
And destin'd Man himself to judge Man fall'n.

   So spake the Father, and unfoulding bright
Toward the right hand his Glorie, on the Son

Blaz'd forth unclouded Deitie; he full
Resplendent all his Father manifest
Express'd, and thus divinely answer'd milde.
    Father Eternal, thine is to decree,
Mine both in Heav'n and Earth to do thy will
Supream, that thou in mee thy Son belov'd   70
Mayst ever rest well pleas'd. I go to judge
On Earth these thy transgressors, but thou knowst,
Whoever judg'd, the worst on mee must light,
When time shall be, for so I undertook
Before thee; and not repenting, this obtaine
Of right, that I may mitigate thir doom
On me deriv'd, yet I shall temper so
Justice with Mercie, as may illustrate most
Them fully satisfied, and thee appease.
Attendance none shall need, nor Train, where none   80
Are to behold the Judgement, but the judg'd,
Those two; the third best absent is condemn'd,
Convict by flight, and Rebel to all Law
Conviction to the Serpent none belongs.
    Thus saying, from his radiant Seat he rose
Of high collateral glorie: him Thrones and Powers,
Princedoms, and Dominations ministrant
Accompanied to Heaven Gate, from whence
Eden and all the Coast in prospect lay.
Down he descended strait; the speed of Gods   90
Time counts not, though with swiftest minutes wing'd.
Now was the Sun in Western cadence low
From Noon, and gentle Aires due at thir hour
To fan the Earth now wak'd, and usher in
The Eevning coole when he from wrauth more coole
Came the mild Judge and Intercessor both
To sentence Man: the voice of God they heard
Now walking in the Garden, by soft windes
Brought to thir Ears, while day declin'd, they heard
And from his presence hid themselves among   100
The thickest Trees, both Man and Wife, till God
Approaching, thus to *Adam* call'd aloud.
    Where art thou *Adam*, wont with joy to meet
My coming seen far off? I miss thee here,
Not pleas'd, thus entertaind with solitude,
Where obvious dutie erewhile appear'd unsaught:
Or come I less conspicuous, or what change
Absents thee, or what chance detains? Come forth.
He came, and with him *Eve*, more loth, though first
To offend, discount'nanc't both, and discompos'd;   110

Love was not in thir looks, either to God
Or to each other, but apparent guilt,
And shame, and perturbation, and despaire,
Anger, and obstinacie, and hate, and guile.
Whence *Adam* faultring long, thus answer'd brief.
   I heard thee in the Garden, and of thy voice
Affraid, being naked, hid my self. To whom
The gracious Judge without revile repli'd.
   My voice thou oft hast heard, and hast not fear'd,
But still rejoyc't, how is it now become   120
So dreadful to thee? that thou art naked, who
Hath told thee? hast thou eaten of the Tree
Whereof I gave thee charge thou shouldst not eat?
   To whom thus *Adam* sore beset repli'd.
O Heav'n! in evil strait this day I stand
Before my Judge, either to undergoe
My self the total Crime, or to accuse
My other self, the partner of my life;
Whose failing, while her Faith to me remaines,
I should conceal, and not expose to blame   130
By my complaint; but strict necessitie
Subdues me, and calamitous constraint,
Least on my head both sin and punishment,
However insupportable, be all
Devolv'd; though should I hold my peace, yet thou
Wouldst easily detect what I conceale.
This Woman whom thou mad'st to be my help,
And gav'st me as thy perfet gift, so good,
So fit, so acceptable, so Divine,
That from her hand I could suspect no ill,   140
And what she did, whatever in it self,
Her doing seem'd to justifie the deed;
Shee gave me of the Tree, and I did eate.
   To whom the sovran Presence thus repli'd.
Was shee thy God, that her thou didst obey
Before his voice, or was shee made thy guide,
Superior, or but equal, that to her
Thou did'st resigne thy Manhood, and the Place
Wherein God set thee above her made of thee,
And for thee, whose perfection farr excell'd   150
Hers in all real dignitie: Adornd
She was indeed, and lovely to attract
Thy Love, not thy Subjection, and her Gifts
Were such as under Government well seem'd,
Unseemly to beare rule, which was thy part
And person, had'st thou known thy self aright.

So having said, he thus to *Eve* in few:
Say Woman, what is this which thou hast done?
   To whom sad *Eve* with shame nigh overwhelm'd,
Confessing soon, yet not before her Judge   160
Bold or loquacious, thus abasht repli'd.
The Serpent me beguil'd and I did eate.
   Which when the Lord God heard, without delay
To Judgement he proceeded on th' accus'd
Serpent though brute, unable to transferre
The Guilt on him who made him instrument
Of mischief, and polluted from the end
Of his Creation; justly then accurst,
As vitiated in Nature: more to know
Concern'd not Man (since he no further knew)   170
Nor alter'd his offence; yet God at last
To Satan first in sin his doom apply'd
Though in mysterious terms, judg'd as then best:
And on the Serpent thus his curse let fall.
   Because thou hast done this, thou art accurst
Above all Cattel, each Beast of the Field;
Upon thy Belly groveling thou shalt goe,
And dust shalt eat all the days of thy Life.
Between Thee and the Woman I will put
Enmitie, and between thine and her Seed;   180
Her Seed shall bruise thy head, thou bruise his heel.
   So spake this Oracle, then verifi'd
When *Jesus* son of *Mary* second *Eve*,
Saw Satan fall like Lightning down from Heav'n,
Prince of the Aire; then rising from his Grave
Spoild Principalities and Powers, triumpht
In open shew, and with ascention bright
Captivity led captive through the Aire,
The Realme it self of Satan long usurpt,
Whom he shall tread at last under our feet;   190
Eevn hee who now foretold his fatal bruise,
And to the Woman thus his Sentence turn'd.
   Thy sorrow I will greatly multiplie
By thy Conception; Childern thou shalt bring
In sorrow forth, and to thy Husbands will
Thine shall submit, hee over thee shall rule.
   On *Adam* last thus judgement he pronounc'd.
Because thou has heark'nd to the voice of thy Wife,
And eaten of the Tree concerning which
I charg'd thee, saying: Thou shalt not eate thereof, 200
Curs'd is the ground for thy sake, thou in sorrow
Shalt eate thereof all the days of thy Life;

Thornes also and Thistles it shall bring thee forth
Unbid, and thou shalt eate th' Herb of th' Field,
In the sweat of thy Face shalt thou eate Bread,
Till thou return unto the ground, for thou
Out of the ground wast taken, know thy Birth,
For dust thou art, and shalt to dust returne.
    So judg'd he Man, both Judge and Saviour sent,
And th' instant stroke of Death denounc't that day   *210*
Remov'd farr off; then pittying how they stood
Before him naked to the aire, that now
Must suffer change, disdain'd not to begin
Thenceforth the forme of servant to assume,
As when he wash'd his servants feet, so now
As Father of his Familie he clad
Thir nakedness with Skins of Beasts, or slain,
Or as the Snake with youthful Coate repaid;
And thought not much to cloath his Enemies:
Nor hee thir outward oncly with the Skins   *220*
Of Beasts, but inward nakedness, much more
Opprobrious, with his Robe of righteousness,
Araying cover'd from his Fathers sight.
To him with swift ascent he up return'd,
Into his blissful bosom reassum'd
In glory as of old, to him appeas'd
All, though all-knowing, what had past with Man
Recounted, mixing intercession sweet.
Meanwhile ere thus was sin'd and judg'd on Earth,
Within the Gates of Hell sate Sin and Death,   *230*
In counterview within the Gates, that now
Stood open wide, belching outrageous flame
Farr into *Chaos*, since the Fiend pass'd through,
Sin opening, who thus now to Death began.
    O Son, why sit we here each other viewing
Idlely, while Satan our great Author thrives
In other Worlds, and happier Seat provides
For us his ofspring deare? It cannot be
But that success attends him; if mishap,
Ere this he had return'd, with fury driv'n   *240*
By his Avenger, since no place like this
Can fit his punishment, or their revenge.
Methinks I feel new strength within me rise,
Wings growing, and Dominion giv'n me large
Beyond this Deep; whatever drawes me on,
Or sympathie, or som connatural force
Powerful at greatest distance to unite
With secret amity things of like kinde

By secretest conveyance. Thou my Shade
Inseparable must with mee along:
For Death from Sin no power can separate.
But least the difficultie of passing back
Stay his returne perhaps over this Gulfe
Impassable, impervious, let us try
Adventrous work, yet to thy power and mine
Not unagreeable, to found a path
Over this Maine from Hell to that new World
Where Satan now prevailes, a Monument
Of merit high to all th' infernal Host,
Easing thir passage hence, for intercourse,
Or transmigration, as thir lot shall lead.
Nor can I miss the way, so strongly drawn
By this new felt attraction and instinct.
   Whom thus the meager Shadow answerd soon.
Goe whither Fate and inclination strong
Leads thee, I shall not lag behinde, nor erre
The way, thou leading, such a sent I draw
Of carnage, prey innumerable, and taste
The savour of Death from all things there that live:
Nor shall I to the work thou enterprisest
Be wanting, but afford thee equal aid.
   So saying, with delight he snuff'd the smell
Of mortal change on Earth. As when a flock
Of ravenous Fowl, though many a League remote,
Against the day of Battel, to a Field,
Where Armies lie encampt, come flying, lur'd
With sent of living Carcasses design'd
For death, the following day, in bloodie fight.
So sented the grim Feature, and upturn'd
His Nostril wide into the murkie Air,
Sagacious of his Quarrey from so farr.
Then Both from out Hell Gates into the waste
Wide Anarchie of *Chaos* damp and dark
Flew divers, & with Power (thir Power was great)
Hovering upon the Waters; what they met
Solid or slimie, as in raging Sea
Tost up and down, together crowded drove
From each side shoaling towards the mouth of Hell.
As when two Polar Winds blowing adverse
Upon the *Cronian* Sea, together drive
Mountains of Ice, that stop th' imagin'd way
Beyond *Petsora* Eastward, to the rich
Cathaian Coast. The aggregated Soyle
Death with his Mace petrific, cold and dry,

As with a Trident smote, and fix't as firm
As *Delos* floating once; the rest his look
Bound with *Gorgonian* rigor not to move,
And with *Asphaltic* slime; broad as the Gate,
Deep to the Roots of Hell the gather'd beach
They fasten'd, and the Mole immense wraught on   *300*
Over the foaming deep high Archt, a Bridge
Of length prodigious joyning to the Wall
Immoveable of this now fenceless world
Forfeit to Death; from hence a passage broad,
Smooth, easie, inoffensive down to Hell.
So, if great things to small may be compar'd,
Xerxes, the *Libertie* of *Greece* to yoke,
From *Susa* his *Memnonian* Palace high
Came to the Sea, and over *Hellespont*
Bridging his way, *Europe* with *Asia* joyn'd,   *310*
And scourg'd with many a stroak th' indignant waves.
Now had they brought the work by wondrous Art
Pontifical, a ridge of pendent Rock
Over the vext Abyss, following the track
Of *Satan*, to the self same place where hee
First lighted from his Wing, and landed safe
From out of *Chaos* to the outside bare
Of this round World: with Pinns of Adamant
And Chains they made all fast, too fast they made
And durable; and now in little space   *320*
The Confines met of Empyrean Heav'n
And of this World, and on the left hand Hell
With long reach interpos'd; three sev'ral wayes
In sight, to each of these three places led.
And now thir way to Earth they had descri'd,
To Paradise first tending, when behold
Satan in likeness of an Angel bright
Betwixt the *Centaure* and the *Scorpion* stearing
His *Zenith*, while the Sun in *Aries* rose:
Disguis'd he came, but those his Childern dear   *330*
Thir Parent soon discern'd, though in disguise.
Hee, after *Eve* seduc't, unminded slunk
Into the Wood fast by, and changing shape
To observe the sequel, saw his guileful act
By *Eve*, though all unweeting, seconded
Upon her Husband, saw thir shame that sought
Vain covertures; but when he saw descend
The Son of God to judge them, terrifi'd
Hee fled, not hoping to escape, but shun
The present, fearing guiltie what his wrauth   *340*

Might suddenly inflict; that past, return'd
By Night, and listning where the hapless Paire
Sate in thir sad discourse, and various plaint,
Thence gatherd his own doom, which understood
Not instant, but of future time. With joy
And tidings fraught, to Hell he now return'd,
And at the brink of *Chaos*, neer the foot
Of this new wondrous Pontifice, unhop't
Met who to meet him came, his Ofspring dear.
Great joy was at thir meeting, and at sight 350
Of that stupendious Bridge his joy encreas'd.
Long hee admiring stood, till Sin, his faire
Inchanting Daughter, thus the silence broke.

   O Parent, these are thy magnific deeds,
Thy Trophies, which thou view'st as not thine own,
Thou art thir Author and prime Architect:
For I no sooner in my Heart divin'd,
My Heart, which by a secret harmonie
Still moves with thine, joyn'd in connexion sweet,
That thou on Earth hadst prosper'd, which thy looks 360
Now also evidence, but straight I felt
Though distant from thee Worlds between, yet felt
That I must after thee with this thy Son;
Such fatal consequence unites us three:
Hell could no longer hold us in her bounds,
Nor this unvoyageable Gulf obscure
Detain from following thy illustrious track.
Thou hast atchiev'd our libertie, confin'd
Within Hell Gates till now, thou us impow'rd
To fortifie thus farr, and overlay 370
With this portentous Bridge the dark Abyss.
Thine now is all this World, thy vertue hath won
What thy hands builded not, thy Wisdom gain'd
With odds what Warr hath lost, and fully aveng'd
Our foile in Heav'n; here thou shalt Monarch reign,
There didst not; there let him still Victor sway,
As Battel hath adjudg'd, from this new World
Retiring, by his own doom alienated,
And henceforth Monarchie with thee divide
Of all things, parted by th' Empyreal bounds, 380
His Quadrature, from thy Orbicular World,
Or trie thee now more dang'rous to his Throne.

   Whom thus the Prince of Darkness answerd glad.
Fair Daughter, and thou Son and Grandchild both,
High proof ye now have giv'n to be the Race
Of *Satan* (for I glorie in the name,

Antagonist of Heav'ns Almightie King)
Amply have merited of me, of all
Th' Infernal Empire, that so neer Heav'ns dore
Triumphal with triumphal act have met,   *390*
Mine with this glorious Work, & made one Realm
Hell and this World, one Realm, one Continent
Of easie thorough-fare. Therefore while I
Descend through Darkness, on your Rode with ease
To my associate Powers, them to acquaint
With these successes, and with them rejoyce,
You two this way, among those numerous Orbs
All yours, right down to Paradise descend;
There dwell & Reign in bliss, thence on the Earth
Dominion exercise and in the Aire,   *400*
Chiefly on Man, sole Lord of all declar'd,
Him first make sure your thrall, and lastly kill.
My Substitutes I send ye, and Create
Plenipotent on Earth, of matchless might
Issuing from mee: on your joynt vigor now
My hold of this new Kingdom all depends,
Through Sin to Death expos'd by my exploit.
If your joynt power prevaile, th' affaires of Hell
No detriment need feare, goe and be strong.

  So saying he dismiss'd them, they with speed   *410*
Thir course through thickest Constellations held
Spreading thir bane; the blasted Starrs lookt wan,
And Planets, Planet-strook, real Eclips
Then sufferd. Th' other way *Satan* went down
The Causey to Hell Gate; on either side
Disparted *Chaos* over built exclaimd,
And with rebounding surge the barrs assaild,
That scorn'd his indignation: through the Gate,
Wide open and unguarded, *Satan* pass'd,
And all about found desolate; for those   *420*
Appointed to sit there, had left thir charge,
Flown to the upper World; the rest were all
Farr to the inland retir'd, about the walls
Of *Pandæmonium*, Citie and proud seate
Of *Lucifer*, so by allusion calld,
Of that bright Starr to *Satan* paragond.
There kept thir Watch the Legions, while the Grand
In Council sate, sollicitous what chance
Might intercept thir Emperiour sent, so hee
Departing gave command, and they observ'd.   *430*
As when the *Tartar* from his *Russian* Foe
By *Astracan* over the Snowie Plaines

Retires, or *Bactrian* Sophi from the hornes
Of *Turkish* Crescent, leaves all waste beyond
The Realme of *Aladule*, in his retreate
To *Tauris* or *Casbeen*. So these the late
Heav'n-banisht Host, left desert utmost Hell
Many a dark League, reduc't in careful Watch
Round thir Metropolis, and now expecting
Each hour thir great adventurer from the search   *440*
Of Forrein Worlds: he through the midst unmarkt,
In shew plebeian Angel militant
Of lowest order, past; and from the dore
Of that *Plutonian* Hall, invisible
Ascended his high Throne, which under state
Of richest texture spred, at th' upper end
Was plac't in regal lustre. Down a while
He sate, and round about him saw unseen:
At last as from a Cloud his fulgent head
And shape Starr-bright appeer'd, or brighter, clad   *450*
With what permissive glory since his fall
Was left him, or false glitter: All amaz'd
At that so sudden blaze the *Stygian* throng
Bent thir aspect, and whom they wish'd beheld,
Thir mighty Chief returnd: loud was th' acclaime:
Forth rush'd in haste the great consulting Peers,
Rais'd from thir dark *Divan*, and with like joy
Congratulant approach'd him, who with hand
Silence, and with these words attention won.

   Thrones, Dominations, Princedoms, Vertues, Powers,
For in possession such, not onely of right,   *461*
I call ye and declare ye now, returnd
Successful beyond hope, to lead ye forth
Triumphant out of this infernal Pit
Abominable, accurst, the house of woe,
And Dungeon of our Tyrant: Now possess,
As Lords, a spacious World, to our native Heaven
Little inferiour, by my adventure hard
With peril great atchiev'd. Long were to tell
What I have don, what sufferd, with what paine   *470*
Voyag'd th' unreal, vast, unbounded deep
Of horrible confusion, over which
By Sin and Death a broad way now is pav'd
To expedite your glorious march; but I
Toild out my uncouth passage, forc't to ride
Th' untractable Abysse, plung'd in the womb
Of unoriginal *Night* and *Chaos* wilde,
That jealous of thir secrets fiercely oppos'd

My journey strange, with clamorous uproare
Protesting Fate supreame; thence how I found 480
The new created World, which fame in Heav'n
Long had foretold, a Fabrick wonderful
Of absolute perfection, therein Man
Plac't in a Paradise, by our exile
Made happie: Him by fraud I have seduc'd
From his Creator, and the more to increase
Your wonder, with an Apple; he thereat
Offended, worth your laughter, hath giv'n up
Both his beloved Man and all his World,
To Sin and Death a prey, and so to us, 490
Without our hazard, labour, or allarme,
To range in, and to dwell, and over Man,
To rule, as over all he should have rul'd.
True is, mee also he hath judg'd, or rather
Mee not, but the brute Serpent in whose shape
Man I deceav'd: that which to mee belongs,
Is enmity, which he will put between
Mee and Mankinde; I am to bruise his heel;
His Seed, when is not set, shall bruise my head:
A World who would not purchase with a bruise, 500
Or much more grievous pain? Ye have th' account
Of my performance: What remaines, ye Gods,
But up and enter now into full bliss.
   So having said, a while he stood, expecting
Thir universal shout and high applause
To fill his eare, when contrary he hears
On all sides, from innumerable tongues
A dismal universal hiss, the sound
Of public scorn; he wonderd, but not long
Had leasure, wondring at himself now more; 510
His Visage drawn he felt to sharp and spare,
His Armes clung to his Ribs, his Leggs entwining
Each other, till supplanted down he fell
A monstrous Serpent on his Belly prone,
Reluctant, but in vaine, a greater power
Now rul'd him, punisht in the shape he sin'd,
According to his doom: he would have spoke,
But hiss for hiss returnd with forked tongue
To forked tongue, for now were all transform'd
Alike, to Serpents all as accessories 520
To his bold Riot: dreadful was the din
Of hissing through the Hall, thick swarming now
With complicated monsters, head and taile,
Scorpion and Asp, and *Amphisbæna* dire,

Cerastes hornd, *Hydrus*, and *Ellops* drear,
And *Dipsas* (Not so thick swarm'd once the Soil
Bedropt with blood of *Gorgon*, or the Isle
Ophiusa) but still greatest hee the midst,
Now Dragon grown, larger then whom the Sun
Ingenderd in the *Pythian* Vale on slime,   *530*
Huge *Python*, and his Power no less he seem'd
Above the rest still to retain; they all
Him follow'd issuing forth to th' open Field,
Where all yet left of that revolted Rout
Heav'n-fall'n, in station stood or just array,
Sublime with expectation when to see
In Triumph issuing forth thir glorious Chief;
They saw, but other sight instead, a crowd
Of ugly Serpents; horror on them fell,
And horrid sympathie; for what they saw,   *540*
They felt themselvs now changing; down thir arms,
Down fell both Spear and Shield, down they as fast,
And the dire hiss renew'd, and the dire form
Catcht by Contagion, like in punishment,
As in thir crime. Thus was th' applause they meant,
Turnd to exploding hiss, triumph to shame
Cast on themselves from thir own mouths. There stood
A Grove hard by, sprung up with this thir change,
His will who reigns above, to aggravate
Thir penance, laden with fair Fruit, like that   *550*
Which grew in Paradise, the bait of *Eve*
Us'd by the Tempter: on that prospect strange
Thir earnest eyes they fix'd, imagining
For one forbidden Tree a multitude
Now ris'n, to work them furder woe or shame;
Yet parcht with scalding thurst and hunger fierce,
Though to delude them sent, could not obstain,
But on they rould in heaps, and up the Trees
Climbing, sat thicker than the snakie locks
That curld *Megæra*: greedily they pluck'd   *560*
The Frutage fair to sight, like that which grew
Neer that bituminous Lake where *Sodom* flam'd;
This more delusive, not the touch, but taste
Deceav'd; they fondly thinking to allay
Thir appetite with gust, instead of Fruit
Chewd bitter Ashes, which th' offended taste
With spattering noise rejected: oft they assayd,
Hunger and thirst constraining, drugd as oft,
With hatefullest disrelish writh'd thir jaws
With soot and cinders fill'd; so oft they fell   *570*

Into the same illusion, not as Man
Whom they triumph'd once lapst. Thus were they
    plagu'd
And worn with Famin, long and ceasless hiss,
Till thir lost shape, permitted, they resum'd,
Yearly enjoynd, some say, to undergo
This annual humbling certain number'd days,
To dash thir pride, and joy for Man seduc't.
However some tradition they dispers'd
Among the Heathen of thir purchase got,
And Fabl'd how the Serpent, whom they calld   580
Ophion with *Eurynome*, the wide-
Encroaching *Eve* perhaps, had first the rule
Of high *Olympus*, thence by *Saturn* driv'n
And *Ops*, ere yet *Dictæan Jove* was born.
Mean while in Paradise the hellish pair
Too soon arriv'd, *Sin* there in power before,
Once actual, now in body, and to dwell
Habitual habitant; behind her *Death*
Close following pace for pace, not mounted yet
On his pale Horse: to whom *Sin* thus began.   590
    Second of *Satan* sprung, all conquering *Death*,
What thinkst thou of our Empire now, though earnd
With travail difficult, not better farr
Then stil at Hels dark threshold to have sate watch,
Unnam'd, undreaded, and thy self half starv'd?
    Whom thus the Sin-born Monster answerd soon.
To mee, who with eternal Famin pine,
Alike is Hell, or Paradise, or Heaven,
There best, where most with ravin I may meet;
Which here, though plenteous, all too little seems   600
To stuff this Maw, this vast unhide-bound Corps.
    To whom th' incestuous Mother thus repli'd.
Thou therefore on these Herbs, and Fruits, & Flours
Feed first, on each Beast next, and Fish, and Fowle,
No homely morsels, and whatever thing
The Sithe of Time mowes down, devour unspar'd,
Till I in Man residing through the Race,
His thoughts, his looks, words, actions all infect,
And season him thy last and sweetest prey.
    This said, they both betook them several wayes,   610
Both to destroy, or unimmortal make
All kinds, and for destruction to mature
Sooner or later; which th' Almightie seeing
From his transcendent Seat the Saints among,
To those bright Orders uttered thus his voice.

See with what heat these Dogs of Hell advance
To waste and havoc yonder World, which I
So fair and good created, and had still
Kept in that state, had not the folly of Man
Let in these wastful Furies, who impute   *620*
Folly to mee, so doth the Prince of Hell
And his Adherents, that with so much ease
I suffer them to enter and possess
A place so heav'nly, and conniving seem
To gratifie my scornful Enemies,
That laugh, as if transported with some fit
Of Passion, I to them had quitted all,
At random yeilded up to their misrule;
And know not that I call'd and drew them thither
My Hell-hounds, to lick up the draff and filth   *630*
Which mans polluting Sin with taint hath shed
On what was pure, till cramm'd and gorg'd, nigh burst
With suckt and glutted offal, at one sling
Of thy victorious Arm, well-pleasing Son,
Both *Sin*, and *Death*, and yawning *Grave* at last
Through *Chaos* hurld, obstruct the mouth of Hell
For ever, and seal up his ravenous Jawes.
Then Heav'n and Earth renewd shall be made pure
To sanctitie that shall receive no staine:
Till then the Curse pronounc't on both precedes.   *640*
   Hee ended, and the heav'nly Audience loud
Sung *Halleluia*, as the sound of Seas,
Through multitude that sung: Just are thy ways,
Righteous are thy Decrees on all thy Works;
Who can extenuate thee? Next, to the Son,
Destin'd restorer of Mankind, by whom
New Heav'n and Earth shall to the Ages rise,
Or down from Heav'n descend. Such was thir song,
While the Creator calling forth by name
His mightie Angels gave them several charge,   *650*
As sorted best with present things. The Sun
Had first his precept so to move, so shine,
As might affect the Earth with cold and heat
Scarce tollerable, and from the North to call
Decrepit Winter, from the South to bring
Solstitial summers heat. To the blanc Moone
Her office they prescrib'd, to th' other five
Thir planetarie motions and aspects
In *Sextile*, *Square*, and *Trine*, and *Opposite*,
Of noxious efficacie, and when to joyne   *660*
In Synod unbenigne, and taught the fixt

Thir influence malignant when to showre,
Which of them rising with the Sun, or falling,
Should prove tempestuous: To the Winds they set
Thir corners, when with bluster to confound
Sea, Aire, and Shoar, the Thunder when to rowle
With terror through the dark Aereal Hall.
Some say he bid his Angels turne ascanse
The Poles of Earth twice ten degrees and more
From the Suns Axle; they with labour push'd   670
Oblique the Centric Globe: Som say the Sun
Was bid turn Reines from th' Equinoctial Rode
Like distant breadth to *Taurus* with the Seav'n
Atlantick Sisters, and the *Spartan* Twins
Up to the *Tropic* Crab; thence down amaine
By *Leo* and the *Virgin* and the *Scales*,
As deep as *Capricorne*, to bring in change
Of Seasons to each Clime; else had the Spring
Perpetual smil'd on Earth with vernant Flours,
Equal in Days and Nights, except to those   680
Beyond the Polar Circles; to them Day
Had unbenighted shon, while the low Sun
To recompence his distance, in thir sight
Had rounded still th' *Horizon*, and not known
Or East or West, which had forbid the Snow
From cold *Estotiland*, and South as farr
Beneath *Magellan*. At that tasted Fruit
The Sun, as from *Thyestean* Banquet, turn'd
His course intended; else how had the World
Inhabited, though sinless, more then now,   690
Avoided pinching cold and scorching heate?
These changes in the Heav'ns, though slow, produc'd
Like change on Sea and Land, sideral blast,
Vapour, and Mist, and Exhalation hot,
Corrupt and Pestilent: Now from the North
Of *Norumbega*, and the *Samoed* shoar
Bursting thir brazen Dungeon, armd with ice
And snow and haile and stormie gust and flaw,
Boreas and *Cæcias* and *Argestes* loud
And *Thrascias* rend the Woods and Seas upturn;   700
With adverse blast up-turns them from the South
Notus and *Afer* black with thundrous Clouds
From *Serraliona;* thwart of these as fierce
Forth rush the *Levant* and the *Ponent* Windes
Eurus and *Zephir* with thir lateral noise,
Sirocco, and *Libecchio*. Thus began
Outrage from liveless things; but Discord first

Daughter of Sin, among th' irrational,
Death introduc'd through fierce antipathie:
Beast now with Beast gan war, & Fowle with Fowle, 710
And Fish with Fish; to graze the Herb all leaving,
Devour'd each other; nor stood much in awe
Of Man, but fled him, or with count'nance grim
Glar'd on him passing: these were from without
The growing miseries, which *Adam* saw
Alreadie in part, though hid in gloomiest shade,
To sorrow abandond, but worse felt within,
And in a troubl'd Sea of passion tost,
Thus to disburd'n sought with sad complaint.
   O miserable of happie! is this the end 720
Of this new glorious World, and mee so late
The Glory of that Glory, who now becom
Accurst of blessed, hide me from the face
Of God, whom to behold was then my highth
Of happiness: yet well, if here would end
The miserie, I deserv'd it, and would beare
My own deservings; but this will not serve;
All that I eate or drink, or shall beget,
Is propagated curse. O voice once heard
Delightfully, *Encrease and multiply*, 730
Now death to heare! for what can I encrease
Or multiplie, but curses on my head?
Who of all Ages to succeed, but feeling
The evil on him brought by me, will curse
My Head, Ill fare our Ancestor impure,
For this we may thank *Adam*; but his thanks
Shall be the execration; so besides
Mine own that bide upon me, all from mee
Shall with a fierce reflux on mee redound,
On mee as on thir natural center light 740
Heavie, though in thir place. O fleeting joyes
Of Paradise, deare bought with lasting woes!
Did I request thee, Maker, from my Clay
To mould me Man, did I sollicite thee
From darkness to promote me, or here place
In this delicious Garden? as my Will
Concurd not to my being, it were but right
And equal to reduce me to my dust,
Desirous to resigne, and render back
All I receav'd, unable to performe 750
Thy terms too hard, by which I was to hold
The good I sought not. To the loss of that,
Sufficient penaltie, why hast thou added

The sense of endless woes? inexplicable
Thy Justice seems; yet to say truth, too late,
I thus contest; then should have been refusd
Those terms whatever, when they were propos'd:
Thou didst accept them; wilt thou enjoy the good,
Then cavil the conditions? and though God
Made thee without thy leave, what if thy Son   760
Prove disobedient, and reprov'd, retort,
Wherefore didst thou beget me? I sought it not:
Wouldst thou admit for his contempt of thee
That proud excuse? yet him not thy election,
But Natural necessity begot.
God made thee of choice his own, and of his own
To serve him, thy reward was of his grace,
Thy punishment then justly is at his Will.
Be it so, for I submit, his doom is fair,
That dust I am, and shall to dust returne: 770
O welcom hour whenever! why delayes
His hand to execute what his Decree
Fixd on this day? why do I overlive,
Why am I mockt with death, and length'nd out
To deathless pain? how gladly would I meet
Mortalitie my sentence, and be Earth
Insensible, how glad would lay me down
As in my Mothers lap? there I should rest
And sleep secure; his dreadful voice no more
Would Thunder in my ears, no fear of worse   780
To mee and to my ofspring would torment me
With cruel expectation. Yet one doubt
Pursues me still, least all I cannot die,
Least that pure breath of Life, the Spirit of Man
Which God inspir'd, cannot together perish
With this corporeal Clod; then in the Grave,
Or in some other dismal place, who knows
But I shall die a living Death? O thought
Horrid, if true! yet why? it was but breath
Of Life that sinn'd; what dies but what had life   790
And sin? the Bodie properly hath neither.
All of me then shall die: let this appease
The doubt, since humane reach no further knows.
For though the Lord of all be infinite,
Is his wrauth also? be it, man is not so,
But mortal doom'd. How can he exercise
Wrath without end on Man whom Death must end?
Can he make deathless Death? that were to make
Strange contradiction, which to God himself

Impossible is held, as Argument 800
Of weakness, not of Power. Will he draw out,
For angers sake, finite to infinite
In punisht man, to satisfie his rigour
Satisfi'd never; that were to extend
His Sentence beyond dust and Natures Law,
By which all Causes else according still
To the reception of thir matter act,
Not to th' extent of thir own Spheare. But say
That Death be not one stroak, as I suppos'd,
Bereaving sense, but endless miserie 810
From this day onward, which I feel begun
Both in me, and without me, and so last
To perpetuitie; Ay me, that fear
Comes thundring back with dreadful revolution
On my defensless head; both Death and I
Am found Eternal, and incorporate both,
Nor I on my part single, in mee all
Posteritie stands curst: Fair Patrimonie
That I must leave ye, Sons; O were I able
To waste it all my self, and leave ye none! 820
So disinherited how would ye bless
Me now your Curse! Ah, why should all mankind
For one mans fault thus guiltless be condemn'd,
If guiltless? But from mee what can proceed,
But all corrupt, both Mind and Will deprav'd,
Not to do onely, but to will the same
With me; how can they acquitted stand
In sight of God? Him after all Disputes
Forc't I absolve: all my evasions vain
And reasonings, though through Mazes, leads me still 830
But to my own conviction: first and last
On mee, mee onely, as the sourse and spring
Of all corruption, all the blame lights due;
So might the wrauth. Fond wish! couldst thou support
That burden heavier then the Earth to bear,
Then all the World much heavier, though divided
With that bad Woman? Thus what thou desir'st,
And what thou fearst, alike destroyes all hope
Of refuge, and concludes thee miserable
Beyond all past example and future, 840
To *Satan* onely like both crime and doom.
O Conscience, into what Abyss of fears
And horrors hast thou driv'n me; out of which
I find no way, from deep to deeper plung'd!
   Thus *Adam* to himself lamented loud

Through the still Night, not now, as ere man fell,
Wholsom and cool, and mild, but with black Air
Accompanied, with damps and dreadful gloom,
Which to his evil Conscience represented
All things with double terror: On the ground   *850*
Outstretcht he lay, on the cold ground, and oft
Curs'd his Creation, Death as oft accus'd
Of tardie execution, since denounc't
The day of his offence. Why comes not Death,
Said hee, with one thrice acceptable stroke
To end me? Shall Truth fail to keep her word,
Justice Divine not hast'n to be just?
But Death comes not at call, Justice Divine
Mends not her slowest pace for prayers or cries.
O Woods, O Fountains, Hillocks, Dales and Bowrs, *860*
With other echo late I taught your Shades
To answer, and resound farr other Song.
Whom thus afflicted when sad *Eve* beheld,
Desolate where she sate, approaching nigh,
Soft words to his fierce passion she assay'd:
But her with stern regard he thus repell'd.

   Out of my sight, thou Serpent, that name best
Befits thee with him leagu'd, thy self as false
And hateful; nothing wants, but that thy shape,
Like his, and colour Serpentine may shew   *870*
Thy inward fraud, to warn all Creatures from thee
Henceforth; least that too heav'nly form, pretended
To hellish falshood, snare them. But for thee
I had persisted happie, had not thy pride
And wandring vanitie, when lest was safe,
Rejected my forewarning, and disdain'd
Not to be trusted, longing to be seen
Though by the Devil himself, him overweening
To over-reach, but with the Serpent meeting
Fool'd and beguil'd, by him thou, I by thee,   *880*
To trust thee from my side, imagin'd wise,
Constant, mature, proof against all assaults,
And understood not all was but a shew
Rather then solid vertu, all but a Rib
Crooked by nature, bent, as now appears,
More to the part sinister from me drawn,
Well if thrown out, as supernumerarie
To my just number found. O why did God,
Creator wise, that peopl'd highest Heav'n
With Spirits Masculine, create at last   *890*
This noveltie on Earth, this fair defect

Of Nature, and not fill the World at once
With Men as Angels without Feminine,
Or find some other way to generate
Mankind? this mischief had not then befall'n,
And more that shall befall, innumerable
Disturbances on Earth through Femal snares,
And straight conjunction with this Sex: for either
He never shall find out fit Mate, but such
As some misfortune brings him, or mistake,   *900*
Or whom he wishes most shall seldom gain
Through her perverseness, but shall see her gaind
By a farr worse, or if she love, withheld
By Parents, or his happiest choice too late
Shall meet, alreadie linkt and Wedlock-bound
To a fell Adversarie, his hate or shame:
Which infinite calamitie shall cause
To Humane life, and houshold peace confound.

   He added not, and from her turn'd, but *Eve*
Not so repulst, with Tears that ceas'd not flowing,   *910*
And tresses all disorderd, at his feet
Fell humble, and imbracing them, besaught
His peace, and thus proceeded in her plaint.

   Forsake me not thus, *Adam*, witness Heav'n
What love sincere, and reverence in my heart
I beare thee, and unweeting have offended,
Unhappilie deceav'd; thy suppliant
I beg, and clasp thy knees; bereave me not,
Whereon I live, thy gentle looks, thy aid,
Thy counsel in this uttermost distress,   *920*
My onely strength and stay: forlorn of thee,
Whither shall I betake me, where subsist?
While yet we live, scarse one short hour perhaps,
Between us two let there be peace, both joyning,
As joyn'd in injuries, one enmitie
Against a Foe by doom express assign'd us,
That cruel Serpent: On me exercise not
Thy hatred for this miserie befall'n,
On me already lost, mee, then thy self
More miserable; both have sin'd, but thou   *930*
Against God onely, I against God and thee,
And to the place of judgement will return,
There with my cries importune Heaven, that all
The sentence from thy head remov'd may light
On me, sole cause to thee of all this woe,
Mee mee onely just object of his ire.

   She ended weeping, and her lowlie plight,

Immoveable till peace obtain'd from fault
Acknowledg'd and deplor'd, in *Adam* wraught
Commiseration; soon his heart relented
Towards her, his life so late and sole delight,
Now at his feet submissive in distress,
Creature so faire his reconcilement seeking,
His counsel whom she had displeas'd, his aide;
As one disarm'd, his anger all he lost,
And thus with peaceful words uprais'd her soon.

    Unwarie, and too desirous, as before,
So now of what thou knowst not, who desir'st
The punishment all on thy self; alas,
Beare thine own first, ill able to sustaine
His full wrauth whose thou feelst as yet lest part,
And my displeasure bearst so ill. If Prayers
Could alter high Decrees, I to that place
Would speed before thee, and be louder heard,
That on my head all might be visited,
Thy frailtie and infirmer Sex forgiv'n,
To me committed and by me expos'd.
But rise, let us no more contend, nor blame
Each other, blam'd enough elsewhere, but strive
In offices of Love, how we may light'n
Each others burden in our share of woe;
Since this days Death denounc't, if ought I see,
Will prove no sudden, but a slow-pac't evill,
A long days dying to augment our paine,
And to our Seed (O hapless Seed!) deriv'd.

    To whom thus *Eve*, recovering heart, repli'd.
Adam, by sad experiment I know
How little weight my words with thee can finde,
Found so erroneous, thence by just event
Found so unfortunate; nevertheless,
Restor'd by thee, vile as I am, to place
Of new acceptance, hopeful to regaine
Thy Love, the sole contentment of my heart,
Living or dying from thee I will not hide
What thoughts in my unquiet brest are ris'n,
Tending to som relief of our extremes,
Or end, though sharp and sad, yet tolerable,
As in our evils, and of easier choice.
If care of our descent perplex us most,
Which must be born to certain woe, devourd
By Death at last, and miserable it is
To be to others cause of misery,
Our own begotten, and of our Loines to bring

Into this cursed World a woful Race,
That after wretched Life must be at last
Food for so foule a Monster, in thy power
It lies, yet ere Conception to prevent
The Race unblest, to being yet unbegot.
Childless thou art, Childless remaine:
So Death shall be deceav'd his glut, and with us two   *990*
Be forc'd to satisfie his Rav'nous Maw.
But if thou judge it hard and difficult,
Conversing, looking, loving, to abstain
From Loves due Rites, Nuptial embraces sweet,
And with desire to languish without hope,
Before the present object languishing
With like desire, which would be miserie
And torment less then none of what we dread,
Then both our selves and Seed at once to free
From what we fear for both, let us make short,   *1000*
Let us seek Death, or hee not found, supply
With our own hands his Office on our selves;
Why stand we longer shivering under feares,
That shew no end but Death, and have the power,
Of many wayes to die the shortest choosing,
Destruction with destruction to destroy.
  She ended heer, or vehement despaire
Broke off the rest; so much of Death her thoughts
Had entertaind, as di'd her Cheeks with pale.
But *Adam* with such counsel nothing sway'd,   *1010*
To better hopes his more attentive minde
Labouring had rais'd, and thus to *Eve* repli'd.
  Eve, thy contempt of life and pleasure seems
To argue in thee somthing more sublime
And excellent then what thy minde contemnes;
But self-destruction therefore saught, refutes
That excellence thought in thee, and implies,
Not thy contempt, but anguish and regret
For loss of life and pleasure overlov'd.
Or if thou covet death, as utmost end   *1020*
Of miserie, so thinking to evade
The penaltie pronounc't, doubt not but God
Hath wiselier arm'd his vengeful ire then so
To be forestall'd; much more I fear least Death
So snatcht will not exempt us from the paine
We are by doom to pay; rather such acts
Of contumacie will provoke the highest
To make death in us live: Then let us seek
Som safer resolution, which methinks

I have in view, calling to minde with heed   *1030*
Part of our Sentence, that thy Seed shall bruise
The Serpents head; piteous amends, unless
Be meant, whom I conjecture, our grand Foe
Satan, who in the Serpent hath contriv'd
Against us this deceit: to crush his head
Would be revenge indeed; which will be lost
By death brought on our selves, or childless days
Resolv'd, as thou proposest; so our Foe
Shall scape his punishment ordain'd, and wee
Instead shall double ours upon our heads.   *1040*
No more be mention'd then of violence
Against our selves, and wilful barrenness,
That cuts us off from hope, and savours onely
Rancor and pride, impatience and despite,
Reluctance against God and his just yoke
Laid on our Necks. Remember with what mild
And gracious temper he both heard and judg'd
Without wrauth or reviling; wee expected
Immediate dissolution, which we thought
Was meant by Death that day, when lo, to thee   *1050*
Pains onely in Child-bearing were foretold,
And bringing forth, soon recompenc't with joy,
Fruit of thy Womb: On mee the Curse aslope
Glanc'd on the ground, with labour I must earne
My bread; what harm? Idleness had bin worse;
My labour will sustain me; and least Cold
Or Heat should injure us, his timely care
Hath unbesaught provided, and his hands
Cloath'd us unworthie, pitying while he judg'd;
How much more, if we pray him, will his ear   *1060*
Be open, and his heart to pitie incline,
And teach us further by what means to shun
Th' inclement Seasons, Rain, Ice, Hail and Snow,
Which now the Skie with various Face begins
To shew us in this Mountain, while the Winds
Blow moist and keen, shattering the graceful locks
Of these fair spreading Trees; which bids us seek
Som better shroud, som better warmth to cherish
Our Limbs benumm'd, ere this diurnal Starr
Leave cold the Night, how we his gather'd beams   *1070*
Reflected, may with matter sere foment,
Or by collision of two bodies grinde
The Air attrite to Fire, as late the Clouds
Justling or pusht with Winds rude in thir shock
Tine the slant Lightning, whose thwart flame driv'n down

Kindles the gummie bark of Firr or Pine,
And sends a comfortable heat from farr,
Which might supply the Sun: such Fire to use,
And what may else be remedie or cure
To evils which our own misdeeds have wrought, *1080*
Hee will instruct us praying, and of Grace
Beseeching him, so as we need not fear
To pass commodiously this life, sustain'd
By him with many comforts, till we end
In dust, our final rest and native home.
What better can we do, then to the place
Repairing where he judg'd us, prostrate fall
Before him reverent, and there confess
Humbly our faults, and pardon beg, with tears
Watering the ground, and with our sighs the Air *1090*
Frequenting, sent from hearts contrite, in sign
Of sorrow unfeign'd, and humiliation meek.
Undoubtedly he will relent and turn
From his displeasure; in whose look serene,
When angry most he seem'd and most severe,
What else but favor, grace, and mercie shon?
 So spake our Father penitent, nor *Eve*
Felt less remorse: they forthwith to the place
Repairing where he judg'd them prostrate fell
Before him reverent, and both confess'd *1100*
Humbly thir faults, and pardon beg'd, with tears
Watering the ground, and with thir sighs the Air
Frequenting, sent from hearts contrite, in sign
Of sorrow unfeign'd, and humiliation meek.

BOOK XI

THE ARGUMENT

The Son of God presents to his Father the Prayers of our first Parents now repenting, and intercedes for them: God accepts them, but declares that they must no longer abide in Paradise; sends Michael *with a Band of Cherubim to dispossess them; but first to reveal to* Adam *future things:* Michaels *coming down.* Adam *shews to* Eve *certain ominous signs; he discerns* Michaels *approach, goes out to meet him: the Angel denounces thir departure.* Eve's *Lamentation.* Adam *pleads, but submits: The Angel leads him up to a high Hill, sets before him in vision what shall happ'n till the Flood.*

THUS they in lowliest plight repentant stood
Praying, for from the Mercie-seat above
Prevenient Grace descending had remov'd
The stonie from thir hearts, and made new flesh
Regenerate grow instead, that sighs now breath'd
Unutterable, which the Spirit of prayer
Inspir'd, and wing'd for Heav'n with speedier flight
Then loudest Oratorie: yet thir port
Not of mean suiters, nor important less
Seem'd thir Petition, then when th' ancient Pair   10
In Fables old, less ancient yet then these,
Deucalion and chaste *Pyrrha* to restore
The Race of Mankind drownd, before the Shrine
Of *Themis* stood devout. To Heav'n thir prayers
Flew up, nor missd the way, by envious windes
Blow'n vagabond or frustrate: in they passd
Dimentionless through Heav'nly dores; then clad
With incense, where the Golden Altar fum'd,
By thir great Intercessor, came in sight
Before the Fathers Throne: Them the glad Son   20
Presenting, thus to intercede began.

See Father, what first fruits on Earth are sprung
From thy implanted Grace in Man, these Sighs
And Prayers, which in this Golden Censer, mixt
With Incense, I thy Priest before thee bring,
Fruits of more pleasing savour from thy seed
Sow'n with contrition in his heart, then those
Which his own hand manuring all the Trees
Of Paradise could have produc't, ere fall'n
From innocence. Now therefore bend thine eare   30
To supplication, heare his sighs though mute;
Unskilful with what words to pray, let mee

299

Interpret for him, mee his Advocate
And propitiation, all his works on mee
Good or not good ingraft, my Merit those
Shall perfet, and for these my Death shall pay.
Accept me, and in mee from these receave
The smell of peace toward Mankinde, let him live
Before thee reconcil'd, at least his days
Numberd, though sad, till Death, his doom (which I   40
To mitigate thus plead, not to reverse)
To better life shall yeeld him, where with mee
All my redeemd may dwell in joy and bliss,
Made one with me as I with thee am one.
    To whom the Father, without Cloud, serene.
All thy request for Man, accepted Son,
Obtain, all thy request was my Decree:
But longer in that Paradise to dwell,
The Law I gave to Nature him forbids:
Those pure immortal Elements that know   50
No gross, no unharmoneous mixture foule,
Eject him tainted now, and purge him off
As a distemper, gross to aire as gross,
And mortal food, as may dispose him best
For dissolution wrought by Sin, that first
Distemperd all things, and of incorrupt
Corrupted. I at first with two fair gifts
Created him endowd, with Happiness
And Immortalitie: that fondly lost,
This other serv'd but to eternize woe;   60
Till I provided Death; so Death becomes
His final remedie, and after Life
Tri'd in sharp tribulation, and refin'd
By Faith and faithful works, to second Life,
Wak't in the renovation of the just,
Resignes him up with Heav'n and Earth renewd.
But let us call to Synod all the Blest
Through Heavn's wide bounds; from them I will not hide
My judgments, how with Mankind I proceed,
As how with peccant Angels late they saw;   70
And in thir state, though firm, stood more confirmd.
    He ended, and the Son gave signal high
To the bright Minister that watch'd, hee blew
His Trumpet, heard in *Oreb* since perhaps
When God descended, and perhaps once more
To sound at general doom. Th' Angelic blast
Filld all the Regions: from thir blissful Bowrs

Of *Amarantin* Shade, Fountain or Spring,
By the waters of Life, where ere they sate
In fellowships of joy: the Sons of Light   *80*
Hasted, resorting to the Summons high,
And took thir Seats; till from his Throne supream
Th' Almighty thus pronounc'd his sovran Will.

   O Sons, like one of us Man is become
To know both Good and Evil, since his taste
Of that defended Fruit; but let him boast
His knowledge of Good lost, and Evil got,
Happier, had it suffic'd him to have known
Good by it self, and Evil not at all.
He sorrows now, repents, and prayes contrite,   *90*
My motions in him, longer then they move,
His heart I know, how variable and vain
Self-left. Least therefore his now bolder hand
Reach also of the Tree of Life, and eat,
And live for ever, dream at least to live
For ever, to remove him I decree,
And send him from the Garden forth to Till
The Ground whence he was taken, fitter soile.

   Michael, this my behest have thou in charge,
Take to thee from among the Cherubim   *100*
Thy choice of flaming Warriours, least the Fiend
Or in behalf of Man, or to invade
Vacant possession som new trouble raise:
Hast thee, and from the Paradise of God
Without remorse drive out the sinful Pair,
From hallowd ground th' unholie, and denounce
To them and to thir Progenie from thence
Perpetual banishment. Yet least they faint
At the sad Sentence rigorously urg'd,
For I behold them soft'nd and with tears   *110*
Bewailing thir excess, all terror hide.
If patiently thy bidding they obey,
Dismiss them not disconsolate; reveale
To *Adam* what shall come in future dayes,
As I shall thee enlighten, intermix
My Cov'nant in the Womans seed renewd;
So send them forth, though sorrowing, yet in peace:
And on the East side of the Garden place,
Where entrance up from *Eden* easiest climbes,
Cherubic watch, and of a Sword the flame   *120*
Wide waving, all approach farr off to fright,
And guard all passage to the Tree of Life:
Least Paradise a receptacle prove

To Spirits foule, and all my Trees thir prey,
With whose stol'n Fruit Man once more to delude.
   He ceas'd; and th' Archangelic Power prepar'd
For swift descent, with him the Cohort bright
Of watchful Cherubim; four faces each
Had, like a double *Janus*, all thir shape
Spangl'd with eyes more numerous then those   *130*
Of *Argus*, and more wakeful then to drouze,
Charm'd with *Arcadian* Pipe, the Pastoral Reed
Of *Hermes*, or his opiate Rod. Mean while
To resalute the World with sacred Light
Leucothea wak'd, and with fresh dews imbalmd
The Earth, when *Adam* and first Matron *Eve*
Had ended now thir Orisons, and found,
Strength added from above, new hope to spring
Out of despaire, joy, but with fear yet linkt;
Which thus to *Eve* his welcome words renewd.   *140*
   Eve, easily may Faith admit, that all
The good which we enjoy, from Heav'n descends
But that from us ought should ascend to Heav'n
So prevalent as to concerne the mind
Of God high-blest, or to incline his will,
Hard to belief may seem; yet this will Prayer,
Or one short sigh of humane breath, up-borne
Ev'n to the Seat of God. For since I saught
By Prayer th' offended Deitie to appease,
Kneel'd and before him humbl'd all my heart,   *150*
Methought I saw him placable and mild,
Bending his eare; perswasion in me grew
That I was heard with favour; peace return'd
Home to my brest, and to my memorie
His promise, that thy Seed shall bruise our Foe;
Which then not minded in dismay, yet now
Assures me that the bitterness of death
Is past, and we shall live. Whence Haile to thee
Eve rightly call'd, Mother of all Mankind,
Mother of all things living, since by thee   *160*
Man is to live, and all things live for Man.
   To whom thus *Eve* with sad demeanour meek.
Ill worthie I such title should belong
To me transgressour, who for thee ordaind
A help, became thy snare; to mee reproach
Rather belongs, distrust and all dispraise:
But infinite in pardon was my Judge,
That I who first brought Death on all, am grac't
The sourse of life; next favourable thou,

Who highly thus to entitle me voutsaf'st, *170*
Farr other name deserving. But the Field
To labour calls us now with sweat impos'd,
Though after sleepless Night; for see the Morn,
All unconcern'd with our unrest, begins
Her rosie progress smiling; let us forth,
I never from thy side henceforth to stray,
Wherere our days work lies, though now enjoind
Laborious, till day droop; while here we dwell,
What can be toilsom in these pleasant Walkes?
Here let us live, though in fall'n state, content. *180*

   So spake, so wish'd much humbl'd *Eve*, but Fate
Subscrib'd not; Nature first gave Signs, imprest
On Bird, Beast, Aire, Aire suddenly eclips'd
After short blush of Morn; nigh in her sight
The Bird of *Jove*, stoopt from his aerie tour,
Two Birds of gayest plume before him drove:
Down from a Hill the Beast that reigns in Woods,
First Hunter then, pursu'd a gentle brace,
Goodliest of all the Forrest, Hart and Hinde;
Direct to th' Eastern Gate was bent thir flight. *190*
Adam observ'd, and with his Eye the chase
Pursuing, not unmov'd to *Eve* thus spake.

   O *Eve*, some furder change awaits us nigh,
Which Heav'n by these mute signs in Nature shews
Forerunners of his purpose, or to warn
Us haply too secure of our discharge
From penaltie, because from death releast
Some days; how long, and what till then our life,
Who knows, or more then this, that we are dust,
And thither must return and be no more. *200*
Why else this double object in our sight
Of flight pursu'd in th' Air and ore the ground
One way the self-same hour? why in the East
Darkness ere Dayes mid-course, and Morning light
More orient in yon Western Cloud that draws
O're the blew Firmament a radiant white,
And slow descends, with somthing heav'nly fraught.

   He err'd not, for by this the heav'nly Bands
Down from a Skie of Jasper lighted now
In Paradise, and on a Hill made alt, *210*
A glorious Apparition, had not doubt
And carnal fear that day dimm'd *Adams* eye.
Not that more glorious, when the Angels met
Jacob in *Mahanaim*, where he saw
The field Pavilion'd with his Guardians bright;

Nor that which on the flaming Mount appeerd
In *Dothan*, cover'd with a Camp of Fire,
Against the *Syrian* King, who to surprize
One man, Assassin-like had levied Warr,
Warr unproclam'd. The Princely Hierarch   220
In thir bright stand, there left his Powers to seise
Possession of the Garden; hee alone,
To finde where *Adam* shelterd, took his way,
Not unperceav'd of *Adam*, who to *Eve*,
While the great Visitant approachd, thus spake.
   Eve, now expect great tidings, which perhaps
Of us will soon determin, or impose
New Laws to be observ'd; for I descrie
From yonder blazing Cloud that veils the Hill
One of the heav'nly Host, and by his Gate   230
None of the meanest, some great Potentate
Or of the Thrones above, such Majestie
Invests him coming; yet not terrible,
That I should fear, nor sociably mild,
As *Raphael*, that I should much confide,
But solemn and sublime, whom not to offend,
With reverence I must meet, and thou retire.
He ended; and th' Arch-Angel soon drew nigh,
Not in his shape Celestial, but as Man
Clad to meet Man; over his lucid Armes   240
A militarie Vest of purple flowd
Livelier then *Melibæan*, or the graine
Of *Sarra*, worn by Kings and Hero's old
In time of Truce; *Iris* had dipt the wooff;
His starrie Helme unbuckl'd shew'd him prime
In Manhood where Youth ended; by his side
As in a glistering *Zodiac* hung the Sword,
Satans dire dread, and in his hand the Spear.
Adam bowd low, hee Kingly from his State
Inclin'd not, but his coming thus declar'd.   250
   Adam, Heav'ns high behest no Preface needs:
Sufficient that thy Prayers are heard, and Death,
Then due by sentence when thou didst transgress,
Defeated of his seisure many dayes
Giv'n thee of Grace, wherein thou may'st repent,
And one bad act with many deeds well done
Mayst cover: well may then thy Lord appeas'd
Redeem thee quite from Deaths rapacious claime;
But longer in this Paradise to dwell
Permits not; to remove thee I am come,   260
And send thee from the Garden forth to till

The ground whence thou wast tak'n, fitter Soile.
   He added not, for *Adam* at the newes
Heart-strook with chilling gripe of sorrow stood,
That all his senses bound; *Eve*, who unseen
Yet all had heard, with audible lament
Discover'd soon the place of her retire.
   O unexspected stroke, worse then of Death!
Must I thus leave thee Paradise? thus leave
Thee Native Soile, these happie Walks and Shades,   270
Fit haunt of Gods? where I had hope to spend,
Quiet though sad, the respit of that day
That must be mortal to us both. O flours,
That never will in other Climate grow,
My early visitation, and my last
At Eev'n, which I bred up with tender hand
From the first op'ning bud, and gave ye Names,
Who now shall reare ye to the Sun, or ranke
Your Tribes, and water from th' ambrosial Fount?
Thee lastly nuptial Bowre, by mee adornd   280
With what to sight or smell was sweet; from thee
How shall I part, and whither wander down
Into a lower World, to this obscure
And wilde, how shall we breath in other Aire
Less pure, accustomd to immortal Fruits?
   Whom thus the Angel interrupted milde.
Lament not *Eve*, but patiently resigne
What justly thou hast lost; nor set thy heart,
Thus over fond, on that which is not thine;
Thy going is not lonely, with thee goes   290
Thy Husband, him to follow thou art bound;
Where he abides, think there thy native soile.
   Adam by this from the cold sudden damp
Recovering, and his scatterd spirits returnd,
To *Michael* thus his humble words addressd.
   Celestial, whether among the Thrones, or nam'd
Of them the Highest, for such of shape may seem
Prince above Princes, gently hast thou tould
Thy message, which might else in telling wound,
And in performing end us; what besides   300
Of sorrow and dejection and despair
Our frailtie can sustain, thy tidings bring,
Departure from this happy place, our sweet
Recess, and onely consolation left
Familiar to our eyes, all places else
Inhospitable appeer and desolate,
Nor knowing us nor known: and if by prayer

Incessant I could hope to change the will
Of him who all things can, I would not cease
To wearie him with my assiduous cries: 310
But prayer against his absolute Decree
No more availes then breath against the winde,
Blown stifling back on him that breaths it forth:
Therefore to his great bidding I submit.
This most afflicts me, that departing hence,
As from his face I shall be hid, deprivd
His blessed count'nance; here I could frequent,
With worship, place by place where he voutsaf'd
Presence Divine, and to my Sons relate;
On this Mount he appeerd, under this Tree 320
Stood visible, among these Pines his voice
I heard, here with him at this Fountain talk'd:
So many grateful Altars I would reare
Of grassie Terfe, and pile up every Stone
Of lustre from the brook, in memorie,
Or monument to Ages, and thereon
Offer sweet smelling Gumms & Fruits and Flours:
In yonder nether World where shall I seek
His bright appearances, or footstep trace?
For though I fled him angrie, yet recall'd 330
To life prolongd and promisd Race, I now
Gladly behold though but his utmost skirts
Of glory, and farr off his steps adore.
    To whom thus *Michael* with regard benigne.
Adam, thou know'st Heav'n his, and all the Earth,
Not this Rock onely; his Omnipresence fills
Land, Sea, and Aire, and every kinde that lives,
Fomented by his virtual power and warmd:
All th' Earth he gave thee to possess and rule,
No despicable gift; surmise not then 340
His presence to these narrow bounds confin'd
Of Paradise or *Eden:* this had been
Perhaps thy Capital Seate, from whence had spred
All generations, and had hither come
From all the ends of th' Earth, to celebrate
And reverence thee thir great Progenitor.
But this præeminence thou hast lost, brought down
To dwell on eeven ground now with thy Sons:
Yet doubt not but in Vallie and in Plaine
God is as here, and will be found alike 350
Present, and of his presence many a signe
Still following thee, still compassing thee round
With goodness and paternal Love, his Face

Express, and of his steps the track Divine.
Which that thou mayst beleeve, and be confirmd,
Ere thou from hence depart, know I am sent
To shew thee what shall come in future dayes
To thee and to thy ofspring; good with bad
Expect to hear, supernal Grace contending
With sinfulness of Men; thereby to learn   360
True patience, and to temper joy with fear
And pious sorrow, equally enur'd
By moderation either state to beare,
Prosperous or adverse: so shalt thou lead
Safest thy life, and best prepar'd endure
Thy mortal passage when it comes. Ascend
This Hill; let *Eve* (for I have drencht her eyes)
Here sleep below while thou to foresight wak'st,
As once thou slepst, while Shee to life was formd.
   To whom thus *Adam* gratefully repli'd.   370
Ascend, I follow thee, safe Guide, the path
Thou lead'st me, and to the hand of Heav'n submit,
However chast'ning, to the evil turne
My obvious breast, arming to overcom
By suffering, and earne rest from labour won,
If so I may attain. So both ascend
In the Visions of God: It was a Hill
Of Paradise the highest, from whose top
The Hemisphere of Earth in cleerest Ken
Stretcht out to amplest reach of prospect lay.   380
Not higher that Hill nor wider looking round,
Whereon for different cause the Tempter set
Our second *Adam* in the Wilderness,
To shew him all Earths Kingdomes and thir Glory.
His Eye might there command wherever stood
City of old or modern Fame, the Seat
Of mightiest Empire, from the destind Walls
Of *Cambalu*, seat of *Cathaian Can*
And *Samarchand* by *Oxus*, *Temirs* Throne,
To *Paquin* of *Sinæan* Kings, and thence   390
To *Agra* and *Lahor* of great *Mogul*
Down to the golden *Chersonese*, or where
The *Persian* in *Ecbatan* sate, or since
In *Hispahan*, or where the *Russian Ksar*
In *Mosco*, or the Sultan in *Bizance*,
Turchestan-born; nor could his eye not ken
Th' Empire of *Negus* to his utmost Port
Ercoco and the less Maritime Kings
Mombaza, and *Quiloa*, and *Melind*,

And *Sofala* thought *Ophir*, to the Realme 400
Of *Congo*, and *Angola* fardest South;
Or thence from *Niger* Flood to *Atlas* Mount
The Kingdoms of *Almansor*, *Fez* and *Sus*,
Marocco and *Algiers*, and *Tremisen;*
On *Europe* thence, and where *Rome* was to sway
The World: in Spirit perhaps he also saw
Rich *Mexico* the seat of *Motezume*,
And *Cusco* in *Peru*, the richer seat
Of *Atabalipa*, and yet unspoil'd
Guiana, whose great Citie *Geryons* Sons 410
Call *El Dorado:* but to nobler sights
Michael from *Adams* eyes the Filme remov'd
Which that false Fruit that promis'd clearer sight
Had bred; then purg'd with Euphrasie and Rue
The visual Nerve, for he had much to see;
And from the Well of Life three drops instill'd.
So deep the power of these Ingredients pierc'd,
Eeven to the inmost seat of mental sight,
That *Adam* now enforc't to close his eyes,
Sunk down and all his Spirits became intranst: 420
But him the gentle Angel by the hand
Soon rais'd, and his attention thus recall'd.
   Adam, now ope thine eyes, and first behold
Th' effects which thy original crime hath wrought
In some to spring from thee, who never touch'd
Th' excepted Tree, nor with the Snake conspir'd,
Nor sinn'd thy sin, yet from that sin derive
Corruption to bring forth more violent deeds.
   His eyes he op'nd, and beheld a field,
Part arable and tilth, whereon were Sheaves 430
New reapt, the other part sheep-walks and foulds;
Ith' midst an Altar as the Land-mark stood
Rustic, of grassie sord; thither anon
A sweatie Reaper from his Tillage brought
First Fruits, the green Eare, and the yellow Sheaf,
Uncull'd, as came to hand; a Shepherd next
More meek came with the Firstlings of his Flock
Choicest and best; then sacrificing, laid
The Inwards and thir Fat, with Incense strew'd,
On the cleft Wood, and all due Rites perform'd. 440
His Offring soon propitious Fire from Heav'n
Consum'd with nimble glance, and grateful steame;
The others not, for his was not sincere;
Whereat hee inlie rag'd, and as they talk'd,
Smote him into the Midriff with a stone

That beat out life; he fell, and deadly pale
Groand out his Soul with gushing bloud effus'd.
Much at that sight was *Adam* in his heart
Dismai'd, and thus in haste to th' Angel cri'd.
    O Teacher, some great mischief hath befall'n   *450*
To that meek man, who well had sacrific'd;
Is Pietie thus and pure Devotion paid?
    T' whom *Michael* thus, hee also mov'd, repli'd.
These two are Brethren, *Adam*, and to come
Out of thy loyns; th' unjust the just hath slain,
For envie that his Brothers Offering found
From Heav'n acceptance; but the bloodie Fact
Will be aveng'd, and th' others Faith approv'd
Loose no reward, though here thou see him die,
Rowling in dust and gore. To which our Sire.   *460*
    Alas, both for the deed and for the cause!
But have I now seen Death? Is this the way
I must return to native dust? O sight
Of terrour, foul and ugly to behold,
Horrid to think, how horrible to feel!
    To whom thus *Michael*. Death thou hast seen
In his first shape on man; but many shapes
Of Death, and many are the wayes that lead
To his grim Cave, all dismal; yet to sense
More terrible at th' entrance then within.   *470*
Some, as thou saw'st, by violent stroke shall die,
By Fire, Flood, Famin, by Intemperance more
In Meats and Drinks, which on the Earth shal bring
Diseases dire, of which a monstrous crew
Before thee shall appear; that thou mayst know
What miserie th' inabstinence of *Eve*
Shall bring on men. Immediately a place
Before his eyes appeard, sad, noysom, dark,
A Lazar-house it seemd, wherein were laid
Numbers of all diseas'd, all maladies   *480*
Of gastly Spasm, or racking torture, qualmes
Of heart-sick Agonie, all feavorous kinds,
Convulsions, Epilepsies, fierce Catarrhs,
Intestin Stone and Ulcer, Colic pangs,[1]
Dropsies, and Asthma's, and Joint-racking Rheums.
Dire was the tossing, deep the groans, despair
Tended the sick busiest from Couch to Couch;

---

[1] After this line, *1674* adds:
  Dæmoniac Phrenzie, moaping Melancholie
  And Moon struck madness, pining Atrophie,
  Marasmus, and wide wasting Pestilence,

And over them triumphant Death his Dart
Shook, but delaid to strike, though oft invok't
With vows, as thir chief good, and final hope. 490
Sight so deform what heart of Rock could long
Drie-ey'd behold? *Adam* could not, but wept,
Though not of Woman born; compassion quell'd
His best of Man, and gave him up to tears
A space, till firmer thoughts restraind excess,
And scarce recovering words his plaint renew'd.
   O miserable Mankind, to what fall
Degraded, to what wretched state reserv'd!
Better end heer unborn. Why is life giv'n
To be thus wrested from us? rather why 500
Obtruded on us thus? who if we knew
What we receive, would either not accept
Life offer'd, or soon beg to lay it down,
Glad to be so dismist in peace. Can thus
Th' Image of God in man created once
So goodly and erect, though faultie since,
To such unsightly sufferings be debas't
Under inhuman pains? Why should not Man,
Retaining still Divine similitude
In part, from such deformities be free, 510
And for his Makers Image sake exempt?
   Thir Makers Image, answer'd *Michael*, then
Forsook them, when themselves they villifi'd
To serve ungovern'd appetite, and took
His Image whom they serv'd, a brutish vice,
Inductive mainly to the sin of *Eve*.
Therefore so abject is thir punishment,
Disfiguring not Gods likeness, but thir own,
Or if his likeness, by themselves defac't
While they pervert pure Natures healthful rules 520
To loathsom sickness, worthily, since they
Gods Image did not reverence in themselves.
   I yeild it just, said *Adam*, and submit.
But is there yet no other way, besides
These painful passages, how we may come
To Death, and mix with our connatural dust?
   There is, said *Michael*, if thou well observe
The rule of not too much, by temperance taught
In what thou eatst and drinkst, seeking from thence
Due nourishment, not gluttonous delight, 530
Till many years over thy head return:
So maist thou live, till like ripe Fruit thou drop
Into thy Mothers lap, or be with ease

Gatherd, not harshly pluckt, for death mature:
This is old age; but then thou must outlive
Thy youth, thy strength, thy beauty, which will change
To withered weak & gray; thy Senses then
Obtuse, all taste of pleasure must forgoe,
To what thou hast, and for the Aire of youth
Hopeful and cheerful, in thy blood will reigne 540
A melancholly damp of cold and dry
To waigh thy spirits down, and last consume
The Balme of Life. To whom our Ancestor.
   Henceforth I flie not Death, nor would prolong
Life much, bent rather how I may be quit
Fairest and easiest of this combrous charge,
Which I must keep till my appointed day
Of rendring up, *Michael* to him repli'd.
   Nor love thy Life, nor hate; but what thou livst
Live well, how long or short permit to Heav'n: 550
And now prepare thee for another sight.
   He lookd and saw a spacious Plaine, whereon
Were Tents of various hue; by some were herds
Of Cattel grazing: others, whence the sound
Of Instruments that made melodious chime
Was heard, of Harp and Organ; and who moovd
Thir stops and chords was seen: his volant touch
Instinct through all proportions low and high
Fled and pursu'd transverse the resonant fugue.
In other part stood one who at the Forge 560
Labouring, two massie clods of Iron and Brass
Had melted (whether found where casual fire
Had wasted woods on Mountain or in Vale,
Down to the veins of Earth, thence gliding hot
To som Caves mouth, or whether washt by stream
From underground) the liquid Ore he dreind
Into fit moulds prepar'd; from which he formd
First his own Tooles; then, what might else be wrought
Fusil or grav'n in mettle. After these,
But on the hether side a different sort 570
From the high neighbouring Hills, which was thir Seat,
Down to the Plain descended: by thir guise
Just men they seemd, and all thir study bent
To worship God aright, and know his works
Not hid, nor those things last which might preserve
Freedom and Peace to men: they on the Plain
Long had not walkt, when from the Tents behold
A Bevie of fair Women, richly gay
In Gems and wanton dress; to the Harp they sung

Soft amorous Ditties, and in dance came on: 580
The Men though grave, ey'd them, and let thir eyes
Rove without rein, till in the amorous Net
Fast caught, they lik'd, and each his liking chose;
And now of love they treat till th' Eevning Star
Loves Harbinger appeerd; then all in heat
They light the Nuptial Torch, and bid invoke
Hymen, then first to marriage Rites invok't;
With Feast and Musick all the Tents resound.
Such happy interview and fair event
Of love & youth not lost, Songs, Garlands, Flours, 590
And charming Symphonies attach'd the heart
Of *Adam*, soon enclin'd to admit delight,
The bent of Nature; which he thus express'd.
   True opener of mine eyes, prime Angel blest,
Much better seems this Vision, and more hope
Of peaceful dayes portends, then those two past;
Those were of hate and death, or pain much worse,
Here Nature seems fulfilld in all her ends.
   To whom thus *Michael*. Judg not what is best
By pleasure, though to Nature seeming meet, 600
Created, as thou art, to nobler end
Holie and pure, conformitie divine.
Those Tents thou sawst so pleasant, were the Tents
Of wickedness, wherein shall dwell his Race
Who slew his Brother; studious they appere
Of Arts that polish Life, Inventers rare,
Unmindful of thir Maker, though his Spirit
Taught them, but they his gifts acknowledg'd none.
Yet they a beauteous ofspring shall beget;
For that fair femal Troop thou sawst, that seemd 610
Of Goddesses, so blithe, so smooth, so gay,
Yet empty of all good wherein consists
Womans domestic honour and chief praise;
Bred onely and completed to the taste
Of lustful appetence, to sing, to dance,
To dress, and troule the Tongue, and roule the Eye.
To these that sober Race of Men, whose lives
Religious titl'd them the Sons of God,
Shall yeild up all thir vertue, all thir fame
Ignobly, to the traines and to the smiles 620
Of these fair Atheists, and now swim in joy,
(Erelong to swim at larg) and laugh; for which
The world erelong a world of tears must weepe.
   To whom thus *Adam* of short joy bereft.
O pittie and shame, that they who to live well

Enterd so faire, should turn aside to tread
Paths indirect, or in the mid way faint!
But still I see the tenor of Mans woe
Holds on the same, from Woman to begin.
   From Mans effeminate slackness it begins,   630
Said th' Angel, who should better hold his place
By wisdome, and superiour gifts receavd.
But now prepare thee for another Scene.
   He lookd and saw wide Territorie spred
Before him, Towns, and rural works between,
Cities of Men with lofty Gates and Towrs,
Concours in Arms, fierce Faces threatning Warr,
Giants of mightie Bone, and bould emprise;
Part wield thir Arms, part courb the foaming Steed,
Single or in Array of Battel rang'd   640
Both Horse and Foot, nor idely mustring stood;
One way a Band select from forage drives
A herd of Beeves, faire Oxen and faire Kine
From a fat Meddow ground; or fleecy Flock,
Ewes and thir bleating Lambs over the Plaine,
Thir Bootie; scarce with Life the Shepherds flye,
But call in aide, which tacks a bloody Fray;
With cruel Tournament the Squadrons joine;
Where Cattel pastur'd late, now scatterd lies
With Carcasses and Arms th' ensanguind Field   650
Deserted: Others to a Citie strong
Lay Siege, encampt; by Batterie, Scale, and Mine,
Assaulting; others from the Wall defend
With Dart and Jav'lin, Stones and sulfurous Fire;
On each hand slaughter and gigantic deeds.
In other part the scepter'd Haralds call
To Council in the Citie Gates: anon
Grey-headed men and grave, with Warriours mixt,
Assemble, and Harangues are heard, but soon
In factious opposition, till at last   660
Of middle Age one rising, eminent
In wise deport, spake much of Right and Wrong,
Of Justice, of Religion, Truth and Peace,
And Judgement from above: him old and young
Exploded, and had seiz'd with violent hands,
Had not a Cloud descending snatch'd him thence
Unseen amid the throng: so violence
Proceeded, and Oppression, and Sword-Law
Through all the Plain, and refuge none was found.
Adam was all in tears, and to his guide   670
Lamenting turnd full sad; O what are these,

Deaths Ministers, not Men, who thus deal Death
Inhumanly to men, and multiply
Ten thousand fould the sin of him who slew
His Brother; for of whom such massacher
Make they but of thir Brethren, men of men?
But who was that Just Man, whom had not Heav'n
Rescu'd, had in his Righteousness bin lost?
    To whom thus *Michael;* These are the product
Of those ill-mated Marriages thou saw'st;   680
Where good with bad were matcht, who of themselves
Abhor to joyn; and by imprudence mixt,
Produce prodigious Births of bodie or mind.
Such were these Giants, men of high renown;
For in those dayes Might onely shall be admir'd,
And Valour and Heroic Vertu call'd;
To overcome in Battel, and subdue
Nations, and bring home spoils with infinite
Man-slaughter, shall be held the highest pitch
Of human Glorie, and for Glorie done   690
Of triumph, to be styl'd great Conquerours,
Patrons of Mankind, Gods, and Sons of Gods,
Destroyers rightlier call'd and Plagues of men.
Thus Fame shall be achiev'd, renown on Earth,
And what most merits fame in silence hid.
But hee the seventh from thee, whom thou beheldst
The onely righteous in a World perverse,
And therefore hated, therefore so beset
With Foes for daring single to be just,
And utter odious Truth, that God would come   700
To judge them with his Saints: Him the most High
Rapt in a balmie Cloud with winged Steeds
Did, as thou sawst, receave, to walk with God
High in Salvation and the Climes of bliss,
Exempt from Death; to shew thee what reward
Awaits the good, the rest what punishment;
Which now direct thine eyes and soon behold.
    He look'd, & saw the face of things quite chang'd;
The brazen Throat of Warr had ceast to roar,
All now was turn'd to jollitie and game,   710
To luxurie and riot, feast and dance,
Marrying or prostituting, as befell,
Rape or Adulterie, where passing faire
Allurd them; thence from Cups to civil Broiles.
At length a Reverend Sire among them came,
And of thir doings great dislike declar'd,
And testifi'd against thir wayes; hee oft

Frequented thir Assemblies, whereso met,
Triumphs or Festivals, and to them preachd
Conversion and Repentance, as to Souls 720
In prison under Judgements imminent:
But all in vain: which when he saw, he ceas'd
Contending, and remov'd his Tents farr off;
Then from the Mountain hewing Timber tall,
Began to build a Vessel of huge bulk,
Measur'd by Cubit, length, & breadth, and highth,
Smeard round with Pitch, and in the side a dore
Contriv'd, and of provisions laid in large
For Man and Beast: when loe a wonder strange!
Of everie Beast, and Bird, and Insect small 730
Came seavens, and pairs, and enterd in, as taught
Thir order; last the Sire, and his three Sons
With thir four Wives; and God made fast the dore.
Meanwhile the Southwind rose, & with black wings
Wide hovering, all the Clouds together drove
From under Heav'n; the Hills to their supplie
Vapour, and Exhalation dusk and moist,
Sent up amain; and now the thick'nd Skie
Like a dark Ceeling stood; down rush'd the Rain
Impetuous, and continu'd till the Earth 740
No more was seen; the floating Vessel swum
Uplifted; and secure with beaked prow
Rode tilting o're the Waves, all dwellings else
Flood overwhelmd, and them with all thir pomp
Deep under water rould; Sea cover'd Sea,
Sea without shoar; and in thir Palaces
Where luxurie late reign'd, Sea-monsters whelp'd
And stabl'd; of Mankind, so numerous late,
All left, in one small bottom swum imbark't.
How didst thou grieve then, *Adam*, to behold 750
The end of all thy Ofspring, end so sad,
Depopulation; thee another Floud,
Of tears and sorrow a Floud thee also drown'd,
And sunk thee as thy Sons; till gently reard
By th' Angel, on thy feet thou stoodst at last,
Though comfortless, as when a Father mourns
His Children, all in view destroyd at once;
And scarce to th' Angel utterdst thus thy plaint.
   O Visions ill foreseen! better had I
Liv'd ignorant of future, so had borne 760
My part of evil onely, each dayes lot
Anough to bear; those now, that were dispenst
The burd'n of many Ages, on me light

At once, by my foreknowledge gaining Birth
Abortive, to torment me ere thir being,
With thought that they must be. Let no man seek
Henceforth to be foretold what shall befall
Him or his Children, evil he may be sure,
Which neither his foreknowing can prevent,
And hee the future evil shall no less   770
In apprehension then in substance feel
Grievous to bear: but that care now is past,
Man is not whom to warne: those few escap't
Famin and anguish will at last consume
Wandring that watrie Desert: I had hope
When violence was ceas't, and Warr on Earth,
All would have then gon well, peace would have crownd
With length of happy days the race of man;
But I was farr deceav'd; for now I see
Peace to corrupt no less then Warr to waste.   780
How comes it thus? unfould, Celestial Guide,
And whether here the Race of man will end.
To whom thus *Michael*. Those whom last thou sawst
In triumph and luxurious wealth, are they
First seen in acts of prowess eminent
And great exploits, but of true vertu void;
Who having spilt much blood, and don much waste
Subduing Nations, and achievd thereby
Fame in the World, high titles, and rich prey,
Shall change thir course to pleasure, ease, and sloth, 790
Surfet, and lust, till wantonness and pride
Raise out of friendship hostil deeds in Peace.
The conquerd also, and enslav'd by Warr
Shall with thir freedom lost all vertu loose
And feare of God, from whom thir pietie feign'd
In sharp contest of Battel found no aide
Against invaders; therefore coold in zeale
Thenceforth shall practice how to live secure,
Worldlie or dissolute, on what thir Lords
Shall leave them to enjoy; for th' Earth shall bear   800
More than anough, that temperance may be tri'd:
So all shall turn degenerate, all deprav'd,
Justice and Temperance, Truth and Faith forgot;
One Man except, the onely Son of light
In a dark Age, against example good,
Against allurement, custom, and a World
Offended; fearless of reproach and scorn,
Or violence, hee of thir wicked wayes
Shall them admonish, and before them set

The paths of righteousness, how much more safe,   810
And full of peace, denouncing wrauth to come
On thir impenitence; and shall returne
Of them derided, but of God observd
The one just Man alive; by his command
Shall build a wondrous Ark, as thou beheldst,
To save himself and houshold from amidst
A World devote to universal rack.
No sooner hee with them of Man and Beast
Select for life shall in the Ark be lodg'd,
And shelterd round, but all the Cataracts   820
Of Heav'n set open on the Earth shall powre
Raine day and night, all fountaines of the Deep
Broke up, shall heave the Ocean to usurp
Beyond all bounds, till inundation rise
Above the highest Hills: then shall this Mount
Of Paradise by might of Waves be moovd
Out of his place, pushd by the horned floud,
With all his verdure spoil'd, and Trees adrift
Down the great River to the op'ning Gulf,
And there take root an Iland salt and bare,   830
The haunt of Seales and Orcs, and Sea-mews clang.
To teach thee that God attributes to place
No sanctitie, if none be thither brought
By Men who there frequent, or therein dwell.
And now what further shall ensue, behold.

  He lookd, and saw the Ark hull on the floud,
Which now abated, for the Clouds were fled,
Drivn by a keen North-winde, that blowing drie
Wrinkl'd the face of Deluge, as decai'd;
And the cleer Sun on his wide watrie Glass   840
Gaz'd hot, and of the fresh Wave largely drew,
As after thirst, which made thir flowing shrink
From standing lake to tripping ebbe, that stole
With soft foot towards the deep, who now had stopt
His Sluces, as the Heav'n his windows shut.
The Ark no more now flotes, but seems on ground
Fast on the top of som high mountain fixt.
And now the tops of Hills as Rocks appeer;
With clamor thence the rapid Currents drive
Towards the retreating Sea thir furious tyde.   850
Forthwith from out the Arke a Raven flies,
And after him, the surer messenger,
A Dove sent forth once and agen to spie
Green Tree or ground whereon his foot may light;
The second time returning, in his Bill

An Olive leafe he brings, pacific signe:
Anon drie ground appeers, and from his Arke
The ancient Sire descends with all his Train;
Then with uplifted hands, and eyes devout,
Grateful to Heav'n, over his head beholds 860
A dewie Cloud, and in the Cloud a Bow
Conspicuous with three listed colours gay,
Betok'ning peace from God, and Cov'nant new.
Whereat the heart of *Adam* erst so sad
Greatly rejoyc'd, and thus his joy broke forth.
   O thou that future things canst represent
As present, Heav'nly instructer, I revive
At this last sight, assur'd that Man shall live
With all the Creatures, and thir seed preserve.
Farr less I now lament for one whole World 870
Of wicked Sons destroyd, then I rejoyce
For one Man found so perfet and so just,
That God voutsafes to raise another World
From him, and all his anger to forget.
But say, what mean those coloured streaks in Heavn,
Distended as the Brow of God appeas'd,
Or serve they as a flourie verge to binde
The fluid skirts of that same watrie Cloud,
Least it again dissolve and showr the Earth?
   To whom th' Archangel. Dextrously thou aim'st; 880
So willingly doth God remit his Ire,
Though late repenting him of Man deprav'd,
Griev'd at his heart, when looking down he saw
The whole Earth fill'd with violence, and all flesh
Corrupting each thir way; yet those remoov'd,
Such grace shall one just Man find in his sight,
That he relents, not to blot out mankind,
And makes a Covenant never to destroy
The Earth again by flood, nor let the Sea
Surpass his bounds, nor Rain to drown the World 890
With Man therein or Beast; but when he brings
Over the Earth a Cloud, will therein set
His triple-colour'd Bow, whereon to look
And call to mind his Cov'nant: Day and Night,
Seed time and Harvest, Heat and hoary Frost
Shall hold thir course, till fire purge all things new,
Both Heav'n and Earth, wherein the just shall dwell.

BOOK XII

THE ARGUMENT

The Angel Michael *continues from the Flood to relate what shall succeed; then, in the mention of* Abraham, *comes by degrees to explain, who that Seed of the Woman shall be, which was promised* Adam *and* Eve *in the Fall; his Incarnation, Death, Resurrection, and Ascension; the state of the Church till his second Coming.* Adam *greatly satisfied and recomforted by these Relations and Promises descends the Hill with* Michael; *wakens* Eve, *who all this while had slept, but with gentle dreams compos'd to quietness of mind and submission.* Michael *in either hand leads them out of Paradise, the fiery Sword waving behind them, and the Cherubim taking thir Stations to guard the Place.*

[AS ONE who in his journey bates at Noone,
Though bent on speed, so heer the Archangel paus'd
Betwixt the world destroy'd and world restor'd,
If *Adam* aught perhaps might interpose;
Then with transition sweet new Speech resumes.] [1]
 Thus thou hast seen one World begin and end;
And Man as from a second stock proceed.
Much thou hast yet to see, but I perceave
Thy mortal sight to faile; objects divine
Must needs impaire and wearie human sense: *10*
Henceforth what is to com I will relate,
Thou therefore give due audience, and attend.
This second sours of Men, while yet but few,
And while the dread of judgement past remains
Fresh in thir mindes, fearing the Deitie,
With some regard to what is just and right
Shall lead thir lives, and multiplie apace,
Labouring the soile, and reaping plenteous crop,
Corn wine and oyle; and from the herd or flock,
Oft sacrificing Bullock, Lamb, or Kid,   *20*
With large Wine-offerings pour'd, and sacred Feast
Shal spend thir dayes in joy unblam'd, and dwell
Long time in peace by Families and Tribes
Under paternal rule; till one shall rise
Of proud ambitious heart, who not content
With fair equalitie, fraternal state,
Will arrogate Dominion undeserv'd
Over his brethren, and quite dispossess
Concord and law of Nature from the Earth;

[1] The five bracketed lines were added in the second edition (1674), when the original Book x was divided into Book xi and Book xii.

Hunting (and Men not Beasts shall be his game) 30
With Warr and hostile snare such as refuse
Subjection to his Empire tyrannous:
A mightie Hunter thence he shall be styl'd
Before the Lord, as in despite of Heav'n,
Or from Heav'n claming second Sovrantie;
And from Rebellion shall derive his name,
Though of Rebellion others he accuse.
Hee with a crew, whom like Ambition joyns
With him or under him to tyrannize,
Marching from *Eden* towards the West, shall finde 40
The Plain, wherein a black bituminous gurge
Boiles out from under ground, the mouth of Hell;
Of Brick, and of that stuff they cast to build
A Citie & Towre, whose top may reach to Heav'n;
And get themselves a name, least far disperst
In foraign Lands thir memorie be lost,
Regardless whether good or evil fame.
But God who oft descends to visit men
Unseen, and through thir habitations walks
To mark thir doings, them beholding soon, 50
Comes down to see thir Citie, ere the Tower
Obstruct Heav'n Towrs, and in derision sets
Upon thir Tongues a various Spirit to rase
Quite out thir Native Language, and instead
To sow a jangling noise of words unknown:
Forthwith a hideous gabble rises loud
Among the Builders; each to other calls
Not understood, till hoarse, and all in rage,
As mockt they storm; great laughter was in Heav'n
And looking down, to see the hubbub strange 60
And hear the din; thus was the building left
Ridiculous, and the work Confusion nam'd.
 Whereto thus *Adam* fatherly displeas'd.
O execrable Son so to aspire
Above his Brethren, to himself assuming
Authoritie usurpt, from God not giv'n:
He gave us onely over Beast, Fish, Fowl
Dominion absolute; that right we hold
By his donation; but Man over men
He made not Lord; such title to himself 70
Reserving, human left from human free.
But this Usurper his encroachment proud
Stayes not on Man; to God his Tower intends
Siege and defiance: Wretched man! what food
Will he convey up thither to sustain

Himself and his rash Armie, where thin Aire
Above the Clouds will pine his entrails gross,
And famish him of Breath, if not of Bread?
    To whom thus *Michael*. Justly thou abhorr'st
That Son, who on the quiet state of men   *80*
Such trouble brought, affecting to subdue
Rational Libertie; yet know withall,
Since thy original lapse, true Libertie
Is lost, which alwayes with right Reason dwells
Twinn'd, and from her hath no dividual being:
Reason in man obscur'd, or not obeyd,
Immediately inordinate desires
And upstart Passions catch the Government
From Reason, and to servitude reduce
Man till then free. Therefore since hee permits   *90*
Within himself unworthie Powers to reign
Over free Reason, God in Judgement just
Subjects him from without to violent Lords;
Who oft as undeservedly enthrall
His outward freedom: Tyrannie must be,
Though to the Tyrant thereby no excuse.
Yet somtimes Nations will decline so low
From vertue, which is reason, that no wrong,
But Justice, and some fatal curse annext
Deprives them of thir outward libertie,   *100*
Thir inward lost; Witness th' irreverent Son
Of him who built the Ark, who for the shame
Don to his Father, heard this heavie curse,
Servant of Servants, on his vitious Race.
Thus will this latter, as the former World,
Still tend from bad to worse, till God at last
Wearied with their iniquities, withdraw
His presence from among them, and avert
His holy Eyes; resolving from thenceforth
To leave them to thir own polluted wayes;   *110*
And one peculiar Nation to select
From all the rest, of whom to be invok'd,
A Nation from one faithful man to spring:
Him on this side *Euphrates* yet residing,
Bred up in Idol-worship; O that men
(Canst thou believe?) should be so stupid grown,
While yet the Patriark liv'd, who scap'd the Flood,
As to forsake the living God, and fall
To worship thir own work in Wood and Stone
For Gods! yet him God the most High voutsafes   *120*
To call by Vision from his Fathers house,

His kindred and false Gods, into a Land
Which he will shew him, and from him will raise
A mightie Nation, and upon him showre
His benediction so, that in his Seed
All Nations shall be blest; hee straight obeys,
Not knowing to what Land, yet firm believes:
I see him, but thou canst not, with what Faith
He leaves his Gods, his Friends, and native Soile
Ur of *Chaldæa*, passing now the Ford   *130*
To *Haran*, after him a cumbrous Train
Of Herds and Flocks, and numerous servitude;
Not wandring poor, but trusting all his wealth
With God, who call'd him, in a land unknown.
Canaan he now attains, I see his Tents
Pitcht about *Sechem*, and the neighbouring Plaine
Of *Moreh;* there by promise he receaves
Gift to his Progenie of all that Land;
From *Hamath* Northward to the Desert South
(Things by thir names I call, though yet unnam'd)   *140*
From *Hermon* East to the great Western Sea,
Mount *Hermon*, yonder Sea, each place behold
In prospect, as I point them; on the shoare
Mount *Carmel;* here the double-founted stream
Jordan, true limit Eastward; but his Sons
Shall dwell to *Senir*, that long ridge of Hills.
This ponder, that all Nations of the Earth
Shall in his Seed be blessed; by that Seed
Is meant thy great deliverer, who shall bruise
The Serpents head; whereof to thee anon   *150*
Plainlier shall be reveald. This Patriarch blest,
Whom *faithful Abraham* due time shall call,
A Son, and of his Son a Grand-childe leaves,
Like him in faith, in wisdom, and renown;
The Grandchilde with twelve Sons increast, departs
From *Canaan*, to a land hereafter call'd
Egypt, divided by the River *Nile;*
See where it flows, disgorging at seaven mouthes
Into the Sea: to sojourn in that Land
He comes invited by a yonger Son   *160*
In time of dearth, a Son whose worthy deeds
Raise him to be the second in that Realme
Of *Pharao:* there he dies, and leaves his Race
Growing into a Nation, and now grown
Suspected to a sequent King, who seeks
To stop thir overgrowth, as inmate guests
Too numerous; whence of guests he makes them slaves

Inhospitably, and kills thir infant Males:
Till by two brethren (those two brethren call
Moses and *Aaron*) sent from God to claime
His people from enthralment, they return
With glory and spoile back to thir promis'd Land.
But first the lawless Tyrant, who denies
To know thir God, or message to regard,
Must be compelld by Signes and Judgements dire;
To blood unshed the Rivers must be turnd,
Frogs, Lice and Flies must all his Palace fill
With loath'd intrusion, and fill all the land;
His Cattel must of Rot and Murren die,
Botches and blaines must all his flesh imboss,
And all his people; Thunder mixt with Haile,
Haile mixt with fire must rend th' *Egyptian* Skie
And wheel on th' Earth, devouring where it rouls;
What it devours not, Herb, or Fruit, or Graine,
A darksom Cloud of Locusts swarming down
Must eat, and on the ground leave nothing green:
Darkness must overshadow all his bounds,
Palpable darkness, and blot out three dayes;
Last with one midnight stroke all the first-born
Of *Egypt* must lie dead. Thus with ten wounds
This River-dragon tam'd at length submits
To let his sojourners depart, and oft
Humbles his stubborn heart, but still as Ice
More hard'nd after thaw, till in his rage
Pursuing whom he late dismissd, the Sea
Swallows him with his Host, but them lets pass
As on drie land between two christal walls,
Aw'd by the rod of *Moses* so to stand
Divided, till his rescu'd gain thir shoar:
Such wondrous power God to his Saint will lend,
Though present in his Angel, who shall goe
Before them in a Cloud, and Pillar of Fire,
By day a Cloud, by night a Pillar of Fire,
To guide them in thir journey, and remove
Behinde them, while th' obdurat King pursues:
All night he will pursue, but his approach
Darkness defends between till morning Watch;
Then through the Firey Pillar and the Cloud
God looking forth will trouble all his Host
And craze thir Chariot wheels: when by command
Moses once more his potent Rod extends
Over the Sea; the Sea his Rod obeys;
On thir imbattelld ranks the Waves return,

And overwhelm thir Warr: the Race elect
Safe towards *Canaan* from the shoar advance
Through the wilde Desert, not the readiest way,
Least entring on the *Canaanite* allarmd
Warr terrifie them inexpert, and feare
Return them back to *Egypt*, choosing rather
Inglorious life with servitude; for life   220
To noble and ignoble is more sweet
Untraind in Armes, where rashness leads not on.
This also shall they gain by thir delay
In the wide Wilderness, there they shall found
Thir government, and thir great Senate choose
Through the twelve Tribes, to rule by Laws ordaind:
God from the Mount of *Sinai*, whose gray top
Shall tremble, he descending, will himself
In Thunder Lightning and loud Trumpets sound
Ordaine them Lawes; part such as appertaine   230
To civil Justice, part religious Rites
Of sacrifice, informing them, by types
And shadowes, of that destind Seed to bruise
The Serpent, by what meanes he shall achieve
Mankinds deliverance. But the voice of God
To mortal eare is dreadful; they beseech
That *Moses* might report to them his will,
And terror cease; he grants them thir desire,
Instructed that to God is no access
Without Mediator, whose high Office now   240
Moses in figure beares, to introduce
One greater, of whose day he shall foretell,
And all the Prophets in thir Age, the times
Of great *Messiah* shall sing. Thus Laws and Rites
Establisht, such delight hath God in Men
Obedient to his will, that he voutsafes
Among them to set up his Tabernacle,
The holy One with mortal Men to dwell:
By his prescript a Sanctuary is fram'd
Of Cedar, overlaid with Gold, therein   250
An Ark, and in the Ark his Testimony,
The Records of his Cov'nant, over these
A Mercie-seat of Gold between the wings
Of two bright Cherubim, before him burn
Seaven Lamps as in a Zodiac representing
The Heav'nly fires; over the Tent a Cloud
Shall rest by Day, a fierie gleame by Night,
Save when they journie, and at length they come,
Conducted by his Angel to the Land

Promisd to *Abraham* and his Seed: the rest 260
Were long to tell, how many Battels fought,
How many Kings destroyd, and Kingdoms won,
Or how the Sun shall in mid Heav'n stand still
A day entire, and Nights due course adjourne,
Mans voice commanding, Sun in *Gibeon* stand,
And thou Moon in the vale of *Aialon*,
Till *Israel* overcome; so call the third
From *Abraham*, Son of *Isaac*, and from him
His whole descent, who thus shall *Canaan* win.

    Here *Adam* interpos'd. O sent from Heav'n, 270
Enlightner of my darkness, gracious things
Thou hast reveald, those chiefly which concerne
Just *Abraham* and his Seed: now first I finde
Mine eyes true op'ning, and my heart much eas'd,
Erwhile perplext with thoughts what would becom
Of mee and all Mankind; but now I see
His day, in whom all Nations shall be blest,
Favour unmerited by me, who sought
Forbidd'n knowledge by forbidd'n means.
This yet I apprehend not, why to those 280
Among whom God will deigne to dwell on Earth
So many and so various Laws are giv'n;
So many Laws argue so many sins
Among them; how can God with such reside?

    To whom thus *Michael*. Doubt not but that sin
Will reign among them, as of thee begot;
And therefore was Law given them to evince
Thir natural pravitie, by stirring up
Sin against Law to fight; that when they see
Law can discover sin, but not remove, 290
Save by those shadowie expiations weak,
The bloud of Bulls and Goats, they may conclude
Some bloud more precious must be paid for Man,
Just for unjust, that in such righteousness
To them by Faith imputed, they may finde
Justification towards God, and peace
Of Conscience, which the Law by Ceremonies
Cannot appease, nor Man the moral part
Perform, and not performing cannot live.
So Law appears imperfet, and but giv'n 300
With purpose to resign them in full time
Up to a better Cov'nant, disciplin'd
From shadowie Types to Truth, from Flesh to Spirit,
From imposition of strict Laws, to free
Acceptance of large Grace, from servil fear

To filial, works of Law to works of Faith.
And therefore shall not *Moses*, though of God
Highly belov'd, being but the Minister
Of Law, his people into *Canaan* lead;
But *Joshua* whom the Gentiles *Jesus* call,   *310*
His Name and Office bearing, who shall quell
The adversarie Serpent, and bring back
Through the worlds wilderness long wanderd man
Safe to eternal Paradise of rest.
Meanwhile they in thir earthly *Canaan* plac't
Long time shall dwell and prosper, but when sins
National interrupt thir public peace,
Provoking God to raise them enemies:
From whom as oft he saves them penitent
By Judges first, then under Kings; of whom   *320*
The second, both for pietie renownd
And puissant deeds, a promise shall receive
Irrevocable, that his Regal Throne
For ever shall endure; the like shall sing
All Prophecie, That of the Royal Stock
Of *David* (so I name this King) shall rise
A Son, the Womans Seed to thee foretold,
Foretold to *Abraham*, as in whom shall trust
All Nations, and to Kings foretold, of Kings
The last, for of his Reign shall be no end.   *330*
But first a long succession must ensue,
And his next Son for Wealth and Wisdom fam'd,
The clouded Ark of God till then in Tents
Wandring, shall in a glorious Temple enshrine.
Such follow him, as shall be registerd
Part good, part bad, of bad the longer scrowle,
Whose foul Idolatries, and other faults
Heapt to the popular summe, will so incense
God, as to leave them, and expose thir Land,
Thir Citie, his Temple, and his holy Ark   *340*
With all his sacred things, a scorn and prey
To that proud Citie, whose high Walls thou saw'st
Left in confusion, *Babylon* thence call'd.
There in captivitie he lets them dwell
The space of seventie years, then brings them back,
Remembring mercie, and his Cov'nant sworn
To *David*, stablisht as the dayes of Heav'n.
Returnd from *Babylon* by leave of Kings
Thir Lords, whom God dispos'd, the house of God
They first re-edifie, and for a while   *350*
In mean estate live moderate, till grown

In wealth and multitude, factious they grow;
But first among the Priests dissension springs,
Men who attend the Altar, and should most
Endeavour Peace: thir strife pollution brings
Upon the Temple it self: at last they seise
The Scepter, and regard not *Davids* Sons,
Then loose it to a stranger, that the true
Anointed King *Messiah* might be born
Barr'd of his right; yet at his Birth a Starr   360
Unseen before in Heav'n proclaims him com,
And guides the Eastern Sages, who enquire
His place, to offer Incense, Myrrh, and Gold;
His place of birth a solemn Angel tells
To simple Shepherds, keeping watch by night;
They gladly thither haste, and by a Quire
Of squadrond Angels hear his Carol sung.
A Virgin is his Mother, but his Sire
The Power of the most High; he shall ascend
The Throne hereditarie, and bound his Reign   370
With earths wide bounds, his glory with the Heav'ns.

    He ceas'd, discerning *Adam* with such joy
Surcharg'd, as had like grief bin dew'd in tears,
Without the vent of words, which these he breathd.

    O Prophet of glad tidings, finisher
Of utmost hope! now clear I understand
What oft my steddiest thoughts have searcht in vain,
Why our great expectation should be call'd
The seed of Woman: Virgin Mother, Haile,
High in the love of Heav'n, yet from my Loynes   380
Thou shalt proceed, and from thy Womb the Son
Of God most High; So God with man unites.
Needs must the Serpent now his capital bruise
Expect with mortal paine: say where and when
Thir fight, what stroke shall bruise the Victors heel.

    To whom thus *Michael*. Dream not of thir fight,
As of a Duel, or the local wounds
Of head or heel: not therefore joynes the Son
Manhood to God-head, with more strength to foil
Thy enemie; nor so is overcome   390
Satan, whose fall from Heav'n, a deadlier bruise,
Disabl'd not to give thee thy deaths wound:
Which hee, who comes thy Saviour, shall recure,
Not by destroying *Satan*, but his works
In thee and in thy Seed: nor can this be,
But by fulfilling that which thou didst want,
Obedience to the Law of God, impos'd

On penaltie of death, and suffering death,
The penaltie to thy transgression due,
And due to theirs which out of thine will grow: 400
So onely can high Justice rest appaid.
The Law of God exact he shall fulfill
Both by obedience and by love, though love
Alone fulfill the Law; thy punishment
He shall endure by coming in the Flesh
To a reproachful life and cursed death,
Proclaming Life to all who shall believe
In his redemption, and that his obedience
Imputed becomes theirs by Faith, his merits
To save them, not thir own, though legal works. 410
For this he shall live hated, be blasphem'd,
Seis'd on by force, judg'd, and to death condemnd
A shameful and accurst, naild to the Cross
By his own Nation, slaine for bringing Life;
But to the Cross he nailes thy Enemies,
The Law that is against thee, and the sins
Of all mankinde, with him there crucifi'd,
Never to hurt them more who rightly trust
In this his satisfaction; so he dies,
But soon revives, Death over him no power 420
Shall long usurp; ere the third dawning light
Returne, the Starres of Morn shall see him rise
Out of his grave, fresh as the dawning light,
Thy ransom paid, which Man from death redeems,
His death for Man, as many as offerd Life
Neglect not, and the benefit imbrace
By Faith not void of workes: this God-like act
Annuls thy doom, the death thou shouldst have dy'd,
In sin for ever lost from life; this act
Shall bruise the head of *Satan*, crush his strength 430
Defeating Sin and Death, his two maine armes,
And fix farr deeper in his head thir stings
Then temporal death shall bruise the Victors heel,
Or theirs whom he redeems, a death like sleep,
A gentle wafting to immortal Life.
Nor after resurrection shall he stay
Longer on Earth then certaine times to appeer
To his Disciples, Men who in his Life
Still follow'd him; to them shall leave in charge
To teach all nations what of him they learn'd 440
And his Salvation, them who shall beleeve
Baptizing in the profluent streame, the signe
Of washing them from guilt of sin to Life

Pure, and in mind prepar'd, if so befall,
For death, like that which the redeemer dy'd.
All Nations they shall teach; for from that day
Not onely to the Sons of *Abrahams* Loines
Salvation shall be Preacht, but to the Sons
Of *Abrahams* Faith wherever through the world;
So in his seed all Nations shall be blest.   *450*
Then to the Heav'n of Heav'ns he shall ascend
With victory, triumphing through the aire
Over his foes and thine; there shall surprise
The Serpent, Prince of aire, and drag in Chaines
Through all his realme, & there confounded leave;
Then enter into glory, and resume
His Seat at Gods right hand, exalted high
Above all names in Heav'n; and thence shall come,
When this worlds dissolution shall be ripe,
With glory and power to judge both quick & dead   *460*
To judge th' unfaithful dead, but to reward
His faithful, and receave them into bliss,
Whether in Heav'n or Earth, for then the Earth
Shall all be Paradise, far happier place
Then this of *Eden*, and far happier daies.
    So spake th' Archangel *Michael*, then paus'd,
As at the Worlds great period; and our Sire
Replete with joy and wonder thus repli'd.
    O goodness infinite, goodness immense!
That all this good of evil shall produce,   *470*
And evil turn to good; more wonderful
Then that by which creation first brought forth
Light out of darkness! full of doubt I stand,
Whether I should repent me now of sin
By mee done and occasiond, or rejoyce
Much more, that much more good thereof shall spring,
To God more glory, more good will to Men
From God, and over wrauth grace shall abound.
But say, if our deliverer up to Heav'n
Must reascend, what will betide the few   *480*
His faithful, left among th' unfaithful herd,
The enemies of truth; who then shall guide
His people, who defend? will they not deale
Wors with his followers then with him they dealt?
    Be sure they will, said th' Angel; but from Heav'n
Hee to his own a Comforter will send,
The promise of the Father, who shall dwell
His Spirit within them, and the Law of Faith
Working through love, upon thir hearts shall write,

To guide them in all truth, and also arme 490
With spiritual Armour, able to resist
Satans assaults, and quench his fierie darts,
What Man can do against them, not affraid,
Though to the death, against such cruelties
With inward consolations recompenc't,
And oft supported so as shall amaze
Thir proudest persecuters: for the Spirit
Powrd first on his Apostles, whom he sends
To evangelize the Nations, then on all
Baptiz'd, shall them with wondrous gifts endue 500
To speak all Tongues, and do all Miracles,
As did thir Lord before them. Thus they win
Great numbers of each Nation to receave
With joy the tidings brought from Heav'n: at length
Thir Ministry perform'd, and race well run,
Thir doctrine and thir story written left,
They die; but in thir room, as they forewarne,
Wolves shall succeed for teachers, grievous Wolves,
Who all the sacred mysteries of Heav'n
To thir own vile advantages shall turne 510
Of lucre and ambition, and the truth
With superstitions and traditions taint,
Left onely in those written Records pure,
Though not but by the Spirit understood.
Then shall they seek to avail themselves of names,
Places and titles, and with these to joine
Secular power, though feigning still to act
By spiritual, to themselves appropriating
The Spirit of God, promisd alike and giv'n
To all Beleevers; and from that pretense, 520
Spiritual Lawes by carnal power shall force
On every conscience; Laws which none shall finde
Left them inrould, or what the Spirit within
Shall on the heart engrave. What will they then
But force the Spirit of Grace it self, and binde
His consort Libertie; what, but unbuild
His living Temples, built by Faith to stand,
Thir own Faith not anothers: for on Earth
Who against Faith and Conscience can be heard
Infallible? yet many will presume: 530
Whence heavie persecution shall arise
On all who in the worship persevere
Of Spirit and Truth; the rest, farr greater part,
Will deem in outward Rites and specious formes
Religion satisfi'd; Truth shall retire

Bestuck with slandrous darts, and works of Faith
Rarely be found: so shall the World goe on,
To good malignant, to bad men benigne,
Under her own waight groaning, till the day
Appeer of respiration to the just,   *540*
And vengeance to the wicked, at return
Of him so lately promiss'd to thy aid,
The Womans seed, obscurely then foretold,
Now amplier known thy Saviour and thy Lord,
Last in the Clouds from Heav'n to be reveald
In glory of the Father, to dissolve
Satan with his perverted World, then raise
From the conflagrant mass, purg'd and refin'd,
New Heav'ns, new Earth, Ages of endless date
Founded in righteousness and peace and love,   *550*
To bring forth fruits Joy and eternal Bliss.

  He ended; and thus *Adam* last reply'd.
How soon hath thy prediction, Seer blest,
Measur'd this transient World, the Race of time,
Till time stand fixt: beyond is all abyss,
Eternitie, whose end no eye can reach.
Greatly instructed I shall hence depart.
Greatly in peace of thought, and have my fill
Of knowledge, what this vessel can containe;
Beyond which was my folly to aspire.   *560*
Henceforth I learne, that to obey is best,
And love with feare the onely God, to walk
As in his presence, ever to observe
His providence, and on him sole depend,
Merciful over all his works, with good
Still overcoming evil, and by small
Accomplishing great things, by things deemd weak
Subverting worldly strong, and worldly wise
By simply meek; that suffering for Truths sake
Is fortitude to highest victorie,   *570*
And to the faithful Death the Gate of Life;
Taught this by his example whom I now
Acknowledge my Redeemer ever blest.

  To whom thus also th' Angel last repli'd:
This having learnt, thou hast attained the summe
Of wisdom; hope no higher, though all the Starrs
Thou knewst by name, and all th' ethereal Powers,
All secrets of the deep, all Natures works,
Or works of God in Heav'n, Air, Earth, or Sea,
And all the riches of this World enjoydst,   *580*
And all the rule, one Empire; onely add

Deeds to thy knowledge answerable, add Faith,
Add Vertue, Patience, Temperance, add Love,
By name to come call'd Charitie, the soul
Of all the rest: then wilt thou not be loath
To leave this Paradise, but shalt possess
A Paradise within thee, happier farr.
Let us descend now therefore from this top
Of Speculation; for the hour precise
Exacts our parting hence; and see the Guards,   *590*
By mee encampt on yonder Hill, expect
Thir motion, at whose Front a flaming Sword,
In signal of remove, waves fiercely round;
We may no longer stay: go, waken *Eve*;
Her also I with gentle Dreams have calm'd
Portending good, and all her spirits compos'd
To meek submission: thou at season fit
Let her with thee partake what thou hast heard,
Chiefly what may concern her Faith to know,
The great deliverance by her Seed to come   *600*
(For by the Womans Seed) on all Mankind.
That ye may live, which will be many dayes,
Both in one Faith unanimous though sad,
With cause for evils past, yet much more cheer'd
With meditation on the happie end.
   He ended, and they both descend the Hill;
Descended, *Adam* to the Bowre where *Eve*
Lay sleeping ran before, but found her wak't;
And thus with words not sad she him receav'd.
   Whence thou returnst, & whither wentst, I know;   *610*
For God is also in sleep, and Dreams advise,
Which he hath sent propitious, some great good
Presaging, since with sorrow and hearts distress
Wearied I fell asleep: but now lead on;
In mee is no delay; with thee to goe,
Is to stay here; without thee here to stay,
Is to go hence unwilling; thou to mee
Art all things under Heav'n, all places thou,
Who for my wilful crime art banisht hence.
This further consolation yet secure   *620*
I carry hence; though all by mee is lost,
Such favour I unworthie am voutsaft,
By mee the Promis'd Seed shall all restore.
   So spake our Mother *Eve*, and *Adam* heard
Well pleas'd, but answer'd not; for now too nigh
Th' Archangel stood, and from the other Hill
To thir fixt Station, all in bright array

The Cherubim descended; on the ground
Gliding meteorous, as Ev'ning Mist
Ris'n from a River o're the marish glides, 630
And gathers ground fast at the Labourers heel
Homeward returning. High in Front advanc't,
The brandisht Sword of God before them blaz'd
Fierce as a Comet; which with torrid heat,
And vapour as the *Libyan* Air adust,
Began to parch that temperate Clime; whereat
In either hand the hastning Angel caught
Our lingring Parents, and to th' Eastern Gate
Led them direct, and down the Cliff as fast
To the subjected Plaine; then disappeer'd. 640
They looking back, all th' Eastern side beheld
Of Paradise, so late thir happie seat,
Wav'd over by that flaming Brand, the Gate
With dreadful Faces throng'd and fierie Armes:
Som natural tears they drop'd, but wip'd them soon;
The World was all before them, where to choose
Thir place of rest, and Providence thir guide:
They hand in hand with wandring steps and slow,
Through *Eden* took thir solitarie way.

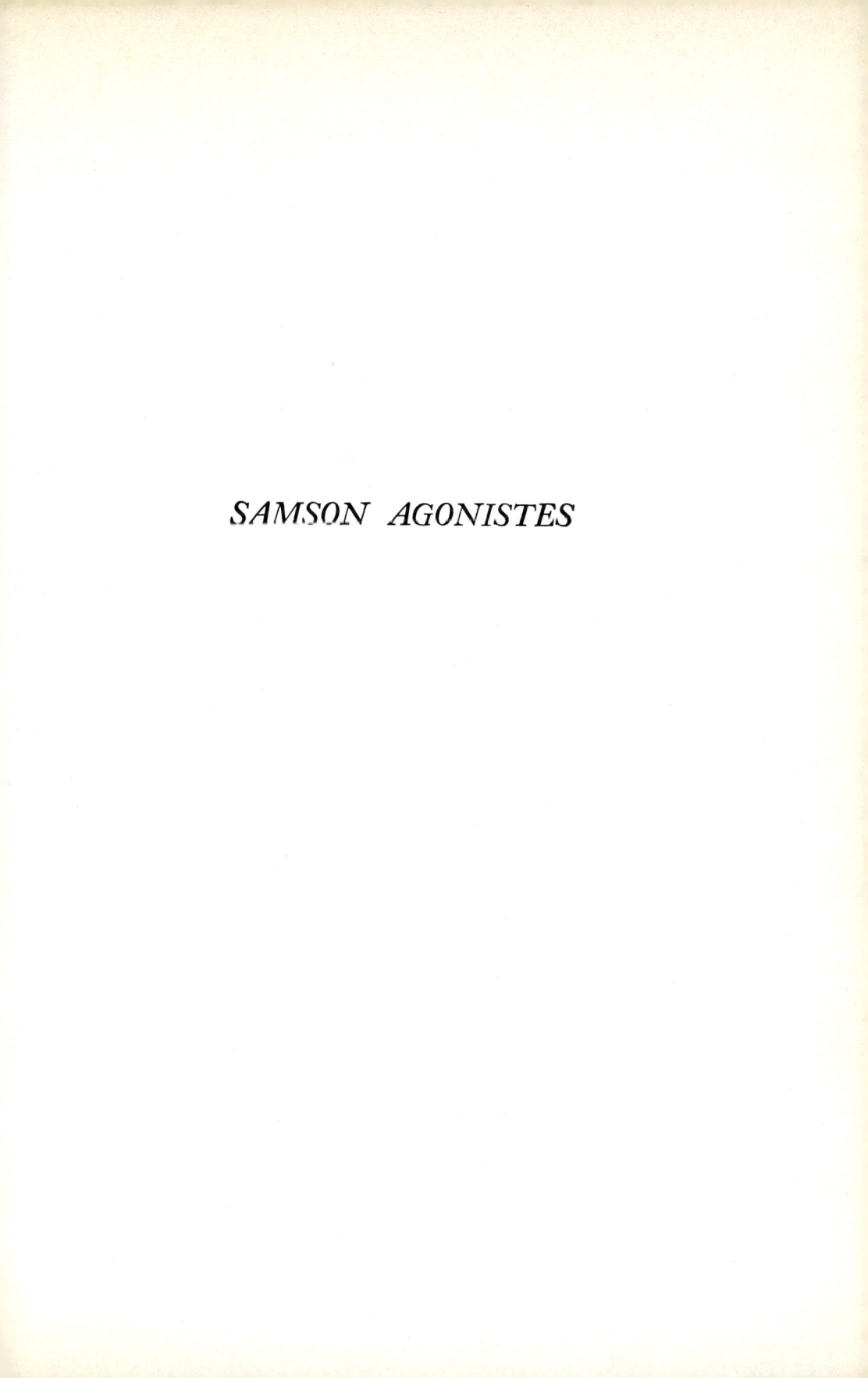

SAMSON AGONISTES

Of that sort of Dramatic Poem which is call'd Tragedy

TRAGEDY, as it was antiently compos'd, hath been ever held the gravest, moralest, and most profitable of all other Poems: therefore said by *Aristotle* to be of power by raising pity and fear, or terror, to purge the mind of those and such like passions, that is to temper and reduce them to just measure with a kind of delight, stirr'd up by reading or seeing those passions well imitated. Nor is Nature wanting in her own effects to make good his assertion: for so in Physic things of melancholic hue and quality are us'd against melancholy, sowr against sowr, salt to remove salt humours. Hence Philosophers and other gravest Writers, as *Cicero*, *Plutarch* and others, frequently cite out of Tragic Poets, both to adorn and illustrate thir discourse. The Apostle *Paul* himself thought it not unworthy to insert a verse of *Euripides* into the Text of Holy Scripture, 1 *Cor.* 15. 33. and *Pareus* commenting on the *Revelation*, divides the whole Book as a Tragedy, into Acts distinguisht each by a Chorus of Heavenly Harpings and Song between. Heretofore Men in highest dignity have labour'd not a little to be thought able to compose a Tragedy. Of that honour *Dionysius* the elder was no less ambitious, then before of his attaining to the Tyranny. *Augustus Cæsar* also had begun his *Ajax*, but unable to please his own judgment with what he had begun, left it unfinisht. *Seneca* the Philosopher is by some thought the Author of those Tragedies (at lest the best of them) that go under that name. *Gregory Nazianzen* a Father of the Church, thought it not unbeseeming the sanctity of his person to write a Tragedy, which he entitl'd, *Christ suffering*. This is mention'd to vindicate Tragedy from the small esteem, or rather infamy, which in the account of many it undergoes at this day with other common Interludes; hap'ning through the Poets error of intermixing Comic stuff with Tragic sadness and gravity; or introducing trivial and vulgar persons, which by all judicious hath bin counted absurd; and brought in without discretion, corruptly to gratifie the people. And though antient Tragedy use no Prologue, yet using sometimes, in case of self defence, or explanation, that which *Martial* calls an Epistle; in behalf of this Tragedy coming forth after the antient manner, much different from what among us passes for best, thus much before-hand may be Epistl'd; that *Chorus* is here introduc'd after the Greek manner, not antient only but modern, and still in use among the *Italians*. In the modelling therefore of this Poem, with good reason, the Antients and

Italians are rather follow'd, as of much more authority and fame. The measure of Verse us'd in the Chorus is of all sorts, call'd by the Greeks *Monostrophic*, or rather *Apolelymenon*, without regard had to *Strophe*, *Antistrophe* or *Epod*, which were a kind of Stanza's fram'd only for the Music, then us'd with the Chorus that sung; not essential to the Poem, and therefore not material; or being divided into Stanza's or Pauses, they may be call'd *Allæostropha*. Division into Act and Scene referring chiefly to the Stage (to which this work never was intended) is here omitted.

It suffices if the whole Drama be found not produc't beyond the fift Act, of the style and uniformitie, and that commonly call'd the Plot, whether intricate or explicit, which is nothing indeed but such œconomy, or disposition of the fable as may stand best with verisimilitude and decorum; they only will best judge who are not unacquainted with *Æschulus, Sophocles,* and *Euripides,* the three Tragic Poets unequall'd yet by any, and the best rule to all who endeavour to write Tragedy. The circumscription of time wherein the whole Drama begins and ends, is according to antient rule, and best example, within the space of 24 hours.

SAMSON AGONISTES

THE ARGUMENT

Samson *made Captive, Blind, and now in the Prison at Gaza, there to labour as in a common work-house, on a Festival day, in the general cessation from labour, comes forth into the open Air, to a place nigh, somewhat retir'd there to sit a while and bemoan his condition. Where he happens at length to be visited by certain friends and equals of his tribe, which make the Chorus, who seek to comfort him what they can; then by his old Father* Manoa, *who endeavours the like, and withal tells him his purpose to procure his liberty by ransom; lastly, that this Feast was proclaim'd by the* Philistins *as a day of Thanksgiving for thir deliverance from the hands of* Samson, *which yet more troubles him.* Manoa *then departs to prosecute his endeavour with the* Philistian *Lords for* Samson's *redemption; who in the mean while is visited by other persons; and lastly by a publick Officer to require his coming to the Feast before the Lords and People, to play or shew his strength in thir presence; he at first refuses, dismissing the publick Officer with absolute denyal to come; at length perswaded inwardly that this was from God, he yields to go along with him, who came now the second time with great threatnings to fetch him; the Chorus yet remaining on the place,* Manoa *returns full of joyful hope, to procure e're long his Sons deliverance: in the midst of which discourse an Ebrew comes in haste confusedly at first; and afterward more distinctly relating the Catastrophe, what* Samson *had done to the* Philistins, *and by accident to himself; wherewith the Tragedy ends.*

The Persons

Samson.
Manoa *the Father of* Samson.
Dalila *his Wife.*
Harapha *of Gath.*
Publick Officer. Messenger.
Chorus *of* Danites.

The Scene before the Prison in Gaza.

SAMS. A little onward lend thy guiding hand
To these dark steps, a little further on;
For yonder bank hath choice of Sun or shade,
There I am wont to sit, when any chance
Relieves me from my task of servile toyl,
Daily in the common Prison else enjoyn'd me,
Where I a Prisoner chain'd, scarce freely draw
The air imprison'd also, close and damp,
Unwholsom draught: but here I feel amends,
The breath of Heav'n fresh-blowing, pure and sweet,   *10*
With day-spring born; here leave me to respire.
This day a solemn Feast the people hold
To *Dagon* thir Sea-Idol, and forbid
Laborious works, unwillingly this rest

Thir Superstition yields me; hence with leave
Retiring from the popular noise, I seek
This unfrequented place to find some ease,
Ease to the body some, none to the mind
From restless thoughts, that like a deadly swarm
Of Hornets arm'd, no sooner found alone,   20
But rush upon me thronging, and present
Times past, what once I was, and what am now.
O wherefore was my birth from Heaven foretold
Twice by an Angel, who at last in sight
Of both my Parents all in flames ascended
From off the Altar, where an Off'ring burn'd,
As in a fiery column charioting
His Godlike presence, and from some great act
Or benefit reveal'd to *Abraham's* race?
Why was my breeding order'd and prescrib'd   30
As of a person separate to God,
Design'd for great exploits; if I must dye
Betray'd, Captiv'd, and both my Eyes put out,
Made of my Enemies the scorn and gaze;
To grind in Brazen Fetters under task
With this Heav'n-gifted strength? O glorious strength
Put to the labour of a Beast, debas't
Lower then bondslave! Promise was that I
Should *Israel* from *Philistian* yoke deliver;
Ask for this great Deliverer now, and find him   40
Eyeless in *Gaza* at the Mill with slaves,
Himself in bonds under *Philistian* yoke;
Yet stay, let me not rashly call in doubt
Divine Prediction; what if all foretold
Had been fulfilld but through mine own default,
Whom have I to complain of but my self?
Who this high gift of strength committed to me,
In what part lodg'd, how easily bereft me,
Under the Seal of silence could not keep,
But weakly to a woman must reveal it   50
O'recome with importunity and tears.
O impotence of mind, in body strong!
But what is strength without a double share
Of wisdom, vast, unwieldy, burdensom,
Proudly secure, yet liable to fall
By weakest suttleties, not made to rule,
But to subserve where wisdom bears command.
God, when he gave me strength, to shew withal
How slight the gift was, hung it in my Hair.
But peace, I must not quarrel with the will   60

Of highest dispensation, which herein
Happ'ly had ends above my reach to know:
Suffices that to me strength is my bane,
And proves the sourse of all my miseries;
So many, and so huge, that each apart
Would ask a life to wail, but chief of all,
O loss of sight, of thee I most complain!
Blind among enemies, O worse then chains,
Dungeon, or beggery, or decrepit age!
Light the prime work of God to me is extinct,   70
And all her various objects of delight
Annull'd, which might in part my grief have eas'd,
Inferiour to the vilest now become
Of man or worm; the vilest here excel me,
They creep, yet see, I dark in light expos'd
To daily fraud, contempt, abuse and wrong,
Within doors, or without, still as a fool,
In power of others, never in my own;
Scarce half I seem to live, dead more then half.
O dark, dark, dark, amid the blaze of noon,   80
Irrecoverably dark, total Eclipse
Without all hope of day!
O first created Beam, and thou great Word,
Let there be light, and light was over all;
Why am I thus bereav'd thy prime decree?
The Sun to me is dark
And silent as the Moon,
When she deserts the night
Hid in her vacant interlunar cave.
Since light so necessary is to life,   90
And almost life itself, if it be true
That light is in the Soul,
She all in every part; why was the sight
To such a tender ball as th' eye confin'd?
So obvious and so easie to be quench't,
And not as feeling through all parts diffus'd,
That she might look at will through every pore?
Then had I not been thus exil'd from light;
As in the land of darkness yet in light,
To live a life half dead, a living death,   100
And buried; but O yet more miserable!
My self, my Sepulcher, a moving Grave,
Buried, yet not exempt
By priviledge of death and burial
From worst of other evils, pains and wrongs,
But made hereby obnoxious more

To all the miseries of life,
Life in captivity
Among inhuman foes.
But who are these? for with joint pace I hear   *110*
The tread of many feet stearing this way;
Perhaps my enemies who come to stare
At my affliction, and perhaps to insult,
Thir daily practice to afflict me more.
    Chor. This, this is he; softly a while,
Let us not break in upon him;
O change beyond report, thought, or belief!
See how he lies at random, carelessly diffus'd,
With languish't head unpropt,
As one past hope, abandon'd   *120*
And by himself given over;
In slavish habit, ill-fitted weeds
O're worn and soild;
Or do my eyes misrepresent? Can this be hee,
That Heroic, that Renown'd,
Irresistible *Samson?* whom unarm'd
No strength of man, or fiercest wild beast could with-
    stand;
Who tore the Lion, as the Lion tears the Kid,
Ran on embattelld Armies clad in Iron,
And weaponless himself,   *130*
Made Arms ridiculous, useless the forgery
Of brazen shield and spear, the hammer'd Cuirass,
Chalybean temper'd steel, and frock of mail
Adamantean Proof;
But safest he who stood aloof,
When insupportably his foot advanc't,
In scorn of thir proud arms and warlike tools,
Spurn'd them to death by Troops. The bold
    Ascalonite
Fled from his Lion ramp, old Warriors turn'd
Thir plated backs under his heel;   *140*
Or grovling soiled thir crested helmets in the dust.
Then with what trivial weapon came to hand,
The Jaw of a dead Ass, his sword of bone,
A thousand fore-skins fell, the flower of *Palestin*
In *Ramath-lechi* famous to this day:
Then by main force pull'd up, and on his shoulders
    bore
The Gates of *Azza*, Post, and massie Bar
Up to the Hill by *Hebron*, seat of Giants old,
No journey of a Sabbath day, and loaded so;

Like whom the Gentiles feign to bear up Heav'n. *150*
Which shall I first bewail,
Thy Bondage or lost Sight,
Prison within Prison
Inseparably dark?
Thou art become (O worst imprisonment!)
The Dungeon of thy self; thy Soul
(Which Men enjoying sight oft without cause complain)
Imprison'd now indeed,
In real darkness of the body dwells,
Shut up from outward light *160*
To incorporate with gloomy night;
For inward light alas
Puts forth no visual beam.
O mirror of our fickle state,
Since man on earth unparallel'd!
The rarer thy example stands,
By how much from the top of wondrous glory,
Strongest of mortal men,
To lowest pitch of abject fortune thou art fall'n.
For him I reckon not in high estate *170*
Whom long descent of birth
Or the sphear of fortune raises;
But thee whose strength, while vertue was her mate
Might have subdu'd the Earth,
Universally crown'd with highest praises.
    Sam. I hear the sound of words, thir sense the air
Dissolves unjointed e're it reach my ear.
    Chor. Hee speaks, let us draw nigh. Matchless in might,
The glory late of *Israel*, now the grief;
We come thy friends and neighbours not unknown *180*
From *Eshtaol* and *Zora's* fruitful Vale
To visit or bewail thee, or if better,
Counsel or Consolation we may bring,
Salve to thy Sores, apt words have power to swage
The tumors of a troubl'd mind,
And are as Balm to fester'd wounds.
    Sam. Your coming, Friends, revives me, for I learn
Now of my own experience, not by talk,
How counterfeit a coin they are who friends
Bear in their Superscription (of the most *190*
I would be understood) in prosperous days
They swarm, but in adverse withdraw their head
Not to be found, though sought. Yee see, O friends,
How many evils have enclos'd me round;
Yet that which was the worst now least afflicts me,

Blindness, for had I sight, confus'd with shame,
How could I once look up, or heave the head,
Who like a foolish Pilot have shipwrack't,
My Vessel trusted to me from above,
Gloriously rigg'd; and for a word, a tear,   *200*
Fool, have divulg'd the secret gift of God
To a deceitful Woman: tell me Friends,
Am I not sung and proverbd for a Fool
In every street, do they not say, how well
Are come upon him his deserts? yet why?
Immeasurable strength they might behold
In me, of wisdom nothing more then mean;
This with the other should, at least, have paird,
These two proportiond ill drove me transverse.

  Chor. Tax not divine disposal, wisest Men   *210*
Have err'd, and by bad Women been deceiv'd;
And shall again, pretend they ne're so wise.
Deject not then so overmuch thy self,
Who hast of sorrow thy full load besides;
Yet truth to say, I oft have heard men wonder
Why thou shouldst wed *Philistian* women rather
Then of thine own Tribe fairer, or as fair,
At least of thy own Nation, and as noble.

  Sam. The first I saw at *Timna*, and she pleas'd
Mee, not my Parents, that I sought to wed,   *220*
The daughter of an Infidel: they knew not
That what I motion'd was of God; I knew
From intimate impulse, and therefore urg'd
The Marriage on; that by occasion hence
I might begin *Israel's* Deliverance,
The work to which I was divinely call'd;
She proving false, the next I took to Wife
(O that I never had! fond wish too late)
Was in the Vale of *Sorec*, *Dalila*,
That specious Monster, my accomplisht snare.   *230*
I thought it lawful from my former act,
And the same end; still watching to oppress
Israel's oppressours: of what now I suffer
She was not the prime cause, but I my self,
Who vanquisht with a peal of words (O weakness!)
Gave up my fort of silence to a Woman.

  Chor. In seeking just occasion to provoke
The *Philistine*, thy Countries Enemy,
Thou never wast remiss, I bear thee witness:
Yet *Israel* still serves with all his Sons.   *240*

  Sam. That fault I take not on me, but transfer

On *Israel*'s Governours, and Heads of Tribes,
Who seeing those great acts which God had done
Singly by me against their Conquerours
Acknowledg'd not, or not at all consider'd
Deliverance offerd: I on th' other side
Us'd no ambition to commend my deeds,
The deeds themselves, though mute, spoke loud the
    dooer;
But they persisted deaf, and would not seem
To count them things worth notice, till at length   250
Thir Lords the *Philistines* with gather'd powers
Enterd *Judea* seeking mee, who then
Safe to the rock of *Etham* was retir'd,
Not flying, but fore-casting in what place
To set upon them, what advantag'd best;
Mean while the men of *Judah* to prevent
The harrass of thir Land, beset me round;
I willingly on some conditions came
Into thir hands, and they as gladly yield me
To the uncircumcis'd a welcom prey,   260
Bound with two cords; but cords to me were threds
Toucht with the flame: on thir whole Host I flew
Unarm'd, and with a trivial weapon fell'd
Thir choicest youth; they only liv'd who fled.
Had *Judah* that day join'd, or one whole Tribe,
They had by this possess'd the Towers of *Gath*,
And lorded over them whom now they serve;
But what more oft in Nations grown corrupt,
And by thir vices brought to servitude,
Then to love Bondage more then Liberty,   270
Bondage with ease then strenuous liberty;
And to despise, or envy, or suspect
Whom God hath of his special favour rais'd
As thir Deliverer; if he aught begin,
How frequent to desert him, and at last
To heap ingratitude on worthiest deeds?
    Chor. Thy words to my remembrance bring
How *Succoth* and the Fort of *Penuel*
Thir great Deliverer contemn'd,
The matchless *Gideon* in pursuit   280
Of *Madian* and her vanquisht Kings:
And how ingrateful *Ephraim*
Had dealt with *Jephtha*, who by argument,
Not worse then by his shield and spear
Defended *Israel* from the *Ammonite*,
Had not his prowess quell'd thir pride

In that sore battel when so many dy'd
Without Reprieve adjudg'd to death,
For want of well pronouncing *Shibboleth*.
   Sam. Of such examples adde mee to the roul,   *290*
Mee easily indeed mine may neglect,
But Gods propos'd deliverance not so.
   Chor. Just are the ways of God,
And justifiable to Men;
Unless there be who think not God at all,
If any be, they walk obscure;
For of such Doctrine never was there School,
But the heart of the Fool,
And no man therein Doctor but himself.
   Yet more there be who doubt his ways not just,   *300*
As to his own edicts, found contradicting,
Then give the rains to wandring thought,
Regardless of his glories diminution;
Till by thir own perplexities involv'd
They ravel more, still less resolv'd,
But never find self-satisfying solution.
   As if they would confine th' interminable,
And tie him to his own prescript,
Who made our Laws to bind us, not himself,
And hath full right to exempt   *310*
Whom so it pleases him by choice
From National obstriction, without taint
Of sin, or legal debt;
For with his own Laws he can best dispence.
   He would not else who never wanted means,
Nor in respect of the enemy just cause
To set his people free,
Have prompted this Heroic *Nazarite*,
Against his vow of strictest purity,
To seek in marriage that fallacious Bride,   *320*
Unclean, unchaste.
   Down Reason then, at least vain reasonings down,
Though Reason here aver
That moral verdit quits her of unclean:
Unchaste was subsequent, her stain not his.
   But see here comes thy reverend Sire
With careful step, Locks white as doune,
Old *Manoah:* advise
Forthwith how thou oughtst to receive him.
   Sam. Ay me, another inward grief awak't,   *330*
With mention of that name renews th' assault.
   Man. Brethren and men of *Dan*, for such ye seem,

Though in this uncouth place; if old respect,
As I suppose, towards your once gloried friend,
My Son now Captive, hither hath inform'd
Your younger feet, while mine cast back with age
Came lagging after; say if he be here.
  Chor. As signal now in low dejected state,
As earst in highest, behold him where he lies.
  Man. O miserable change! is this the man,   340
That invincible *Samson*, far renown'd,
The dread of *Israel*'s foes, who with a strength
Equivalent to Angels walk'd thir streets,
None offering fight; who single combatant
Duell'd thir Armies rank't in proud array,
Himself an Army, now unequal match
To save himself against a coward arm'd
At one spears length. O ever failing trust
In mortal strength! and oh what not in man
Deceivable and vain! Nay what thing good   350
Pray'd for, but often proves our woe, our bane?
I pray'd for Children, and thought barrenness
In wedlock a reproach; I gain'd a Son,
And such a Son as all Men hail'd me happy;
Who would be now a Father in my stead?
O wherefore did God grant me my request,
And as a blessing with such pomp adorn'd?
Why are his gifts desirable, to tempt
Our earnest Prayers, then giv'n with solemn hand
As Graces, draw a Scorpions tail behind?   360
For this did the Angel twice descend? for this
Ordain'd thy nurture holy, as of a Plant;
Select, and Sacred, Glorious for a while,
The miracle of men: then in an hour
Ensnar'd, assaulted, overcome, led bound,
Thy Foes derision, Captive, Poor, and Blind
Into a Dungeon thrust, to work with Slaves?
Alas methinks whom God hath chosen once
To worthiest deeds, if he through frailty err,
He should not so o'rewhelm, and as a thrall   370
Subject him to so foul indignities,
Be it but for honours sake of former deeds.
  Sam. Appoint not heavenly disposition, Father,
Nothing of all these evils hath befall'n me
But justly; I my self have brought them on,
Sole Author I, sole cause: if aught seem vile,
As vile hath been my folly, who have profan'd
The mystery of God giv'n me under pledge

Of vow, and have betray'd it to a woman,
A *Canaanite*, my faithless enemy.   380
This well I knew, nor was at all supris'd,
But warn'd by oft experience: did not she
Of *Timna* first betray me, and reveal
The secret wrested from me in her highth
Of Nuptial Love profest, carrying it strait
To them who had corrupted her, my Spies,
And Rivals? In this other was there found
More Faith? who also in her prime of love,
Spousal embraces, vitiated with Gold,
Though offer'd only, by the sent conceiv'd   390
Her spurious first-born; Treason against me?
Thrice she assay'd with flattering prayers and sighs,
And amorous reproaches to win from me
My capital secret, in what part my strength
Lay stor'd in what part summ'd, that she might know:
Thrice I deluded her, and turn'd to sport
Her importunity, each time perceiving
How openly, and with what impudence
She purpos'd to betray me, and (which was worse
Then undissembl'd hate) with what contempt   400
She sought to make me Traytor to my self;
Yet the fourth time, when mustring all her wiles,
With blandisht parlies, feminine assaults,
Tongue-batteries, she surceas'd not day nor night
To storm me over-watch't, and wearied out.
At times when men seek most repose and rest,
I yielded, and unlock'd her all my heart,
Who with a grain of manhood well resolv'd
Might easily have shook off all her snares:
But foul effeminacy held me yok't   410
Her Bond-slave; O indignity, O blot
To Honour and Religion! servil mind
Rewarded well with servil punishment!
The base degree to which I now am fall'n,
These rags, this grinding, is not yet so base
As was my former servitude, ignoble,
Unmanly, ignominious, infamous,
True slavery, and that blindness worse then this,
That saw not how degenerately I serv'd.

   Man. I cannot praise thy Marriage choises, Son,   420
Rather approv'd them not; but thou didst plead
Divine impulsion prompting how thou might'st
Find some occasion to infest our Foes.
I state not that; this I am sure; our Foes

Found soon occasion thereby to make thee
Thir Captive, and thir triumph; thou the sooner
Temptation found'st, or over-potent charms
To violate the sacred trust of silence
Deposited within thee; which to have kept
Tacit, was in thy power; true; and thou bear'st   *430*
Enough, and more the burden of that fault;
Bitterly hast thou paid, and still art paying
That rigid score. A worse thing yet remains,
This day the *Philistines* a popular Feast
Here celebrate in *Gaza*; and proclaim
Great Pomp, and Sacrifice, and Praises loud
To *Dagon*, as their God who hath deliver'd
Thee *Samson* bound and blind into thir hands,
Them out of thine, who slew'st them many a slain.
So *Dagon* shall be magnifi'd, and God,   *440*
Besides whom is no God, compar'd with Idols,
Disglorifi'd, blasphem'd, and had in scorn
By th' Idolatrous rout amidst thir wine;
Which to have come to pass by means of thee,
Samson, of all thy sufferings think the heaviest,
Of all reproach the most with shame that ever
Could have befall'n thee and thy Fathers house.
   Sam. Father, I do acknowledge and confess
That I this honour, I this pomp have brought
To *Dagon*, and advanc'd his praises high   *450*
Among the Heathen round; to God have brought
Dishonour, obloquie, and op't the mouths
Of Idolists, and Atheists; have brought scandal
To *Israel*, diffidence of God, and doubt
In feeble hearts, propense anough before
To waver, or fall off and joyn with Idols:
Which is my chief affliction, shame and sorrow,
The anguish of my Soul, that suffers not
Mine eie to harbour sleep, or thoughts to rest.
This only hope relieves me, that the strife   *460*
With me hath end; all the contest is now
'Twixt God and *Dagon; Dagon* hath presum'd,
Me overthrown, to enter lists with God,
His Deity comparing and preferring
Before the God of *Abraham*. He, be sure,
Will not connive, or linger, thus provok'd,
But will arise and his great name assert:
Dagon must stoop, and shall e're long receive
Such a discomfit, as shall quite despoil him
Of all these boasted Trophies won on me,   *470*

And with confusion blank his Worshippers.
    Man. With cause this hope relieves thee, and these words
I as a Prophecy receive: for God,
Nothing more certain, will not long defer
To vindicate the glory of his name
Against all competition, nor will long
Endure it, doubtful whether God be Lord,
Or *Dagon.* But for thee what shall be done?
Thou must not in the mean while here forgot
Lie in this miserable loathsom plight   *480*
Neglected. I already have made way
To some *Philistian* Lords, with whom to treat
About thy ransom: well they may by this
Have satisfi'd thir utmost of revenge
By pains and slaveries, worse then death inflicted
On thee, who now no more canst do them harm.
    Sam. Spare that proposal, Father, spare the trouble
Of that sollicitation; let me here,
As I deserve, pay on my punishment;
And expiate, if possible, my crime,   *490*
Shameful garrulity. To have reveal'd
Secrets of men, the secrets of a friend,
How hainous had the fact been, how deserving
Contempt, and scorn of all, to be excluded
All friendship, and avoided as a blab,
The mark of fool set on his front?
But I Gods counsel have not kept, his holy secret
Presumptuously have publish'd, impiously,
Weakly at least, and shamefully: A sin
That Gentiles in thir Parables condemn   *500*
To thir abyss and horrid pains confin'd.
    Man. Be penitent and for thy fault contrite,
But act not in thy own affliction, Son,
Repent the sin, but if the punishment
Thou canst avoid, self-preservation bids;
Or th' execution leave to high disposal,
And let another hand, not thine, exact
Thy penal forfeit from thy self; perhaps
God will relent, and quit thee all his debt;
Who evermore approves and more accepts   *510*
(Best pleas'd with humble and filial submission)
Him who imploring mercy sues for life,
Then who self-rigorous chooses death as due;
Which argues over-just, and self-displeas'd
For self-offence, more then for God offended.

Reject not then what offerd means, who knows
But God hath set before us, to return thee
Home to thy countrey and his sacred house,
Where thou mayst bring thy off'rings, to avert
His further ire, with praiers and vows renew'd.   *520*
    Sam. His pardon I implore; but as for life,
To what end should I seek it? when in strength
All mortals I excell'd, and great in hopes
With youthful courage and magnanimous thoughts
Of birth from Heav'n foretold and high exploits,
Full of divine instinct, after some proof
Of acts indeed heroic, far beyond
The Sons of *Anac*, famous now and blaz'd,
Fearless of danger, like a petty God
I walk'd about admir'd of all and dreaded   *530*
On hostile ground, none daring my affront.
Then swoll'n with pride into the snare I fell
Of fair fallacious looks, venereal trains,
Softn'd with pleasure and voluptuous life;
At length to lay my head and hallow'd pledge
Of all my strength in the lascivious lap
Of a deceitful Concubine who shore me
Like a tame Weather, all my precious fleece,
Then turn'd me out ridiculous, despoil'd,
Shav'n, and disarm'd among my enemies.   *540*
    Chor. Desire of wine and all delicious drinks,
Which many a famous Warriour overturns,
Thou couldst repress, nor did the dancing Rubie
Sparkling, out-pow'rd, the flavor, or the smell,
Or taste that cheers the heart of Gods and men,
Allure thee from the cool Crystalline stream.
    Sam. Where ever fountain or fresh current flow'd
Against the Eastern ray, translucent, pure,
With touch ætherial of Heav'ns fiery rod
I drank, from the clear milkie juice allaying   *550*
Thirst, and refresht; nor envy'd them the grape
Whose heads that turbulent liquor fills with fumes.
    Chor. O madness, to think use of strongest wines
And strongest drinks our chief support of health,
When God with these forbid'n made choice to rear
His mighty Champion, strong above compare,
Whose drink was only from the liquid brook.
    Sam. But what avail'd this temperance, not compleat
Against another object more enticing?
What boots it at one gate to make defence   *560*
And at another to let in the foe

Effeminatly vanquish't? by which means,
Now blind, disheartn'd, sham'd, dishonour'd, quell'd,
To what can I be useful, wherein serve
My Nation, and the work from Heav'n impos'd,
But to sit idle on the houshold hearth,
A burdenous drone; to visitants a gaze,
Or pitied object, these redundant locks
Robustious to no purpose clustring down,
Vain monument of strength; till length of years   570
And sedentary numness craze my limbs
To a contemptible old age obscure.
Here rather let me drudge and earn my bread,
Till vermin or the draff of servil food
Consume me, and oft-invocated death
Hast'n the welcom end of all my pains.
   Man. Wilt thou then serve the *Philistines* with that gift
Which was expresly giv'n thee to annoy them?
Better at home lie bed-rid, not only idle,
Inglorious, unimploy'd, with age out-worn.   580
But God who caus'd a fountain at thy prayer
From the dry ground to spring, thy thirst to allay
After the brunt of battel, can as easie
Cause light again within thy eies to spring,
Wherewith to serve him better then thou hast;
And I perswade me so; why else this strength
Miraculous yet remaining in those locks?
His might continues in thee not for naught,
Nor shall his wondrous gifts be frustrate thus.
   Sam. All otherwise to me my thoughts portend,   590
That these dark orbs no more shall treat with light,
Nor th' other light of life continue long,
But yield to double darkness nigh at hand:
So much I feel my genial spirits droop,
My hopes all flat, nature within me seems
In all her functions weary of herself;
My race of glory run, and race of shame,
And I shall shortly be with them that rest.
   Man. Believe not these suggestions which proceed
From anguish of the mind and humours black,   600
That mingle with thy fancy. I however
Must not omit a Fathers timely care
To prosecute the means of thy deliverance
By ransom or how else: mean while be calm,
And healing words from these thy friends admit.
   Sam. O that torment should not be confin'd
To the bodies wounds and sores

With maladies innumerable
In heart, head, brest, and reins;
But must secret passage find   *610*
To th' inmost mind,
There exercise all his fierce accidents,
And on her purest spirits prey,
As on entrails, joints, and limbs,
With answerable pains, but more intense,
Though void of corporal sense.
   My griefs not only pain me
As a lingring disease,
But finding no redress, ferment and rage,
Nor less then wounds immedicable   *620*
Ranckle, and fester, and gangrene,
To black mortification.
Thoughts my Tormenters arm'd with deadly stings
Mangle my apprehensive tenderest parts,
Exasperate, exulcerate, and raise
Dire inflammation which no cooling herb
Or medcinal liquor can asswage,
Nor breath of Vernal Air from snowy *Alp*.
Sleep hath forsook and giv'n me o're
To deaths benumming Opium as my only cure.   *630*
Thence faintings, swounings of despair,
And sense of Heav'ns desertion.
   I was his nursling once and choice delight,
His destin'd from the womb,
Promisd by Heavenly message twice descending.
Under his special eie
Abstemious I grew up and thriv'd amain;
He led me on to mightiest deeds
Above the nerve of mortal arm
Against the uncircumcis'd, our enemies.   *640*
But now hath cast me off as never known,
And to those cruel enemies,
Whom I by his appointment had provok't,
Left me all helpless with th' irreparable loss
Of sight, reserv'd alive to be repeated
The subject of thir cruelty, or scorn.
Nor am I in the list of them that hope;
Hopeless are all my evils, all remediless;
This one prayer yet remains, might I be heard,
No long petition, speedy death,   *650*
The close of all my miseries, and the balm.
   Chor. Many are the sayings of the wise
In antient and in modern books enroll'd;

Extolling Patience as the truest fortitude;
And to the bearing well of all calamities,
All chances incident to mans frail life
Consolatories writ
With studied argument, and much perswasion sought
Lenient of grief and anxious thought,
But with th' afflicted in his pangs thir sound   *660*
Little prevails, or rather seems a tune,
Harsh, and of dissonant mood from his complaint,
Unless he feel within
Some sourse of consolation from above;
Secret refreshings, that repair his strength,
And fainting spirits uphold.
   God of our Fathers, what is man!
That thou towards him with hand so various,
Or might I say contrarious,
Temperst thy providence through his short course,   *670*
Not evenly, as thou rul'st
The Angelic orders and inferiour creatures mute,
Irrational and brute.
Nor do I name of men the common rout,
That wandring loose about
Grow up and perish, as the summer flie,
Heads without name no more rememberd,
But such as thou hast solemnly elected,
With gifts and graces eminently adorn'd
To some great work, thy glory,   *680*
And peoples safety, which in part they effect:
Yet toward these thus dignifi'd, thou oft
Amidst thir highth of noon,
Changest thy countenance, and thy hand with no regard
Of highest favours past
From thee on them, or them to thee of service.
   Nor only dost degrade them, or remit
To life obscur'd, which were a fair dismission,
But throw'st them lower then thou didst exalt them high,
Unseemly falls in human eie,   *690*
Too grievous for the trespass or omission,
Oft leav'st them to the hostile sword
Of Heathen and prophane, thir carkasses
To dogs and fowls a prey, or else captiv'd:
Or to the unjust tribunals, under change of times,
And condemnation of the ingrateful multitude.
If these they scape, perhaps in poverty
With sickness and disease thou bow'st them down,
Painful diseases and deform'd,

In crude old age; 700
Though not disordinate, yet causless suffring
The punishment of dissolute days, in fine,
Just or unjust, alike seem miserable,
For oft alike, both come to evil end.
   So deal not with this once thy glorious Champion,
The Image of thy strength, and mighty minister.
What do I beg? how hast thou dealt already?
Behold him in this state calamitous, and turn
His labours, for thou canst, to peaceful end.
   But who is this, what thing of Sea or Land? 710
Femal of sex it seems,
That so bedeckt, ornate, and gay,
Comes this way sailing
Like a stately Ship
Of *Tarsus*, bound for th' Isles
Of *Javan* or *Gadier*
With all her bravery on, and tackle trim,
Sails fill'd, and streamers waving,
Courted by all the winds that hold them play,
An Amber sent of odorous perfume 720
Her harbinger, a damsel train behind;
Some rich *Philistian* Matron she may seem,
And now at nearer view, no other certain
Than *Dalila* thy wife.
   Sam. My Wife, my Traytress, let her not come near me.
   Cho. Yet on she moves, now stands & eies thee fixt,
About t' have spoke, but now, with head declin'd
Like a fair flower surcharg'd with dew, she weeps
And words addrest seem into tears dissolv'd,
Wetting the borders of her silk'n veil: 730
But now again she makes address to speak.
   Dal. With doubtful feet and wavering resolution
I came, still dreading thy displeasure, *Samson*,
Which to have merited, without excuse,
I cannot but acknowledge, yet if tears
May expiate (though the fact more evil drew
In the perverse event then I foresaw)
My penance hath not slack'n'd, though my pardon
No way assur'd. But conjugal affection
Prevailing over fear, and timerous doubt 740
Hath led me on desirous to behold
Once more thy face, and know of thy estate.
If aught in my ability may serve
To light'n what thou suffer'st, and appease

Thy mind with what amends is in my power,
Though late, yet in some part to recompense
My rash but more unfortunate misdeed.
    Sam. Out, out *Hyæna*; these are thy wonted arts,
And arts of every woman false like thee,
To break all faith, all vows, deceive, betray,   750
Then as repentant to submit, beseech,
And reconcilement move with feign'd remorse,
Confess, and promise wonders in her change,
Not truly penitent, but chief to try
Her husband, how far urg'd his patience bears,
His vertue or weakness which way to assail:
Then with more cautious and instructed skill
Again transgresses, and again submits;
That wisest and best men full oft beguil'd
With goodness principl'd not to reject   760
The penitent, but ever to forgive,
Are drawn to wear out miserable days,
Entangl'd with a poysnous bosom snake,
If not by quick destruction soon cut off
As I by thee, to Ages an example.
    Dal. Yet hear me *Samson*; not that I endeavour
To lessen or extenuate my offence,
But that on th' other side if it be weigh'd
By it self, with aggravations not surcharg'd,
Or else with just allowance counterpois'd   770
I may, if possible, thy pardon find
The easier towards me, or thy hatred less.
First granting, as I do, it was a weakness
In me, but incident to all our sex,
Curiosity, inquisitive, importune
Of secrets, then with like infirmity
To publish them, both common female faults:
Was it not weakness also to make known
For importunity, that is for naught,
Wherein consisted all thy strength and safety?   780
To what I did thou shewdst me first the way.
But I to enemies reveal'd, and should not.
Nor shouldst thou have trusted that to womans frailty
E're I to thee, thou to thy self wast cruel.
Let weakness then with weakness come to parl
So near related, or the same of kind,
Thine forgive mine; that men may censure thine
The gentler, if severely thou exact not
More strength from me, then in thy self was found.
And what if Love, which thou interpret'st hate,   790

The jealousie of Love, powerful of sway
In human hearts, nor less in mine towards thee,
Caus'd what I did? I saw thee mutable
Of fancy, feard lest one day thou wouldst leave me
As her at *Timna*, sought by all means therefore
How to endear, and hold thee to me firmest:
No better way I saw then by importuning
To learn thy secrets, get into my power
Thy key of strength and safety: thou wilt say,
Why then reveal'd? I was assur'd by those 800
Who tempted me, that nothing was design'd
Against thee but safe custody, and hold:
That made for me, I knew that liberty
Would draw thee forth to perilous enterprises,
While I at home sate full of cares and fears
Wailing thy absence in my widow'd bed;
Here I should still enjoy thee day and night
Mine and Loves prisoner, not the *Philistines*,
Whole to my self, unhazarded abroad,
Fearless at home of partners in my love. 810
These reasons in Loves law have past for good,
Though fond and reasonless to some perhaps:
And Love hath oft, well meaning, wrought much wo,
Yet always pity or pardon hath obtain'd.
Be not unlike all others, not austere
As thou art strong, inflexible as steel.
If thou in strength all mortals dost exceed,
In uncompassionate anger do not so.
  Sam. How cunningly the sorceress displays
Her own transgressions, to upbraid me mine! 820
That malice not repentance brought thee hither,
By this appears: I gave, thou say'st, th' example,
I led the way; bitter reproach, but true,
I to my self was false e're thou to me,
Such pardon therefore as I give my folly,
Take to thy wicked deed: which when thou seest
Impartial, self-severe, inexorable,
Thou wilt renounce thy seeking, and much rather
Confess it feign'd, weakness is thy excuse,
And I believe it, weakness to resist 830
Philistian gold: if weakness may excuse,
What Murtherer, what Traytor, Parricide,
Incestuous, Sacrilegious, but may plead it?
All wickedness is weakness: that plea therefore
With God or Man will gain thee no remission.
But Love constrain'd thee; call it furious rage

To satisfie thy lust: Love seeks to have Love;
My love how couldst thou hope, who tookst the way
To raise in me inexpiable hate,
Knowing, as needs I must, by thee betray'd?   *840*
In vain thou striv'st to cover shame with shame,
Or by evasions thy crime uncoverst more.
    Dal. Since thou determinst weakness for no plea
In man or woman, though to thy own condemning,
Hear what assaults I had, what snares besides,
What sieges girt me round, e're I consented;
Which might have aw'd the best resolv'd of men,
The constantest to have yielded without blame.
It was not gold, as to my charge thou lay'st,
That wrought with me: thou know'st the Magistrates *850*
And Princes of my countrey came in person,
Sollicited, commanded, threatn'd, urg'd,
Adjur'd by all the bonds of civil Duty
And of Religion, press'd how just it was,
How honourable, how glorious to entrap
A common enemy, who had destroy'd
Such numbers of our Nation: and the Priest
Was not behind, but ever at my ear,
Preaching how meritorious with the gods
It would be to ensnare an irreligious   *860*
Dishonourer of *Dagon:* what had I
To oppose against such powerful arguments?
Only my love of thee held long debate;
And combated in silence all these reasons
With hard contest: at length that grounded maxim
So rife and celebrated in the mouths
Of wisest men; that to the public good
Private respects must yield; with grave authority
Took full possession of me and prevail'd;
Vertue, as I thought, truth, duty so enjoyning.   *870*
    Sam. I thought where all thy circling wiles would end;
In feign'd Religion, smooth hypocrisie.
But had thy love, still odiously pretended,
Bin, as it ought, sincere, it would have taught thee
Far other reasonings, brought forth other deeds.
I before all the daughters of my Tribe
And of my Nation chose thee from among
My enemies, lov'd thee, as too well thou knew'st,
Too well, unbosom'd all my secrets to thee,
Not out of levity, but over-powr'd   *880*
By thy request, who could deny thee nothing;
Yet now am judg'd an enemy. Why then

Didst thou at first receive me for thy husband?
Then, as since then, thy countries foe profest:
Being once a wife, for me thou wast to leave
Parents and countrey; nor was I their subject,
Nor under their protection but my own,
Thou mine, not theirs: if aught against my life
Thy countrey sought of thee, it sought unjustly,
Against the law of nature, law of nations,   *890*
No more thy countrey, but an impious crew
Of men conspiring to uphold thir state
By worse than hostile deeds, violating the ends
For which our countrey is a name so dear;
Not therefore to be obey'd. But zeal mov'd thee;
To please thy gods thou didst it; gods unable
To acquit themselves and prosecute their foes
But by ungodly deeds, the contradiction
Of their own deity, Gods cannot be:
Less therefore to be pleas'd, obey'd, or fear'd,   *900*
These false pretexts and varnish'd colours failing,
Bare in thy guilt how foul must thou appear?
   Dal. In argument with men a woman ever
Goes by the worse, whatever be her cause.
   Sam. For want of words no doubt, or lack of breath,
Witness when I was worried with thy peals.
   Dal. I was a fool, too rash, and quite mistaken
In what I thought would have succeeded best.
Let me obtain forgiveness of thee, *Samson*,
Afford me place to shew what recompence   *910*
Towards thee I intend for what I have misdone,
Misguided: only what remains past cure
Bear not too sensibly, nor still insist
To afflict thy self in vain: though sight be lost,
Life yet hath many solaces, enjoy'd
Where other senses want not their delights
At home in leisure and domestic ease,
Exempt from many a care and chance to which
Eye sight exposes daily men abroad.
I to the Lords will intercede, not doubting   *920*
Thir favourable ear, that I may fetch thee
From forth this loathsom prison-house, to abide
With me, where my redoubl'd love and care
With nursing diligence, to me glad office,
May ever tend about thee to old age
With all things grateful chear'd, and so suppli'd,
That what by me thou hast lost thou least shalt miss.
   Sam. No, no, of my condition take no care;

It fits not; thou and I long since are twain;
Nor think me so unwary or accurst   930
To bring my feet again into the snare
Where once I have been caught; I know thy trains
Though dearly to my cost, thy ginns, and toyls;
Thy fair enchanted cup, and warbling charms
No more on me have power, their force is null'd,
So much of Adders wisdom I have learn't
To fence my ear against thy sorceries.
If in my flower of youth and strength, when all men
Lov'd, honour'd, fear'd me, thou alone could hate me
Thy Husband, slight me, sell me, and forgo me;   940
How wouldst thou use me now, blind, and thereby
Deceiveable, in most things as a child
Helpless, thence easily contemn'd, and scorn'd,
And last neglected? How wouldst thou insult
When I must live uxorious to thy will
In perfet thraldom, how again betray me,
Bearing my words and doings to the Lords
To gloss upon, and censuring, frown or smile?
This Gaol I count the house of Liberty
To thine whose doors my feet shall never enter.   950
   Dal. Let me approach at least, and touch thy hand.
   Sam. Not for thy life, lest fierce remembrance wake
My sudden rage to tear thee joint by joint.
At distance I forgive thee, go with that;
Bewail thy falshood, and the pious works
It hath brought forth to make thee memorable
Among illustrious women, faithful wives:
Cherish thy hast'n'd widowhood with the gold
Of Matrimonial treason: so farwel.
   Dal. I see thou art implacable, more deaf   960
To prayers, then winds and seas, yet winds to seas
Are reconcil'd at length, and Sea to Shore:
Thy anger, unappeasable, still rages,
Eternal tempest never to be calm'd.
Why do I humble thus my self, and suing
For peace, reap nothing but repulse and hate?
Bid go with evil omen and the brand
Of infamy upon my name denounc't?
To mix with thy concernments I desist
Henceforth, nor too much disapprove my own.   970
Fame if not double-fac't is double-mouth'd,
And with contrary blast proclaims most deeds,
On both his wings, one black, th' other white,
Bears greatest names in his wild aerie flight.

My name perhaps among the Circumcis'd
In *Dan*, in *Judah*, and the bordering Tribes,
To all posterity may stand defam'd,
With malediction mention'd, and the blot
Of falshood most unconjugal traduc't.
But in my countrey where I most desire,   *980*
In *Ecron*, *Gaza*, *Asdod*, and in *Gath*
I shall be nam'd among the famousest
Of Women, sung at solemn festivals,
Living and dead recorded, who to save
Her countrey from a fierce destroyer, chose
Above the faith of wedlock-bands, my tomb
With odours visited and annual flowers.
Not less renown'd then in Mount *Ephraim*,
Jael, who with inhospitable guile
Smote *Sisera* sleeping through the Temples nail'd.   *990*
Nor shall I count it hainous to enjoy
The public marks of honour and reward
Conferr'd upon me, for the piety
Which to my countrey I was judg'd to have shewn.
At this who ever envies or repines
I leave him to his lot, and like my own.
    Chor. She's gone, a manifest Serpent by her sting
Discover'd in the end, till now conceal'd.
    Sam. So let her go, God sent her to debase me,
And aggravate my folly who committed   *1000*
To such a viper his most sacred trust
Of secresie, my safety, and my life.
    Chor. Yet beauty, though injurious, hath strange power,
After offence returning, to regain
Love once possest, nor can be easily
Repuls't, without much inward passion felt
And secret sting of amorous remorse.
    Sam. Love-quarrels oft in pleasing concord end,
Not wedlock-trechery endangering life.
    Chor. It is not vertue, wisdom, valour, wit,   *1010*
Strength, comliness of shape, or amplest merit
That womans love can win or long inherit;
But what it is, hard is to say,
Harder to hit,
(Which way soever men refer it)
Much like thy riddle, *Samson*, in one day
Or seven, though one should musing sit;
    If any of these or all, the *Timnian* bride
Had not so soon preferr'd
Thy Paranymph, worthless to thee compar'd,   *1020*

Successour in thy bed,
Nor both so loosly disally'd
Thir nuptials, nor this last so trecherously
Had shorn the fatal harvest of thy head.
Is it for that such outward ornament
Was lavish't on thir Sex, that inward gifts
Were left for hast unfinish't, judgment scant,
Capacity not rais'd to apprehend
Or value what is best
In choice, but oftest to affect the wrong? *1030*
Or was too much of self-love mixt,
Of constancy no root infixt,
That either they love nothing, or not long?
   What e're it be, to wisest men and best
Seeming at first all heavenly under virgin veil,
Soft, modest, meek, demure,
Once join'd, the contrary she proves, a thorn
Intestin, far within defensive arms
A cleaving mischief, in his way to vertue
Adverse and turbulent, or by her charms *1040*
Draws him awry enslav'd
With dotage, and his sense deprav'd
To folly and shameful deeds which ruin ends.
What Pilot so expert but needs must wreck
Embarqu'd with such a Stears-mate at the Helm?
   Favour'd of Heav'n who finds
One vertuous rarely found,
That in domestic good combines:
Happy that house! his way to peace is smooth:
But vertue which breaks through all opposition, *1050*
And all temptation can remove,
Most shines and most is acceptable above.
   Therefore Gods universal Law
Gave to the man despotic power
Over his female in due awe,
Nor from that right to part an hour,
Smile she or lowre:
So shall he least confusion draw
On his whole life, not sway'd
By female usurpation, nor dismay'd. *1060*
  But had we best retire, I see a storm?
  Sam. Fair days have oft contracted wind and rain.
  Chor. But this another kind of tempest brings.
  Sam. Be less abstruse, my riddling days are past.
  Chor. Look now for no inchanting voice, nor fear
The bait of honied words; a rougher tongue

Draws hitherward, I know him by his stride,
The Giant *Harapha* of *Gath*, his look
Haughty as is his pile high-built and proud.
Comes he in peace? what wind hath blown him hither
I less conjecture then when first I saw 1071
The sumptuous *Dalila* floating this way:
His habit carries peace, his brow defiance.
    Sam. Or peace or not, alike to me he comes.
    Chor. His fraught we soon shall know, he now arrives.
    Har. I come not *Samson*, to condole thy chance,
As these perhaps, yet wish it had not been,
Though for no friendly intent. I am of *Gath*,
Men call me *Harapha*, of stock renown'd
As *Og* or *Anak* and the *Emims* old 1080
That *Kiriathaim* held, thou knowst me now
If thou at all art known. Much I have heard
Of thy prodigious might and feats perform'd
Incredible to me, in this displeas'd,
That I was never present on the place
Of those encounters, where we might have tri'd
Each others force in camp or listed field:
And now am come to see of whom such noise
Hath walk'd about, and each limb to survey,
If thy appearance answer loud report. 1090
    Sam. The way to know were not to see but taste.
    Har. Dost thou already single me; I thought
Gives and the Mill had tam'd thee? O that fortune
Had brought me to the field where thou art fam'd
To have wrought such wonders with an Asses Jaw;
I should have forc'd thee soon with other arms,
Or left thy carkass where the Ass lay thrown:
So had the glory of Prowess been recover'd
To *Palestine*, won by a *Philistine*
From the unforeskinn'd race, of whom thou bear'st 1100
The highest name for valiant Acts, that honour
Certain to have won by mortal duel from thee,
I lose, prevented by thy eyes put out.
    Sam. Boast not of what thou wouldst have done, but do
What then thou would'st, thou seest it in thy hand.
    Har. To combat with a blind man I disdain,
And thou hast need much washing to be toucht.
    Sam. Such usage as your honourable Lords
Afford me assassinated and betray'd,
Who durst not with thir whole united powers 1110
In fight withstand me single and unarm'd,
Nor in the house with chamber Ambushes

Close-banded durst attaque me, no not sleeping,
Till they had hir'd a woman with their gold
Breaking her Marriage Faith to circumvent me.
Therefore without feign'd shifts let be assign'd
Some narrow place enclos'd, where sight may give thee,
Or rather flight, no great advantage on me;
Then put on all thy gorgeous arms, thy Helmet
And Brigandine of brass, thy broad Habergeon,   *1120*
Vant-brass and Greves, and Gauntlet, add thy Spear
A Weavers beam, and seven-times-folded shield,
I only with an Oak'n staff will meet thee,
And raise such out-cries on thy clatter'd Iron,
Which long shall not with-hold mee from thy head,
That in a little time while breath remains thee,
Thou oft shalt wish thy self at *Gath* to boast
Again in safety what thou wouldst have done
To *Samson*, but shalt never see *Gath* more.

   Har. Thou durst not thus disparage glorious arms *1130*
Which greatest Heroes have in battel worn,
Thir ornament and safety, had not spells
And black enchantments, some Magicians Art
Arm'd thee or charm'd thee strong, which thou from
    Heaven
Feigndst at thy birth was giv'n thee in thy hair,
Where strength can least abide, though all thy hairs
Were bristles rang'd like those that ridge the back
Of chaf't wild Boars, or ruffl'd Porcupines.

   Sam. I know no Spells, use no forbidden Arts;
My trust is in the living God who gave me   *1140*
At my Nativity this strength, diffus'd
No less through all my sinews, joints and bones,
Then thine, while I preserv'd these locks unshorn,
The pledge of my unviolated vow.
For proof hereof, if *Dagon* be thy god,
Go to his Temple, invocate his aid
With solemnest devotion, spread before him
How highly it concerns his glory now
To frustrate and dissolve these Magic spells,
Which I to be the power of *Israel's* God   *1150*
Avow, and challenge *Dagon* to the test,
Offering to combat thee his Champion bold,
With th' utmost of his Godhead seconded:
Then thou shalt see, or rather to thy sorrow
Soon feel, whose God is strongest, thine or mine.

   Har. Presume not on thy God, what e're he be,
Thee he regards not, owns not, hath cut off

Quite from his people, and delivered up
Into thy Enemies hand, permitted them
To put out both thine eyes, and fetter'd send thee   *1160*
Into the common Prison, there to grind
Among the Slaves and Asses thy comrades,
As good for nothing else, no better service
With those thy boyst'rous locks, no worthy match
For valour to assail, nor by the sword
Of noble Warriour, so to stain his honour,
But by the Barbers razor best subdu'd.
  Sam. All these indignities, for such they are
From thine, these evils I deserve and more,
Acknowledge them from God inflicted on me   *1170*
Justly, yet despair not of his final pardon
Whose ear is ever open; and his eye
Gracious to re-admit the suppliant;
In confidence whereof I once again
Defie thee to the trial of mortal fight,
By combat to decide whose god is God,
Thine or whom I with *Israel's* Sons adore.
  Har. Fair honour that thou dost thy God, in trusting
He will accept thee to defend his cause,
A Murtherer, a Revolter, and a Robber.   *1180*
  Sam. Tongue-doubtie Giant, how dost thou prove me these?
  Har. Is not thy Nation subject to our Lords?
Thir Magistrates confest it, when they took thee
As a League-breaker and deliver'd bound
Into our hands: for hadst thou not committed
Nortorious murder on those thirty men
At *Askalon*, who never did thee harm,
Then like a Robber stripdst them of thir robes?
The *Philistines*, when thou hadst broke the league,
Went up with armed powers thee only seeking,   *1190*
To others did no violence nor spoil.
  Sam. Among the Daughters of the *Philistines*
I chose a Wife, which argu'd me no foe;
And in your City held my Nuptial Feast:
But your ill-meaning Politician Lords,
Under pretence of Bridal friends and guests,
Appointed to await me thirty spies,
Who threatning cruel death constrain'd the bride
To wring from me and tell to them my secret,
That solv'd the riddle which I had propos'd.   *1200*
When I perceiv'd all set on enmity,
As on my enemies, where ever chanc'd,

I us'd hostility, and took thir spoil
To pay my underminers in thir coin.
My Nation was subjected to your Lords.
It was the force of Conquest; force with force
Is well ejected when the Conquer'd can.
But I a private person, whom my Countrey
As a league-breaker gave up bound, presum'd
Single Rebellion and did Hostile Acts. *1210*
I was no private but a person rais'd
With strength sufficient and command from Heav'n
To free my Countrey; if their servile minds
Me their Deliverer sent would not receive,
But to thir Masters gave me up for nought,
Th' unworthier they; whence to this day they serve.
I was to do my part from Heav'n assign'd,
And had perform'd it if my known offence
Had not disabl'd me, not all your force:
These shifts refuted, answer thy appellant *1220*
Though by his blindness maim'd for high attempts,
Who now defies thee thrice to single fight,
As a petty enterprise of small enforce.
    Har. With thee a Man condemn'd, a Slave enrol'd,
Due by the Law to capital punishment?
To fight with thee no man of arms will deign.
    Sam. Cam'st thou for this, vain boaster, to survey me,
To descant on my strength, and give thy verdit?
Come nearer, part not hence so slight inform'd;
But take good heed my hand survey not thee. *1230*
    Har. O *Baal-zebub!* can my ears unus'd
Hear these dishonours, and not render death?
    Sam. No man with-holds thee, nothing from thy hand
Fear I incurable; bring up thy van,
My heels are fetter'd, but my fist is free.
    Har. This insolence other kind of answer fits.
    Sam. Go baffl'd coward, lest I run upon thee,
Though in these chains, bulk without spirit vast,
And with one buffet lay thy structure low,
Or swing thee in the Air, then dash thee down *1240*
To the hazard of thy brains and shatter'd sides.
    Har. By *Astaroth* e're long thou shalt lament
These braveries in Irons loaden on thee.
    Chor. His Giantship is gone somewhat crestfall'n,
Stalking with less unconsci'nable strides,
And lower looks, but in a sultrie chafe.
    Sam. I dread him not, nor all his Giant-brood,
Though Fame divulge him Father of five Sons

All of Gigantic size, *Goliah* chief.
    Chor. He will directly to the Lords, I fear,   *1250*
And with malitious counsel stir them up
Some way or other yet further to afflict thee.
    Sam. He must allege some cause, and offer'd fight
Will not dare mention, lest a question rise
Whether he durst accept the offer or not,
And that he durst not plain enough appear'd.
Much more affliction then already felt
They cannot well impose, nor I sustain;
If they intend advantage of my labours
The work of many hands, which earns my keeping   *1260*
With no small profit daily to my owners.
But come what will, my deadliest foe will prove
My speediest friend, by death to rid me hence,
The worst that he can give, to me the best.
Yet so it may fall out, because thir end
Is hate, not help to me, it may with mine
Draw thir own ruin who attempt the deed.
    Chor. Oh how comely it is and how reviving
To the Spirits of just men long opprest!
When God into the hands of thir deliverer   *1270*
Puts invincible might
To quell the mighty of the Earth, th' oppressour,
The brute and boist'rous force of violent men
Hardy and industrious to support
Tyrannic power, but raging to pursue
The righteous and all such as honour Truth;
He all thir Ammunition
And feats of War defeats
With plain Heroic magnitude of mind
And celestial vigour arm'd,   *1280*
Thir Armories and Magazins contemns,
Renders them useless, while
With winged expedition
Swift as the lightning glance he executes
His errand on the wicked, who surpris'd
Lose thir defence distracted and amaz'd
    But patience is more oft the exercise
Of Saints, the trial of thir fortitude,
Making them each his own Deliverer,
And Victor over all   *1290*
That tyrannie or fortune can inflict,
Either of these is in thy lot,
Samson, with might endu'd
Above the Sons of men; but sight bereav'd

May chance to number thee with those
Whom Patience finally must crown.
This Idols day hath bin to thee no day of rest,
   Labouring thy mind
More then the working day thy hands,
And yet perhaps more trouble is behind.   *1300*
For I descry this way
Some other tending, in his hand
A Scepter or quaint staff he bears,
Comes on amain, speed in his look.
By his habit I discern him now
A Public Officer, and now at hand.
His message will be short and voluble.
   Off. *Ebrews*, the Pris'ner *Samson* here I seek.
   Chor. His manacles remark him, there he sits.
   Off. Samson, to thee our Lords thus bid me say;   *1310*
This day to *Dagon* is a solemn Feast,
With Sacrifices, Triumph, Pomp, and Games;
Thy strength they know surpassing human rate,
And now some public proof thereof require
To honour this great Feast, and great Assembly;
Rise therefore with all speed and come along,
Where I will see thee heartn'd and fresh clad
To appear as fits before th' illustrious Lords.
   Sam. Thou knowst I am an *Ebrew*, therefore tell them,
Our Law forbids at thir Religious Rites   *1320*
My presence; for that cause I cannot come.
   Off. This answer, be assur'd, will not content them.
   Sam. Have they not Sword-players, and ev'ry sort
Of Gymnic Artists, Wrestlers, Riders, Runners,
Juglers and Dancers, Antics, Mummers, Mimics,
But they must pick me out with shackles tir'd,
And over-labour'd at thir publick Mill,
To make them sport with blind activity?
Do they not seek occasion of new quarrels
On my refusal to distress me more,   *1330*
Or make a game of my calamities?
Return the way thou cam'st, I will not come.
   Off. Regard thy self, this will offend them highly.
   Sam. My self? my conscience and internal peace.
Can they think me so broken, so debas'd
With corporal servitude, that my mind ever
Will condescend to such absurd commands?
Although thir drudge, to be thir fool or jester,
And in my midst of sorrow and heart-grief
To shew them feats, and play before thir god,   *1340*

The worst of all indignities, yet on me
Joyn'd with extream contempt? I will not come.
   Off. My message was impos'd on me with speed,
Brooks no delay: is this thy resolution?
   Sam. So take it with what speed thy message needs.
   Off. I am sorry what this stoutness will produce.
   Sam. Perhaps thou shalt have cause to sorrow indeed.
   Chor. Consider, *Samson;* matters now are strain'd
Up to the highth, whether to hold or break;
He's gone, and who knows how he may report   *1350*
Thy words by adding fuel to the flame?
Expect another message more imperious,
More Lordly thund'ring then thou well wilt bear.
   Sam. Shall I abuse this Consecrated gift
Of strength, again returning with my hair
After my great transgression, so requite
Favour renew'd, and add a greater sin
By prostituting holy things to Idols;
A *Nazarite* in place abominable
Vaunting my strength in honour to thir *Dagon?*   *1360*
Besides, how vile, contemptible, ridiculous,
What act more execrably unclean, prophane?
   Chor. Yet with this strength thou serv'st the *Philistines,*
Idolatrous, uncircumcis'd, unclean.
   Sam. Not in thir Idol-worship, but by labour
Honest and lawful to deserve my food
Of those who have me in thir civil power.
   Chor. Where the heart joins not, outward acts defile not.
   Sam. Where outward force constrains, the sentence holds;
But who constrains me to the Temple of *Dagon,*   *1370*
Not dragging? the *Philistian* Lords command.
Commands are no constraints. If I obey them,
I do it freely; venturing to displease
God for the fear of Man, and Man prefer,
Set God behind: which in his jealousie
Shall never, unrepented, find forgiveness.
Yet that he may dispense with me or thee
Present in Temples at Idolatrous Rites
For some important cause, thou needst not doubt.
   Chor. How thou wilt here come off surmounts my reach.
   Sam. Be of good courage, I begin to feel   *1381*
Some rouzing motions in me which dispose
To something extraordinary my thoughts.
I with this Messenger will go along,
Nothing to do, be sure, that may dishonour
Our Law, or stain my vow of *Nazarite.*

If there be aught of presage in the mind,
This day will be remarkable in my life
By some great act, or of my days the last.
    Chor. In time thou hast resolv'd, the man returns.   *1390*
    Off. Samson, this second message from our Lords
To thee I am bid say. Art thou our Slave,
Our Captive, at the public Mill our drudge,
And dar'st thou at our sending and command
Dispute thy coming? come without delay;
Or we shall find such Engines to assail
And hamper thee, as thou shalt come of force,
Though thou wert firmlier fastn'd then a rock.
    Sam. I could be well content to try thir Art,
Which to no few of them would prove pernicious.   *1400*
Yet knowing thir advantages too many,
Because they shall not trail me through thir streets
Like a wild Beast, I am content to go.
Masters commands come with a power resistless
To such as owe them absolute subjection;
And for a life who will not change his purpose?
(So mutable are all the ways of men)
Yet this be sure, in nothing to comply
Scandalous or forbidden in our Law.
    Off. I praise thy resolution, doff these links: *1410*
By this compliance thou wilt win the Lords
To favour, and perhaps to set thee free.
    Sam. Brethren farewel, your company along
I will not wish, lest it perhaps offend them
To see me girt with Friends; and how the sight
Of me as of a common Enemy,
So dreaded once, may now exasperate them
I know not. Lords are Lordliest in thir wine;
And the well-feasted Priest then soonest fir'd
With zeal, if aught Religion seem concern'd: *1420*
No less the people on thir Holy-days
Impetuous, insolent, unquenchable;
Happ'n what may, of me expect to hear
Nothing dishonourable, impure, unworthy
Our God, our Law, my Nation, or my self,
The last of me or no I cannot warrant.
    Chor. Go, and the Holy One
Of *Israel* be thy guide
To what may serve his glory best, & spread his name
Great among the Heathen round: *1430*
Send thee the Angel of thy Birth, to stand
Fast by thy side, who from thy Fathers field

Rode up in flames after his message told
Of thy conception, and be now a shield
Of fire; that Spirit that first rusht on thee
In the camp of *Dan*
Be efficacious in thee now at need.
For never was from Heaven imparted
Measure of strength so great to mortal seed,
As in thy wond'rous actions hath been seen. *1440*
But wherefore comes old *Manoa* in such hast
With youthful steps? much livelier than e're while
He seems: supposing here to find his Son,
Or of him bringing to us some glad news?

   Man. Peace with you brethren; my inducement hither
Was not at present here to find my Son,
By order of the Lords new parted hence
To come and play before them at thir Feast.
I heard all as I came, the City rings
And numbers thither flock, I had no will, *1450*
Lest I should see him forc't to things unseemly.
But that which moved my coming now, was chiefly
To give ye part with me what hope I have
With good success to work his liberty.

   Chor. That hope would much rejoyce us to partake
With thee; say reverend Sire, we thirst to hear.

   Man. I have attempted one by one the Lords
Either at home, or through the high street passing,
With supplication prone and Fathers tears
To accept of ransom for my Son thir pris'ner, *1460*
Some much averse I found and wondrous harsh,
Contemptuous, proud, set on revenge and spite;
That part most reverenc'd *Dagon* and his Priests,
Others more moderate seeming, but thir aim
Private reward, for which both God and State
They easily would set to sale, a third
More generous far and civil, who confess'd
They had anough reveng'd, having reduc't
Thir foe to misery beneath thir fears,
The rest was magnanimity to remit, *1470*
If some convenient ransom were propos'd.
What noise or shout was that? it tore the Skie.

   Chor. Doubtless the people shouting to behold
Thir once great dread, captive, & blind before them,
Or at some proof of strength before them shown.

   Man. His ransom, if my whole inheritance
May compass it, shall willingly be paid
And numberd down: much rather I shall chuse

To live the poorest in my Tribe, then richest,
And he in that calamitous prison left. *1480*
No, I am fixt not to part hence without him.
For his redemption all my Patrimony,
If need be, I am ready to forgo
And quit: not wanting him, I shall want nothing.
   Chor. Fathers are wont to lay up for thir Sons,
Thou for thy Son art bent to lay out all;
Sons wont to nurse thir Parents in old age,
Thou in old age car'st how to nurse thy Son,
Made older then thy age through eye-sight lost.
   Man. It shall be my delight to tend his eyes, *1490*
And view him sitting in the house, enobl'd
With all those high exploits by him atchiev'd,
And on his shoulders waving down those locks,
That of a Nation arm'd the strength contain'd:
And I perswade me God had not permitted
His strength again to grow up with his hair
Garrison'd round about him like a Camp
Of faithful Souldiery, were not his purpose
To use him further yet in some great service,
Not to sit idle with so great a gift *1500*
Useless, and thence ridiculous about him.
And since his strength with eye-sight was not lost,
God will restore him eye-sight to his strength.
   Chor. Thy hopes are not ill founded nor seem vain
Of his delivery, and thy joy thereon
Conceiv'd, agreeable to a Fathers love,
In both which we, as next participate.
   Man. I know your friendly minds and—O what noise!
Mercy of Heav'n what hideous noise was that!
Horribly loud unlike the former shout. *1510*
   Chor. Noise call you it or universal groan
As if the whole inhabitation perish'd,
Blood, death, and deathful deeds are in that noise,
Ruin, destruction at the utmost point.
   Man. Of ruin indeed methought I heard the noise,
Oh it continues, they have slain my Son.
   Chor. Thy Son is rather slaying them, that outcry
From slaughter of one foe could not ascend.
   Man. Some dismal accident it needs must be;
What shall we do, stay here or run and see? *1520*
   Chor. Best keep together here, lest running thither
We unawares run into dangers mouth.
This evil on the *Philistines* is fall'n,
From whom could else a general cry be heard?

The sufferers then will scarce molest us here,
From other hands we need not much to fear.
What if his eye-sight (for to *Israels* God
Nothing is hard) by miracle restor'd,
He now be dealing dole among his foes,
And over heaps of slaughter'd walk his way?   1530
   Man. That were a joy presumptuous to be thought.
   Chor. Yet God hath wrought things as incredible
For his people of old; what hinders now?
   Man. He can I know, but doubt to think he will;
Yet Hope would fain subscribe, and tempts Belief.
A little stay will bring some notice hither.
   Chor. Of good or bad so great, of bad the sooner;
For evil news rides post, while good news baits.
And to our wish I see one hither speeding,
An *Ebrew*, as I guess, and of our Tribe.   1540
   Mess. O whither shall I run, or which way flie
The sight of this so horrid spectacle
Which earst my eyes beheld and yet behold;
For dire imagination still persues me.
But providence or instinct of nature seems,
Or reason though disturb'd, and scarse consulted
To have guided me aright, I know not how,
To thee first reverend *Manoa*, and to these
My Countreymen, whom here I knew remaining,
As at some distance from the place of horrour,   1550
So in the sad event too much concern'd.
   Man. The accident was loud, & here before thee
With rueful cry, yet what it was we hear not,
No Preface needs, thou seest we long to know.
   Mess. It would burst forth, but I recover breath
And sense distract, to know well what I utter.
   Man. Tell us the sum, the circumstance defer.
   Mess. Gaza yet stands, but all her Sons are fall'n,
All in a moment overwhelm'd and fall'n.
   Man. Sad, but thou knowst to *Israelites* not saddest   1560
The desolation of a Hostile City.
   Mess. Feed on that first, there may in grief be surfet.
   Man. Relate by whom. *Mess.* By *Samson.*
      Man. That still lessens
The sorrow, and converts it nigh to joy.
   Mess. Ah *Manoa* I refrain, too suddenly
To utter what will come at last too soon;
Lest evil tidings with too rude irruption
Hitting thy aged ear should pierce too deep.
   Man. Suspense in news is torture, speak them out.

    Mess. Then take the worst in brief, *Samson* is dead. *1570*
    Man. The worst indeed, O all my hope's defeated
To free him hence! but death who sets all free
Hath paid his ransom now and full discharge.
What windy joy this day had I conceiv'd
Hopeful of his Delivery, which now proves
Abortive as the first-born bloom of spring
Nipt with the lagging rear of winters frost.
Yet e're I give the rains to grief, say first,
How dy'd he? death to life is crown or shame.
All by him fell thou say'st, by whom fell he,   *1580*
What glorious hand gave *Samson* his deaths wound?
    Mess. Unwounded of his enemies he fell.
    Man. Wearied with slaughter then or how? explain.
    Mess. By his own hands. *Man.* Self-violence? what cause
Brought him so soon at variance with himself
Among his foes? *Mess.* Inevitable cause
At once both to destroy and be destroy'd;
The Edifice where all were met to see him
Upon thir heads and on his own he pull'd.
    Man. O lastly over-strong against thy self!   *1590*
A dreadful way thou took'st to thy revenge.
More than anough we know; but while things yet
Are in confusion, give us if thou canst,
Eye-witness of what first or last was done,
Relation more particular and distinct.
    Mess. Occasions drew me early to this City,
And as the gates I enter'd with Sun-rise,
The morning Trumpets Festival proclaim'd
Through each high street: little I had dispatch't
When all abroad was rumour'd that this day   *1600*
Samson should be brought forth to shew the people
Proof of his mighty strength in feats and games;
I sorrow'd at his captive state, but minded
Not to be absent at that spectacle.
The building was a spacious Theatre
Half round on two main Pillars vaulted high,
With seats where all the Lords and each degree
Of sort, might sit in order to behold,
The other side was op'n, where the throng
On banks and scaffolds under Skie might stand;   *1610*
I among these aloof obscurely stood.
The Feast and noon grew high, and Sacrifice
Had fill'd thir hearts with mirth, high chear, & wine,
When to thir sports they turn'd. Immediately
Was *Samson* as a public servant brought,

In thir state Livery clad; before him Pipes
And Timbrels, on each side went armed guards,
Both horse and foot before him and behind
Archers, and Slingers, Cataphracts and Spears.
At sight of him the people with a shout   *1620*
Rifted the Air clamouring thir god with praise,
Who had made thir dreadful enemy thir thrall.
He patient but undaunted where they led him,
Came to the place, and what was set before him
Which without help of eye, might be assay'd,
To heave, pull, draw, or break, he still perform'd
All with incredible, stupendious force,
None daring to appear Antagonist.
At length for intermission sake they led him
Between the pillars; he his guide requested   *1630*
(For so from such as nearer stood we heard)
As over-tir'd to let him lean a while
With both his arms on those two massie Pillars
That to the arched roof gave main support.
He unsuspitious led him; which when *Samson*
Felt in his arms, with head a while enclin'd,
And eyes fast fixt he stood, as one who pray'd,
Or some great matter in his mind revolv'd.
At last with head erect thus cryed aloud,
Hitherto, Lords, what your commands impos'd   *1640*
I have perform'd, as reason was, obeying,
Not without wonder or delight beheld.
Now of my own accord such other tryal
I mean to shew you of my strength, yet greater;
As with amaze shall strike all who behold.
This utter'd, straining all his nerves he bow'd,
As with the force of winds and waters pent,
When Mountains tremble, those two massie Pillars
With horrible convulsion to and fro,
He tugg'd, he shook, till down thy came and drew   *1650*
The whole roof after them, with burst of thunder
Upon the heads of all who sate beneath,
Lords, Ladies, Captains, Councellors, or Priests,
Thir choice nobility and flower, not only
Of this but each *Philistian* City round
Met from all parts to solemnize this Feast.
Samson with these immixt, inevitably
Pulld down the same destruction on himself;
The vulgar only scap'd who stood without.
    Chor. O dearly-bought revenge, yet glorious!   *1660*
Living or dying thou hast fulfill'd

The work for which thou wast foretold
To *Israel*, and now ly'st victorious
Among thy slain self-kill'd
Not willingly, but tangl'd in the fold
Of dire necessity, whose law in death conjoin'd
Thee with thy slaughter'd foes in number more
Then all thy life had slain before.
    Semichor. While thir hearts were jocund and sublime,
Drunk with Idolatry, drunk with Wine,   *1670*
And fat regorg'd of Bulls and Goats,
Chaunting thir Idol, and preferring
Before our living Dread who dwells
In *Silo* his bright Sanctuary:
Among them he a spirit of phrenzie sent,
Who hurt thir minds,
And urg'd them on with mad desire
To call in hast for thir destroyer;
They only set on sport and play
Unweetingly importun'd   *1680*
Thir own destruction to come speedy upon them.
So fond are mortal men
Fall'n into wrath divine,
As thir own ruin on themselves to invite,
Insensate left, or to sense reprobate,
And with blindness internal struck.
    Semichor. But he though blind of sight,
Despis'd and thought extinguish't quite,
With inward eyes illuminated
His fierie vertue rouz'd   *1690*
From under ashes into sudden flame,
And as an ev'ning Dragon came,
Assailant on the perched roosts,
And nests in order rang'd
Of tame villatic Fowl; but as an Eagle
His cloudless thunder bolted on thir heads.
So vertue giv'n for lost,
Deprest, and overthrown, as seem'd,
Like that self-begott'n bird
In the *Arabian* woods embost,   *1700*
That no second knows nor third,
And lay e're while a Holocaust,
From out her ashie womb now teem'd
Revives, reflourishes, then vigorous most
When most unactive deem'd,
And though her body die, her fame survives,
A secular bird ages of lives.

Man. Come, come, no time for lamentation now,
Nor much more cause, *Samson* hath quit himself
Like *Samson*, and heroicly hath finish'd   1710
A life Heroic, on his Enemies
Fully reveng'd, hath left them years of mourning,
And lamentation to the Sons of *Caphtor*
Through all *Philistian* bounds. To *Israel*
Honour hath left, and freedom, let but them
Find courage to lay hold on this occasion,
To himself and Fathers house eternal fame;
And which is best and happiest yet, all this
With God not parted from him, as was feard,
But favouring and assisting to the end.   1720
Nothing is here for tears, nothing to wail
Or knock the breast, no weakness, no contempt,
Dispraise, or blame, nothing but well and fair,
And what may quiet us in a death so noble.
Let us go find the body where it lies
Sok't in his enemies blood, and from the stream
With lavers pure and cleansing herbs wash off
The clotted gore. I with what speed the while
(*Gaza* is not in plight to say us nay)
Will send for all my kindred, all my friends   1730
To fetch him hence and solemnly attend
With silent obsequie and funeral train
Home to his Fathers house: there will I build him
A Monument, and plant it round with shade
Of Laurel ever green, and branching Palm,
With all his Trophies hung, and Acts enroll'd
In copious Legend, or sweet Lyric Song.
Thither shall all the valiant youth resort,
And from his memory inflame thir breasts
To matchless valour, and adventures high: 1740
The Virgins also shall on feastful days
Visit his Tomb with flowers, only bewailing
His lot unfortunate in nuptial choice,
From whence captivity and loss of eyes.
    Chor. All is best, though we oft doubt,
What th' unsearchable dispose
Of highest wisdom brings about,
And ever best found in the close.
Oft he seems to hide his face,
But unexpectedly returns   1750
And to his faithful Champion hath in place
Bore witness gloriously; whence *Gaza* mourns
And all that band them to resist

His uncontroulable intent,
His servants he with new acquist
Of true experience from this great event
With peace and consolation hath dismist,
And calm of mind all passion spent.

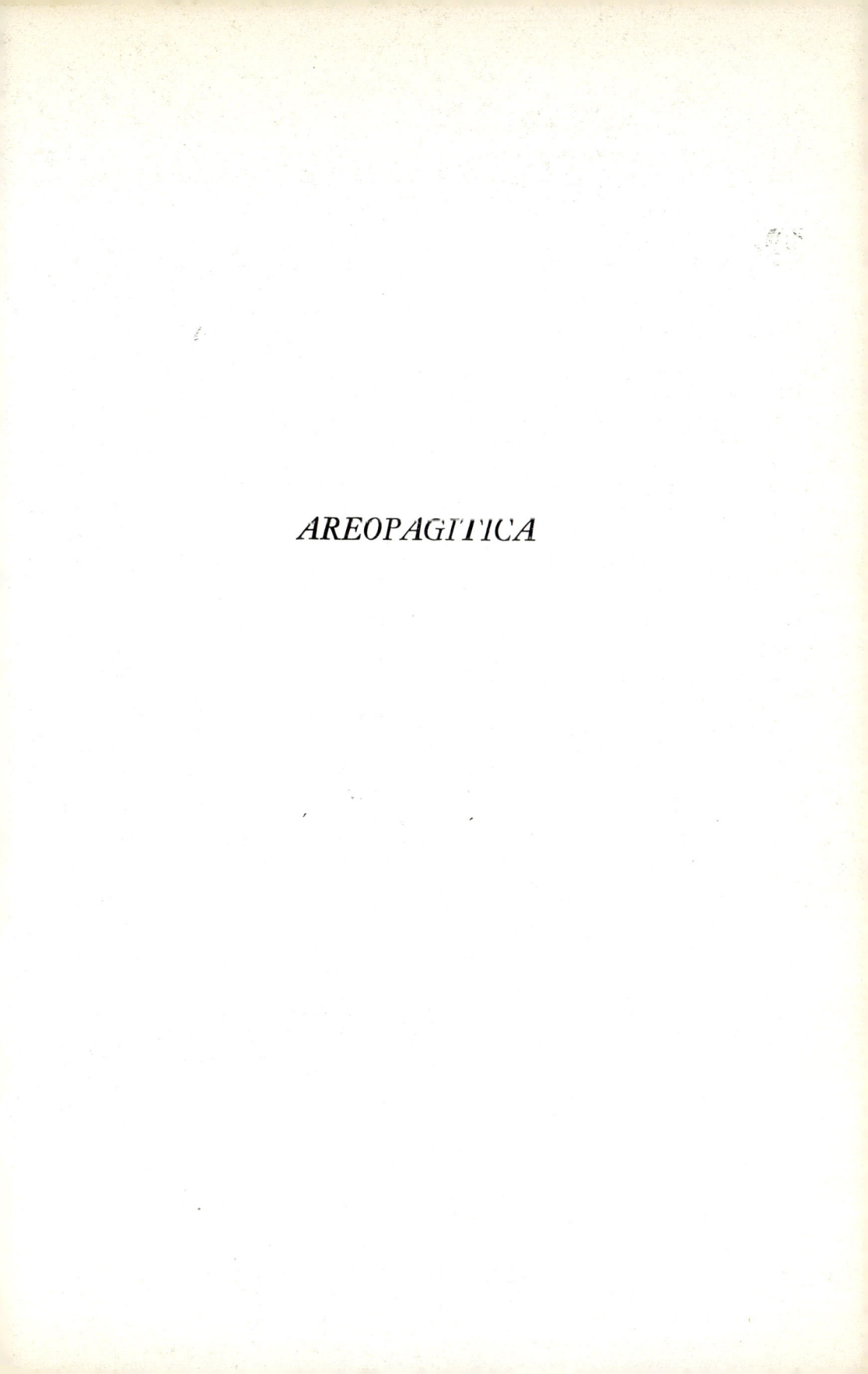

AREOPAGITICA

AREOPAGITICA

*Analysis of the Order of Parliament (June 14, 1643),
Against which the Areopagitica was Directed*

1. The Preamble recounts that "many false ... scandalous, seditious, and libellous" works have lately been published, "to the great defamation of Religion and government"; that many private printing-presses have been set up; and that "divers of the Stationers' Company" have infringed the rights of the Company.

2. "It is therefore ordered by the Lords and Commons In Parliament," (1) that no Order "of both or either House shall be printed" except by command; (2) *that no Book, etc., "shall from henceforth be printed or put to sale, unless the same be first approved of and licensed by such person or persons as both or either of the said Houses shall appoint for the licensing of the same"*; (3) that no book, of which the copyright has been granted to the Company, "for their relief and the maintenance of their poor," be printed by any person or persons "without the license and consent of the Master, Warden, and assistants of the said Company"; (4) that no book, "formerly printed here," be imported from beyond seas, "upon pain of forfeiting the same to the Owner" of the Copyright, "and such further punishment as shall be thought fit."

3. The Stationers' Company and the officers of the two Houses are authorised to search for unlicensed Presses, and to break them up; to search for unlicensed Books, etc., and confiscate them; and to "apprehend all authors, printers and others" concerned in publishing unlicensed books and to bring them before the Houses "or the Committee of Examination" for "further punishments," such persons not to be released till they have given satisfaction and also "sufficient caution not to offend in like sort for the future."

4. "All Justices of the Peace, Captains, Constables and other officers" are ordered to give aid in the execution of the above.

A SPEECH FOR THE LIBERTY OF UNLICENSED PRINTING, TO THE PARLIAMENT OF ENGLAND (1644)

THEY, who to states and governors of the Commonwealth direct their speech, High Court of Parliament, or, wanting such access in a private condition, write that which they foresee may advance the public good; I suppose them, as at the beginning of no mean endeavour, not a little altered and moved inwardly in their minds: some with doubt of what will be the success, others with fear of what will be the censure; some with hope, others with confidence of what they have to speak. And me perhaps each of these dispositions, as the subject was whereon I entered, may have at other times variously affected; and likely might in these foremost expressions now also disclose which of them swayed most, but that the very attempt of this address thus made, and the thought of whom it hath recourse to, hath got the power within me to a passion, far more welcome than incidental to a preface.

Which though I stay not to confess ere any ask, I shall be blameless, if it be no other than the joy and gratulation which it brings to all who wish and promote their country's liberty; whereof this whole discourse proposed will be a certain testimony, if not a trophy. For this is not the liberty which we can hope, that no grievance ever should arise in the Commonwealth—that let no man in this world expect; but when complaints are freely heard, deeply considered and speedily reformed, then is the utmost bound of civil liberty attained that wise men look for. To which if I now manifest by the very sound of this which I shall utter, that we are already in good part arrived, and yet from such a steep disadvantage of tyranny and superstition grounded into our principles as was beyond the manhood of a Roman recovery, it will be attributed first, as is most due, to the strong assistance of God our deliverer, next to your faithful guidance and undaunted wisdom, Lords and Commons of England. Neither is it in God's esteem the diminution of His glory, when honourable things are spoken of good men and worthy magistrates; which if I now first should begin to do, after so fair a progress of your laudable deeds, and such a long obligement upon the whole realm to your indefatigable virtues, I might be justly reckoned among the tardiest, and the unwillingest of them that praise ye.

Nevertheless there being three principal things, without which all praising is but courtship and flattery: First, when that only is praised which is solidly worth praise: next, when greatest likelihoods are brought that such things are truly and really in those persons to whom they are ascribed: the other, when he who praises, by showing that such his actual persuasion is of whom he writes, can demonstrate that he flatters not; the former two of these I have heretofore endeavoured, rescuing the employment from him who went about to impair your merits with a trivial and malignant encomium; the latter as belonging chiefly to mine own acquittal, that whom I so extolled I did not flatter, hath been reserved opportunely to this occasion.

For he who freely magnifies what hath been nobly done, and fears not to declare as freely what might be done better, gives ye the best covenant of his fidelity; and that his loyalist affection and his hope waits on your proceedings. His highest praising is not flattery, and his plainest advice is a kind of praising. For though I should affirm and hold by argument, that it would fare better with truth, with learning and the Commonwealth, if one of your published Orders, which I should name, were called in; yet at the same time it could not but much redound to the lustre of your mild and equal government, whenas private persons are hereby animated to think ye better pleased with public advice, than other statists have been delighted heretofore with public flattery. And men will then see what difference there is between the magnanimity of a triennial Parliament, and that jealous haughtiness of prelates and Cabin Counsellors that usurped of late, whenas they shall observe ye in the midst of your victories and successes more gently brooking written exceptions against a voted Order than other Courts, which had produced nothing worth memory but the weak ostentation of wealth, would have endured the least signified dislike at any sudden Proclamation.

If I should thus far presume upon the meek demeanour of your civil and gentle greatness, Lords and Commons, as what your published Order hath directly said, that to gainsay, I might defend myself with ease, if any should accuse me of being new or insolent, did they but know how much better I find ye esteem it to imitate the old and elegant humanity of Greece, than the barbaric pride of a Hunnish and Norwegian stateliness. And out of those ages, to whose polite wisdom and letters we owe that we are not yet Goths and Jutlanders, I could name him who from his private house wrote that discourse to the Parliament of Athens, that persuades them to change the form of democraty which was then established. Such honour was done in those days to men who professed the study of wisdom and eloquence, not only in their own country, but in other lands, that cities and signiories heard them gladly, and with great respect, if they had aught in public to admonish the state. Thus did Dion Prusæus, a stranger and a private orator, counsel the Rhodians against a former edict; and I abound with other like examples, which to set here would be superfluous.

But if from the industry of a life wholly dedicated to studious labours, and those natural endowments haply not the worse for two and fifty degrees of northern latitude, so much must be derogated, as to count me not equal to any of those who had this privilege, I would obtain to be thought not so inferior, as yourselves are superior to the most of them who received their counsel: and how far you excel them, be assured, Lords and Commons, there can no greater testimony appear, than when your prudent spirit acknowledges and obeys the voice of reason from what quarter soever it be heard speaking; and renders ye as willing to repeal any Act of your own setting forth, as any set forth by your predecessors.

If ye be thus resolved, as it were injury to think ye were not, I know not what should withhold me from presenting ye with a fit instance wherein to show both that love of truth which ye eminently profess, and that uprightness of your judgment which is not wont to be partial to yourselves; by judging over again that Order which ye have ordained to regulate Printing:—that no book, pamphlet, or paper shall be henceforth printed, unless the same be first approved and licensed by such, or at least one of such, as shall be thereto appointed. For that part which preserves justly every man's copy to himself, or provides for the poor, I touch not, only wish they be not made pretences to abuse and persecute honest and painful men, who offend not in either of these particulars. But that other clause of Licensing Books, which we thought had died with his brother quadragesimal and matrimonial when the prelates expired, I shall now attend with such a homily, as shall lay before ye, first the inventors of it to be those whom ye will be loth to own; next what is to be thought in general of reading, whatever sort the books be; and that this Order avails nothing to the suppressing of scandalous, seditious, and libellous books, which were mainly intended to be suppressed. Last, that it will be primely to the discouragement of all learning, and the stop of Truth, not only by disexercising and blunting our abilities in what we know already, but by hindering and cropping the discovery that might be yet further made both in religious and civil Wisdom.

I deny not, but that it is of greatest concernment in the Church and Commonwealth, to have a vigilant eye how books demean themselves as well as men; and thereafter to confine, imprison, and do sharpest justice on them as malefactors. For books are not absolutely dead things, but do contain a potency of life in them to be as active as that soul was whose progeny they are; nay, they do preserve as in a vial the purest efficacy and extraction of that living intellect that bred them. I know they are as lively, and as vigorously productive, as those fabulous dragon's teeth; and being sown up and down, may chance to spring up armed men. And yet, on the other hand, unless wariness be used, as good almost kill a man as kill a good book. Who kills a man kills a reasonable creature, God's image; but he who destroys a good book, kills reason itself, kills the image of God, as it were in the eye. Many a man lives a burden to the earth; but a good book is the precious life-blood of a master spirit, embalmed and treasured up on purpose to a life beyond life. 'Tis true, no age can restore a life, whereof perhaps there is no great loss; and revolutions of ages do not oft recover the loss of a rejected truth, for the want of which whole nations fare the worse.

We should be wary therefore what persecution we raise against the living labours of public men, how we spill that seasoned life of man, preserved and stored up in books; since we see a kind of homicide may be thus committed, sometimes a martyrdom, and if it extend to the whole impression, a kind of massacre; whereof the execution ends not in the slaying of an elemental life, but strikes at that ethereal and fifth essence, the breath of reason itself, slays an immortality rather than a life. But lest I should be condemned of introducing licence, while I oppose licensing, I refuse not the pains to be so much historical, as will serve to show what hath been done by ancient and famous commonwealths against this disorder, till the very time that this project of licensing crept out of the inquisition, was catched up by our prelates, and hath caught some of our presbyters.

In Athens, where books and wits were ever busier than in any other part of Greece, I find but only two sorts of writings which the magistrate cared to take notice of; those either blasphemous and atheistical, or libellous. Thus the books of Protagoras were by the judges of Areopagus commanded to be burnt, and himself banished the territory for a discourse begun with his confessing not to know "whether there were gods, or whether not." And against defaming, it was agreed that none should be traduced by name, as was the manner of Vetus Comœdia, whereby we may guess how they censured libelling. And this course was quick enough, as Cicero writes, to quell both the desperate wits of other atheists, and the open way of defaming, as the event showed. Of other sects and opinions, though tending to voluptuousness, and the denying of Divine Providence, they took no heed.

Therefore we do not read that either Epicurus, or that libertine school of Cyrene, or what the Cynic impudence uttered, was ever questioned by the laws. Neither is it recorded that the writings of those old comedians were suppressed, though the acting of them were forbid; and that Plato commended the reading of Aristophanes, the loosest of them all, to his royal scholar Dionysius, is commonly known, and may be excused, if holy Chrysostom, as is reported, nightly studied so much the same author and had the art to cleanse a scurrilous vehemence into the style of a rousing sermon.

That other leading city of Greece, Lacedæmon, considering that Lycurgus their lawgiver was so addicted to elegant learning, as to have been the first that brought out of Ionia the scattered works of Homer, and sent the poet Thales from Crete to prepare and mollify the Spartan surliness with his smooth songs and odes, the better to plant among them law and civility, it is to be wondered how museless and unbookish they were, minding nought but the feats of war. There needed no licensing of books among them; for they disliked all but their own laconic apothegms, and took a slight occasion to chase Archilochus out of their city, perhaps for composing in a higher strain than their own soldierly ballads and roundels could reach to. Or if it were for his broad verses, they were not therein so cautious but they were as dissolute in their promiscuous conversing; whence Euripides affirms in *Andromache*, that their women were all unchaste. Thus much may give us light after what sort of books were prohibited among the Greeks.

The Romans also, for many ages trained up only to a military roughness resembling most the Lacedæmonian guise, knew of learning little but what their twelve Tables, and the Pontific College with their augurs and flamens taught them in religion and law, so unacquainted with other learning, that when Carneades and Critolaus, with the Stoic Diogenes coming ambassadors to Rome, took thereby occasion to give the city a taste of their philosophy, they were suspected for seducers by no less a man than Cato the Censor, who moved it in the Senate to dismiss them speedily, and to banish all such Attic babblers out of Italy. But Scipio and others of the noblest senators withstood him and his old Sabine austerity; honoured and admired the men; and the censor himself at last, in his old age, fell to the study of what whereof before he was so scrupulous. And yet at the same time, Nævius and Plautus, the first Latin comedians, had filled the city with all the borrowed scenes of Menander and Philemon. Then began to be considered there also what was to be done to libellous books and authors; for Nævius was quickly cast into prison for his unbridled pen, and released by the tribunes upon his recantation; we read also that libels were burnt, and the makers punished by Augustus. The like severity, no doubt, was used, if aught were impiously written against their esteemed gods. Except in these two points, how the world went in books, the magistrate kept no reckoning.

And therefore Lucretius without impeachment versifies his Epicurism to

Memmius, and had the honour to be set forth the second time by Cicero, so great a father of the commonwealth; although himself disputes against that opinion in his own writings. Nor was the satirical sharpness or naked plainness of Lucilius, or Catullus, or Flaccus, by any order prohibited. And for matters of state, the story of Titus Livius, though it extolled that part which Pompey held, was not therefore suppressed by Octavius Cæsar of the other faction. But that Naso was by him banished in his old age, for the wanton poems of his youth, was but a mere covert of state over some secret cause: and besides, the books were neither banished nor called in. From hence we shall meet with little else but tyranny in the Roman empire, that we may not marvel, if not so often bad as good books were silenced. I shall therefore deem to have been large enough, in producing what among the ancients was punishable to write; save only which, all other arguments were free to treat on.

By this time the emperors were become Christians, whose discipline in this point I do not find to have been more severe than what was formerly in practice. The books of those whom they took to be grand heretics were examined, refuted, and condemned in the general Councils; and not till then were prohibited, or burnt, by authority of the emperor. As for the writings of heathen authors, unless they were plain invectives against Christianity, as those of Porphyrius and Proclus, they met with no interdict that can be cited, till about the year 400, in a Carthaginian Council, wherein bishops themselves were forbid to read the books of Gentiles, but heresies they might read: while others long before them, on the contrary, scrupled more the books of heretics than of Gentiles. And that the primitive Councils and bishops were wont only to declare what books were not commendable, passing no further, but leaving it to each one's conscience to read or to lay by, till after the year 800, is observed already by Padre Paolo, the great unmasker of the Trentine Council.

After which time the Popes of Rome, engrossing what they pleased of political rule into their own hands, extended their dominion over men's eyes, as they had before over their judgments, burning and prohibiting to be read what they fancied not; yet sparing in their censures, and the books not many which they so dealt with: till Martin V., by his bull, not only prohibited, but was the first that excommunicated the reading of heretical books; for about that time Wickliffe and Huss, growing terrible, were they who first drove the Papal Court to a stricter policy of prohibiting. Which course Leo X. and his successors followed, until the Council of Trent and the Spanish Inquisition engendering together brought forth, or perfected, those Catalogues and expurging Indexes, that rake through the entrails of many an old good author, with a violation worse than any could be offered to his tomb. Nor did they stay in matters heretical, but any subject that was not to their palate, they either condemned in a Prohibition, or had it straight into the new Purgatory of an Index.

To fill up the measure of encroachment, their last invention was to ordain that no book, pamphlet, or paper should be printed (as if St. Peter had bequeathed them the keys of the press also out of *Paradise*) unless it were approved and licensed under the hands of two or three glutton friars. For example:

> Let the Chancellor Cini be pleased to see if in this present work be contained aught that may withstand the printing.
> Vincent Rabbatta, Vicar of Florence.

> I have seen this present work, and find nothing athwart the Catholic faith and good manners: in witness whereof I have given, etc.
> Nicolo Cini, Chancellor of Florence.

> Attending the precedent relation, it is allowed that this present work of Davanzati may be printed. Vincent Rabbatta, etc.

> It may be printed, July 15.
> Friar Simon Mompei d'Amelia, Chancellor of the holy office in Florence.

Sure they have a conceit, if he of the bottomless pit had not long since broke prison, that this quadruple exorcism would bar him down. I fear their next design will be to get into their custody the licensing of that which they say Claudius intended, but went not through with. Vouchsafe to see another of their forms, the Roman stamp:

> Imprimatur, If it seem good to the reverend master of the holy Palace.
> Belcastro, Vicegerent.
> Imprimatur, Friar Nicolo Rodolphi, Master of the holy Palace.

Sometimes five Imprimaturs are seen together dialogue-wise in the piazza of one title-page, complimenting and ducking each to other with their shaven reverences, whether the author, who stands by in perplexity at the foot of his epistle, shall to the press or to the sponge. These are the pretty responsories, these are the dear antiphonies, that so bewitched of late our Prelates and their chaplains with the goodly echo they made; and besotted us to the gay imitation of a lordly Imprimatur, one from Lambeth House, another from the west end of Paul's; so apishly romanising, that the word of command still was set down in Latin; as if the learned grammatical pen that wrote it would cast no ink without Latin; or perhaps, as they thought, because no vulgar tongue was worthy to express the pure conceit of an Imprimatur; but rather, as I hope, for that our English, the language of men, ever famous and foremost in the achievements of liberty, will not easily find servile letters enow to spell such a dictatory presumption English.

And thus ye have the inventors and the original of book-licensing ripped up and drawn as lineally as any pedigree. We have it not, that can be heard of, from any ancient state, or polity or church; nor by any statute left us by our ancestors elder or later; nor from the modern custom of any reformed city or church abroad; but from the most anti-christian council and the most tyrannous inquisition that ever inquired. Till then books were ever as freely admitted into the world as any other birth; the issue of the brain was no more stifled than the issue of the womb: no envious Juno sat cross-legged over the nativity of any man's intellectual offspring; but if it proved a monster, who denies, but that it was justly burnt, or sunk into the sea? But that a book, in worse condition than a peccant soul, should be to stand before a jury ere it be born to the world, and undergo yet in darkness the judgment of Radamanth and his colleagues, ere it can pass the ferry backward into light, was never heard before, till that mysterious iniquity, provoked and troubled at the first entrance of Reformation, sought out new limbos and new hells wherein they might include our books also within the number of their damned. And this was the rare morsel so officiously snatched up, and so ill-favouredly imitated by our inquisiturient bishops, and the attendant minorities their chaplains. That ye like not now these most certain authors of this licensing order, and that all sinister intention was far distant from your thoughts, when ye were importuned the passing it, all men who know the integrity of your actions, and how ye honour Truth, will clear ye readily.

But some will say, What though the inventors were bad, the thing for all that may be good? It may be so; yet if that thing be no such deep invention, but obvious, and easy for any man to light on, and yet best and wisest commonwealths through all ages and occasions have foreborne to use it, and falsest seducers and oppressors of men were the first who took it up, and to no other purpose but to obstruct and hinder the first approach of Reformation; I am of those who believe it will be a harder alchymy than Lullius ever knew, to sublimate any good use out of such an invention. Yet this only is what I request to gain from this reason, that it may be held a dangerous and suspicious fruit, as certainly it deserves, for the tree that bore it, until I can dissect one by one the properties it has. But I have first to finish, as was propounded, what is to be thought in general of reading books, whatever sort they be, and whether be more the benefit or the harm that thence proceeds?

Not to insist upon the examples of Moses, Daniel, and Paul, who were skilful in all the learning of the Egyptians, Chaldeans, and Greeks, which could not probably be without reading their books of all sorts; in Paul especially, who thought it no defilement to insert into Holy Scripture the sentences of three Greek poets, and one of them a tragedian; the question was notwithstanding sometimes controverted among the primitive doctors, but with great odds on that side which affirmed it both lawful and profitable; as was then evidently perceived, when Julian the Apostate and subtlest enemy to our faith made a decree forbidding Christians the study of heathen learning: for, said he, they wound us with our own weapons, and with our own arts and sciences they overcome us. And indeed the Christians were put so to their shifts by this crafty means, and so much in danger to decline into all ignorance, that the two Apollinarii were fain, as a man may say, to coin all the seven liberal sciences out of the Bible, reducing it into divers forms of orations, poems, dialogues, even to the calculating of a new Christian grammar. But, saith the historian Socrates, the providence of God provided better than the industry of Apollinarius and his son, by taking away that illiterate law with the life of him who devised it. So great an injury they then held it to be deprived of Hellenic learning; and thought it a persecution more undermining, and secretly decaying the Church, than the open cruelty of Decius or Diocletian.

And perhaps it was the same politic drift that the devil whipped St. Jerome in a Lenten dream, for reading Cicero; or else it was a phantasm bred by the fever which had then seized him. For had an angel been his discipliner, unless it were for dwelling too much upon Ciceronianisms, and had chastised the reading, not the vanity, it had been plainly partial; first to correct him for grave Cicero, and not for scurril Plautus, whom he confesses to have been reading, not long before; next to correct him only, and let so many more ancient fathers wax old in those pleasant and florid studies without the lash of such a tutoring apparition; insomuch that Basil teaches how some good use may be made of Margites, a sportful poem, not now extant, writ by Homer; and why not then of Morgante, an Italian romance much to the same purpose?

But if it be agreed we shall be tried by visions, there is a vision recorded by Eusebius, far ancienter than this tale of Jerome to the nun Eustochium, and, besides, has nothing of a fever in it. Dionysius Alexandrinus was about the year 240 a person of great name in the Church for piety and learning, who had wont to avail himself much against heretics by being conversant in their books; until a certain presbyter laid it scrupulously to his conscience, how he durst venture himself among those defiling volumes. The worthy man, loth to give offence, fell into a new debate with himself what was to be thought; when suddenly a vision sent from God (it is his own epistle that so avers it) confirmed him in these words: Read any books whatever come to thy hands, for thou art sufficient both to judge aright, and to examine each matter. To this revelation he assented the sooner, as he confesses, because it was answerable to that of the Apostle to the Thessalonians, Prove all things, hold fast that which is good. And he might have added another remarkable saying of the same author: To the pure, all things are pure; not only meats and drinks, but all kind of knowledge whether of good or evil; the knowledge cannot defile, nor consequently the books, if the will and conscience be not defiled.

For books are as meats and viands are; some of good, some of evil substance; and yet God, in that unapocryphal vision, said without exception, Rise, Peter, kill and eat, leaving the choice to each man's discretion. Wholesome meats to a vitiated stomach differ little or nothing from unwholesome; and best books to a naughty mind are not unappliable to occasions of evil. Bad meats will scarce breed good nourishment in the healthiest concoction; but herein the difference is of bad books, that they to a discreet and judicious reader serve in many respects to discover, to confute, to forewarn, and to illustrate. Whereof what better witness can ye expect I should produce, than one of your own now sitting in Parliament, the chief of learned men reputed in this land, Mr. Selden; whose volume of natural and national laws proves, not only by great authorities brought together, but by exquisite reasons and theorems almost mathematically demonstrative, that all opinions, yea errors, known, read, and collated, are of main service and assistance toward the speedy attainment of what is truest. I conceive, therefore, that when God did enlarge the universal diet of man's body, saving ever the rules of temperance, He then also, as before, left arbitrary the dieting and repasting of our minds; as wherein every mature man might have to exercise his own leading capacity.

How great a virtue is temperance, how much of moment through the whole life of man! Yet God commits the managing so great a trust, without particular law or prescription, wholly to the demeanour of every grown man. And therefore when He Himself tabled the Jews from heaven, that omer, which was every man's daily portion of manna, is computed to have been more than might have well sufficed the heartiest feeder thrice as many meals. For those actions which enter into a man, rather than issue out of him, and therefore defile not, God uses not to captivate under a perpetual childhood of prescription, but trusts him with the gift of reason to be his own chooser; there were but little work left for preaching, if law and compulsion should grow so fast upon those things which heretofore were governed only by exhortation. Solomon informs us, that much reading is a weariness to the flesh; but neither he nor other inspired author tells us that such or such reading is unlawful: yet certainly had God thought good to limit us herein, it had been much more expedient to have told us what was unlawful than what was wearisome. As for the burning of those Ephesian books by St. Paul's converts; 'tis replied the books were magic, the Syriac so renders them. It was a private act, a voluntary act, and leaves us to a voluntary imitation: the men in remorse burnt those books which were their own; the magistrate by this example is not appointed; these men practised the books, another might perhaps have read them in some sort usefully.

Good and evil we know in the field of this world grow up together almost inseparably; and the knowledge of good is so involved and interwoven with the knowledge of evil, and in so many cunning resemblances hardly to be discerned, that those confused seeds which were imposed upon Psyche as an incessant labour to cull out, and sort asunder, were not more intermixed. It was from out the rind of one apple tasted, that the knowledge of good and evil, as two twins cleaving together, leaped forth into the world. And perhaps this is that doom which Adam fell into of knowing good and evil, that is to say of knowing good by evil. As therefore the state of man now is; what wisdom can there be to choose, what continence to forbear without the knowledge of evil? He that can apprehend and consider vice with all her baits and seeming pleasures, and yet abstain, and yet distinguish, and yet prefer that which is truly better, he is the true wayfaring Christian.

I cannot praise a fugitive and cloistered virtue, unexercised and unbreathed, that never sallies out and sees her adversary, but slinks out of the race, where that immortal garland is to be run for, not without dust and heat. Assuredly we bring not innocence into the world, we bring impurity much rather; that which purifies us is trial, and trial is by what is contrary. That virtue therefore which is but a youngling in the contemplation of evil, and knows not the utmost that vice promises to her followers, and rejects it, is but a blank virtue, not a pure; her whiteness is but an excremental whiteness. Which was the reason why our sage and serious poet Spenser, whom I dare be known to think a better teacher than Scotus or Aquinas, describing true temperance under the person of Guion, brings him in with his palmer through the cave of Mammon, and the bower of earthly bliss, that he might see and know, and yet abstain. Since therefore the knowledge and survey of vice is in this world so necessary to the constituting of human virtue, and the scanning of error to the confirmation of truth, how can we more safely, and with less danger, scout into the regions of sin and falsity than by reading all manner of tractates and hearing all manner of reason? And this is the benefit which may be had of books promiscuously read.

But of the harm that may result hence three kinds are usually reckoned. First, is feared the infection that may spread; but then all human learning and controversy in religious points must remove out of the world, yea the Bible itself; for that ofttimes relates blasphemy not nicely, it describes the carnal sense of wicked men not unelegantly, it brings in holiest men passionately murmuring against Providence through all the arguments of Epicurus: in other great disputes it answers dubiously and darkly to the common reader. And ask a Talmudist what ails the modesty of his marginal Keri, that Moses and all the prophets cannot persuade him to pronounce the textual Chetiv. For these causes we all know the Bible itself put by the Papist into the first rank of prohibited books. The ancientest fathers must be next removed, as Clement of Alexandria, and that Eusebian book of Evangelic preparation, transmitting our ears through a hoard of heathenish obscenities to receive the Gospel. Who finds not that Irenæus, Epiphanius, Jerome, and others discover more heresies than they well confute, and that oft for heresy which is the truer opinion?

Nor boots it to say for these, and all the heathen writers of greatest infection, if it must be thought so, with whom is bound up the life of human learning, that they writ in an unknown tongue, so long as we are sure those languages are known as well to the worst of men, who are both most able, and most diligent to instil the poison they suck, first into the courts of princes, acquainting them with the choicest delights and criticisms of sin. As perhaps did that Petronius whom Nero called his Arbiter, the master of his revels; and the notorious ribald of Arezzo, dreaded and yet dear to the Italian courtiers. I name not him for posterity's sake, whom Henry VIII. named in merriment his Vicar of hell. By which compendious way all the contagion that foreign books can infuse will find a passage to the people far easier and shorter than an Indian voyage, though it could be sailed either by the north of Cataio eastward, or of Canada westward, while our Spanish licensing gags the English press never so severely.

But on the other side that infection which is from books of controversy in religion is more doubtful and dangerous to the learned than to the ignorant; and yet those books must be permitted untouched by the licenser. It will be hard to instance where any ignorant man hath been ever seduced by papistical book in English, unless it were commended and expounded to him by some of that clergy: and indeed all such tractates, whether false or true, are as the prophecy of Isaiah was to the eunuch, not to be understood without a guide. But of our priests and doctors how many have been corrupted by studying the comments of Jesuits and Sorbonists, and how fast they could transfuse that corruption into the people, our experience is both late and sad. It is not forgot, since the acute and distinct Arminius was perverted merely by the perusing of a nameless discourse written at Delft, which at first he took in hand to confute.

Seeing, therefore, that those books, and those in great abundance, which are likeliest to taint both life and doctrine, cannot be suppressed without the fall of learning and of all ability in disputation, and that these books of either sort are most and soonest catching to the learned, from whom to the common people whatever is heretical or dissolute may quickly be conveyed, and that evil manners are as perfectly learnt without books a thousand other ways which cannot be stopped, and evil doctrine not with books can propagate, except a teacher guide, which he might also do without writing, and so beyond prohibiting, I am not able to unfold, how this cautelous enterprise of licensing can be exempted from the number of vain and impossible attempts. And he who were pleasantly disposed could not well avoid to liken it to the exploit of that gallant man who thought to pound up the crows by shutting his park gate.

Besides another inconvenience, if learned men be the first receivers out of books and dispreaders both of vice and error, how shall the licensers themselves be confided in, unless we can confer upon them, or they assume to themselves above all others in the land, the grace of infallibility and uncorruptedness? And again, if it be true that a wise man, like a good refiner, can gather gold out of the drossiest volume, and that a fool will be a fool with the best book, yea or without book; there is no reason that we should deprive a wise man of any advantage to his wisdom, while we seek to restrain from a fool, that which being restrained will be no hindrance to his folly. For if there should be so much exactness always used to keep that from him which is unfit for his reading, we should in the judgment of Aristotle not only, but of Solomon and of our Saviour, not vouchsafe him good precepts, and by consequence not willingly admit him to good books; as being certain that a wise man will make better use of an idle pamphlet, than a fool will do of sacred Scripture.

'Tis next alleged we must not expose ourselves to temptations without necessity, and next to that, not employ our time in vain things. To both these objections one answer will serve, out of the grounds already laid, that to all men such books are not temptations, nor vanities, but useful drugs and materials wherewith to temper and compose effective and strong medicines, which man's life cannot want. The rest, as children and childish men, who have not the art to qualify and prepare these working minerals, well may be exhorted to forbear, but hindered forcibly they cannot be by all the licensing that Sainted Inquisition could ever yet contrive. Which is what I promised to deliver next, That this order of licensing conduces nothing to the end for which it was framed; and hath almost prevented me by being clear already while thus much hath been explaining. See the ingenuity of Truth, who, when she gets a free and willing hand, opens herself faster than the pace of method and discourse can overtake her.

It was the task which I began with, to show that no nation, or well-instituted state, if they valued books at all, did ever use this way of licensing; and it might be answered, that this is a piece of prudence lately discovered. To which I return, that as it was a thing slight and obvious to think on, so if it had been difficult to find out, there wanted not among them long since who suggested such a course; which they not following, leave us a pattern of their judgment that it was not the not knowing, but the not approving, which was the cause of their not using it.

Plato, a man of high authority, indeed, but least of all for his commonwealth, in the book of his Laws, which no city ever yet received, fed his fancy by making many edicts to his airy burgomasters, which they who otherwise admire him wish had been rather buried and excused in the genial cups of an Academic night sitting. By which laws he seems to tolerate no kind of learning but by unalterable decree, consisting most of practical traditions, to the attainment whereof a library of smaller bulk than his own Dialogues would be abundant. And there also enacts, that no poet should so much as read to any private man what he had written, until the judges and law-keepers had seen it, and allowed it. But that Plato meant this law peculiarly to that commonwealth which he had imagined, and to no other, is evident. Why was he not else a lawgiver to himself, but a transgressor, and to be expelled by his own magistrates; both for the wanton epigrams and dialogues which he made, and his perpetual reading of Sophron Mimus and Aristophanes, books of grossest infamy, and also for commending the latter of them, though he were the malicious libeller of his chief friends, to be read by the tyrant Dionysius, who had little need of such trash to spend his time on? But that he knew this licensing of poems had reference and dependence to many other provisos there set down in his fancied republic, which in this world could have no place: and so neither he himself, nor any magistrate, or city ever imitated that course, which, taken apart from those other collateral injunctions, must needs be vain and fruitless. For if they fell upon one kind of strictness, unless their care were equal to regulate all other things of like aptness to corrupt the mind, that single endeavour they knew would be but a fond labour; to shut and fortify one gate against corruption, and be necessitated to leave others round about wide open.

If we think to regulate printing, thereby to rectify manners, we must regulate all recreations and pastimes, all that is delightful to man. No music must be heard, no song be set or sung, but what is grave and Doric. There must be licensing dancers, that no gesture, motion, or deportment be taught our youth but what by their allowance shall be thought honest; for such Plato was provided of; it will ask more than the work of twenty licensers to examine all the lutes, the violins, and the guitars in every house; they must not be suffered to prattle as they do, but must be licensed what they may say. And who shall silence all the airs and madrigals that whisper softness in chambers? The windows also, and the balconies must be thought on; there are shrewd books, with dangerous frontispieces, set to sale; who shall prohibit them, shall twenty licensers? The villages also must have their visitors to inquire what lectures the bagpipe and the rebeck reads, even to the ballatry and the gamut of every municipal fiddler, for these are the countryman's Arcadias, and his Monte Mayors.

Next, what more national corruption, for which England hears ill abroad, than household gluttony: who shall be the rectors of our daily rioting? And what shall be done to inhibit the multitudes that frequent those houses where drunkenness is sold and harboured? Our garments also should be referred to the licensing of some more sober workmasters to see them cut into a less wanton garb. Who shall regulate all the mixed conversation of our youth, male and female together, as is the fashion of this country? Who shall still appoint what shall be discoursed, what presumed, and no further? Lastly, who shall forbid and separate all idle resort, all evil company? These things will be, and must be; but how they shall be least hurtful, how least enticing, herein consists the grave and governing wisdom of a state.

To sequester out of the world into Atlantic and Utopian polities which never can be drawn into use, will not mend our condition; but to ordain wisely as in this world of evil, in the midst whereof God hath placed us unavoidably. Nor is it Plato's licensing of books will do this, which necessarily pulls along with it so many other kinds of licensing, as will make us all both ridiculous and weary, and yet frustrate; but those unwritten, or at least unconstraining, laws of virtuous education, religious and civil nurture, which Plato there mentions as the bonds and ligaments of the commonwealth, the pillars and the sustainers of every written statute; these they be which will bear chief sway in such matters as these, when all licensing will be easily eluded. Impunity and remissness, for certain, are the bane of a commonwealth; but here the great art lies, to discern in what the law is to bid restraint and punishment, and in what things persuasion only is to work.

If every action, which is good or evil in man at ripe years, were to be under pittance and prescription and compulsion, what were virtue but a name, what praise could be then due to well-doing, what gramercy to be sober, just, or continent? Many there be that complain of Divine Providence for suffering Adam to transgress; foolish tongues! When God gave him reason, He gave him freedom to choose, for reason is but choosing;

he had been else a mere artificial Adam, such an Adam as he is in the motions. We ourselves esteem not of that obedience, or love, or gift, which is of force: God therefore left him free, set before him a provoking object, ever almost in his eyes; herein consisted his merit, herein the right of his reward, the praise of his abstinence. Wherefore did He create passions within us, pleasures round about us, but that these rightly tempered are the very ingredients of virtue?

They are not skilful considerers of human things, who imagine to remove sin by removing the matter of sin; for, besides that it is a huge heap increasing under the very act of diminishing, though some part of it may for a time be withdrawn from some persons, it cannot from all, in such a universal thing as books are; and when this is done, yet the sin remains entire. Though ye take from a covetous man all his treasure, he has yet one jewel left, ye cannot bereave him of his covetousness. Banish all objects of lust, shut up all youth into the severest discipline that can be exercised in any hermitage, ye cannot make them chaste, that came not thither so: such great care and wisdom is required to the right managing of this point. Suppose we could expel sin by this means; look how much we thus expel of sin, so much we expel of virtue: for the matter of them both is the same; remove that, and ye remove them both alike.

This justifies the high providence of God, who, though He commands us temperance, justice, continence, yet pours out before us, even to a profuseness, all desirable things, and gives us minds that can wander beyond all limit and satiety. Why should we then affect a rigour contrary to the manner of God and of nature, by abridging or scanting those means, which books freely permitted are, both to the trial of virtue and the exercise of truth? It would be better done, to learn that the law must needs be frivolous, which goes to restrain things, uncertainly and yet equally working to good and to evil. And were I the chooser, a dram of well-doing should be preferred before many times as much the forcible hindrance of evil-doing. For God sure esteems the growth and completing of one virtuous person more than the restraint of ten vicious.

And albeit whatever thing we hear or see, sitting, walking, travelling, or conversing, may be fitly called our book, and is of the same effect that writings are, yet grant the thing to be prohibited were only books, it appears that this order hitherto is far insufficient to the end which it intends. Do we not see, not once or oftener, but weekly, that continued court-libel against the Parliament and City, printed, as the wet sheets can witness, and dispersed among us, for all that licensing can do? yet this is the prime service a man would think, wherein this Order should give proof of itself. If it were executed, you'll say. But certain, if execution be remiss or blindfold now, and in this particular, what will it be hereafter and in other books? If then the Order shall not be vain and frustrate, behold a new labour, Lords and Commons, ye must repeal and proscribe all scandalous and unlicensed books already printed and divulged; after ye have drawn them up into a list, that all may know which are condemned, and which not; and ordain that no foreign books be delivered out of custody, till they have been read over. This office will require the whole time of not a few overseers, and those no vulgar men. There be also books which are partly useful and excellent, partly culpable and pernicious; this work will ask as many more officials, to make expurgations and expunctions, that the Commonwealth of Learning be not damnified. In fine, when the multitude of books increase upon their hands, ye must be fain to catalogue all those printers who are found frequently offending, and forbid the importation of their whole suspected typography. In a word, that this your Order may be exact and not deficient, ye must reform it perfectly according to the model of Trent and Seville, which I know ye abhor to do.

Yet though ye should condescend to this, which God forbid, the Order still would be but fruitless and defective to that end whereto ye meant it. If to prevent sects and schisms, who is so unread or so uncatechised in story, that hath not heard of many sects refusing books as a hindrance, and preserving their doctrine unmixed for many ages, only by unwritten traditions? The Christian faith, for that was once a schism, is not unknown to have spread all over Asia, ere any Gospel or Epistle was seen in writing. If the amendment of manners be aimed at, look into Italy and Spain, whether those places be one scruple the better, the honester, the wiser, the chaster, since all the inquisitional rigour that hath been executed upon books.

Another reason, whereby to make it plain that this Order will miss the end it seeks, consider by the quality which ought to be in every licenser. It cannot be denied but that he who is made judge to sit upon the birth or death of books, whether they may be wafted into this world or not, had need to be a man above the common measure, both studious, learned, and judicious; there may be else no mean mistakes in the censure of what is passable or not; which is also no mean injury. If he be of such worth as behoves him, there cannot be a more tedious and unpleasing journey-work, a greater loss of time levied upon his head, than to be made the perpetual reader of unchosen books and pamphlets, ofttimes huge volumes. There is no book that is acceptable unless at certain seasons; but to be enjoined the reading of that at all times, and in a hand scarce legible, whereof three pages would not down at any time in the fairest print, is an imposition which I cannot believe how he that values time and his own studies, or is but of a sensible nostril, should be able to endure. In this one thing I crave leave of the present licensers to be pardoned for so thinking; who doubtless took this office up, looking on it through their obedience to the Parliament, whose command perhaps made all things seem easy and unlaborious to them; but that this short trial hath wearied them out already, their own expressions and excuses to them who make so many journeys to solicit their licence are testimony enough. Seeing therefore those who now possess the employment by all evident signs wish themselves well rid of it; and that no man of worth, none that is not a plain unthrift of his own hours is ever likely to succeed them, except he mean to put himself to the salary of a press corrector; we may easily foresee what kind of licensers we are to expect hereafter, either ignorant, imperious, and remiss, or basely pecuniary. This is what I had to show, wherein this Order cannot conduce to that end whereof it bears the intention.

I lastly proceed from the no good it can do, to the manifest hurt it causes, in being first the greatest discouragement and affront that can be offered to learning, and to learned men.

It was the complaint and lamentation of prelates, upon every least breath of a motion to remove pluralities, and distribute more equally Church revenues, that then all learning would be for ever dashed and discouraged. But as for that opinion, I never found cause to think that the tenth part of learning stood or fell with the clergy: nor could I ever but hold it for a sordid and unworthy speech of any churchman who had a competency left him. If therefore ye be loth to dishearten heartily and discontent, not the mercenary crew of false pretenders to learning, but the free and ingenuous sort of such as evidently were born to study, and love learning for itself, not for lucre or any other end but the service of God and of truth, and perhaps that lasting fame and perpetuity of praise which God and good men have consented shall be the reward of those whose published labours advance the good of mankind, then know that, so far to distrust the judgment and the honesty of one who hath but a common repute in learning, and never yet offended, as not to count him fit to print his mind without a tutor and examiner, lest he should drop a schism, or something of corruption, is the greatest displeasure and indignity to a free and knowing spirit that can be put upon him.

What advantage is it to be a man over it is to be a boy at school, if we have only escaped the ferula to come under the fescue of an Imprimatur, if serious and elaborate writings, as if they were no more than the theme of a grammar-lad under his pedagogue, must not be uttered without the cursory eyes of a temporising and extemporising licenser? He who is not trusted with his own actions, his drift not being known to be evil, and standing to the hazard of law and penalty, has no great argument to think himself reputed in the Commonwealth, wherein he was born, for other than a fool or a foreigner. When a man writes to the world, he summons up all his reason and deliberation to assist him; he searches, meditates, is industrious, and likely consults and confers with his judicious friends; after all which done he takes himself to be informed in what he writes, as well as any that writ before him. If, in this the most consummate act of his fidelity and ripeness, no years, no industry, no former proof of his abilities can bring him to that state of maturity, as not to be still mistrusted and suspected, unless he carry all his considerate diligence, all his midnight watchings and expense of Palladian oil, to the hasty view of an unleisured licenser, perhaps much his younger, perhaps far his inferior in judgment, perhaps one who never knew the labour of bookwriting, and if he be not repulsed or slighted, must appear in print like a puny with his guardian, and his censor's hand on the back of his title to be his bail and surety that he is no idiot or seducer, it cannot be but a dishonour and derogation to the author, to the book, to the privilege and dignity of Learning.

And what if the author shall be one so copious of fancy, as to have many things well worth the adding come into his mind after licensing, while the book is yet under the press, which not seldom happens to the best and diligentest writers; and that perhaps a dozen times in one book? The printer dares not go beyond his licensed copy; so often then must the author trudge to his leave-giver, that those his new insertions may be viewed; and many a jaunt will be made, ere that licenser, for it must be the same man, can either be found, or found at leisure; meanwhile either the press must stand still, which is no small damage, or the author lose his accuratest thoughts, and send the book forth worse than he had made it, which to a diligent writer is the greatest melancholy and vexation that can befall.

And how can a man teach with authority, which is the life of teaching, how can he be a doctor in his book as he ought to be, or else had better be silent, whenas all he teaches, all he delivers, is but under the tuition, under the correction of his patriarchal licenser to blot or alter what precisely accords not with the hidebound humour which he calls his judgment? When every acute reader, upon the first sight of a pedantic licence, will be ready with these like words to ding the book a quoit's distance from him: I hate a pupil teacher, I endure not an instructor that comes to me under the wardship of an overseeing fist. I know nothing of the licenser, but that I have his own hand here for his arrogance; who shall warrant me his judgment? The State, sir, replies the stationer, but has a quick return: The State shall be my governors, but not my critics; they may be mistaken in the choice of a licenser, as easily as this licenser may be mistaken in an author; this is some common stuff; and he might add from Sir Francis Bacon, That such authorised books are but the language of the times. For though a licenser should happen to be judicious more than ordinary, which will be a great jeopardy of the next succession, yet his very office and his commission enjoins him to let pass nothing but what is vulgarly received already.

Nay, which is more lamentable, if the work of any deceased author, though never so famous in his lifetime and even to this day, come to their hands for licence to be printed, or reprinted, if there be found in his book one sentence of a venturous edge, uttered in the height of zeal and who knows whether it might not be the dictate of a divine spirit, yet not suiting with every low decrepit humour of their own, though it were Knox himself, the Reformer of a Kingdom, that spake it, they will not pardon him their dash: the sense of that great man shall to all posterity be lost, for the fearfulness or the presumptuous rashness of a perfunctory licenser. And to what an author this violence hath been lately done, and in what book of greatest consequence to be faithfully published, I could now instance, but shall forbear till a more convenient season.

Yet if these things be not resented seriously and timely by them who have the remedy in their power, but that such iron moulds as these shall have authority to gnaw out the choicest periods of exquisitest books, and to commit such a treacherous fraud against the orphan remainders of worthiest men after death, the more sorrow will belong to that hapless race of men, whose misfortune it is to have understanding. Henceforth let no man care to learn, or care to be more than worldly-wise; for certainly in higher matters to be ignorant and slothful, to be a common steadfast dunce, will be the only pleasant life, and only in request.

And as it is a particular disesteem of every knowing person alive, and most injurious to the written labours and monuments of the dead, so to me it seems an undervaluing and vilifying of the whole Nation. I cannot set so light by all the invention, the art, the wit, the grave and solid judgment which is in England, as that it can be comprehended in any twenty capacities how good soever, much less that it should not pass except their superintendence be over it, except it be sifted and strained with their strainers, that it should be uncurrent without their manual stamp. Truth and understanding are not such wares as to be monopolised and traded in by tickets and statutes and standards. We must not think to make a staple commodity of all the knowledge in the land, to mark and licence it like our broadcloth and our woolpacks. What is it but a servitude like that imposed by the Philistines, not to be allowed the sharpening of our own axes and coulters, but we must repair from all quarters to twenty licensing forges? Had anyone written and divulged erroneous things and scandalous to honest life, misusing and forfeiting the esteem had of his reason among men, if after conviction this only censure were adjudged him that he should never henceforth write but what were first examined by an appointed officer, whose hand should be annexed to pass his credit for him that now he might be safely read; it could not be apprehended less than a disgraceful punishment. Whence to include the whole Nation, and those that never yet thus offended, under such a diffident and suspectful prohibition, may plainly be understood what a disparagement it is. So much the more, whenas debtors and delinquents may walk abroad without a keeper, but unoffensive books must not stir forth without a visible jailer in their title.

Nor is it to the common people less than a reproach; for if we be so jealous over them, as that we dare not trust them with an English pamphlet, what do we but censure them for a giddy, vicious, and ungrounded people; in such a sick and weak state of faith and discretion, as to be able to take nothing down but through the pipe of a licenser? That this is care or love of them, we cannot pretend, whenas, in those popish places where the laity are most hated and despised, the same strictness is used over them. Wisdom we cannot call it, because it stops but one breach of licence, nor that neither: whenas those corruptions, which it seeks to prevent, break in faster at other doors which cannot be shut.

And in conclusion it reflects to the disrepute of our Ministers also, of whose labours we should hope better, and of the proficiency which their flock reaps by them, than that after all this light of the Gospel which is, and is to be, and all this continual preaching, they should still be frequented with such an unprincipled, unedified and laic rabble, as that the whiff of every new pamphlet should stagger them out of their catechism, and Christian walking. This may have much reason to discourage the Ministers when such a low conceit is had of all their exhortations, and the benefiting of their hearers, as that they are not thought fit to be turned loose to three sheets of paper without a licenser; that all the sermons, all the lectures preached, printed, vented in such numbers, and such volumes, as have now well nigh made all other books unsaleable, should not be armour enough against one single Enchiridion, without the castle of St. Angelo of an Imprimatur.

And lest some should persuade ye, Lords and Commons, that these arguments of learned men's discouragement at this your Order are mere flourishes, and not real, I could recount what I have seen and heard in other countries, where this kind of inquisition tyrannises; when I have sat among their learned men, for that honour I had, and been counted happy to be born in such a place of philosophic freedom, as they supposed England was, while themselves did nothing but bemoan the servile condition into which learning amongst them was brought; that this was it which had damped the glory of Italian wits; that nothing had been there written now these many years but flattery and fustian. There it was that I found and visited the famous Galileo, grown old a prisoner to the Inquisition, for thinking in astronomy otherwise than the Franciscan and Dominican licensers thought.

And though I knew that England then was groaning loudest under the prelatical yoke, nevertheless I took it as a pledge of future happiness, that other nations were so persuaded of her liberty. Yet was it beyond my hope that those Worthies were then breathing in her air, who should be her leaders to such a deliverance, as shall never be forgotten by any revolution of time that this world hath to finish. When that was once begun, it was as little in my fear that, what words of complaint I heard among learned men of other parts uttered against the Inquisition, the same I should hear by as learned men at home uttered in time of Parliament against an order of licensing; and that so generally that, when I had disclosed myself a companion of their discontent, I might say, if without envy, that he whom an honest quæstorship had endeared to the Sicilians was not more by them importuned against Verres, than the favourable opinion which I had among many who honour ye, and are known and respected by ye, loaded me with entreaties and persuasions, that I would not despair to lay together that which just reason should bring into my mind, toward the removal of an undeserved thraldom upon learning. That this is not therefore the disburdening of a particular fancy, but the common grievance of all those who had prepared their minds and studies above the vulgar pitch to advance truth in others, and from others to entertain it, thus much may satisfy.

And in their name I shall for neither friend nor foe conceal what the general murmur is; that if it come to inquisitioning again and licensing, and that we are so timorous of ourselves, and so suspicious of all men, as to fear each book and the shaking of every leaf, before we know what the contents are; if some who but of late were little better than silenced from preaching shall come now to silence us from reading, except what they please, it cannot be guessed what is intended by some but a second tyranny over learning: and will soon put it out of controversy, that Bishops and Presbyters are the same to us, both name and thing. That those evils of Prelaty, which before from five or six and twenty sees were distributively charged upon the whole people, will now light wholly upon learning, is not obscure to us: whenas now the Pastor of a small unlearned Parish on the sudden shall be exalted Archbishop over a large diocese of books, and yet not remove, but keep his other cure too, a mystical pluralist. He who but of late cried down the sole ordination of every novice Bachelor of Art, and denied sole jurisdiction over the simplest parishioner, shall now at home in his private chair assume both these over worthiest and excellentest books and ablest authors that write them.

This is not, ye Covenants and Protestations that we have made! this is not to put down Prelaty; this is but to chop an Episcopacy; this is but to translate the Palace Metropolitan from one kind of dominion into another; this is but an old canonical sleight of commuting our penance. To startle thus betimes at a mere unlicensed pamphlet will after a while be afraid of every conventicle, and a while after will make a conventicle of every Christian meeting. But I am certain that a State governed by the rules of justice and fortitude, or a Church built and founded upon the rock of faith and true knowledge, cannot be so pusillanimous. While things are yet not constituted in Religion, that freedom of writing should be restrained by a discipline imitated from the Prelates and learnt by them from the Inquisition, to shut us up all again into the breast of a licenser, must needs give cause of doubt and discouragement to all learned and religious men.

Who cannot but discern the fineness of this politic drift, and who are the contrivers; that while Bishops were to be baited down, then all Presses might be open; it was the people's birthright and privilege in time of Parliament, it was the breaking forth of light? But now, the Bishops abrogated and voided out the Church, as if our Reformation sought no more but to make room for others into their seats under another name, the episcopal arts begin to bud again, the cruse of truth must run no more oil, liberty of Printing must be enthralled again under a prelatical commission of twenty, the privilege of the people nullified, and, which is worse, the freedom of learning must groan again, and to her old fetters: all this the Parliament yet sitting. Although their own late arguments and defences against the Prelates might remember them, that this obstructing violence meets for the most part with an event utterly opposite to the end which it drives at: instead of suppressing sects and schisms, it raises them and invests them with a reputation. "The punishing of wits enhances their authority," said the Viscount St. Albans; "and a forbidden writing is thought to be a certain spark of truth that flies up in the faces of them who seek to tread it out."

This Order, therefore, may prove a nursing-mother to sects, but I shall easily show how it will be a stepdame to Truth: and first by disenabling us to the maintenance of what is known already.

Well knows he who uses to consider, that our faith and knowledge thrives by exercise, as well as our limbs and complexion. Truth is compared in Scripture to a streaming fountain; if her waters flow not in a perpetual progression, they sicken into a muddy pool of conformity and tradition. A man may be a heretic in the truth; and if he believe things only because his Pastor says so, or the Assembly so determines, without knowing other reason, though his belief be true, yet the very truth he holds becomes his heresy.

There is not any burden that some would gladlier post off to another than the charge and care of their Religion. There be—who knows not that there be?—of Protestants and professors who live and die in as arrant an implicit faith as any lay Papist of Loretto. A wealthy man, addicted to his pleasure and to his profits, finds Religion to be a traffic so entangled, and of so many piddling accounts, that of all mysteries he cannot skill to keep a stock going upon that trade. What should he do? fain he would have the name to be religious, fain he would bear up with his neighbours in that. What does he therefore, but resolve to give over toiling, and to find himself out some factor, to whose care and credit he may commit the whole managing of his religious affairs? some Divine of note and estimation that must be. To him he adheres, resigns the whole warehouse of his religion, with all the locks and keys, into his custody; and indeed makes the very person of that man his religion; esteems his associating with him a sufficient evidence and commendatory of his own piety. So that a man may say his religion is now no more within himself, but is become a dividual movable, and goes and comes near him, according as that good man frequents the house. He entertains him, gives him gifts, feasts him, lodges him; his religion comes home at night, prays, is liberally supped, and sumptuously laid to sleep, rises, is saluted, and after the malmsey, or some well-spiced brewage, and better breakfasted than he whose morning appetite would have gladly fed on green figs between Bethany and Jerusalem, his Religion walks abroad at eight, and leaves his kind entertainer in the shop trading all day without his Religion.

Another sort there be who, when they hear that all things shall be ordered, all things regulated and settled, nothing written but what passes through the custom-house of certain Publicans that have the tonnaging and poundaging of all free-spoken truth, will straight give themselves up into your hands, make 'em and cut 'em out what religion ye please: there be delights, there be recreations and jolly pastimes that will fetch the day about from sun to sun, and rock the tedious year as in a delightful dream. What need they torture their heads with that which others have taken so strictly and so unalterably into their own purveying? These are the fruits which a dull ease and cessation of our knowledge will bring forth among the people. How goodly and how to be wished were such an obedient unanimity as this, what a fine conformity would it starch us all into! Doubtless a staunch and solid piece of framework, as any January could freeze together.

Nor much better will be the consequence even among the clergy themselves. It is no new thing never heard of before, for a parochial Minister, who has his reward and is at his Hercules' pillars in a warm benefice, to be easily inclinable, if he have nothing else that may rouse up his studies, to finish his circuit in an English Concordance and a topic folio, the gatherings and savings of a sober graduateship, a Harmony and a Catena; treading the constant round of certain common doctrinal heads, attended with the uses, motives, marks, and means, out of which, as out of an alphabet, or sol-fa, by forming and transforming, joining and disjoining variously, a little bookcraft, and two hours' meditation, might furnish him unspeakably to the performance of more than a weekly charge of sermoning: not to reckon up the infinite helps of interlinearies, breviaries, synopses, and other loitering gear. But as for the multitude of sermons ready printed and piled up, on every text that is not difficult, our London trading St. Thomas in his vestry, and add to boot St. Martin and St. Hugh, have not within their hallowed limits more vendible ware of all sorts ready made: so that penury he never need fear of pulpit provision, having where so plenteously to refresh his magazine. But if his rear and flanks be not impaled, if his back door be not secured by the rigid licenser, but that a bold book may now and then issue forth and give the assault to some of his old collections in their trenches, it will concern him then to keep waking, to stand in watch, to set good guards and sentinels about his received opinions, to walk the round and counter-round with his fellow inspectors, fearing lest any of his flock be seduced, who also then would be better instructed, better exercised and disciplined. And God send that the fear of this diligence, which must then be used, do not make us affect the laziness of a licensing Church.

For if we be sure we are in the right, and do not hold the truth guiltily, which becomes not, if we ourselves condemn not our own weak and frivolous teaching, and the people for an untaught and irreligious gadding rout, what can be more fair than when a man judicious, learned, and of a conscience, for aught we know, as good as theirs that taught us what we know, shall not privily from house to house, which is more dangerous, but openly by writing publish to the world what his opinion is, what his reasons, and wherefore that which is now thought cannot be sound? Christ urged it as wherewith to justify himself, that he preached in public; yet writing is more public than preaching; and more easy to refutation, if need be, there being so many whose business and profession merely it is to be the champions of Truth; which if they neglect, what can be imputed but their sloth, or unability?

Thus much we are hindered and disinured by this course of licensing, toward the true knowledge of what we seem to know. For how much it hurts and hinders the licensers themselves in the calling of their ministry, more than any secular employment, if they will discharge that office as they ought, so that of necessity they must neglect either the one duty or the other, I insist not, because it is a particular, but leave it to their own conscience, how they will decide it there.

There is yet behind of what I proposed to lay open, the incredible loss and detriment that this plot of incensing puts us to; more than if some enemy at sea should stop up all our havens and ports and creeks, it hinders and retards the importation of our richest Merchandise, Truth; nay, it was first established and put in practice by Antichristian malice and mystery on set purpose to extinguish, if it were possible, the light of Reformation, and to settle falsehood; little differing from that policy wherewith the Turk upholds his Alcoran, by the prohibition of Printing. 'Tis not denied, but gladly confessed, we are to send our thanks and vows to Heaven louder than most of nations, for that great measure of truth which we enjoy, especially in those main points between us and the Pope, with his appurtenances the Prelates: but he who thinks we are to pitch our tent here, and have attained the utmost prospect of reformation that the mortal glass wherein we contemplate can show us, till we come to beatific vision, that man by this very opinion declares that he is yet far short of Truth.

Truth indeed came once into the world with her Divine Master, and was a perfect shape most glorious to look on: but when He ascended, and His Apostles after Him were laid asleep, then straight arose a wicked race of deceivers, who, as that story goes of the Egyptian Typhon with his conspirators, how they dealt with the good Osiris, took the virgin Truth, hewed her lovely form into a thousand pieces, and scattered them to the four winds. From that time ever since, the sad friends of Truth, such as durst appear, imitating the careful search that Isis made for the mangled body of Osiris, went up and down gathering up limb by limb, still as they could find them. We have not yet found them all, Lords and Commons, nor ever shall do, till her Master's second coming; He shall bring together every joint and member, and shall mould them into an immortal feature of loveliness and perfection. Suffer not these licensing prohibitions to stand at every place of opportunity, forbidding and disturbing them that continue seeking, that continue to do our obsequies to the torn body of our martyred saint.

We boast our light; but if we look not wisely on the Sun itself, it smites us into darkness. Who can discern those planets that are oft combust, and those stars of brightest magnitude that rise and set with the Sun, until the opposite motion of their orbs bring them to such a place in the firmament, where they may be seen evening or morning? The light which we have gained was given us, not to be ever staring on, but by it to discover onward things more remote from our knowledge. It is not the unfrocking of a priest, the unmitring of a bishop, and the removing him from off the presbyterian shoulders, that will make us a happy Nation. No, if other things as great in the Church, and in the rule of life both economical and political, be not looked into and reformed, we have looked so long upon the blaze that Zuinglius and Calvin hath beaconed up to us, that we are stark blind.

There be who perpetually complain of schisms and sects, and make it such a calamity that any man dissents from their maxims. 'Tis their own pride and ignorance which causes the disturbing, who neither will hear with meekness, nor can convince; yet all must be suppressed which is not found in their Syntagma. They are the troublers, they are the dividers of unity, who neglect and permit not others to unite those dissevered pieces which are yet wanting to the body of Truth. To be still searching what we know not by what we know, still closing up truth to truth as we find it (for all her body is homogeneal and proportional), this is the golden rule in theology as well as in arithmetic, and makes up the best harmony in a Church; not the forced and outward union of cold and neutral, and inwardly divided minds.

Lords and Commons of England, consider what Nation it is whereof ye are, and whereof ye are the governors: a Nation not slow and dull, but of a quick, ingenious and piercing spirit, acute to invent, subtle and sinewy to discourse, not beneath the reach of any point, the highest that human capacity can soar to. Therefore the studies of Learning in her deepest sciences have been so ancient and so eminent among us, that writers of good antiquity and ablest judgment have been persuaded that even the school of Pythagoras and the Persian wisdom took beginning from the old philosophy of this island. And that wise and civil Roman, Julius Agricola, who governed once here for Cæsar, preferred the natural wits of Britain before the laboured studies of the French. Nor is it for nothing that the grave and frugal Transylvanian sends out yearly from as far as the mountainous borders of Russia, and beyond the Hercynian wilderness, not their youth, but their staid men, to learn our language and our theologic arts.

Yet that which is above all this, the favour and the love of Heaven, we have great argument to think in a peculiar manner propitious and propending towards us. Why else was this Nation chosen before any other, that out of her, as out of Sion, should be proclaimed and sounded forth the first tidings and trumpet of Reformation to all Europe? And had it not been the obstinate perverseness of our prelates against the divine and admirable spirit of Wickliff, to suppress him as a schismatic and innovator, perhaps neither the Bohemian Huss and Jerome, no nor the name of Luther or of Calvin, had been ever known: the glory of reforming all our neighbours had been completely ours. But now, as our obdurate clergy have with violence demeaned the matter, we are become hitherto the latest and backwardest scholars, of whom God offered to have made us the teachers. Now once again by all concurrence of signs, and by the general instinct of holy and devout men, as they daily and solemnly express their thoughts, God is decreeing to begin some new and great period in His Church, even to the reforming of Reformation itself: what does He then but reveal Himself to His servants, and as His manner is, first to His Englishmen? I say, as His manner is, first to us, though we mark not the method of His counsels, and are unworthy.

Behold now this vast City: a city of refuge, the mansion house of liberty, encompassed and surrounded with His protection; the shop of war hath not there more anvils and hammers waking, to fashion out the plates and instruments of armed Justice in defence of beleaguered Truth, than there be pens and heads there, sitting by their studious lamps, musing, searching, revolving new notions and ideas wherewith to present, as with their homage and their fealty, the approaching Reformation: others as fast reading, trying all things, assenting to the force of reason and convincement. What could a man require more from a Nation so pliant and so prone to seek after knowledge? What wants there to such a towardly and pregnant soil, but wise and faithful labourers, to make a knowing people, a Nation of Prophets, of Sages, and of Worthies? We reckon more than five months yet to harvest; there need not be five weeks; had we but eyes to lift up, the fields are white already.

Where there is much desire to learn, there of necessity will be much arguing, much writing, many opinions; for opinion in good men is but knowledge in the making. Under these fantastic terrors of sect and schism, we wrong the earnest and zealous thirst after knowledge and understanding which God hath stirred up in this city. What some lament of, we rather should rejoice at, should rather praise this pious forwardness among men, to reassume the ill-reputed care of their Religion into their own hands again. A little generous prudence, a little forbearance of one another, and some grain of charity might win all these diligences to join, and unite in one general and brotherly search after Truth; could we but forego this prelatical tradition of crowding free consciences and Christian liberties into canons and precepts of men. I doubt not, if some great and worthy stranger should come among us, wise to discern the mould and temper of a people, and how to govern it, observing the high hopes and aims, the diligent alacrity of our extended thoughts and reasonings in the pursuance of truth and freedom, but that he would cry out as Pyrrhus did, admiring the Roman docility and courage: If such were my Epirots, I would not despair the greatest design that could be attempted, to make a Church or Kingdom happy.

Yet these are the men cried out against for schismatics and sectaries; as if, while the temple of the Lord was building, some cutting, some squaring the marble, others hewing the cedars, there should be a sort of irrational men who could not consider there must be many schisms and many dissections made in the quarry and in the timber, ere the house of God can be built. And when every stone is laid artfully together, it cannot be united into a continuity, it can but be contiguous in this world; neither can every piece of the building be of one form; nay rather the perfection consists in this, that, out of many moderate varieties and brotherly dissimilitudes that are not vastly disproportional, arises the goodly and the graceful symmetry that commends the whole pile and structure.

Let us therefore be more considerate builders, more wise in spiritual architecture, when great reformation is expected. For now the time seems come, wherein Moses the great prophet may sit in heaven rejoicing to see that memorable and glorious wish of his fulfilled, when not only our seventy Elders, but all the Lord's people, are become prophets. No marvel then though some men, and some good men too perhaps, but young in goodness, as Joshua then was, envy them. They fret, and out of their own weakness are in agony, lest these divisions and subdivisions will undo us. The adversary again applauds, and waits the hour: When they have branched themselves out, saith he, small enough into parties and partitions, then will be our time. Fool! he sees not the firm root, out of which we all grow, though into branches: nor will be ware until he see our small divided maniples cutting through at every angle of his ill-united and unwieldy brigade. And that we are to hope better of all these supposed sects and schisms, and that we shall not need that solicitude, honest perhaps though over-timorous of them that vex in this behalf, but shall laugh in the end at those malicious applauders of our differences, I have these reasons to persuade me.

First, when a City shall be as it were besieged and blocked about, her navigable river infested, inroads and incursions round, defiance and battle oft rumoured to be marching up even to her walls and suburb trenches, that then the people, or the greater part, more than at other times, wholly taken up with the study of highest and most important matters to be reformed, should be disputing, reasoning, reading, inventing, discoursing, even to a rarity and admiration, things not before discoursed or written of, argues first a singular goodwill, contentedness and confidence in your prudent foresight and safe government, Lords and Commons; and from thence derives itself to a gallant bravery and well-grounded contempt of their enemies, as if there were no small number of as great spirits among us, as his was, who when Rome was nigh besieged by Hannibal, being in the city, bought that piece of ground at no cheap rate, whereon Hannibal himself encamped his own regiment.

Next, it is a lively and cheerful presage of our happy success and victory. For as in a body, when the blood is fresh, the spirits pure and vigorous, not only to vital but to rational faculties, and those in the acutest and the pertest operations of wit and subtlety, it argues in what good plight and constitution the body is so when the cheerfulness of the people is so sprightly up, as that it has not only wherewith to guard well its own freedom and safety, but to spare, and to bestow upon the solidest and sublimest points of controversy and new invention, it betokens us not degenerated, nor drooping to a fatal decay, but casting off the old and wrinkled skin of corruption to outlive these pangs and wax young again, entering the glorious ways of truth and prosperous virtue, destined to become great and honourable in these latter ages. Methinks I see in my mind a noble and puissant nation rousing herself like a strong man after sleep, and shaking her invincible locks. Methinks I see her as an eagle mewing her mighty youth, and kindling her undazzled eyes at the full midday beam; purging and unscaling her long-abused sight at the fountain itself of heavenly radiance; while the whole noise of timorous and flocking birds, with those also that love the twilight, flutter about, amazed at what she means, and in their envious gabble would prognosticate a year of sects and schisms.

What would ye do then? should ye suppress all this flowery crop of knowledge and new light sprung up and yet springing daily in this city? should ye set an oligarchy of twenty engrossers over it, to bring a famine upon our minds again, when we shall know nothing but what is measured to us by their bushel? Believe it, Lords and Commons, they who counsel ye to such a suppressing do as good as bid ye suppress yourselves; and I will soon show how. If it be desired to know the immediate cause of all this free writing and free speaking, there cannot be assigned a truer than your own mild and free and humane government. It is the liberty, Lords and Commons, which your own valorous and happy counsels have purchased us, liberty which is the nurse of all great wits; this is that which hath rarefied and enlightened our spirits like the influence of heaven; this is that which hath enfranchised, enlarged and lifted up our apprehensions degrees above themselves.

Ye cannot make us now less capable, less knowing, less eagerly pursuing of the truth, unless ye first make yourselves, that made us so, less the lovers, less the founders of our true liberty. We can grow ignorant again, brutish, formal and slavish, as ye found us; but you then must first become that which ye cannot be, oppressive, arbitrary and tyrannous, as they were from whom ye have freed us. That our hearts are now more capacious, our thoughts more erected to the search and expectation of greatest and exactest things, is the issue of your own virtue propagated in us; ye cannot suppress that, unless ye reinforce an abrogated and merciless law, that fathers may despatch at will their own children. And who shall then stick closest to ye, and excite others? not he who takes up arms for coat and conduct, and his four nobles of Danegelt. Although I dispraise not the defence of just immunities, yet love my peace better, if that were all. Give me the liberty to know, to utter, and to argue freely according to conscience, above all liberties.

What would be best advised, then, if it be found so hurtful and so unequal to suppress opinions for the newness or the unsuitableness to a customary acceptance, will not be my task to say. I only shall repeat what I have learned from one of your own honourable number, a right noble and pious lord, who, had he not sacrificed his life and fortunes to the Church and Commonwealth, we had not now missed and bewailed a worthy and undoubted patron of this argument. Ye know him, I am sure; yet I for honour's sake, and may it be eternal to him, shall name him, the Lord Brook. He writing of Episcopacy and by the way treating of sects and schisms, left ye his vote, or rather now the last words of his dying charge, which I know will ever be of dear and honoured regard with ye, so full of meekness and breathing charity, that next to His last testament, who bequeathed love and peace to His disciples, I cannot call to mind where I have read or heard words more mild and peaceful. He there exhorts us to hear with patience and humility those, however they be miscalled, that desire to live purely, in such a use of God's ordinances, as the best guidance of their conscience gives them, and to tolerate them, though in some disconformity to ourselves. The book itself will tell us more at large, being published to the world, and dedicated to the Parliament by him who, both for his life and for his death, deserves that what advice he left be not laid by without perusal.

And now the time in special is, by privilege to write and speak what may help to the further discussing of matters in agitation. The temple of Janus with his two controversial faces might now not unsignificantly be set open. And though all the winds of doctrine were let loose to play upon the earth, so Truth be in the field, we do injuriously, by licensing and prohibiting, to misdoubt her strength. Let her and Falsehood grapple; who ever knew Truth put to the worse, in a free and open encounter? Her confuting is the best and surest suppressing. He who hears what praying there is for light and clearer knowledge to be sent down among us, would think of other matters to be constituted beyond the discipline of Geneva, framed and fabricked already to our hands. Yet when the new light which we beg for shines in upon us, there be who envy and oppose, if it come not first in at their casements. What a collusion is this, whenas we are exhorted by the wise man to use diligence, to seek for wisdom as for hidden treasures early and late, that another order shall enjoin us to know nothing but by statute? When a man hath been labouring the hardest labour in the deep mines of knowledge; hath furnished out his findings in all their equipage; drawn forth his reasons as it were a battle ranged; scattered and defeated all objections in his way; calls out his adversary into the plain, offers him the advantage of wind and sun, if he please, only that he may try the matter by dint of argument: for his opponents then to skulk, to lay ambushments, to keep a narrow bridge of licensing where the challenger should pass, though it be valour enough in soldiership, is but weakness and cowardice in the wars of Truth.

For who knows not that Truth is strong, next to the Almighty? She needs no policies, nor stratagems, nor licensings to make her victorious; those are the shifts and the defences that error uses against her power. Give her but room, and do not bind her when she sleeps, for then she speaks not true, as the old Proteus did, who spake oracles only when he was caught and bound, but then rather she turns herself into all shapes, except her own, and perhaps tunes her voice according to the time, as Micaiah did before Ahab, until she be adjured into her own likeness. Yet is it not impossible that she may have more shapes than one. What else is all that rank of things indifferent, wherein Truth may be on this side or on the other, without being unlike herself? What but a vain shadow else is the abolition of those ordinances, that hand-writing nailed to the cross? What great purchase is this Christian liberty which Paul so often boasts of? His doctrine is, that he who eats or eats not, regards a day or regards it not, may do either to the Lord. How many other things might be tolerated in peace, and left to conscience, had we but charity, and were it not the chief stronghold of our hypocrisy to be ever judging one another?

I fear yet this iron yoke of outward conformity hath left a slavish print upon our necks; the ghost of a linen decency yet haunts us. We stumble and are impatient at the least dividing of one visible congregation from another, though it be not in fundamentals; and through our forwardness to suppress, and our backwardness to recover any enthralled piece of truth out of the gripe of custom, we care not to keep truth separated from truth, which is the fiercest rent and disunion of all. We do not see that, while we still affect by all means a rigid external formality, we may as soon fall again into a gross conforming stupidity, a stark and dead congealment of wood and hay and stubble, forced and frozen together, which is more to the sudden degenerating of a Church than many subdichotomies of petty schisms.

Not that I can think well of every light separation, or that all in a Church is to be expected gold and silver and precious stones: it is not possible for man to sever the wheat from the tares, the good fish from the other fry; that must be the Angels' Ministry at the end of mortal things. Yet if all cannot be of one mind—as who looks they should be?—this doubtless is more wholesome, more prudent, and more Christian that many be tolerated, rather than all compelled. I mean not tolerated popery, and open superstition, which, as it extirpates all religions and civil supremacies, so itself should be extirpate, provided first that all charitable and compassionate means be used to win and regain the weak and the misled: that also which is impious or evil absolutely either against faith or manners no law can possibly permit, that intends not to unlaw itself: but those neighbouring differences, or rather indifferences, are what I speak of, whether in some point of doctrine or of discipline, which, though they may be many, yet need not interrupt the unity of Spirit, if we could but find among us the bond of peace.

In the meantime if any one would write, and bring his helpful hand to the slow-moving Reformation which we labour under, if Truth have spoken to him before others, or but seemed at least to speak, who hath so bejesuited us that we should trouble that man with asking licence to do so worthy a deed? and not consider this, that if it come to prohibiting, there is not aught more likely to be prohibited than truth itself; whose first appearance to our eyes, bleared and dimmed with prejudice and custom, is more unsightly and unplausible than many errors, even as the person is of many a great man slight and contemptible to see to. And what do they tell us vainly of new opinions, when this very opinion of theirs, that none must be heard, but whom they like, is the worst and newest opinion of all others; and is the chief cause why sects and schisms do so much abound, and true knowledge is kept at distance from us; besides yet a greater danger which is in it?

For when God shakes a Kingdom with strong and healthful commotions to a general reforming, 'tis not untrue that many sectaries and false teachers are then busiest in seducing; but yet more true it is, that God then raises to His own work men of rare abilities, and more than common industry, not only to look back and revise what hath been taught heretofore, but to gain further and go on some new enlightened steps in the discovery of truth. For such is the order of God's enlightening His Church, to dispense and deal out by degrees His beam, so as our earthly eyes may best sustain it.

Neither is God appointed and confined, where and out of what place these His chosen shall be first heard to speak; for He sees not as man sees, chooses not as man chooses, lest we should devote ourselves again to set places, and assemblies, and outward callings of men; planting our faith one while in the old Convocation house, and another while in the Chapel at Westminster; when all the faith and religion that shall be there canonised is not sufficient without plain convincement, and the charity of patient instruction to supple the least bruise of conscience, to edify the meanest Christian, who desires to walk in the Spirit, and not in the letter of human trust, for all the number of voices that can be there made; no, though Harry VII. himself there, with all his liege tombs about him, should lend them voices from the dead, to swell their number.

And if the men be erroneous who appear to be the leading schismatics, what withholds us but our sloth, our self-will, and distrust in the right cause, that we do not give them gentle meeting and gentle dismissions, that we debate not and examine the matter thoroughly with liberal and frequent audience; if not for their sakes, yet for our own? seeing no man who hath tasted learning, but will confess the many ways of profiting by those who, not contented with stale receipts, are able to manage and set forth new positions to the world. And were they but as the dust and cinders of our feet, so long as in that notion they may yet serve to polish and brighten the armoury of Truth, even for that respect they were not utterly to be cast away. But if they be of those whom God hath fitted for the special use of these times with eminent and ample gifts, and those perhaps neither among the Priests nor among the Pharisees, and we in the haste of a precipitant zeal shall make no distinction, but resolve to stop their mouths, because we fear they come with new and dangerous opinions, as we commonly forejudge them ere we understand them, no less than woe to us, while, thinking thus to defend the Gospel, we are found the persecutors.

There have been not a few since the beginning of this Parliament, both of the Presbytery and others, who by their unlicensed books, to the contempt of an Imprimatur, first broke that triple ice clung about our hearts, and taught the people to see day. I hope that none of those were the persuaders to renew upon us this bondage which they themselves have wrought so much good by contemning. But if neither the check that Moses gave to young Joshua, nor the countermand which our Saviour gave to young John, who was so ready to prohibit those whom he thought unlicensed, be not enough to admonish our Elders how unacceptable to God their testy mood of prohibiting is, if neither their own remembrance what evil hath abounded in the Church by this let of licensing, and what good they themselves have begun by transgressing it, be not enough, but that they will persuade and execute the most Dominican part of the Inquisition over us, and are already with one foot in the stirrup so active at suppressing, it would be no unequal distribution in the first place to suppress the suppressors themselves: whom the change of their condition hath puffed up, more than their late experience of harder times hath made wise.

And as for regulating the Press, let no man think to have the honour of advising ye better than yourselves have done in that Order published next before this, "that no book be Printed, unless the Printer's and the Author's name, or at least the Printer's, be registered." Those which otherwise come forth, if they be found mischievous and libellous, the fire and the executioner will be the timeliest and the most effectual remedy that man's prevention can use. For this authentic Spanish policy of licensing books, if I have said aught, will prove the most unlicensed book itself within a short while; and was the immediate image of a Star Chamber decree to that purpose made in those very times when that Court did the rest of those her pious works, for which she is now fallen from the stars with Lucifer. Whereby ye may guess what kind of state prudence, what love of the people, what care of Religion or good manners there was at the contriving, although with singular hypocrisy it pretended to bind books to their good behaviour. And how it got the upper hand of your precedent Order so well constituted before, if we may believe those men whose profession gives them cause to enquire most, it may be doubted there was in it the fraud of some old patentees and monopolisers in the trade of bookselling; who under pretence of the poor in their Company not to be defrauded, and the just retaining of each man his several copy, which God forbid should be gainsaid, brought divers glosing colours to the House, which were indeed but colours, and serving to no end except it be to exercise a superiority over their neighbours; men who do not therefore labour in an honest profession to which learning is indebted, that they should be made other men's vassals. Another end is thought was aimed at by some of them in procuring by petition this Order, that, having power in their hands, malignant books might the easier scape abroad, as the event shows.

But of these sophisms and elenchs of merchandise I skill not. This I know, that errors in a good government and in a bad are equally almost incident; for what Magistrate may not be misinformed, and much the sooner, if Liberty of Printing be reduced into the power of a few? But to redress willingly and speedily what hath been erred, and in highest authority to esteem a plain advertisement more than others have done a sumptuous bribe, is a virtue (honoured Lords and Commons) answerable to your highest actions, and whereof none can participate but greatest and wisest men.

PRINTED IN THE U.S.A.

THE GREAT IDEAS, Volumes 2 and 3

ANGEL
ANIMAL
ARISTOCRACY
ART
ASTRONOMY
BEAUTY
BEING
CAUSE
CHANCE
CHANGE
CITIZEN
CONSTITUTION
COURAGE
CUSTOM AND
  CONVENTION
DEFINITION
DEMOCRACY
DESIRE
DIALECTIC
DUTY
EDUCATION
ELEMENT
EMOTION
ETERNITY
EVOLUTION
EXPERIENCE

FAMILY
FATE
FORM
GOD
GOOD AND EVIL
GOVERNMENT
HABIT
HAPPINESS
HISTORY
HONOR
HYPOTHESIS
IDEA
IMMORTALITY
INDUCTION
INFINITY
JUDGMENT
JUSTICE
KNOWLEDGE
LABOR
LANGUAGE
LAW
LIBERTY
LIFE AND DEATH
LOGIC
LOVE
MAN
MATHEMATICS